Corruption, Protection and Justice in Medieval Europe

What was an "advocate" (Latin: *advocatus*; German: *Vogt*) in the Middle Ages? What responsibilities came with the position and how did they change over time? With this groundbreaking study, Jonathan R. Lyon challenges the standard narrative of a "medieval" Europe of feudalism and lordship being replaced by a "modern" Europe of government, bureaucracy and the state. By focusing on the position of advocate, he argues for continuity in corrupt practices of justice and protection between 750 and 1800. This book traces the development of the role of church advocate from the Carolingian period onward and explains why this position became associated with the violent abuse of power on churches' estates. When other types of advocates became common in and around Germany after 1250, including territorial and urban advocates, they were not officeholders in developing bureaucracies. Instead, they used similar practices to church advocates to profit illicitly from their positions, which calls into question scholarly arguments about the decline of violent lordship and the rise of governmental accountability in European history.

Jonathan R. Lyon is Professor of History at the University of Chicago, where he specializes in the history of the Holy Roman Empire. He has previously held fellowships from the Humboldt Foundation and the Austrian Science Fund. He is the author of *Princely Brothers and Sisters: The Sibling Bond in German Politics, 1100–1250* (2013), which won the 2017 John Nicholas Brown Prize from the Medieval Academy of America, and *Noble Society: Five Lives from Twelfth-Century Germany* (2017).

Corruption, Protection and Justice in Medieval Europe

A Thousand-Year History

Jonathan R. Lyon

University of Chicago

CAMBRIDGE
UNIVERSITY PRESS

CAMBRIDGE
UNIVERSITY PRESS

University Printing House, Cambridge CB2 8BS, United Kingdom

One Liberty Plaza, 20th Floor, New York, NY 10006, USA

477 Williamstown Road, Port Melbourne, VIC 3207, Australia

314–321, 3rd Floor, Plot 3, Splendor Forum, Jasola District Centre,
New Delhi – 110025, India

103 Penang Road, #05–06/07, Visioncrest Commercial, Singapore 238467

Cambridge University Press is part of the University of Cambridge.

It furthers the University's mission by disseminating knowledge in the pursuit of
education, learning, and research at the highest international levels of excellence.

www.cambridge.org
Information on this title: www.cambridge.org/9781316513743
DOI: 10.1017/9781009075961

First published 2023

Printed in the United Kingdom by TJ Books Limited, Padstow Cornwall

A catalogue record for this publication is available from the British Library.

Library of Congress Cataloging-in-Publication Data
Names: Lyon, Jonathan Reed, author.
Title: Corruption, protection and justice in Medieval Europe : a thousand year history /
Jonathan R. Lyon, University of Chicago.
Description: Cambridge, United Kingdom ; New York, NY : Cambridge University
Press, 2022. | Includes bibliographical references and index.
Identifiers: LCCN 2022004705 (print) | LCCN 2022004706 (ebook) | ISBN
9781316513743 (hardback) | ISBN 9781009075961 (ebook)
Subjects: LCSH: Law, Medieval. | Justice, Administration of – Europe – History – To
1500. | Patron and client – Europe – History – To 1500. | Europe – Politics and
government – 476-1492.
Classification: LCC KJ147 .L96 2022 (print) | LCC KJ147 (ebook) | DDC 340.5/5–
dc23/eng/20220531
LC record available at https://lccn.loc.gov/2022004705
LC ebook record available at https://lccn.loc.gov/2022004706

ISBN 978-1-316-51374-3 Hardback

For my parents

Contents

Maps and Figures

Acknowledgments

I was immensely fortunate to have completed almost all of the research for this book before the COVID-19 pandemic limited travel and access to libraries and archives. In 2013–14, a Lise Meitner Fellowship from the Austrian Science Fund (Project # M 1534-G18) enabled me to spend a year at the Institute of Austrian Historical Research in Vienna. In 2017–18, an Alexander von Humboldt Research Fellowship for Experienced Researchers provided me with the opportunity to spend a year at the University of Heidelberg. To be sure, because so many source editions and archival materials have been digitized and made available online, I probably could have written a version of this book sitting on my couch at home in Chicago. However, this is a much better book because of the time I was able to spend in Europe, not only working in archives and libraries but also meeting with friends and colleagues and presenting my work. There is simply no way for me to thank here everyone who helped me with this project by suggesting a source, asking me a difficult question or offering words of encouragement. I have done my best in the footnotes to acknowledge those whose guidance on particular issues was especially valuable.

In both Vienna and Heidelberg, I was made to feel at home by scholarly communities who were remarkably generous with their time. My host in Vienna, Christina Lutter, has helped me with this project from the start, sponsoring my fellowship, discussing advocates with me over many a lunch and reading various drafts of my work. I am also grateful to Thomas Winkelbauer, Elisabeth Gruber, Herwig Weigl, Brigitte Merta and the other members of the Institute of Austrian Historical Research for their hospitality. My host in Heidelberg, Bernd Schneidmüller, has been a mentor to me since we first met in Bamberg in the year 2000 while I was a graduate student; he has always made me feel welcome, and my family's time in Heidelberg was wonderful because of his warmth and kindness. I also cannot thank enough for their hospitality and support in Heidelberg Nikolas Jaspert, Julia Burkhardt and the many other members of the Historisches Seminar, including my research assistant, Isabel Kimpel.

The University of Chicago's Social Sciences Division and Department of History have given me that most precious of scholarly gifts: time. Their generous leave policy and humane teaching load have given me the opportunity to read and reread my sources and to write and revise this book at my own pace over the last eight years. My friend Jimmy Mixson willingly gave some of his own precious time to read a complete draft of the manuscript and offer invaluable feedback; this is a much better book because of his many suggestions and his keen eye for weak arguments. I also thank Paul Cheney, Daisy Delogu, Daniel Frey, Herbert Krammer, Allie Locking, David Nirenberg, Lucy Pick and John Van Engen for reading parts of the manuscript. Levi Roach and Björn Weiler, the two readers for Cambridge University Press, gave expert advice and much encouragement. My research assistant at the University of Chicago, Tristan Sharp, was a great help in the early stages of this project.

When I first began researching medieval advocates eight years ago, I had no idea how vast the source base would prove to be. My wife, Brooke, and our son, Henry, have saved me countless times from falling into the bottomless pit of this project by distracting me from my work. My parents, John and Jan Lyon, are the ones who first prepared for me for this undertaking – and for life – by being supportive in more ways than I can possibly list here. I dedicate this book to them.

Abbreviations

AHR	*The American Historical Review*
BUB	*Urkundenbuch zur Geschichte der Babenberger in Österreich*
CDS I A	*Codex Diplomaticus Saxoniae Regiae*, Part I, Section A
CDS I B	*Codex Diplomaticus Saxoniae Regiae*, Part I, Section B
CDS II	*Codex Diplomaticus Saxoniae Regiae*, Part II
DA	*Deutsches Archiv für Erforschung des Mittelalters*
EHR	*The English Historical Review*
MGH	Monumenta Germaniae Historica
(MGH) Capit.	*Capitularia regum Francorum*
(MGH) Conc.	*Concilia Aevi Karolini*
(MGH) Const.	*Constitutiones et acta publica imperatorum et regum*
(MGH) DD	Diplomata
(MGH) DD Arn	*Die Urkunden Arnolfs*
(MGH) DD Arnulf.	*Die Urkunden der Arnulfinger*
(MGH) DD F I	*Die Urkunden Friedrichs I.*
(MGH) DD F II	*Die Urkunden Friedrichs II.*
(MGH) DD H I	*Die Urkunden Konrad I., Heinrich I. und Otto I.* [Charters of Henry I]
(MGH) DD H II	*Die Urkunden Heinrichs II.*
(MGH) DD H III	*Die Urkunden Heinrichs III.*
(MGH) DD H IV	*Die Urkunden Heinrichs IV.*
(MGH) DD H V	*Die Urkunden Heinrichs V.* (online)
(MGH) DD H VI	*Die Urkunden Heinrichs VI.* (online)
(MGH) DD Ka III	*Die Urkunden Karls III.*
(MGH) DD Karol. I	*Die Urkunden Pippins, Karlmanns und Karls des Grossen*

(MGH) DD Km	*Die Urkunden Ludwigs des Deutschen, Karlmanns und Ludwigs des Jüngeren* [Charters of Karlmann]
(MGH) DD Ko I	*Die Urkunden Konrad I., Heinrich I. und Otto I.* [Charters of Conrad I]
(MGH) DD Ko II	*Die Urkunden Konrads II.*
(MGH) DD Ko III	*Die Urkunden Konrads III.*
(MGH) DD LdD	*Die Urkunden Ludwigs des Deutschen, Karlmanns und Ludwigs des Jüngeren* [Charters of Louis the German]
(MGH) DD LdF	*Die Urkunden Ludwigs des Frommen*
(MGH) DD LdJ	*Die Urkunden Ludwigs des Deutschen, Karlmanns und Ludwigs des Jüngeren* [Charters of Louis the Younger]
(MGH) DD LdK	*Die Urkunden Zwentibolds und Ludwigs des Kindes* [Charters of Louis the Child]
(MGH) DD Lo I	*Die Urkunden Lothars I. und Lothars II.* [Charters of Lothar I]
(MGH) DD Lo III	*Die Urkunden Lothars III.*
(MGH) DD Lu II	*Die Urkunden Ludwigs II.*
(MGH) DD Merov.	*Die Urkunden der Merowinger*
(MGH) DD O I	*Die Urkunden Konrad I., Heinrich I. und Otto I* [Charters of Otto I]
(MGH) DD O II	*Die Urkunden Otto des II.*
(MGH) DD O III	*Die Urkunden Otto des III.*
(MGH) DD Phil	*Die Urkunden Philipps von Schwaben*
(MGH) DD Rudolf.	*Die Urkunden der burgundischen Rudolfinger*
(MGH) DD Wilh	*Die Urkunden Heinrich Raspes und Wilhelms von Holland* [Charters of William of Holland]
(MGH) DD Zwent	*Die Urkunden Zwentibolds und Ludwigs des Kindes* [Charters of Zwentibold]
(MGH) Epp.	Epistolae
(MGH) Epp. saec. XIII	Epistolae Saeculi XIII e Regestis Pontificum Romanorum
(MGH) Epp. sel.	Epistolae selectae
(MGH) SS	Scriptores
(MGH) SSrG	Scriptores rerum Germanicarum
(MGH) SSrG NS	Scriptores rerum Germanicarum, Nova series
MIÖG	*Mitteilungen des Instituts für österreichische Geschichtsforschung*

NCMH	*The New Cambridge Medieval History*
Tr. Freising	*Die Traditionen des Hochstifts Freising*
UB St. Gall	*Urkundenbuch der Abtei Sanct Gallen*
UB Strassburg	*Urkundenbuch der Stadt Strassburg*
ZRG GA	*Zeitschrift der Savigny-Stiftung für Rechtsgeschichte, Germanistische Abteilung*
ZRG KA	*Zeitschrift der Savigny-Stiftung für Rechtsgeschichte, Kanonistische Abteilung*
ZWLG	*Zeitschrift für Württembergische Landesgeschichte*

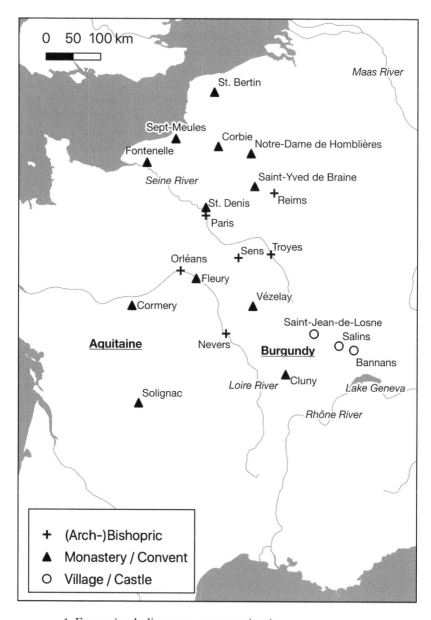

1 France (excluding easternmost regions)

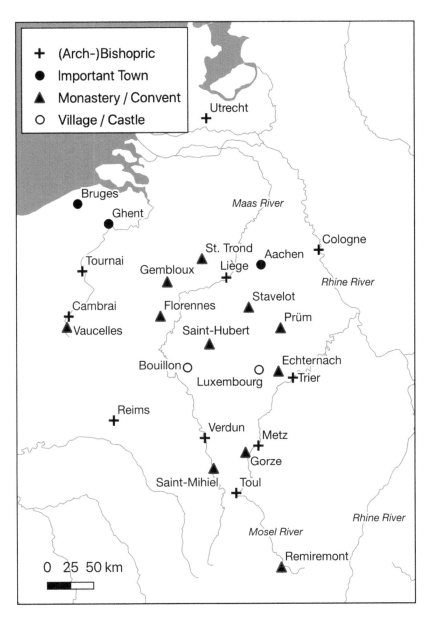

Legend:
- **+** (Arch-)Bishopric
- **●** Important Town
- **▲** Monastery / Convent
- **○** Village / Castle

Utrecht

Bruges

Ghent

Maas River

St. Trond   Aachen   Cologne

Tournai   Gembloux   Liège   *Rhine River*

Cambrai   Florennes   Stavelot

Vaucelles   Saint-Hubert   Prüm

Bouillon○   ○   Echternach
            Luxembourg   Trier

Reims

Verdun   Metz

Saint-Mihiel   Toul   Gorze

Mosel River   *Rhine River*

Remiremont

0 25 50 km

2 Lotharingia and environs

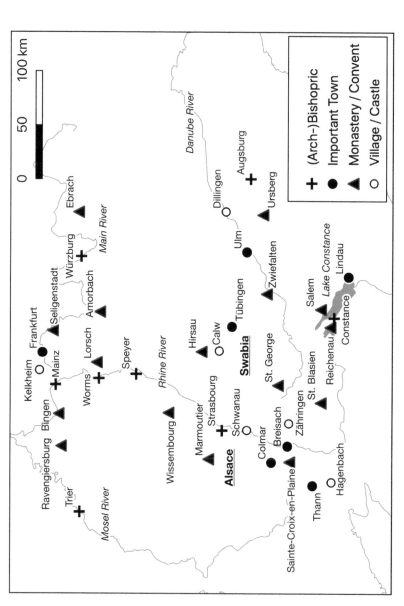

3 Alsace and southwestern Germany

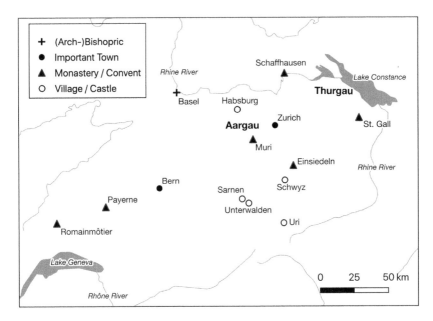

4 Switzerland

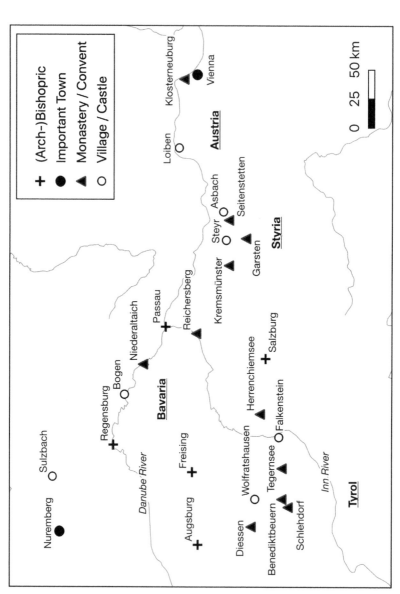

5 Southeastern Germany and Austria

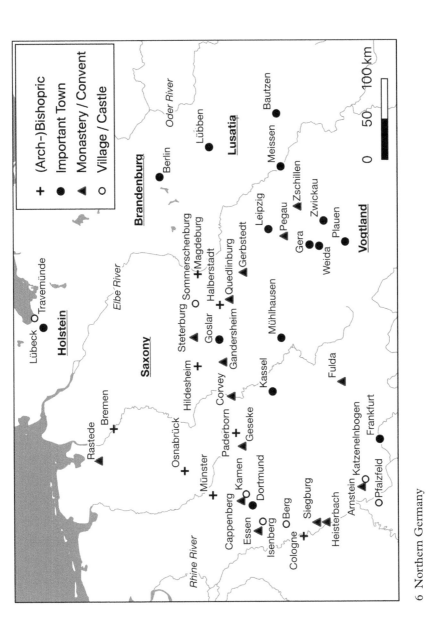

6 Northern Germany

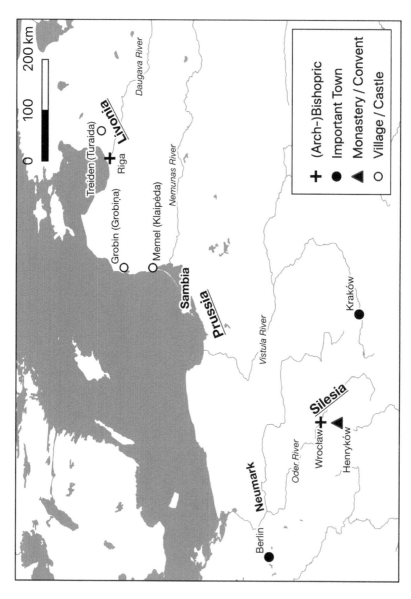

7 The southern Baltic region

Introduction

> He wanted to know the history of the country. He had a college text-book, a big thick one. Years later, showing it to me, he prodded it with his finger, and said, "I durn near memorized every durn word in it. I could name you every name. I could name you every date." Then he prodded it again, this time contemptuously, and said, "And the fellow that wrote it didn't know a God-damned thing. About how things were. He didn't know a thing. I bet things were just like they are now. A lot of folks wrassling round." – Robert Penn Warren, *All the King's Men*[1]

This book argues that during a millennium of European history, from roughly 750 to 1800 CE, a lot of folks were *wrassling round*. If this phrase seems to lack scholarly precision, that is exactly why I find it useful. I employ it here as a synonym for a set of practices that historians have more commonly labeled with such terms as *feudalism, lordship, government, officeholding, bureaucracy* and *state-building*. In more traditional academic phrasing, my argument is this: For centuries, members of ruling elites – from emperors and kings to petty aristocrats and urban oligarchs – competed to profit from other people's property and its inhabitants by providing protection and exercising justice; whether we call them violent feudal lords or accountable state officials, they employed a set of coercive strategies that proved to be remarkably consistent across 1,000 years of European history. This is, however, rather dense verbiage. The words that Robert Penn Warren puts into the mouth of his corrupt Governor Willie Stark summarize this book succinctly. In his frank assessment of the history of the United States of America as *a lot of folks wrassling round*, Willie lays bare a reality we do not typically like to acknowledge: No matter how many myths we weave around our leaders and institutions, great and small, governance has always been a contact sport.

I start in this unconventional fashion in order to avoid a terminological and conceptual trap. Most historians of the so-called European "middle ages" now prefer to avoid the word feudalism because it assumes too rigid and oversimplified a model of socioeconomic relationships in the past.

---

[1] Warren, *All the King's Men*, 67.

1

But the terms lordship, government, officeholding, bureaucracy and state-building are all used routinely in the early twenty-first century to convey (intentionally or not) a teleology about European power structures and processes between 750 and 1800. To be sure, these terms have been defined and employed in so many different ways, in so many different contexts – not only by historians but also by scholars in other fields in the humanistic social sciences – that consensus on their precise meanings has become increasingly difficult to find.[2] However, regardless of which definitions one chooses to use, they all assume a historical narrative that I will argue here has become increasingly untenable: namely, that feudalism and lordship belonged to the bad old days of a "medieval" Europe, which developing governments, bureaucracies and states defeated in order to give birth to a more "modern" Europe.[3]

Why do we need to rethink this narrative? For much of the second half of the twentieth century, studies of politics and government in the social sciences had a tendency to be state-centric, with a narrow focus on strong institutions as the primary drivers of society, politics and economics in the modern world.[4] Since then, however, American and European efforts to create Western-style governments and institutions in developing countries have floundered, in part because of false assumptions about the inevitability of the centralized nation-state. As a result, scholars are increasingly paying attention to various groups of people whom the modern state had supposedly eliminated from the world stage: warlords, strongmen, mercenaries, gangs, cartels and mafias. Some of these groups have acquired new names in recent studies – nonstate actors, violent entrepreneurs, specialists in violence – which are sufficiently imprecise to allow for comparisons across time and around the globe.[5] One of the overarching arguments of much of this work, regardless of the terms employed, is that protection and justice remain privatized in the twenty-first-century, not only in Latin America, Africa and the former Soviet Union but also in the United States and Europe, to an extent that generations of twentieth-century scholars locked in a triumphalist statist teleology of public power and authority never could have imagined.[6]

---

[2] See the next section.
[3] For critiques of the "medieval/modern" periodization scheme, see Fasolt, "Hegel's Ghost"; Davis, *Periodization*; Symes, "Modernity"; Le Goff, *History*; Kaminsky, "Lateness."
[4] As noted by Strange, *Retreat*, 32; Chittolini, "Private," S35–36.
[5] Volkov, "Political Economy"; Marten, *Warlords*; Ahram and King, "Warlord"; Collins, "Patrimonial Alliances."
[6] Eloquent on this issue is Cordelli, *Privatized State*, 1–13. See also Tilly, *Coercion*, 204; Mehlum, Moene, and Torvik, "Plunder"; Arias, "Dynamics"; Owens, "Distinctions"; Joireman, *Government*; Konrad and Skaperdas, "Market."

Many of these arguments about the privatization of various types of authority have turned to the "medieval" Europe of feudalism and lordship as a historical example of a weak state system.[7] To look to "medieval" Europe to understand how privatized, arbitrary forms of power came to be replaced by accountable government, bureaucracy and the state is to assume, however, that "modern" Europe was successful in supplanting these forms of power with public authority. To a significant extent, this is unquestionably true. Nevertheless, many people now recognize that European nation-states have not been as successful as once thought at controlling gangs, cartels, mafias, and other nonstate actors.[8] Gone are the days when people could argue, as they did in the 1960s and 1970s, that many European states had eliminated corruption from within their borders and that only "backward" or "immature" countries still had to confront this problem.[9] At the level of the European Union, too, the extent of corruption is coming into sharper focus. A 2019 investigative report by the *New York Times* found that "corrupt ties between government officials and agricultural businessmen" had led to gross abuses of the EU's farm subsidies in many countries, with oligarchs and the mafia profiting handsomely from programs intended to help small farmers (I highlight this example because siphoning money and goods away from agriculturalists is a central theme of this book).[10] Thus, even in the heart of Europe, skepticism is growing about the grand narrative of the success and stability of Western political structures.

As a result, a reassessment of historical practices of authority in Europe is necessary, one that avoids relying on assumptions about European progress. Put simply, we need to think differently about the people who exercised power in the millennium between 750 and 1800 if we are to understand the lessons this period can teach us. Here, I will argue that by focusing on two of the basic building blocks of how authority is manifested in human society – namely, providing protection and exercising justice – we can peel back some of the layers of accumulated misunderstanding around feudalism, lordship, government, officeholding, bureaucracy and state-building and start anew. My approach is one that has long been central to the historian's craft: set aside older assumptions, return to the sources and retell a story we thought we knew, but in a different way.

In arguing that the standard medieval-to-modern teleology of European history is problematic for the study of protection and justice,

---

[7] North, Wallis, and Weingast, *Violence*, 62–69; Marten, "Warlordism," 48–50; Teschke, "Geopolitical."
[8] Strange, *Retreat*, 91–99.   [9] As noted by Hough, *Corruption*, 13–14, 100–01.
[10] Gebrekidan, Apuzzo and Novak, "The Money Farmers."

I adopt here an unconventional methodology to distance myself from traditional narratives. Throughout the pages that follow, the focus will remain squarely on a term that appears in tens of thousands of surviving sources from across many regions of Europe between 750 and 1800 – and yet has attracted almost no attention in English-language scholarly debates about feudalism, lordship, government, officeholding, bureaucracy and state-building. This is the Latin noun *advocatus* and its German vernacular equivalent *Vogt*, both of which I will translate throughout as "advocate."

In a broad sense, an *advocatus/Vogt* was someone who acted on another's behalf, who performed various functions that the other was unable or unwilling to perform himself or herself. Many readers will be familiar with "advocate" as an occupation comparable to lawyer or barrister today in countries whose legal systems are based on traditions of Roman law.[11] Between 750 and 1800, however, some advocates held other types of responsibilities. Crucial to my argument here is that, in many parts of Europe, advocates were tasked with providing protection and exercising justice on other people's property, most often church property.[12] In this capacity, they frequently disputed with property holders over the proper limits of their authority and employed a variety of (sometimes violent) tactics to profit in whatever way they could from their positions. These advocates illuminate a set of practices of protection and justice across a millennium of European history that were fundamentally corrupt: that is, designed to benefit the advocate, his family and his followers rather than the property holder he represented or the people he was assigned to protect and judge.[13]

As my emphasis on the vernacular word *Vogt* indicates, the advocates that are my focus here were especially common in the German-speaking lands of the Holy Roman Empire (modern Austria, Germany and Switzerland). This book therefore further distances itself from traditional arguments about European progress in anglophone scholarship by rethinking the imagined geography of the continent. The collapse of the nation-state paradigm at the start of the twenty-first century means that medieval England and France – the essential sites for the "origins of the modern state" teleology – can be marginalized, and other regions can

---

[11] "Advocate, n.," *Oxford English Dictionary* online.
[12] The terms *advocatio/advocatia* and *Vogtei* ("advocacy") became commonplace after the turn of the first millennium to describe, either in abstract terms or in more concrete territorial ones, the scope of advocates' authority to judge and protect.
[13] For the various ways of understanding corruption today and historically, see Kroeze, Vitória, and Geltner, "Introduction," 1–6; Hough, *Corruption*, 2–4; Waquet, *Corruption*, 1–18.

become the focus of new narratives of European history.[14] As I will argue here, the German-speaking lands sit at the center of a history of justice, protection, power and authority between 750 and 1800 that shares little in common with the standard English and French version of the making of Europe.[15]

Scholars of German history are familiar with the notion of a German political "special path" (*Sonderweg*), a historiographical argument that sought to explain why Germany developed differently than England and France and was slow to become a nation-state. In German-language scholarship, it has long been recognized that state-building in the Holy Roman Empire took place at the level of the territorial principalities (Bavaria, Saxony, Brandenburg, etc.). According to this work, government, officeholding and bureaucracy were all more visible at this level of political life than the national one.[16] The "special path" argument tended to frame this narrative in negative terms as a story of structural fragmentation and of the failure of the centralized state.[17] However, because it has become clear in the twenty-first century that the Western-style nation-state is not the *sine qua non* of political life, that there is nothing inevitable or permanent about its institutions, the German "special path" looks significantly less special than it once did. Politically heterogeneous empires with shared and overlapping sovereignty regimes (such as the Holy Roman Empire) have proven far more durable than many unitary kingdoms and nation-states, and they therefore have important lessons to teach us.[18]

Thus, the fragmented nature of power and authority in the German-speaking lands prior to the nineteenth century means that these regions lend themselves to comparison with the many modern polities where state-building has failed to live up to the expectations of the nation-state paradigm. As I will argue here, the position of the *advocatus/Vogt* can help us to grasp what a comparison of this sort might look like, because advocates are one of the key reasons why protection and justice in many localities remained outside of the effective control of any centralizing,

---

[14] For the standard narrative, see Strayer, *Medieval Origins* and the next section. For the need to decenter France and England in our narratives of European history, see Reuter, "Debate," 187–95; Taylor, "Formalising," 35–38.

[15] I use *Europe* in this sentence as a "hyperreal term" and a "figure of the imagination" that exerts enormous influence on how we write history; see Chakrabarty, *Provincializing Europe*, 27–28. See also Davis, *Periodization*, 4–6; cf. Bartlett, *Europe*, 1–3.

[16] Moraw, *Verfassung*, 183–94; Schubert, *Fürstliche Herrschaft*; Whaley, *Germany*, 1:1–14; Loud, "Political"; and various articles in *Deutsche Territorialstaat*.

[17] As noted by Wilson, *Heart of Europe*, 3; Scales, *German Identity*, 1–40; Reuter, "Sonderweg"; Schneidmüller, "Konsensuale Herrschaft," 61–64. For the older, negative view: Barraclough, *Origins*, 454–55; Thompson, *Feudal Germany*, xv–xvi.

[18] Burbank and Cooper, *Empires*, 16–17.

sovereign authority between 750 and 1800. For a millennium, advocates blurred the lines between lordship and government, public and private authority and state and nonstate actors. The study of advocates, therefore, does not lead us down a "special path" but rather a much more "normal" one from a global historical perspective, challenging many standard teleologies of European history.[19]

As the following chapters will demonstrate, the role of advocate was prone to abuse from the beginning, and for centuries, the people who held the position – from rulers to minor nobles to townspeople – found creative ways to benefit from it. The *advocatus/Vogt* was part-police officer, part-judge, part-tax collector – a combination of roles that, for very good reasons, modern states have tried to keep separate. From demanding extra payments when presiding over village courts, to unjustly imprisoning farmers who could not pay judicial fines, to going door-to-door in communities and demanding exactions beyond what locals rightfully owed for their "protection," advocates acted in many ways that will look familiar to social scientists who work in places around the globe today where the state is weak. One of the best examples of the quintessential bad *advocatus/Vogt* can be found in the Swiss legend of William Tell, where advocates spark a peasant uprising by violently seizing livestock and other property, running castle-prisons where they lock up anyone who challenges their authority and sexually assaulting young girls and married women alike.[20] The hero William Tell and his antagonists may have been fictional, but there is little reason to question the reality of advocatial misbehavior at the core of the myth. Tracing the long history of such abuses will show why we need to move beyond the triumphalist medieval-to-modern narrative of European progress if we are to address the problem of corrupt practices of protection and justice today.

The people labeled "advocate" in the surviving sources appeared in such a variety of different settings between 750 and 1800 that it can be difficult to see the wearers of this label as a single, coherent group. Indeed, while my focus is the German-speaking lands, I will draw examples in this book from places that belong today to a dozen different European countries from France in the west to Latvia in the east. Nevertheless, across this millennium and wide landscape, there is enough consistency in the basic role of the *advocatus* and *Vogt* as defender and judge that the position can serve as a stable core for my argument. As I will demonstrate here, analyzing continuities and changes in advocates' activities across European history challenges many traditional scholarly categories and

---

[19] I draw inspiration here from Pomeranz, *Great Divergence*. Cf. Mitterauer, *Why Europe?*
[20] See Chapter 15.

grand narratives about transitions from arbitrary lordship to accountable government, private to public administration and patrimonial officeholding to bureaucratic officialdom. From the level of the individual household, village and town to that of the principality and kingdom, a study of advocates highlights some of the enduring features of the relationship between property and its inhabitants, on the one side, and the many people who sought to profit from them by providing protection and exercising justice, on the other.

Scholarly Divides

Collectively, feudalism, lordship, government, officeholding, bureaucracy and state-building comprise an enormous subject with a vast scholarship. I understand these concepts first and foremost through the lens of my own training as a historian of the European Middle Ages.[21] However, historians of this time and place – and historians more generally – do not have a monopoly on these terms and concepts. Numerous other social-scientific fields are also actively debating key issues surrounding them. Fruitful exchanges across the disciplines do occur, of course, and historians have a long tradition of learning from the other social sciences.[22] Nevertheless, even in this digital age, it is impossible for scholars in one discipline to follow all the important debates in other fields. As a result, as historians of medieval Europe employ these key terms and concepts to suit their own needs, and other historians and social scientists do likewise, the gulf between different fields' understandings of feudalism, lordship, government, officeholding, bureaucracy and state-building steadily grows wider – without practitioners in these different fields necessarily realizing it.

Three aspects of this scholarly divide must be emphasized at the outset to explain why I will focus here on the *advocatus* and *Vogt* while setting aside more popular scholarly approaches to past and present practices of protection and justice. The first concerns issues internal to the discipline of medieval history; the second concerns the broader medieval-to-modern teleology as understood by historians of Europe; and the third concerns how this teleology shapes arguments in some of the other social sciences.

---

[21] Because the term "medieval historian" is the common designation for historians who study the European Middle Ages, I will use it for clarity's sake in this Introduction, despite my unease with the label "medieval."

[22] The work of anthropologists is central to medievalists' discussions of both conflict resolution and kinship: Brown and Górecki, "What Conflict Means," 6–10; Hummer, *Visions*, 11–94. Closer to my topic here, the historical sociologist Michael Mann's arguments about social power have also been influential; see Taylor, *State*, 449–51.

Within the field of medieval history, different scholars have long defined and understood feudalism, lordship, government, office-holding, bureaucracy and state-building differently. This has led to very different narratives of the period. As noted above, feudalism does not appear as often as it once did in works in the field. One reason for this is the recognition that there has never been a broad consensus on what the term means; some use it narrowly for the relationship between lords and vassals, while others prefer to understand it as a more general term for the overarching political and social structures of the medieval period.[23] Significantly, in this latter sense feudalism has frequently had a negative connotation, with French Revolutionaries using it to describe everything wrong with the *Ancien Régime*, and Karl Marx arguing that "the political spirit" of the people had "been dissolved, fragmented and lost in the various culs-de-sac of feudal society."[24] Thus, another reason why medievalists have shied away from the term is that, for too many people, it conjures an image of bad lords and abused peasants that is (while not necessarily incorrect) a caricature when it becomes the one descriptor for the whole of medieval history.[25]

Lordship – *Herrschaft* in German, *seigneurie banale* in French – is the label that many historians now use instead of feudalism for the most common form of political authority in Europe between the tenth and thirteenth centuries.[26] As ubiquitous as the term is in modern scholarship, however, it too lacks a clear and consistent definition. Some historians rely to varying degrees, either consciously or unconsciously, on Max Weber's definition of *Herrschaft* (which can also be translated as "domination").[27] These scholars argue that the people in medieval society who exercised lordship were the ones who could constrain others and make dependents obey their commands. Other historians take different approaches to the term, using other modern conceptual frameworks, or

---

[23] Wickham, "Feudal Economy," 3, n. 1, and more generally, Bloch, *Feudal Society*; Ganshof, *Feudalism*; Strayer, "Feudalism"; Cheyette, "Introduction"; Brown, "Tyranny"; Reynolds, *Fiefs*, esp. 1–3; Patzold, *Lehnswesen*. Cf. Anderson, *Passages*, 147–53.

[24] Marx and Engels, *Reader*, 45. See also Ganshof, *Feudalism*, xv; Davis, *Periodization*, 7–11.

[25] Patzold, *Lehnswesen*, 6; Reynolds, *Fiefs*, 1.

[26] Here again, the scholarship on the topic is vast. Useful overviews include Schreiner, "Grundherrschaft"; Reuter, "Forms"; Hechberger, *Adel*, 226–45. Georges Duby provides the clearest descriptions of what is meant by *seigneurie banale*: Duby, *Early Growth*, 172–74; Duby, *Guerriers*, 248–60. For critiques, see below and Cheyette, "Duby's *Mâconnais*."

[27] Weber, *Economy*, 53. For the challenge of translating Weber's *Herrschaft* into English, see ibid., 61–62, n. 31 and Goetz, *Moderne Mediävistik*, 194. For Weber's enduring influence on the study of medieval history, see Brunner, *Land*, 96; Bosl, "Ruler," 359; Reynolds, *Fiefs*, 27; Reuter, "All Quiet," 437; Sabapathy, *Officers*, 20–21; Taylor, *State*, 2–3.

preferring instead to tie lordship more closely to distinctly medieval aspects of power, such as castles.[28] Regardless of how one understands the term, like feudalism it typically carries a negative connotation: lordship is the coercive, violent and arbitrary exercise of power by elites over subject populations.[29]

What medieval historians mean by government, officeholding, bureaucracy and state-building can be equally difficult to pin down, because scholars have widely diverging opinions on the extent to which strong institutional and administrative structures existed in different places at different times during the Middle Ages. Thus, while some historians are comfortable writing about English and French government developing in the twelfth century – or even about Carolingian and Ottonian government existing in earlier periods – other scholars prefer the term governance to suggest less rigid forms of authority and to avoid the modernizing implications of the word government.[30] Like government, the terms officeholding and bureaucracy frequently go undefined, especially in scholarship on the thirteenth to fifteenth centuries. Although Weber's definitions of these terms were closely tied to his ideas about modernity and do not transfer easily into the medieval setting, many historians are nevertheless quick to describe medieval governments in Weberian terms as being staffed by professional bureaucrats who understood their positions as public offices.[31] Not surprisingly, some scholars have taken this one step further and argued that the state existed in the Middle Ages and already possessed institutions that were forerunners to modern state structures. Other historians, however, are equally insistent on a definition of the state that is unique to the medieval European context in order to escape teleological modes of thinking. Still others

---

[28] For definitions, see Bisson, *Crisis*, 3; Barton, *Lordship*, 7; West, *Reframing*, 84; Eldevik, *Episcopal Power*, 14. Other historians who have pointed out the challenges of the word lordship include West, "Lordship," 4–7, 33–38; Veach, *Lordship*, 6; Reynolds, "States," 554; Arnold, *Princes*, 65–68. German scholarship has also called attention to the variety of meanings of the term *Herrschaft*: Goetz, *Moderne Mediävistik*, 193–98; Kroeschell, "Herrschaft."

[29] Influential here is Bisson, "Medieval Lordship." For the "Feudal Revolution" debate, which also shapes conceptions of lordship, see the next section of the Introduction.

[30] Green, *Government*; Baldwin, *Government*; Hollister and Baldwin, "Rise"; Leyser, "Ottonian Government"; Ganshof, *Frankish Institutions*. For the relationship between lordship and government, see Strayer, "Feudalism," 14; Reynolds, "Government," 86–87; Bisson, *Crisis*, 17–19. For governance, see Davis, *Practice*, 7–23; Patzold, "Human Security."

[31] For Weber's bureaucratic ideal type in the medieval context, see Brunner, "Feudalism," 52–54. For uses of the terms bureaucracy and office in the medieval period, see Kittell, *Ad Hoc*; Watts, *Polities*, 238–44; Clanchy, *Memory*, 64–70; Firnhaber-Baker, *Violence*, 90–91; Howe, *Before*, 63; Wolter, "Verwaltung."

choose to avoid the term altogether.[32] The result is a cacophony of disparate voices.

How medieval historians understand and use these terms shapes the broader issue of the medieval-to-modern teleology of European progress. Did Charlemagne (768–814) and his immediate descendants preside over a strong Carolingian state aided by a service aristocracy and public officials?[33] Did their successors in the East Frankish kingdom, the Ottonians (919–1024), have an effective government – or, were they rulers without a state?[34] Scholars' answers to these questions inevitably influence not only narratives of the ninth and tenth centuries but also those of the eleventh and twelfth, the high point of feudalism and lordship according to most historians. The level of government and state-building ascribed to the Carolingians and Ottonians directly impacts the level of disorder that ought to be ascribed to the period of feudal lordship. The less well governed the Frankish lands were in the ninth and tenth centuries, the less dramatic the transition; the better developed the Carolingian and Ottonian states were, the more anarchic the decades after the year 1000 look.[35]

These issues, in turn, feed directly into the question of when feudalism and lordship were replaced by government, accountable officeholding and bureaucracy in the "origins of the modern state" narrative. To speak already in the twelfth century of government in England and France is to suggest that these kingdoms began to free themselves from "feudal" and "medieval" structures of power quite early and to progress along the proper European historical track faster than other parts of the continent. In contrast, since scholars are largely in agreement that the German kings and emperors of the same period did *not* preside over a government that was in any way comparable, it can easily look like Germany was already lagging behind its European rivals centuries before it lost two world wars.[36] If, instead of focusing on the twelfth century, historians push the origins of government and the state into the thirteenth or fourteenth centuries, the twelfth century moves firmly into the category of the age of feudal lordship, making it a period of crisis and instability and

---

[32] Key for the history of the medieval state is Strayer, *Medieval Origins*. For this work's significance, see Freedman and Spiegel, "Medievalisms," 686–90. See also Guenée, *States*, 4–6; Powicke, "Presidential Address"; Reynolds, "Historiography"; Goetz, *Moderne Mediävistik*, 180–85; Davies, "Medieval State"; Reynolds, "States"; Pohl, "Staat"; Watts, *Polities*, 23–42.

[33] Airlie, "Aristocracy." More generally, Hechberger, *Adel*, 194–201. See also Chapter 1.

[34] Leyser, "Ottonian Government"; Althoff, *Ottonen*. See also Chapter 3.

[35] Buc, "What Is Order?" See also the next section of this Introduction and Chapter 4.

[36] For the nature of German "government," see Freed, *Frederick Barbarossa*, 89–110; Weiler, "King as Judge." See also Chapters 8 and 12.

thus slowing the progress narrative of the whole continent.[37] Of course, this teleology looks even slower if one takes the position that European states did not begin to emerge until the "Renaissance" of the fifteenth and sixteenth centuries at the earliest – an argument which squarely fits the idea that Europe had to shed its "medieval" youth and be reborn before it could obtain its mature, "modern" forms (including that of the nation-state).[38]

While this last stance on government and the state is more common-place among Renaissance and early modern historians than medieval ones, it is important to note that there are equally lively debates about all of these concepts in the scholarship on the fifteenth to eighteenth centuries.[39] However, these debates have gone largely unnoticed by medievalists (just as medievalists' debates have gone largely unnoticed by early modernists), further complicating any attempt to summarize succinctly what these terms mean when applied to Europe between 750 and 1800.[40] Thus, while some medieval historians are comfortable with the idea of thirteenth- and fourteenth-century bureaucracies, many early modernists prefer not to speak of professional bureaucracies and public officials existing anywhere in Europe between 1500 and 1800, emphasiz-ing instead that patron–client relationships and patrimonial forms of officeholding were the norm.[41] This begs the question: Were the advanced bureaucratic systems that supposedly developed in Europe between 1250 and 1500 somehow lost to subsequent generations for three centuries? Or, is it more likely that medievalists define the term bureaucracy differently than their modernist colleagues?

Here, we see clearly how the sharp dividing line drawn around the year 1500 in European periodization schemes has made it difficult to have a common conversation about feudalism, lordship, government, officehold-ing, bureaucracy and state-building. More generally, the well-entrenched logic of the medieval-to-modern teleology means that, wherever one places the break between nonstate and state, between private power and public authority, a much larger set of assumptions about progress in European history inevitably comes with it. This is one of the principal reasons why my

---

[37] Bisson, *Crisis*. See also Cheyette, "Reflections," 248–49.

[38] For ca. 1500 as the key period for European state formation, see Tilly, *Coercion*, 36, 76–84; Hont, "Permanent Crisis," 178.

[39] See, for example, Gamberini and Lazzarini, "Introduction"; Burbank and Cooper, *Empires*, 219–50; Holenstein, "Introduction"; Chittolini, "Private"; Hont, "Permanent Crisis." See also Chapter 14.

[40] Fasolt, "Hegel's Ghost," 346; Lyon, "State." Useful as a comparison is Rustow, *Lost Archive*, 103–6.

[41] Adams, *Familial State*; Fritz, "Diener"; Reinhard, "Introduction," 13. See also Chapter 14.

focus here will be on the *advocatus* and *Vogt* – specifically, on what these advocates are described as doing in our sources across a millennium – and why I will consciously avoid referencing lordship and government when framing the actions of individual advocates. Through this approach, I will show that beneath the surface of traditional narratives of European progress is a substratum, a long history of corrupt practices of protection and justice, that defies medieval/modern periodization and other teleologies. Not only the typical division drawn ca. 1500 but also the dividing lines historians like to draw ca. 1000 and ca. 1250 – and, I will suggest at the end, ca. 1800 as well – look much less significant from this perspective than generations of historians have been trained to expect.

The third and final reason why I set aside feudalism, lordship, government, officeholding, bureaucracy and state-building in the pages that follow concerns the enduring impact of the medieval-to-modern teleology on arguments in some of the other social sciences. Medieval historians' lively debates around all of these concepts in recent decades have led to important reconsiderations of the nature of power and authority in Europe. However, these debates have not necessarily resonated outside the field. The traditional narrative arc that sees the rise of government and the state defeating the forces of feudalism and lordship by 1500 remains commonplace in many social-scientific discussions. This narrative unquestionably serves a useful purpose; by studying the interrelationship between weak governmental institutions and violence in the Middle Ages, scholars seek to develop a better understanding of some of the challenges facing weak states today.[42] Unfortunately, work in this field tends to rely on the arguments of mid-twentieth-century medieval historians – Marc Bloch, François Louis Ganshof, Walter Ullmann, Georges Duby, Brian Tierney, Ernst Kantorowicz and Joseph Strayer – when explaining how medieval society and political institutions supposedly worked.[43] Strayer's *On the Medieval Origins of the Modern State* (published in 1970), in particular, remains one of the most important pieces of scholarship written by a medieval historian for social scientists seeking a quick overview of the supposed transition from lordship to government.[44] Twenty-first-century scholarship by

---

[42] See, for example, Marten, *Warlords*, 20–24; North, Wallis, and Weingast, *Violence*, 91–106.

[43] De Long and Shleifer, "Princes," 681; Teschke, "Geopolitical"; Volkov, "Who Is Strong," 81–84; North, Wallis, and Weingast, *Violence*, 62–69; Blaydes and Chaney, "Feudal Revolution"; Mungiu-Pippidi, *Quest*, 61–62. What is striking about much of this work is how few medieval historians are cited at all. Norbert Elias's *The Civilizing Process* (originally published in 1939) and more recent works by Charles Tilly and Hendrik Spruyt are cited much more often than works by scholars trained as medieval historians.

[44] Strayer, *Medieval Origins*. Later editions include a foreword by Charles Tilly. See also the foreword by William Chester Jordan, esp. xix–xx.

medieval historians, on the other hand, is rarely cited in works in other fields – despite its many reassessments of older claims.[45]

Thus, outside of the academic field of medieval history, the European Middle Ages as a whole remain in many ways the anarchic, decentralized opposite of modernity. We can still read of "the problems of feudal particularism" and the "feudal maladies" that Europe needed to overcome in order to progress.[46] In one study of warlordism in a global historical perspective, in which warlordism is essentially synonymous with lordship, the author argues that "warlordism ... in medieval Europe ... lasted for several centuries: from the fall of the Carolingian (or Frankish) empire at the turn of the first millennium until the emergence of sovereign kings in France during the Renaissance in the 1400s."[47] In another study, "the fragmentation of political power" between 950 and 1150 is described as leading to a period of lordship and "*personalized anarchy*," which then gave way to a "feudal state system" between 1150 and 1450 characterized by the territorialization of "public power."[48] My point here is not to critique any of these scholars; rather, it is to highlight how disparate our understandings of the teleological narrative of European history are across the social sciences. At this point, a common conversation is only possible if we stop assuming that feudalism, lordship, government, officeholding, bureaucracy and statebuilding still have explanatory force and instead seek to understand, at a more basic level, how power and authority work(ed).[49] An important aim of this book is to invite readers to see how a careful analysis of historical sources on the *advocatus* and *Vogt* – one that is conversant with both older and newer scholarship on European history – can illuminate potential paths forward.

A New Conversation

To further dismantle the dominant paradigm of European progress from a "medieval" to a "modern" period, I rely here on various strands of early twenty-first-century scholarship on governance and authority in the near-contemporary and contemporary worlds. This does not mean that I will

[45] Among medieval historians, the shift away from Strayer's model came in the closing years of the twentieth century: Freedman and Spiegel, "Medievalisms," 689–90. Nevertheless, the entire debate about the so-called Feudal Revolution has garnered relatively little attention beyond the confines of the field of medieval history (for this debate, see the next section). For one reason why this might be, see Ferguson et al., "Polity," 11.
[46] Spruyt, "Institutional Selection," 539; Graulau, *Underground*, 73.
[47] Marten, "Warlordism," 48.   [48] Teschke, "Geopolitical," 349–52 (italics in original).
[49] For experiments with this sort of conversation, see Patzold, "Human Security," 420–22; Esders and Scheppert, *Mittelalterliches Regieren*.

introduce a new scholarly jargon to the history of the period between 750 and 1800. That would only deepen the morass. Rather, this scholarship will form a (mostly) invisible substructure to my argument, a substructure designed to replace the unseen assumptions attached to feudalism, lordship, government, officeholding, bureaucracy and state-building. This work thus provides a set of concepts that my audience should keep in mind while reading the chapters that follow, even though I will rarely reference these concepts directly. Two strands of social-scientific scholarship are especially important.

The first concerns violence. For generations, medieval historians have debated ideas about "violent lordship" and the so-called Feudal Revolution around the year 1000. According to older scholarship, the growth of hereditary lordship and the privatization of violence in the wake of the Carolingian empire's collapse led to a period of political fragmentation, violent exploitation of local populations and statelessness in Western Europe.[50] Since the later twentieth century, however, scholars have been carefully reassessing just how reliable the sources for endemic violence truly are. Historians influenced by anthropology have emphasized the ways in which violence, as well as threats of violence, could be one strategy among many in dispute-resolution processes.[51] Viewed from this perspective, violence was neither anarchic nor uncontrolled but had specific uses, which members of local elites – both those committing acts of violence and those experiencing them – understood to be components of a broader set of legal and extralegal negotiations about property rights and related issues.

Late twentieth- and twenty-first-century scholarship in other fields has drawn similar conclusions, most compellingly in work on people and organizations that the modern world typically see as perpetrators of casual violence. Studies of both the Sicilian mafia and Russian street gangs have emphasized that there is a logic to criminal protection rackets and other illegal operations and that the mafia and gangs use violence strategically, in a limited fashion, because profits are more stable when criminal enterprises can develop strong networks and relationships.[52] Thus, both medievalists and scholars in other social-scientific fields are in many ways confronting similar problems and asking similar questions as they

---

[50] See, for example, Below, *Deutsche Staat*, 342–50; Bloch, *Feudal Society* (esp. vol. 2).
[51] For the crux of the debate, see Poly and Bournazel, *Feudal Transformation*; Bisson, "Feudal Revolution"; Barthélemy, "Debate"; White, "Debate"; Reuter, "Debate"; Wickham, "Debate"; Bisson, "Debate"; Barthélemy, *Serf*; Bisson, *Crisis*. For violence in particular, see Brown, *Violence*, 1–30; White, "Repenser."
[52] Gambetta, *Sicilian Mafia*, 2; Stephenson, *Gangs*, 67. See also North, Wallis, and Weingast, *Violence*, 274; Mehlum, Moene, and Torvik, "Plunder"; Vinci, "Worms."

increasingly recognize the importance of understanding – rather than merely criticizing – "nonstate actors" and the coercive strategies they employ(ed) in order to be successful. This convergence creates an opportunity for medieval historians to learn from scholars who are exploring logics of violence not only in other preindustrial societies but also in places where the modern state has proven unable to control organized violence within its own borders.[53] Advocates fit well within this framework, because for a millennium accusations of violence leveled against them frequently revolved around protection and justice – two functions that social scientists have long recognized as being tied to the extraction of profits from local populations by both legitimate and illegitimate means.[54]

The second, related argument concerns the distinction between lordly and official behavior, between nonbureaucratic and bureaucratic agents and officials. Medieval historians have shown an increased interest in the rise of accountable officeholding from the thirteenth century onwards. English-language scholarship in this field has tended to focus on England and France, but there is a rich historiography in German about the German-speaking lands as well.[55] Even those scholars who caution against the idea that impersonal bureaucracies had already developed by the fourteenth and fifteenth centuries can find it difficult to escape teleologies that equate accountability with state formation. As a result, historians sometimes struggle to reconcile the abundant evidence for all sorts of official corruption with arguments about the growth of government.[56] Work in other social-scientific disciplines has confronted similar challenges – and offers a useful set of arguments for readers to keep in mind.

I follow, in particular, studies that call into question traditional (especially statist) categories by emphasizing the lack of clear-cut distinctions in many parts of the world between state and nonstate actors.[57] Recent work has shown how the same person can be recognized as legitimate by some people and illegitimate by others, as a "strongman governor" or a "warlord-bureaucrat," who combines both lordly and official behavior,

---

[53] Older work on violence in medieval Europe tended to draw on anthropological studies of "stateless societies" rather than studies of modern states' struggles to exert effective control; see Brown and Górecki, "What Conflict Means," 6–10.

[54] For the connections between protection, justice, and profit, see Lane, "Economic"; Bloch, *Feudal Society*, 2:359–60, 365; Duby, "Evolution"; Harding, *Medieval Law*, 48–54; Poly and Bournazel, *Feudal Transformation*, 31. German scholars have long argued about the extent to which advocacy touches on the history of taxation: Waas, *Vogtei*; Isenmann, "Holy Roman Empire."

[55] Hesse, *Amtsträger*; Schubert, *Fürstliche Herrschaft*, 14–19; *Deutsche Verwaltungsgeschichte*. See also Chapters 12 and 13.

[56] Sabapathy, *Officers*, 248–53; Carpenter and Mattéoni, "Offices," 91.

[57] Stephenson, *Gangs*, 1; Tilly, *Coercion*, 204.

both formal and informal power networks.[58] Other scholars have suggested, along similar lines, that there can be "a symbiotic relationship
between extortionists and state officials" and that state officials can abandon their allegiance to "the state's power, in favor of cooperation with
sources of privatized power."[59] The numerous cases from around the globe
of police officers colluding with – or competing against – local gangs to
profit from criminal activities are well-known examples of the gray area in
which "state" or "public" officials sometimes operate.[60] Viewed from this
perspective, we must be cautious with narratives of European history that
suggest forms of violent and exploitative lordship were eventually replaced
with the norms of accountable officeholding by 1500 or 1800.[61] Instead,
we must be attuned to the possibility that advocates (and others tasked with
providing justice and protection) consistently learned to blur the lines
between lordship and government, public and private authority, and state
and nonstate actors; as those lines shifted over the centuries from 750 to
1800, there were always advocates able to find new, creative ways to locate
and profit from the spaces in between.

While none of these arguments drawn from other disciplines are entirely
new to medieval scholarship, they have not been combined and featured in
a rigorous study that consciously aims to offer a detailed reassessment of
the nature of practices of authority across a millennium of European
history.[62] Admittedly, some readers may find my arguments overly pro-
vocative or too cynical; my drawing of inspiration from research on the
Sicilian mafia, Russian gangs and Afghani warlords is a clear indication that
this book's narrative is not one that aims to glorify Europe's past.[63]
Nevertheless, to bring the study of protection and justice in Europe more
fully into focus and more readily into conversation with other times and
places, we must be prepared to abandon some long-cherished beliefs about
the uniqueness of the European historical trajectory.[64]

---

[58] Mukhopadhyay, *Warlords*, 4–6, 317–18; Marten, *Warlords*, 25; Rustow, *Lost Archive*,
197. For a similar point in the medieval context, see Patzold, "Warlords," 15.
[59] Meloy, "Privatization," 198.
[60] Venkatesh, *Gang Leader*, 230–31; Arias, "Dynamics," 303–07; Stephenson, *Gangs*,
76–80.
[61] For an especially careful consideration of accountable officeholding in the Middle Ages,
see Sabapathy, *Officers*. Cf. Strayer, *Medieval Origins*; Bisson, *Crisis*. For the observation
that scholars no longer assume that the "state" automatically brought "order" with it, see
Buc, "What Is Order?," 294–300. I am also influenced here by Smail, *Legal Plunder*, esp.
160–61.
[62] Gelting, "Reflections," 263–66.
[63] I am not the first to draw inspiration of this sort: Wickham, *Framing*, 330–31; Wickham,
Sleepwalking, 204–05; Reuter, "Nobles," 114.
[64] For similar observations, see Wickham, "Feudal Economy," 39–40; Tilly, "War
Making," 169–70.

My goal is not to paint medieval Europe in an overly negative light either. Other historians who have suggested that medieval lordship – and medieval advocacy, in particular – should be understood as a mafia-style "protection racket" tend to mean this as a sharp critique, as a way to emphasize these institutions' illegitimacy as forms of authority.[65] I see protection rackets, similar to *a lot of folks wrassling round*, as a way to force scholars (myself included) to read our sources in new ways. After all, not everyone who pays for protection in a protection racket thinks it a bad system, and even the modern state has been described as nothing more than a large-scale protection racket.[66] Following scholarship that takes "violent entrepreneurs" and "warlord-bureaucrats" as serious categories of analysis throughout history and across the globe can move European history further away from the stale teleology that privatized feudal lordship inevitably gave way to something better, namely Western-style nation-states and public institutions. My aim here is to suggest a new, more plausible explanation for why it has proven so difficult and unusual for impersonal forms of government and bureaucracy to emerge and endure in modern times – including in European countries with a reputation for strong state structures today.

Advocatus and *Vogt*

How can the study of advocates redirect scholars' approaches to feudalism, lordship, government, officeholding, bureaucracy and state-building? Two answers to this question justify the arguments of this book. First, despite the fact that the advocates who are my focus here have not been discussed extensively in English-language scholarship, they were an important feature of local landscapes in many regions of Europe, especially parts of the German-speaking lands, for at least a millennium. As a result, the seeming obscurity of this subject should not be taken to mean that the *advocatus* and *Vogt* were somehow insignificant; I will demonstrate here that they can bring us to the heart of European political, social and economic life. Second, although the advocates I am discussing here were much more commonplace than many readers may realize, the lack of scholarship on them in English nevertheless presents an invaluable opportunity to further distance readers from the familiar old narratives of the period. In other words, the *advocatus* and *Vogt* offer a surprisingly vast and untouched

---

[65] See, for example, Wood, *Proprietary Church*, 330; Huyghebaert, "Pourquoi," 42; Bouchard, *Strong*, 58.
[66] Tilly, "War Making." See also Brown, *Violence*, 14–15.

canvas on which to paint a new picture of European practices of power, authority, protection and justice.[67]

The Latin word *advocatus* has deep roots as someone who speaks for another in a court of law. The Roman orator Marcus Tullius Cicero (d. 43 BCE) was an advocate of this sort and used his skills as a rhetorician to plead on behalf of clients. As the volume of legal business grew during the later centuries of the Roman Empire, so too did the number of advocates (and their status), thus embedding this form of legal advocacy in the social and cultural fabric of the empire in Late Antiquity.[68] Unsurprisingly, therefore, legal advocates became associated with Christianity as well. In the Latin Vulgate's First Epistle of John we read, "But if any man sin, we have an advocate (*advocatum habemus*) with the Father, Jesus Christ the just" (1 John 2:1).[69]

More important for my argument here than John's letter is the apostle Paul's insistence that God's soldiers should avoid becoming entangled in secular affairs.[70] This became the theological basis for the idea of the ecclesiastical advocate. In the late fourth and early fifth centuries, the Christianization of the Roman Empire prompted members of the rapidly expanding Church to raise questions about the proper relationship between the ecclesiastical hierarchy and the Roman civil court system. In response, both the 407 Council of Carthage and the Theodosian Code decreed that clerics were to be represented in civil matters by advocates (*advocati*) or defenders (*defensores*).[71] The centuries-old Roman office of the legal advocate who handled lawsuits for clients and spoke on their behalf thus provided the solution to the new problem of keeping ecclesiastics free from secular business.[72]

---

[67] One work that integrates advocates into a broad argument about European history is Mitterauer, *Why Europe?*, 99–143. My argument differs significantly from his, however.

[68] Brundage, *Medieval Origins*, 23–45; Humfress, "Advocates"; Crook, *Legal Advocacy*.

[69] *Douay-Rheims Bible* online; *Biblia Sacra*, 1874. The idea that Christ (or occasionally the Holy Spirit or Mary) was sinners' advocate with God was common in Late Antiquity and the Middle Ages; see, for example, Ambrose of Milan, *De Officiis*, 1:254, I.48.239; Augustine of Hippo, *Enarrationes*, 76, LI.13; Caesarius of Arles, *Sermones*, 449–50, CVIII.5; Isidore of Seville, *Etymologiae VII*, 33, VII.2.30; Bede, *Expositio*, 516, II.6.46 (quoting Ambrose).

[70] 2 Tim 2:4; *Biblia Sacra*, 1837. For the many ways of interpreting *saecularia negotia*, see Heydemann, "Nemo Militans."

[71] *Concilia Africae*, 215, chap. 97 (see also 202, chap. 75); *Theodosiani Libri XVI*, 848, XVI.2.38. For the Late Antique terms *advocatus* and *defensor*, see Humfress, "Defensor Ecclesiae."

[72] On this point, see *Theodosian Code*, 447, n. 111, where the translator refers to Late Antique ecclesiastical advocates as "trained professional lawyers." Other scholars are more cautious about the office: Willoweit, "Römische," 30. See also Magnou-Nortier, *Code Théodosien*, 158–60.

The question of whether Roman legal advocates survived the end of Roman imperial rule in Western Europe will be addressed in the first chapter. Regardless, later sources show that from the twelfth century onward, as ancient Roman law began to play a steadily expanding role in the legal life of many parts of Europe, advocates who pleaded on behalf of clients in courts increased noticeably in number and prominence. At the papal curia in Rome, hiring a legal advocate to assist in maneuvering one's case through the system of church courts became essential for success – especially for someone coming from north of the Alps who was completely unfamiliar with the inner workings of the Roman Church's legal apparatus.[73] The German-speaking lands also knew this kind of legal advocate from the thirteenth century onward; however, a different vernacular word came to be used to refer to them: *Advokat* – not *Vogt*.[74] The fact that the German language has two different words deriving from the Latin *advocatus* is important for readers to keep in mind; the advocates at the heart of this study were *not* the ancestors of modern lawyers and barristers.

The type of advocate that is my focus here first surfaces in sources written in eighth-century Francia, in the decades before Charlemagne came to rule over an expansive Frankish empire.[75] Many scholarly definitions of the term *advocatus* during the Carolingian period follow the idea that these advocates were similar to ancient Roman ones, that they "were secular legal representatives for those who could or should not represent themselves, notably clerics."[76] Other definitions emphasize their role within immunities, places where royal agents – especially counts – were not to exercise judicial authority or collect revenues but where agents of the property holder (usually a church or monastery) were permitted to carry out these functions instead.[77] For historians who emphasize the strong institutional framework undergirding law and justice in the Carolingian empire, eighth- and ninth-century advocates held an office (German, *Amt*) and had a specific set of roles to fulfill within the legal

---

[73] Brundage, *Medieval Origins*, 346–47. The papal curia of the Renaissance period is where the office of *advocatus diaboli*, the "devil's advocate" (now known as the "promoter of the faith"), originated. For advocates at other ecclesiastical courts, see Brundage, *Canon Law*, 134–37.

[74] Kluge and Seebold, *Etymologisches Wörterbuch*, 18 (*Advokat*) and 962 (*Vogt*). *Vogt* appears in Old High German as early as the eighth century. *Advokat* first appears in Middle High German in the fourteenth century. See also Chapter 11.

[75] What follows is only a brief outline of the history of advocacy; I expand greatly on this narrative in the chapters that follow.

[76] West, "Significance," 187. For others who make this argument, see Chapter 1.

[77] The immunity will be discussed in Chapter 2. For an example of an immunity-based definition, see Kaminsky and Melton's entry for *Vogt, Vogtei* in the glossary of their translation of Brunner, *Land*, 367–68.

system.[78] Although some scholars have questioned the traditional picture of a sophisticated Carolingian government, this understanding of the Carolingian advocate has remained largely unchallenged since the late nineteenth century.

According to many historians, the collapse of the Carolingian empire and the subsequent political fragmentation led to significant changes in the role of the *advocatus*. For some, the Carolingian-style legal advocate faded into insignificance in the tenth century, or disappeared altogether; for others, advocates survived, but they gradually ceased to be holders of a legal office. As a result, historians sometimes insist on drawing a clear distinction between the Carolingian officeholding type of advocate and later advocates.[79] In this version of events, advocates began to behave more like lords from the tenth century onward: that is, like local power brokers who had seized for themselves rights that had been "public" under the Carolingians but that had become "privatized" – especially rights relating to the protection of churches and the carrying out of justice over churches' dependents.[80] In studies that seek to contextualize advocacy within a wider European framework, advocates are frequently compared to the castellans and seigneurial lords of rural France and the bailiffs and reeves of England.[81] As with these other types of local power holders, ecclesiastical authors often described the church advocates of the eleventh and twelfth centuries in decidedly critical terms – as robbers, plunderers and even tyrants who abused their positions for their own benefit.[82]

In the thirteenth century, as critiques of church advocates reached a crescendo, many ecclesiastical communities began to rid themselves

---

[78] Brunner, *Deutsche Rechtsgeschichte*, 2:308; Senn, *L'Institution*, 1; Hirsch, *Klosterimmunität*, 6; Dopsch, "Grundherrlichkeit," 42; Ganshof, *Frankish Institutions*, 48–50; Pitz, *Verfassungslehre*, 441.

[79] For the argument that Carolingian advocacy was a different phenomenon from later forms of advocacy, see, Aubin, *Entstehung*, 318; Waas, *Vogtei*, 1:44; Mayer, *Fürsten*, 4; and more recently McNair, "Governance," 203; West, "Significance," 204.

[80] The idea that protection and justice were "public" functions that became "private" when the Carolingian empire collapsed is central to many narratives about the rise of feudal lordship. In particular, the argument that "high justice," that is justice over crimes punishable by death (*Blutgerichtsbarkeit*), passed out of the hands of the king and his officials into the hands of others was central to many classic models of feudalism: Bloch, *Feudal Society*, 2:364–65; Below, *Deutsche Staat*, 259–61; Duby, "Evolution." See also Reuter, *Germany*, 219.

[81] Reuter, *Germany*, 230–31; Poly and Bournazel, *Feudal Transformation*, 34–39; West, *Reframing*, 253–54; more generally, Bisson, *Crisis*.

[82] Stieldorf, "Klöster"; Tebruck, "Kirchenvogtei"; Lyon, "Tyrants." For debates about violent lords more generally in this period, see McHaffie, "Law"; Brown, *Violence*, 99–132; Magnou-Nortier, "Enemies." See also the debate on the Feudal Revolution above and Chapters 4 and 7 below.

of their lordly advocates, either by purchasing advocacies and keeping them more tightly under their own control, or by supporting the acquisition of advocacies by increasingly powerful territorial rulers. Historians have referred to this latter process, namely princes' procurement of advocates' "private" rights of protection and justice over churches, as *Entvogtung*.[83] In this scholarly tradition, advocacies play a central role in the history of the rise of princely administrations because many ecclesiastical advocacies formed the cores of later princely territorial states.[84] Although church advocates did not disappear entirely during the fourteenth and fifteenth centuries, there is no question that there were far fewer than there had been in the twelfth century. For this reason, the vast majority of modern scholarship on church advocates concerns the period from roughly 1000 to 1250 rather than subsequent centuries.[85]

This does not mean that the position of *advocatus* ceased to be important after 1250, however. From the twelfth century onward, sources begin to provide glimpses of secular elites' attitudes toward the role of the advocate, allowing us to see the history of advocacy through a different lens than that of ecclesiastical sources. This evidence reveals that, from rulers and prominent nobles to local lords and even leading burghers, the position of advocate – and especially the opportunities for profit that came with it – was viewed in decidedly positive terms. In the centuries after 1250, a wide range of secular property holders gave the label *advocatus*, and increasingly its German equivalent *Vogt*, to various types of agents who worked for them and performed functions that in many ways paralleled the roles of church advocates as providers of protection and justice. The "territorial advocate" (*advocatus terrae, Landvogt*) and "urban advocate" (*advocatus civitatis, Stadtvogt*) are only two of the new positions that proliferated from the thirteenth century onward. Both medieval sources and modern historiography frequently describe these forms of advocacy as offices (*Ämter*) within the military and legal administrations of German principalities and towns.[86]

---

[83] For an overview of the history of the term *Entvogtung*, see Reichert, *Landesherrschaft*, 128–35.

[84] The connection between advocacy and the rise of territorial lordship is one of the bedrocks of German "constitutional history" (*Verfassungsgeschichte*): Waitz, *Deutsche Verfassungsgeschichte*, 7:320–21; Mayer, *Fürsten*, 276–301; Schlesinger, *Entstehung*, 203–8; Simon, *Grundherrschaft*, 41–42.

[85] I will discuss this scholarship in more detail in the chapters that follow. For a similar narrative to the one I have just provided, see Margue, "Klostervogtei," 383–89.

[86] Schubert, *Fürstliche Herrschaft*, 15; Moraw, *Verfassung*, 189–91; Brunner, *Land*, 255–58. Encyclopedia entries are the best place to find church advocates discussed alongside other types of advocates; see, for example, Schmidt, "Vogt, Vogtei." Some historians have argued that the countless people who appear over the centuries with the label *advocatus*

Thus, even if the terms *advocatus* and *Vogt* are not well known in English-language studies on the period from 750 to 1800, the narrative arc of the history of advocates outlined here is one that should look familiar to many readers. The people who appear in the surviving sources with the label "advocate" had official roles to play within the public legal institutions of the Carolingian empire, became private power holders and local troublemakers between the tenth and early thirteenth centuries and then gradually became integrated into the burgeoning princely administrations from the late thirteenth century onward. As I will argue in the pages that follow, each of the various elements of this grand narrative is in need of significant reassessment. To analyze, across a millennium, individual advocates' roles in providing protection and exercising justice is to understand how local elites could – time and again – find creative means to benefit from other people's property and dependents in ways that defy easy categorization and resist our standard histories.

Plan of the Book

My argument unfolds chronologically across the first fourteen chapters. Chapters 1 to 4 cover the period from roughly 750 to 1050, Chapters 5 to 10 the period 1050 to 1250 and Chapters 11 to 14 the period 1250 to 1800. The fifteenth and final chapter offers a wide-ranging assessment of the cultural significance of advocacy across European history. I will introduce the types of sources that are central to my arguments as they become important in the various chapters. Similarly, the shifting geography of advocacy over time will be explained as those shifts become significant. Regardless of time period, place and source material, my focus throughout the following pages will center, as much as possible, on the agency of the individual actors – advocates, ecclesiastics, rulers, princes, burghers and peasants – who were drawn into the often-violent competition over the profits to be had from providing protection and exercising justice.

shared little if anything in common: Aubin, *Entstehung*, 320; Clauss, *Untervogtei*, 18–19; Wood, *Proprietary Church*, 328. Claiming that all advocates were different has tended to justify local studies and microhistories rather than broader, synthetic arguments; on this point, see also Heilmann, *Klostervogtei*, 14–15; Stengel, "Zur Geschichte," 121–22. My arguments here directly challenge this assumption of difference.

1   The First "Medieval" Advocates

On June 20, 751, the mayor of the palace and future Frankish King Pippin III presided over the resolution of a dispute between two religious communities. The original parchment charter preserving the settlement reports that Abbot Fulrad of St. Denis came before Pippin at a palace near Reims to bring suit against a man named Legitemus, the advocate (*advocatus*) of Abbess Ragana of Sept-Meules. Fulrad claimed that Ragana and her convent's agents unjustly held properties that rightfully belonged to St. Denis, and the abbot presented Pippin with a document confirming the properties had previously been given to his monastery. But Legitemus had also brought a document with him to court; his stated that the property had previously been granted to the convent of Sept-Meules. Pippin inquired about the veracity of the competing claims, and when pressed, Legitemus conceded that he had nothing that could disprove the truth of Fulrad's document. The mayor of the palace and the members of his court then found in favor of St. Denis. They decreed that Fulrad and his successors should hold the properties by unchallengeable right against Abbess Ragana and the convent's agents, against Legitemus and against all their successors.[1]

When we set aside all the documents that modern scholars have identified as forgeries, and then go one step further and also set aside seemingly authentic documents that only survive in later copies, leaving us to rely on the small corpus of original documents that historians accept as genuine, then Legitemus is the first post-Roman *advocatus* we know by name. There are a few texts, mostly ninth-century narrative sources and copies of documents preserved in later cartularies, that allow us to identify

---

[1] DD Arnulf., 48–50, no. 22; Sonzogni, *Actes*, 135–36, no. 86; *Chartae Latinae Antiquiores*, 15:12–13, no. 597. See also Peters, *Entwicklung*, 41, 146–47; Stoclet, "Evindicatio," 126. Because the language of dispute settlement documents of this sort (*placita*) is formulaic, the repeated appearances of certain words in these documents are important for my argument. I translate the verb *interpellare* here and elsewhere as "to bring suit against"; *in presente adistabat* as "present at court"; *agentes* as "agents"; and *habiat evindicatas adque elidiatas* as "should hold by unchallengeable right." For this last translation, I follow Fouracre, "Placita," 29, 245.

with at least some confidence a small number of people labeled advocates during the first half of the eighth century.[2] But this source material is meager at best, and it permits few if any firm conclusions about the development of the role of the *advocatus* after the collapse of Roman imperial authority in Western Europe. With Legitemus, the advocate seems to appear almost Athena-like on the scene, bursting forth fully formed from some unseen head, requiring no introduction to his contemporaries. Who was Legitemus? Unfortunately, his biography is impossible to reconstruct. No other sources for him survive, leaving us entirely dependent on what this one document reveals.[3] The most that can be said is that, as *advocatus* for Abbess Ragana, he was present at Pippin's court to respond to the legal suit initiated by Abbot Fulrad, offered evidence in support of the abbess's property claims, and after losing the case was included in the list of people against whom the decision had been made.

As to the questions of whether this was a common role for Legitemus to play or a singular act; whether he had other responsibilities at Sept-Meules or elsewhere; or whether there was more to his position of advocate than what this text describes – none of this can be known. Despite these difficulties, I begin with Legitemus, because we must focus on the people who are explicitly labeled advocates in our sources if we are to understand advocacy's central role in the long European history of corrupt practices of protection and justice.

Rewriting the Early History of Church Advocates

Standard accounts of church advocacy do not start with (or even mention) Legitemus. Most prefer to open the story by looking back to the fifth-century Roman empire, when both church councils and Roman law addressed the problem of ecclesiastics becoming distracted by secular affairs by insisting that they be represented by advocates or defenders.[4] From there, it is a relatively short leap to the appearance of the term *advocatus* at a church

---

[2] See the section "Advocates at Work" in this chapter. My methodology throughout this book is to rely on evidence from original documents whenever possible. I use later copies of documents when the general scholarly consensus is that they are authentic. The reason for this cautious approach, as I will discuss in later chapters, is that forgeries are a significant issue in the history of advocates. Monks and nuns – and by the fourteenth century, nobles as well – routinely forged and manipulated documents in their efforts to alter advocatial rights.

[3] This is his only appearance in Hennebicque-Le Jan, "Prosopographica," 258, no. 200. This is also the only entry for a "Legitemus" in the "Nomen et Gens" database.

[4] See the Introduction for more on this point. Works that begin the history of church advocacy with its Roman roots include Brunner, *Deutsche Rechtsgeschichte*, 2:302–11; Senn, *L'Institution*, 3–4; Starflinger, *Entwickelung*, 7–8; Waas, *Vogtei*, 1:27–28; Naz, "Avouerie, Avoué"; Schmidt, "Vogt, Vogtei," 1811; Willoweit, "Vogt, Vogtei," 933;

council held between 673 and 675 at Saint-Jean-de-Losne in Burgundy; in the presence of the Merovingian Frankish King Childeric II, the council decreed "That no bishop should conduct lawsuits except through an advocate (*per advocatum*), lest he be seen to grow angry while he labors to attend to the commotions of lawsuits."[5] Although this would suggest that there must have been many Frankish advocates before Legitemus, no one appears with the label *advocatus* in other surviving sources from sixth- and seventh-century Francia. Whether this church council reflected or shaped legal practice under the Merovingian rulers is therefore unclear. More generally, the scant surviving evidence does not point to the institutional framework of Late Antique Roman advocacy persisting after 500 CE north of the Alps.[6] To be sure, ancient Roman legal traditions unquestionably influenced the later position of the advocate – not, however, in the ways that most historians have assumed.

Because there are so few sources for advocates before the mid-eighth century, many scholars argue that Charlemagne (768–814) was the first to establish church advocacy as a stable institution, through his efforts to implement wide-ranging judicial and administrative reforms across his empire.[7] In making this claim, historians rely less on the sources for individual advocates' activities during his reign than on the many capitularies (royal legislation) Charlemagne issued that reference advocates.[8] One, from around 789, is the earliest capitulary for the Frankish lands as a whole to mention advocates, listing them alongside a range of other

Clauss, *Untervogtei*, 1–2. Other scholars have linked the origins of the Carolingian advocate more directly to ecclesiastical immunity; for this argument, see Chapter 2. I know of no evidence to support the argument that advocacy also had its roots in Germanic traditions of *Schutzherrschaft* or *Muntherrschaft*: cf. Störmer, *Früher Adel*, 2:424–25; Willoweit, "Römische," 21. Also unconvincing is Pitz, *Verfassungslehre*, 441.

[5] *Concilia Galliae*, 314–17; here, 315, chap. 3. See also Wood, *Merovingian Kingdoms*, 224–29.

[6] Willoweit, "Römische," 31–32. He and others cite Marculf's Formulary – which has been dated to the late seventh century – as additional early evidence because one entry includes the word *advocatus*: *Marculfi Formulae*, 66, chap. 36. However, the earliest manuscripts with this text date from the Carolingian period – after the legal role of the *advocatus* had become more commonplace. For the difficulties of relying on this formulary, see Rio, *Legal Practice*, 59; Brown, "Laypeople," 128–33; West, "Significance," 188. Even the canons of the council at Saint-Jean-de-Losne only survive in one ninth-century manuscript, and there is little indication that the council was important for the subsequent history of canon law.

[7] Mayer, *Fürsten*, 4; Ganshof, *Frankish Institutions*, 48–49; Willoweit, "Vogt, Vogtei," 933. Cf. Dopsch, "Grundherrlichkeit," 19–20. For a more cautious assessment of arguments about the innovative nature of Charlemagne's administration, see Costambeys, Innes and MacLean, *Carolingian World*, 191.

[8] Older scholarship that relies almost entirely on the capitulary evidence to make institutional arguments about advocates includes Waitz, *Deutsche Verfassungsgeschichte*, 4:392–400; Senn, *L'Institution*, 11–84; Ganshof, *Frankish Institutions*, 48–50. For more recent perspectives on the use (and misuse) of capitulary evidence, see McKitterick, *Charlemagne*, 233–37; Costambeys, Innes and MacLean, *Carolingian World*, 182–89.

categories of people expected to appear at judicial assemblies.[9] According to the general capitulary of 802, "bishops, abbots and abbesses should have advocates," and advocates are included among those who should "know the law and love justice" and benefit the Church.[10] Another capitulary from 809 explains that advocates, judges and other judicial figures are to be "of a very good sort ... [who] fear God, and they should be appointed to exercise their ministries."[11] This and comparable language has led many scholars to argue that the position of advocate was, by the early ninth century, a public office in the newly developing Carolingian administration.[12]

While Charlemagne's capitularies are central to arguments about early advocates, the clearest description of the role dates from a few years after his death. One of the canons issued by a papal synod in Rome in 826, entitled "That bishops and all priests should have advocates," decrees:

> Because bishops and all priests are placed in office for the sole purpose of praising God and his good works, each of them therefore should have an advocate, both for ecclesiastical lawsuits and for their own, excepting of course public crime – an advocate not suspected of a bad reputation but found to be of good opinion and praiseworthy skill – lest, while they are attending to human profits, they lose their eternal rewards.[13]

Lucid and concise, the language of this canon strongly suggests that the origins of church advocacy are to be found in prohibitions against ecclesiastics representing themselves before secular courts.[14] The advocate of the Carolingian period thus looks to have had a similar role to that of the ancient Roman advocate – or the modern lawyer or barrister.[15]

---

[9] Capit. 1:67, no. 25, chap. 4. I follow Davis, *Practice*, 288 for the date. There is no reference to advocates in the 789 *Admonitio generalis*, and the early capitularies for Saxony are also silent on the subject.

[10] Capit. 1:93, no. 33, chap. 13: "Ut episcopi, abbates adque abbatissae advocatos ... legem scientes et iustitiam diligentes ... habeant." This is one of the most oft-cited capitularies about advocates: Mayer, *Fürsten*, 4; West, "Significance," 187; Willoweit, "Römische," 33–34. For a reassessment of this capitulary: Davis, *Practice*, 132, 352–54.

[11] Capit. 1:149, no. 61, chap. 11: "ad sua ministeria exercenda."

[12] See, for example, Senn, *L'Institution*, 1; Mayer, *Fürsten*, 4; Ganshof, *Frankish Institutions*, 48–49. For the language of "ministry," see Esders, "Amt und Bann," 263; Davis, *Practice*, 118–27; Sassier, *Royauté*, 143–47; West, "Significance," 206; Zotz, "Amt und Würden," 12–14; Störmer, *Früher Adel*, 2:426. See also *Mediae Latinitatis Lexicon Minus*, 895, which translates *ministerium* as "public office," citing this capitulary. For my uneasiness with this translation, see p. 40.

[13] Conc. 2.2:575, no. 46, chap. 19. The next canon of the council's proceedings continues on this theme: "Concerning those who are unable to find advocates" (575–76, chap. 20). See also Conc. 2.1:264, no. 36, chap. 12.

[14] For modern definitions of the *advocatus* influenced by this language, see Brown, *Unjust Seizure*, 75, n. 6; Clauss, *Untervogtei*, 2.

[15] Brundage, *Medieval Origins*, 62 (though he notes that not all early advocates can be characterized in this way).

Capitularies, canons of church councils and other prescriptive texts tell only part of the story, however. They are statements of top-down ideals rather than descriptions of practice and local conditions. This is not to diminish the significance of these sources for the perspectives they provide on advocates. Nevertheless, it is problematic to rely on them as heavily as much older scholarship has. Because these sources have been the foundation for the modern study of advocacy since the late nineteenth and early twentieth centuries, the standard account of the Frankish *advocatus* is one that rarely – if ever – mentions any advocates by name.[16] This historiographical tradition stands in sharp contrast to much of the scholarship on the period 1000 to 1250, where advocacy is frequently discussed in the context of individual advocates, their familial connections and their local authority.[17] Most work on advocates thus leaves the impression that Carolingian advocacy was an impersonal, quasi-bureaucratic legal institution that had nothing in common with the more intimate, individualized, "lordly" advocacy of later centuries. But this impression is false.

We need only take a closer look at Pippin III's 751 charter to see that the decrees of prescriptive texts do not always reflect legal and social practices on the ground. While this document unquestionably describes Legitemus acting as Abbess Ragana's legal representative in a property dispute, it also describes the winner of the suit, Abbot Fulrad of St. Denis, representing himself. Fulrad had almost certainly been chosen as abbot by Pippin himself because of his early support for the mayor of the palace, and he was a much more prominent figure in Frankish court politics during the early 750s than the otherwise unknown Ragana and Legitemus.[18] As a result, the abbot's personal presence seems to have mattered more for the outcome of this case than the abbess's conformity to good legal form by using an advocate. In other words, once we introduce people into the equation, capitularies and the canons of church councils start to lose some of their seemingly authoritative status.

---

[16] See, for example, Senn, *L'Institution*; Waas, *Vogtei*; Mayer, *Fürsten*. While more recent scholarship is better in this regard, attempts to reconstruct the biographies of individual advocates remain rare. One of the few exceptions is Dohrmann, *Vögte*.

[17] See especially Chapters 5 and 6.

[18] Fulrad would serve as court chaplain for more than thirty years under Pippin and his sons Carloman and Charlemagne: Semmler, "Verdient"; Semmler, "Saint-Denis," 94–97; Stoclet, "Fulrad"; Peters, *Entwicklung*, 46–63. In contrast, nothing is known about the Amalbert who is identified as abbot of St. Denis in 748: Semmler, "Saint-Denis," 93–94. Nor do we know anything about the abbess Ragana of Sept-Meules named in the 751 document; no other source provides any information about the convent of Sept-Meules, which would be destroyed by Vikings: Verdon, "Recherches," 57.

Other types of sources, too, hint at the gap between prescriptive texts and local practices. According to a miracle story told by the monk Adrevald of Fleury (Saint-Benoît-sur-Loire) around 870, a dispute arose in the 830s between Fleury's *advocatus* Eptagius and the advocate of another (unnamed) monastery over a large number of dependents.[19] The advocate of the other monastery went to the local royal agent and "corrupting him with money, bent him from the law of equity."[20] On the day when the lawsuit was to be decided by this royal agent, the abbot of Fleury sent two monks to him, along with two heavy silver vessels as "gifts" (*dona*). But because the royal agent had already been corrupted by the other advocate's bribe, he spurned the monks of Fleury and told them to go back to their monastery, because none of the dependents would be given to them. Immediately thereafter, however, he was tossed from his horse and badly injured; three days later, he died. Adrevald ends the story by noting, "Then, the advocate of Fleury ... brought the suit to the judges, and after receiving the dependents by their legal judgment, he returned home."[21] Regardless of whether or not bribing royal agents was a normal part of the job for Carolingian advocates, this story demonstrates the dangers of assuming that justice functioned according to a formal, institutional framework in eighth- or ninth-century Francia.[22] If we focus on what advocates did, not what they were supposed to do, they begin to look less like bureaucratic officeholders and more like wrestlers over local resources.

Advocates at Work

The 751 charter that names Legitemus was preserved in the archive of the religious community of St. Denis, one of the most important repositories of early Frankish documents in Western Europe.[23] Because of this monastery's close ties to the Frankish rulers from the seventh century onward, many extant records for judicial proceedings at the Merovingian and early

---

[19] *Miracula Sancti Benedicti*, 152–55, I.24. For this source, see Vidier, *L'Historiographie*, 151–64. For this miracle, see Depreux, "Ausprägungen," 362–63; Nelson, "Dispute Settlement," 45. For other references to advocates at Fleury in this period: Prou and Vidier, eds., *Recueil*, 78–79, no. 28 and 83–85, no. 30.

[20] *Miracula Sancti Benedicti*, 152, I.24. "datoque munere corrumpens, ab aequitatis jure deflexit."

[21] Ibid., 154, I.24. Other stories told by Adrevald also mentions advocates: ibid., 154–55, I.25 and 184–85, I.38. See also Head, *Hagiography*, 138–52.

[22] Fouracre, "Carolingian Justice," esp. 800; Esders, "Amt und Bann," 296–97. For a Carolingian-era story of someone trying to bribe an advocate, see Ratpert, *Casus*, 156, chap. 2.

[23] For the significance of the St. Denis archive, see Fouracre, "Placita"; Ganz and Goffart, "Charters"; Brühl, *Studien*, 137–201.

Carolingian courts survive in the rich corpus of texts that was housed there. Unsurprisingly, therefore, two additional early pieces of evidence for the term *advocatus* can also be found in this collection. The first is a document from 748, which scholars judge to be authentic, though the earliest surviving copy is from the thirteenth century. According to it, Pippin III was hearing cases when a woman named Christiana brought suit against "a certain man by the name of Hrodgarius, advocate of St. Denis, and against Abbot Amalbert," claiming that St. Denis unjustly held an estate in a certain village.[24] The second charter, this one an original, is from 759, when Pippin was ruling Francia as king. It reports that two advocates of St. Denis, named Aderulfus and Rodegarius, came before Pippin and brought suit against a count over who had the right to collect a toll in Paris.[25]

These three documents involving Pippin and St. Denis offer the best entry point to the history of the term *advocatus* in the Frankish world because no comparable cluster of evidence from previous decades survives.[26] Given that the reference to an advocate in the 748 text is the first appearance of an advocate anywhere in the extant corpus of authentic texts from St. Denis – which includes documents from the preceding century – comparable sources from earlier years may never have existed at this monastery.[27] Thus, the early Carolingian court is most likely to be the place where the position of advocate first gained a foothold in Europe.[28] Considering this, it is worth noting that the St. Denis advocate "Hrodgarius" of the 748 text may well be the same person as the advocate "Rodegarius" of the 759 document, and this may also be the same person as the "Rotgarius" who appears as one of Pippin's faithful followers (*fideles*) in a dispute settlement from 752 concerning St. Denis property.[29] If these are all the same person, then the first known advocate

---

[24] DD Arnulf., 41–42, no. 18; Sonzogni, *Actes*, 130–31, no. 83.
[25] DD Karol. I, 17–18, no. 12; Sonzogni, *Actes*, 153–55, no. 98; *Chartae Latinae Antiquiores*, 26–29, no. 600.
[26] To this cluster of evidence from Pippin III's reign can also be added Conc. 2.1:62, no. 11, a document from the year 757 for the monastery of Gorze (but preserved in a twelfth-century cartulary). The list of subscribers includes a "Rothingo advocato."
[27] Peters, *Entwicklung*, 144. The only two Merovingian royal charters to reference advocates are both known to be later forgeries: DD Merov., 1:158–62, no. 64 and 1:173–77, no. 69.
[28] I am confident that this statement holds for Europe north of the Alps. The use of the term *advocatus* in Italy is a complicated issue, which I will discuss in Chapters 2–4. In general, however, the term *defensor*, not *advocatus*, was used in early medieval Italy for those who oversaw churches' legal rights at the local level: Noble, *Republic*, 217, 222; Fischer, "Entwicklung." I have not found evidence in the *Codice diplomatico Longobardo* to suggest that advocates were common in the Lombard kingdom prior to Charlemagne's conquest; on this point, see also Albertoni, "Evangelium," 329.
[29] DD Karol. I, 3–4, no. 1.

for St. Denis was someone with a close relationship to the first Carolingian king.[30]

Two other references to named advocates in the first half of the eighth century would seem to support this argument for the centrality of the early Carolingian court to the history of advocacy. Both concern Pippin's father, Charles Martel. The *Chronicle of the Abbots of Fontenelle* (St. Wandrille) reports that in 723, "Abbot Benignus obtained a judgment in his favor against Count Bertharius concerning an estate ... before the mayor of the palace Charles, with his advocate Rotbert mediating."[31] Three years later, in 726, Charles Martel issued a privilege recording his gift of an estate to Willibrord – abbot of Echternach, missionary bishop to Frisia and future saint – for the church in Utrecht. The men who gave their mark to confirm the gift included Erkanfridus, "who was the bishop's advocate and received this document in his own hand with his lord."[32] Both of these texts are problematic; the *Chronicle of the Abbots of Fontenelle* was written in the ninth century, and the 726 charter only survives in manuscripts copied in later centuries. As a result, the fact that the word *advocatus* appears in these two sources may be attributable to scribal interventions made later on, during periods when advocacy was more commonplace.[33] However, if we choose to accept this evidence as reliable, then the courts of the father–son Carolingian mayors of the palace, Charles Martel and Pippin III, emerge as the focal point of the early history of church advocates.

This is plausible, given the accepted narrative of the rise of the Carolingians. Both Charles Martel and Pippin III pursued strategies designed to bring bishoprics and monasteries – and their ecclesiastical properties – under their influence. This proved to be an effective way for them to strengthen their own positions while simultaneously weakening support for the Merovingian rulers.[34] That St. Denis plays a prominent

---

[30] Hennebicque-Le Jan, "Prosopographica," 255, no. 172, where all three are identified as the same person.

[31] Pradié, ed., *Chronique*, 54, III.5.

[32] DD Arnulf., 30–32, no. 13: "qui advocatus fuit episcopi et hanc traditionem manu propria cum domno suo recepit."

[33] The *Chronicle of the Abbots of Fontenelle* is usually dated to the mid-ninth century, but many scholars regard it as a reliable source for earlier years because its author used now-lost archival material: Fouracre, *Charles Martel*, 141; Wood, *Merovingian Kingdoms*, 214 and 277–78. The earliest surviving copies of the 726 charter are in eleventh- and twelfth-century cartularies. Interestingly, this Erkanfridus is identified as a count in two of the surviving copies of the text, which suggests he may have been of high status; see also West, "Significance," 188, n. 9; Ebling, *Prosopographie*, 136–37, no. 155.

[34] Nelson, "Kingship," 388–90; Costambeys, Innes and MacLean, *Carolingian World*, 39; Fouracre, *Charles Martel*, 121–54; Reuter, "Kirchenreform," 43–51; Dierkens, "Carolus," 291–93.

role in this early cluster of evidence for advocates is especially significant, because Pippin's control of this monastery proved important during his *coup d'état* against the last Merovingian king in 751.[35] Viewed from this perspective, it is the property disputes at the heart of the 748, 751 and 759 documents, not theological and legal concerns about ecclesiastics attending secular courts, that become the key to understanding the earliest references to named advocates.

Here, it is worth recalling that Pippin's 751 charter decrees that St. Denis should hold the disputed properties by unchallengeable right against not only Abbess Ragana *but also* Legitemus. In similar fashion, his 748 document, after finding against the woman who brought the suit, states that the St. Denis advocate "Hrodgarius should hold the [disputed] estate … for all time by unchallengeable right … against Christiana on behalf of St. Denis."[36] Both texts suggest that these advocates were not simply ad hoc legal representatives at court; they also had ties to the properties in these lawsuits. The first church advocates thus step out from the shadows as people who were personally invested in the competition over property rights at the local level. Given the enormous amount of property held by many ecclesiastical communities throughout the period from 750 to 1800, this early connection between advocates and religious houses' property regimes is essential for understanding advocacy's existence across a millennium of European history.[37]

The privilege issued by King Pippin in 759 also situates early advocates within the context of local ecclesiastical rights – but in ways that hint at more complex roles. The two men who are identified as the advocates of St. Denis in this text, Aderulfus and Rodegarius, are initially labeled as "agents" (*agentes*) of St. Denis when they are described as coming before King Pippin to bring suit against the count. According to the document, Aderulfus and Rodegarius claimed that the disputed toll in Paris had always been collected by agents of St. Denis, but the count replied that his predecessors had always possessed this toll. The two men then presented a Merovingian royal privilege that confirmed the monastery's possession of the toll. Still, the count refused to relent. The hearing was therefore adjourned until a few days later, when the aforesaid "envoys and advocates (*missi et advocati*) of St. Denis, Aderulfus and Rodegarius,"

---

[35] Charles Martel had already established close ties to St. Denis when consolidating his authority in the area around Paris. He defended its property rights, chose to be buried there and had his son Pippin raised there: Semmler, "Saint-Denis," 93; Peters, *Entwicklung*, 46; Stoclet, "Evindicatio," 132–34.

[36] DD Arnulf., 41–42, no. 18.

[37] For the extensive landholdings of ecclesiastical institutions in this period, see Morris, "Problems"; Herlihy, "Church Property"; De Jong, "Carolingian Monasticism."

came before the king and presented witnesses, who confirmed that the toll belonged to St. Denis. At this point, members of Pippin's court found in favor of St. Denis and its advocates (*advocati*).[38]

All of this suggests that the term *advocatus* was related to other labels for local actors involved in competitions and disputes over property rights. Unlike *advocatus*, however, the two terms *agentes* and *missi* both appear regularly in Frankish documents from before 748. In a privilege issued in the name of King Chlothar III (657–673), for example, agents from St. Denis came to the royal court and alleged that a bishop held properties that rightfully belonged to the monastery.[39] An original charter from the reign of King Childebert III (695–711) describes how the abbot of another monastery went to court to complain that Drogo – the son of the mayor of the palace, Pippin II – had seized a property belonging to that monastery. It reports that "the agents for the aforesaid Drogo had wrongfully taken control [of the property] away from [the abbot] and his monastery, and after that, they had devastated it and despoiled it of its dependents, money and many other advantages." Later, when describing the restitution Drogo was required to pay, the document states that Drogo ought to restore the property's "fruits, that is the vines, grain and profits, which his envoys had damaged there."[40] Here, *agentes* and *missi* are synonymous, as in Pippin III's 759 charter. This raises the possibility that the St. Denis advocates Aderulfus and Rodegarius were also the agents responsible for collecting the disputed toll mentioned in the document. If so, some of the first named advocates were already connected to churches' local rights and economic interests in ways that would persist in many places into the eighteenth century.[41]

In light of this evidence, it is clear that St. Paul's concerns about God's soldiers becoming involved in secular affairs, and Late Antique decrees

[38] DD Karol. I, 17–18, no. 12. For the context of this dispute: Fouracre, *Charles Martel*, 163–65.
[39] DD Merov., 1:243–46, no. 95. See also 1:200–02, no. 79; 1:239–41, no. 93; and 1:391–93, no. 157. For another similar term, *actores*, see 1:227–29, no. 88. See also Fouracre, "Placita."
[40] DD Merov., 1:374–76, no. 149. See also 1:346–48, no. 137 (translated in Fouracre, "Placita," 27). See also Semmler, "Saint-Denis," 119; Fouracre, *Charles Martel*, 50; Wood, *Merovingian Kingdoms*, 262–63. Also interesting in this context is an episcopal charter from 693: Weidemann, *Geschichte*, 2:220–21, no. 12. The chronicler Flodoard of Reims (d. 966), in various stories he tells about the seventh century, refers to the bishops of Reims as having *agentes* and *actores*: Flodoard of Reims, *Historia*, 154–55, II.10 (*agentes*) and 145, II.5 and 169, II.17 (*actores*). He first mentions advocates under Bishop Wulfar (803–816): 172, II.18.
[41] While other scholars have also drawn the connection between *advocatus* and these other terms (West, "Significance," 188; Willoweit, "Vogt, Vogtei," 933), it is important to note that *advocatus* seems to replace the other ones – at least in the context of churches' legal disputes about property – during the early decades of the ninth century.

that ecclesiastics avoid secular courts, cannot fully explain the activities of these earliest church advocates. Factors more firmly rooted in local practices of authority in the early Carolingian empire also played important roles in these activities.

These practical dimensions of the advocatial position are even more pronounced in one of the first of Charlemagne's charters to reference an advocate. In 781, "the advocate of St. Denis and Abbot Fulrad, named Ado," attended a judicial assembly (*mallus publicus*), presided over by a count, in order to bring suit against several people whom he claimed were in possession of a piece of property that rightfully belonged to St. Denis. After winning the suit and receiving a document from the count confirming that St. Denis held the property by unchallengeable right, the advocate Ado traveled to Charlemagne's court, where the count confirmed his decision in the king's presence.[42] Charlemagne then ordered that "the advocate of St. Denis should hold by unchallengeable right for all time [the disputed property] on behalf of St. Denis against the aforesaid men."

Two points are worth emphasizing about this charter, one specific and one general. By 781, Fulrad of St. Denis had been active in Carolingian politics for more than thirty years. The aged abbot, who had represented himself in multiple lawsuits involving St. Denis property in earlier years, may no longer have been healthy enough to attend both a comital court and Charlemagne's court over a single property dispute.[43] If this is the case, then the advocate Ado was a proxy for an ecclesiastic who was unable for physical reasons (not religious ones) to manage a lawsuit himself. Fulrad chose to use an advocate who presumably had more time and energy to pursue the suit vigorously – Ado's incentive apparently being that, if he won the case, he would be the one to hold the disputed property on behalf of St. Denis.[44]

The specific details of this case point to a general trend as well. The reference to a count's judicial assembly in the charter calls attention to the

---

[42] Charlemagne then issued the document that preserves all of these details (though it only survives in a later copy): DD Karol. I, 188–89, no. 138.

[43] Stoclet, "Evindicatio," 127–28.

[44] Two of Charlemagne's charters from the year 775 are additional evidence along these lines. In the first, Abbot Fulrad of St. Denis and the bishop of Paris went to the royal court because of a dispute, but there is no mention of advocates: DD Karol. I, 146–47, no. 102. In the second, the monastery of Honau's advocate and two advocates of the monastery of Corbie came before Charlemagne to settle a property dispute: DD Karol. I, 155–56, no. 110. It is unclear why the churchmen used advocates in the second case but not the first. For more on the first charter: Fouracre, "Carolingian Justice," 793–94; Davis, "Settlement," 163–64. At the end of the second charter, Charlemagne sides with Honau "*contra supradictum Agiserium et Aldradum* [the two advocates of Corbie] *eorumque heredes.*" See Levillain, *Examen*, 84, for an interpretation of this clause.

increasing significance of judicial assemblies at the regional level in the late eighth century.[45] As Charlemagne expanded the administrative reach of his rule throughout his territories, these comital courts – as well as courts presided over by his itinerant representatives (often a count and a bishop) – became key sites for handling property disputes and other lawsuits. Sources from this period and the early ninth century routinely describe advocates as being present at these assemblies across the Carolingian empire.[46] One reason for advocates' active roles at these court gatherings must be that an abbot, abbess or bishop could not possibly have attended every regional judicial assembly where their church held estates while also fulfilling the myriad of other responsibilities that came with their role. As a result, some of the people who were already responsible for local oversight of church properties, *agentes* and *missi*, were given a new label – *advocatus* – to designate them as the legal proxy at court and the principal preserver of property rights at the local level.

By conceiving of advocates in these practical terms, the capitulary evidence that has for so long been the centerpiece of the histories of Frankish advocates can be read in a different light. For example, one of Charlemagne's earliest capitularies for Italy from the early-to-mid-780s, following his successful conquest of the Lombard kingdom, includes the chapter: "Wherever a bishop has property, he should have an advocate in that county, who should give and receive justice without delay."[47] Three decades later, a capitulary issued at Aachen at the close of Charlemagne's reign begins by stating "that bishops and abbots should have advocates, and they [the advocates] should have their own property in that county."[48] The emphasis in both of these prescriptive texts is on the

---

[45] For the different types of judicial authority in this period, see Davis, *Practice*, 50–51. The increasing number of references to the regional *mallus publicus* corresponds to a decline, starting in the same period, in the number of dispute settlement documents (*placita*) issued in the name of the Carolingian rulers at their courts: Kölzer, *Kaiser Ludwig*, 26–27; Dickau, "Studien," 12–14; Stieldorf, "Verschwinden," 1–4.

[46] The rich archive of the bishopric of Lucca in northern Italy preserves a document that mentions an *advocatus* appearing in 785 at an assembly presided over by a duke: *I placiti*, 14–18, no. 6. This text includes (admittedly formulaic) dialogue between the disputants, a characteristic much more typical of Italian documents than those from north of the Alps. Other evidence from before 800 for advocates being involved in ecclesiastics' legal disputes includes Poupardin, ed., *Recueil*, 35–36, no. 22. and Conc. 2.1:167, chap. 8.

[47] Capit. 1:192, no. 91, chap. 6: "ubicumque pontifex substantiam habuerit, advocatum [h]abeat in ipsu comitatu, qui absque tarditate iustitias faciat et suscipiat." These early Italian capitularies frequently prefigured later capitularies intended for the Frankish empire more broadly: Davis, *Practice*, 281. For the dating of the early capitularies, see ibid., 288. See also: McKitterick, "Charlemagne's *Missi*," 256.

[48] Capit. 1:172, no. 77, chap. 14. See also Davis, *Practice*, 53; Fouracre, "Carolingian Justice," 792.

advocate as an agent who was readily available to oversee a church's local legal interests.[49]

Significantly, these local agents came to represent not just ecclesiastics but also laywomen, counts and even kings during the late eighth and ninth centuries.[50] An early capitulary for Italy, probably issued in 781, includes the statement: "the count, or his advocate, should be able to confirm through an oath that he will not be negligent in the conduct of justice."[51] This decree finds confirmation in a small number of charters where counts are represented by advocates in disputes.[52] Another Italian capitulary, this one from the early ninth century, reads, "Our vassals in our ministries should have respect and full justice, as is fitting, and if they are unable to be present, they should have their advocates, who should be able to defend their properties before the count and render justice, whatever the complaint against them."[53] And according to a text from 863 concerning a dispute over a monastery between a West Frankish bishop and King Charles the Bald (d. 877), "The bishop's advocate, Haldricus, brought suit [at the king's court] against the king's advocate, Wido."[54] All of this is additional evidence that religious prohibitions against ecclesiastics attending secular courts were not the principal reason why advocates began to appear in greater numbers over the course of the Carolingian period. Prominent landholders, both religious and secular, needed someone who was familiar with and able to defend their legal rights at the local level, since they could not be everywhere at once.

[49] The necessity of a readily available advocate to attend judicial assemblies may be the reason why an 825 capitulary allows bishops, abbots and abbesses to have two advocates, who were freed from military service as long as they held their *advocatio* (Capit. 1:326, no. 163, chap. 4).

[50] For laywomen, who sometimes have advocates when granting property, see for example UB St. Gall, 1:257–58, no. 273; 1:293–94, no. 317; and 1:354–55, no. 380; Tr. Freising, 1:412, no. 481 and 1:439, no. 515. See also West, "Significance," 187, n. 2.

[51] Capit. 1:190, no. 90, chap. 3. For this capitulary, see Davis, *Practice*, 281–82.

[52] See, for example Prou and Vidier, eds., *Recueil*, 28–30, nos. 12–13. In 822, Emperor Louis the Pious decreed that the losing side in a case was to return the disputed properties "to Count Matfrid or his advocate (*vel eius advocato*)": *Formulae Imperiales*, 321–22, no. 46. This Matfrid was acting as abbot for St. Lifard (Meung-sur-Loire) at the time, and the advocate is also identified in the text as the monastery's *advocatus*, suggesting that a count, in his capacity as lay abbot, might employ an advocate. See also Felten, *Äbte*, 287.

[53] Capit. 1:210, no. 102, chap. 10. For advocates in the capitularies for Italy, see also Albertoni, "Evangelium."

[54] Tessier, ed., *Recueil*, 2:81–86, no. 258. An *advocatus* for the monastery of St. Denis appeared at Charles the Bald's court in 868 when bringing suit; in that year, Charles the Bald was lay abbot for St. Denis and held the monastery under his direct control: ibid., 2:192–96, no. 314. See also Nelson, *Charles the Bald*, 214; Peters, *Entwicklung*, 195–201. In a charter of Emperor Louis II concerning ownership of the wife of one of Louis's *servi*, "our *vassus* Roteri was advocate on our behalf": DD Lu II, 71–72, no. 3.

None of this means that we should simply ignore ecclesiastical decrees about advocates representing religious at secular courts. There was unquestionably a tradition in the Church, dating back to the fifth century, that insisted clerics should not represent themselves in secular lawsuits.[55] Into the twelfth and thirteenth centuries, some monastic authors would continue to argue that advocates had come into existence to handle legal matters that ecclesiastics should avoid. Moreover, throughout much of the period from the eighth to at least the fourteenth century, the volume of sources for church advocates far exceeds the evidence for secular advocates of any sort, a clear indication that the *advocatus* was most prevalent within the ecclesiastical context.[56] Nevertheless, arguments about the religious necessity of church advocates cannot, by themselves, explain the origins of advocacy. Neither Charlemagne nor other Frankish rulers prevented high ecclesiastics from attending secular courts or managing their own legal affairs.[57] Indeed, it is not until the 860s that we find the most forceful statement from within the Carolingian empire that bishops had to be represented by advocates at secular courts, and even this statement seems to have had little effect.[58] As a result, already with the first references to named advocates in the mid-eighth century, it is essential to recognize that the advocatial role was being shaped by practical demands as much as – if not more so than – religious ideals.

---

[55] A canon law collection from the time of Charlemagne includes a copy of the decree of the Council of Carthage concerning the use of advocates in ecclesiastical cases: *Collectio Dacheriana*, 541, II.75. See also Davis, *Practice*, 60–61.

[56] See subsequent chapters for more on these points.

[57] Davis, *Practice*, 62. For Carolingian era debates on ecclesiastics and secular courts: Heydemann, "*Nemo militans.*" In the capitularies, the rationale for advocates is occasionally framed in religious terms but never as explicitly as in the conciliar decrees. See, for example, Capit. 1:201, no. 95, chap. 3. On this capitulary chapter: Pitz, *Verfassungslehre*, 441. See also Capit. 1:196, no. 93, chap. 1.

[58] In 868, in several treatises known collectively as *Pro ecclesiae libertatum defensione*, Hincmar of Reims argued that a bishop could not be forced to appear personally before secular courts and insisted, here and elsewhere, on the use of ecclesiastical advocates; see, for example, Hincmar of Reims, *Quaterniones*, 1048a. However, neither Roman law nor canon law offered precedents that unequivocally supported his position: Schmitz, "Wucher," 553–54; West, "Significance," 189–92; Corcoran, "Hincmar"; McKeon, *Hincmar of Laon*, 24–27. One source Hincmar used was the canons of the 853 Roman synod: Hincmar of Reims, *De presbiteris criminosis*, 105, chap. 11. This synod repeated the 826 Roman synod's decree that all bishops and priests have advocates (see the previous section, "Rewriting the Early History of Church Advocates"). Archbishop Hincmar was an important figure in circulating the canons of the 853 synod within the Frankish world (where the canons of the 826 Roman synod had previously met with little response; see Noble, "Place," 446). All of this suggests that Hincmar was making a novel argument, at least from the perspective of the Carolingian empire, on the necessity of church advocates – more than a century after advocates first appear in Frankish sources.

Toward a History of "Wrassling Round"

The eighth-century sources that have been my focus to this point offer only tantalizing clues about who the first advocates were and what they did. By the early ninth century, however, it becomes possible to situate some advocates more convincingly into local networks of influence and authority.[59] The rich archival sources from Bavaria are especially valuable for this. In the opening decade of the ninth century, Charlemagne's representative in Bavaria, Archbishop Arn of Salzburg (785–821), presided over several dispute settlements, and the records of these disputes reference numerous advocates.[60] This material is vital for understanding how the people who are labeled *advocatus* in our sources fit into church property regimes and into the local competition for lands and rights.

One advocate, in particular, deserves close scrutiny. In June of 802, the archbishop was hearing cases when a woman and her brother brought suit against one of Bishop Atto of Freising's advocates, Kaganhart. The source preserving this dispute reports, "They said that his bishop unjustly possessed part of their paternal inheritance ... But Kaganhart gave this response: 'The property you seek was granted to us years ago by a distinguished man named [gap in manuscript], and for this reason we possess it in our share by right of our church.'"[61] Read in isolation, this text could be taken as an ideal example of what a Carolingian advocate was supposed to do. Although Bishop Atto of Freising is listed as a witness to this dispute settlement, his advocate represented him – we even have a record here of what he supposedly said on his behalf – and zealously

[59] Given that references to advocates start to appear in the 790s at the monasteries of St. Gall and Fulda and the bishopric of Freising, this seems to be the decade when the term first started to find its way into documents being written for local purposes in East Francia: UB St. Gall, 1:118–119, no. 126 and 1:132–133, no. 141; Tr. Freising, 1:168, no. 173; Stengel, ed., *Urkundenbuch*, 1:330, no. 229 and 346–50, nos. 241–43. After this cluster of references from the mid-790s, advocates are largely absent from the Fulda material during the ninth century, which suggests that this initial impulse toward the use of advocates (or at least toward recording their names in texts) gained less traction there than it did at St. Gall and Freising. For the early sources from Fulda, see Raaijmakers, *Making*, 198–201; Declercq, "Originals," 150, 153–54.

[60] For Arn, who was a Bavarian noble who became one of Charlemagne's most loyal supporters in the region, see Brown, *Unjust Seizure*, 102–23; Davis, *Practice*, 64–77; Schneider, "Kapitularien," 480–84. The Bavarian evidence survives mostly in the form of books of short tradition notices (*Traditionsbücher*); for these sources, see Declercq, "Originals"; Redlich, "Traditionsbücher." For early examples of advocates in these Bavarian sources, see Heuwieser, ed., *Traditionen*, 46, no. 54 and 65–66, no. 78; and Widemann, ed., *Traditionen*, 13–15, nos. 14–15 and 23–27, nos. 19–20. Other types of local evidence besides tradition notices confirm how commonplace advocates became in the early ninth century; see, for example, *Formulae Salicae*, 282, no. 21, and for the complex background to this collection, Rio, *Legal Practice*, 101–10.

[61] Tr. Freising, 1:174, no. 183: The use of direct speech is much more common in Italian documents from this period than ones from north of the Alps (see above, n. 46).

defended the church's property rights. However, when this document is read alongside other Freising tradition notices (short records of property transactions and disputes) from around 800, the advocate Kaganhart emerges as a figure whose role extended well beyond his performance at this one judicial assembly.

Although it can be difficult to say with certainty that every Kaganhart who appears in a Freising source from this period must have been the same person, the name features so prominently in numerous tradition notices from a narrow time frame that it is very likely we are dealing with one Kaganhart, who had very close ties to Bishop Atto.[62] Other Freising tradition notices from the first decade of the ninth century also mention an advocate Kaganhart, who is surely the same person.[63] A Kaganhart also appears in the witness lists of several other documents from this period.[64] These tradition notices preserve agreements that were made in numerous different places in and around Freising, which suggests that this Kaganhart was a regular member of Bishop Atto's entourage during these years – and perhaps even traveled around the diocese with him. If this is also the same Kaganhart who donated property to Freising on the day he died, according to a text from 820, then he spent at least two decades embedded in the bishopric's local networks.[65]

The connection between the sometimes-advocate Kaganhart and Bishop Atto of Freising becomes even more intriguing when we examine another cluster of tradition notices. Before becoming bishop in 783, Atto had been abbot of the monastery of Schlehdorf; this monastery had very close ties to the bishopric of Freising, and Atto probably belonged to the founding family.[66] Already in the year 776, the name Kaganhart begins to appear in documents concerning the earliest donations to Schlehdorf.[67] Then, in 794 and 799, just before the densest cluster of references to the advocate Kaganhart, a Kaganhart twice witnessed grants to the monastery of Schlehdorf.[68] When a dispute broke out in the year 802 between Bishop Atto and a man named Lantfrid concerning a property that had been granted to Schlehdorf, Kaganhart was present, appearing with the

---

[62] On the people who appear in this Bavarian source material, see Kohl, "Kleinfamilien," 163–64.
[63] Tr. Freising, 1:219–20, no. 240 and 237, no. 267.
[64] See, for example, ibid., 1:173, no. 182; 182, no. 192; 201–04, nos. 213–17; and 206–07, nos. 221–23.
[65] Ibid., 1:373, no. 435a. For another advocate who seems to have traveled widely with a bishop of Freising, see DD LdD, 90–92, no. 66 and Tr. Freising, 1:607–08, no. 730.
[66] Brown, *Unjust Seizure*, 75–83.
[67] Tr. Freising, 1: 99–102, nos. 75–77. This may not be the same Kaganhart as the advocate of the early ninth century, but the name suggests a close kin connection.
[68] Ibid., 1:166–67, no. 171 and 170–71, no. 177.

label *advocatus* in the witness list of both surviving accounts of the settlement.[69] In other words, Kaganhart was not someone brought in from outside the bishop's personal networks to serve as advocate on an ad hoc basis; he was an insider – possibly even a relative of Bishop Atto – and may have had connections of his own to some of the property disputes in which he was involved.[70]

This evidence cautions against relying on institutional arguments that assume an advocate like Kaganhart was a public officeholder. His role as advocate was only one of the ways in which he was intimately associated with local networks around the bishop of Freising. His strong connections to Atto, rather than any specific set of professional qualifications, were the reason why the bishop chose him as an advocate for particular disputes. If, as some of the capitularies insist, it was the ruler's itinerant representatives – in this case, Arn of Salzburg – who had to appoint the advocate, then the archbishop as the agent of royal authority clearly allowed Atto to pick someone whom he trusted from within his own entourage.[71] At the local level, there was apparently some flexibility in interpreting the prescriptive sources emanating from the Carolingian court. It is therefore unsurprising that there may also have been some flexibility in how local elites understood the role of the advocate.

A case from 818 involving Bishop Atto's successor provides additional evidence along these lines. Bishop Hitto of Freising and a count were hearing cases when the bishop's own advocate, Wichart, brought suit against a man named Waldker, accusing him of entering an estate that belonged to Freising and beating one of the church's dependents. Waldker claimed the estate rightfully belonged to him, which led the bishop and the count to summon those men who best knew the situation. These men, after swearing on relics to tell the truth, explained that the estate had belonged to the bishops of Freising until the time that Waldker had "unjustly" dispossessed the church of it. The people present therefore confirmed that Bishop Hitto and Wichart should be in possession of the estate.[72] Thus, a court overseen by the bishop of Freising found in favor of the bishop in a suit brought by the bishop's own advocate. To describe Wichart as Hitto's legal representative is too simplistic a view of his role here. He was aggressively pursuing a claim against a local rival in order to

---

[69] Ibid., 1:175, no. 184. The relationship between Lantfrid and Atto is discussed in Brown, *Unjust Seizure*, 75–83; Pearson, *Conflicting Loyalties*, 170–72.

[70] Jahn, *Ducatus*, 435–36; Störmer, *Früher Adel*, 1:103–104; Brown, *Unjust Seizure*, 86. See also Tr. Freising, 1:178–79, nos. 186–87.

[71] Capit. 1:115, no. 40, chap. 3. For the close connection between Atto and Arn, see Fouracre, "Carolingian Justice," 784–86.

[72] Tr. Freising, 1:344–45, no. 401a. See also Kohl, "Besitzübertragungen," 74–75.

help the bishop protect Freising's territorial interests. Regardless of what the capitularies decreed about advocates' formal responsibilities and their "ministry" (*ministerium*), local actors had their own strategies and ambitions – and their own ideas about how to use advocates in the give-and-take of local property disputes.[73]

A final example is worth considering briefly because it concerns one of the most famous figures of the first half of the ninth century: Einhard, Charlemagne's first biographer. His many surviving letters are invaluable sources for the political culture of the Carolingian empire. One, written during the late 820s or the 830s and addressed to an unnamed count, concerns Einhard's religious foundation at Seligenstadt near Frankfurt. The letter references "certain dependents . . . whom our current advocate N. sought before you and whom he hopes to be able to acquire, if he should have your help. In the same manner, we entreat your kindness that you might deign to help him not only in this case but also with other properties."[74] Einhard's entreaty offers a rare glimpse at the sorts of personal persuasion – in this case, bending the count's ear to gain an advantage for one's own advocate – that could shape the proceedings of suits that might come before local judges and judicial assemblies.[75]

This letter, alongside the evidence from Freising and the story told by Adrevald of Fleury about a bribe, highlights the danger of relying on the standard definition that "[a]dvocates were secular legal representatives for those who could or should not represent themselves, notably clerics."[76] Such a description fails to capture the many ways in which the first people to be labeled *advocatus* were enmeshed in local power networks that operated through informal means, not rigid institutional structures, in order to advance their interests. Indeed, such a wide variety of sources reveal advocates' activities as extending beyond the setting of the formal judicial assembly that we might ask whether scholars have been looking in the right place for the origins of church advocacy. In what other contexts might the term *advocatus* have been known in circles around the Carolingian court in the eighth and early ninth centuries?

[73] Fouracre, "Carolingian Justice," 785; Cheyette, "Reflections," 253–54; Brown, *Unjust Seizure*, 100. See also Tr. Freising, 1:483–84, no. 563. For another example of an aggressive advocate, this one from the other side of the empire, see Becquet, ed., *Actes*, 20–22, no. 2. For more on this point, see Chapter 2.

[74] Einhard, *Briefe*, 202–03, no. 50. Because some of the words can no longer be read in the manuscript (ibid., 34), the precise context is unclear, but these dependents were probably residing – willingly or unwillingly – in one of the count's monasteries. For this letter, see Mersiowsky, "Regierungspraxis," 146. For Einhard as lay abbot: Patzold, *Ich*, 131–231; Felten, *Äbte*, 283–86; De Jong, "Carolingian Monasticism," 634–35.

[75] Innes, *State*, 124; Brown, "Conflict," 333–44.

[76] West, "Significance," 187. See also McNair, "Governance," 201–06.

An Alternative Origin Story

Historians interested in church advocacy have tended to draw attention to the passages in Late Antique Roman law where advocates are described as legal representatives for ecclesiastics.[77] However, advocates appear elsewhere in Roman law as well. In the Frankish world, knowledge of Roman law survived through copies of the Theodosian Code as well as the Visigothic Breviary of Alaric, which included various abridged versions of the Theodosian Code alongside other Roman legal texts.[78] Seventh- and eighth-century copies of both the Code and the Breviary are extant in several manuscripts from across the Frankish lands, and we know they were read.[79] It is therefore important to consider whether other uses of the term *advocatus* in Roman law might have influenced advocatial roles under the Carolingians.

Intriguingly, the term *advocatus* frequently appears in both the Theodosian Code and the Breviary of Alaric in discussions about the Late Antique Roman office of the *advocatus fisci*: "advocate of the fisc" or "fiscal advocate." Advocates of the fisc specialized in administrative law and oversaw legal matters relating to the imperial properties and rights in a specific district of the Roman empire.[80] One aspect of their role was unquestionably to plead cases before Roman judges, specifically cases concerning the emperor's fiscal interests.[81] Litigation around the collection of taxes, for example, and investigations concerning the rightful ownership of property, lay in their purview.[82] This meant that they were active at the local level in pursuing cases, making them a type of advocate who had a range of responsibilities that combined legal, economic and administrative elements. Neither the Theodosian Code nor the Breviary of Alaric provides a lengthy and detailed description of the role of the *advocatus fisci*, but scattered throughout both texts are numerous references to these local, property-oriented functions.[83]

---

[77] See the Introduction. There is also a great deal of material in the Theodosian Code about the roles of advocates in the Roman legal system more generally; see, for example, *Theodosiani Libri XVI*, II.10.4.

[78] *Breviarium Alaricianum*. The Breviary was the law code used by the Visigothic populations in Aquitaine and southern France and was transmitted from there to Francia. Note that *Theodosiani Libri XVI*, XVI.2.38, on ecclesiastics needing advocates (see the Introduction), is not preserved in the Breviary; in fact, very little of Book 16 on ecclesiastical matters was included in it: Corcoran, "Hincmar," 133; Magnou-Nortier, *Code Théodosien*, 47–48, n. 100.

[79] McKitterick, "Law-Books," 15; Brundage, *Medieval Origins*, 56–57; McKitterick, *Carolingians*, 44, 46 and Table A; Wood, "Code"; Corcoran, "Hincmar."

[80] Humfress, "Advocates," 278; Crook, *Legal Advocacy*, 152, 190; Brunt, "Fiscus," 76–86; Hirschfeld, *Verwaltungsbeamten*, 48–52.

[81] See, for example, *Theodosiani Libri XVI*, X.10.3; X.15.3; and XI.30.41.

[82] Harries, *Law*, 94.

[83] See, for example, *Theodosiani Libri XVI*, X.15 (X.7 in the *Breviarium Alaricianum*), which is titled "De advocatis fisci."

Various sources hint that Carolingian rulers might have been familiar with the Late Antique "advocate of the fisc." In a privilege for Solignac in Aquitaine issued by King Pippin II shortly after the death of his father, Pippin I, in 838, the king took the monastery under royal protection: "Just as the properties of our fisc are defended and secured by our advocates, so should the properties of the said monastery be defended and secured by its advocates."[84] There is little evidence to suggest that the practice of labeling certain people as advocates for the imperial fisc was common in this period – either in Aquitaine or anywhere else.[85] Regardless, this text complements the earliest references to named advocates, because it clearly points to a Carolingian understanding of the role of the advocate that extended beyond judicial assemblies to include a broader set of responsibilities related to church property. While the paucity of the evidence prevents firm conclusions, it is possible that Charles Martel and his son Pippin already saw the position of ecclesiastical advocate as similar to that of the Late Antique Roman fiscal advocate as it was presented in Roman legal texts: in other words, as a position tasked with overseeing the extensive landed interests of important bishoprics and monasteries.

The specific sections of the Theodosian Code and the Breviary of Alaric in which the term *advocatus fisci* appears also point to another significant feature of this Late Antique position: It was prone to misuse. Thus, the Theodosian Code warns, "The advocate of the fisc must beware, under the fear of punishment, that he shall not conceal any advantage of the fisc and that he shall not dare in the name of the fisc to bring false charges against private citizens when no case exists."[86] This passage is preserved in copies of the Breviary as well, where in some early manuscripts it is followed by one of the Breviary's added interpretations of the Roman law: "These men (*advocati fisci*), who should look after the interests and profits of our fisc, must take measures, lest they appear neglectful concerning those things, which are owed to us by law, and

---

[84] Levillain, ed., *Recueil*, 185–98, no. 49: "Et, sicut res fiscorum nostrorum a nostris defenduntur aut adquiruntur advocatis, ita et res ejusdem mona[sterii ab advocatis adquira]ntur eorum aut defendantur" (197–98). For the complicated background to this charter: Koziol, *Politics*, 101–05. Similar language also appears in Levillain, ed., *Recueil*, 207–14, no. 53; 242–46, no. 59; and 248–68, no. 61 (though for this last charter, see Koziol, *Politics*, 35, n. 55). For these documents, see also Depreux, "Ausprägungen," 350–51 and more generally Wood, *Proprietary Church*, 256–57.

[85] DD LdF, 1–5, no. 1, includes a lengthy list of different groups of people under Louis's authority as ruler of Aquitaine (*comitibus, vicariis, centenariis*, etc.) without any mention of advocates; for this charter, see Dickau, "Studien," 25–37. Brunner, "Zeugen- und Inquisitionsbeweis," 158–60, argues that some references to royal advocates and comital advocates are examples of advocates representing the fisc, even if the term *advocatus fisci* is not explicitly used.

[86] *Theodosiani Libri XVI*, X.15.1 (English translation: *Theodosian Code*, trans. Pharr, 281).

lest they show themselves to be perverters of the law by unjustly demanding something from the local people in the name of the fisc."[87] As the remainder of this book will show, these Late Antique concerns about advocates taking advantage of their positions for their own benefit would be repeated across the millennium of European history from 750 to 1800.

Conclusion

Historians in the early twenty-first century are more skeptical than previous generations once were about the reach of top-down practices of Carolingian authority. Many have argued that the sprawling Frankish empire was "under-governed," with significant variation at the regional level in how decrees issued by the center were implemented at the periphery.[88] Nevertheless, the idea that, across the empire, the Carolingian advocate was first and foremost a legal representative at court – because that is what the capitularies tell us he was – remains dominant in the scholarship. As I have argued in this chapter, however, if we focus on what individual, named advocates are described as doing in the sources, rather than what prescriptive texts claim they were supposed to do, a different picture emerges. From the beginning, the people labeled *advocatus* did much more than simply initiate and respond to lawsuits in secular courts; they had multifaceted links to churches' territorial interests and property regimes. As a result, we must look on the ground, at the level of the village and estate, to understand why and how advocacy became so closely associated with corrupt practices of protection and justice.

---

[87] *Breviarium Alaricianum*, X.7.1. Munich, Bayerische Staatsbibliothek, Clm 22501 is a manuscript that scholars have dated to the seventh century and localized to southern France, possibly Lyons; it was probably already in the library at the cathedral in Würzburg in the ninth century. It includes the sections of the Breviary on *De erroribus advocatorum* (II.11) and *De advocato fisci* (X.7). For this manuscript: Esders, *Römische Rechtstradition*, 53–54; Bierbrauer, *Vorkarolingischen*, 1:13, no. 1; Bischoff, *Manuscripts*, 4; Gaudemet, "Bréviaire," 13. Wolfenbüttel, Herzog August Bibliothek, Cod. Guelf. 97 Weiss., which McKitterick dates to ca. 770 and localizes to northern or northeastern France (McKitterick, *Carolingians*, 48) is a much more abbreviated version of the Breviary than the Munich manuscript, but it also contains shortened entries for *De erroribus advocatorum* and *De advocato fisci*.
[88] Goldberg, *Struggle*, 206–07; Davis, *Practice*, 338–40. Cf. Costambeys, Innes and MacLean, *Carolingian World*, 191–94.

2 Putting Down Roots in Ninth-Century Francia

When the St. Gall monk Notker "the Stammerer" wrote his *Deeds of Charlemagne* in the mid-880s for Charlemagne's great-grandson, Emperor Charles the Fat (d. 888), his aim was not historical accuracy as we understand that concept today. Many of the text's humorous anecdotes and quasi-legendary stories comment on late ninth-century politics, not on the events of Charlemagne's reign. Among other goals, Notker sought to connect Charles the Fat to his illustrious great-grandfather in a narrative of Carolingian world empire.[1] In one story, the St. Gall monk describes the diplomacy between Charlemagne and the Muslim caliph Harun al-Rashid, as a way to highlight Carolingian greatness. After the caliph gave the Frankish ruler an elephant, among other gifts, Charlemagne sent Harun al-Rashid horses, textiles and hunting dogs.[2] The caliph, anxious to see the dogs in action, rode out with them and the Frankish envoys. When the dogs caught a lion and the Franks promptly killed it with their swords, Harun al-Rashid was so impressed that he was immediately convinced of Charlemagne's superiority:

What therefore can I possibly give him worthily, since he has taken such care to honor me so? If I give him the land promised to Abraham and shown to Joshua, he cannot defend it from the barbarians, because he is so far away; or if he undertook to defend it with his greatness of soul, I fear that the provinces bordering on the kingdom of the Franks would fall away from his command. So in the end I am tempted to make good on his generosity in this way: I will give the land into his power, and I will be his advocate (*advocatus*) over it. He himself, whenever it shall seem most opportune, may direct envoys to me, and he will find me a most faithful steward of the income of this very province.[3]

That the caliph would offer to be Charlemagne's advocate for the Holy Land sounds outlandish today. Nevertheless, Notker, whose monastery of St. Gall preserves one of the richest surviving source bases for the

---

[1] MacLean, *Kingship*, 222–27.
[2] For Einhard's version of this story: Einhard, *Vita Karoli*, 19, chap. 16.
[3] Notker, *Deeds*, 100, II.9 (Latin edition: Notker, *Gesta Karoli*, 64): "*dabo quidem illam in eius potestatem et ego advocatus eius ero super eam.*"

activities of advocates in the ninth-century Carolingian empire, provides
here invaluable insight into the ideal role of the advocate.[4] Tellingly, he
makes no mention of legal representation at court. Rather, he describes
the advocate as a defender of distant properties and a collector of owed
revenues. In the approximately 125 years since named advocates had first
begun to appear with some frequency, the scope of advocatial responsibilities had seemingly expanded dramatically. As I will argue here, a wide
range of sources from the mid- and late ninth century corroborate
Notker's depiction and reveal advocates who were increasingly figures
of local significance on ecclesiastical estates – in some places, even dis-
pensing justice for churches' dependents.

Advocates and Property

Formal judicial assemblies were never the only place where Carolingian-
era advocates worked. The eighth- and early ninth-century sources suggest that, from the beginning, advocates had strong local ties to the people
they represented; in some cases, they had interests of their own in the
properties and rights they went to law courts to dispute.[5] We catch only
glimpses of these local connections under the early Carolingians.
Beginning in the 820s, however, the volume of extant evidence for advocates' activities expands rapidly across the Frankish empire, and a much
clearer picture of the *advocatus* as a figure of local authority and influence
emerges.

One of the most striking descriptions of a village-level perspective on an
advocate appears in a document issued in the name of Charlemagne's
grandson King Pippin I of Aquitaine in 828. While the king was holding
court, a group of peasants came to court to complain about the abbot of
Cormery, to whom their village belonged, and about the abbot's advocate, Agenus,

on the grounds that the abbot and his envoys had demanded and exacted from
them more in rent and renders than they ought to pay and hand over ... Agenus
the advocate and Magenar the provost of the monastery were present there, and
they made a statement rebutting that claim, as follows: neither the abbot nor they

---

[4] St. Gall's approximately 800 extant documents from the period between the mid-eighth
century and 920 are the most important charter collection for this period from north of the
Alps. They have been discussed by numerous scholars; see, for example, McKitterick,
Carolingians, 77–134; Mersiowsky, *Urkunde*, 1:278–418; Heidecker, "Charters"; Zeller,
"Writing Charters." There are more than twenty-five documents from St. Gall dated to
the 880s, when Notker was writing, that reference advocates; see, for example, UB
St. Gall, 2:254–55, no. 650 and 259–60, nos. 655–56. I thank Bernhard Zeller for
discussing the St. Gall charters with me.
[5] See Chapter 1.

themselves had exacted, or ordered to be exacted, any dues or renders other than their predecessors had paid to the monastery's representatives for thirty years.[6]

The advocate and provost then presented an estate survey that listed the peasants' traditional obligations. When the peasants were unable to counter this, Pippin and his court found in favor of the monastery, and Pippin ordered "that ... the advocate Agenus and the provost Magenar should on behalf of that house of God receive a record of it."

As in Notker's story in his *Deeds of Charlemagne*, there is a clear connection here between the position of advocate and revenue collection on particular estates. In this case, the document explicitly describes Agenus as having a role to play in keeping track of what dependents were legally obligated to pay their landlord. If we take the complaints of the monastery's dependents seriously, this text also suggests that advocates could be involved in seeking to increase those revenues in ways that could bring them into conflict with the people working the land. This is not the last time that we will see a church's dependents complain about their advocates in these terms; however, comparable evidence from the Carolingian period is sparse.[7] It is not until roughly 200 years after King Pippin's document that comparable accusations of advocatial abuses become commonplace.[8] Nevertheless, there is abundant ninth-century evidence for advocates operating at the local level and having responsibilities that brought them into close contact with those who labored on ecclesiastical estates.

Beginning in the 810s and 820s, many local source collections call attention to advocates' involvement in donations to churches as well as purchases and exchanges of ecclesiastical property.[9] Thus, a tradition notice from the Bavarian bishopric of Freising dated to 815 concerns "the purchase agreement that Sindeo, advocate of Bishop Hitto, made on Bishop Hitto's command with a certain man named Lantfrid. Lantfrid handed over [a section of forest] into the hands of Bishop Hitto's aforesaid advocate and received from him as payment a horse."[10] Similarly, a charter from the mid-810s from the monastery of St. Gall records

---

[6] I follow here the translation in Nelson, "Dispute Settlement," 49 (with a few minor changes). Latin editions: *Settlement of Disputes*, 246–47, Appendix 8; Levillain, ed., *Recueil*, 44–47, no. 12. See also Costambeys, Innes, and MacLean, *Carolingian World*, 266.

[7] One capitulary that raises the issue of bishops, abbots and their advocates despoiling the poor is Capit. 1:165, no. 73, chap. 2.

[8] See Chapter 4.

[9] Some of the most important source collections for this section are discussed at length in the articles in *Tauschgeschäft und Tauschurkunde*; see especially Kasten and Gross, "Prekarieurkunden," 360.

[10] Tr. Freising, 1:283–84, no. 332.

a property agreement between the abbot and a man who gave the monastery his possessions in a particular village and received certain rights in return; the text explains that the agreement was made "with the hand" of the abbot's advocate.[11] While not every extant document that records a property agreement mentions the involvement of an advocate, the frequent references to advocates taking property into their hands (*in manum/manus, cum manu/manibus* or *per manum/manus*) suggest that they were often present for gifts, purchases and exchanges.[12]

What did this language of property passing into or through the hands of an advocate mean? Obviously, it cannot be taken literally. However, a donor typically placed on the altar some kind of object that symbolically represented the property as a whole.[13] That advocates had a part in this symbolic transfer and presumably took the object into their own hands is evidence for their direct involvement in confirming these sorts of agreements. In other words, advocates did not only become involved with churches' property rights when those rights were being contested at judicial assemblies; they were also present at other moments when the legal status of ecclesiastical properties was at stake.

The broader significance of all of this is suggested by a Freising tradition notice from the year 828. After describing how a husband and wife made a donation on the altar, it reports that "Bishop Hitto sent his advocate Reginbert" to the estate that had been gifted to the church, "in order that he might legally receive possession of the property."[14] This text clearly positions the advocate at the local level, on a specific property, in the role of asserting the bishop's claims of jurisdiction. That advocates could have such personal connections to properties that came into a church's possession is essential context for understanding the long history of advocacy's links to corrupt practices of protection and justice.

Beginning in the 820s, a pattern emerges in the St. Gall charter material that reinforces the argument that advocates were closely connected to churches' local property interests. The monastery made large numbers of precarial agreements, in which the abbot and the community received a property and then granted it back to the donor on revocable tenure,

---

[11] UB St. Gall, 1:207, no. 217.

[12] Not only prelates but also priests are sometimes identified as giving property "with the hand of my advocate" (see, for example, UB St. Gall, 1:311, no. 337 and 339–40, no. 365; Tr. Freising, 1:168, no. 173); however, at other times the sources describe priests making grants without any reference to an *advocatus* (see, for example, UB St. Gall, 1:206–7, no. 216; Tr. Freising, 1:156–57, no. 156 and 182, no. 192). See also Goetz, "Tauschurkunden," 183.

[13] Kohl, *Lokale Gesellschaften*, 77–78; Kohl, "Besitzübertragungen," 80–81; Zeller, "Writing Charters," 27–29.

[14] Tr. Freising, 1:478–79, no. 556c. See also Kohl, *Lokale Gesellschaften*, 81.

usually in return for a rent or service of some kind.[15] The documents recording this type of arrangement routinely mention advocates. For example, a charter from 821 preserves a record of a man and his son granting land to the monastery; Abbot Cozbert then gave the land back to them for their use in return for an annual payment, and the list of signatories at the end of the document begins, "Abbot Cozbert, who wanted this precarial agreement to be made and made it with the hand of his advocate Panto."[16] Eight years later in 829, the abbot made a precarial agreement with another man "with the consent of our brothers and of our advocate Ruodin."[17] The numerous surviving precarial documents of this sort point to advocates having direct knowledge of the complex set of rights that held together a church's patchwork of estates and other properties.

One of the most striking features of the St. Gall charter collection is that many different advocates are named in these documents. In the decade of the 820s alone, we encounter monastic advocates named Gisalfrid, Lantbert, Panto, Switgar, Tagobert, Ruodin, Isker, Wolfhart and Puato.[18] Research into the locations of the properties named in these charters and the identities of the various advocates has demonstrated that St. Gall in this period offers the best evidence from anywhere in the Frankish world for different advocates operating in different regions where the monastery possessed estates.[19] Genealogical studies suggest that many of these advocates belonged to prominent local families with properties of their own in those same regions.[20] A St. Gall advocate named Ruadpert, for example, appears in several charters from the mid-ninth century concerning properties in the region west of the monastery; his father was also active as an advocate in the same region, and there were St. Gall monks with the name Ruadpert who may well have been relatives

---

[15] *Settlement of Disputes*, 273; Hedwig, "Precaria." For St. Gall in particular, see Goetz, "Tauschurkunden"; Dohrmann, *Vögte*, 76–86.
[16] UB St. Gall, 1:254–55, no. 269.
[17] Ibid., 1:301–302, no. 327. References to advocates as signatories and/or consenters to these kinds of precarial arrangements are commonplace at St. Gall throughout the ninth century; see, for example, ibid., 1:266–67, no. 285; 1:338–39, no. 364; and 2:196, no. 583. This is formulaic language, as evidenced by the fact that it also appears in a St. Gall formulary collection: *Collectio Sangallensis*, 401, no. 7; 402–03, no. 9; and 404, no. 11 (on this point, see also Dohrmann, *Vögte*, 82–85). Formulary collections from the neighboring monastery of Reichenau have almost nothing to say about the use of advocates in precarial agreements, which suggests the St. Gall evidence should not be taken as the basis for broader regional conclusions: In *Formulae Augiensis* a *vendicio* (353–54, no. 13) mentions advocates, but two *precaria* (352, no. 7 and 355, no. 17) do not.
[18] UB St. Gall, 1:236–37, no. 245; 253–55, nos. 268–69; 258–59, no. 274; 266–67, no. 285; 276, no. 298; 281, no. 304; 283, no. 306; and 302–3, no. 328.
[19] Dohrmann, *Vögte*, 87–119. Cf. Starflinger, *Entwickelung*, 12–13.
[20] Dohrmann, *Vögte*, 120–45.

of his.[21] As with the Freising advocate Kaganhart discussed in the previous chapter, we should not understand Ruadpert's relationship to the monastery solely from the perspective of his position as advocate; he was clearly connected to the monastery in multiple ways.

That both Ruadpert and his father were named as advocates for St. Gall does not necessarily mean that the position of advocate was hereditary by the mid-ninth century. It is more likely that the monastery chose to draw its advocates from a relatively small pool of prominent local families who had their own property interests in the regions where St. Gall had estates.[22] Sources from the bishopric of Freising point in this direction as well. A man who occasionally served as an advocate for the bishops between 829 and 851, Pilgrim of Allershausen, belonged to the upper stratum of property owners in the region just to the west of Freising.[23] His father, Cotaperht, had made small donations to the church of Freising in earlier years, not only for the sake of his soul but also presumably to bring his family to the bishops' attention.[24] The strategy seems to have worked, because Pilgrim's connections to the church of Freising were extensive; he was not only an advocate but also witnessed numerous property agreements and made donations of his own to further bind his family to the bishopric.[25] Ecclesiastical advocates emerge from these sources as members of leading local families who knew the extent of a church's properties in their own neighborhoods and who had the standing to intervene in the church's legal affairs concerning those properties when necessary.

The sources from Freising and St. Gall are the best ninth-century evidence from north of the Alps for connecting named advocates to specific church properties.[26] Nevertheless, by mid-century, texts composed at various other religious communities provide glimpses of comparable situations elsewhere in the Frankish lands – especially in the eastern half of the empire.[27] At the monastery of Wissembourg (Weissenburg),

[21] Ibid., 134, 158–63. The advocate Ruadpert appears between the 840s and 860s.
[22] Kohl, *Lokale Gesellschaften*, 322–23; West, "Significance," 193.
[23] See, for example, Tr. Freising, 1:502, no. 586; 551–52, no. 654; and 605–06, no. 727. For Pilgrim: Kohl, "Kleinfamilien," 164–68.
[24] Kohl, *Lokale Gesellschaften*, 169–70.
[25] Tr. Freising, 1:499–500, no. 583; 522–23, no. 609; 546, no. 644; and 555–56, no. 660.
[26] See, for example, ibid., 1:660–61, no. 822; 666–67, no. 834; 734–35, nos. 960–61; UB St. Gall, 2:78–80, nos. 462–63; and 112–15, nos. 497–500. In the 870s and 880s, there are also numerous references to advocates in the tradition notices from the Bavarian bishopric of Regensburg: Widemann, ed., *Traditionen*, 71–111, nos. 78–137.
[27] The best ninth-century source collections tend to be from bishoprics and imperial monasteries, making it difficult to know whether other communities, such as noble foundations and monasteries under diocesan authority, had advocates in the ninth century – as we know many did in the tenth (see Chapter 3).

there are no references to an advocate in any of its extant documents until the year 830, when the list of witnesses to a precarial agreement includes the advocate Gebolt.[28] This man belonged to a family that had been prominent in the surrounding region for more than a century and had longstanding, close connections to the monastery.[29] Similarly, the Folcnand who appears as advocate in documents from both Fulda and Seligenstadt in the second half of the ninth century was a leading landholder in the area where he lived, someone who used his position as advocate to expand his own influence.[30] In both of these cases, as at Freising and St. Gall, a focus on regional social networks and power dynamics – rather than top-down legal and institutional structures – reveals advocates to be members of local elites with the status and authority to help churches oversee their property rights.[31]

"Policing" Powers

By the 820s at the latest, church advocates appear in local settings far more often than they do at regional judicial assemblies. This does not mean, however, that we should downplay the significance of their responsibilities representing religious communities in lawsuits. Rather, it means that – whatever the origins of the Frankish advocate might have been – the position had by this time become one rooted in churches' property interests. Increasingly, even the capitularies issued by the Carolingian rulers reflected the bottom-up needs of churches over the top-down goals of the royal court. A capitulary issued by Emperor Louis the Pious (814–40) in the year 821, for example, decrees, "If dependents, either ecclesiastical ones or those of any free men, flee to our fisc, and their lords (*domini*) or their advocates demand them back, if the agent of our fisc sees that he cannot hold them justly in our power, he should expel them from the fisc, and their lords should receive them."[32] Thus, advocates were tasked with

---

[28] *Traditiones Wizenburgenses*, 406–09, no. 198.
[29] Hummer, *Politics*, 70, 200. The only other advocate to be identified by name in this collection of tradition notices, a Rodoin in the early 860s, belonged to the same kin group: *Traditiones Wizenburgenses*, 515–16, no. 272.
[30] Innes, *State*, 44–45. The evidence is problematic, however. The only text to identify Folcnand as an *advocatus* for Fulda survives in a twelfth-century copy: DD LdD, 271–72, no. 185a. The Seligenstadt text that explicitly mentions an *advocatus* Folcnand is undated: Schmidt, "Mittheilungen," 612–13.
[31] Cf. West, "Significance," 203.
[32] *Kapitulariensammlung*, 621, 4.3. For similar language, see Flodoard of Reims, *Historia*, 172, II.18 and 175, II.19. Another unusually detailed capitulary about advocates from Louis the Pious's reign concerns the giving of false testimony in court: *Kapitulariensammlung*, 633–34, 4.22; on this passage, see Schmitz, "Capitulary," 433–34.

handling a wide range of legal issues tied to churches' properties – including churches' dependents.[33]

Other sources provide additional evidence for advocates' increasingly multifaceted responsibilities related to ecclesiastical lands and rights. Especially detailed is a formulary collection which was probably written at Sens in West Francia soon after 818.[34] Like many such collections, this one's context was local rather than pan-imperial; it may have initially been intended for a particular count or religious community. Some of its entries indicate that abbots could attend judicial assemblies in this period, with or without advocates, and could bring suit themselves.[35] However, one section also explains at great length how an advocate "should without hindrance be able to pursue and defend all cases, which he is obliged to undertake or refute." It continues with a formula for appointing a new episcopal advocate: "I, bishop of saint x and church x enjoin, order and through this document charge that you, my faithful x, should investigate, examine, pursue and bring suit concerning the properties of saint x located in district x, ... in judicial assemblies, villages, fortifications, towns and cities, and even, if necessary, in a palace, before [royal agents] and before all judges."[36] In this formula, the role of the advocate is clearly framed within the context of property and any legal issues that might arise because of it. Significantly, the text also suggests that advocates had a great deal of latitude to initiate and aggressively pursue claims concerning ecclesiastical property rights; theirs was a decidedly active, not reactive, role.[37]

The language of this formulary parallels the language of mid-ninth-century documents concerning the inquest (*inquisitio*). Permission to conduct an inquest, when granted by a ruler, enabled churches to investigate property losses and to initiate property disputes by taking sworn evidence from witnesses.[38] Although Emperor Louis the Pious granted the right of inquest to a few churches in the empire, the majority of his

---

[33] On this point, see also Chapter 1.

[34] *Formulae Senonenses Recentiores*. For discussions of this collection, see Rio, *Legal Practice*, 121–26; Mordek, *Bibliotheca capitularium*, 482–84.

[35] *Formulae Senonenses Recentiores*, 212–13, nos. 3–4 and 214, no. 7. See also Rio, *Legal Practice*, 123.

[36] *Formulae Senonenses Recentiores*, 216, no. 10: "*investigare, inquirere, prosequi et admallare debeas.*"

[37] This is further suggested by Carolingian royal privileges that decree that the advocates for some monasteries would not face fines for losing lawsuits they had brought before judicial assemblies. See, for example, Levillain, ed., *Recueil*, 133–51, no. 32 (here p. 150). For this charter, see Koziol, *Politics*, 99–101. See also Tessier, ed., *Recueil*, 3:236–39.

[38] *Settlement of Disputes*, 272 (and various articles in the same volume). For inquests more generally, see Schmitz, "Capitulary," 434–35; Bachrach, "Inquisitio"; Brunner, "Zeugen- und Inquisitionsbeweis," 146–247.

charters do not explicitly reference advocates as having any role in the process.[39] Beginning in the 830s, however, especially in the Italian kingdom, subsequent generations of Carolingian rulers issued charters drawing direct connections between advocates and the legal process of inquest. In King Lothar I's charter of 837 for one Italian bishop, he ordered that wherever necessary, because of losses that had been suffered to the bishopric's property, "a very exacting and most prudent inquest about the church's properties and household should be conducted through suitable men, whom the bishop or the church's advocate should summon to appear."[40] Sixteen years later in 853, Lothar's son Louis II ordered bishops, counts and other royal agents to support an Italian monastery, and in particular its advocates, as they sought to restore properties that had been lost.[41] Thus, the right of inquest gave the advocates of some churches another opportunity to associate themselves with ecclesiastical property interests, further evidence that the *advocatus* was someone with extensive knowledge of churches' local rights.

Advocates' steadily expanding local roles may be one reason why the middle decades of the ninth century are the period when the term *advocatio*, "advocacy," first appeared. In some cases, the term seems to be referring to the collective set of responsibilities that came with the position of advocate.[42] In others, there may well be a geographical component too. In a capitulary of 861, for example, the West Frankish king Charles the Bald decreed that an advocate should take legal action against any dependents "from his advocacy" who refused to accept royal money.[43] These earliest uses of the term are too infrequent to reveal whether it had a technical meaning in this period, but its appearance points to the deep roots that the position of advocate had acquired over the course of a few decades. In some places, especially in the German-speaking lands, the

---

[39] Exceptions to this general rule include two of his charters for the southern French monastery of Aniane: DD LdF, 464–65, no. 188 and 879–81, no. 353 (though both only survive in twelfth-century copies). See also DD Lo I, 155–56, no. 54, for Saint-Mihiel, which claims to be a copy of a lost Louis the Pious charter; it too mentions advocates in connection with the right of inquest but only survives in a later copy (see also Gillen, *Saint-Mihiel*, 122–23).

[40] DD Lo I, 111–12, no. 34. See also UB St. Gall, 2:393–94, no. 15, from the reign of Louis the Pious, which preserves the record of an inquest concerning some of the monastery's properties in Italy and mentions an *advocatus* for some of these Italian estates. For the Italian context: Screen, "Lothar I."

[41] DD Lu II, 87, no. 12; see also 174–75, no. 55.

[42] For example, DD Lo I, 165–66, no. 59; Capit., 2:94–96, no. 218, chap. 1.

[43] Capit., 2:301–2, no. 271. See also Tessier, ed., *Recueil*, 2:81–86, no. 258; 2:192–194, no. 314; and 2:334–336, no. 375. The term *advocatio* seems not to have been as common in East Francia as it was in West Francia or Northern Italy in the mid-ninth century.

foundations laid in this period were the basis for a continuous thousand-year history of advocacy.[44]

All of this evidence for the intensification of local advocatial responsi-bilities reflects the fact that – contrary to some historians' arguments about strong institutional and governmental structures under the Carolingians – administrative positions were fluid and flexible in this period. Rulers, religious communities and local elites all seem to have construed the role of the advocate in broad terms, as encompassing a range of legal matters pertaining to land, its income and its dependents. This diversity is reflected in scholarship that suggests advocates per-formed not only "lawyer-like" functions for churches but also acquired "policing" responsibilities on ecclesiastical estates.[45] Their roles pursuing escaped dependents, investigating cases concerning church property and organizing inquests all point in this direction.

We must be cautious, however, to define our terms when ascribing policing powers to Carolingian advocates. Police forces first emerged in Europe during the fourteenth and fifteenth centuries, not the ninth.[46] Moreover, twenty-first-century social scientists studying various coun-tries across the world do not consider "policing" a neutral concept, or as an impartial or accountable form of governmental intervention into local life. In many places, "legitimate" police forces can be virtually indistin-guishable from "illegitimate" criminal gangs; moreover, police officials are frequently connected through informal networks to a wide range of criminal groups and illegal operations.[47] As a result, to explain ninth-century Frankish advocacy in terms of policing is only helpful if this is understood to mean something more than an official set of responsibilities that everyone with the label *advocatus* dutifully performed. Modern scholarship on policing suggests, on the contrary, that advocates would have had the opportunity to be aggressive enforcers of rights on ecclesias-tical estates – and might have frequently abused their powers for the church's, or their own, benefit.

"Policing," broadly defined, thus formed only one aspect of a portfolio of responsibilities that linked advocates to ecclesiastical lands, rights and

<hr>

[44] Noteworthy here is the story of an advocate accompanying churchmen to collect a saint's relics and bring them to Saxony in 836: Erconrad of Le Mans, *Translatio*, 76–81 (also pp. 19–20). On this story: Goffart, *Forgeries*, 327–34; Röckelein, *Reliquientranslationen*, 155–62, 328–29. For similar examples of advocates serving as escorts, see subsequent chapters.
[45] For this language: West, "Significance," 198; Wood, *Proprietary Church*, 328–29; Senn, *L'Institution*, 93; Brunner, *Deutsche Rechtsgeschichte*, 308.
[46] Zorzi, "Justice," 501.
[47] Venkatesh, *Gang Leader*, 230–33; Arias, "Dynamics," 305–06; Stephenson, *Gangs*, 77–80.

dependents in multiple, potentially self-serving ways. Combined with advocates' roles relating to lawsuits at judicial assemblies and to property donations and exchanges, these policing functions helped to create a powerful and influential position, one that gave local elites various opportunities to benefit from their access to the enormous amounts of property held by religious communities in the Carolingian empire. But the list of advocatial roles does not end there. Especially in the eastern parts of the Frankish world, advocates from the mid-ninth century onward were also sometimes called upon to exercise justice on ecclesiastical estates.

Advocates and Immunities in the East Frankish Kingdom

In the ninth-century Carolingian empire, counts were the main figures responsible for representing royal authority and administering justice at the regional level. While the size of the counties overseen by counts varied considerably across the different regions of the empire, counts' chief responsibilities were fairly consistent everywhere: They presided over their county's judicial assembly (*mallus publicus*), kept the peace, collected dues and mustered troops for the royal army.[48] In return, they held benefices from the Carolingian rulers, from which they drew much of their income – though they also profited from their position in other ways, such as by fining criminals and anyone who failed to appear when summoned.[49] Despite the wide-ranging scope of comital authority, some properties and local populations in the empire were not subject to a count, because a ruler had granted a landholder – most often an ecclesiastical community – an "immunity." To follow the history of advocacy from the ninth century onward, it is essential to understand how such an immunity worked.

As is the case with advocacy, older generations of scholars approaching the subject of this type of immunity from the perspectives of legal and constitutional history wanted to see it as an institution framed by a clear set of rules and expectations. Recent historians have been far more cautious, however, and recognize that immunities could vary in character across time and place, as both rulers and ecclesiastics shaped the concept to suit their own needs.[50] For my purpose here, a basic description will

---

[48] Goldberg, *Struggle*, 216–17. The count has long been central to questions about the size and scope of Carolingian government: Hechberger, *Adel*, 194–201.

[49] For the issue of how counts profited from their position, see Esders, "Amt und Bann," 296–97; Bachrach, "Benefices," 18–28. See also Innes, *State*, 124.

[50] For the classic older model, see Brunner, *Deutsche Rechtsgeschichte*, 2:307–11; Senn, *L'Institution*, 12–17; Mayer, *Fürsten*, 2–4; Ganshof, *Frankish Institutions*, 47–50. For

suffice by way of introduction: when a ruler granted a church an immunity, he was exempting the territories of that church (either specific properties or the church's holdings as a whole) from interference by royal agents – especially counts – who were not permitted to access those estates to exercise justice or collect dues and services from the church's dependents.[51]

For many scholars, the history of church advocacy was inextricably intertwined with the history of the ecclesiastical immunity from the beginning. According to these historians, the advocate came into being as the legal agent responsible for performing within ecclesiastical immunities those functions that would otherwise have been carried out by royal officials.[52] This argument is problematic, however. The earliest references to advocates do not mention them operating within the framework of the church immunity, and projecting the ideas present in later texts backward in time is a flawed approach. As the previous section has shown, advocates gradually accumulated more and more responsibilities over the course of the Carolingian period; their ties to the immunity are best understood as an outgrowth of their expanding roles.

I take this position because advocates and immunities begin to be referenced together on a consistent basis in a specific place at a specific time: the East Frankish Kingdom of Louis "the German" (826–76) during the 850s. The corpus of extant, original charters issued by Louis's father, Emperor Louis the Pious, does not refer to advocates acting in immunities, nor do the early charters of Louis's brothers, who ruled other parts of the Carolingian empire.[53] During the 820s and 830s, the young Louis's own charters for his East Frankish lands make no mention of advocacy at all. Only from the late 840s do his documents start to reference advocates with any frequency. While some of these charters borrow their language about advocates from earlier documents, others suggest that Louis's court was experimenting with new ideas about

more recent perspectives, see Fouracre, "Eternal Light"; Rosenwein, *Negotiating Space*, 3–9; Koziol, *Politics*, 30–31. For the period under consideration here: Goldberg, *Struggle*, 219–20.

[51] I take this basic definition from *Settlement of Disputes*, 272. From Charlemagne's time onward, rulers frequently granted royal protection and immunity to churches and monasteries: Semmler, "Traditio," 1–16; Fouracre, "Eternal Light," 58.

[52] Senn, *L'Institution*, 12; Ganshof, *Frankish Institutions*, 48–49; Fouracre, "Eternal Light," 64. Some scholars, in contrast, have downplayed the significance of the connection between the immunity and advocacy: Willoweit, "Vogt, Vogtei," 934; West, "Significance," 198–201.

[53] I stress here extant, original charters, because many later forgers added clauses about advocates to the immunities granted by Carolingian rulers. See, for example, DD LdF, 1011–14, no. 409 and compare Tessier, ed., *Recueil*, 1:111–15, no. 41 and 1:343–48, no. 131.

advocatial roles and responsibilities.[54] It is in this context that the connection between advocates and immunities first emerges definitively.

For example, in a privilege from 853 for the monastery of St. Emmeram in Bavaria, Louis the German confirmed the community's possession of certain properties and insisted that "no public judge (*iudex publicus*) nor any other power" was to exercise jurisdiction over any of the people on those properties; if anyone sought justice against those people, "then the advocates and ministers of the monastery ... should strive diligently to investigate the truth of the matter and correct it."[55] The text also makes it clear that no public judge could compel those people to go to court, "so long as the advocates of the same monastery should want to exercise justice." A royal charter from a few months later concerning a property grant to the newly founded convent of Sts. Felix and Regula in Zurich includes similar language.[56] The connection between immunity and advocacy is even more explicit in Louis's 857 privilege for the monastery of Niederaltaich in Bavaria, which concerns all the community's possessions. It is worth quoting at length, because much of the language in it is critical to understanding the next 900 years of the history of advocacy:

We order ... that no public judge, or anyone else with judicial power, or any of our faithful men in the present or future – neither counts nor [other royal agents] – should dare ... to enter into the churches, manors, fields or any of the other possessions, which [that monastery] justly and legally holds and possesses at this time [or acquires in the future] in ... our kingdom for the purpose of hearing cases, collecting fines and rents, taking sureties, or prosecuting justly or unjustly the men of that monastery (both the free ones and also the unfree, the Slavs and tenants living upon its land). Nor should they dare to enter for the purpose of taking payments or meals, making overnight stays, or demanding unlawful exactions.[57]

The privilege then turns to the monastery's rights in the immunity:

But let it be permitted to [the abbot] and his successors that they possess in quiet order and tranquil security [all] the possessions of the aforesaid monastery ... under the protection of our defense and immunity, far removed from the disturbance and vulgar action of every judicial power. And the advocates of this church should judge and bring to an end every case that has to be investigated and tried.

---

[54] For conventional language in his charters, see for example DD LdD, 101–02, no. 72; 126–27, no. 88; 170–71, no. 121; 213–14, no. 151; and 222–224, nos. 159–60. Cf. ibid., 63–64, no. 47; 80–82, nos. 59–60; and 85–86, no. 62. For the significance of the late 840s and early 850s for Louis's reign, see Goldberg, "*Dominus Hludowicus*," 195; Depreux, "Development," 49–50.

[55] DD LdD, 87–89, no. 64. Also important is Louis's 851 privilege for the convent of Herford: ibid., 83–84, no. 81. For this Herford privilege: Pitz, *Verfassungslehre*, 440–41. For the increasingly formulaic language concerning advocates in immunities from this period, see Stengel, *Diplomatik*, 110–14.

[56] DD LdD, 92–94, no. 67.   [57] Ibid., 116–17, no. 80.

Much of the language here that bars counts and other royal agents from entering onto a church's properties in order to judge cases, collect fines, eat meals and stay overnight was already present in immunities issued in the name of Louis the German's father, Louis the Pious.[58] However, these earlier immunities did not explain who was to perform these functions in their place. That the advocate is explicitly tasked in this privilege with fulfilling the role of judge on the monastery's lands is therefore significant.[59] In the East Frankish Kingdom of the mid-ninth century, the ruler was imbuing advocates with even more legitimate local authority than they already possessed, intensifying their connections to ecclesiastical property interests and rights.

A contemporary narrative source suggests that Louis the German and his court were aware that expanding the scope of advocates' activities into the judicial sphere raised potential problems. Under the year 852, the *Annals of Fulda* report that the king decreed at a royal assembly that counts and other local royal agents should not, within their own district, undertake to conduct a lawsuit for someone else under the name of advocate – but that they could do so in other districts.[60] Some scholars have suggested that Louis the German was trying here to close a known "loophole" in court proceedings by making it clear that no one could be judge and advocate in the same case.[61] However, there is almost certainly more at stake here than a concern for courtroom ethics. By granting advocates judicial authority within ecclesiastical immunities, Louis the German was effectively limiting the authority of counts and other royal agents within the regions under their control; however, those counts and royal agents could regain that authority by claiming to be the advocates for immune churches. In ninth-century East Francia, there is little evidence for counts acting as advocates in this way, which suggests that Louis's decree was respected.[62] In subsequent

---

[58] See, for example, DD LdF, 144–46, no. 57; 329–32, no. 130; and 581–84, no. 234.

[59] The pairing of the roles of advocate and judge appears early in the Christian tradition in the idea that Christ was not only humanity's advocate but also its judge (see the Introduction). This idea is echoed in some Carolingian-era sources that describe the ruler as a church's advocate and judge: see, for example, MGH Epp. 5:309–10, no. 7.

[60] *Annales Fuldenses*, 43 (English: *Annals of Fulda*, 34). This follows some earlier capitulary material from the time of Louis the Pious: *Kapitulariensammlung*, 655, 4.60.

[61] Goldberg, "*Dominus Hludowicus*," 192; Pitz, *Verfassungslehre*, 442–43; Goldberg, *Struggle*, 228–29. The Theodosian Code (*Theodosiani Libri XVI*, II.10.5; *Breviarium Alaricianum*, II.10.2) forbade the same person from acting as both advocate and judge in the same case.

[62] One possible exception is a text from Corvey dated to 826–76, which only survives in a fifteenth-century manuscript: Honselmann, ed., *Mönchslisten*, 126, no. 257 ("Bardoni comiti aduocato nostro"). See also Mersiowsky, "Tauschgeschäfte," 251–54; Rembold, *Conquest*, 177–78. Another possible exception survives in the twelfth-century *Codex Eberhardi*, 296, no. 31 ("Nordalah comes et *advocatus*"); see also Koch, ed., *Oorkondenboek*, 1:12–19, no. 7, where this is dated to the early ninth century.

centuries, however, many counts would seek to expand their power and influence by claiming the advocacies for neighboring churches in possession of immunities.[63]

A closer look at the language of East Frankish immunities brings into sharper focus the significance of this expansion of advocatial authority from the 850s onward. Soon after Louis the German's death, his son Louis III the Younger issued a privilege in 877 for the Saxon convent of Gandersheim, which includes the decree that "no count or any other royal agent may presume to hold judicial power, collect judicial fines, stay overnight or demand meals in the said monastery except by the consent and request of the monastery's abbess."[64] It then continues, "And the men of that abbess, whether free or servile, may not be coerced by any judicial power, but they should obtain their justice and should execute justice toward others in the presence of the abbess's advocate." While this charter does not explicitly state that the advocate was to replace the count as the one who could collect judicial fines, stay overnight and demand food within the immunity, it is essential to recognize that justice and profit were inextricably linked in this way throughout most of European history. Some scholars have even suggested that "exercising justice" was synonymous with collecting revenue.[65] This is an extreme position, but there is no question that anyone who presided over judicial assemblies had numerous opportunities (some more ethical than others) to benefit from the role.[66]

The potential advantages to be gained from exercising justice point to a broader issue. As with royal agents, it is difficult to know from the surviving Carolingian evidence how churches remunerated advocates for fulfilling their responsibilities. Historians who have addressed this issue have tended to draw attention to the small number of sources that indicate some advocates held a small amount of property from the churches they served.[67] That the position of advocate came with property may help to explain its attractiveness for local elites, but it is impossible to determine how much of an advocate's income came from such a benefice as opposed to other sources.[68] The language of some immunities about

---

[63] This issue will be discussed at length in Chapters 3, 5, 7 and elsewhere.

[64] DD LdJ, 335–37, no. 3.

[65] Magnou-Nortier, "Note," 263. For a critique of Magnou-Nortier, see Fouracre, "Carolingian Justice," 801–02. For the significance of justice as a source of revenue more generally, see Carocci and Collavini, "Cost," 135–38.

[66] Reuter, *Germany*, 28–29. See also Chapter 1.

[67] McNair, "Governance," 210; West, "Significance," 193. See also Capit. 1:151, no 62, chap. 23; DD Arn, 41–42, no. 28; Guérard, ed., *Polyptyque*, 93, XXVI, no. 1; and *Diplomata Belgica*, 67–69, no. 37.

[68] Some of Charlemagne's capitularies already express concerns about greedy advocates harming monasteries: Capit. 1:93, no. 33, chap. 13 and 124, no. 44, chap. 12. The Freising tradition notices suggest that advocates might hold on behalf of the bishopric the

collecting judicial fines, staying overnight and demanding food is important in this context. In subsequent centuries, advocates would routinely claim that, when they came onto ecclesiastical estates to hold court, they were to receive a portion of the fines and were to be fed and housed at the religious community's expense.[69] Although there is little explicit evidence from the Carolingian period for advocates benefitting in this way, the subsequent nine centuries of the history of advocacy would prove that access to ecclesiastical property brought many opportunities of this kind for advocates to profit from their position.

Diverging Paths

As my focus on the East Frankish kingdom in the previous section indicates, mid-ninth-century sources from the various parts of the Carolingian empire reveal that advocatial roles had begun to diverge at the regional level by this period. Differences in the types of surviving evidence from West Francia, East Francia and Northern Italy may make these variations appear more significant than they actually were, but advocates were clearly engaging in different sorts of activities in different places.

Royal and imperial charters from the closing decades of the century demonstrate this trend. After King Louis the German died in 876 and his younger half-brother Emperor Charles the Bald died the following year, Charlemagne's grandsons were gone from the stage of European history. Both rulers had multiple sons who divided the empire, but during the next few years, all but one of their legitimate heirs died. Thus, in the mid-880s, Louis the German's last surviving son, Emperor Charles the Fat, briefly brought the different kingdoms together in his own hands – before he too died in 888. Sources from the short period when he ruled in East Francia, Northern Italy and West Francia are especially valuable in terms of understanding the diverging histories of advocacy in the different kingdoms.

In West Francia, references to advocates in royal privileges are much rarer than they are in the privileges from either Northern Italy or East Francia. The charters issued by the West Frankish rulers immediately prior to Charles the Fat – Louis II the Stammerer (d. 879) and his sons Louis (d. 882) and Carloman (d. 884) – are noteworthy for the paucity of their references to advocates.[70] Moreover, although almost half of the

---

properties they have successfully won for the church in lawsuits – a potentially potent incentive for them to pursue cases aggressively whenever they could: see, for example, Tr. Freising, 1:344–45, no. 401a; 432–33, no. 507; and 483–84, no. 563.

[69] See Chapter 6.

[70] One exception is Carloman's 881 charter for the abbot of Saint-Florent: Grat et al., eds., *Recueil*, 140–44, no. 55 (though it only survives in later copies). Another, which only

surviving original charters issued by Charles the Fat are for West Frankish recipients, advocates are absent from these documents as well.[71] The local evidence is not significantly better. By this period, the St. Denis archive is not as rich a source for advocates as it had been in the eighth or early ninth centuries.[72] Narrative texts – including the miracle collection written at the monastery of Fleury in the late ninth century – occasionally show advocates assisting ecclesiastical communities in property disputes or other legal matters, but such evidence is rare.[73] As we will see in subsequent chapters, there continued to be advocates for St. Denis, Fleury and a few other Carolingian-era West Frankish religious communities into the twelfth and thirteenth centuries. However, on the whole, by 900, advocacy seems to have been a more limited phenomenon in West Francia than elsewhere.[74]

In contrast, Charles the Fat's charters issued for Northern Italian ecclesiastical communities follow earlier Italian scribal practices and reference advocates when discussing inquests, disputes settlements at court and occasionally immunities as well.[75] Many of the advocates named in Italian sources from this period were deeply embedded in the legal culture of the judicial assemblies; several are even identified as holding other law-court-related positions – including that of notary – simultaneously with their advocatial roles.[76] As a result, to read the late ninth-century Northern Italian evidence for advocates is to be left with the distinct impression that the term advocate meant something different south of the Alps in this period than it did further north. This is not to suggest that the position of advocate was more bureaucratic or official in

survives in a seventeenth-century copy, references the *advocatus* Adalmar of the monastery of St. Martin in Tours and dates from the early 890s. It concerns properties that had supposedly been unjustly seized from the monastery and includes a passage in which the abbot tells Adalmar: "You are their advocate. If it is necessary, you will fight for them" (*advocatus eorum es. Et si necesse fuerit, tu pugnabis pro eis*). See *Recueil des actes de Robert 1ᵉʳ*, 139–41, no. 37. For this Adalmar, see McNair, "Governance," 209–10.

[71] For these West Frankish charters, see MacLean, *Kingship*, 100–01.

[72] There is an overall decline after the reign of Charles the Bald in the number of extant documents concerning St. Denis's property holdings: Peters, *Entwicklung*, 211.

[73] For Fleury, see Chapter 1. See also Flodoard of Reims, *Historia*, 256–57, III.18 and 340, III.26. For other discussions of advocates in West Francia in the later ninth century, see West, "Significance," 195–98; Depreux, "Ausprägungen," 348–51.

[74] For more on this point, see subsequent chapters and Senn, *L'Institution*, 95–109; West, "Monks," 388–93.

[75] See, for example, DD Ka III, 51–54, no. 31; 76–79, no. 47; 81–83, no. 49; and 252–53, no. 156. The word *advocator*, which appears only in the Italian context, is used in some of these documents. For this term, see Riedmann, "Vescovi e Avvocati," 39–40.

[76] See, for example, *I Placiti*, 221–23, no. 61 and 229–34, no. 64; DD Ka III, 41–43, no. 25. The distinctive language of the Italian evidence can also be seen in DD Lo I, 66–69, no. 7; *I Placiti*, 1:254–60, no. 71; *Chronicon Farfense*, 168–69, 171–73.

Italy than it was elsewhere, only that the language of the sources is quite distinctive and points to a different framework for advocates' activities.[77]

East Frankish royal privileges continue to make frequent references to advocates after 875 – and continue to show advocates as active in a variety of settings. The charters issued by Charles the Fat's brothers, Karlmann (d. 880) and Louis III the Younger (d. 882), mention advocates in the context of property exchanges and immunities.[78] One of Charles the Fat's documents from 883 includes what was by this time well-established formal language for Bavarian property exchanges; a churchman "gave his properties to [the monastery of] St. Emmeram . . . with the hand of his advocate Otnand and with the consent and counsel of the most venerable Bishop Ambricho of Regensburg and his advocates."[79] More generally, source collections in Bavaria, at St. Gall and elsewhere in East Francia also show advocates as active figures throughout the late 870s and 880s in various types of local agreements.[80]

A small group of sources from Zurich and its environs offers an especially vivid picture of the prominent role of an advocate in this period. Louis the German founded the convent of Sts. Felix and Regula in Zurich in 853; he made his own daughter the first head of the community and granted it royal estates around Zurich.[81] From the beginning, therefore, this new community was closely tied to royal interests in the East Frankish kingdom. There was also a community of male canons at Zurich (Grossmünster), and from this community there survives a roll (*rotulus*) preserving copies of some of the late-ninth- and tenth-century documents for the house. These include a text concerning an agreement made between 876 and 880 "with the permission of Willeharius, advocate of King Charles [the Fat]."[82] The precise role of this royal advocate is unclear, but other sources provide additional evidence for his activities. In 873, he is named second in the list of signatories to an agreement made at Zurich, in which one of Louis the German's men exchanged properties with St. Gall.[83] Then, in a charter from 876, Willeharius is identified as the *advocatus* for the abbess of the convent of Sts. Felix and Regula.[84] In 883, he appears again as this community's advocate in a property exchange.[85] Taken together, these

---

[77] See subsequent chapters for more on this point.
[78] DD Km, 305–06, no. 15; DD LdJ, 335–37, no. 3; 340–42, no. 6; and 359–60, no. 19. For LdJ, no. 6, see Pitz, *Verfassungslehre*, 441.
[79] DD Ka III, 120–21, no. 73. See also ibid., 122–23, no. 75.   [80] See above.
[81] Goldberg, *Struggle*, 238–39; Zotz, "*Turegum nobilissimum*," 340–43.
[82] Steiner, *Alte Rotuli*, 296–97, R9.   [83] UB St. Gall, 2:188–89, no. 576.
[84] Escher and Schweizer, eds., *Urkundenbuch*, 52–53, no. 130. When the abbess was at Cham instead of Zurich in 877, her *advocatus* was a man named Adalbert, and Willehar was a witness: ibid., 53–54, no. 131.
[85] Ibid., 62–63, no. 145.

references suggest that Willeharius was one of the leading figures in and around Zurich for at least a decade.[86] Though his wide-ranging authority does not seem to have been typical for advocates of the late ninth century, he is nevertheless evidence for advocacy's expanding scope in the East Frankish kingdom of his day.

Conclusion

During the ninth century, advocates appear more often in East Frankish sources than they do in the sources from other parts of the Carolingian empire. Given that advocacy would survive in the German-speaking lands longer than it would elsewhere, this suggests that advocates were already fulfilling an important role in East Frankish society from a very early point in their history.[87] What was this role? The answer brings us back to Notker the Stammerer, with whom this chapter began. Writing at the monastery of St. Gall in the 880s, he was clearly familiar with the position of the advocate as it was understood in East Francia during his lifetime. For him and his fellow monks, the advocate was a figure with broad judicial and administrative authority at the local level. Viewed from this perspective, historians who suggest a dichotomy between Carolingian "official" advocates and later "lordly" ones are misguided because advocates would continue to be found acting locally, especially on churches' estates, for the next 900 years. The important question, therefore, is not when advocates ceased being officers at law courts; that was never their most prominent role in the Carolingian empire. Rather, the important question is why, in the tenth century, advocacy increasingly attracted the interest of leading members of the secular elite, who had the power and influence to shape the advocate's role at the local level to suit their own interests.

---

[86] Steiner, *Alte Rotuli*, 343. See also Fischer, "Monasterium," 168–70.

[87] It is beyond my scope here to consider whether other sorts of local agents played comparable roles in other parts of the Carolingian empire. My own sense is that the *advocatus* became more entrenched in East Francia because it was imported into the region at the same time that the Church's infrastructure more generally was being established east of the Rhine. West Francia and Northern Italy had other, older traditions for administering church property at the local level.

3   The "Aristocratization" of Post-Carolingian Advocacy

On November 26, 1740, Abbess Maria Elizabeth of the 800-year-old convent at Quedlinburg in Saxony issued a charter formally enfeoffing King Frederick the Great of Prussia with the advocacy (*Vogtey*) over her community (see Figure 3.1).[1] Unlike most of the archival material preserved from eighteenth-century Prussia, this document was not written on sheets of paper but an unusually large piece of parchment – approximately 2½ x 1½ feet. Two ornate red wax seals, one belonging to the abbess and the other to the convent, still hang from it. The charter was clearly designed to impress its viewers and to call attention to the high status of the community, which had become, in the midst of the Reformation, a house for Lutheran aristocratic women living pious lives.[2] This document is also tangible evidence of the enduring significance of advocacy across almost a millennium of European history, because in order to explain why a Protestant abbess was enfeoffing a Prussian king with Quedlinburg's advocacy, it is necessary to look back to the tenth century, to the earliest reference to an *advocatus* for this community.

In 936, the East Frankish king and future emperor Otto I (936–73) issued a privilege to the new convent at Quedlinburg, which was located on the site where his father, King Henry I (919–36), had recently been buried.[3] This charter, probably the first issued by Otto after he had succeeded his father, is mostly a list of the convent's property holdings and rights. Near the end, however, it shifts to another subject. The privilege explains that any of Otto's descendants who become kings in Francia and Saxony should have power over and defend the religious house and the women living there. However, if someone else should be

---

[1] Berlin, Geheimes Staatsarchiv Preußischer Kulturbesitz, VII. HA, Geistliche Fürsten, Abtei Quedlinburg, No. 27.

[2] Wiesner-Hanks, "Ideology"; Küppers-Braun, "Kanonissin." For a more detailed discussion of Frederick the Great and Quedlinburg, see Chapter 14.

[3] On the foundation and early history of Quedlinburg, see Greer, *Commemorating Power*, 103–40; Bernhardt, *Itinerant*, 138–49; Althoff, "Gandersheim"; Leyser, *Rule*, 63–73.

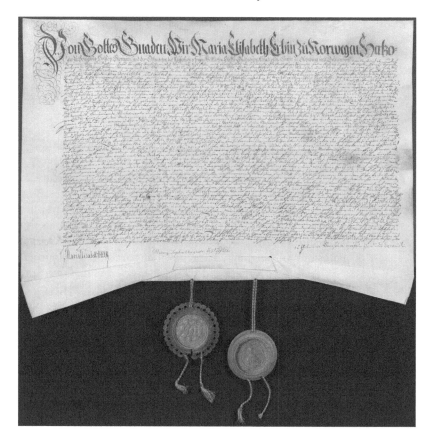

Figure 3.1 Abbess Maria Elizabeth of Quedlinburg's privilege from 1740 enfeoffing King Frederick the Great of Prussia with the advocacy for her community. Berlin, GStA PK, VII, Geistliche Fürsten, Abtei Quedlinburg, No. 27.

chosen as king, "whoever of our kin is the most powerful (*potentissimus*) should be had as advocate of this place and of the community."[4]

From the perspective of the Carolingian evidence for advocates, the language of this privilege is unexpected. It suggests that the new king

---

[4] DD O I, 89–90, no. 1: " ... *nostrae namque cognationis qui potentissimus sit, advocatus habeatur et loci praedicti et eiusdem catervae.*" Historians have offered various translations and interpretations of this passage: Greer, *Commemorating Power*, 108–09; Wood, *Proprietary Church*, 283–84; Körntgen, "Zwischen," 10–11; Mayer, *Fürsten*, 218; Semmler, "Traditio," 16; Krumwiede, *Fischbeck*, 90–92; Schlesinger, *Entstehung*, 207; Bernhardt, *Itinerant*, 6–7.

considered the role of advocate sufficiently important and prestigious that the position's heritability within his family needed to be established in writing. Otto's insistence that the most powerful of his kin were to be advocates of Quedlinburg in the future further implies that the position came with significant responsibilities. But what exactly did the term *advocatus* mean here, given that no eighth- or ninth-century source ascribes comparable eminence to the role of monastic advocate? Why did the issue of who should be advocate merit this kind of attention in a royal charter? And why was possession of the advocacy for this convent of such importance that, more than 800 years after Otto's original charter, it was still the centerpiece of a document issued by an abbess to a Prussian king? As I will argue here, just as the ninth century witnessed a trend toward advocates becoming increasingly involved in religious houses' property interests, the tenth century saw the position of advocate become increasingly pivotal to the relationship between noble elites and ecclesiastical communities across broad stretches of Europe. In the process, advocates took on the roles of judge and defender in ways that would fundamentally shape local power dynamics for centuries.

The Social Status of Tenth-Century Advocates

The tenth century is a notoriously difficult period for anyone writing the history of Europe. The fragmentation of political authority that accompanied Carolingian dynastic decline has led historians to portray this century in sharply different ways.[5] Narratives of the collapse of the Carolingian "state" and the rise of "feudal lordship" have proven especially durable and continue to exert influence over scholarly discussions.[6] Other historians, however, have argued for much more gradual transformations in political, social and economic life. As a result, alongside arguments for "stateless" political communities that relied on rituals to rule, there also appear arguments for robust administrative structures and governmental systems surviving from the Carolingian period into the tenth century.[7] Careful analysis of the position of advocate in the ninth- and tenth-century sources suggests it is best to take a middle road. On the one hand, there is clear continuity in many advocatial responsibilities across this period. At the same time, the social status of the people using the label "advocate" changed significantly.

---

[5] For general overviews, see Howe, *Before*, 57–66; Reuter, "Introduction."
[6] For an early version of this narrative, see Below, *Deutsche Staat*, 342–50. See the Introduction and Chapter 4 for the Feudal Revolution debate.
[7] Cf. Althoff, *Ottonen* and Bachrach, "Exercise." For this debate, see also Wangerin, *Kingship*, 4–12.

The first point to emphasize is that advocates continue to be well represented in a variety of sources throughout the tenth century. There is no indication that the end of the Carolingian empire meant the end of church advocates.[8] They are named in hundreds of texts from the Loire valley in the west to the Elbe river in the east, from the North Sea and Baltic Sea coasts to central Italy. In Bavaria and Swabia in the south of the East Frankish kingdom, where some of the most important ninth-century evidence for advocates has been preserved, sources remain abundant throughout the century. In Lotharingia, which lay between the West and East Frankish kingdoms and was fought over by their kings for several decades before coming under more durable East Frankish control after 923, there is a significant increase in the number of references to advocates by mid-century.[9] Thus, from a bird's-eye perspective, the volume of tenth-century sources that mention advocacy in general or name specific advocates looks imposing.

But the devil is in the details – or rather, the lack thereof. There are, at best, only a handful of surviving sources from the tenth century for most religious communities, and there are few opportunities to corroborate archival documents with contemporary narrative texts, or vice versa. As a result, the majority of the material concerning advocates lacks density; it is widely dispersed, both geographically and chronologically, clustering only rarely in ways that allow for detailed analysis of any one advocate or advocacy. Moreover, the overwhelming majority of references to advocates in extant sources are frustratingly brief. We rarely get a clear sense of what advocates were doing in any given place at any given time. The evidence for advocacy from these years thus gives the impression of being the small tip of a very large iceberg. Mentions of advocates are so commonplace, across such broad stretches of the former Carolingian empire, that there can be no doubt that advocacy was just as significant – if not more so – than it was during the ninth century. However, crafting a coherent narrative of the role of the *advocatus* at the local level is exceedingly difficult.

The challenges posed by the source material are evident in the numerous documents that name advocates in signatory and witness lists – but that otherwise tell us nothing about these people or their responsibilities.

---

[8] Cf. West, "Significance," 204–06; West, "Monks," 376, n. 10. While sources referencing advocates are rare in West Francia in the middle decades of the tenth century (Depreux, "Ausprägungen," 353–54; McNair, "Governance," 213–22), the source material from East Francia remains rich, as this chapter will show.

[9] For discussions of tenth-century advocates in this region: Boshof, "Untersuchungen"; Genicot, "Vocabulaire"; Dierkens and Devroey, "L'avouerie"; Parisse, "Noblesse"; Margue, "Klostervogtei." For the complicated political history of Lotharingia in this period: MacLean, "Shadow Kingdom"; Parisse, "Lotharingia."

At one Lotharingian monastery, the first mention of an advocate is in a document from the year 981, where the eighth person named as a signatory is the advocate Thierry.[10] This is all the text reveals about Thierry, and the next reference to an advocate in sources from this community is in the signatory list of a charter from almost fifty years later in 1028, making it impossible to say anything conclusive about the early history of advocacy at this monastery.[11] Similarly, one of the most important surviving sources for social networks in tenth-century Europe, the memorial book from the convent at Remiremont, includes several references to advocates, yet most of them are only names in the lengthy signatory lists of property transactions.[12] Comparable examples abound.[13]

Adding to the difficulty is the formulaic nature of many tenth-century sources' references to advocates. The language of property moving into or out of a church's possession via the hand(s) of an advocate is even more commonplace than it was under the Carolingians.[14] The tradition notices preserved at Bavarian religious communities continue to name advocates in clauses of this sort in especially large numbers. For the episcopacy of Bishop Wolfram of Freising (926–37), a half-dozen different Freising advocates are named in thirty-eight of the forty surviving tradition notices.[15] However, the language of all of these documents is repetitive

---

[10] Despy, ed. *Chartes*, 332–33, no. 7 (Diplomata Belgica Online, ID 1308). See also Dierkens and Devroey, "L'avouerie," 54–55, 90–91.

[11] Despy, ed., *Chartes*, 333–34, no. 8 (Diplomata Belgica Online, ID 1326). See also Dierkens and Devroey, "L'avouerie," 90.

[12] *Liber Memorialis von Remiremont*, 1:40 (2:19r, I); 1:90 (2:41v, IV); 1:146 (68v, I); and 1:146 (69r). For the dating of some of these entries: Hlawitschka, *Studien*, 48–53 (see also 141, no. 87). For an advocate making a grant, see *Liber Memorialis von Remiremont*, 1:145 (68r). See also Boshof, "Untersuchungen," 82–83.

[13] See, for example, for the monastery of Gorze: d'Herbomez, ed., *Cartulaire*, 190–91, no. 104; 204–05, no. 111; 207–09, no. 114; and 214–15, no. 118; Nightingale, *Monasteries*, 83–84. For the bishopric of Cambrai: Diplomata Belgica Online, ID 207; Despy, "Serfs," 1142–43. For the bishopric of Verdun: Évrard, ed., *Actes*, 62–64, no. 26; Évrard, "Les avoueries," 176–77; Barth, *Herzog*, 86. For the monastery of St. Peter (Blandigni) in Ghent: *Diplomata Belgica*, 143–46, no. 53 (Diplomata Belgica Online, ID 538); Vanderputten, *Monastic Reform as Process*, 32–33. For the monastery of Gembloux: Roland, ed., *Recueil*, 12–15, nos. 3–4 and 19–21, no. 7 (Diplomata Belgica Online, ID 1281, 1284 and 1297). For the monastery of Echternach: Wampach, *Geschichte*, 259–60, no. 167; Boshof, "Untersuchungen," 81. Boshof links the relative lack of evidence for advocates at Echternach to the lay abbots there, but lay abbots elsewhere employed advocates (see Chapter 2). Interpreting the sources from the kingdom of Burgundy is equally challenging; see, for example, Roth, ed., *Cartulaire*, 3, no. 10; 87–88, no. 41; 96–97, nos. 51–52; and 301–02, no. 338; see also Endemann, *Vogtei*, 19–20.

[14] See Chapter 2.

[15] Tr. Freising, 2:1–29, nos. 1047–1086. Many of these same names also appear frequently in the witness lists of these documents, which suggests that all of these advocates were closely connected to the church of Freising.

and rarely provides any details about a specific advocate beyond his name.[16]

As frustrating as much of this evidence is, when we sift through the formulaic language and the great jumble of names in signatory and witness lists, two clear trends emerge. Both point unmistakably to the steadily expanding prominence of advocacy during the tenth century.

First, it becomes increasingly common to find one person designated as advocate for the same religious community and its properties across several years, even decades. This is especially clear at St. Gall, where the ninth-century charters name a dizzying array of advocates.[17] Around 900, in contrast, the advocate Eskeric appears much more often than anyone else.[18] Then, in the early tenth century, the advocate Amalung is named in numerous St. Gall documents; his wide-ranging activities suggest that the regional division of advocates had begun to break down at St. Gall and that a single advocate was now responsible for overseeing the monastery's property rights.[19] The newfound importance of the roles played by Eskeric and Amalung is evident in the monastery's necrologies, where they are the earliest two people explicitly labeled *advocatus* in the entries recording the days of their deaths.[20] The monks thus saw their advocatial positions as the defining feature of their relationships with the monastic community.[21]

At the bishopric of Freising, a similar pattern is discernible. The advocate Ratolt appears more frequently than other advocates in the middle decades of the tenth century. In one tradition notice, he is even labeled "arch-advocate" (*archiadvocatus*).[22] The advocate Pabo then predominates in the tradition notices from the first two decades of the episcopacy

---

[16] See, similarly, Widemann, ed., *Traditionen*, 124–44, nos. 162–92 and 183–219, nos. 201–62; Heuwieser, ed., *Traditionen*, 71–72, no. 86; 76–77, nos. 89–90; *Salzburger Urkundenbuch*, 67–85, nos. 1–20 and 168–87, nos. 1–24. See also Martin, "Vogtei," 346–49. Occasionally, there are interesting variations in the formulaic language: Thiel and Engels, ed., *Traditionen*, 5–6, no. 3.

[17] See Chapter 2.

[18] For Eskeric, see UB St. Gall, 2:280–81, no. 679; 301–302, no. 699; 313–16, nos. 712–13; 317, no. 715; and 323–24, no. 721. He also witnessed other agreements.

[19] See, for example, UB St. Gall, 2:352–54, nos. 750–52; 359–61, nos. 758–59; 364–65, no. 763; 367, no. 766; 369–70, no. 768; 371–72, nos. 770–71; and 374–76, nos. 774–75. See also Dohrmann, *Vögte*, 114–15.

[20] Dohrmann, *Vögte*, 120; 363–64, n. 137; and 387, n. 416; Dümmler and Wartmann, "Todtenbuch," 31 (27.1: "*Obitus Eskerici advocati*") and 43 (5.6: "*Obitus Amalungi advocati*").

[21] This shift is even more pronounced in the second half of the century, when a man named Wito is the only advocate to appear in St. Gall's charters: UB St. Gall, 3:21–28, nos. 802–12; 30–31, no. 815; and 32, no. 817. For the rising social status of advocates at St. Martin in Tours in this period, see McNair, "Governance," 210–12.

[22] Tr. Freising, 2:79–80, no. 1153. See Kohl, *Lokale Gesellschaften*, 317. A "Ratolt" is also identified as *defensor ecclesię* in Tr. Freising, 2:5–6, no. 1053 in the *cum manu* formula,

of Bishop Abraham (957–94), appearing once as "principal advocate" (*principalis advocatus*).[23] Both the terms "arch-advocate" and "principal advocate" leave little doubt that a single *advocatus* was coming to play a more active role than other advocates at Freising – though, admittedly, the terse tradition notices from the bishopric do not explain what this might have meant in practice.[24]

For most other religious communities, there is not enough evidence spanning the Carolingian and post-Carolingian periods to observe with this level of clarity a steady decline in the number of different advocates. Nevertheless, the surviving tenth-century sources from most churches typically name only one or two advocates across many years or even decades, suggesting a comparable trend.[25] At the monastery of St. Maximin in Trier, for example, the advocate Hilderad appears more often than any other advocate during the second half of the tenth century.[26] Thus, while the formulaic language of many of these sources is similar to the language of the Carolingian-era sources, this continuity obscures important changes to the holders of the position of advocate.

The second trend that emerges from a closer examination of the ninth-century evidence helps to explain the first: Many of the advocates named in the sources were high-ranking members of local elites.[27] In one of the first surviving tradition notices from the archbishopric of Salzburg, the auxiliary bishop made a grant in 927 "with the hand of his advocate, Duke

---

which suggests that *defensor* here is a synonym for *advocatus* (for more on this point, see n. 72 below).

[23] Tr. Freising, 2:81–152, nos. 1155–1250. No. 1226b (pp. 136–37) labels him *principalis advocatus*, but this version dates from the first half of the eleventh century; 1226a, the older version of the same agreement, does not use this language. After Pabo, Odalschalk was the most frequent advocate for Abraham: Tr. Freising, 2:152–93, nos. 1251–1312; Kohl, *Lokale Gesellschaften*, 316–17. For all the Freising advocates in this period, see Stahleder, *Hochstift Freising*, 42–49, who suggests Odalschalk might have been Pabo's son.

[24] For a similar decline in the number of different people named as Salzburg advocates around the same time, see Martin, "Vogtei," 348–49. For the same trend at Brixen under Bishop Albuin (ca. 975–1006), Redlich, ed., *Traditionsbücher*, 3–5, nos. 6–10; 6–7, nos. 13–15; and 9, no. 19.

[25] At the monastery of St. Bertin, the surviving evidence mentions only one *advocatus*, Everard, during the middle decades of the century: Folcuin, *Gesta*, 628 and 632; Halphen, ed., *Actes*, 32–35, no. 15 (Diplomata Belgica Online, ID 6352). At St. Peter in Ghent, an Ingelbert is listed more frequently than others: Diplomata Belgica Online, ID 4578, 4582–84, 4589–90 and 4594.

[26] Wampach, ed., *Quellenbuch*, 210–13, no. 166; 216–219, no. 168; 224–27, no. 171; and 231–36, no. 173. See also Boshof, "Untersuchungen," 83–84; Schroeder, "Avoués," 190–93. For the problem of St. Maximin forgeries, see Kölzer, *Studien*, 274.

[27] Some historians have argued for the high status of specific advocates by studying naming patterns. See, for example, Boshof, "Untersuchungen," 60–61; Oostebrink, "Drache," 198–210. However, constructing reliable genealogies on the basis of tenth-century sources is difficult, and I am skeptical of many of these arguments.

Berthold."[28] Several decades later, Archbishop Frederick of Salzburg (958–91) granted property "with the hand of his advocate, Count Hartwig."[29] On the other end of the East Frankish kingdom, at the monastery of Stavelot in Lotharingia, a husband and wife made a donation in 966 "with the authority and attestation of the count and advocate Gozilo."[30]

Counts, in particular, appear as advocates with increasing frequency over the course of the tenth century.[31] As discussed in the previous chapter, the East Frankish king Louis the German had decreed in the 850s that counts were not to serve as advocates in the regions where they held authority.[32] By 900, however, this decree seems to have carried little weight. Tellingly, even royal charters refer to counts acting as advocates – without any indication that the kings considered this a problem.[33] In other words, there is no indication that noble elites were usurping advocatial positions to which they had no legitimate claims; the rulers accepted their expanded roles (at least initially).[34] This may help to explain King Otto I's willingness in his 936 Quedlinburg privilege to use the term *advocatus* for members of his own family, whose ancestors had been counts and dukes in Saxony.[35] For the East Frankish kingdom's secular elites, it was rapidly becoming desirable to claim the position of advocate

---

[28] *Salzburger Urkundenbuch*, 68–69, no. 2. This is the younger brother of Duke Arnulf, who held authority over the eastern frontiers of Bavaria during this period: Fräss-Ehrfeld, *Geschichte Kärntens*, 100. For comparable examples, see Depreux, "Ausprägungen," 352 and Gillen, *Saint-Mihiel*, 123.

[29] *Salzburger Urkundenbuch*, 186, no. 23.

[30] Halkin and Roland, eds., *Recueil*, 183–85, no. 82. For more on this document and Gozilo, see below. Count Gozilo is first named advocate in 965 (ibid., 180–81, no. 80). In the late 950s, the advocate for the monastery had been Erenfrid (ibid., 172–73, no. 75 and 175–76, no. 77). Then, in a document from 960 (ibid., 177–78, no. 78) there is an advocate named Bernard, and in another from the same year (ibid., 179–80, no. 79), there are two advocates named Lambert and Hubert. Carré, "Avoueries," 7–8, argues one of these two advocates is the advocate for the bishop of Liège, who issued the charter (making this the earliest extant reference to an advocate for Liège). The presence of multiple advocates for Stavelot in such a short span of time suggests that after Erenfrid died there was uncertainty surrounding the role for a few years until Count Gozilo acquired the advocacy. See Petit, "L'avouerie," 136–42.

[31] Tr. Freising, 1:788–89, no. 1045; *Salzburger Urkundenbuch*, 86–88, nos. 21–23 and 168–70, no. 2; *Rheinisches Urkundenbuch*, 2:116–18, no. 206; d'Herbomez, ed., *Cartulaire*, 177–79, no. 96; and UB St. Gall, 2:362–63, no. 761.

[32] See Chapter 2.

[33] See, for example, DD O I, 409, no. 292; DD O III, 517–18, no. 106 and 676–77, no. 259. As early as 904, an agreement made at the royal court refers to a count-advocate: *Codex Laureshamensis*, 1:342–43, no. 59.

[34] For similar observations, see Nieus, "Avouerie" (in press) and Holzfurtner, "Ebersberg," 573–74.

[35] Althoff, *Ottonen*, 16–28.

for ecclesiastical communities and their properties, regardless of one's rank.[36]

Because the tenth-century source material is so fragmentary, even these high-ranking advocates are not well documented. As a result, their advocatial functions are frequently just as obscure as those of the lower-status advocates of the ninth century.[37] Nevertheless, as the above examples demonstrate, the evidence suggests that these advocates of elite status were playing roles similar to those of Carolingian-era church advocates.[38] We therefore must avoid viewing the advocates of the tenth century as significantly different from earlier ones. Continuity and change are both evident, gradually intermixing over the course of the century to shape the long history of advocacy.

Old Roles, New Opportunities

Royal privileges follow a similar pattern. As noted in the previous chapter, East Frankish royal charters were already referencing advocates more often than royal charters from elsewhere in the Carolingian empire in the mid-ninth century. This trend accelerates around 900. The East Frankish king and emperor Arnulf (887–99), as well as his immediate successors, tied the advocates of various churches closely to those communities' property interests.[39] Some privileges from this period also point to these rulers issuing immunities to a gradually expanding pool of churches – and granting advocates judicial authority over the people living within those immunities.[40] St. Gall, for example, received privileges from King Louis the Child (900–11), King Conrad I (911–18) and the first Ottonian ruler, Henry I, all of which made the monastery's

---

[36] There is a chicken-and-egg problem here. In the extant sources from before the year 936, the pattern I have just described – fewer advocates, many of whom belonged to the uppermost elite – is not yet definitive; there are only a handful of texts from across the East Frankish kingdom that are starting to point in this direction. The question, therefore, is whether Otto I was an influential figure in elevating the status of the position of *advocatus*, or whether he was responding to a trend that was already taking shape – but which is not yet perceptible to historians at this early date.

[37] On this point, see also Margue, "Klostervogtei," 403–06; Martin, "Vogtei," 349–50.

[38] Advocates in the East Frankish kingdom continued to occasionally represent ecclesiastics in property disputes at lawcourts; Dohrmann, *Vögte*, 117; Heidecker, "Charters," 51–53; *Codex Laureshamensis*, 2:145–46, no. 532; Fleck, *Leben*, 146–49, chap. 16; and for a general statement, Regino of Prüm, *De Ecclesiasticis Disciplinis*, cols. 347–48, chap. 334.

[39] DD Arn, 114–15, no. 76 and 163–64, no. 111; DD LdK, 156–57, no. 39. For this last charter, see also Brunner, *Österreichische Geschichte*, 61, where the advocate is identified as the father of a count and grandfather of an archbishop of Salzburg.

[40] DD Arn, 85–87, no. 59; DD Zwent, 51–53, no. 19; DD Ko I, 14, no. 14; and DD H I, 41–42, no. 3.

advocates responsible for handling cases concerning St. Gall's property.[41]

In contrast, the few references to advocates and advocacies in tenth-century West Frankish royal sources show less variation, and they mostly concern well-established churches and monasteries rather than newer foundations like Quedlinburg.[42] Along the fluid frontier between the West and East Frankish kingdoms, advocates are named more often in East Frankish royal charters than West Frankish ones.[43] In the Northern Italian kingdom, there is more evidence for advocates in royal charters than in West Francia, but here, too, there is less variety in the language of advocacy than in East Francia.[44] Even after Otto I began to exercise royal authority south of the Alps in the 950s, references to advocates in documents from this region differ noticeably from Ottonian charters from north of the Alps.[45]

The increasing distinctiveness of advocacy in the East Frankish kingdom is evident in a privilege for one of the most famous monasteries in all of Latin Christendom, Cluny, which was founded by the duke of Aquitaine in 909/910. Historians have long debated whether or not Cluny had advocates, because the word *advocatus* rarely appears in the vast collection of surviving documents from this community.[46] The

[41] DD LdK, 105–7, no. 8 and 140–41, no. 29; DD Ko I, 5–6, no. 5; and DD H I, 48–49, no. 12.

[42] Lauer, ed., *Recueil*, 246–49, no. 104; *Recueil des actes de Robert 1er*, 101–02, no. 24; Halphen, ed., *Recueil*, 32–35, no. 15; 43–45, no. 21; and 169–73, no. 69. Otto I's contemporary King Louis IV (936–54) issued no extant privileges that mention advocates. References to advocates are also uncommon in the charters of the kings of Burgundy; see DD Rudolf., 153–55, no. 39; 242–45, no. 91; 336–38, no. 156 and 347–48, no. 168.

[43] Bernhardt, *Itinerant*, 108–09, nevertheless argues for the influence of West Frankish charter traditions in Lotharingia. For the language of advocacy in royal privileges for St. Peter's in Ghent, for example, see DD O I, 431, no. 317; Halphen, ed., *Recueil*, 43–49, nos. 21–22; and DD O II, 163–64, no. 145.

[44] *I Diplomi di Guido*, 27–32, no. 11 and 94–96, no. 10; *I Diplomi Italiani*, 10–15, no. 4. The evidence is much richer in the charters of Berengar I (888–924); see, for example, *I Diplomi di Berengario I*, 188–92, no. 70; 222–24, no. 83; 235–39, no. 88; 302–08, no. 117; and 338–40, no. 131. For references to advocates under Berengar I's successors, between 926 and 961, see *I Diplomi di Ugo*, 133–35, no. 44; 174–78, no. 59; 184–89, no. 63; 267–70, no. 8; 274–76, no. 10; 304–08, no. 5; and 319–25, no. 10. See also Albertoni, "Evangelium."

[45] See, for example, DD O I, 383–85, no. 269; 464–66, no. 340; 484–85, no. 352; 495–96, no. 360; DD O II, 295–97, no. 255; and DD O III, 653–55, no. 237. See also Osheim, *Italian Lordship*, 32; Bougard, "Public Power," 52–53. For an especially interesting privilege in light of my arguments in subsequent chapters, see DD O I, 448–49, no. 334; Manganaro, "Forme," 40–41.

[46] Constable, "Cluny," 403–04 and 420; West, "Monks," 398–99; Bouchard, *Sword*, 126. Because the tenth-century evidence for advocates in West Francia is so limited, it is difficult to know how unusual Cluny's lack of advocates was. We know the monastery of Saint-Pierre de Gigny near Cluny had an advocate, because the abbot of Cluny brought suit against him in 925: *Recueil des actes de Robert 1er*, 48, no. 3. For the nearby bishop of Autun's advocate in 916, see ibid., 201–03, no. 50.

silence of the sources suggests that the monastery did not rely on advocates for its extensive property interests in West Francia. However, this is not the case if we consider Cluny's holdings further east. In 983, Emperor Otto II (973–83) issued an immunity for Payerne (Peterlingen) in today's Switzerland, a priory of Cluny, and gave Abbot Maiolus of Cluny and the monks of Payerne the right to choose their own advocate.[47] Two other prominent West Frankish monasteries, St. Denis and St. Remi at Reims, similarly received from the Ottonians the right to appoint their own advocates for their estates in the East Frankish realm.[48]

Thus, for reasons dating back to at least the reign of King Louis the German in the mid-ninth century, the linkage between advocates and ecclesiastical property rights was stronger and more widespread in regions under the influence and authority of the East Frankish rulers than anywhere else. This is not to suggest that church advocates disappeared completely from West Francia and Northern Italy in the tenth and eleventh centuries (as will become clear from subsequent chapters), only that the evidence for both continuity and change is more abundant in East Francia across this period.

Beginning with Otto I, the increasing number of royal charters enables us to discern a pattern that would persist for several centuries. Monasteries and bishoprics frequently sent representatives to a new king early in his reign to ask him for a new privilege confirming the rights granted by earlier rulers (and often also to request additional rights). Because many East Frankish charters of the late ninth and early tenth centuries referenced advocacy, the new privileges issued by Otto I and his successors regularly did so as well. Thus, soon after becoming king, Otto I confirmed for the Saxon monastery of Corvey earlier royal privileges that had granted the community's advocates the right to hear cases concerning its dependents.[49] In 940, he also confirmed St. Gall's rights, including the community's use of advocates within its immunity.[50] Otto I confirmed similar immunities for numerous other churches during his reign, ensuring the enduring importance of the advocate's role as judge on ecclesiastical estates in the East Frankish kingdom.[51] Otto's immediate successors

---

[47] DD O II, 364, no. 307. See also DD Ko II, 1–2, no. 1 (English translation: Hill, Jr., *Medieval Monarchy*, 201–02, no. 32). For the story of an abbot of Cluny becoming directly involved in a dispute with an advocate, see Chapter 4.

[48] For St. Denis, DD O II, 260–61, no. 232; for St. Remi, DD O I, 400–01, no. 286 and DD H II, 18–19, no. 16. See also Roberts, "Hegemony," 166–67; Nieus, "Vicomte," 119.

[49] DD O I, 92, no. 3.   [50] Ibid., 111–12, no. 25.

[51] See, for example, ibid., 98–99, no. 11; 101–02, no. 14; and 111, no. 24. Confirmations continue, though not with the same frequency, into the later years of his rule: ibid., 227, no. 146; 255–56, no. 174; and 439–40, no. 325. See Manganaro, "Forme," who emphasizes the plasticity of the immunity under Otto I.

followed suit, oftentimes copying verbatim the formulae from older privileges into their charters.[52]

Over the course of the tenth century, new language about advocates also proliferates in Ottonian immunities, further distancing East Frankish advocacy from advocacy elsewhere. Especially significant is the language relating to advocates' judicial authority. In the tenth century, East Frankish rulers increasingly granted to advocates the ban (*bannus*) – a term which referred to the ruler's role as protector as well as his judicial authority, in particular his authority over the most egregious criminal cases (capital crimes).[53] For example, five years after Otto I made Magdeburg on the Elbe frontier in Saxony the seat of a new archbishopric in 968, his son and heir Otto II issued a charter concerning advocates' responsibilities in the town of Magdeburg itself:

[N]o count or judge … should hold any power or the ban in the city of Magdeburg or its territories except the advocate chosen freely by the archbishop of that church. The merchants and Jews living there and all the households of dependents, slaves and Slavs belonging to that place may be prosecuted by, and suffer judicial sentences from, no one except the same advocate, according to the law.[54]

Thus, in the town of Magdeburg, the advocate was the chief judicial figure.

The Ottonians gave other advocates comparable authority over towns and markets held by churches. Otto I's privilege of 969 for the bishopric of Speyer granted the bishop and his advocate expansive judicial authority within the town.[55] King Otto III (983–1002) issued a privilege in 994 for the community of canonesses at Quedlinburg, in which he established a market at Quedlinburg, described its borders and made this market district immune from all judicial authority except that of the advocate chosen by the community of canonesses.[56] This connection between advocates and various towns and markets would have long-term consequences because in later centuries many of these places would become

---

[52] See, for example, DD O II, 54–55, no. 45 and 58–59, no. 49; DD O III, 428–29, no. 29 and 431–32, no. 32.

[53] Scheyhing, "Bann"; Hechberger, *Adel*, 256. For *capitale crimen*, see DD O II, 215–16, no. 189.

[54] DD O II, 38–39, no. 29. Cf. DD O I, 415–16, no. 300. For similar language, see DD LdK, 102–03, no. 6; DD O I, 157, no. 77; and DD O II, 225, no. 198.

[55] DD O I, 520–21, no. 379. See also DD O II, 108–09, no. 94 and 103–04, no. 89.

[56] DD O III, 566–57, no. 155. See also ibid., 473–74, no. 66; 545–46, no. 135; and 552–53, no. 142. Also interesting in this context is ibid., 419–20, no. 21.

wealthy and populous cities where the leading burghers did not necessarily want to be under the authority of church-appointed advocates.[57]

As different as some of this language may look from that of Carolingian-era privileges, it clearly follows from the judicial authority granted to advocates in immunities since the mid-ninth century. In contrast, other new language in Ottonian privileges seems to be the product of developments and concerns that have no obvious antecedents in earlier sources. For example, in 952, Otto I gave a privilege to the convent at Geseke, which had been founded a short time earlier by a man named Hoholt and his three siblings.[58] Otto first took the community into his royal protection.[59] He then granted it an immunity, freeing it from everyone holding judicial authority "except this Hoholt, who [will be] advocate up to the end of his life, and after his death, if he has a son, [the son will be advocate]. If he does not have a son, his brother's son [will be advocate], and so, as long as this world lasts, we decree that the advocate will be from his descent."[60] Otto III's charter from 991 for the nuns of another community, this one founded by a noble husband and wife, similarly insists that the advocacy remain in the founders' family.[61] Both of these privileges parallel Otto I's privilege for Quedlinburg in declaring that prominent families could maintain hereditary control over their foundations' advocacies. The East Frankish rulers clearly wanted religious houses to have powerful and wealthy advocates who could oversee justice and keep the peace on their properties.

In the mid-tenth century, noble founders were not the only people interested in receiving royal privileges that clarified how a religious community's advocate was to be selected. Bishops, abbots and abbesses also went to the Ottonian kings seeking such documents.[62] Otto II's privilege of 976 for one convent is especially noteworthy because the community's right to choose its own advocate is paired with its right to choose its own abbess; in this case, the privilege references the importance of an apt and suitable abbess and a useful (*utilis*) advocate.[63] Given the many different

---

[57] See Chapters 12–14.
[58] DD O I, 239–40, no. 158. For the numerous women's communities founded in this period by noble families, see Greer, *Commemorating Power*, 17–38; Leyser, *Rule*, 63–73; Althoff, "Gandersheim," 123–24.
[59] This was common practice in this period for religious communities founded by other members of the secular elite: Leyser, *Rule*, 68–69.
[60] DD O I, 239–40, no. 158. Early the next century, according to the *Life* of Bishop Meinwerk of Paderborn (1009–36), the *advocatus* for this convent (Gesecke) was the nephew of the abbess, evidence of the tight kin networks at family foundations like this one: *Vita Meinwerci*, 224–27, chap. 194.
[61] DD O III, 475–76, no. 68.
[62] See, for example, DD O I, 570–71, no. 418; DD O II, 12, no. 3 and 263, no. 234.
[63] DD O II, 159–60, no. 142. See also, ibid., 253–54, no. 225. For the word *utilis*, see Chapter 4.

types of religious communities in the East Frankish kingdom (imperial houses dating to the Carolingian period or earlier, newer Ottonian royal foundations and noble foundations, communities under episcopal control, etc.), it is unsurprising that rulers and communities increasingly considered it necessary to specify who had the right to appoint the advocate for a particular church or property.[64]

The language of these privileges is significant, because the Ottonian rulers established and maintained close ties to a large number of bishoprics, monasteries and convents across their kingdom. As historians have long argued, the Ottonians sought to ensure that churches managed their affairs properly not only for spiritual reasons but also for practical ones; the rulers relied on the extensive properties held by churches to support their itinerant lifestyle and their military campaigns.[65] Prelates therefore had prominent secular roles in the East Frankish kingdom, and like their Carolingian predecessors, they had too many responsibilities to oversee all their estates themselves. Both rulers and prelates thus saw in the position of advocate a way to ensure law and order on ecclesiastical property. When Otto III, in a 988 privilege for one bishop, referred to the bishop's right to choose his own advocate to preside over an advocatial court (*placitum advocati*) as "the custom in other bishoprics in our kingdom," it is evidence that advocates had become the chief providers of justice for churches at the local level in East Francia.[66] Who appointed these advocates was therefore a key question.

Given this, it is noteworthy that the mid-tenth century sees one of the earliest cases (if not *the* earliest) of a monk trying to alter the language of royal documents to give his religious community the right to appoint its own advocate. Otto I founded the monastery of St. Maurice in Magdeburg in 937 and made numerous property donations to the community in subsequent years.[67] One of the first monks of St. Maurice also served as a scribe in Otto's chancery in the 940s and 950s and was responsible for writing (and forging) royal privileges issued in favor of

---

[64] See, for example, DD O II, 366–67, no. 310 and DD O III, 422–23, no. 24. In the early eleventh century, the number of immunities giving communities the right to pick their own advocates increases; see, for example, DD H II, 136–37, no. 111; 157–58, no. 131; and DD Ko II, 174–75, no. 129.

[65] Older scholarship drew a direct connection between the so-called Imperial Church System (*Reichskirchensystem*) of the Ottonians and advocacy: see, for example, Otto, *Entwicklung*, 1; Schlesinger, *Entstehung*, 203–04. While the idea of a *Reichskirchensystem* has come under critique (Reuter, "Imperial Church System"), the East Frankish kings maintained much more control over many bishoprics and royal monasteries than the West Frankish kings did in the tenth century: Hoffmann, "König"; Vogtherr, *Reichsabteien*, 274–82; Bernhardt, *Itinerant*, 30–31.

[66] DD O III, 449–50, no. 48. See, similarly, DD H II, 259–60, no. 223.

[67] Greer, *Commemorating Power*, 112–21.

his community. On three separate occasions, he reworked earlier authentic documents to include the sentence: "We [Otto I] have granted to them [the monks] the right of electing their abbot and advocate themselves, whomever they want, provided the abbot is worthy."[68] While this addition did not initially find its way into authentic records, in 948 the monk-scribe succeeded in acquiring for St. Maurice a formal privilege containing this language.[69] As subsequent chapters will show, concerns over who had the right to choose advocates would persist for centuries – and lead to more overt attempts at forgery and document manipulation.[70]

The middle decades of the tenth century are also when the issue of protection begins to appear regularly in royal charters concerning advocates. This is additional evidence that these were crucial years for the history of advocacy in the East Frankish kingdom. Some scholars have argued that advocates' roles protecting monasteries emerged earlier, as a result of the Viking invasions. This is certainly plausible, but the extant evidence does not point unequivocally in that direction.[71] In contrast, Otto I's privilege of 955 for a newly founded convent explicitly labels the king the community's advocate when explaining that the women there "should be subject to no secular dominion except ours, because we want to be their advocate and defender."[72] The charter then states in the context of the immunity "that no public judge nor anyone else with judicial power should presume to prosecute unjustly the men of the aforesaid church ... in any case except that place's advocate."[73] Whether the advocate in this second passage should also be understood to be the king is unclear; regardless, this document clearly points to the idea of the advocate as both defender and judge.

One of the richest narrative sources for advocacy in the tenth century also highlights the importance of protection. The *Life* of Bishop Ulrich of Augsburg (923–73), written in the 980s or early 990s by the Augsburg

[68] DD O I, 103–05 no. 16; 108–09, no. 21; and 179–81, no. 97. For a discussion of the complexities surrounding these three documents, see the editor's comments in the MGH edition and Beumann and Schlesinger, "Urkundenstudien," 183–86.

[69] DD O I, 179–81, no. 97b. I am grateful to Levi Roach for calling this evidence to my attention. For forgeries more generally in this period, see Roach, *Forgery*.

[70] See especially Chapter 8.

[71] Cf. Huyghebaert, "Pourquoi," 35–36. For the difficulty of understanding what is meant by "protection" in documents from this period, see Manganaro, "Rulership," 171–72.

[72] DD O I, 255–56, no. 174. For the king as *defensor* in earlier sources, see for example Capit., 1:93, no. 33, ch. 5; MGH Epp. 5:309–10, no. 7; and DD Arn, 149–52, no. 103. Other tenth-century sources, especially Bavarian tradition notices, occasionally use the term *defensor* in property transaction formulae where one would expect to find *advocatus*, suggesting that some scribes considered the words synonymous: Tr. Freising, 2:5–6, no. 1053; 2:51, no. 1116; and 2:64–66, nos. 1133–34; Widemann, ed., *Traditionen*, 135, no. 180; 139, no. 185; and 141, no. 189. For more on this point, see Chapter 4.

[73] DD O I, 255–56, no. 174; Krumwiede, *Fischbeck*, 79, 97.

cathedral canon Gerhard, contains several references to the bishopric's advocates in various contexts.[74] In one passage, when questions swirled around who would succeed as bishop after Ulrich's death, "Certain churchmen, led by the advocate and some other troops of the same bishopric, set out to make a journey to the emperor's court, bringing the episcopal scepter with them."[75] The advocate appears here as the head of the military retinue supplying protection to the traveling churchmen.

Another passage is equally noteworthy. After celebrating Easter, Bishop Ulrich visited various places in his diocese, including five monasteries under episcopal authority. As Gerhard explains, "He never gave them [i.e., the monasteries] as a benefice to laymen. But, he would grant [as a benefice] to someone from the district, where the monastery was located, some of the more distant places belonging to those monasteries, so that he could have a monastic advocate there to defend the church's properties."[76] Gerhard then continues, "However, [Bishop Ulrich] kept in his own power all the best places, namely for this reason: so that he would be able to visit them, and stay there, and make the necessary improvements for their upkeep." In this passage, Gerhard makes it clear that every estate did not have an advocate; the bishop kept the best of his monasteries' properties for himself rather than granting them as a benefice to an advocate to defend. That said, he also recognizes the practical problem of a church community trying to administer distant estates and emphasizes the advocate's role in protecting these properties. Significantly, Gerhard also suggests that the bishop could not visit or stay on the properties held by advocates. In other words, someone who held the advocacy for a property had greater access to it than the bishop did.

This is surely another factor behind the "aristocratization" of advocacy in this period and adds context to the word *potentissimus* in Otto's 936 privilege for Quedlinburg. If physical defense of ecclesiastical communities and their properties was becoming an increasingly important responsibility for advocates, it follows that rulers and ecclesiastics would want as locally powerful an advocate as they could find. This may be one reason why counts and other nobles increasingly held the position in the tenth century; they were the people with the military resources to defend churches and lands that lay close to their own centers of authority.[77] In

---

[74] For traditional advocatial roles in his text, see Gerhard of Augsburg, *Vita*, 150–53, I.7 and 320–27, I.28.

[75] Ibid., 302–03, I.28.

[76] Ibid., 136–39, I.5. There is very little documentary evidence from Augsburg in this period, but for a *defensor* and an *advocatus*, see Feist and Helleiner, "Urkundenwesen," 46–47.

[77] My language here is intentionally vague. Our evidence does not indicate how often counts and other leading nobles were appointed as advocates in the ways described in Ottonian

the process, these high-ranking members of the secular elite gained access to the properties where they maintained peace and order. What, precisely, this access entailed will be explored in subsequent chapters. As many readers may have already surmised, having the most powerful local figure as advocate could be helpful in some circumstances – but could also lead to conflict if prelate and advocate did not see eye to eye on the scope of the advocate's responsibilities.

The Trouble with Categories

As the previous sections have shown, even though the tenth-century sources for advocates lack density and detail, there is abundant evidence that advocacy was a widespread phenomenon in this period.[78] This material is sufficiently diverse that historians have been reluctant to offer a single definition of the term *advocatus* for the post-Carolingian era. Earlier generations of German and Austrian scholars, in an effort to impose order on the disparate evidence, preferred to identify different categories of advocates. In the process, they created a set of advocatial institutions that continue to influence how historians think about advocacy.

For example, King Otto I's 936 charter for Quedlinburg has been linked to the institution of the so-called "protector-advocate" (*Schirmvogt*), a type of advocate that would exist into the eighteenth century and that was legally obligated to defend a religious community from harm.[79] Scholars have argued that this is a different type of advocate than the ninth-century "officer-advocate" (*Beamtenvogt*), who belonged to the Carolingian administration, or the "court-advocate" (*Gerichtsvogt*), who exercised judicial authority on properties in immunities.[80] According to some historians, the tenth century also saw the emergence of the institution of the "main advocate" (*Obervogt* or *Hochvogt*), who held the advocacy for the religious community itself and the lands immediately

privileges or Ulrich's *Life* – versus how often they may have forced themselves into the position (see Chapter 4).

[78] In addition, other types of advocates besides church advocates also appear in the sources. For heavenly advocates, see DD H I, 41–42, no. 3 and Widukind of Corvey, *Rerum Gestarum Saxonicarum Libri Tres*, 48, I.34. For elite women's advocates: DD Ko I, 19–20, no. 20; DD H I, 54–55, no. 19; and Redlich, ed., *Traditionsbücher*, 1–2, nos. 1–3. For a royal follower's advocate, see DD Arn, 47–48, no. 32. For counts and dukes having advocates of their own: Thiel and Engels, ed., *Traditionen*, 14, no. 10; Widemann, ed., *Traditionen*, 195, no. 214.

[79] For this label for some advocates, see especially Pitz, *Verfassungslehre*, 443–44 and in older scholarship Otto, *Entwicklung*, 109; Aubin, *Entstehung*, 298.

[80] Otto, *Entwicklung*, 109, and in a twelfth-century context Liebhart, "*Advocatiae*," 173. For a more cautious approach to these terms, Brunner, *Österreichische Geschichte*, 43–44.

around its physical buildings – in contrast to "local advocates" (*Nebenvögte, Ortsvögte* or *Bezirksvögte*), who operated on ecclesiastical estates in more distant regions.[81] If this "main advocate" was a count or duke, the difference between Carolingian and post-Carolingian advocacy becomes even more pronounced, since scholars consider this "seigneurial-advocacy" or "lordly-advocacy" (*Herrenvogtei*) a very different phenomenon from the "officer-advocacy" of the earlier period.[82]

The desire to wrestle the thousands of references to advocates into some sort of logical framework is understandable. As noted above, some tenth-century authors and scribes had already begun to address the proliferation of advocates in the world around them by using such terms as "arch-advocate" and "principal advocate" to distinguish between different advocates.[83] Similarly, when Emperor Otto II issued a charter in 981 for the abbot of Prüm, he confirmed a property exchange made through the hands of two "advocates of the same monastery, namely the advocate *edilis*, Harpernus, and the advocate *pagensis*, Volpert."[84] The word *edilis* seems to describe the advocate of the monastic community itself (perhaps a synonym of sorts for "arch-advocate") and is presumably used here to help distinguish Harpernus from another advocate with more localized responsibilities at the regional level (the *pagus*).[85]

None of these terms, however, suggests a rigid category. Given how unusual such compound labels are for advocates in the sources from the tenth century (or subsequent ones), I am skeptical that contemporaries understood these terms to be referring to distinct forms of advocacy. One example does not an institution make. Some advocates were responsible for monastic communities and some were responsible for specific properties, some may have had roles that emphasized protection and others roles that emphasized exercising justice, but none of this means there were structurally different advocatial positions.[86] As a result, attempts to guess

---

[81] For these and other terms, see Krumwiede, *Fischbeck*, 84–97; Hechberger, *Adel*, 255–56; Otto, *Entwicklung*, 9–10.

[82] Boshof, "Untersuchungen," 89–90; Fichtenau, *Lebensordnungen*, 1:316 (English translation: Fichtenau, *Living*, 236). For a more nuanced discussion of the early medieval idea of "office," see Zotz, "Amt und Würden." For another skeptical view of the traditional categories, see Margue, "Klostervogtei."

[83] In the early eleventh century, a Tegernsee notice mentions a *fiscalis advocatus* participating in a property exchange: Acht, ed., *Traditionen*, 1–2, no. 1; see also ibid., 7–9, no. 8 (DD Ko II, 289–90, no. 212) and Tr. Freising, 2:292–94, no. 1438b (DD Ko II, 290–91, no. 213). A charter from Stavelot mentions an *advocatus altaris*: Halkin and Roland, ed. *Recueil*, 201–02, no. 93.

[84] DD O II, 286–87, no. 252.

[85] I take this explanation for *edilis* from *Mediae Latinitatis Lexicon Minus*, 481. However, the translation there is based solely on this same charter.

[86] Otto I's charters for Quedlinburg and Fischbeck refer to advocates for the women of the community and advocates for the place, which certainly implies two different senses of

what "type" of advocate someone might have been – when, for example, a document simply states the name of an advocate in a witness list – are misguided.[87] Categories can be useful; however, we cannot simply impose them on evidence that resists our desire for categorization.

I read the diversity of language around church advocates in tenth-century sources as a sign of the rapid and organic expansion of the use of the term *advocatus* in this period. From kings and emperors, to bishops and other ecclesiastics, to members of noble elites, different people saw in the position of advocate different opportunities. As churches continued to possess and acquire vast amounts of property across many parts of Europe, the label *advocatus* proved in many ways to be an empty vessel. By 900, for a century and a half the advocate had been a local, secular agent who could access ecclesiastical estates to watch over the church's property rights. In the East Frankish kingdom, the important judicial roles assigned to advocates within ecclesiastical immunities further expanded the role. The idea that these holders of judicial authority, who increasingly belonged to noble elites, might also physically defend a church's people and property soon followed. However, none of this happened by design. "Top-down" concerns about securing the resources on ecclesiastical property and the "bottom-up" necessity of maintaining law and order on that property led advocacy to grow to fill a variety of practical needs for church communities.

Viewing advocates' roles in flexible rather than rigid terms restores agency to the rulers, ecclesiastics and secular elites who sought to make advocacy work for them. On the one hand, given the extent and significance of church property, it is understandable that prelates wanted to exert as much influence as possible over their advocates. That Bishop Ulrich of Augsburg decided for himself which of his estates required advocates and which he would keep more tightly under his own control is unsurprising. Equally understandable is the image of advocacy depicted in a document of 926 from the monastery of St. Maximin in Trier, which includes in its signatory list "the advocate Folmar, to whom the office of the advocacy (*officium aduocationis*) was given by the East Frankish king Henry [I] in a judicial assembly at Worms."[88] This language of royal

the term, one more closely linked to people and the other to property. However, this sort of distinction is not drawn in most sources from this period. Cf. Stengel, *Diplomatik*, 514–15.

[87] The difficulties that can follow from this sort of rigid typology can be seen clearly in Resmini, *St. Maximin*, 573–74, where the idea that Archbishop Brun of Cologne was St. Maximin's first "Obervogt" is discussed. See also Wampach, *Quellenbuch*, 307, no. 217.

[88] Beyer, ed. *Urkundenbuch*, 230–31, no. 166. (*S. Uuolmari aduocati. cui Uuormatię. in publico mallo officium aduocationis traditum est ab Henrico rege*). In another copy, 231–32,

"office" reflects the perspectives of both the king and the monastic community; they expected advocates to do a job, to perform specific duties for churches. We must be careful not to over-interpret the spare language of this one text, however, nor use it to characterize tenth-century advocacy everywhere as a formal "office" controlled entirely by rulers and prelates.

Indeed, other sources suggest that noble elites had different ideas and expectations for the role of advocate. Royal privileges acknowledging that the advocacies for some monastic communities were to be hereditary within the founding family point in this direction rather than toward ideas of accountable office-holding. A set of documents from the monastery of Stavelot highlights noble perspectives too. As noted above, a 966 donation to this community and its abbot was made "with the authority and attestation of the count and advocate Gozilo." Significantly, this text also includes in the signatory list a "Bernulf, who was present there in place of the advocate (*vice advocati*)."[89] This Bernulf appears again in a 968 document from Stavelot, this time as "Bernulf, who acted as advocate in place of Count Gozilo."[90]

Were this document from a century later, many historians would probably box Bernulf into the category of "subadvocate" (*subadvocatus* or *Untervogt*).[91] However, this sort of institutional framework is unnecessary – and almost certainly misleading. The sources point to an ad hoc case of delegation that echoes, in many ways, the Carolingian origins of advocacy. Just as high-ranking ecclesiastics needed advocates because they had too many other responsibilities to manage all of their property rights themselves, so the "aristocratization" of advocacy in the tenth century began to give rise to a comparable issue. High-ranking advocates (such as counts) also had many other responsibilities and needed agents to fulfill their advocatial responsibilities for them. Advocacy was expanding, organically, in ways that would have long-term, unintended consequences.

Emphasizing individual agency and the differing perspectives that rulers, ecclesiastics and nobles had toward the position of advocate challenges traditional narratives of a Feudal Revolution. Central to these narratives is

---

no. 167, the word is not *officium* but *ministerium*, which echoes the terminology of some Carolingian capitularies. For Folmar, see also, ibid., 227–28, no. 163 and 234–35, no. 170. This case has been much discussed in the scholarship: Nightingale, *Monasteries*, 199–200; Kölzer, *Studien*, 296; Barth, *Herzog*, 65; Schroeder, "Avoués," 190–91; Le Jan, "L'Aristocratie," 87–88; Resmini, *St. Maximin*, 574; and Boshof, "Untersuchungen," 85.

[89] Halkin and Roland, ed. *Recueil*, 183–85, no. 82.

[90] Ibid., 185–87, no. 83. He is "*Bernulfi advocati*" as signatory. See also ibid., 194–95, no. 88.

[91] See Chapters 5 and 7.

the question of when Carolingian forms of public authority declined and were replaced by private forms of lordly power.[92] For historians of West Francia, answers focus on the disappearance of the formal judicial assembly presided over by the count (the *mallus publicus*) and the rise of informal processes of dispute settlement.[93] While the Feudal Revolution debate is not as central to scholarship on the East Frankish kingdom, there are similar questions about when the position of count became hereditary and based more on a lineage's own properties and rights than on public authority granted by the ruler.[94] However, much of this work – on both kingdoms – presumes a sharp distinction between the public and the private, the official and the lordly, that the sources for advocacy do not support.

Evidence from in and around Zurich is especially helpful here. The tenth-century roll preserved at the community of male canons in Zurich (Grossmünster) includes copies of several documents that point to the existence of an advocate with wide-ranging authority.[95] This was a man named Kerhard, who was active in the 920s and 930s.[96] Following the order of the documents copied into the roll, he is first named in a text that references a property dispute involving the male canons, which at some earlier point had led them to go "to the town of Zurich to the legitimate judicial assembly of the advocate Kerhard."[97] Another entry likewise concerns a property dispute heard "in the public judicial assembly of the advocate Kerhard."[98] This Kerhard seems to have been blending advocatial and comital authority in ways that blur the line between the two roles. Strengthening this interpretation, a generation later a charter from 955 opens by stating "how Burchard, advocate of the castle of Zurich," sought a disputed tithe from some

[92] For other aspects of this debate, see Chapter 4.
[93] Especially germane to my arguments here is Duby, "Evolution." For critiques, see Cheyette, "Duby's *Mâconnais*"; White, "Courts"; West, *Reframing*.
[94] For a survey of scholarship on this topic, see Bachrach, "Benefices." See also Hechberger, *Adel*, 254–63; Reuter, *Germany*, 218–20; Arnold, *Princes*, 112–20; Holzfurtner, "Ebersberg." This is a parallel development to the supposed shift from the *Beamtenvogt* to the *Herrenvogt* discussed earlier in this chapter.
[95] I discussed this *rotulus* in Chapter 2.
[96] Steiner, *Alte Rotuli*, 301–02, no. R15 and 294–96, no. R8. See also Escher and Schweizer, ed., *Urkundenbuch*, 1:79–80, no. 188 and 86–87, no. 194.
[97] Steiner, *Alte Rotuli*, 291–92, no. R5. Later in this text, the canons went "to the legitimate judicial assembly of Liuto, count and advocate" ("*in legitimum concilium Liutoni comitis et aduocati*"). See also ibid., 293, no. R6 and pp. 58–60.
[98] Ibid., 293–94, no. R7 and pp. 59–60. See also ibid., 297, no. R10 and p. 61. For comparable language in charters from nearby St. Gall in the same period, see UB St. Gall, 3:17, no. 797 and 3:28, no. 812. The dating clause of the first of these documents refers to the document being drawn up "under Count Berengar," which suggests that the advocate had not usurped his judicial authority. See also Steiner, *Alte Rotuli*, 298, no. R11; 302–304, no. R16; and 304–06, no. R17.

villagers.[99] This same Burchard is labeled a count in other documents from this period and oversees a "public judicial assembly" in one.[100] The language of these sources suggests that, as high-ranking members of secular elites acquired church advocacies, they combined advocatial rights and responsibilities with other sorts of claims to power and authority without drawing sharp lines between them.[101] That so many Ottonian privileges assigned advocates judicial authority – and granted prominent nobles hereditary control of advocacies – indicates that the East Frankish rulers supported these developments, at least to a certain extent. If a royal grant of immunity to a church shifted large amounts of property outside of the local count's authority, but that count then acquired the advocacy over those church properties, this count-advocate cannot possibly be described as "the private count of the ecclesiastical immunist."[102] Rather than a clear transition from public to private forms of justice, it seems more likely that the "aristocratization" of advocacy belongs to a broader trend of local power holders, especially dukes and counts, gradually acquiring whatever local rights they could.[103]

From a tenth-century perspective, there is no reason to judge this trend in negative terms. While arguments from silence are dangerous, it is noteworthy that critiques of advocates are rare in the extant sources. Some of the best-known narrative works of this period make no mention of advocates in their accounts of the century's many conflicts.[104] Indeed, there is little evidence to suggest that the "aristocratization" of advocacy was a source of anxiety for those who lived through it.[105] The position of advocate even has a positive reputation in a miracle collection preserved at the monastery of Gorze.[106] When one of the monastery's most difficult

---

[99] Escher and Schweizer, ed., *Urkundenbuch*, 95–96, no. 203. See also Steiner, *Alte Rotuli*, 211–13; Fischer, "Monasterium," 170–75.

[100] Escher and Schweizer, ed., *Urkundenbuch*, 98, no. 208. Otto I had visited Zurich in 952, which suggests he had a role to play in this arrangement. For the "Ämterkombination" under Burchard, see Steiner, *Alte Rotuli*, 212.

[101] Another possibility is a conservative scribal culture using terminology that no longer accurately reflects practices on the ground; see Cheyette, "Duby's *Mâconnais*," 304–05. This does not seem to be the case here, however.

[102] Reuter, *Germany*, 219.

[103] For the complexity of this issue, see also Margue, "Klostervogtei," 403–04; Wood, *Proprietary Church*, 329–30.

[104] I know of no references to advocates in the historical works of Regino of Prüm and Liudprand of Cremona, nor in the *Lives* of Empress Matilda. Widukind of Corvey uses the term, but not for church advocates (48, I.34 and 96, II.36). See also Margue, "Klostervogtei," 389–92.

[105] One exception is a miracle story written shortly after the year 946 at the monastery of St. Bavo in Ghent. See Chapter 15 for this story.

[106] For the Gorze source material, see Nightingale, *Monasteries*, 82–84; Flammarion, "Sources"; Boshof, "Untersuchungen," 72–73; Parisse, "Restaurer."

rivals, a count Boso, refused to return properties that rightly belonged to Gorze, he became ill to the point of death.[107] Only when he agreed to restore the properties did he begin to recover. As a result, after acknowledging the power of the community's patron saint, he declared, "If it is pleasing, have me hereafter as a most faithful advocate, whom you had until now as a most dreadful attacker."[108] What better defender of church property could there be than a faithful count-advocate?

Conclusion

When we stop trying to fit all the references to advocates in tenth-century sources into modern categories and instead recognize the ability of individuals to shape advocacy at the local level, we can begin to appreciate how providing protection and exercising justice could open a world of possibilities for how secular elites interacted with church property. As fragmentary as the source base is, a close reading of the evidence nevertheless illuminates a trend toward the growing interdependency of nobles, ecclesiastical communities and church property. Put simply, rulers and prelates turned to members of local secular elites to provide protection and justice on ecclesiastical estates, because powerful local nobles were the people best suited to fill the expanding role of the advocate. In the process, these nobles gained access to churches' estates and dependents and extended their local influence and authority. In tenth-century sources, there is little indication that this interdependency generated serious tensions or disputes. Everyone seems to have recognized the advantages of the "aristocratization" of advocacy. In the early eleventh century, however, many ecclesiastics' attitudes toward their advocates would change rapidly.

---

[107] For context, see Nightingale, *Monasteries*, 16–17, 47–50.

[108] Jacobsen, ed., *Miracula*, 122–23, chap. 12: "*Unde deinceps me advocatum habetote, si placet, fidissimum, quem hactenus habuistis pervasorem atrocissimum.*" There is also a Latin-French edition of this text published only a year after the Latin–German: *Miracles de Saint Gorgon*, 174–77, chap. 14. The miracles were compiled at Gorze between 982 and ca. 1015. In the *vita* of Abbot John of Gorze from a few years earlier (ca. 980), the word *patronus* is used instead in this story: Jacobsen, ed., *Leben*, 392–405, chaps. 104–09 (this is also Parisse, ed., *La vie de Jean*, 132–37). See also Nightingale, *Monasteries*, 87–88, 152. The only person labeled an *advocatus* in the *vita* is the advocate for a widowed countess: Jacobsen, ed., *Leben*, 386–93, chaps. 101–02.

4 Elite Competition at the Turn of the First Millennium

Dietrich of Amorbach, also known as Thierry of Fleury, was an unusually well-traveled monk for the decades around the year 1000. Probably born sometime around 950, he entered the monastery of Fleury in the Loire valley in the 980s or early 990s. From there, he traveled to Italy, including Rome and Montecassino, before crossing the Alps northward in or around 1006 to settle in the German-speaking lands, spending time at Trier and the monastery of Amorbach.[1] Around the year 1010, Dietrich wrote the *Illatio sancti Benedicti*, dedicating it to the abbot of Amorbach. In this work, he recounts various miracles performed by St. Benedict in defense of Fleury, which housed the saint's relics. One of these miracles supposedly occurred in the later ninth century.

When a band of Vikings arrived at Fleury one night, the helpless monks could do nothing to stop them from ransacking the monastery. However, St. Benedict intervened to help his flock: "The most blessed father Benedict appeared to the most powerful Count Gislolf, who was the advocate and defender of that monastery, and said to him: 'Hey, brother, why are you so overcome by cowardice and fear that you forsake the noblest place of your advocacy (*tuae advocationis*), Fleury, which has been devastated by a pagan horde and left undefended ...?'"[2] The saint then urged the count to gather his troops and pursue the Vikings. Gislolf, startled by his unexpected guest, replied by explaining he could not possibly call together an army quickly enough. But St. Benedict assured the advocate that he would support and protect him if he rode out with the few men available to him. Three days later, Count Gislolf and his followers were victorious against the Vikings, freeing many captives while suffering no injuries. News of this great victory soon reached the king of

---

[1] The details of his biography are difficult to piece together; see Hoffmann, "Theoderich"; Bern of Reichenau, *Tractatus liturgici*, xxi–xxii.

[2] Dietrich von Amorbach [Thierry de Fleury], *Illatio*, 364–65. An earlier version, which is much shorter, calls him only count: *Miracula Sancti Benedicti*, 194–95, I.41. A later version closely follows Dietrich's: Hugh of Fleury, *Opera Historica*, 379–80. For the legendary qualities of this story, see Dümmler, "Leben," 7–9; Vidier, *L'Historiographie*, 170–76.

West Francia, who wanted to know "how Count Gislolf, advocate of St. Benedict, had struck down such a great host with only a few men." When the count came to the royal court and explained how the saint had fought at his side, the king was so impressed that he traveled to Fleury and gave lavish gifts to help restore it.

Because of St. Benedict's importance for the Latin Christian monastic tradition, Dietrich of Amorbach's *Illatio sancti Benedicti* circulated widely. By the late twelfth century, it was being copied into a massive hagiographical collection compiled in Austria, more than 1,000 kilometers from its setting of Fleury.[3] Count Gislolf's miraculous victory may therefore have been one of the better-known stories about an advocate among the educated elites of subsequent centuries. If so, one wonders what this audience might have thought of it. On the one hand, the advocate defeats the Vikings and recovers the monastery's property; on the other hand, St. Benedict was the real hero, the one who first had to rouse Gislolf and convince him to help – before personally fighting alongside him. As I will argue here, Dietrich of Amorbach's rather uninspiring depiction of Fleury's reluctant advocate fits a broader pattern that developed around the year 1000. It is in this period that many ecclesiastical communities became increasingly critical of their advocates' behavior, giving us our first unequivocal evidence for advocates' corrupt practices of justice and protection.

Out of the Shadows

The story of the count-advocate Gislolf riding into battle against the Vikings with St. Benedict at his side is remarkable for many reasons. One is the story's length, for there is no comparably detailed account of the actions of an advocate in any source from the previous quarter-millennium of the history of church advocacy. In general, the decades around the year 1000 witnessed important changes in the production of local sources; not only do more texts survive from these years than from the early and mid-tenth century, but the sources become richer and more diverse as well.[4] It is therefore unsurprising, given the ubiquity of church advocacy across wide swaths of Europe by the year 1000, that many texts

---

[3] For this hagiographical collection, the *Magnum Legendarium Austriacum* (MLA), see Ó Riain, "*Legendarium.*" The *Illatio* can be found in the MLA in, for example, Zwettl, Stiftsbibliothek, Cod. 15, fols. 46v–49r (digitized). My thanks to Diarmuid Ó Riain for discussing the manuscripts of this collection with me. For the *Illatio*'s audience, see also Head, *Hagiography*, 126.

[4] For the challenges posed by these sources, see Geary, *Phantoms*, 178–79; Bedos-Rezak, "Diplomatic Sources"; Barthélemy, *Serf*, 9–10; Buc, "What Is Order?," 284–85.

begin to provide a level of specificity about the roles of advocates that simply cannot be found in earlier sources.

Before turning to critiques of advocates in some of this material, I first must stress that much of the evidence from this period points to continuity with earlier sources for advocacy. The Ottonian rulers of the East Frankish kingdom continued to issue privileges to monasteries and bishoprics that borrowed language from older documents and confirmed advocates' responsibilities in ecclesiastical immunities. The last of the Ottonian emperors, Henry II (1002–24), issued roughly seventy-five charters that reference advocates, approximately 15 percent of the total known output from his reign, and none suggests these advocates had significantly different responsibilities than their predecessors.[5] At the local level, the documents written at many religious communities continued to employ the language of property passing through the hands of advocates when those communities received, granted or exchanged property.[6] As more churches and monasteries were founded in the kingdom and as the kingdom expanded eastward – especially down the Danube River valley and into other parts of today's Austria – advocacy traveled to these places as well; the advocates named in sources from these new foundations played familiar roles.[7]

Continuity does not mean stasis, however. Three trends already evident in the tenth century accelerated in the decades after the year 1000, helping to reshape the relationships between many advocates and religious communities.

First, there are fewer references to advocates arguing cases on behalf of ecclesiastics. One reason for this is the limited evidence for comital courts and other judicial assemblies in the East Frankish kingdom by the late

---

[5] See DD H II. Many churches I have discussed in the preceding chapters, including St. Gall, St. Maximin in Trier and the bishopric of Speyer, received new privileges in this period.

[6] For the continuing use of *cum manu/in manum/per manum* clauses in the early eleventh century, see for example: Heuwieser, ed., *Traditionen*, 82–83, no. 94; 86, no. 100; and 91–92, no. 110; Tr. Freising, 2:206–07, no. 1324; 238, no. 1371; and 255–56, nos. 1394–95; and *Salzburger Urkundenbuch*, 211–23, nos. 1–26 and 224–28, nos. 28–36. For more examples, see below.

[7] For the newly founded bishopric of Bamberg, see DD H II, 560–61, no. 438; for the newly founded convent of Göss in Styria, see DD H II, 548–49, no. 428; for the newly founded monastery of Deutz, see Oediger, ed., *Regesten*, 180, no. 600 and 194–97, no. 658; and for the bishopric of Brandenburg along the Elbe frontier further north, see DD H II, 259–60, no. 223. In the patriarchate of Aquileia, on the frontier between East Frankish and northern Italian documentary cultures, advocates appear in signatory lists and can also be found speaking at judicial assemblies in language typical of Italian sources: *Die älteren Urkunden des Klosters S. Maria*, 73–75, no. 1 and MGH DD Ko II, 125–27, no. 92 (English translation: Hill, Jr., *Medieval Monarchy*, 202–05, no. 33); see also Riedmann, "Vescovi e Avvocati," 52–55.

tenth century.[8] However, as noted in previous chapters, arguing court cases was never the only role played by earlier advocates either. The rich sources for advocates acting at the local level on church property in the years around 1000 indicate that, by this period at the latest, providing protection and exercising justice had become the true focal points of advocatial responsibilities.

Second, an increasing number of the advocates named in extant sources are dukes, counts or other members of the upper echelons of the secular elite.[9] The *Life* of Bishop Meinwerk of Paderborn (1009–36) is noteworthy in this context, because the bishop's advocate, the local count Amalung, is named in more than thirty documents copied into the text.[10] According to the record of one arrangement between the bishop and a local monastery, "Count Amalung, the highest advocate of the mother church, took this agreement in his hand from the altar and confirmed it by the ban of royal power in his comital authority."[11] Here, Amalung is described as possessing not only advocatial authority but also royally delegated comital authority, highlighting the dangers of drawing sharp distinctions between the position of advocate and nobles' other roles in this period.

Third, and following closely on this second point, the hereditary circulation of church advocacies was becoming commonplace. Already under the Carolingians, evidence indicates that (at least in some regions) advocates were drawn from leading local families across multiple generations.[12] In the tenth century, a few Ottonian royal charters explicitly describe the advocacies of monasteries founded by prominent nobles as hereditary.[13] The first half of the eleventh century then sees a much more expansive source base for this trend, pointing clearly to local nobles understanding the position of *advocatus* as a family possession.[14]

[8] Reuter, "Property Transactions," 187–88. For an exception to this general pattern, see *Miracula Sancti Benedicti*, 352–55, VI.3. As in previous periods, the sources for advocates speaking at *placita* are best in northern Italy (see Chapters 1 and 3).
[9] On this point, see also Margue, "Klostervogtei," esp. the map on p. 405; Bloch, *Feudal Society*, 2:404–05. For specific examples in the sources: Bloch, ed. "Urkunden," 426–27, no. 26; *Chronicon Benedictoburanum*, 222; DD H II, 211–13, nos. 177–78; 265–67, no. 230; and 287–89, no. 250; and *Annales Hildesheimenses*, 44. See also Dopsch, "Grafen," 511; Hemmerle, *Benediktbeuern*, 201.
[10] *Vita Meinwerci*. This *Life* was written in the twelfth century, but there is no reason to believe that its author altered these eleventh-century tradition notices: Reuter, "Property Transactions," 166–67. For Meinwerk's career, see Balzer, "Vornehm."
[11] *Vita Meinwerci*, 240, chap. 211: "*summus matris ecclesie advocatus.*" For the ban in this period, see McHaffie, "Law," 27–28. For other references to Amalung, see for example, *Vita Meinwerci*, 110–11, chap. 29 (with n. 247); 124–27, chap. 49; and 132–33, chap. 66.
[12] See Chapter 2.   [13] See Chapter 3.
[14] Vanderputten, "Fulcard's Pigsty," 95–96; Vanderputten, "Monks," 589–90.

This last trend would profoundly impact the subsequent history of advocacy by blurring the line between churches' properties and nobles' properties. When, for example, as in one charter from ca. 1020, the witness list includes not only a monastery's advocate but also his sons listed immediately after him, it suggests that familial interests were becoming entangled with the advocate's formal responsibilities.[15] Similarly, a document written around 1045 describes a gift given to the monastery of Stavelot in the presence of "the lord abbot Poppo and Adelard, son of the advocate Boso."[16] Around the same time, the monk Gonzo of Florennes referred to "our *advocatrix* Gisela," which may be the earliest use of this term for a woman of the secular elite.[17] If, as seems most likely, she was given this label as the wife of the advocate – or perhaps as a widow and the mother of a minor heir – then this is additional evidence of advocacy being perceived as a possession to be safeguarded by the whole family.[18]

Closely tied to this hereditary aspect is the growing number of multigenerational noble families who held more than one advocacy. Count Siegfried of Luxembourg and his descendants offer an especially well-attested example of this trend. He is named as advocate of Echternach in 997, and his son, Henry I, had already appeared a year earlier as advocate for St. Maximin in Trier.[19] In the next generation, Henry II was also advocate for St. Maximin and Echternach – and his brother, Frederick, was advocate of Stavelot.[20] Three generations, three monastic advocacies in close proximity to the family's seat of power at Luxembourg. Unlike the tenth century, when the scattered references to advocates are difficult to piece together into a coherent picture of family relations, these counts demonstrate how a lineage used the position of advocate to build its influence and authority. In subsequent decades, other comital lineages would follow suit, relying heavily on church advocacies to expand their power and territorial reach.[21]

---

[15] Bloch, ed., "Urkunden," 428–30, no. 28.

[16] Halkin and Roland, ed., *Recueil*, 220–21, no. 104.

[17] Gonzo of Florennes, *Ex Miraculis S. Gengulfi*, 796, chap. 36. Around the same time at Benediktbeuern, there is a reference to a "*Iudita duxatrix defensatrix huius loci*": *Chronicon Benedictoburanum*, 221.

[18] For Gisela, see Dierkens and Devroey, "L'avouerie," 78. For women as advocates more generally, Lyon, "Advocata." For another example of multiple family members tied to an advocacy, see *Diplomata Belgica*, 362–63, no. 214.

[19] Wampach, ed., *Quellenbuch*, 289–93, no. 207. See also Kölzer, *Studien*, 274.

[20] Wampach, ed., *Quellenbuch*, 347–52, no. 248a, where the two brothers are identified in a property agreement involving the two monasteries as "*advocatis locorum predictis comitibus Heinrico sive Friderico*." For the importance of advocacies to the counts of Luxembourg, see Margue, "Klostervogtei," 388; Twellenkamp, "Luxemburger"; Schroeder, "Avoués," esp. 193–95.

[21] See, for example, Stahleder, *Hochstift Freising*, 53–56. More generally: Hechberger, *Adel*, 255–56. For a cautionary note on this topic: Clauss, "Vogteibündelung," 171–79. For the significance of advocacy for noble lineages, see also Chapter 5.

Practical challenges arose from counts and dukes accumulating advocacies. As noted in the previous chapter, some high-ranking advocates had already begun by the mid-tenth century to delegate their authority, and this trend takes on clearer contours in the early eleventh century. When granting property in 1033, the count of Metz explained that he was giving the monastery all his rights on the said properties "except the protection of an advocate, which [protection] I have retained for the sake of my soul's health, so that the [monastery] might always have on these properties a protector and defender from my own heirs." However, the count then "entrusted the performance of this protection to a certain one of our faithful men, named Gerard, because he lived nearer to the place."[22] This is an unusually direct acknowledgment that the protection of monastic properties was physical; that it necessitated a defender who was available on short notice to fulfill the role effectively.

This period also sees the earliest appearances of the term "subadvocate" (*subadvocatus*), which further suggests that noble advocates increasingly required someone to help them fulfill their local advocatial responsibilities.[23] Indeed, subadvocates are evidence that people understood the advocatial roles of providing protection and exercising justice in practical, not abstract, terms.[24] Churches permitted advocates to access their property, because someone had to judge criminals and physically defend ecclesiastical estates; if churches could not do it themselves, they needed to find someone else who could. This may seem like an obvious point, but sources written prior to the year 1000 rarely provide direct evidence for what advocates did *in practice* at the local level on ecclesiastical estates. As this starts to change in the early eleventh century, numerous sources offer more detailed descriptions of advocates' responsibilities. This evidence demonstrates the growing influence that advocates held over churches' property and dependents.

As Dietrich of Amorbach's story of the Viking raid and Fleury's advocate indicates, defending religious communities and their estates from outside invaders emerged as a key advocatial role in this period. The monk Froumund from the Bavarian monastery of Tegernsee compiled an especially informative collection of letters for this issue.[25] In one, an abbot wrote to a local bishop to complain about the many injuries his

[22] Chevrier and Chaume, eds., *Chartes et documents*, 92–94, no. 313: "*Cujus tutele functionem cuidam nostro fideli, Gerardo nomine, quia vicinior erat, ...* " For a similar example, see *Cartulary of Montier-en-Der*, 121–23, no. 34.
[23] Bloch, ed., "Urkunden," 426–27, no. 26 and 443–44, no. 37. See also Clauss, *Untervogtei*, 153–54. The term becomes much more common from 1075 (see Chapters 5 and 7).
[24] For more on this point, see Chapter 5.   [25] Schmeidler, "Briefsammlungen," 223.

community had suffered at the hands of a local man's son, explaining, "We have no defender against all these things, because the business of other affairs continually adds to your labor, and our advocate, occupied in every direction by the traps of our enemies, is being torn to pieces."[26] In another, the monks at Tegernsee wrote to their abbot, "You must appoint an advocate for us without delay, for we are despoiled from all sides by many men, and what we have is carried off by thieves."[27] Later in this chapter I will address the question of whether church property was really under such constant threat of attack in this period. Here, what is important to note is that as advocates gained more and more access to ecclesiastical property, expectations grew that they would physically defend the community, its estates and its dependents whenever necessary.[28]

Other early eleventh-century evidence points to advocates having additional responsibilities on churches' estates. The monk Ekkehard IV (d. 1057), who continued the rich tradition of history writing at the oft-mentioned monastery of St. Gall, recounts a lengthy story set in the 910s during the reign of the East Frankish king Conrad I. It concerns a conflict between the abbot of St. Gall and two brothers responsible for overseeing parts of the royal fisc.[29] The background to the conflict lay in King Conrad I's decision in 912 to give those fisc lands to St. Gall, making the donation "into the advocate's hand upon the altar."[30] Soon thereafter, the abbot, "with his advocate," traveled to the newly granted lands, where for three days, as was their right according to local law, "they claimed the men of the fisc by oaths."[31] Thus, an advocate was present on a newly acquired monastic property, actively involved in integrating the estate's inhabitants into the religious community's property regime. If other advocates did something similar every time the surviving sources describe property

---

[26] Froumund, *Briefsammlung*, 14–15, no. 13. In the early eleventh century, numerous other sources also pair *advocatus* and *defensor/defensio*, evidence for the growing significance of advocates' roles providing protection. See, for example, Tr. Freising, 2:278–79, no. 1422; Widemann, ed., *Traditionen*, 247, no. 328; Acht, ed., *Traditionen*, 7–9, no. 8; and Richer of Saint-Rémi, *Historiae*, 307, 4.108. Especially interesting is language in charters from St. Peter (Ghent); in grants to the monastery of people, especially women and children, the monastery's *advocatus* was to be responsible for their protection and defense (*mundeburdem quoque et defensionem*): *Diplomatica Belgica Online*, ID 540, 571, 578 and 640.

[27] Froumund, *Briefsammlung*, 60–61, no. 51.

[28] For an excellent discussion of the ideal role of the advocate as protector, see Lauwers, "Vie."

[29] Ekkehard IV, *Casus*, 162–69, chaps. 16–17. I place this story here, rather than in the previous chapter, because the language almost certainly reflects eleventh-century norms rather than those of a century earlier; see also Zotz, "Burg und Amt," 142–43.

[30] Ekkehard IV, *Casus*, 164–65, chap. 16.

[31] Ibid., 166–69, chap. 17. See Chapter 2 for a reference to a Freising advocate being sent to a newly acquired property, which suggests a similar role.

passing through their hands to a church, then many advocates must have been well-known figures to the inhabitants of ecclesiastical estates.[32]

Sources from this period also provide evidence of the practical aspects of advocates' judicial responsibilities. In one letter in Froumund's collection, a man went before the abbot of Tegernsee and the community's advocate in a dispute over a tithe, giving us a glimpse of an advocate as judge in a local dispute.[33] More revealing is a charter from 1023, in which Emperor Henry II confirmed an agreement between two longstanding territorial rivals, the bishopric of Worms and the monastery of Lorsch, about crimes committed by members of one of their households against members of the other's household.[34] It decrees that any injustice that has remained uncorrected for a long time "should be fully corrected by their advocates on both sides." Henry II then explains that if any new dispute should arise, the advocates "should come together and should correct it as quickly as possible." The privilege is even more specific about the advocates' roles in homicide cases, where a member of one household killed a member of the other household: "The advocate in whose advocacy this should happen should carry out the punishment ..., with the bishop and abbot's knowledge ... And if the murderer is from the bishop's household and the advocate is not able to apprehend him or does not wish to do so, let the faithful men of the abbot apprehend him, if they are able."[35] To label these advocates judges is clearly insufficient; as with some Carolingian advocates, they also had policing responsibilities and meted out punishments, which suggests an expansive role.[36]

Although the sources from the first half of the eleventh century are more detailed than those from previous periods, they are still too scattered and fragmentary to determine whether all advocates combined all of these roles of legal overseer of property rights, possessor of judicial authority and military defender.[37] Regardless, there is no question that advocates'

---

[32] Helpful here is McHaffie, "Law," 30–33. Ekkehard goes on to explain that the advocate subsequently struggled in his role as protector: Ekkehard IV, *Casus*, 168–69, chap. 17.

[33] Froumund, *Briefsammlung*, 83, no. 73. See also ibid., 12–13, no. 12 and 120, no. 113. For advocates presiding over *placita*, see also two charters from Trier: Beyer, *Urkundenbuch*, 357–58, no. 305 and 365–66, no. 310.

[34] DD H II, 639–41, no. 501. For Worms and Lorsch, see Roach, *Forgery*, 22–23. For advocates at Lorsch, see also *Codex Laureshamensis*, 1:387, no. 120. For advocates at Worms, see also the *Lex familiae Wormatiensis ecclesie* of Bishop Burchard of Worms (1000–25): Weinrich, ed., *Quellen*, 96–97, chap. 21.

[35] Similar language appears in another of Henry II's charters: DD H II, 648–50, no. 507 (English translation: Hill, *Medieval Monarchy*, 190–92, no. 30).

[36] There are parallels here with the ninth-century evidence for advocates having a role to play as the pursuers of escaped dependents; see Chapter 2.

[37] Regional variation in advocatial responsibilities continued in this period. Sources from Flanders, in particular, point in this direction; see Nieus, "Avouerie," in press. For

scope of action relating to churches and church property, which was already quite extensive by the late ninth and early tenth centuries, was continuing to expand around 1000. To be an advocate was to have access to ecclesiastical estates and dependents for any number of purposes. With the claim to hold an advocacy therefore came a variety of opportunities – not only to serve local church communities but also to take advantage of whatever their properties and rights had to offer.

Critiques of Advocacy in the West Frankish Kingdom

Dietrich of Amorbach was not the only author writing in the decades around 1000 to suggest that advocates did not always do their jobs as well as ecclesiastics would have liked. Accusations against advocates, many of them much harsher than his critique of the count-advocate Gislolf's slow response to the Viking threat, became increasingly common in this period. Indeed, critical comments about advocates proliferate so quickly in the late tenth and early eleventh centuries that this was clearly a crucial moment in the history of advocacy. These years mark the beginning of the centuries-long adversarial dynamic that would come to define many ecclesiastical communities' relationships with their advocates.

To chart the rise in complaints about advocates, it is necessary to pay close attention to geographical variations for reasons that will become clear. Let us begin, therefore, in the West Frankish kingdom, where critiques of advocacy have been viewed through the lens of the scholarly debate over a Feudal Revolution/Transformation/Mutation around the year 1000. At the core of this debate is the question of whether this period witnessed the rapid expansion of decentralized, private – and frequently anarchic – forms of power.[38] For some scholars, who read the many complaints about endemic violence in the French countryside as accurate reflections of what was happening on the ground, local lords aggressively attacked the peasantry and churches "in a crescendo of rapine and destruction" as they sought to expand their own power.[39] Weak rulers lacking the governmental and institutional structures of the

---

Burgundy, where providing protection seems to have been a more important role than exercising justice, see Bouchard, *Sword*, 125–30; Endemann, *Vogtei*.

[38] See the Introduction and Chapter 3 for more on this debate. For a brief overview, see Brown, *Violence*, 99–103. For the ways in which arguments for a sharp break ca. 1000 have entered general narratives, see Wickham, *Medieval Europe*, 104–06; Carocci and Collavini, "Cost," 138–41.

[39] Bois, *Transformation*, 136. Admittedly, this is one of the more extreme perspectives in the scholarship, though similar rhetoric can be found in other works; see, for example, Mostert, *Political Theology*, 38. For the argument that the language of violence in the sources should be taken seriously, see especially Bisson, *Crisis*, 41–68.

old Carolingian empire could not provide justice and protection in most places, leaving petty lords in their castles as the de facto local power brokers and the ones who dominated the surrounding landscape.[40] In response, bishops and other ecclesiastics began a movement known as the Peace of God; they held councils in various parts of the kingdom, which issued decrees aimed at protecting churchmen and church property, including livestock (especially cattle), from violence.[41] The threat of divine punishment thus came to replace royal judgment until the kings of France and high-ranking nobles were gradually able to restore a more centralized form of peace and order.

Other scholars question whether the level of violence in the French countryside really rose so dramatically around the year 1000. They have been quick to point out that our sources for lordly violence in this period were all written by monks and other ecclesiastics who were defending their own communities' interests. According to this interpretation, the rhetoric of rapine and destruction was not the product of widespread anarchy at the local level but rather of competition within the elite over property and its rights.[42] Monks were quick to label local lords violent plunderers when those lords claimed what religious communities believed rightly belonged to them. Accusations of abusive behavior were therefore one component of a process of negotiation and dispute resolution whereby church communities and local lords sought to control the narrative around their claims and counterclaims.[43]

Debates about how to interpret the evidence for violence around the year 1000 have a direct bearing on the history of advocacy, because the earliest harsh critiques of advocates appear in West Frankish sources from this period. The timing of these critiques is noteworthy for another reason; they begin in the same period when ecclesiastics were increasingly stressing the advocate's role as protector. Thus, we can easily read Dietrich of Amorbach's story about the count-advocate Gislolf primarily as a lesson about proper advocatial behavior in Dietrich's present rather than as a factual account of what happened during a Viking raid a century earlier. Indeed, if violence was increasing in the countryside, then advocates should have been the ones stepping in to defend churches from

---

[40] Duby, *Early Growth*, 172–74; Poly and Bournazel, *Feudal Transformation*, 35.

[41] For a brief overview, see Koziol, *Peace*, 43–87. The issue of livestock is a key one for reasons that will become clear in subsequent chapters; see also Goetz, "Protection," 267–70.

[42] See especially for this debate Bisson, "Feudal Revolution"; Barthélemy, "Debate"; White, "Debate"; Reuter, "Debate"; Wickham, "Debate"; Bisson, "Debate."

[43] Geary, "Conflicts"; Brown, *Violence*, 107 and 111; Koziol, "Monks"; and more recently, McHaffie, "Law." Cf. Mazel, "Amitié." Comparable discussions are rare in German-language scholarship, but see Fichtenau, *Lebensordnungen*, 1:316–17.

outside enemies. However, the sources suggest this was not always the case; church advocates were sometimes the problem rather than the solution.

When Dietrich was a monk at Fleury, the abbot there was Abbo (988–1004). At the time, this monastery was one of the most prominent religious communities in the West Frankish kingdom, but it was beset by local adversaries.[44] Kings had previously granted Fleury immunity from secular and ecclesiastical judicial authorities, and in 987, King Hugh Capet had confirmed that Fleury was a royal monastery under his protection.[45] Six years later, however, Abbo came into the king's presence to complain about "the bad customs and incessant plundering" carried out by a man named Arnoul, who claimed the advocacy and other rights for some of Fleury's estates.[46] This Arnoul was the nephew of Bishop Arnoul of Orléans, an important ally of the king, and the king therefore negotiated a compromise rather than finding completely in favor of Fleury.[47] This was not a satisfactory conclusion for Abbo. In his *Collection of Canons* (*Collectio Canonum*), addressed to Hugh Capet and his son Robert and probably written between 994–96, he complains in the second chapter about "the defenders of churches and monasteries." It is worth quoting from this passage at length, because readers will encounter similar language for the remainder of this book:

Those who are called today the defenders of churches defend for themselves against the authority of the laws and canons what had rightfully belonged to churches. Inflicting violence against clerics and monks, they plunder the properties of churches and monasteries that they hold in usufruct, drive the peasants into poverty and reduce rather than augment churches' possessions. Those who ought to be their defenders ruin them. [Churches'] abundant possessions are exposed to plunder by every enemy. [The defenders] are not in the least prepared, and they make excuses. They who consider themselves not just advocates but lords (*dominos*) stand back until – after the enemies' departure – they consume whatever is left ... For that reason, we see churches destroyed and monasteries torn apart. Some, which once flourished in great glory through the alms of good men, are reduced to the greatest want, because many men, offering themselves unasked under the pretense of advocacy (*advocationis obtentu*), steal the greatest portion

---

[44] Roach, *Forgery*, 159–63.
[45] Mostert, *Political Theology*, 37; Head, *Hagiography*, 240–50.
[46] Prou and Vidier, ed., *Recueil*, 182–85, no. 70. For "bad customs" (*mali consuetudines*), see Koziol, *Peace*, 20–21, 69–70; Bisson, *Crisis*, 47; Barthélemy, *Serf*, 123–24; Magnou-Nortier, "Enemies," 70–71; Poly and Bournazel, *Feudal Transformation*, 28–34; Mazel, "Amitié," 86–87. For all of this Fleury material, see also Depreux, "Ausprägungen," 362–72; Barthélemy, *Chevaliers*, 114–87.
[47] For this dispute, Roach, *Forgery*, 163–64; Dachowski, *Abbo of Fleury*, 146–50; Rosenwein, Head and Farmer, "Monks," 781–82; Mostert, *Political Theology*, 38–39.

from the possessions, income and gifts, which the ecclesiastics ought to have enjoyed.[48]

Given the absence of any comparably harsh rhetoric about advocates in sources written during the preceding 250 years, Abbo's long list of complaints is striking. His outburst does not read like a spontaneous rant – or the result of one specific incident – but as the product of years of frustration. This raises the obvious, though unanswerable, question of how long simmering tensions between the monastery and its advocates might have been building before finally bursting into the open shortly before 1000. The early eleventh century saw growing concern about advocatial misbehavior toward religious communities across such broad swaths of Europe that Fleury's situation seems to be typical, not exceptional, which suggests a deeper, older set of problems between churches and advocates. If Abbo's complaints reflect a set of conflict points that had existed for years, even decades, prior to the year 1000, this would greatly strengthen my main arguments about the long history of corrupt practices of protection and justice in Europe between 750 and 1800. However, the extant sources simply do not permit definitive conclusions along these lines.

That said, I am hesitant to see Abbo's critiques of advocates as nothing more than a product of the rising tensions between churches and all sorts of local lords around the year 1000.[49] There is more to the abbot's attacks on advocates and defenders than just generic accusations of "violence" and "plunder." Some of his complaints are specific to the role of the advocate, which suggests we cannot simply shrug off his dramatic rhetoric as evidence for a general atmosphere of feudal anarchy. Advocates were abusing their positions in ways that make sense if we consider the development of the position since the ninth (and possibly the eighth) century. The key underlying issues for Abbo include the failure of advocates/defenders to protect church property (here, we see language that might have influenced Dietrich of Amorbach's work a few years later) and the misuse of ecclesiastical property for advocates' personal gain. The complaint that these men "consider themselves not just advocates but lords" is especially revealing, because Abbo is implying that advocates were treating ecclesiastical property as if it belonged to them; they were not

---

[48] Abbo of Fleury, *Canones*, cols. 476–77, chap. 2. See also Mostert, *Political Theology*, 52–54; Dachowski, *Abbo of Fleury*, 161–63, 171–72; Rosenwein, Head, and Farmer, "Monks," 783. It is difficult to assess the influence of Abbo's collection, because only one manuscript survives (Mostert, *Political Theology*, p. 53). The compiler of at least one later canon law collection did know the work: Rolker, "Collection," 63–64.

[49] I am skeptical, in particular, that this new rhetoric reflects new, apocalyptic concerns tied to the year 1000 and the hope that the unjust and violent were about to have their comeuppance; cf. Landes, "Fear," 103, 129.

acting as agents of the church community but instead had come to view Fleury's lands as their own. By exercising justice and providing protection, advocates had acquired sufficient authority and influence over ecclesiastical estates and dependents that, by the year 1000 at the latest, they had begun directly challenging churches' rights as property holders.

Abbot Abbo soon inspired others at his monastery to follow in his rhetorical footsteps. Aimo of Fleury (d. between 1008 and 1020), author of Abbo's *Life* and one of the contributors to Fleury's miracle collections, also wrote critically of the monastery's advocates.[50] At one point in his *Life* of Abbo, Aimo describes the abbot as visiting Duke William V of Aquitaine (993–1030) and asking him for assistance with one of the monastery's possessions, "which was strongly oppressed by the malicious actions of its advocates."[51] In his miracle collection, he tells the story of St. Benedict intervening for a village belonging to the monastery, "which the advocate Gauzfredus, while he defended it exceedingly well from outsiders, actually devastated more violently than any outsider."[52] The insider/outsider distinction here is a crucial one: Advocates had the right to access ecclesiastical estates and were therefore not external invaders but agents of a church abusing their delegated authority for their own benefit.

The monastery of St. Denis, the most important site for understanding the emergence of advocates in the mid-eighth century, provides similar evidence. One early eleventh-century text, which includes a long list of complaints about Heilo, the advocate for two of its villages north of Paris, explains, "He called all of them [the dependents of St. Denis] together at [his] castle and rendered justice there. He compelled all of them to dig the moat for that castle . . . He made their oxen till for his own benefit, and he took whatever of their wine and corn that he wanted."[53] The final comment is tied to the common complaint about excessive demands, but the other complaints show advocates doing much more than simply plundering ecclesiastical estates indiscriminately; these are sustained efforts to make a church's dependents work for the advocate. Especially noteworthy is the claim that this advocate exercised justice in a place where he could control the proceedings, because it is echoed in a story from Fleury about the aforementioned Gauzfredus, who "forced the dependents of St. Benedict within the halls of his house, [and] presiding over the court,

---

[50] Vidier, *L'Historiographie*, 181–95.   [51] Aimo of Fleury, *Vita*, 110–11, chap. 17.
[52] *Miracula Sancti Benedicti*, 272–75, III.13; "*quam advocatus vocabulo Gauzfredus, quamvis ab extraneis defenderet, violentius quam quilibet externus vastabat.*" For the details of this miracle, which was retold even more vividly by Andrew of Fleury a generation later, see Chapter 15.
[53] Liebaert, "Règlement," 72–73.

issued public judgments against them. He attacked [them] with cunning tricks and then, having ripped away the monks' rights, joined [them] little by little to his will."[54]

A close reading of the West Frankish evidence from the years around 1000 demonstrates that we cannot simply lump critiques of advocates in with every other story about lordly "violence," "plunder" and "bad customs." The ecclesiastical authors of our sources were much more discerning than that.[55] They understood that advocates were increasingly taking advantage of their rightful roles as defenders and judges in ways that other neighboring power holders could not. This looks less like a dramatic Feudal Revolution than a case of local agents gradually coming to realize that there was no one who could prevent them from pushing the boundaries of their delegated authority. As advocate, why not demand extra grain and livestock from a monastery's dependents in order to help feed your own entourage? Why not put those dependents to work on your own lands? After all, they only enjoyed relative peace and order because of you.

Critiques of Advocacy in the East Frankish Kingdom

The geographical focal point of the debate about the rise of violent lordship around the year 1000 has always been the French-speaking parts of Europe. Historians of the East Frankish kingdom have no need for a Feudal Revolution in this period, because the Ottonians emerged by the mid-tenth century as a relatively strong royal dynasty able to exert effective authority across much of the realm.[56] That some of the earliest examples of harsh critiques of advocacy come from Fleury and St. Denis – two of the leading monasteries in the West Frankish kingdom – fits well this narrative that West Francia suffered more than East Francia from a lack of centralized government.[57] Also fitting with this narrative is the fact that the dramatic rhetoric of violent advocates first appears in the East Frankish kingdom in Lotharingia along the frontier with West Francia. The *Deeds of the Bishops of Cambrai*, for example, note how a man named "Heriward took for himself the advocacies of numerous estates, as if for their defense, but more so as a hostile plunderer; he devastated them with

---

[54] *Miracula Sancti Benedicti*, 352–53, VI.3.

[55] Cf. Little, *Benedictine Maledictions*, 207–08.

[56] Reuter, "Debate," 187–89. See also Buc, "What Is Order?," 281–82. For a different regional perspective, West, *Reframing*.

[57] To be fair, not every reference to an advocate in a West Frankish source from this period is critical. See, for example, Chevrier and Chaume, eds., *Chartes et documents*, 17, no. 215 and 71, no. 282.

continuous exactions."[58] The *Chronicle of Saint-Mihiel* begins a story about the bad duke-advocates of certain estates belonging to the monastery by explaining how "the dukes, who were seen as the defenders of the [estates] – called patrons or advocates – seized [them], retaining some for themselves and giving others to their armed retainers in benefice."[59] As in the West Frankish sources, these advocates from the far west of the East Frankish kingdom are described as doing whatever they wanted on churches' properties.[60]

We must be careful, however, not to be misled by the language of our sources. A close reading of the evidence from other parts of the East Frankish kingdom shows that the period around 1000 witnessed just as significant a turning point in the history of advocatial abuses there, despite the relative strength of Ottonian kingship.

Consider, for example, a privilege issued by King Otto III in 994 – around the time that Abbo of Fleury was composing his *Collection of Canons*. It explains that no one could be constituted advocate of one women's religious community in southwest Germany,

except one whom the abbess of that convent, with the counsel of the entire community, chose for themselves as being apt and useful (*aptum et utilem*). And if, unknowingly and without sufficient caution they should acquire for themselves an advocate who is not good (*non bonum*), having recognized the situation, let them have the power to cast him off and replace him with another who is more useful (*utiliorem*) to them.[61]

Similarly, in 997 Otto III gifted a church a piece of property and decreed that no one should hold any power over that property "except the aforesaid brothers [of the church] and the advocate whom they should choose for it. [The advocate] should always preserve and care for that property for the [church], unless by chance the brothers, sound of mind, should find it more desirable to change to a more useful one (*utilius*)."[62] And in

---

[58] *Gesta Episcoporum Cameracensium*, 442, 1.99. My translation is based partially on *Deeds of the Bishops of Cambrai*, 99. Later in the *Gesta*, there is another harsh critique of an advocate (p. 490, chap. 2). The charters of the mid-eleventh-century bishops of Cambrai reveal little about individual advocates or advocacy more generally: Van Mingroot, ed., *Chartes*.

[59] Lesort, ed., *Chronique*, 30, chap. 32: "*loci defensores, patroni dicti vel advocati.*" See also Gillen, *Saint-Mihiel*, 123–25; Boshof, "Untersuchungen," 75, 78–79.

[60] Imperial charters from the first half of the eleventh century use rhetoric similar to Fleury's and Cambrai's for communities west of the Rhine before they use it for communities further east; see, for example, DD H III, 64–66, no. 51.

[61] DD O III, 568–69, no. 157. This charter survives in the original. DD O II, 342–43, no. 290 is an earlier example of a reference to advocates who behave *inutiliter*, but it only survives in a fourteenth-century copy.

[62] DD O III, 665–66, no. 249.

a privilege from 1009, King Henry II acknowledged that the advocate appointed by the archbishops of Magdeburg for certain properties might not do his job properly: "If, may it not happen, the advocate there should unjustly and presumptuously act in any way contrary to the law, let him be brought to the assembly in our palace and let the matter be settled through a just examination."[63]

While the language of these texts is not as dramatic as the rhetoric of violence and plunder in contemporary sources from further west, it is nonetheless significant when considered in comparison to the previous two centuries of royal privileges for religious communities. The long narrative arc of immunities and the language they use when discussing the position of advocate is striking. Emperor Louis the Pious's grants of immunity in the early ninth century tend to say nothing about advocates or, more broadly, about who was to exercise authority within the immunity instead of counts and other royal agents. In the mid-ninth century, many of Louis the German's charters clarify this issue by stating that the church's advocate should exercise judicial authority, but neither his privileges nor those of his immediate successors clearly state who was to appoint the advocate. Not until the reign of Otto I in the mid-tenth century does it become common for East Frankish privileges to explicitly lay out the procedures for the selection of an advocate. There is, in other words, a gradual trend across more than a century of immunities toward an increasing level of detail about church advocates, and around 1000 this trend enters a new phase with the emergence of a new question: What happens if an advocate, after being properly chosen, does not do his job and needs to be replaced?

The timing of this trend is clearly no coincidence. Although these privileges are not explicit about the types of bad behavior tied to advocacy, the emerging concern about advocates being "useful" (*utilis*) to religious communities is significant. The word is a common one in sources from this period, and its meaning is not as vague as one might think. In a letter of 1021 from Fulbert of Chartres to Duke William V of Aquitaine, a letter well known to specialists for its place in histories of feudalism, Fulbert notes that a vassal who swears fidelity to his lord should remember, among other things, to be "useful"; as Fulbert then explains, "Useful, [that is,] not to cause him any loss as regards his possessions."[64] Viewed from this perspective, the useless (*inutilis*) advocate is one who fails to provide proper protection and/or fails to render everything that is due the religious community from its estates. Thus, we

---

[63] DD H II, 233, no. 199. See also ibid., 28–29, no. 25.
[64] Fulbert of Chartres, *Letters*, 90–93, no. 51; Ganshof, *Feudalism*, 76.

cannot assume that the East Frankish kingdom around 1000 lacked problems with church advocates comparable to those in West Francia. Indeed, if we cast a wide net, we discover a variety of sources that expand on the concerns recorded in these Ottonian privileges.

Let us return to Emperor Henry II's aforementioned charter regulating crimes committed by members of the households of the bishop of Worms and abbot of Lorsch. After decreeing that the advocate, in whose advocacy a fight or a homicide occurred, was to mete out the punishment, the charter notes, "If, however, the advocate, having profited from a bribe or being moved by pity, should wish to turn away from this decree by any artfulness, he will lose our grace and his advocacy, if he does not undertake to swear upon sacred relics that he was not able to apprehend the murderer or attacker anywhere."[65] This is evidence for the kinds of small-scale advocatial abuses that were apparently becoming more common-place around the year 1000; advocates could take advantage of their judicial authority by accepting bribes rather than vigorously pursuing criminal cases. In other words, justice was no more impartial in the East Frankish kingdom in this period than it was in West Francia or in the earlier Carolingian empire; it was about friendship, negotiation and intrigue.[66]

Evidence for increasing problems with advocates can also be found in the aforementioned collection of letters compiled by the Tegernsee monk Froumund. While some of his letters take a positive view of the role of the advocate in defending his religious community and its property rights, others are more critical. For Froumund, many of the problems center on a man named Penno, the retainer of a Count "O" (probably the local nobleman Odalrich). Because the letters in the collection are undated and not necessarily preserved in chronological order, the precise sequence of events is difficult to reconstruct. It seems clear, however, that Penno's misbehavior as Tegernsee's advocate drove Abbot Gotthard (1001–02) to remove him from the position. According to a letter written by Abbot Eberhard of Tegernsee (1002–03) to his predecessor, "We lament . . . that our fellow citizen (*concivem*) Penno brings much persecution upon us"; because Gotthard had taken the advocacy (*advocatio*) away from him, "he does to us and to our household every calumny and injury, which he is able to contrive."[67]

Soon thereafter, Abbot Eberhard wrote to the lord count "O" to explain that he had appointed a man named Sigihard as advocate after

---

[65] DD H II, 639–41, no. 501. Cf. note 34 above.
[66] Koziol, "Monks," 247–48. See also Chapter 1.
[67] Froumund, *Briefsammlung*, 70–71, no. 62.

consulting with the duke of Bavaria, the monks of the community and the monastic household. Because Count "O" had not been involved in the decision, the abbot sought his approval of the choice. He then continued, "Also, we seek your mercy. Order your retainer Penno to return to us the servants and dependents of [our monastery] who belong to us. If he says we have some from his benefice, we will return them to him willingly."[68] The situation apparently remained unsettled, however, because in another letter, this one to Duke Henry of Bavaria, the abbot writes, "We ask … that you give us with your powerful hand Count Odalrich as advocate of the monastery. The brothers are suffering such great scarcity of necessities, I am ashamed to speak openly to them. For I fear to profess to you everything, as it is."[69] This rapid change in advocates – at least three, apparently, in the span of only a year or two – did not improve matters for Tegernsee. Eberhard's successor, Abbot Beringer, wrote to King Henry II at some point in the ensuing years: "We suffer excessive persecution from our fellow citizens (concivium), especially from our former advocates, who are moved by the greatest anger and hatred against us, because they were thoroughly stripped of the properties of the monastery."[70]

In many ways, the rhetoric of persecution and injury employed here parallels the language used by contemporary monks in West Francia.[71] Churches in the East Frankish kingdom struggled just as much as those further west to find advocates willing to defend their properties and rights without making excessive demands in return for providing protection. Especially striking in the letters from Tegernsee is the repeated use of the term concivis, because it emphasizes the interconnectedness of a monastic house and its advocates. They were neighbors from the monks' perspective, members of the same local community, which made churches' rising number of conflicts with their advocates all the more frustrating to ecclesiastical authors.

Reframing the Year 1000

How should we understand the increasing level of concern about advocatial abuses, given that these concerns appear almost simultaneously in

[68] Ibid., 67–68, no. 59.   [69] Ibid., 69, no. 61.
[70] Ibid., 89–90, no. 83. Beringer also wrote to the count "O," asking him to intervene on their behalf with Penno and threatening to bring the case to the duke if the count failed to help: ibid., 92, no. 87. For these letters, see also Bernhardt, Itinerant, 55–56.
[71] Another important piece of evidence comes from the monastery of Benediktbeuern near Tegernsee. A mid-eleventh-century roll contains a list of bishops and leading nobles with the explanation: "These are [the people] who received St. Benedict's estates in benefice or who were its defenders, bad or good (mali vel boni)." See Chronicon Benedictoburanum, 221; Geary, Phantoms, 116–19; Störmer, Früher Adel, 2:452–54.

sources from both the East and West Frankish kingdoms? Clearly, debates about the collapse of public authority in West Francia and about the relative strength of Ottonian kingship in East Francia are unconstructive; the explanation cannot be found in top-down models that focus on the existence or nonexistence of the state and centralized government in one place or another. Advocates everywhere were operating at such a local level – on individual ecclesiastical estates, in small villages – that it is unrealistic to expect any king to have been able to regulate their activities. At a time when kings across Europe ruled from the saddle, traveling continuously to exert their authority effectively, such small-scale abuses of power would have been almost impossible to stop.[72] To be sure, there were attempts to hold advocates accountable; Emperor Otto III's privileges giving religious communities the right to replace advocates who were not "useful" are clear evidence that rulers around the year 1000 recognized there were problems with some advocates' behavior. But enforcing such a right, especially when the misbehaving advocate was a duke or count who had multidimensional relationships with both the ruler and the religious community, was inevitably going to be difficult.[73]

Thus, it was the widespread process of "aristocratization," which had started to shift more advocacies into the hands of the leading members of the secular elites from the tenth century onward, that best explains the increasing critiques of advocates in both East and West Francia. Everywhere, noble advocates were altering the power dynamics between themselves and religious communities by seeking to expand their access to ecclesiastical rights and properties. While some scholars have been inclined to describe what these advocates were doing as a new form of lordship, this is misleading.[74] In many cases, the roles being performed by these advocates were not significantly different from those performed by earlier advocates. Moreover, it is not at all clear that their actions were initially opposed by either kings or religious communities, who recognized the advantages of having prominent nobles as the local protectors of ecclesiastical estates. What seems new in the years around 1000 is that our sources begin to render more visible the competition between churches

---

[72] For the itinerant nature of kingship, see Bernhardt, *Itinerant*, 45–70; Leyser, *Rule*, 102–05. Itinerant kingship was not new in the ninth and tenth centuries. It was crucial to Carolingian rule as well; see Goldberg, *Struggle*, 222–26. Nevertheless, as the sources for local societies improve around the year 1000, it is easier to see the limited reach of royal authority in most parts of Europe.

[73] The dispute between Fleury and the local noble Arnoul cited above in the section "Critiques of Advocacy in the West Frankish Kingdom" is a good example of the networks of kinship and alliance that bound together members of the ruling elite.

[74] See the Introduction and Chapter 3.

and advocates over where, precisely, the limits of the position of advocate lay.

Nowhere were kings strong enough to enforce top-down resolutions to these disputes; they had to be settled locally. Whatever "gentlemen's agreements" might have governed the relationships between advocates and religious communities in earlier decades, by the years around 1000 it had clearly become necessary to define advocatial expectations and responsibilities more formally.[75] Thus, when a count donated an estate to the monastery of St. Vanne in Verdun in 1020, he included all his rights to the estate but retained the advocacy for his heirs "on this condition: that they should take nothing, nor should they, in the three judicial assemblies (*placitis*) per year, as is done in other advocacies, extort anything from the poor or claim anything for themselves."[76] As we will see in subsequent chapters, regulations of this sort become much more commonplace after 1050, but this early example shows that what was customary and acceptable advocatial income, and what was excessive, could be open to interpretation and increasingly had to be negotiated between the advocate and the religious community.[77]

If this document from St. Vanne demonstrates that the two sides could sometimes find middle ground, other sources suggest that the competition over advocatial rights could last years, if not decades. A dispute involving the monastery of Romainmôtier in the kingdom of Burgundy is revealing in this context. During this period, the abbots of Cluny were also the abbots of Romainmôtier, and it was under Abbot Odilo (994–1049) that a disagreement first arose concerning the monastery's property rights in Bannans, approximately forty kilometers northwest of the monastery.[78] As early as 1001, there is evidence for the sons of a count named Gaucher (I) causing trouble there.[79] One of these sons, Humbert II, abandoned his claims in Bannans shortly before his death in 1028.[80]

---

[75] For "gentlemen's agreements" in this context, see Barthélemy, *Chevaliers*, 147. For churches paying more attention to defining the extent of their rights and properties in this period, see Mazel, *L'évêque*, 211–15, 221–27.

[76] Bloch, ed., "Urkunden," 427–28, no. 27. On this document, see also Boshof, "Untersuchungen," 91. For a similar agreement, see *Cartulary of Montier-en-Der*, 121–23, no. 34; Depreux, "Ausprägungen," 365–67, 373. For other pre-1050 examples of efforts to regulate advocatial income, see Boussard, "Actes royaux," 103–05; Vanderputten, "Fulcard's Pigsty," 96. Also interesting in this context is *Annales Sancti Quintini*, 508 (year 994).

[77] Brown, *Violence*, 102–03.

[78] For Odilo as abbot of Romainmôtier, see Endemann, *Vogtei*, 14–15.

[79] Pahud, ed., *Cartulaire*, 155–56, no. 48. This Gaucher and his sons were based at Salins-les-Bains, approximately 35 kilometers west of Bannans, meaning that Bannans lay roughly halfway between Romainmôtier and this family's center of power.

[80] Ibid., 149–50, no. 44.

However, property rights at Bannans remained a point of tension into the next generation.[81]

According to one text, around 1045, "Gaucher (II) . . . proclaimed that he held the advocacy on the estate of Bannans and on the other estates belonging to it."[82] Gaucher claimed that Abbot Maiolus of Cluny and Romainmôtier had given the advocacy to his father and that Abbot Odilo of Cluny and Romainmôtier had given it to him (Gaucher II). When Abbot Odilo passed through the region, however, "the dependents of [Romainmôtier] rushed to him, complaining about the evils that Gaucher had done to them, that there were too many to endure."[83] The complaint was eventually heard before the count of Burgundy. Although Abbot Odilo was prevented by illness from going, he sent two monks and another agent, who swore an oath that the advocacy had not been given to either the father or the son.[84] Only then did Gaucher abandon his claim.[85]

While the precise details of the story are difficult to reconstruct, the question of whether or not Gaucher had ever possessed the advocacy at all shows how the position of advocate had become a focal point for competitions between nobles and religious communities like never before. There are echoes here of Abbo of Fleury's complaint that local power holders offered "themselves unasked under the pretense of advocacy" as defenders.[86] Entrepreneurial nobles were increasingly using advocacy as a way to claim access to ecclesiastical estates. Abbots Odilo and Abbo responded by insisting that these nobles were usurpers. Whether such disputes would be settled peacefully or erupt into violence differed from case to case, because around the year 1000 – and for centuries to come – the nature and extent of advocates' authority were open to negotiation, not rigidly defined.[87]

Conclusion

By the early eleventh century, there was a *can't live with them, can't live without them* quality to religious communities' relationships with their advocates. On their numerous and scattered estates, ecclesiastical houses had to rely on nobles (and their followers), because they were the people with sufficient skill and authority to pursue and prosecute criminals and to defend a church's property and dependents from outsiders. As a result,

---

[81] For this dispute, see Endemann, *Vogtei*, 20–21; Vregille, "Moines," 111–14.
[82] Pahud, ed. *Cartulaire*, 121–23, no. 27.   [83] Ibid.   [84] Ibid.   [85] Ibid., 177–78, no. 67.
[86] See the section "Critiques of Advocacy in the West Frankish Kingdom."
[87] For pertinent observations along these lines, see Pischek, *Vogtgerichtsbarkeit*, 101; McHaffie, "Law," 34–35.

over the course of the quarter-millennium after 750, advocates became an essential feature of many local landscapes across Europe. In the process, however, nobles learned that there were opportunities to profit from their role as advocates; that they could challenge religious communities over questions of how much access they could have to ecclesiastical property and the income produced by it. Around 1000, the sources for this competition between religious communities and advocates are not abundant enough to suggest that conflict was commonplace. In the ensuing decades, however, calls to reform the Church and to improve religious life led to a surge in new ecclesiastical foundations and property donations to churches – throwing fuel on the long-smoldering fire of church–advocate relations.

5   The Limits of Church Reform

The conflict with the German king Henry IV (1056–1106) over the appointment and investiture of bishops has made Gregory VII (1073–85) one of the best-known popes of the Middle Ages. From his reception of the excommunicated Henry at the snow-covered castle of Canossa to his flight into exile before the same ruler's troops at Rome a few years later, he seems to have spent much of his time as pope moving from one dramatic event to the next. In October of 1074, however, before the great clashes of his papacy had begun, Gregory wrote a letter about an issue that hardly seems worthy of the famed pope's attention: the inheritance of a monastic advocacy. Addressed to two bishops, the short letter attempts to intercede on behalf of a small convent in Alsace, Sainte-Croix-en-Plaine (Heiligkreuz). As it explains, two relatives, "Hugo and Gerard, seeking their own things rather than those of God, . . . while they fight one another over the advocacy, destroy the goods of the monastery. Those things, which have been established for the support of the nuns of God, they turn into plunder for their knights through their impious attacks."[1] Gregory then asks the bishops to help settle the dispute, noting that Gerard seems to be the one who ought to have the advocacy since as the pope understands it, he is the older of the two.

Why did Pope Gregory VII take such an interest in this monastic advocacy? The answer lies at the intersection of local history and the early papal reform efforts of the mid-eleventh century. Sainte-Croix-en-Plaine had been founded in the opening decades of the eleventh century by a count named Hugh and his wife, Heilwig, at Woffenheim, not far from their castle of Eguisheim. A typical noble foundation of its day, there is no reason to think that it would have attracted much notice outside of its immediate neighborhood if not for the fact that one of Hugh and Heilwig's sons, Bruno, became Pope Leo IX (1048–54). Previously bishop of Toul, Bruno was a central figure in the initial reform push at

---

[1] *Register Gregors VII.*, 146–47, II.14. The community is also sometimes called Woffenheim; for this community, see Hummer, "Reform."

Rome against simony and clerical marriage.[2] Nevertheless, he also remained a member of his family, and after the deaths of his brothers, he inherited his parents' rights over Sainte-Croix-en-Plaine. In 1049, seeking to regulate the community's future status, the new pope decreed that he was placing the convent

under our apostolic see ... in order to defend it against all men who oppose it or undertake to oppose it, so that no one might usurp for themselves the exercising of any power there or in the places belonging to it. It should always remain peaceful and free ... [in] complete liberty and subject to no one except the apostolic see.[3]

Despite such grand rhetoric of papal protection and monastic liberty, Pope Leo IX did not envision that the convent would be separated entirely from the world around it. His privilege discusses the community's advocacy at great length. Although the text never explains what this advocacy was – or what, exactly, the advocatial role might have entailed – it announces that Leo IX granted the advocacy to his nephew Henry and Henry's heirs, privileging the eldest.[4] It is this clause that Pope Gregory VII would reference twenty-five years later when intervening in the dispute between the two kinsmen over the advocacy. The calls for church reform and monastic liberty that were growing louder in the mid-eleventh century had thus brought questions about advocates to the threshold of St. Peter's. Less than two years after becoming pope, Gregory had learned an essential lesson: No one who took an interest in protecting churches' properties and rights could avoid becoming entangled in advocacy's intricate web.

Theory and Practice

Beginning in the second half of the eleventh century, the volume of evidence for advocates and advocacy in the German kingdom becomes overwhelming – and remains so until the end of the eighteenth century.[5] One reason for this is the overall increase in the number of sources that survive in comparison to earlier periods; there is simply more material for many of the churches and monasteries discussed in the previous chapters.[6] But this is only one reason. New calls to reform and improve

---

[2] For Leo, see Smith, "Leo IX"; Zey, *Investiturstreit*, 36–39; Howe, *Before*, 297–313; Tellenbach, *Church*, 146–47.

[3] Leo IX, *Epistolae*, cols. 635–37, no. 30.

[4] For more on this clause, see the next section, "Theory and Practice."

[5] I will start to use "German kingdom" rather than "East Frankish kingdom" in this chapter, because the term *regnum Teutonicum* first came into regular use after 1050; see Arnold, *Medieval Germany*, 4–12.

[6] Mancia, "Sources."

the spiritual life in Latin Christendom prompted waves of new religious foundations, and the period from approximately 1050 to 1150 witnessed the establishment of the largest number of new ecclesiastical communities that most parts of Europe had ever seen.[7]

This trend is first evident in the various Benedictine reform efforts radiating outward from such places as Hirsau and Siegburg.[8] By the period around 1100, new communities of Augustinian canons and canonesses – and soon thereafter, Premonstratensian canons and canonesses – were also being founded across Europe. In the German kingdom, many of these foundations had advocates from the beginning, in contrast to new religious houses in other parts of Europe (including France), where advocacy was not as closely linked to reform. Even Cistercian houses east of the Rhine, although far less inclined in the long term than other religious communities to accept local nobles as advocates, had to confront the issue of advocacy in the early decades of their existence.[9]

The general label of "reform" that historians use to explain this surge in new religious houses and orders is a contested one. Ecclesiastical authors of the eleventh and twelfth centuries did indeed employ the term *reformatio*, because many people were self-consciously trying to improve the religious life and spiritual commitment of all Christians in Europe.[10] Nevertheless, ideas of reform touched upon so many different themes – accession to church offices, clerical and lay marriage, liturgy, monastic regimens, lay spirituality and the relationship between imperial and papal authority – that scholars have cautioned against imagining a monolithic concept shared by everyone who thought of himself or herself as a reformer.[11] For the history of advocacy, this cautionary note is essential because the sources discuss advocates and advocacies in a variety of ways between approximately 1050 and 1150. Amidst the whirl of ideas circulating in these years, the overwhelming majority of ecclesiastics in the German kingdom never seriously questioned the need for advocates to provide protection and justice for their communities. Opinions differed, however, about the proper relationship between church and advocate in this age of rethinking the relationships between the Church and society at large.

---

[7] Venarde, *Women's Monasticism*, 10, 181; Weinfurter, "Die kirchliche Ordnung," 304; Vanderputten, "Crises," 262–63; Lyon, "Nobility," 849–53.

[8] See the next two sections of this chapter, "New Foundations, New Orders, New Advocates," and "Ecclesiastical Office, Noble Asset."

[9] For overviews of the various new forms of monasticism in this period, see Melville, *Monasticism*; Vones-Liebenstein, "Similarities."

[10] Constable, *Reformation*, 3.

[11] Vanderputten, "Monastic Reform"; Beach, *Trauma*; Barrow, "Ideas."

To understand the impact of reform ideas on the history of advocacy, the reigns of the first two rulers of the Salian dynasty of the German kingdom, Emperor Conrad II (1027–39) and his son Emperor Henry III (1039–56), are critical. Following a pattern that was already evident under the Ottonians, both Conrad and Henry issued numerous privileges at the start of their rule confirming the rights of royal protection and immunity granted by their predecessors to existing monastic houses. These documents routinely reference the position of advocate in ways that echo tenth-century usage.[12] However, in contrast to the Ottonian period, by the second quarter of the eleventh century, the founders of new religious communities had begun to show less interest in seeking privileges of royal protection and immunity from the German rulers. By the 1040s at the latest, times were clearly changing.[13]

This decline in privileges granting royal protection coincided with a surge in the number of papal privileges placing religious communities under the protection of the Roman See. Papal protection was not a new concept in this period, but its popularity grew as church reformers emphasized the need to limit secular authorities' influence over the religious life.[14] Emperor Henry III, who was interested in promoting some reform ideas, helped to spur this trend by installing the reform-minded Bishop Bruno of Toul as Pope Leo IX.[15] Already as bishop, Bruno had sought to improve monastic life in his diocese.[16] He was guided in part by ideals emanating from the monastery of Cluny, which had been granted to the papacy for protection at the time of its foundation in the tenth century. The idea of distancing a monastic house from both diocesan authority and secular control in order to give its members more freedom to pursue their spiritual goals quickly became popular with monks and founders alike.

Thus, Leo IX's 1049 privilege for his family foundation at Sainte-Croix-en-Plaine was just one of several documents the new pope issued to bring religious houses more firmly into the papal fold. The same year, his

---

[12] See, for example, DD Ko II, 2–3, no. 2; 11–12, no. 10; and H III, 1–3, nos. 1–2.

[13] Scholars have long recognized Henry III's 1045 privilege for the community of canons at Beromünster as marking the end of traditional grants of royal protection: DD H III, 160–61, no. 129; see also 162–63, no. 130. On this point, see Wood, *Proprietary Church*, 366–69; Schmid, "Adel," 306–07; Semmler, "Traditio," 21. The extended minority of Henry III's son and heir, Henry IV, played a role in this trend; see Robinson, *Henry IV*, 19–62; Vogtherr, "Die Reichsklöster," 436–48.

[14] There is an enormous body of scholarship on the development of the ideas of papal protection and monastic liberty; see Rennie, *Freedom*; Wood, *Proprietary Church*, 839–47; Tellenbach, *Libertas*, esp. 140–47; Hirsch, "Constitutional History," 134–37.

[15] Weinfurter, *Salian Century*, 93–96.

[16] *Life of Pope Leo*, 117–18, I.12 and 139–40, II.12. For Bruno and church advocacy while he was bishop, see Boshof, "Untersuchungen," 100.

privilege for another convent similarly confirmed that the noble founder had given the house to the Roman Church – and, as at Sainte-Croix-en-Plaine, detailed how the founder and his heirs would be the advocates.[17] Leo also encouraged one of his nephews, Count Adalbert II of Calw, to re-establish the monastery of Hirsau in Swabia; under its abbot William (1069–91), it emerged as one of the most important centers east of the Rhine for the dissemination of ideas about papal protection and monastic liberty.[18] The monastery of All Saints (Allerheiligen) in Schaffhausen in today's Switzerland, another noble foundation supported by Pope Leo IX, likewise became prominent in reform circles.[19] Especially in the southwest of the German kingdom, strong connections between Pope Leo IX, local nobles and monastic reformers helped to spread ideas of papal protection – while preserving the centuries-old tradition of church advocacy.

The close connections that Pope Leo IX and some of his immediate successors had with the noble founders of new communities did not go unchallenged by subsequent generations of reformers. In 1080, six years after Gregory VII intervened on the question of who the rightful advocate for Sainte-Croix-en-Plaine was, the same pope wrote a letter to Abbot William of Hirsau about the monastery of Schaffhausen, in which he offered a different opinion about the heritability of church advocacies. He insisted "that no [one] … may presume to claim for himself any provisions of ownership in that place, nor a hereditary right, a right of advocacy, a right of investiture, nor any power whatsoever, which may harm the liberty of the monastery."[20] His concern was not with advocacy itself but unjust claims to it, because he then noted, "[T]he abbot may choose as advocate whomever he wants; and if he afterwards should not be useful (*utilis*) to the monastery, the abbot may constitute another after he has been removed." Gregory then goes one step further, explaining that "a privilege, which our predecessor of good memory Alexander [Pope Alexander II (1061–73)], persuaded by deceit and deception, made for that place …, in which he conceded to Count Herward and his heirs the advocacy and the power of appointing the abbot and the administration of all property, we … invalidate [and] make null and void."

Some historians have read this letter as an extreme reformist position; as a radical attempt to eliminate completely secular influence over

---

[17] Leo IX, *Epistolae*, cols. 637–39, no. 32. See also Regesta Imperii Online, RI III, 5, 2 no. 716.
[18] Janssen, "Papst Leo IX," 61–64.
[19] Beach, *Trauma*, 17; Schmid, "Adel," 301; Jakobs, *Hirsauer*, 57–58.
[20] *Register Gregors VII.*, 2:502–05, 7.24.

a monastic community.[21] But as dramatic as Pope Gregory VII's rhetoric is here, his position is not a new one. German royal privileges from the mid-tenth century onward had already addressed the question of how advocates were to be selected, with some decreeing advocacies to be hereditary and others giving abbots or abbesses the right to choose – and replace – their advocates.[22] The papal chancery's use of the word *utilis* here is especially telling because the German royal chancery had been employing this term in reference to advocates for almost a century by the time of Gregory's letter.[23] In other words, this document demonstrates that the papacy in the final quarter of the eleventh century found itself faced with the same set of basic issues about advocacy that the rulers of the German kingdom had already been confronting for decades.

Sources from many of the newly founded monasteries in the southwest of the German kingdom show church reformers' efforts to align advocacy with the ideals of monastic liberty and papal protection. When Count Adalbert of Calw re-established the monastery of Hirsau with Pope Leo IX's support, he did so by endowing it with lands and rights from his own holdings. Initially, he maintained control of these properties, and he is thus described as possessing the monastery "in his own right."[24] Under the influence of Abbot William of Hirsau, however, Adalbert and his wife and children decided to renounce all their rights over the monastery and to grant it full liberty; Abbot William then traveled to Rome, where Pope Gregory VII gave him a privilege confirming the monastery's new status.[25] Clearly, reform ideals could inspire even high-ranking nobles to abandon their traditional claims to their religious foundations' properties and rights.

Nevertheless, the privilege known as the "Hirsau Formulary" – which would prove to be one of the most influential documents in German monastic reform circles in subsequent decades – demonstrates that church advocacy still had a role to play. Dated 1075 and issued in King Henry IV's name, it confirms that Adalbert and his wife and children did indeed renounce every power and right they held over the monastery. However, it then goes on to explain,

---

[21] Wood, *Proprietary Church*, 843–44; Tellenbach, *Church*, 299–300; Hirsch, "Constitutional History," 145–48. See also Rennie, *Freedom*, 177–78.

[22] See Chapters 3 and 4.   [23] See Chapter 3.

[24] Haimo of Hirsau, *Vita*, 212, chap. 2. See also Tellenbach, *Church*, 299. I will avoid here debates about the *Eigenkirche* in the Middle Ages, because while it is connected to the issue of advocacy, it is a modern category rather than a medieval one. See Wood, *Proprietary Church*, 1.

[25] Berthold of Reichenau, *Chronicon*, 233–34 (English translation: Berthold of Reichenau, *Chronicle*, 141).

The count grants to [Hirsau] that any advocate be made from his heirs, provided that the abbot, with the brothers' counsel, should find such a person among them, who (just like the count now) is not roused by earthly opportunity but by heavenly reward and who wants to defend zealously the monastery's goods and its established liberty and privilege; if not, the abbot may choose an apt and useful advocate from wherever he pleases.[26]

The Hirsau Formulary then details the advocate's rights, explaining for example that the advocate, with the abbot's support, "should receive the legitimate ban from the king, and three times a year, if necessary, either in the monastery or wherever and whenever it pleases the abbot, he should come when invited by the abbot and exercise justice properly."[27]

While much of this language is new, the advocate's well-established responsibilities of providing protection and exercising justice are nevertheless front and center. In fact, the pairing of the demand for a pious and zealous defender with an explicit statement about the hereditary nature of the advocacy suggests Count Adalbert had not given away as much in the name of monastic liberty as it might initially appear. The abbot and monks would effectively have to disinherit one of Adalbert's descendants before they could select an advocate from outside his lineage – a potentially dangerous step to take. The section on advocatial justice can likewise be read as Adalbert maintaining significant influence over his foundation. Although the document insists that the advocate's judicial authority came from the king (not from Adalbert's familial claims to Hirsau and its estates), the privilege nevertheless makes it clear that Adalbert as advocate was the person with the power to access the monastery's property to hold court.

Thus, as the Hirsau Formulary clearly shows, whatever one might want to imagine monastic liberty to mean in our sources, in the German kingdom it ran up against the entrenched position of the advocate. Advocacy had developed over the course of the Carolingian and post-Carolingian periods to address two inescapable problems: Somebody needed to keep order on churches' estates and provide justice for their dependents, and somebody needed to *physically* protect ecclesiastical communities and their properties from external threats. So long as the popes resided in Rome, the theory of papal protection could never compensate entirely for the practical necessities of religious communities.[28] Freeing a monastery completely from secular authority would have

---

[26] DD H IV, 357–62, no. 280 (here, p. 360). This is an oft-discussed document; see Stieldorf, "Klöster," 53–54, 62–63; Melville, *Monasticism*, 87; Wood, *Proprietary Church*, 843; Jakobs, *Hirsauer*, 17–23; Scheyhing, *Eide*, 200–07; Mayer, *Fürsten*, 50–62.
[27] DD H IV, 360, no. 280. For the ban, see Chapter 3 and Scheyhing, *Eide*, 205–09.
[28] Weinfurter, *Salzburger Bistumsreform*, 121; Hirsch, "Constitutional History," 147–49.

placed the responsibility for protection and justice in the hands of the monastic community and its local agents (who lacked the resources and clout of leading nobles like Count Adalbert of Calw) – or in the hands of the king. However, in the German kingdom of the late eleventh century, the king was the reformers' principal concern because of the rulers' traditional claims to wide-ranging authority over bishoprics and monasteries.[29] At Hirsau, therefore, the need for a local protector and judge was solved – as it had been at many other noble foundations since the time of Otto I's foundation of Quedlinburg – by making the advocacy hereditary. The case of Sainte-Croix-en-Plaine has already shown, however, that even when the rules of inheritance were clearly spelled out in writing, disputes over which family member was to receive an advocacy could lead to violence and damage monastic properties.

As a result, there was also another strand of reform – as evidenced by Pope Gregory VII's above-quoted letter to Abbot William of Hirsau about Schaffhausen – that insisted religious communities should have the right to choose their own advocates. But this was not a panacea either. Here too, reformist ideals quickly ran up against practical realities on the ground.

The best late-eleventh-century evidence for the problems that could arise when communities chose their advocates freely comes from the monastery of Muri in modern Switzerland. It had been founded around 1027 by members of the family that would later be known as the Habsburgs.[30] In 1082, Count Werner (of Habsburg), like many of his contemporaries in the southwest of the German kingdom, asked Abbot William of Hirsau and other reformers to improve the religious life in his family's foundation. Monks from the nearby monastery of St. Blasien therefore came to Muri.[31] Keeping with the reform ideals of the day, Count Werner issued a privilege that same year declaring the community completely free and granting to the monks "that they should elect an advocate for themselves, whomever they want."[32]

Another document describes the history of the advocacy over the next several years: "[T]he entire community chose as advocate for themselves ... Liudolf [of Regensberg] ..., and they commended to him the place and all its appurtenances. After he had presided over this place for a short time, on account of the war between Count Werner and his

---

[29] Weinfurter, *Salian Century*, 151–53.

[30] For the early history of Muri and the most important source collection for the monastery's first years, see *Acta Murensia*; Meier, *Gründung*, 35–40; Jakobs, *Adel*, 43–65.

[31] Jakobs, *Adel*, 49–52.

[32] *Acta Murensia*, 26, no. 10: "*ut eligerent sibi advocatum quemcumque vellent.*" See also Meier, *Gründung*, 167; Wood, *Proprietary Church*, 844–46.

nephews from Lenzburg, he renounced the advocacy and advised the brothers to provide another advocate for themselves."[33] Liudolf, who was already involved in various local conflicts because of his position as advocate of St. Gall in this same period, apparently wanted to avoid being in the middle of a family dispute.[34] As a result, the Muri monks "designated for themselves this time a certain Richwin of Rüsegg as advocate .... [But] because Richwin was unable to protect the place properly, the brothers very often complained about their problems and needs to Count Werner." As a result, Werner, "with the brothers' encouragement and at their request (and also because he wanted to do it) gave a certain [estate] ... to the same Richwin and received from him the advocacy into his own power."[35]

Thus, the ineffectiveness of two consecutive advocates from outside the founding family prompted the monks to seek out the count who had reformed their community as its new advocate. Moreover, the abbot and monks of Muri decreed that, after Werner, "his eldest son should receive the advocacy from the abbot, not on account of any right of his own or by hereditary right but according to the contents of the privilege [of 1082]."[36] At least as the story is told here, Count Werner was willing – initially – to renounce his claims to the advocacy of Muri in order to follow reform ideals and give the monastery true liberty. However, when the outsiders chosen as advocates proved unable to serve as effective defenders, Werner acquired the advocacy for himself. The count and the abbot then agreed to keep the advocacy in his lineage – but without explicitly acknowledging it to be hereditary. Free elections of advocates, which permitted monasteries to bring in someone other than the founder and his family, might have been great in theory but they were deeply flawed in practice, especially if the freely elected advocates did not have the local influence and authority to protect the community and its properties.[37]

With this in mind, let us return a final time to Pope Leo IX's family foundation of Sainte-Croix-en-Plaine. According to his privilege for the convent, "After my nephew Henry dies, the advocacy ought to belong to

---

[33] *Acta Murensia*, 26–29, no. 11. The reasons for Count Werner's conflict with his sister's sons are not entirely clear, but inheritance rights in and around Muri may have been a factor: Meier, *Gründung*, 167–68; Jakobs, *Adel*, 57–60.
[34] For Liudolf as advocate of St. Gall, see *Casuum S. Galli Continuatio II*, 156–57 and 159; Jakobs, *Adel*, 57, n. 50.
[35] *Acta Murensia*, 26–29, no. 11: "*advocaciam in suam potestatem.*"
[36] Ibid. See also Meier, *Gründung*, 171–74.
[37] Meier, *Gründung*, 168. For an example of papal and imperial privileges offering different perspectives on whether a monastic advocacy was hereditary in the founding family, see Stephan, ed., *Urkunden*, 3–20, nos. 1–5 and 25–28, no. 9. For this community, see also Lyon, "Noble Lineages."

whomever is eldest among the possessors of the . . . castle [of Eguisheim], if there should be several."[38] Here, Leo does more than simply decree that the advocacy was heritable within his family; he links the inheritance of the convent's advocacy directly to the inheritance of the neighboring family castle.[39] This is a clear acknowledgment that the person best able to be advocate and to defend an ecclesiastical community was the nobleman in possession of the nearest fortified site. While some church reformers insisted that local nobles ought to have as little authority as possible as advocates, Pope Leo IX – clearly shaped by his own family background – seems to have had an especially keen sense of the limits of monastic liberty. As the number of new religious foundations exploded across the German kingdom in the late eleventh and twelfth centuries, the need for effective protection and justice at the local level ensured that advocacy would continue to have a vital role to play.

New Foundations, New Orders, New Advocates

While my focus to this point has been the southwest of the German kingdom, the numerous and varied waves of reform that swept through Europe in the late eleventh and early twelfth centuries led advocacy to expand in other regions as well. Everywhere in the German kingdom, the noble couples and families who established and endowed new religious houses sought to maintain possession of the advocacies for their foundations. Archbishops and bishops – who were also driving forces in the reform movements of the day – were equally interested in asserting their authority over the advocates of the new communities belonging to their churches. At older houses too, including those founded in the Carolingian and Ottonian periods, the issue of advocacy frequently generated new questions around 1100 as these houses came under the influence of new reforming ideals.

The reforms that had taken root at the monastery of Hirsau proved influential across the German kingdom.[40] In eastern Saxony during the closing years of the eleventh century, a local nobleman named Wiprecht founded and endowed a monastery at Pegau near his castle of Groitzsch; he asked the abbot of Corvey, whose monastery played a central role in disseminating Hirsau's reform ideas to the northeast of the German kingdom,

---

[38] Leo IX, *Epistolae*, cols. 635.–37, no. 30. See also Zotz, "Burg und Amt," 148–49.
[39] Hummer, "Reform," 80–84. As historians of the medieval nobility have noted, this period increasingly saw noble lineages naming themselves after specific castles as these castles became important for family identity; see especially Schmid, "Problematik."
[40] Jakobs, *Hirsauer*. For the sometimes-contentious implementation of these reforms, see Beach, *Trauma*.

for monks for his new community.[41] According to a twelfth-century account
of Pegau's history, Wiprecht also decided to give the monastery to "the
apostolic see in perpetuity"; he therefore sent a trusted agent to Rome "to
bind that monastery to the Roman liberty."[42] In 1106, Pope Paschal II issued
a privilege for Pegau, recognizing the community to be under Rome's
authority but also noting, in language that echoes the Hirsau Formulary,

> The lord Wiprecht nevertheless made an exception of the advocacy, which he was
> prepared to hold himself. After him, the first born of his posterity, if indeed he
> should want to preside over the church justly and beneficially, should be advocate;
> if, however, his posterity should fail – may God avert it! – the abbot of that place,
> with the sounder advice of his brothers, should choose whomever he wants as an
> advocate advantageous to him and to the church.[43]

Elsewhere in the German kingdom, too, new communities were adopting
similar language about their advocacies.[44]

Another of the most important early centers for monastic reform lay along
the middle Rhine River. The monastery of Siegburg, founded in 1064 by
Archbishop Anno II of Cologne (1056–75), offers a different perspective on
the constantly evolving dynamic between a religious community and its
advocates.[45] Anno's 1075 privilege for his new monastery established four
regionally distinct advocacies for Siegburg and granted each to a different
advocate. The archbishop seems to have intentionally assigned advocates
whose own territorial strongholds were *not* situated close to the advocacies
for which they were responsible. Moreover, he avoided giving any of the
advocacies to the most powerful nobles in the region around Siegburg, most
notably the counts of Berg.[46] In his attempts to limit the influence and
authority of the monastery's advocates, he also defined their responsibilities
narrowly: "We establish concerning the advocates, whom we have provided
to be defenders of that church, that once per year at the places pre-
determined for them they should come and should hold judicial assemblies
for the purpose of issuing judgments." He then explained that they were to
judge "with the abbot's counsel assault, theft, breaking the peace and
inheritance disputes ... The settling of all other cases they relinquish to
the judgment of the abbot and his household."[47] As impressive as all this

[41] *Deeds of Margrave Wiprecht*, 65–67.   [42] Ibid., 71.
[43] CDS I A, 2:8–9, no. 8. See also *Deeds of Margrave Wiprecht*, 71–72.
[44] For similar language in a privilege for the newly founded Benedictine community at
Bosau near Pegau, see Rosenfeld and Schulze, eds., *Urkundenbuch*, 1:105–07, no. 123.
[45] This monastery features prominently in one of the most important studies of advocates in
this period: Clauss, *Untervogtei*, 223–27.
[46] Ibid., 225.
[47] Wisplinghoff, ed., *Urkunden*, 12–16, no. 8. See also Stieldorf, "Klöster," 62–63. For the
types of cases advocates were expected to judge, see Chapter 6.

sounds, Anno's elaborate attempts to divide and restrict the power of Siegburg's advocates were successful for, at most, fifty years. By the 1120s at the latest, the counts of Berg seem to have acquired control over the advocacy – and they would maintain it for the next century.[48] As at Muri, it was easier said than done to keep the most powerful noble families from gaining influence and control over local advocacies.

The monastic reforms that radiated out from Hirsau and Siegburg in the late eleventh and early twelfth centuries were largely phenomena of the German kingdom. Given that advocacy had flourished for more than two centuries in precisely those regions where these new traditions developed and spread, it is unsurprising that reformers in these circles accepted advocates. But there were also pan-European reform movements during this period, many of which began in places where advocacy was not as firmly embedded in local societies as it was in the German-speaking lands. Significantly, when communities belonging to these new orders were founded in the German kingdom, they too recognized the need to address the issue of church advocacy.

Houses of Augustinian canons and canonesses, for example, quickly adopted the language of advocacy that was already commonplace in other types of communities.[49] In the archdiocese of Salzburg, where numerous Augustinian houses were established from around 1100, privileges for some new communities insisted on the community's free choice of its advocates, while others acknowledged that local nobles and their heirs were to be the advocates for the communities they founded and endowed.[50] Further west, phrasing similar to that found in the documents discussed in this chapter appears in one of Archbishop Adalbert I of Mainz's charters from the year 1130. After a count gave the archbishopric the house of Augustinian canons he had established, the archbishop confirmed that

[A]s long as the count lives, he will hold the right of advocacy. When he dies, if his inheritance should by chance be divided between two heirs, the one who possesses by hereditary right – not by usurpation – those estates pertaining to the castle of Dill should be invested as advocate by us or one of our successors without any objection.[51]

Elsewhere, a privilege for a new Augustinian community stated that an advocate would only serve as long as it pleased the provost and it

---

[48] Nikolay-Panter, "Siegburg," 208–09; Berner, *Kreuzzug*, 188–89; Clauss, "Vogteibündelung," 179–88.

[49] For Augustinian canons, see Vones-Liebenstein, "Similarities"; Melville, *Monasticism*, 125–35.

[50] Weinfurter, *Salzburger Bistumsreform*, 143–51. See also Gilcher, ed., *Traditionen*, 124*–131*.

[51] *Mainzer Urkundenbuch*, 1:482–83, no. 567.

benefitted the community.[52] Thus, the Augustinian canons and canonesses of the German kingdom were just as embedded in the culture of advocacy as the religious communities of the preceding decades and centuries.

The Premonstratensians, or Norbertines (after the movement's founder, Norbert of Xanten), followed the Augustinian rule for canons as well, and their numbers grew rapidly during the second quarter of the twelfth century.[53] Premonstratensian foundations offer especially good evidence in terms of understanding the geography of advocacy because privileges for new communities in the German kingdom have much more to say on the topic than privileges for the communities appearing simultaneously in France. After Count Ludwig of Arnstein and his wife Guda made the decision to found a Premonstratensian house at their castle of Arnstein east of the Rhine and to dedicate themselves to the religious life, Pope Innocent II, in his privilege of 1142 for the new community, decreed, "No one may presume to take hold of or make use of the advocacy of your place except him whom the abbot and brothers provide through election according to God's will and for the place's advantage."[54] In contrast, five years later in 1147, Pope Eugenius III's privilege for the new Premonstratensian community of Saint-Yved de Braine in France – 350 kilometers west of Arnstein – makes no mention of advocacy.[55] The longstanding tradition of church advocacy in the German kingdom thus continued to exert a powerful pull, one which pan-European religious orders could not ignore.

Of the major new reform movements and religious orders to sweep across the German kingdom in the century after 1050, the one that had the most complicated relationship with advocacy was unquestionably the Cistercians.[56] From the beginning, Cistercian leaders were anxious to limit the influence of local secular elites over their communities.[57]

---

[52] CDS I A, 2:51–53, no. 59.

[53] For the Premonstratensians, Melville, *Monasticism*, 158–63; Vones-Liebenstein, "Similarities," 774.

[54] Herquet, ed. *Urkundenbuch*, 1–3, no. 1. See also *Deeds of Count Ludwig*, 237. Other Premonstratensian communities also provide good evidence for advocates; see, for example, Horstkötter, ed., *Urkundenbuch*, 1:1–13, no. 1; Weissthanner, ed., *Urkunden*, 1–3, no. 1 and 15–16, no. 10; *Fundatio Monasterii Gratiae Dei*, 689.

[55] Guyotjeannin, ed., *Chartrier*, 135–37, no. 1. The Premonstratensian house of Ninove in Flanders had the counts of Flanders as its advocates: Bijsterveld, "Conflict," 173–74.

[56] For the early years of the order, see Newman, "Foundation." For the difficulties of generalizing about Cistercian advocacy, see Hirsch, "Studien."

[57] Melville, *Monasticism*, 146–51. Although Bernard of Clairvaux complained about bad advocates, he was referring to legal advocates of the Roman legal tradition, who were becoming increasingly common in some places (especially Italy) by the mid-twelfth century: Bernard of Clairvaux, *De Consideratione*, 408–09, 1.10. On these legal advocates, see Chapter 8.

However, by the time the Cistercians began to gain popularity in the German kingdom in the second quarter of the twelfth century, it was impossible to simply ignore advocacy. At Ebrach, which was founded in 1127 as the first Cistercian monastery east of the Rhine, early documents recording grants of property to the community frequently had to insist that no advocate would have any rights over the communities' properties.[58] Even as far west as the bishopric of Cambrai, the bishop confirmed in his 1133 privilege for the new community of Vaucelles that the founders "had freed [the monastery and its properties] from every advocacy."[59] Thus, early Cistercian communities had to be explicit about their intention of limiting advocatial authority.

In the German kingdom, declaring a community free from local advocates raised the obvious question of who would defend the religious house and its estates and exercise justice over its dependents. One of the most common ways for Cistercian houses to address the issue of advocacy was to ask the ruler to be advocate. In 1155, Emperor Frederick I issued a charter for the Cistercian house at Salem, which included the statement, "Because the brothers of that order look to the Roman Church, whose special advocates and defenders we are, for the special status of their humble obedience, we prohibit ... any person from holding or usurping the office of advocacy (officium advocatię) there, preserving for us alone and our successors in perpetuity this office of defense (defensionis officium)."[60] Almost a century later, this idea comes across as firmly entrenched in a 1240 privilege issued by King Conrad IV for the monastery of Ebrach: "Just as the Cistercian order has always been free and immune from every type of advocate, so it follows that [Ebrach] may be subject to absolutely no advocates except only the emperor of the Romans – unless it should subject itself voluntarily to one[.]"[61]

While this sounds definitive, a closer look at the twelfth-century evidence indicates that all houses belonging to the Cistercian order did not have blanket freedom from local advocates. Indeed, the language of the 1240 privilege was almost certainly provided to the imperial chancery by the monastery of Ebrach in an attempt, more than a century after its foundation, to make its status clear in the face of continuing questions

---

[58] Goez, ed., *Urkunden*, 1:16–18, no. 5 and 34–41, no. 16. See also Waas, *Vogtei*, 2:43–53.
[59] Tock, ed. *Chartes*, 58–60, no. 2.
[60] DD F I, 216–17, no. 129. For this passage, see also Hirsch, "Studien," 33–34. The following year, Frederick I issued a charter for Cistercian Maulbronn with similar language: DD F I, 222–23, no. 132. For the emperors as "special advocates" of the Roman Church, see Chapter 11.
[61] Goez, ed., *Urkunden*, 1:354–58, no. 174 (the editor's notes are essential). For the context of this 1240 privilege, see also ibid., 192–95, no. 91; 198–201, no. 95; and 241–44, no. 115. See also Hirsch, "Studien," 22–25.

about an advocacy for the community. At many other Cistercian houses in the German kingdom, dukes and other leading nobles routinely claimed to be the advocates.[62] East of the Elbe, in particular, a region where the German rulers had little direct influence, it was even more commonplace to find the advocacies for Cistercian communities shaped by the interests of the leading nobles.[63] The picture becomes even more complicated when we consider early women's houses. In 1147, for example, the noblewoman Friderun and her son Markward II of Grumbach founded a community of Cistercian nuns.[64] The archbishop of Mainz's privilege for this new foundation includes one of the more remarkable twelfth-century statements about the role of the advocate: "The lady (*domina*) Friderun, with her son Markward, established that the church have as advocate the oldest of their heirs in succession, who moved by the fear of God ought to protect its properties and zealously defend the convent's liberty from the disturbances of the wicked with the shield of his protection."[65] The rhetoric of this document suggests that Cistercian communities could have advocatial relationships that were every bit as complex as the relationships that other types of religious communities had with their advocates.[66]

The Cistercians, more than any of the other new reform movements of the late eleventh and early twelfth centuries, highlight some of the pitfalls of taking too narrow an approach to the study of the advocate. Historians who have examined advocacy in this period have tended to emphasize discontinuity with older (especially Carolingian) forms of advocacy. By focusing in particular on the new monastic reform trends of the period, scholars have tried to paint a picture of post-1050 advocates as a new phenomenon linked to changing conceptions of the ideal role of spiritual communities in Christian society.[67] However, the evidence suggests quite the opposite. Advocates and advocacy were such well-established features

---

[62] See, for example, BUB, 1:74–75, no. 54; Graber, ed., *Urkundenbuch*, 1:11–14, no. 7; *Urkundenbuch des Klosters Frauensee*, 6–7, no. 13.

[63] See, for example, "Chorin" and "Marienwalde," in *Brandenburgisches Klosterbuch*, 335 and 865. More generally for advocacy east of the Elbe, Auge, "Hominium," 211–12. See also Chapter 12.

[64] For Cistercian women's communities in this period, see Freeman, "Nuns," 100–03.

[65] *Mainzer Urkundenbuch*, 2.1:188–92, no. 98. See also DD Ko III, 339–42, no. 188. As with other religious communities, Cistercian houses founded by nobles frequently had to accept the members of the founding family as the community's advocates: Hirsch, "Studien," 13–14.

[66] See also Goez, ed., *Urkunden*, 1: 381–83, no. 188. For an example of a Cistercian monastery being granted the advocacies for certain properties, see DD H VI, 294–96, BB 348.

[67] Cf. Tellenbach, *Church*, 299–303 and West, "Monks." For the significance of the reform period for the relations between nobles and monks, see also Mazel, "Amitié."

of the local noble/ecclesiastical landscape by the mid-eleventh century that no religious communities in the German kingdom – including Cistercian houses – could operate outside the entrenched culture of advocacy. Put simply, the advocates of the reform era do not look very different from the advocates of the century before the papacy of Leo IX.[68] They maintained their wide-ranging responsibilities as secular authority figures able to access religious communities' properties to provide protection and justice.

Ecclesiastical Office, Noble Asset

The reformers of the late eleventh and twelfth centuries insisted that advocates were churches' agents and had a clearly defined set of responsibilities. As we have seen in the previous chapters, however, the "aristocratization" of advocacy in the preceding decades meant that church advocates were not low-status figures. They were frequently dukes and counts and other high-ranking nobles, people who in many cases possessed significantly more power and influence than the ecclesiastical communities – especially the fledgling new foundations – they were to "serve." As a result, reformers' efforts to define advocacy were not entirely successful. There existed in this period a broad spectrum of different perspectives on the proper role of the advocate.

Religious authors sought to attach a strong sense of official duty to the position. The *Deeds* of Archbishop Albero of Trier (1131–52) preserve an especially vivid description of the oath that a count-palatine supposedly swore when he became advocate. While touching a cross containing relics, including a piece of the True Cross, he said, "I give to you, lord archbishop, this Lord, He who was crucified for us, as my guarantor, and I swear to you by His virtue that I shall never do anything against you, and that I shall assist you faithfully in all your interests with all my military forces and with all my strength."[69] The chronicler Ortlieb of Zwiefalten, writing in the 1130s, describes the ideal process for appointing and removing advocates. He praises one advocate, a local count, because

---

[68] In addition, property agreements continue into this period to include references to advocates, whether in witness lists or in *manum/manus* clauses. See, for example, Tr. Tegernsee, 144–45, no. 181 and 254, no. 334; "Benediktbeurer Traditionsbuch," 17–18, no. 29; Pahud, ed., *Cartulaire*, 116–17, no. 23; Hoffmann, *Bücher*, 107, no. 65; Feger, ed., *Chronik*, 162–63, 3.42 and 222–25, 5.24; Krimm-Beumann, ed., *Güterverzeichnisse*, 56–59, no. R 96. See also Lyon, "Tyrants"; Klohn, *Entwicklung*, 29–38. References like these gradually become less common over the course of the twelfth century, but see Chapter 12.

[69] Balderich of Trier, *Warrior Bishop*, 67–68 (Latin: Balderich of Trier, *Gesta Alberonis*, 255–56, chap. 25).

"[u]ntil the day of his death, he took care to defend the monastery in the manner of a pious father." After he died, however, his brother "did not have the strength to bear the burden of this kind of care, because he suffered from the pain of gout." The monks therefore elected Duke Welf (V) of Bavaria to be their advocate "on the condition that the [monastery's] liberty, acquired through privilege, remain inviolate. He [Welf] should know that he only has this charge so long as he is willing to benefit this place."[70] Ortlieb asserts that the monks of Zwiefalten had complete control over their monastery's advocacy, and he clearly positions the advocates as agents who existed to serve the community.

One of the best early-twelfth-century pieces of evidence for an advocate properly carrying out his judicial functions appears in a lengthy miracle story in the *Life* of the aforementioned Archbishop Anno II of Cologne.[71] According to the text, there was a powerful and celebrated nobleman named Arnold who held the castle of Dollendorf (approximately seventy-five kilometers to the south of Cologne): "One time, when he was holding court [as advocate] in those regions, he was judging with judicial severity the diverse cases of those bringing suit. As is fitting of a judge, he turned well-deserved anger toward the guilty and acted more mildly when a very grave crime ought not to have stood in the way of his mercy."[72] His excellence as advocate became even clearer when a madman named Volcbert, who had no respect for justice or reverence for the judge, was summoned to attend one of his court sessions. When it became apparent that Volcbert was possessed by the devil, "the pious advocate" (*religiosus advocatus*) prayed to Anno, who miraculously struck the madman down.[73] While other authors occasionally compliment advocates for their faithful service to their religious communities, the phrase "pious advocate" is unusually high praise.[74] Most religious communities did not describe their advocates so positively.

Ecclesiastics' efforts to depict the ideal advocate as an officeholder beholden to a religious community frequently encountered resistance from the nobles who held the position. To be clear, some nobles willingly

---

[70] *Zwiefalter Chroniken*, 68, chap. 15. For the advocates of Zwiefalten, see also Patzold, "Klösterliches Lehnswesen," 120.

[71] *Vita Annonis Archiepiscopi*, 510–12, 3.24. The same story reappears in the later version of his *Life* from ca. 1180: *Vita Annonis minor*, 142–53, 2.45.

[72] *Vita Annonis Archiepiscopi*, 510. The reference to Arnold hearing cases "*in illis partibus*" highlights his role exercising justice distant from Cologne; a reference to his "*amministratio defensoris*" from his castle further cements the idea of him as a local agent protecting distant properties.

[73] Ibid., 512.

[74] See, for example, Bernold of St. Blasien, *Chronicle*, 292; Herman of Tournai, *Restoration*, 81, chap. 57; Lambert of Ardres, *History*, 143, chap. 112. For the rarity of such compliments, see Tebruck, "Kirchenvogtei," 423.

ceded a great deal of influence to reformers and respected their goals; there were not two permanently rivalrous camps, lay and religious, that could never agree on the proper role of the advocate. That said, many nobles did not understand advocacy as an office under the authority of the Church but as a hereditary possession they controlled.[75] The dueling perspectives on the role of the advocate are laid out plainly in a text from one Bavarian religious community during the opening decades of the twelfth century. Upon choosing an advocate, the community asked the local bishop to make sure that their choice "be entrusted with this office (*hoc officium*), not be granted it as a benefice (*non beneficium*)."[76]

While most of our sources for advocacy from the late eleventh and twelfth centuries were written by ecclesiastics, we can occasionally discern nobles' perspectives. An unusual but nevertheless revealing example dates from 1084, when a man named Gaucher (III) of Salins made a donation to the monastery of Romainmôtier. We met Gaucher's family in the previous chapter when his father became entangled in a dispute with Abbot Odilo of Cluny and Romainmôtier about the advocacy for a place called Bannans. Gaucher (III)'s donation of 1084 was also connected to the ongoing back and forth between his family and Romainmôtier over Bannans, but what is noteworthy about this document is the title that Gaucher uses. It is not his father's title of knight (*miles*) but "I, Gaucher, son of Gaucher son of Humbert, by the grace of God advocate of the town of Salins (*gratia Dei advocatus oppidi Salinensis*)."[77]

To declare oneself in possession of a title or right "by the grace of God" was to state emphatically that you were not someone else's agent or official. Kings, dukes and (increasingly) counts asserted in this period that they held their positions *gratia Dei* to make it clear they were responsible to God alone for their authority.[78] However, at its root, the Latin term *advocatus* refers to someone who is called to do something by somebody else. It follows logically, therefore, that an advocate holds their authority through that person, not God.[79] Gaucher (III), who was at best a middling member of the secular elite, was therefore asserting a dubious claim; he was trying to make himself out to be more than he really was. Whatever his intent, the timing of this language is noteworthy, for it helps us to see that the reform movements of the second half of the

---

[75] See Chapter 4 for early evidence along these lines.

[76] Mai, ed., *Traditionen*, 144–47, nos. 4–5. See also Seibert, "*Non predium*," 147–48, 152–53; Burkhardt, "Ordnungsvorstellungen," 187.

[77] Pahud, ed., *Cartulaire*, 129–30, no. 32. The monks included a copy of this text in their twelfth-century cartulary: ibid., 126–28, no. 30.

[78] Koziol, *Begging*, 27–30, 43–44, 256–57.   [79] For more on this point, see Chapter 11.

eleventh century were not all-encompassing. Away from the papal court and the great reforming monasteries, there were very different ideas circulating – especially within the secular elites – about what an advocate was.

Although the language of Gaucher's document is atypical, the underlying implication that the label *advocatus* was socially prestigious – a highly desirable marker of status and rank within the secular elite – was not. Across the German kingdom, sources show nobles using their advocatial positions to bolster their and their relatives' claims to be prominent figures in society. In 1134, the noblewoman Liutgart, who belonged to the lineage that held the advocacy for the bishopric of Regensburg in Bavaria, made a donation to a monastery as "the lady (*domina*) Liutgart *advocata*, mother of the advocate Frederick the elder."[80] This is a lineage that held no higher title than advocate (such as count). The text's designation of Liutgart as *advocata* therefore should not be read as evidence she was a judge and protector for Regensburg but that this was the title everyone in the family used to assert their noble status.[81] Indeed, the early decades of the twelfth century were a time when it was commonplace for wives, and especially widows, to be designated *advocata*, *advocatrix* or *advocatissa* as a way of proving that their husband's or son's advocacy elevated their own standing as well.[82]

As the previous chapters have argued, from roughly 950 onward the most prominent nobles in the German kingdom increasingly sought to acquire church advocacies and to insist on their heritability. While the counts of Luxembourg offer one of the best examples from the early eleventh century of a lineage accumulating multiple advocacies and holding onto them across multiple generations, by the end of the century most of the leading lineages were pursuing this strategy.[83] According to a chronicle written at Klosterneuburg near Vienna, the eldest son of Margrave Leopold III of Austria (d. 1136) did not inherit his father's march of Austria but rather his advocacies: "The firstborn, named Adalbert, was made advocate of Klosterneuburg and of all the monasteries belonging to the margrave's advocacy (*ad advocatiam marchionis*)."[84] While

---

[80] *Niederösterreichisches Urkundenbuch*, 2.2:664–65, no. 21[20].
[81] For this lineage, Starflinger, *Entwickelung*, 21–25.
[82] For women as advocates, see Lyon, "Advocata."
[83] Clauss, *Untervogtei*, 157–58. Clear evidence for the hereditary nature of one advocacy can be seen in a 1093 charter issued by the abbot of Werden, which notes that a count acted "*uice advocati ecclesię nostrę Adolfi. qui tunc temporis puer erat*" (Lacomblet, ed., *Urkundenbuch*, 1:159–60, no. 247). See for this advocacy Clauss, "Vogteibündelung," 172–73; Milz, "Die Vögte," 205; Finger, "Kloster."
[84] *Annales Austriae*, 610. For Adalbert as *advocatus*, see also BUB, 1:14–16, no. 11; 4.1:53–54, no. 620; 4.1:81–83, no. 674 and 4.1:98, no. 706; Brunner, *Leopold*, 195–96; Reichert, *Landesherrschaft*, 162–63, 191–92.

not a representative example of how most noble lineages managed inheritance, this clearly demonstrates the value of advocacies to even the uppermost echelons of the princely elite. Duke Henry the Lion of Bavaria and Saxony (d. 1195), one of the most powerful nobles of the twelfth-century German kingdom, also sought to accumulate advocacies for his lineage; he possessed more than fifty during his lifetime – including those for older monasteries and newer reformed communities – and fought tenaciously to maintain control of all of them.[85]

The next chapter will examine the economic benefits that nobles could accrue from holding church advocacies. Here, it is important to emphasize that accumulating advocacies was, for many lineages, the cornerstone to their local power and influence.[86] To be clear, not every advocatial position was of equal value. A noble family who founded a monastery on property they donated and retained the advocacy may have gained spiritual benefits but would not have profited economically in any meaningful way; the family members who were the advocates would have continued to provide protection and exercise justice just as they had done when it was the family's property.[87] The real economic benefits came when nobles acquired the advocacies for imperial monasteries and convents, bishoprics, religious communities under episcopal authority, and the noble foundations of other lineages that had become extinct in the male line. In all of these cases, noble advocates gained access to property and rights to which they otherwise would have had no legitimate claim. The twelfth-century counts of Sulzbach in Bavaria, for example, were advocates for so many monasteries and episcopal estates in the region around Sulzbach that they seem to have drawn most of their wealth and authority from these advocacies – not from their rights as counts, about which the surviving sources tell us significantly less.[88]

The dukes of Zähringen, one of the leading lineages of the southwest of the German kingdom from the late eleventh to the early thirteenth century, also relied on advocacies for a significant part of their authority.[89] For example, the dukes acquired the advocacy for the monastery of St. George in the Black Forest after Duke Berthold II (d. 1111) protected the monastery from an attack, which suggests that an informal role as a defender led to the monastery recognizing the lineage as its advocates.[90] In the next generation, Duke Conrad (d. 1152) acquired

---

[85] Clauss, *Untervogtei*, 159–67; Seibert, "*Non predium*," 160. See also Wibald of Stablo, *Briefbuch*, 22–24, no. 12, and the discussion of this letter in Jordan, *Henry the Lion*, 30–31.
[86] For the relationship between church advocacies and "*adlige Herrschaftsbildung*," see now Andermann and Bünz, "Kirchenvogtei."
[87] Küss, *Diepoldinger*, 171–73.   [88] Dendorfer, *Gruppenbildung*, 292–314.
[89] For the history of this lineage, see Zotz, *Zähringer*.   [90] Ibid., 53.

the advocacy for the important reformed monastery of St. Blasien; because its previous advocate had been lax, Emperor Henry V intervened and permitted the abbot to choose another who would be "more useful" (utiliorem).[91] Later, the dukes also sought to become advocates of the oft-mentioned monastery of St. Gall.[92]

The centrality of advocacy for these dukes is best seen in Zurich, where there had been advocates for the convent of Sts. Felix and Regula and the canons of Grossmünster since the late ninth century.[93] In a privilege issued by Duke Berthold V of Zähringen (d. 1218) in 1187 for the canons, he titles himself duke, then rector of Burgundy (a position he had received from Emperor Frederick I), and thereafter, "by the grace of God and imperial grace the legitimate advocate of Zurich, what is called kastfoget."[94] This is another rare example of someone claiming to be advocate "by the grace of God," though in this case Berthold also acknowledges the role of the emperor. More significantly, the duke's use of both the phrase legitimus advocatus and the vernacular term kastfoget in this document indicates that the position was a well-established one; his title of advocate, not his position as duke or rector, gave him authority in Zurich.[95] One historian of the early twentieth century saw the acquisition of all these advocacies as a key component of the "state" constructed by these dukes.[96] While the term "state" is problematic, there is no question that church advocacies were crucial to many nobles' efforts to extend their authority.

As the leading members of the secular elite accumulated advocacies, they further widened the gap between the ecclesiastical ideal of advocates as officeholders and the local practice of advocacy. Dukes, margraves and counts could not personally provide protection and justice in all of the places where they were advocates.[97] They had other rights and properties to oversee as well, and they were also expected to attend the royal court and participate in royal expeditions – including those that crossed the Alps to Italy.[98] As a result, nobles in the decades after 1050 increasingly turned to surrogates to fulfill many of their advocatial responsibilities.

---

[91] Braun, ed., Urkundenbuch, 1:142–48, no. 125. For this and other Zähringer advocacies, see Zotz, Zähringer, 42, 71, 102, 111, 126.

[92] See Chapter 10.   [93] See Chapters 2 and 3.

[94] Parlow, Die Zähringer, 337–38, no. 526. For the term kastfoget, see Chapter 6. For a more detailed discussion of how church advocates could exert authority over entire towns, see Chapter 12.

[95] Zotz, "Zürich," 111–12; Zotz, Zähringer, 126–27, 179–80.

[96] Mayer, "State." For more on the role of advocacies in "state-building," see Chapter 12.

[97] Clauss, Untervogtei, 160–61.

[98] For an example of an advocate writing a letter because he could not be present, see Annales Reicherspergenses, 475.

Members of nobles' entourages therefore began to play more prominent roles in providing protection and exercising justice on ecclesiastical estates – under the designation of "subadvocate" (*subadvocatus*).[99] In the process, advocacy continued to grow organically in new directions, and the question of whether it was an ecclesiastical office or an asset that nobles could use to reward faithful followers grew even more vexed.[100]

Conclusion

During the second half of the eleventh century, church reformers sought to alter the relationship between the spiritual and secular spheres. From the Papal See in Rome to small churches on the fringes of Latin Christendom, they imagined religious communities free from lay influence and the corruption of the world. Religious men and women, not kings and nobles, were to be the true leaders of the Church and spiritual guides for the laity. But local realities complicated universalist ideals. So long as churches remained prominent landholders, secular authority inevitably intruded on the religious life. In those parts of Europe that had been shaped by a continuous tradition of church advocacy since the Carolingian period, reformers knew they could not eliminate advocates; instead, they sought to control them. They emphasized advocates' official functions: The advocate was an agent working at the behest of the religious community, there to provide protection and exercise justice when needed. A few nobles, caught up in the fervor of reform, agreed with this vision of advocacy. Most, however, had different ideas and saw in the position of advocate opportunities to advance their own interests rather than those of churches. What, exactly, were those opportunities? To answer this question, we must take a closer look at the benefits that came with the role of advocate.

---

[99] For this term, see also Chapter 4. One early mention of a *subadvocatus* east of the Rhine is "Benediktbeurer Traditionsbuch," 13, no. 16 (dated 1057). Clauss, *Untervogtei*, 117–19, notes that this is probably a term provided by the mid-twelfth-century scribe; however, this does not mean that some sort of comparable role did not already exist around 1050. For the term *subdefensor*, see Wisplinghoff, ed., *Urkunden*, 45–47, no. 22.

[100] Clauss, *Untervogtei*, 295. For more on this point, see Chapter 7.

6   Pigs and Sheep, Beer and Wine, Pennies and Pounds

The coins minted during the late twelfth and early thirteenth centuries by the monastery of Pegau in Saxony are mostly unspectacular. Silver pennies struck on only one side – a type of coin known as a bracteate – they typically include an image of a large cross, with smaller symbols (a star or a crozier, for example) tucked between its arms.[1] Many of these surviving pennies are in good enough condition that the legend encircling the image is still legible; most often, the name of the presiding abbot of Pegau appears. While some readers may be surprised that a monastery could possess minting rights and be in a position to issue coins of its own design in the name of its abbot (or abbess), this was commonplace in the German kingdom, where numerous ecclesiastical communities and secular princes produced coinage that circulated in their own territories – and also competed with the coins issued by the rulers.[2]

Although the silver pennies minted at Pegau are in many ways quite typical of monastic coinage of the time, a series of surviving bracteates issued at the community in the early thirteenth century demand close attention. On one penny, the legend clearly spells out *not* the name of the abbot but rather "Count Dietrich," and the objects between the arms of the cross include a decidedly un-monastic sword as well as the imperial orb (see Figure 6.1).[3] On another coin, the four fields between the arms of the cross combine to depict a seated man with a sword across his lap.[4] Other issues of pennies at Pegau include one with an image of an eagle, a popular symbol of authority among German

---

[1] Becker, "Pegauer Brakteatenprägung"; Haverkamp, "Jewish Images," 213–16. For bracteates more generally, Svensson, *Renovatio Monetae*; Spufford, *Money*, 104.

[2] Woods, "Charlemagne," 112–13; Steinbach, *Geld*, 26–41; Kamp, *Moneta Regis*. I am grateful to Sebastian Steinbach for discussing medieval coinage with me.

[3] Thieme, *Brakteaten*, 35–36, 168–71; kenom Virtuelles Münzkabinett: www.kenom.de/o bjekt/record_DE-15_kenom_195867/1/-/. Other coin issues with his name: www .kenom.de/objekt/record_DE-15_kenom_195869/1/-/ and www.kenom.de/objekt/recor d_DE-15_kenom_195868/1/-/ (last accessed September 14, 2021).

[4] Kenom Virtuelles Münzkabinett: www.kenom.de/objekt/record_DE-15_kenom_195870/ 1/-/ (last accessed September 14, 2021).

Figure 6.1 Penny from Pegau with the legend "TEODERICVS COMES" ("Count Dietrich"). Universitätsbibliothek Leipzig, Inventar Nummer 1979/0171. www.kenom.de/objekt/record_DE-15_kenom_195867/1/-/

nobles.[5] Combined, all of these bracteates give the strong impression that members of the secular elite exerted significant influence over the mint at Pegau in the decades around 1200.

Written sources rarely provide the necessary context to help us interpret the rich numismatic evidence unearthed by professional archeologists and backyard metal-detector enthusiasts. Fortunately, these Pegau bracteates are an exception. A chronicle written in the early thirteenth century at an ecclesiastical community north of Pegau reports that the German king Philip of Swabia (1198–1208) granted the advocacy of Pegau to Count Dietrich of Sommerschenburg (d. 1207), a member of one of the leading noble lineages in Saxony, the Wettins.[6] Dietrich then "shamelessly made use of it [the advocacy], violently forcing Pegau's inhabitants to serve him. Nor did he refrain from injuring its abbot. For,

[5] Kenom Virtuelles Münzkabinett: www.kenom.de/objekt/record_DE-15_kenom_195872/1/-/ (last accessed September 14, 2021). For the eagle as a popular symbol, see Wilson, *Heart of Europe*, 270–71.
[6] Pätzold, *Wettiner*, 234–35. For this lineage, see also Lyon, *Princely Brothers*.

one time [the abbot] was captured by [the count's] men and was expelled from that church for an entire year."[7] The evidence of the Pegau bracteates stamped with the count's name and symbols of secular authority suggests that Dietrich used this opportunity to seize the monastery's minting rights. This is a good example of the sort of competition that typified many relationships between prelates and advocates in this period, a point to which I will return in subsequent chapters. Here, I want to emphasize that the appearance of Dietrich's name on the pennies minted at Pegau is one of the most tangible pieces of extant evidence for the economic dimensions of the role of the advocate. To understand these economic dimensions – and advocacy more generally after 1050 – it is essential to follow the money.

Profiting from Justice

Why would a member of the secular elite want to be an advocate, to be responsible for exercising justice and providing protection for a religious community? While this question could be approached in a variety of ways, an essential element of any answer is that it paid to be an advocate. Scattered evidence from the ninth and tenth centuries suggests that advocates typically held modest benefices in return for carrying out their responsibilities. Sources from these centuries also occasionally express concerns about advocates becoming greedy and demanding more than they were supposed to receive. None of this material is abundant, however, and there is little to suggest that advocatial compensation was an issue that garnered significant attention from rulers, ecclesiastics or secular elites before the year 1000.[8]

This changed in the early eleventh century, when some ecclesiastical sources began to include language defining not only what advocates were supposed to do but also what they could expect as payment in return for doing it.[9] By the early twelfth century, regulating advocatial income had become one of the most common features of archival documents concerning advocates. These texts leave little doubt that religious communities considered it essential to place clear limitations on payments to advocates in order to prevent abuses. Indeed, as I will discuss later, one of the leading reasons ecclesiastical houses in the German kingdom forged

---

[7] *Chronica Sereni Montis*, 277–78, 345–46. The annals written at Pegau are silent about all of this: *Annales Pegavienses*, 268.

[8] See Chapters 2 and 3.

[9] See Chapter 4. Pope Leo IX's privilege for the women's community of Sainte-Croix-en-Plaine, which I discussed in the previous chapter, includes a detailed section about what the advocates were to be paid: Leo IX, *Epistolae*, cols. 635–37, no. 30.

documents from the late eleventh century onward was to alter the economic terms of their relationships with their advocates.[10] Before considering advocatial abuses and ecclesiastical efforts to counter them,
however, it is first necessary to understand what the accepted economic
benefits were that typically accrued to those who served as advocates.

The most straightforward form of advocatial income was judicial fines.
Presiding over law courts had emerged as one of the central roles of the
advocate during the late ninth and tenth centuries. Carolingian, and especially Ottonian, privileges granting immunities frequently decreed that an
ecclesiastical community's advocate was the one responsible for judging
criminals and meting out punishment.[11] In the decades after 1050, many
church reformers also tied the advocate's judicial authority to the idea that
prelates and other members of the Church should not shed blood. Thus,
writing in the mid-thirteenth century, Abbot Herman of Niederaltaich
explained, "Because it is not of the clerical dignity to administer justice or
blood punishment, the advocate will judge ... thefts, rapes, homicides,
immoderate disputes, arsons and similar cases among the men of the
church. In these cases, a churchman could be made [to act] contrary to
the provisions of canon law, if he should inflict the punishment."[12] Many of
the privileges written during the eleventh and twelfth centuries that detail
the responsibilities of church advocates provide similar lists of the crimes
they were to judge; these too tend to focus on crimes that could lead to
physical forms of punishment, especially execution.[13]

None of this means, however, that we should picture advocates routinely wielding the sword of justice to maim or kill criminals. Contrary to
popular culture's depictions of medieval criminal justice as a gruesome
spectacle, the most common forms of punishment across Europe in this
period – even for violent crimes – were fines and the confiscation of
property.[14] As a result, agreements between churches and advocates
frequently decreed that advocates had the right to one-third of the judicial
fines they collected when holding court.

For example, in a document from 1075 concerning the monastery of
Notre-Dame de Homblières, the count of Vermandois agreed, "if at any
time I will have been [made] advocate by the abbot or his monks for the
purpose of doing justice, then I will receive for myself a one-third part of
that justice."[15] Similarly, at some point between 1071 and 1093, the

---

[10] See Chapter 8.   [11] See Chapters 2 and 3.   [12] *De Advocatis*, 373.
[13] For more examples, see below. Early twentieth-century scholarship abounds with discussions of advocates and *Gerichtsbarkeit*; see Pischek, *Vogtgerichtsbarkeit*; Glitsch,
Untersuchungen; Hirsch, *Klosterimmunität*, 66–98; Aubin, "Immunität."
[14] Dean, *Crime*, 130–31; Smail, *Consumption*, 8–9; Tabuteau, "Punishments," 147–48.
[15] *Cartulary of Notre-Dame of Homblières*, 79–80, no. 31.

abbot of St. Bavo in Ghent made an agreement with the community's advocate; the advocate was to hold three judicial assemblies per year, "and if anyone should fight, or should commit theft or rape, he – sitting with the abbot – should administer justice and ought to receive therefrom the third penny."[16] Further east, Archbishop Anno II of Cologne's 1075 privilege for his new foundation of Siegburg first lists those places where the community's advocates were to hold court before explaining, "Judging, with the abbot's counsel, the shedding of blood, thefts, viola-tion of the peace and inheritance disputes, they should be content with their one-third. And they should not seek one-third except from those cases, which are aired in the advocate's courts or postponed from them."[17] The wide geographical spread of language of this sort by the 1070s is a clear indication that this had become a generally accepted aspect of advocatial income.[18]

The custom that someone who exercised judicial authority on another's behalf had the right to one-third of the fines is already evident in Carolingian sources concerning the judicial authority of counts.[19] This is a reminder of the significance of ninth- and tenth-century grants of immunity for the development of advocates' rights and responsibilities. It is also evidence that the church-reform movements of the decades after 1050 did not significantly alter older traditions of advocatial authority, especially in the German kingdom. Although new foundations were frequently the ones to stipulate that advocates could only hold court one or three times per year and could collect only one-third of the fines when they did so, these were not new ideas developed in reform circles. They were based on the much older tradition that advocates performed the functions of the count on ecclesiastical estates.[20]

From the perspective of pre-Enlightenment conceptualizations of jus-tice, the concern expressed in these documents about the proper division of fines fits other general patterns too. Financial gain was a central feature

---

[16] *Diplomata Belgica*, 251–52, no. 142; see also 213–14, no. 116, concerning St. Peter in Ghent, which explains that the monastery's dependents also had to pay a fixed amount of wine if they went to the advocate's castle to pursue a lawsuit.

[17] Wisplinghoff, ed., *Urkunden*, 15, no. 8.

[18] For other examples, see Dufour-Malbezin, ed., *Actes*, 182–83, no. 103; DD H IV, 360, no. 280 and 657–58, no. 482; *Mainzer Urkundenbuch*, 1:445–46, no. 538; CDS I A, 2:47, no. 55; *Fundatio Monasterii Gratiae Dei*, 689, chap. 8. Some historians argue that advo-cates in the kingdom of France had less judicial authority than advocates in the German kingdom: West, "Monks," 388–93; Bouchard, *Sword*, 125–30; Endemann, *Vogtei*, 45–47. While this may be true generally, advocates did claim judicial authority at some French monasteries (for one example, see Chapter 10).

[19] See, for example, Capit. 1:166, no. 74, chap. 2. For the similarities between advocatial courts and other lawcourts, see Planck, *Gerichtsverfahren*, 1:118, 149–50.

[20] See Chapters 2 and 3.

of judicial practices throughout the millennium under investigation here.[21] While perhaps counterintuitive from a modern perspective, that a judge could profit directly from the cases over which he presided was the norm.[22] This is presumably one reason why nobles would have wanted to serve as church advocates. That said, advocates typically received only one-third of the fines; ecclesiastical communities were the chief financial beneficiaries when their dependents committed crimes. Extant sources do not indicate how much advocates might have earned as judges, but it is difficult to imagine that violent crime was so rampant in the countryside that collecting one-third of the judicial fines at one or three court sessions per year was very lucrative for most advocates.[23] Moreover, there is no reason to think that they successfully collected fines in every case, since the guilty might have fled, hidden their movables or been too poor to pay more than a fraction of what they owed.[24]

Unsurprisingly, therefore, sources regulating the relationships between religious communities and their advocates frequently list additional benefits that the advocate accrued from exercising justice. The most prominent of these benefits concern the food, drink and lodging that the advocate and his entourage were to receive whenever he held court. Thus, the Hirsau Formulary explains that on each of the days of the three court sessions presided over by the advocate, he was to receive nothing except one-third of the fines and certain provisions – including "one measure of grain, one suckling-pig and one measure of wine."[25] The archbishop of Cologne's privilege from 1075 for Siegburg lists "the provisions, which the abbot owes to the advocate on each day of the court: two measures of wheat, one measure of wine, two measures of beer, two pigs worth two shillings, a small pig worth six pennies, two geese, four chickens, twenty eggs and six measures of oats."[26] Elsewhere, the lists of provisions were even more detailed. Documents from two religious communities separated by 600 kilometers, Gerbstedt in Saxony and Marmoutier (Maursmünster) in Alsace, both list different provisions depending on the season when the advocate held his three

[21] Carocci and Collavini, "Cost," 139; Peters, "Prison," 33–34; Duby, *Early Growth*, 172–73.
[22] For the idea that "crimes that men committed were the patrimony of the prince" because of the ubiquity of judicial fines, see from 1764 Beccaria, *On Crimes and Punishments*, 33–35, chap. 17.
[23] For the question of how profitable exercising justice was, see Dean, *Crime*, 133; May, "Index."
[24] Evidence along these lines from the twelfth-century countryside is minimal; I take this point from the later urban context: Smail, *Legal Plunder*, 153–56, 186.
[25] DD H IV, 360, no. 280. For this document, see Chapter 5.
[26] Wisplinghoff, ed., *Urkunden*, 15–16, no. 8.

court sessions.[27] In short, everywhere that advocacy was common, advocates and their entourages typically rode away from their law courts on churches' estates with not only one-third of the judicial fines but also full stomachs.

The word I have translated above as "provisions" is *servitium*, and this term is crucial for understanding the significance of the food, drink and lodging given to advocates when they came onto ecclesiastical estates to hold court. From the Carolingian period onward, the royal *servitium* referred to the rights of lodging and provisions that many ecclesiastical communities owed to the king and his court.[28] As discussed previously, a royal privilege of 877 granting immunity to one convent decreed, among other things, that "no count or any other [royal agent] may presume to hold judicial power, collect judicial fines, stay overnight, or demand food in the said monastery"; it then states that the convent's advocate was responsible for exercising justice.[29] While this privilege does not explicitly state that the advocate was to receive the food and lodging traditionally owed royal agents in return for holding court, by the eleventh century at the latest the *servitium* had unquestionably come to be attached to the role of advocate in this way.[30]

All of this evidence for judicial fines and provisions can be read in two ways. On the one hand, because these benefits parallel the benefits that counts had also received as local judicial authorities since the Carolingian period, they highlight the fact that advocatial authority had deep roots in customary practices of justice. This is further evidence for the inadequacy of "public"/"private" or "official"/"lordly" dichotomies when discussing the nature of authority before and after the year 1000. On the other hand, the fact that so many documents from France to Austria regulate which crimes advocates could judge, what fraction of the fines they could collect and how much they should be fed – *down to the exact number of eggs* – is evidence that churches and their advocates frequently disagreed about the details of those customary practices.[31] Because justice was profitable across the millennium from 750 to 1800, both advocates and religious

---

[27] CDS I A, 2:47, no. 55 and Schöpflin, ed., *Alsatia*, 227, no. 275. See also Schmidt, *Seigneurs*, 91–93.

[28] The term *servitium* had many meanings and, from the Carolingian period, could also refer to the military service required of royal followers; see Bernhardt, *Itinerant*, 75–78; Freed, *Frederick Barbarossa*, 100–02; Brühl, "Servitium Regis." See also Cheyette, *Ermengard*, 158–59.

[29] DD Km, 335–37, no. 3.

[30] In Flanders, churches and advocates also agreed on advocatial payments relating to the advocates' need for supplies when going on military campaign. See Nieus and Vanderputten, "Diplôme princier," 11–12. Nieus, "Avouerie" (in press).

[31] On this point, see Duby, *Guerriers*, 239.

communities competed to benefit as much as possible from holding courts and judging churches' dependents. Tensions were therefore inevitable.

Paying for Protection

In the mid-twelfth century, the margrave of Styria in today's Austria issued a privilege to the monastery of Garsten, which his ancestors had founded earlier in the century. It details the advocate's rights (*ius advocati*), echoing in many places the documents discussed in the previous section. For example, "[t]hree times per year, ... he [the advocate] ought to hold his court, ... where either the abbot himself or his authorized messenger ought to sit at the advocate's side, and from every fine, either for assault or theft, two parts fall to the church, the third to him."[32] It is more specific about the division of the fines in murder cases. If one of the monastery's dependents murdered another dependent, the division of the fine was likewise two-thirds for Garsten and one-third for the advocate; however, if someone from outside the monastery's properties murdered one of Garsten's dependents, the advocate was the one who would receive two-thirds of the fine. This text also notes that the advocate would receive a meal when he held court if he wanted one. It then closes with a list of properties and rights he was to hold "for the advocate's rights."[33]

This final clause begs an obvious question: if the advocate was already being paid through fines and meals for exercising justice, what else was he doing to receive these properties and rights as an added benefit? The evidence from Garsten does not permit a definitive answer. Sources from other religious communities include similar descriptions of advocates holding properties, typically in fief, meaning Garsten was not unusual in remunerating its advocates in this way. At the monastery of Gorze, for example, a privilege from 1095 granted the advocate ten estates in fief while limiting the other types of claims he could make on the monastery's property.[34] As at Garsten, it is unclear what the advocate was expected to do in return, but fiefs of this sort were clearly an important part of the relationship between churches and advocates.[35] Thus, while ecclesiastics frequently insisted that the advocacies for their churches were *not* fiefs,

---

[32] Haider, ed., *Traditionsurkunden*, 84–86, no. K18. For my assessment of this document, which Haider labels a forgery, see Lyon, "Noble Lineages."
[33] Haider, ed., *Traditionsurkunden*, 86, no. K18.
[34] D'Herbomez, ed., *Cartulaire*, 245–48, no. 140.
[35] For fiefs in this period, see Patzold, *Lehnswesen*, 71–86 and the articles in *Das Lehnswesen im Hochmittelalter*.

they willingly gave other properties to their advocates in fief in return for some of the services they provided.[36]

More revealing than grants of fiefs are references to additional types of payments in coin or in kind – or, occasionally, in forced labor – beyond those given when an advocate held court. When Count Baldwin V of Flanders in 1042 settled a dispute between the abbot of St. Bertin and the community's advocate, Gerbode, concerning the advocate's rights in one village, he decreed, "[E]very year, from every piece of cultivated land in that village, he should have a half-measure of oats without any objection, by this agreement and condition: that he should demand or receive nothing more from the same village by any inducement or machination whatsoever and that he should not withdraw suitable aid for its defense."[37] It continues by explaining that the advocate was to receive a measure of grain from the abbot every year at Christmas in return for his leaving in peace the monastic community's dependents living nearby unless any should commit a crime. Here, we see with unusual clarity a monastery paying an advocate for protection.

Though not as explicit, a document from 1080 concerning the advocacies for two villages belonging to the monastery of Saint-Mihiel points in a similar direction. It explains that in one of the villages, "each household" was to give the advocate no more than one measure of oats, one loaf of bread, one chicken, one penny and one small bundle of hay on the feast of St. Martin (November 11); then, on the feast of the purification of the Virgin Mary (February 2), the village as a community was to provide five shillings worth of food or the *servitium* for ten knights for one night.[38] The annual payments from each household hint that this type of advocatial income was not directly related to the advocate's functions holding court but to the defense of the village.[39] The connection between protection and advocates' income is suggested in a different fashion in a document from a monastery near Troyes from around 1126 concerning the advocacy for a village; it explains that, in the month of May, each household had to provide one laborer to do six

---

[36] Schieffer, "Lehnswesen," 83. It was more common for the advocacies for individual ecclesiastical estates to be treated as fiefs; see, for example, *Prümer Urbar*, 200, n. 1 and 237, n. 5.

[37] Nieus and Vanderputten, "Diplôme princier," 11–12, 23–25 and 50–53 (text edition). For this type of document, see also Parisse, "Les règlements."

[38] Lesort, ed., *Chronique*, 159–61, no. 41. The households of the other village did not owe the small bundle of hay – but apparently owed all of the other payments – and only two shillings' worth of food. For this advocacy, see also Boshof, "Untersuchungen," 79–80; Gillen, *Saint-Mihiel*, 128–29.

[39] In other places, it was the monks who were to pay: *Mainzer Urkundenbuch*, 1:445–46, no. 538.

days' work "supplying the castle."[40] Apparently, the advocate's castle kept the churches' dependents safe, so they were obligated to help maintain it.

Given that exercising justice and providing protection were advocates' two main responsibilities by the mid-eleventh century, it follows that these additional types of benefits – everything besides judicial fines and the *servitium* – concerned their roles as protectors. Paying a fixed amount in return for the protection of people and property is essentially a form of taxation, of course, and some scholars have argued that advocacy played a key role in the early history of taxes in parts of Europe.[41] However, distinguishing between plunder, tribute and taxation when discussing local relationships based on the supply of and demand for protection can be difficult. Whether or not the protector is genuinely providing protection against outside threats or is, in fact, himself the principal source of danger to the people paying for protection fundamentally shapes the meaning of these payments.[42] As we will see in the next chapter, the Latin terms for the payments advocates received reflect this ambivalence; *exactiones*, translated neutrally as "exactions," is sometimes better translated as "extortions," sometimes as "taxes," depending on context.[43]

As a result, calling protection payments a form of taxation is to assume a particular understanding of the situation that may not reflect local actors' perceptions. For now, it is best to emphasize instead the term that appears in the margrave of Styria's privilege for Garsten: "right" (*jus*). Regardless of how we label these payments, everyone recognized that advocates had the right to be paid *something* for providing protection. How much they had the right to be paid was an entirely different question.[44]

Some scholars have suggested that the total amount of income nobles received from local payments of this sort was quite small. According to this line of argument, it was less the money, goods or labor services that mattered to the advocate than the claims to authority over the people paying.[45] The payments were thus a way of reminding dependents where

---

[40] *Cartulary of Montier-en-Der*, 294–96, no. 150. See also ibid., 245–48, no. 116; Bur, *Formation*, 259–60, 347–50.

[41] See, for example, Waas, *Vogtei*, 2:73–74; Simon, *Grundherrschaft*, 46–51; Bosl, "Schutz"; Brunner, *Land*, 308–09; Fried, "Steuer."

[42] Helpful here is Freedman, *Peasant Servitude*, 99–103. See Chapter 10 for much more on this point.

[43] See, for example, the aforementioned texts concerning St. Bertin and Montier-en-Der: Nieus and Vanderputten, "Diplôme princier," 50–53; *Cartulary of Montier-en-Der*, 294–96, no. 150.

[44] Instead of *ius*, the term *consuetudo* (custom) is sometimes used; see Chapters 4 and 7.

[45] Cheyette, *Ermengard*, 160–61.

they belonged in the social hierarchy. However, a purely symbolic expla-nation for the growing significance of advocatial income after 1050 is unconvincing.[46] There was too much flexibility in social interactions at the local level to fix a single meaning to these payments. Even if each payment was quite small, a local aristocrat, acting as advocate, was taking income away from the church – income he could then use to show his largesse by distributing food and drink to the members of his own entou-rage. Viewed from this perspective, the symbolic and economic aspects of these payments were intertwined at multiple levels. What might seem like a paltry sum to a prominent noble advocate nevertheless integrated him into the economic regimes of religious communities and gave him the opportunity to reward his local followers from a church's estates rather than his own.

The potential economic significance of these local payments comes into clearer focus when we recall that by the twelfth century many nobles held multiple advocacies.[47] As a result, while the annual payments from one estate might not have been substantial, most advocates exercised justice and provided protection on numerous properties. This can best be seen in one of the few sources from the twelfth-century German kingdom that offers a nobleman's perspective on advocacy. The Falkenstein Codex (*Codex Falkensteinensis*) was commissioned by the Bavarian Count Sigiboto IV of Falkenstein before he departed on Emperor Frederick I's fourth Italian campaign in 1166.[48] It includes a detailed (though incomplete) record of his rights and properties and was apparently intended for his children, so they would understand what they held as his heirs if he died on campaign. Church advocacies play a prominent role in the codex. One entry even explains where two docu-ments concerning Sigiboto's advocatial rights over two monasteries were stored in case they needed to be consulted.[49]

Some of the references to advocacy in the Falkenstein Codex are detailed lists of the count's rights wherever he was advocate. An early entry refers to those things "that pertain to his *servitium*, when he holds a legitimate law court" in one local advocacy.[50] His rights included lodging for the night as well as a meal on the day of the court. The meal was to have an impressive spread: "five pigs (two mature and three young ones); thirty bushels of oats for fodder plus ten bushels for brewing; two bushels of wheat; three bushels of rye; a measure of corn; a measure of mead and a measure of wine; ten geese; thirty chickens; 100 cheeses; one

[46] Buc, "What Is Order?," 289–90.   [47] See Chapter 5.
[48] For background to this codex, see Freed, *Counts*; Freed, "Bavarian Wine."
[49] *Codex Falkensteinensis*, 66–67, no. 103.   [50] Ibid., 11, no. 5.

cow; and thirty eggs." The codex includes similar entries for the count's advocacies on estates belonging to the archbishopric of Salzburg and monastery of Herrenchiemsee.[51] However, it does not list every church advocacy that Sigiboto is known to have held, making it impossible to ascertain the full extent of the income he received as advocate.[52]

Count Sigiboto IV survived Emperor Frederick I's expedition to Italy, and after his return to Bavaria he continued to add material to the codex for the remainder of his life. One of these additional entries, dated to the 1180s or early 1190s, is a listing of the *jus modiorum*, "the right to oats," that Sigiboto had from the advocacy for the Bavarian monastery of Herrenchiemsee: two bushels from one estate, one bushel from another, eight pecks from a third, and so on.[53] An entire page of the manuscript is dedicated to listing the monastery's estates and the amount of oats the advocate was to receive from each one. In total, this entry lists sixty-six bushels that he was to receive annually. To give some context, by one historian's estimate that amount of wheat or rye could have been used to bake approximately 1,650 large loaves of bread.[54] This is clearly not a small, symbolic amount of grain. Indeed, the Falkenstein Codex is clear evidence that Sigiboto wanted his heirs to know exactly how much income they would receive as the monastery's advocates.[55] What mattered first and foremost to the count about his role as advocate was how much he would be paid.[56]

Other sources from this period that provide glimpses into nobles' perspectives on advocacy also point in this direction. The oldest manuscript listing the dues owed in coin and kind to the Wittelsbach dukes of Bavaria (a type of work known as an *Urbar* in German) dates from the 1230s.[57] It contains approximately 2,000 entries from different towns, villages and estates across Bavaria, each one representing a claim to the revenues from a specific right held by the dukes. Roughly 5 percent of these entries are references to advocacies, and the dukes collected from these advocatial rights more than 100 bushels of wheat, 60 bushels of rye,

---

[51] Ibid., 45, no. 72. For the advocacy of Herrenchiemsee in this period, see Wild, "Herrenchiemsee," 140–42.

[52] Freed, "Bavarian Wine," 89–90.   [53] *Codex Falkensteinensis*, 70–71, no. 107.

[54] Using John Freed's calculations from his own detailed analysis of the *Codex Falkensteinensis*: Freed, "Bavarian Wine," 83, n. 45.

[55] It is worth noting that the counts of Falkenstein were not an especially wealthy or prominent comital lineage: Freed, *Counts*.

[56] I know of only one example of a list of what an advocate was expected to provide a religious community rather than what was owed to him: *Solothurner Urkundenbuch*, 13–15, no. 7. Wood sees this as an aspect of lordship rather than advocacy, however: Wood, *Proprietary Church*, 366–69. See also Hirsch, *Die Klosterimmunität*, 3.

[57] For the difficulty of translating the term *Urbar* into English, see Freed, "Bavarian Wine," 71–72, n. 2.

1,000 bushels of oats, cheese, wine, beer, chickens, hundreds of sheep and lambs and more than 50 pounds of silver.[58] While it is impossible to know if the dukes successfully collected all of this each year, the numbers clearly show that being an advocate was profitable. Equally compelling evidence along these lines is the appearance of the vernacular term *Kastvogt* in some documents. In one from 1210, for example, there is a reference to "the advocate, who is commonly called *Kastvogt*."[59] Although the precise meaning of this term is unclear, some have suggested it stems from the boxes or chests in which advocates collected the payments they were owed.[60] If so, advocatial income must have been central to local perceptions of advocates' roles.

The surviving sources from the twelfth and early thirteenth century are much too fragmentary and problematic to be able to calculate what percentage of an aristocrat's total income came from church advocacies.[61] Regardless, the frequency with which advocates' income appears in our sources from the late eleventh century onward is evidence that we need to take this revenue seriously. It clearly paid to be an advocate and to provide justice and protection for religious communities, their estates and their dependents. Here, we see the inadequacy of describing advocacy as simply one aspect of an ill-defined notion of "lordship" during this period. To be a church advocate was not simply to dominate the local countryside. The abundant evidence for churches reaching agreements with their advocates about advocatial income points to advocates fulfilling an essential function by keeping people and property safe – a function that ecclesiastics willingly paid for them to fulfill.

From Memory to Written Record

To this point, it has been necessary to cast a wide net to find sources that reveal advocacy's economic dimensions. For the period before 1200 we are fortunate if we have two or three documents from any given religious community that offer clues about advocatial payments. There are even fewer sources for nobles' perspectives on advocates' rights and sources of

---

[58] Heeg-Engelhart, ed., *Herzogsurbar*. One of the most impressive entries is for the advocacy for Wessobrunn, from which they were to receive 126 bushels of oats a year: ibid., 151, no. 1223. There are also entries for advocacies over individual properties, with some of these including lodging rights: ibid., 210–11, nos. 1471c and 1477. As with the Falkenstein Codex, not every church advocacy is listed: ibid., 125*–127*.

[59] Parlow, *Die Zähringer*, 382–83, no. 582. See also ibid., 337–38, no. 526 and Zotz, *Zähringer*, 126–27.

[60] Stievermann, *Landesherrschaft*, 20. See also the entry for "Kastenvogt" in the online *Deutsches Wörterbuch von Jacob Grimm und Wilhelm Grimm*.

[61] Zehetmayer, "Vogtei," 239–42.

income.[62] To be fair, though, detailed evidence about the local econo-
mies of the late eleventh and twelfth centuries is difficult to find anywhere.
Even places with a reputation for being precocious in developing strong
financial institutions, such as Normandy and Flanders, are lacking in
good sources until the closing years of the twelfth century.[63] When the
evidence improves in the thirteenth, much of it reflects the shift toward
a money economy and the decline in the significance of traditional agrarian profits vis-à-vis newer sources of royal and princely revenue.[64]
Although the income from agricultural estates was increasingly oversha-
dowed by revenues available from expanded trade and manufacturing,
this income nevertheless remained essential for many ecclesiastical communities and nobles.

As a result, many religious houses participated in the general
thirteenth-century trend of producing and preserving detailed written
records relating to their economic interests; these included lists of their
property holdings and incomes – and occasionally of their advocates'
rights.[65] For our purposes, the Bavarian monastery of Niederaltaich
under the above-mentioned Abbot Herman (1242–73) deserves close
attention. Herman was a typical prelate of the mid-thirteenth century,
a keen administrator who dedicated much of his time as abbot to
improving the economic and legal situation of his community.[66]
Unlike many of his contemporaries, however, Herman left behind
a remarkably rich collection of material – including several lengthy
manuscripts – that testifies to his tireless efforts and organizational
skills. This material provides an unusually clear picture of the place
of advocates and advocatial rights in the economic life of a religious
community.

One of Herman's manuscripts, preserved today in Munich, is well
known to historians of advocacy, because it contains a detailed narrative

---

[62] I will discuss a few exceptions in subsequent chapters. In general, the economic aspects of
noble "lordship" have not been studied in detail, as noted by Bünz, "Adlige
Unternehmer?"

[63] Kittell, *Ad Hoc*, 196; Lyon and Verhulst, *Medieval Finance*, 64, 88; Berkhofer, *Day of
Reckoning*, 157–58. See, more generally, Epstein, *Economic*, 122–27.

[64] Lyon and Verhulst, *Medieval Finance*, 94; Duby, *Guerriers*, 241.

[65] Freed, "Bavarian Wine," 73–78. For documentary cultures more generally, Bertrand,
Documenting, 5–6; Clanchy, *Memory*, 94–98; Kittell, *Ad Hoc*. For arguments about the
relationship between writing and the rise of government, see Bisson, *Crisis*, 336–48;
West, *Reframing*, 98–99; Watts, *Polities*, 73; Berkhofer, *Day of Reckoning*, 7–8.
However, as the modern world shows, criminal operations can be just as reliant on
written records as legitimate governments; see Venkatesh, *Gang Leader*, 255–56.

[66] Klose, ed., *Urbare*, 13*–19*; Herzberg-Fränkel, "Wirtschaftsgeschichte," 180–81. One
of Herman's predecessors, Abbot Poppo, had already begun keeping track of debts,
pledges, purchases and other sorts of financial matters: ibid., 181.

about his community's advocates.[67] I will discuss this text in the next chapter. What interests me here is the manuscript in which it appears, because the codex belongs to a group of manuscripts from Herman's time as abbot that contain not only copies of important documents but also detailed accounts of Niederaltaich's property rights and financial situation; it is an *Urbar* like that of the Wittelsbach dukes already discussed in this chapter. Two other Niederaltaich manuscripts housed today in Vienna are similar in many ways.[68] One of these Vienna manuscripts dates from the first years of Herman's abbacy, which suggests that he was anxious from the beginning to gain a clear picture of the monastery's holdings.[69] In the mid-1250s, the abbot and his scribes then compiled the Munich manuscript, which is the most polished and beautiful of the three codices. By the closing years of Herman's abbacy, however, it had apparently become outdated, which prompted the production of the second Vienna manuscript. Though each codex is organized differently, a great deal of material appears in more than one manuscript. When read together, these codices therefore present an extraordinarily rich collection of economic information about the monastery, spanning approximately a quarter-century.[70]

Herman had become abbot around the time when the counts of Bogen, who had been Niederaltaich's advocates for generations, died out in the male line; the Wittelsbach dukes of Bavaria then acquired the advocacy. Unsurprisingly, therefore, all three manuscripts contain sections explicitly dedicated to the economic rights of the monastery's advocates.[71] In the older of the Vienna manuscripts, the caption for this section reads, "In the year of the Lord 1253, in the month of February, by order of the illustrious lord Otto, duke of Bavaria, I, Abbot Herman, after a thorough investigation, wrote down the following concerning the advocate's rights for the estates and men of the monastery Niederaltaich and the cell Rinchnach."[72] This passage points to the necessity for precise

---

[67] This is the so-called *De Advocatis Altahensibus* (*On the Advocates of Niederaltaich*). For this text, see also Dendorfer, "Abtei," 93–106.

[68] These are Munich, Bayerisches Hauptstaatsarchiv, Kl. Niederaltaich Lit. 39 (hereafter Munich ms); Vienna, Haus-, Hof- und Staatsarchiv, Hs. R 83/1 and Hs. R 83/2 (hereafter Vienna ms 1 and Vienna ms 2). A fourth manuscript containing a fragment of an *Urbar* will not be discussed; see Klose, ed., *Urbare*, 1:47*–49*.

[69] For the dating of all the manuscripts, see ibid., 1:24*–46*.

[70] See especially Herzberg-Fränkel, "Wirtschaftsgeschichtlichen Quellen"; Herzberg-Fränkel, "Wirtschaftsgeschichte."

[71] This section is labeled "De iure advocati" in Vienna ms 1, fol. 21v; "Ius advocati" in Vienna ms 2, fol. 109v; and "De iure advocati in prediis nostris" in Munich ms, fol. 120v. See also Klose, ed., *Urbare*, 2:677–78. I follow here my own counting of the folios in the manuscripts, not Klose's.

[72] Vienna ms 1, fol. 21v; Klose, ed., *Urbare*, 2:689, no. 2.

information. Duke Otto had a reputation at Niederaltaich for being a better advocate than his predecessors, but in order to stay within the proper bounds of his advocatial rights, both he and Herman needed to know exactly what those rights were.[73]

What follows in both Vienna manuscripts are lengthy lists of specific places where the monastery's advocates exercised advocatial authority. Initially, the lists simply name those places where the monastery held properties over which the advocates had rights. Then, they record how many bushels of wheat and oats, how many cheeses and how much money were to be given to the advocate from these places.[74] The most common listings are for oats and money. The statement that ends the lists of advocatial rights in all three manuscripts offers an explanation for all of these payments:

The counts of Bogen, with the consent of the abbots, established that the above-written rights of the advocate of the church were to be given in the same way as from antiquity, such that, after these things had been paid, our estates, along with their cultivators and dependents, should suffer thereafter neither [additional] payments (*steuras*), nor lodging, nor expenses for the public law courts, nor any other troubles. The advocate ought to hold a law court with the men of the church three times per year, namely twice in summer and once in winter, and for his expenses for doing this, the "advocate's penny" (*vogtphenning*) and oats for feeding the horses are to be given to him.[75]

The Munich manuscript provides the most straightforward record of these rights. It first lists properties that were to provide a money payment: one talent from one, twelve shillings from another, and so on. This section ends with the note that the sum was twenty pounds, three shillings and nine pennies.[76] There then follows a listing of places that were to provide oats, and how much: fourteen bushels from one, thirteen from another, and so on. This section likewise ends with the total amount.[77] Thus, even more clearly than the Falkenstein Codex, these Niederaltaich manuscripts signal that each of the monastery's estates could make a single,

[73] Herzberg-Fränkel, "Wirtschaftsgeschichte," 183.
[74] Klose, ed., *Urbare*, 2:691, no. 20. The entry notes that three cheeses were equal in value to one penny, which reflects the increasing monetization of the agrarian economy in the thirteenth century; see Spufford, *Money*, 240–48.
[75] Klose, ed., *Urbare*, 2:683, no. 19. Readers may recognize in the term *steuras* the modern German word *Steuer*, "tax." However, I avoid this translation here for reasons explained in the section above, "Paying for Protection."
[76] Ibid., 2:678–681. The Vienna codices confirm some of these entries. For example, "In Vsterling datur advocato talentum" (ibid., 2:679, no. 3) appears in Vienna ms 1, fol. 25r and Vienna ms 2, fol. 113v. This is only one example out of the tangle of entries, but it points to the consistency of the income over several decades.
[77] Klose, ed., *Urbare*, 2:681–682.

fixed annual payment of either coin or grain to the advocate in return for all of his rights and responsibilities.

This bundling of all advocatial income into one payment is evident in the terminology that emerges in the thirteenth century around the economic dimensions of advocacy. Herman's use of the word *Vogtpfennig* – "advocate's penny" – points in this direction. Other entries in his manuscripts use the phrase "*De denariis advocacie*," the Latin equivalent of the *Vogtpfennig*.[78] This vocabulary was not unique to Niederaltaich. A charter from 1287 from another monastery references "7 of the advocate's pennies, which are commonly called *voitespfenning*."[79] Other compound terms from this period – such as *vogetmutte* (the advocate's bushel), *vogdwaiz* (the advocate's wheat) and *vogthuhn* (the advocate's chicken) – are evidence that agricultural products remained an important part of advocatial income into the thirteenth century (and later).[80] Nevertheless, it is the monetization of advocacy that emerges from the sources as the most important economic development in this period.

Indeed, advocates and religious communities increasingly negotiated lump-sum payments in coin.[81] In 1243, for example, Duke Frederick II of Austria confirmed an agreement between Abbot Herman and one of the duke's ministerials for the advocacy of a single village in Lower Austria.[82] The abbot and his successors agreed to give the ministerial eighteen pounds (*libras*) per year; in return, the advocate would hold three law courts per year "with twenty-four mounted men" and would have lodging for him and his men on each of these occasions, "or he will receive five pounds for all of their expenses." Here, the annual payments and the *servitium* when holding court are handled separately, but both are clearly expressed in monetary terms. In 1281, the advocate of Niederaltaich, Duke Henry XIII of Bavaria, went one step further when he explained "that we have been accustomed to receive for every advocatial right (*omni Jure advocatali*) concerning the people and estates of the church of Niederaltaich 100 pounds, and having received them ... are obliged to defend the aforesaid church's estates and people."[83] While the duke

---

[78] Ibid., 2:684, no. 2. See more generally for the significance of this trend, Waas, *Vogtei*, 2:88–91.

[79] Krausen, ed., *Urkunden*, 338, no. 417.

[80] For these terms, see for example Klose, ed., *Urbare*, 2:685, no. 21; Heeg-Engelhart, ed., *Herzogsurbar*, 96, no. 828.

[81] This had already started in the twelfth century. See, for example, *Mainzer Urkundenbuch*, 1:445–46, no. 538 and 2.1:556–58, no. 327; *Cartulary of Montier-en-Der*, 294–96, no. 150. See more generally Spufford, *Money*, 242.

[82] Klose, ed., *Urkunden*, 23–26, no. 128.

[83] *Monumenta Boica*, 11:255–56, no. 118. See also Herzberg-Fränkel, "Wirtschaftsgeschichte," 192.

acknowledges his responsibilities as the church's protector, the language of this document points unmistakably toward a commodification of advocacy.[84]

This document takes us too far afield, chronologically speaking. I will return in subsequent chapters to the developments that transformed advocacy in the decades and centuries after 1250. Here, what is important to emphasize is that this text is, in many ways, the logical outcome of the expanding efforts by secular and ecclesiastical elites to define in detail in writing the economic dimensions of advocacy. From the mid-eleventh century onward, regulating what advocates should be paid for exercising justice and providing protection required a steadily rising volume of ink and parchment, which is a testament to the subject's significance. Payments in pigs, sheep, beer and wine – and increasingly in pennies and pounds – clearly mattered, and as discussions of these payments came to overshadow discussions of the specific rights and responsibilities of advocates, it was only a matter of time before advocacy began to be expressed purely in terms of its monetary value.[85]

The Power of Money

I close this chapter as I began it, with the coins minted and exchanged in the advocate's shadow, in order to emphasize another key aspect of the interrelationship of advocates, justice, protection and money. The bracteates naming Count Dietrich minted at the monastery of Pegau in the early thirteenth century are not the only coins that can be linked directly to advocacy. An even richer collection comes from Quedlinburg in the middle decades of the twelfth century. There, depictions of advocates on several different coin types offer clear visual evidence for the influence that advocates could exert over the economic life of a religious house's properties.

The advocacy for the women's community at Quedlinburg is not easy to follow during the first two centuries of its existence. As already discussed, Otto I's foundation privilege for Quedlinburg stated that the position of advocate was to remain in his family, and this suggests that the other rulers from his Ottonian dynasty held the advocacy until the dynasty's end in 1024.[86] In the written record, there is no reference to another advocate for Quedlinburg until the second quarter of the twelfth century; at some point in the mid-1130s, or perhaps a few years earlier, Frederick of Sommerschenburg, the count-palatine of Saxony, became

---

[84] See subsequent chapters for more on this point.
[85] Cf. Zehetmayer, "Vogtei," 241–43, 254–55.   [86] See Chapter 3.

advocate and held the position until his death in 1162.[87] It then passed to his son Albrecht, who held it from 1162 until 1179.[88] Throughout Albrecht's time as advocate, his sister was the abbess of Quedlinburg: Adelheid III (1161–84). Thus, a religious community that King Otto I had envisioned as being closely tied to his ruling dynasty had, 200 years after his death, moved into the hands of a local noble family – as was the case with many other imperial monasteries too.

The coins minted at Quedlinburg in the eleventh and early twelfth centuries help fill in some of the gaps about the advocates, but the evidence is difficult to interpret.[89] Some historians suggest that the early Salian emperors may have served as advocates in the eleventh century, followed in the early twelfth century by Duke Lothar of Saxony, the future Emperor Lothar III (1125–37).[90] Two different denars (silver pennies struck on both sides) minted under Abbess Gerberga (1126–37) include on one side an image of a bearded man holding a sword and a banner, and scholars have identified this figure as the advocate (probably Count-Palatine Frederick of Saxony).[91] Two different bracteates minted under Gerberga's successor, Abbess Beatrice II (1138–60), depict a pair of figures (Figure 6.2). One is a seated woman, who on one coin holds a palm frond and on the other a staff and lily; next to her on both coins is a standing man with a sword resting on his shoulder. Scholars have consistently identified these figures as the abbess and the advocate.[92] This image could be viewed as menacing – as the advocate threatening the abbess with violence to remind her who holds effective authority over her community and its properties. However, there is no way to determine who designed these coin types. Given that there is no evidence to suggest a serious conflict between the advocate and the religious house (as was the case at Pegau), a more plausible interpretation is that the advocate and abbess are being depicted here as partners, one wielding secular and the other spiritual authority. As these coins circulated on Quedlinburg's estates, they would have been a powerful visual statement of the advocate's role as one who provided justice and protection for the abbess and her dependents.

---

[87] Mehl, *Münzen*, 53–54. A charter from the mid-1130s issued by Abbess Gerberga of Quedlinburg was drawn up "*in presentia nostra & Comitis Palatini, Friderici, aduocati videlicet nostri*" (Erath, ed., *Codex*, 81–82, no. 4). See also ibid., 82, no. 5 and 87–88, no. 11 for Frederick as advocate.

[88] Arnstedt, "Schirmvogtei," 172–73. See also Erath, ed., *Codex*, 93–94, no. 20.

[89] Mehl, *Münzen*, 53–54, 345; Steinbach, *Geld*, 141–46; Kluge, *Deutsche Münzgeschichte*, 68 and 270–71, no. 441.

[90] Mehl, *Münzen*, 52–53.   [91] Ibid., 350–51 and 358, nos. 48–49.

[92] Ibid., 364–65, nos. 55–56. See also p. 383, no. 78, where Mehl suggests that the lettering around the outside of a bracteate originally spelled out the name Frederick. For coin no. 56, see Figure 6.2.

Figure 6.2 Bracteate from Quedlinburg depicting an advocate and abbess. Universitätsbibliothek Leipzig, Inventar Nummer 1987/1454. www.kenom.de/objekt/record_DE-15_kenom_188427/1/-/

Other coin types minted at Quedlinburg in this period seem to suggest that Count-Palatine Frederick and his son Albrecht were more than just the abbesses' partners. One bracteate bearing the name of Abbess Beatrice depicts in a central arch a figure with a sword leaning against the right shoulder while holding a lily in the left hand.[93] From the neck down, the clothing parallels the clothing of the abbess on other coins minted in Beatrice's name, yet the head is clearly that of a man. It appears that whoever designed this coin used a preexisting stamp depicting the abbess and altered it to turn this central figure into the advocate. This interpretation is strengthened by a second surviving bracteate type from this period, which clearly depicts a man seated between two towers, holding a sword and a lily (see Figure 6.3).[94] What has happened to the abbess, and what does it mean that the advocate is so prominently the main figure on a coin minted at Quedlinburg?

Under the next abbess, Adelheid III, who was Count-Palatine Frederick's daughter and Albrecht's sister, there are additional coin types depicting men

[93] Ibid., 384–85, no. 79.   [94] Ibid., 386, no. 80.

Figure 6.3 Bracteate from Quedlinburg depicting an advocate. Universitätsbibliothek Leipzig, Inventar Nummer 1995/1464. www .kenom.de/objekt/record_DE-15_kenom_188456/1/-/

with swords. In some, the abbess is flanked by two male figures, possibly her father and brother (see Figure 6.4) .[95] Another shows abbess and swordsman seated next to each other.[96] A third depicts a man with a sword and a staff, seated between two towers – without the abbess present.[97] Comparable images of advocates on Quedlinburg coins are rare after the deaths of the siblings Albrecht and Adelheid, which suggests that the advocates exerted undue influence over Quedlinburg in this period when there were strong family connections between the counts-palatine and the community.[98] Perhaps we glimpse here evidence of an abbess (willingly or unwillingly) granting her relatives greater access to the economic rights of her community than previous or subsequent abbesses allowed.

[95] Ibid., 401–04, nos. 99–101. Mehl notes that some scholars doubt this interpretation on the grounds that a father and son could not hold an advocacy jointly. However, this was never a hard-and-fast rule.
[96] Ibid., 415, no. 119.   [97] Ibid., 415–16, no. 120.
[98] But see ibid., 458, no. 188, for a bracteate from the first quarter of the thirteenth century depicting abbess and advocate together.

Figure 6.4 Bracteate from Quedlinburg depicting an abbess flanked by two men, possibly father-and-son advocates. Münzkabinett der Staatliche Museen zu Berlin, No.18201075. Photo by Lutz-Jürgen Lübke (Lübke & Wiedemann)

No other religious communities offer comparably rich numismatic evidence for advocates.[99] Nevertheless, the coins from Quedlinburg are a clear indication that advocacy, protection, justice and money were inescapably intertwined by the mid-twelfth century. Viewed symbolically, these coins demonstrate the nature of advocatial authority; the common-place image of the sword on the shoulder points directly to advocates' roles exercising justice and providing protection. Viewed economically, these coins highlight the value and importance of advocatial revenues.[100] When a church's dependents paid fines and made other payments to

[99] What little evidence there is mostly comes from eastern Saxony, where both Quedlinburg and Pegau are located; see, for example, Kluge, *Deutsche Münzgeschichte*, 67–68 and 226–27, nos. 308–10. See also a royal coin from Thuringia depicting King Frederick I, his wife and an advocate: Haussherr and Väterlein, ed., *Zeit*, 1:138, no. 188.25 and 2:Abb. 104.1.

[100] Minting rights were valuable. Bracteates, in particular, were often short-lived coins, with the mint collecting the old coins and issuing new ones regularly. The mint made a profit, because when someone turned in the old coins, they were given fewer of the new ones (four old coins for three new ones, for example); Svensson, *Renovatio Monetae*, 44–49.

advocates using coins on which an image of the advocate appeared, they were acknowledging the right of their advocate to profit from his position.[101]

Conclusion

Advocacy was a complex phenomenon, and scholars can approach it from a variety of different perspectives – for example, the history of law and judicial practices, the history of Church institutions and the history of local property rights. While all of these are unquestionably valid approaches, it is essential to recognize the centrality of the economic dimensions of advocacy, regardless of the perspective one chooses to take. People had to pay (and still do pay, in one way or another) for protection and justice. The position of advocate was therefore a profitable one. This helps to explain why, from the tenth century onward, many of the highest-ranking members of the secular elite in Europe were interested in holding not just one but many advocacies. It also helps to explain why advocacies were a source of tension between nobles and religious communities. Because the two sides did not always agree on the amounts and the sources of advocatial income, disputes – some of them violent – frequently erupted.

---

[101] In one charter from the 1130s, a decade when some Quedlinburg bracteates depicted the advocate, the advocate was to receive three shillings annually from an estate: Erath, ed., *Codex*, 81–82, no. 4.

7   A History of Violence

The earliest sources for advocates at the monastery of Tegernsee in Bavaria date from the years around 1000. As at many other religious houses, the evidence for these first advocates is fragmentary and difficult to interpret; only a few letters suggest that the community's abbots and monks occasionally had to confront problems concerning the advocacy.[1] By the mid-twelfth century, the situation was strikingly different. When the abbot of Tegernsee traveled to the court of Emperor Frederick I Barbarossa (1152–90) in 1157 to complain about his advocates' many abuses, he initiated a phase of intense focus on the advocacy. Monks at the community soon began forging documents that were intended first and foremost to alter the monastery's relationship with its advocates and limit advocatial rights on the monastery's properties. During the 1160s and 1170s, two of Tegernsee's monks, one writing in verse and the other in prose, dedicated entire sections of their hagiographical works about the monastery's patron saint, Quirinus, to stories about the saint punishing the advocates for their many misdeeds.[2] In the 150 years between the early eleventh century and the late twelfth, Tegernsee's advocates had moved from the periphery to the center of the community's attention – for all the wrong reasons.

The anonymous monk who wrote the prose *Passion of St. Quirinus* was especially critical of the noble lineage who held Tegernsee's advocacy from the 1120s to the 1150s, the counts from the nearby castle of Wolfratshausen. He summarizes the offenses perpetrated by Count Otto I of Wolfratshausen (d. 1127) in especially colorful terms: "Count Otto . . . held the Tegernsee advocacy, which he successfully defended from others in every way. But by himself he was more intolerable than everyone else in every way, because in whatever place he was defending, he alone (pretending to be a guardian) took everything – just like the hawk did to the doves in

---

[1] See Chapter 4.
[2] All of these sources will be discussed at greater length later in this chapter and the next.

the fable."[3] The ancient fable of the hawk (or kite) and the doves was well known in the twelfth century, and an author needed to make only a passing reference to it, as here, because he knew his readers would be familiar with the story.[4] For a modern audience it is worth citing in full:

When the doves had often fled from a certain kite and escaped death by the swiftness of their wings the bird of prey turned to treacherous negotiation, using these wily words with which to trick the peaceful clan: "Why do you prefer to live a life of anxiety rather than to make a treaty and choose me as your king? I would keep you safe from every wrong." The doves, believing what he said, entrusted themselves to the kite, who, on obtaining the sovereignty, began to devour them one by one, making his authority felt with cruel talons. Then one of those who were still left remarked: "We deserve the blows we get for having committed our lives to this pirate."[5]

As we shall see in the next chapters, monks were not quite the peace-loving, helpless doves they sometimes portrayed themselves to be in their dealings with their advocates. Nevertheless, this fable is helpful for understanding how religious communities framed their conflicts with their advocates. For the author of the *Passion of St. Quirinus*, advocates were quite simply cunning, violent predators.

The monks at Tegernsee were not alone in characterizing their advocates in this way. Starting in the second half of the eleventh century, the number of complaints about bad advocates explodes everywhere that advocacy was commonplace. One explanation for this trend is that there were quantitatively more church advocates than ever in the decades after 1050 because of the surge in new religious foundations.[6] But this is only a partial explanation. To understand why so many monks and other religious accused their advocates of perpetrating violence, it is necessary to read past the dramatic rhetoric in the sources and to seek the roots of the problem at the intersection of advocacy, justice, protection and the profits to be had from churches' property rights.

Poison Quills and the Rhetoric of Violence

Complaints about advocates appear in an extraordinarily wide range of sources written between roughly 1050 and 1250. While the majority of this material comes from the German kingdom because church advocacy

---

[3] *Passio*, 276–77. This is a key source for my arguments in this and subsequent chapters. While I have consulted the two oldest extant manuscripts (Vorau, Stiftsbibliothek, Cod. 277 and Munich, Bayerische Staatsbibliothek, Clm 18571), I have found the printed edition to be excellent and therefore cite it throughout.
[4] For the medieval reception of this fable, see Wolverton, *Cosmas*, 95–102; Mann, *Aesop*, 62; Dicke and Grubmüller, *Fabeln*, no. 555.
[5] *Babrius and Phaedrus*, 226–29, no. 31.   [6] See Chapter 5.

was more deeply entrenched in this region, a few communities further west also told stories of bad advocates. Chronicles, annals, saints' lives and other hagiographical works, epistolary collections and charters (royal, papal, episcopal, monastic and noble) all offer vivid accusations of advocatial abuses. Occasionally, some of these texts refer to the scourge of advocacy in general terms; a charter issued by the bishop of Hildesheim in 1181 notes, "We cannot ignore the many injuries inflicted on churches, wherever they are established, on account of the intolerable excesses of advocates."[7] In most cases, however, ecclesiastics directed their verbal attacks at the advocates of their own religious communities – and frequently did not hesitate to name names. There are countless examples of criticisms of this sort, far too many to address in a short chapter. Here, a small sample provides a sense of the rich variety of colorful rhetoric that monks and other religious unleashed against their advocates.[8]

Many advocates apparently enjoyed terrorizing religious communities and their dependents whenever they could. At the monastery of Saint-Hubert in the Ardennes, one monk reported in a story set in the late eleventh century how "the abbot shuddered at the barbarity" of the community's advocate Alberic when he heard what Alberic had been doing to the house's dependents.[9] At nearby Gembloux, a chronicler described how, in 1122, a church "with all of its appurtenances, along with the whole village, was consumed by fire because of its rebellious advocate."[10] Three decades later around 1151, Abbot Wibald of Stavelot wrote to one of his monks about the monastery's situation: "Your advocates, committing sins, are not defenders of the poor but the most cruel destroyers and most inimical ambushers of your liberty."[11] And under the entry for the year 1160, the annals of the house of canons at Reichersberg in Bavaria report that an advocate's son, "after his father's death, violently invaded this advocacy ... and then sought to bring about not a few troubles for this church against the will of the provost and brothers."[12] In many other texts, it is the phrase "the violence of advocates" (*violentia advocatorum*) that succinctly summarizes the host of possible advocatial abuses.[13]

---

[7] *Urkundenbuch des Hochstifts Hildesheim*, 391–93, no. 402.
[8] For other discussions of violent advocates, see Stieldorf, "Klöster"; Lauwers, "Vie"; Dupont, "Violence."
[9] Hanquet, ed., *Chronique*, 103, chap. 41. See below for more on this passage.
[10] *Sigeberti Gemblacensis Chronica*, 378.
[11] Wibald of Stablo, *Briefbuch*, 2:612, no. 289. For another letter from this period complaining about an advocate's misbehavior, see *Tegernseer Briefsammlung*, 180–81, no. 151.
[12] *Annales Reicherspergenses*, 467. For another advocate's *multa mala*, see *Chronicon Ottenburanum*, 620.
[13] See, for example, Haider, ed., *Traditionsurkunden*, 84–86, no. K 18; DD Ko III, 47–49, no. 30; DD F I, 274–76, no. 160.

The Tegernsee monk who in the 1160s wrote the verse account of the life, passion, translation and miracles of St. Quirinus was especially fond of colorful rhetoric. The closing section of his work, a series of poems about the community's advocates, is labeled "On the iniquity of judges and advocates."[14] In the first poem, he laments that Tegernsee's advocates, "who knew to spare their own properties, ... plundered the properties of churches in the name of protecting them."[15] In a later poem, one advocate in particular comes in for especially sharp critique; he is described not only as a plunderer but also a butcher and a wolf.[16] A monk at Echternach near Luxembourg employed the same animal metaphor when he complained about "all types of crimes committed against this house and household of God by the wickedest – not so much advocates as – most rapacious wolves."[17] The Tegernsee monk who wrote the prose *Passion of St. Quirinus* and referenced the fable of the kite and the dove also introduced another of the community's advocates by emphasizing his predatory nature: "This young Otto, although he was looking after the advocacy for only a brief time, as if the cub of the mature lion, took after his father. He learned to seize the wealth of the poor household and to seize the goods of the monastery."[18] Here, we find echoes of a biblical proverb: "As a roaring lion, and a hungry bear, so is a wicked prince over the poor people."[19]

For some authors, advocates' many abuses were best summarized with the term "tyranny." The prolific mid-twelfth-century chronicler Otto, bishop of Freising, limits his use of the concept of tyranny among his contemporaries to only the family of his bishopric's advocates: "None of them – or very few – of either sex ... may be found but those who either rage in open tyranny or who, utterly infatuated with and unworthy of every honor both ecclesiastical and secular, devote themselves to thefts and robberies and lead a miserable life begging."[20] Hugh of Poitiers, in his history of the monastery of Vézelay, frequently uses the word "tyrant" to refer to the counts of Nevers during their long-running dispute with the monastery over the community's advocacy.[21] And at Tegernsee, the *Passion of St. Quirinus* begins its discussion of advocates by explaining, "With the

---

[14] Metellus of Tegernsee, *Quirinalien*, 337.   [15] Ibid., 338, no. 1.   [16] Ibid., 342, no. 4.

[17] *Ex Vita Sancti Willibrordi*, 27. For another example of a wolf metaphor, see Depreux, "Ausprägungen," 376.

[18] *Passio*, 283.   [19] Proverbs 28:15 (*Douay-Rheims Bible* online).

[20] Otto of Freising, *Chronica*, 283–84, VI.20 (partly based on the English translation in Otto of Freising, *The Two Cities*, 382). For a more extensive discussion of this passage, see Lyon, "Tyrants."

[21] *Monumenta Vizeliacensia*, 425, 517 and 529–30 (English translation: Hugh of Poitiers, *Vézelay Chronicle*, 168, 233 and 246). I discuss this chronicle at much greater length in Chapter 10.

memory of many who are still living as witness, we celebrate the perpetual victory of our most unconquerable patron over our advocates' tyranny."[22]

None of this language is unique to advocates. It was commonplace in other parts of Europe at this time for other sorts of offenders.[23] In general, the terms used to label advocatial violence and destruction after 1050 are the same terms that historians have emphasized in their arguments about a Feudal Revolution and anarchic lordship around the year 1000.[24] We are therefore confronted with the same question that stands at the center of debates about how dramatic the political and social changes of the turn of the millennium were: Does the language of violence in our sources reflect realities on the ground, or did ecclesiastical authors mostly employ this language for rhetorical reasons to shape the narratives of local disputes to their advantage?

In answering this vexed question, one advantage that historians of the post-1050 period have over scholars of earlier centuries is that our sources are better; texts are frequently more detailed, and in many cases multiple sources discuss the same event or dispute. As a result, it is sometimes easier to determine whether authors employed the language of violence for dramatic effect or because they were reporting actual incidents of abuse or destruction. Let me take one especially shocking example – though not one involving church advocacy – to highlight what I mean. A written account from 1349 of the attack the preceding year on the Jewish community of Tàrrega in Aragon includes the words *violenter, raptores, dampna gravia, injurias* and *molestias* – all of them words routinely used 250 years earlier for advocatial abuses.[25] In this case, while the author unquestionably chose these words to generate sympathy for the community's plight, archeologists have also confirmed that the attack in Tàrrega happened – and killed an estimated 300 members of the Jewish community there.[26] We therefore cannot dismiss this language of violence as mere rhetoric. This is not to suggest that every time a twelfth-century monk accused an advocate of violence that he was referring to the deaths of 300 people; that level of rural depopulation surely would have left a deeper imprint on the historical record.[27] Rather, this example serves as

[22] *Passio*, 275. For the language of tyranny, see also DD H II, 671–73, no. 521; Wibald of Stablo, *Briefbuch*, 2:578, no. 270.
[23] Bisson, *Crisis*, 278–87; Mazel, "Amitié," 82–91.   [24] See Chapter 4.
[25] Colet et al., "Black Death," 71–72. See also Nirenberg, *Communities*, 237–38. More broadly, Nirenberg's approach to understanding violence guides my own work here, especially his insistence that we focus on quotidian and strategic forms of violence rather than only cataclysmic moments (p. 249).
[26] Colet et al., "Black Death."
[27] For the argument that *violentia* could mean bad behavior without physical violence in the twelfth and thirteenth centuries, see Reichert, *Landesherrschaft*, 125. See also Smail, *Legal Plunder*, 242–44.

a reminder that we must look for corroborating evidence whenever we can, reading past the dramatic rhetoric to consider on a case-by-case basis what our sources might be telling us.

This approach suggests that, in some cases, religious communities did exaggerate the extent of advocatial violence in order to gain an advantage in dispute settlements.[28] In 1157, for example, when Emperor Frederick I and the princes in attendance at court heard the dispute between the abbot of Tegernsee and his advocate, Count Henry II of Wolfratshausen (d. 1157), they issued a judgment, which Frederick's chancery then wrote up in the form of an imperial privilege. Although most of the issues discussed in the privilege are quite technical and concern who had the right to judge specific cases on the monastery's estates, the language at the start of the text hints at the ways in which the abbot must have initially framed the dispute to the court: "In our times, we see that the insolence of its advocates and bad custom have greatly diminished the monastery's grace and respect."[29] Another source from this same period offers a different perspective, however. Duke Henry II of Austria wrote a letter to the abbot of Tegernsee cautioning him against risking their friendship by undermining the count's authority: "My most beloved relative, Count Henry of Wolfratshausen, has complained to me that you are eager to take away his judicial authority, which he ought to have over your church from his advocatial right."[30] Here is evidence that this was not a case of egregious advocatial abuses – as the imperial privilege's rhetoric implies – but a dispute that hinged on different understandings of the advocate's rights.[31]

A more challenging example of source interpretation concerns an incident at the monastery of St. Bertin. In a passage of Simon of Ghent's *Deeds of the Abbots of St. Bertin*, written around 1100 but describing an incident from half a century earlier, we learn that "a most serious dispute arose between the lord abbot Bovo and the advocate of this place, Gerbodo."[32] Rather than immediately explaining the details of the conflict, however, the author first frames the incident in order to leave little doubt who was at fault:

Since it concerns the office of advocate (*officium advocati*) to defend ecclesiastical possessions and distant properties from the dangerous attacks of wicked men, when the tables are turned (as happened on this occasion), the church to be

---

[28] For more on this point, see Chapter 4 and White, "Repenser"; Barthélemy, "Debate"; White, "Debate."
[29] DD F I, 274–6, no. 160.   [30] *Tegernseer Briefsammlung*, 295–96, no. 266.
[31] For a similar example, Höppl, ed., *Traditionen*, 13–14, no. 7.
[32] Simon of Ghent, *Gesta*, 638–39, chap. 13. See also Nieus and Vanderputten, "Diplôme princier" and Depreux, "Ausprägungen," 377.

defended is disturbed by [advocates'] passion for greed, and they [advocates] are
wont to be a burden rather than to serve ecclesiastical utility.

At this point, the text turns to the specific dispute: "In [a certain] village of
St. Bertin, Gerbodo declared certain unjust exactions had to be paid.
Usurping for himself the undeserved right over the unfree inhabitants of
St. Bertin, he disturbed everything more oppressively than an enemy."

Simon of Ghent then included a copy of a charter supposedly issued by
Count Baldwin V of Flanders in 1056 to settle this dispute.[33] This
document also employs the generic language of violence and oppression
to cast the advocate in a bad light. However, it also contains a much more
detailed (and graphic) accusation: Some of Gerbodo's men, acting at his
behest, cruelly seized a St. Bertin monk named Alberic when he came to
the village, and castrated him. The specificity of this story strongly suggests that an actual event lay behind this accusation, that acts of advocatial violence could sometimes be very real. That said, like Emperor
Frederick I's privilege of 1157 for Tegernsee, this document is a record
of a compromise orchestrated by the count, not of a clear victory by the
monastery – which suggests that even physical violence against a monk
could be seen by contemporaries as part of the process of disputing rather
than proof that an advocate had acted completely outside the lines of
acceptable behavior.[34]

As these examples show, the question of how to interpret the language
of advocatial violence and tyranny in our sources is not an either/or
question of whether it is overblown rhetoric or accurate reportage. The
previous chapters have demonstrated that the role of the advocate had
been growing organically for three centuries across broad stretches of
Europe before accusations of abusive advocates exploded after the year
1050. Hundreds, if not thousands, of extant documents from the eighth
century onward reveal efforts to define advocates' responsibilities clearly,
an indication that tensions had been lurking beneath the surface long
before the mid-eleventh century. This is unsurprising: Providing protection and exercising justice have always been capacious, flexible spheres of
action. When we add the vexed issue of how – and how much – advocates
were to be paid for fulfilling their responsibilities, it becomes even easier
to understand why disagreements were so common and why violence,
whether rhetorical or real, had a strategic role to play in these disputes.

---

[33] Nieus and Vanderputten, "Diplôme princier," 54–57, no. 2. This charter is one of
a complicated set of forgeries: ibid., 25–27; Vanderputten, "Monks," 585–91; and for
forgeries more generally, Chapter 8.

[34] Brown, *Violence*, 99–132; Vanderputten, "Fulcard's Pigsty," 112–13. See also Stieldorf,
"Klöster," 76–77, who points out that kings frequently sought compromises in these
situations because they needed the support of both nobles and prelates to rule.

Religious communities leveled accusations of violence when they thought their rights were being violated; advocates employed violence when they thought *their* rights were being violated. With no ruler or central authority willing or able to define unequivocally through enforceable laws where the line between appropriate and inappropriate advocatial behavior was to be drawn, local relationships were fluid – and what constituted corruption was very much open to interpretation.

Bad Defenders, Bad Judges

To be an *advocatus* was to have access to someone else's estates and dependents – most commonly before 1250, those of a church – in order to exercise justice and provide protection in return for payment. This basic description of the position of advocate is essential to keep in mind when examining the roots of religious communities' criticisms of their advocates. While generic accusations of violence, tyranny and abuse were directed against countless different groups in Europe between 1050 and 1250, many of the more specific complaints about advocates can, in one way or another, be tied to their responsibilities around protection and justice. It is these critiques that best reveal the issues that could fracture the relationships between religious communities and their advocates.

Complaints about the failure of advocates to provide effective protection abound. I have already cited sources that describe advocates who, instead of being defenders, turned out to be the greatest threats to churches' estates and dependents. Equally common are critiques of advocates who did nothing when others attacked ecclesiastical properties. Sigebert of Gembloux, writing in the 1070s, laments how little his community's advocates did to protect the monastery's rights: "how great was the advocates' impotency and infidelity!"[35] "Infidelity" (*infidelitas*) is an especially telling complaint, as it points to the failure of Gembloux's advocates to do what they had promised to do for the monastery. Other sources tell similar stories about advocates who took an oath to protect the religious community and its properties but then failed to do so.[36] One abbot of St. Trond, writing in the early 1120s, was especially critical of an advocate for his unwillingness to pursue the many people who were unjustly seizing the monastery's goods. Even though the bishop of Metz had ordered the advocate to bring the plunderers to justice, "he did not want to, so we lost everything."[37]

---

[35] *Gesta Abbatum Gemblacensium*, 533, chap. 20.   [36] Lyon, "Tyrants."

[37] Raoul of St. Trond, *Epistulae*, 121–22, no. 3. For another example of an advocate who was apparently uninterested in pursuing justice against someone damaging a monastery's rights, see *Tegernseer Briefsammlung*, 266–67, no. 237.

Ecclesiastical authors were equally disparaging of advocates for the numerous different ways they tried to take advantage of their responsibilities exercising justice on ecclesiastical estates. A privilege issued in the name of King Philip I of France in 1066 for one monastery explains that the abbot had come to the royal court to complain about a nobleman, "who wanted to possess the [monastery's] lands through advocacy and bad custom"; the abbot's first two specific complaints were that "in all the [monastery's] lands everywhere he wants a meal to be prepared for him, and he forces the peasants and inhabitants ... to [come to him] for his justice."[38] In the diocese of Halberstadt in the early 1130s, the advocate was accused of abusing his judicial rights in a different way; he summoned clergy members "to his court sessions [and] strove to subject them to secular justice."[39] The aforementioned charter issued by Emperor Frederick I Barbarossa to Tegernsee in 1157 likewise references complaints about advocatial justice:

> The abbot's officials (cooks, bakers and others accustomed to minister to the abbot and brothers within the monastery's immunity), if they should quarrel, should not be compelled to render account before the advocate. If they should injure one another with blows and should be summoned to a legitimate court proceeding, the advocate ought to impose correction and punishment without hatred and with the abbot's honor preserved.[40]

The Tegernsee monk who wrote the prose *Passion of St. Quirinus* offers some context when he reports about the community's advocate Count Henry II of Wolfratshausen, "In every court session he was threatening more cruelly the men of the church than his own men."[41] Everyone, it seems, could be subject to harsh advocatial justice – whether they were supposed to be tried and judged in advocatial courts or not.

All of this provides context for a privilege granted to the monastery of Garsten in the 1150s, which insisted "the abbot himself or his authorized messenger ought to sit at the advocate's side" when the advocate held court.[42] A local nobleman had too many opportunities when exercising justice over a church's dependents to push the limits of his authority by judging people and crimes he was not supposed to judge and by being overly harsh in his sentences.[43] In both cases, he would receive additional

---

[38] Prou, ed., *Recueil*, 79–83, no. 27. It only survives in a thirteenth-century copy, and the editor argues it shows signs of having been manipulated. However, for my purposes here, this and other possible forgeries are useful for showing what religious communities expected from their advocates. For more on forgeries, see the next chapter.

[39] *Urkundenbuch des Hochstifts Halberstadt*, 1:136–38, no. 167. This text also insists that the advocate only hold court "*in domo episcopali.*"

[40] DD F I, 274–76, no. 160. See also Stieldorf, "Klöster," 76–77.   [41] *Passio*, 284.

[42] Haider, ed., *Traditionsurkunden*, 84–86, no. K 18.

[43] Spiess, "Bäuerliche Gesellschaft," 398–401.

income from the fines, meaning he had little incentive to fulfill his role properly unless the religious community was willing and able to curb his judicial powers. More broadly, ecclesiastical authors' complaints about advocates failing to be good defenders and judges point to the challenge of controlling nobles' behavior whenever they accessed estates that did not belong to them. This was an opportunity for advocates to benefit materially without doing damage to their own rights and properties. It is hardly surprising, therefore, that churches and advocates did not always see eye to eye about what it meant for an advocate to provide protection and exercise justice.

Exactions – and the People Who Exacted Them

As noted in the previous chapter, judicial fines and meals on court days were not the only ways religious communities paid advocates. There were also annual protection payments of various sorts, which over the course of the twelfth and early thirteenth centuries increasingly became a central feature of the many sources that sought to regulate advocatial rights. These payments generated tensions and conflicts between churches and advocates for numerous reasons, and many ecclesiastical authors reserved some of their harshest critiques of advocacy for this subject. It is here that the sources reveal with unusual clarity how the inhabitants of ecclesiastical estates tended to bear the brunt of the burden when churches and their advocates disagreed about the rightful price of protection.

We have already seen how the author of the *Deeds of the Abbots of St. Bertin* lamented that one of his community's advocates "declared certain unjust exactions had to be paid" at one of the monastery's villages.[44] Comparable complaints about "exactions" (*exactiones*) are commonplace. At the monastery of Saint-Hubert, they are referred to as the "advocates' violent exactions."[45] At Tegernsee, the author of the *Passion of St. Quirinus* is equally blunt; the aforementioned Count Otto I of Wolfratshausen was "more intolerable than everyone else in every way," in part because he "harassed our household continuously with harsh exactions."[46] Another advocate was no better, thanks to "the violence and the exactions, with which he ruthlessly oppressed Quirinus' men."[47]

What were these exactions? The numerous attempts to regulate advocatial payments discussed in the previous chapter leave little doubt that

[44] Simon of Ghent, *Gesta*, 638–39, ch. 13.   [45] Hanquet, ed., *Chronique*, 104, chap. 41.
[46] *Passio*, 277, 280.
[47] Ibid., 284. Frederick I's charter refers to unjust exactions and bad customs: DD F I, 274–76, no. 160.

advocates frequently demanded more from ecclesiastical dependents than religious communities deemed appropriate. The term *exactiones*, even without modifiers like "unjust" or "violent," seems to have had sufficiently negative connotations as excessive payments that advocates apparently preferred other terms to justify their actions. A charter issued by the German king Conrad III in 1145 refers to "exactions [and] tallages (*tallias*), which some people call *precarias* or *petitiones*."[48] *Tallias*, like *exactiones*, is a common word for the dues owed by dependents and is frequently defined as a form of arbitrary taxation. *Precarias* and *petitiones* are much vaguer terms, however, and might best be translated as "requests" and "solicitations." Equally revealing is Emperor Frederick I's charter of 1157 for Tegernsee, where he prohibited "to be demanded or offered . . . the gifts (*oblationes*) of bread and other things, which were made to the advocate on Epiphany."[49] "Requests," "solicitations" and "gifts" all sound like euphemisms, like attempts by advocates and their supporters to downplay any coercion they might have used when demanding protection payments from ecclesiastical dependents.[50]

Regardless of the terms used, there were clearly sharp disagreements between advocates and religious communities over the amount of income that advocates collected from churches' dependents. There was no definitive, universally recognized distinction between an illegitimate protection payment demanded by an "abusive" advocate and a legitimate "tax" paid to an advocate acting in his "official" capacity. Instead, religious communities and their advocates wrestled to define good versus bad customs, and traditional rights versus novel demands, across a complex and contested spectrum of possibilities.

The extent of these exactions is only part of the story, however. The strong reactions against *exactiones* in so many sources were also a product of *how* advocates were collecting these payments. At the monastery of Saint-Hubert, "a certain advocate named Alberic, demanding for himself service labor that was not owed, oppressed the church's household so much that one poor man's cow miscarried while plowing, and in its stead, the poor man had to bear its side of the yoke for the whole day."[51] This story is a reminder of the very local, highly personal level at which advocates operated when they accessed a church's property.

Nobles who held numerous advocacies inevitably had to rely on their followers to collect protection payments for them, and these agents' actions were frequent targets of religious communities' complaints about exactions. Thus, the abbot of Prüm complained in the years around

---

[48] DD Ko III, 252–54, no. 140.   [49] DD F I, 274–76, no. 160.
[50] For more on this point, see Chapter 10.   [51] Hanquet, ed., *Chronique*, 103, chap. 41.

1100 that his advocate "openly places his exactors (*exactores*) on our properties to demand his provisions (*servicium*) throughout the year."[52] At Tegernsee, the *Passion of St. Quirinus* reports of one of the community's advocates that "he installed cruel judges (*iudices*), who exacted the count's rights from the commoners by going door to door through every village and house. One of them [the judges], it is said, first started in our household the exaction of having to give cows for slaughter as an advocatial right (*advocatię iure*)."[53] Later, the author returns to this same judge to complain again that he demanded payments "from every single village and house."[54]

While "exactor" and "judge" are the labels in these sources for the advocatial agents who were directly involved in making demands of churches' dependents, the more common term for these local figures was "subadvocate" (*subadvocatus*). As discussed previously, scholars have typically argued that subadvocates became commonplace over the course of the eleventh century, because prominent nobles could not perform their proper functions as advocates everywhere they held advocacies.[55] Subadvocates were therefore proxy defenders and judges. They were typically chosen by the advocate, not the religious community, and this was a frequent point of tension.[56] In those cases where we know the identities of subadvocates, the evidence indicates that they typically came from the region where their subadvocacy was – and may even have held the nearest castle – meaning they were much more likely than a prominent noble advocate to attempt to gain frequent access to the ecclesiastical properties under their subadvocatial authority.[57] It is unsurprising, therefore, that they, rather than the advocate, were often the target of withering critiques by religious authors.

For example, a forged charter supposedly issued by Emperor Henry V in 1106 for one church mentions "the pillaging, attacks and many injuries inflicted by its subadvocates."[58] The monks of Benediktbeuern in Bavaria wrote an unnamed supporter in the 1180s about the "never-ending trouble" in which the community found itself: "For the subadvocate Wal[ter] has reduced [our] household to such great want of things that they cannot and dare not give us any service or help ... He inflicted exactions, blows, and wounds – to the point of drawing blood – [on some of the monastery's servants] ... He wore down our household and forced

[52] DD H IV, 647–50, no. 476. See also Stieldorf, "Klöster," 71–72.   [53] *Passio*, 280.
[54] Ibid.   [55] See Chapter 5. See also Carré, "Avoueries," 229.
[56] Clauss, *Untervogtei*, 57–95. For subadvocates in Flanders, where their origins differed somewhat, see Vanderputten, "Fulcard's Pigsty," 97.
[57] Clauss, *Untervogtei*, 99–122. Cf. Wickham, "Feudal Economy," 32–33.
[58] DD H V, no. 8.

it into flight."[59] The abbot of another monastery "abolished a certain exaction of an unjust *servitium*, which was demanded unjustly by the subadvocate" of one of the church's villages.[60] Thus, while from an advocate's perspective a subadvocate might plausibly be described as a local proxy and tax farmer, from a church's perspective it was just as likely that a subadvocate would be perceived as nothing more than a petty shakedown artist.

Seeing many subadvocates in this light rather than as advocates' formal representatives helps to explain why so many religious communities insisted that their advocates not appoint subadvocates. When the margrave of Styria sought to regulate the advocate's rights at the monastery of Garsten in the mid-twelfth century, he insisted that an advocate "should never consider those helpers or representatives called subadvocates."[61] The Council of Reims (1148) similarly decreed that subadvocates be removed from their positions.[62] Emperor Henry V's privilege of 1114 for Grossmünster in Zurich offers an especially striking solution to the problem of subadvocates: "We command firmly and decree by imperial authority that [the community] is to have only one advocate; if by chance that advocate places any other under himself, he should be deprived of the advocacy . . ., and that subadvocate should receive the ban from the king or emperor."[63] In this way, Henry V sought to limit the abuses that came from multiple (sub)advocates claiming access to ecclesiastical properties and their own share of a church's income.[64]

Religious communities' complaints about exactions and the local actors who came onto their properties to collect them call attention to a key aspect of the history of advocacy. The relationship between a church and its advocate did not only involve bishops, abbots, monks, nuns and canons on the one side and dukes, margraves, counts and other high-ranking nobles on the other. Churches' rural dependents and nobles' armed followers were frequently the ones on the front lines of experiencing and exercising advocatial authority. This was especially the case if the estates lay far from both the religious house and the advocate's main

---

[59] *Tegernseer Briefsammlung*, 309–10, no. 279. This Walter appears twice as *subadvocatus* in "Benediktbeurer Traditionsbuch," 41–43, nos. 97–98. See also Clauss, *Untervogtei*, 118–19.

[60] Lacomblet, ed., *Urkundenbuch*, 4:773–74, no. 623. See also Clauss, *Untervogtei*, 228–30. For another pairing of subadvocates and unjust exactions, see DD F I, 2:195–97, no. 355.

[61] Haider, ed., *Traditionsurkunden*, 84–86, no. K 18.   [62] Clauss, *Untervogtei*, 124–30.

[63] DD H V, no. 124. I thank Thomas Zotz for calling this charter to my attention; see also Zotz, "Zürich," 105–07. For other attempts to limit subadvocates, see DD Lo III, 134–36, no. 86; BUB, 1:47–48, no. 33 and 1:85–90, no. 65.

[64] Clauss, *Untervogtei*, 261–62.

castles, limiting the opportunities that the religious community and its advocates had to intervene directly in the relationship between subadvocates and village communities. Hearing the voices of rural dependents in such situations is difficult because of the nature of the sources.[65] Nevertheless, we must take seriously comments such as this one from the monastery of Garsten: "[The abbot and monks] did not have the strength to endure the complaints and sobs of the poor, who were very frequently lamenting both the damage to their possessions and the injuries to their bodies."[66] As we will see in subsequent chapters, similar critiques of (sub)advocates' relationships with local populations recur across the centuries.

Blurring Property Lines

According to many sources, when advocates and their men accessed ecclesiastical estates and demanded payments in return for justice and protection, this was often the prelude to those advocates treating church property as if it were their own. Such a dramatic form of abuse of the advocate's position had wide-ranging effects. When advocates blurred the lines between what was theirs and what was a church's, they altered local power dynamics and upset their relationships with religious communities in numerous ways.

Advocates who simply took whatever they wanted to take from churches were frequently described as being no better than thieves. Thus, as noted above, the Tegernsee monk who wrote the prose *Passion of St. Quirinus* describes one of his community's advocates as learning, while still young, "how to plunder our impoverished household and destroy the monastery's goods."[67] In a charter from 1133, the bishop of Halberstadt complained "how Werner, our advocate, seduced by the counsel of certain perverse men, ... committed rash violence against the clerics of our city. Namely, he violently seized the property of certain brothers."[68] One of the most problematic advocatial claims to church property appears in a charter issued by Emperor Frederick I to the bishop of Hildesheim at some point around 1160.[69] It begins with the kind of rhetoric that was commonplace on this subject: "We have heard that the

---

[65] For a good discussion of advocacy from the village-level perspective, see Spiess, "Bäuerliche Gesellschaft." The twelfth-century German kingdom lacks the rich sources for local complaints that are central to the arguments in Bisson, *Tormented*.

[66] Haider, ed., *Traditionsurkunden*, 84–86, no. K 18.   [67] *Passio*, 283.

[68] *Urkundenbuch des Hochstifts Halberstadt*, 1:136–38, no. 167. For this Werner, see also ibid., 130–32, no. 159; 138–40, nos. 168–69; and 142–43, no. 171.

[69] DD F I, 2:143–44, no. 320.

church of Hildesheim is greatly disturbed by the violent importunity of its advocates." It then turns to the specific issue, namely that the advocates "claim for themselves the personal goods of dying priests." Frederick decried this practice and sought to ban it, but as we will see, churches would continue to complain about this particular problem for the next half-millennium.[70]

Many accusations of advocates seizing property point to longer-term strategies on their part to benefit from their positions. The house of Augustinian canons at Reichersberg struggled during the 1150s and early 1160s to deal with the problem of its advocates naming subadvocates without the community's permission – and then granting them the advocacy as if it were a benefice.[71] This led Emperor Frederick I in 1162 to ban the practice on the community's properties.[72] Later that same year, when Duke Henry the Lion of Bavaria and Saxony acquired the advocacy for one of Reichersberg's properties, he accepted this and agreed not to grant the advocacy to any subadvocates as a benefice.[73] The flurry of sources around this subject clearly show it was a significant concern. If an advocate treated an advocacy as a benefice, he could grant it to one of his own supporters and shift the properties attached to that advocacy into his own property regime.[74]

The blurring of the line between the property rights pertaining to an advocacy and a nobleman's other property rights frequently led to churches becoming embroiled in their advocates' military conflicts. Duke Henry the Lion of Saxony and Bavaria had to promise the bishop of Freising that no castle would be built on the lands attached to an advocacy without the bishop's consent.[75] That this was a widespread problem is suggested by Emperor Frederick II's *Statute in Favor of the Princes* of 1232; the first clause states that "Neither we nor anyone else, by reason of an advocacy or under any other pretext, may construct a new castle or town on churches' estates."[76]

Ecclesiastical estates could also become a target for advocates' enemies during military conflicts. In 1150, King Conrad III wrote to the bishop of Liège,

It has been made known to us that on account of [your] hatred for Count Henry of Rupe [Laroche], who is advocate of the church of Stavelot, both you and your

---

[70] See Chapter 15 for a seventeenth-century example.
[71] *Annales Reicherspergenses*, 467–68.   [72] DD F I, 2:195–97, no. 355.
[73] *Urkunden Heinrichs des Löwen*, 81–83, no. 57. For a detailed discussion of subadvocacy at Reichersberg, see Clauss, *Untervogtei*, 63–74.
[74] For more on this point, see the next section.
[75] *Urkunden Heinrichs des Löwen*, 153–54, no. 102.
[76] Const., 2:212, no. 171. See also Zehetmayer, "Vogtei," 228–33.

men have set fires and committed acts of robbery on the properties of the same church, although those same goods are to a great extent free from the advocate's *servitium.*[77]

At the monastery of Niederaltaich in Bavaria, a war in the early thirteenth century between the community's advocate and another noble lineage led to the advocate's rivals seizing some of the monastery's cattle and despoiling some of its estates.[78] This general problem also caught Frederick II's attention; in his 1220 *Privilege in Favor of the Ecclesiastical Princes,* he decreed "that no one may inflict damage on the properties of any church because of the advocate of those properties."[79]

While advocates' military conflicts are some of the clearest examples of how churches were impacted by their property being viewed as their advocate's property, the blurring of property lines is evident in other contexts as well. One persistent problem for many church communities was that advocates' relatives sought to benefit from their properties. The *Passion of St. Quirinus* complains that

the advocate Otto ... went to the monastery and earnestly requested that [the community] keep his wife Lauretta there. Because the request of the powerful man was a command, we could not refuse ... [She] remained there, with the brothers serving her entirely at their own expense, until Easter, burdening the place very much with the incessant mob of people coming and going.[80]

Herman of Tournai tells a different kind of story about an advocate and his wife, though here too the fundamental issue is that advocacies were sometimes treated as family property: "[The advocate] Fastrad ... held the lands of this church as a benefice from the bishop's hand. He saw his wife, Ida, ... distributing these lands to his peasants to live on and farm, and he told her that she would be doing an evil thing if she handed out [those] lands to other people."[81]

Given all of this, it is unsurprising that some advocates interfered in churches' internal affairs in order to ensure that the religious communities would not challenge their access to ecclesiastical properties and rights. The annals of Einsiedeln, for example, report that during the twelfth century the monastery's advocates routinely ignored the community's right to elect its own abbot. At one point in the 1170s, the advocate attempted to install as abbot his own brother, a monk at nearby St. Gall,

---

[77] Wibald of Stablo, *Briefbuch,* 2:578–79, no. 271. See also ibid., 1:136–38, no. 78.
[78] Vienna, Österreichische Nationalbibliothek, Cod. 413, fols. 184 and 185v (Printed edition: Braunmüller, "Drangsale"). For this text, see also Dendorfer, "Abtei," 125–26. For a similar story, see *Chronicon Laureshamense,* 436.
[79] Const., 2:89, no. 73.   [80] *Passio,* 280–81.
[81] Herman of Tournai, *Restoration,* 23 (Latin: Herman of Tournai, *Liber,* 45, chap. 9).

in order to have an ally in the position.[82] If advocates could not manipulate elections, they could try to sideline inimical ecclesiastics in other ways. The chronicle written at the monastery of Lorsch describes what happened when the community's abbot, Anselm (d. 1102), "began to support and defend his church's household manfully against its oppressors, especially against the tyranny of the advocate Berthold."[83] The advocate "was able to approach [him in church], when he was unaware and unprepared, . . . and to seize the surprised abbot deceitfully." He then imprisoned him.[84] For many nobles, advocacies were too valuable to allow abbots or other religious to interfere with their goal of transforming their advocatial rights into an integral feature of their own power and authority.

Multigenerational Disputes

The most dramatic forms of advocatial violence were disruptive moments in the life of religious communities. As we will see in the next two chapters, such moments could elicit strong responses from ecclesiastics, and many church advocacies underwent significant changes during the twelfth and thirteenth centuries as communities attempted ever more extreme interventions to limit their advocates' power and influence. However, to focus on advocates' interference in abbatial elections or their imprisonment of abbots is to let extraordinary acts overshadow quotidian ones. In the majority of cases when sources refer to the violence of advocates, they are not referring to brief, intense moments of conflict but to advocatial abuses that extended over years if not decades.

The convent of Remiremont's long-running dispute with its advocates, the dukes of Lotharingia, over the convent's properties and rights is a telling example. In 1123, Pope Calixtus II wrote to the abbess, "It has reached our ears that Duke Thierry [d. 1115/16] and his subadvocates violently seized certain possessions and dues, which are for the use of you and your sisters."[85] The dispute between the convent and the dukes then came before the court of King Conrad III two decades later in the early 1140s; according to the king, "Duke Mathieu [d. 1176] disturbed the

---

[82] *Annalen des Klosters Einsiedeln*, 288–96 (esp. p. 292). The *Passion of St. Quirinus* also complains about the community's advocate trying to interfere in an abbatial election: *Passio*, 284. For other examples see Lyon, "Advocata," 160–66; Arnold, *Count*, 73–75; Wibald of Stablo, *Briefbuch*, 1:192–93, no. 106 and 1:202–10, no. 113.

[83] *Chronicon Laureshamense*, 429.

[84] As noted in the previous chapter, the abbot of Pegau was imprisoned by his advocate a century later.

[85] Bridot, ed., *Chartes*, 109–11, no. 48. The dispute would continue under Thierry's son, Duke Simon I of Lotharingia (1115–39): ibid., 121–24, no. 56.

peace with diverse, unjust exactions and many violent acts against the church."[86] A short time later, between 1147 and 1151, the archbishop of Trier oversaw a peace agreement between Abbess Judith and Duke Mathieu; the numerous terms of the agreement included, "The advocates should not come into possession of any oats, unless they have faithfully renounced their right of pannage and the church receives its full amount of oats for brewing beer. In addition, the cows, which the advocates have recently grown accustomed to receive unjustly in their possession on Christmas, they should not receive at all henceforth."[87] Even this agreement did not end the dispute, however and Pope Hadrian IV threatened the duke with excommunication in 1157 because of the ongoing conflict.[88] There is little evidence to suggest that Remiremont was able to strike the right balance with its advocates. The occasional successful dispute settlement cannot lead us to overlook the sea of evidence for persistent difficulties between religious communities and advocates.

There is no better evidence for this than the works of Abbot Herman of Niederaltaich (1242–73), whom we met in the previous chapter. He is best known to scholars of medieval advocacy for his concise description of the role of the advocate:

[W]hen any estate is assigned to a church, the advocate ought to take it into his protection and to defend it from every person to the extent that justice supports him and the church. Moreover, because it is not of the clerical dignity to administer justice or punishment of blood, the advocate will judge according to customary justice thefts, rapes, homicides, immoderate disputes, arsons and similar cases among the men of the church.[89]

This passage appears in a text known today as *On the Advocates of Niederaltaich* (*De advocatis Altahensibus*). The title is an apt one, but Herman did not give this or any other title to his work; he copied it – without any context or explanation for why it belonged there – onto a blank page in the most polished of the manuscripts he compiled to help him administer his monastery's properties and rights.[90] Herman suggests in the opening sentence that the work emerged from his efforts to gather all the documents he needed for this project: "Having examined the church's privileges from this place and that, and the ancient donations of estates, we were not able to ascertain fully who first constituted which

---

[86] DD Ko III, 132–34, no. 75 (Bridot, ed., *Chartes*, 131–34, no. 60).
[87] Bridot, ed., *Chartes*, 157–59, no. 72.
[88] Ibid., 172–73, no. 77. See also 189–93, nos. 89–90 and 194–96, no. 92.
[89] *De Advocatis*, 373.
[90] Munich, Bayerisches Hauptstaatsarchiv, KL Niederaltaich Lit. 39, fol. 51v. I will discuss the text's placement in the manuscript below.

advocates of this church."[91] He then includes the description of advocacy cited above before providing a brief history of the community's advocates. But the tone of this history differs sharply from the dispassionate opening sentences. Much of *On the Advocates of Niederaltaich* reads like an encyclopedia of advocatial abuses.[92]

Tensions between Niederaltaich and its advocates build slowly in Herman's text. After stating plainly, "We have found that these were the church's advocates," the abbot begins in the deep past, for which he apparently had few sources.[93] Initially, all he gives are names and a few clues to situate them chronologically: for example, "At the time of Duke Arnold [Arnulf] and Abbot Agilolf, Raffold was advocate of the church of Niederaltaich."[94] This entry can be linked to the years around 900, and most of the other names in Herman's opening list of advocates are also from the tenth and early eleventh centuries.[95] Not until he introduces Count Aschwin of Bogen, who was advocate of the monastery in the mid-eleventh century, does his history become more detailed. Aschwin's lineage would hold the advocacy until 1242, and Herman seems to have known this family's genealogy well. He reports that Aschwin's son Adalbert followed him as advocate. Adalbert and his wife had three sons, the third of whom was "Berthold, a peaceful and wealthy man, advocate of the church of Niederaltaich at the time of Abbots Conrad and Boleslaus."[96] With this comment, Herman brings his narrative up to the middle of the twelfth century, approximately 100 years before he was writing.

At this point, the work changes noticeably. Herman shifts to the next generation of the counts of Bogen by explaining, "This man [Berthold] bore from Liutgard Count Albert [III of Bogen]. This Albert was advocate of the church at the time of Abbots Udalrich and Dietmar. He was a savage and warlike man, and on account of this, he became a destroyer of churches and the whole province."[97] The abbot follows this comment with a lengthy and colorful list of complaints about Albert and his descendants. Herman mentions Albert's "harmful persecution" of the monastery; he explains how the community's estates sustained "very many injuries" and how the count "committed very many crimes"; and he notes

[91] *De Advocatis*, 373.
[92] For a lengthy discussion of this text, see Dendorfer, "Abtei," 93–106.
[93] *De Advocatis*, 373. Herman almost certainly based much of this section on a now-lost *Traditionsbuch* for Niederaltaich: Deutinger, "Traditionsbuch." A marginal notation in the manuscript also suggests that Herman knew the name of one early advocate from two charters issued by King Louis the Child in 905: DD LdK, 156–60, nos. 39–40. See Dendorfer, "Abtei," 109.
[94] *De Advocatis*, 373.   [95] Deutinger, "Traditionsbuch."   [96] *De Advocatis*, 373.
[97] Ibid., 373–74.

that Albert's sons acted with "such great fury and malice ... that they made the entire territory of their county almost uninhabitable."[98]

What follows is a much more specific set of complaints, all of which we have already seen in this chapter in sources from other religious communities. The monastery had been impoverished due to wars between the counts of Bogen and other nobles, the illicit construction of castles and "diverse exactions."[99] The abbot explicitly singles out Count Albert III of Bogen when noting, "Under the harmful persecution of this count, our church first began to have subadvocates and to endure the most wicked exactions."[100] According to Herman, Albert III also "offered the right of advocacy in some places to other people in pledge, to others he conceded possession by feudal right." He then lists properties and rights that the advocates had given in fief to their followers.[101]

Significantly, Herman included this work about the advocates in the section of the manuscript set aside to list Niederaltaich's rights in *Mundrichinge* (Mintraching), one of the places mentioned in this passage as having been enfeoffed to a Bernhard of Lerchenfeld.[102] The codicological setting of the text thus suggests that the abbot's sharp critique of the monastery's advocates was related to the loss of specific ecclesiastical properties and incomes. Herman was keeping track of those estates that had slipped from his monastery's control into the hands of his community's advocates and their followers in previous decades. It is hardly surprising, therefore, that Herman saw the extinction of the lineage of the counts of Bogen in 1242 and the passing of the advocacy to the Wittelsbach dukes of Bavaria as an opportunity for a fresh start.[103] After decades of advocatial abuses, it was time to account for all the monastery's lost properties and to reassert the community's rights.

Conclusion

"Tyranny," "barbarity," "cruelty": it can be difficult to dig beneath the surface of the most florid rhetoric of advocatial violence and to grasp the

---

[98] Ibid., 374.   [99] Ibid.
[100] Ibid. Herman uses the phrase "*steurarum exactiones iniquissimas*," which is unusual. For more on the relationship between advocatial exactions and the history of taxes (German: *Steuer*), see Chapter 6.
[101] Ibid. Herman also complains that the advocates "alienated our church's ministerials through external marriages." On this issue, see Stieldorf, "Klöster," 82, and more generally Freed, *Noble Bondsmen*.
[102] Munich, Bayerisches Hauptstaatsarchiv, KL Niederaltaich Lit. 39, fol. 49r. For the advocacy for Mintraching, see also Klose, ed., *Urbare*, 1:433–56. For why the text is in this manuscript, see also Stieldorf, "Klöster," 56–61.
[103] See Chapter 6.

complex forces that shaped the relationships between religious communities and their advocates. When we do so, however, it quickly becomes clear that specific issues lay behind the generic descriptions of advocates' misbehavior. At the core of many disputes and conflicts were disagreements, at a very basic level, about the scope of the position of advocate. Was it an accountable office with clearly defined limits, or were providing protection and exercising justice too dynamic and open-ended to be contained by a strict set of rules? The boundaries between appropriate and inappropriate actions and between just and unjust payments were simply too fluid for religious communities and their advocates to find and maintain consensus on these issues. As a result, both accusations of violence and actual violent acts served as subtle (or, at times, not-so-subtle) attempts for one side or the other to adjust the parameters of the conversation, to alter the nature of the advocatial position to its advantage. As we will see, these attempts were not confined to the period from roughly 1050 to 1250; similar efforts would continue to shape the violent history of advocacy into the eighteenth century.

8   Weapons of the Not-So-Weak

When the famed mystic Hildegard (d. 1179) moved her community of Benedictine nuns from Disibodenberg to the Rupertsberg in Bingen on the River Rhine around the year 1150, she had to attend to various practical matters. According to Hildegard's *Life*, completed by a monk in the 1180s, the abbess first had to acquire all the property on which the new convent would be located, so that no other landowner could interfere with the community in the future.[1] It was also essential, since this was a religious house operating in the German kingdom in the mid-twelfth century, that something be done at the outset about the community's advocacy. As the *Life* explains, Hildegard wanted the community to be free from secular authority and subject only to the protection of the church of Mainz, with the archbishop of Mainz her only defender: "For, if she accepted a lay advocate for herself, she might seem to be introducing a wolf in sheep's clothing. In just that way, a great many churches throughout the world are disturbed and laid waste as by a common disease."[2]

The metaphors of advocate as wolf and advocacy as disease leave little doubt about this author's opinion of church advocates. He frames Hildegard's decision as a product of advocacy's increasingly negative reputation among the religious elites of the later twelfth century. When Emperor Frederick I issued a privilege for the convent in 1163, he also acknowledged some of the dangers of advocacy, decreeing, "lest anyone usurp for himself its advocacy, we receive that place with the nuns and its possessions under our imperial protection, so that it may always be free and secure from all infestations and injuries by the imperial right hand and with the help of the archbishop of Mainz."[3] According to the imperial chancery, the emperor, not the archbishop, was the true defender of the

---

[1] *Vita Sanctae Hildegardis*, 12, I.7. For this text, see *Life of Hildegard*, 118–29.
[2] *Vita Sanctae Hildegardis*, 12–13, I.7: "*laicum aduocatum.*" See also *Life of Hildegard*, 147. For another example from this period of a monastic community trying to avoid lay advocates altogether, see Petersen, "Rechtsstellung," 94–96.
[3] DD F I, 2:274–75, no. 398.

convent's properties and rights – and the one to protect it from the abuses of bad advocates.

Both Hildegard's *Life* and Frederick's privilege call attention to a key theme in the sources for church advocacy between roughly 1050 and 1250, namely efforts to rein in – and, increasingly, to prohibit completely – noble advocates.[4] The years around 1000 had seen rulers attempt to make advocates accountable by granting some religious communities the right to replace advocates who did not prove themselves "useful" (*utilis*).[5] The abundant sources from the eleventh through thirteenth centuries detailing how often advocates could access church properties and how much they could receive as payment for exercising justice and providing protection are further evidence for these regulatory impulses. Nevertheless, as the previous chapter has shown, these efforts frequently proved insufficient. The fact that one of the most detailed surviving accounts of advocatial abuses – Abbot Herman's *On the Advocates of Niederaltaich* – was produced a quarter of a millennium after conflicts between churches and their advocates first surface in extant sources points to the failure of written directives to generate long-term peace and stability.[6] Disputes over advocatial rights often spanned years, decades or even generations despite resolution attempts, which is why Hildegard of Bingen's *Life* could refer so casually to the "common disease" of advocacy – and why the abbess would logically seek to avoid lay advocates altogether.

The seemingly endless litany of complaints about advocates oppressing churches and their dependents might lead one to think that religious communities had limited tools at their disposal to challenge corrupt advocates. Ecclesiastical sources frequently claim that monks, nuns and canons were the weak trying to fend off the strong, the helpless sheep stalked by predatory wolves, the peaceful doves futilely trying to protect themselves from the hawk's talons. However, conflicts over advocacy were fundamentally disputes between different members of the social, political and economic elite – some of them lay nobles, some of them members of the church hierarchy (who were frequently related by blood to those same lay nobles). As a result, if we look past the rhetoric of religious communities' powerlessness, we frequently find churches resisting their advocates, even in places where advocacy had been well entrenched since the ninth and tenth centuries.

These forms of resistance were not the weapons of the weak (foot-dragging, dissimulation, feigned ignorance, slander, sabotage, etc.);

---

[4] Wagner, "Weistum," 84, refers to the *Antivogtprogramme* of reformed monasteries, but the efforts to limit advocatial authority were more ad hoc than programmatic.
[5] See Chapter 4.   [6] See Chapter 7.

religious communities and their leaders belonged to the uppermost echelons of society, not the peasantry.[7] They therefore employed a very different set of strategies as they sought to curtail the power of advocates: they
forged documents, brought their complaints directly to rulers and popes
and purchased their advocacies back from nobles. All of these had the
goal of limiting their advocates' influence – but all of them inevitably left
lingering questions about who would provide effective justice and protection at the local level if not a noble advocate.

Forging Documents

In 1098, the monks of Schaffhausen processed in prayer from their
monastery to their advocate's castle, led by crosses and relics, to protest
their advocate's many misdeeds. They were met with violence: "[A]ll
were ill treated by the [advocate's] knights, some of them killed, some
wounded, and they were forced to return or to be carried home, while the
crosses and relics were smashed to pieces."[8] As shocking as this outcome
is, the monks' initial decision to organize a procession is in many ways just
as surprising. The surviving sources offer few comparable examples of
religious communities directly confronting their advocates in this fashion.
There are occasional references to communal prayers, or the ringing of
bells to publicize advocatial abuses, but even these tactics seem to have
been employed infrequently.[9] In most cases, monastic communities preferred to protest their advocates' actions in other ways. One of their
preferred strategies was to take advantage of their technical expertise in
producing documents.[10]

Ecclesiastical communities, not nobles and their entourages, wrote the
majority of sources that survive for advocates and advocacy before 1250.
Even many of the imperial and papal privileges issued for religious houses
show signs that the scribes who wrote them relied heavily on language
given to them by members of the communities seeking the privileges.[11] As

---

[7] For this list, see Scott, *Weapons*, 29, 36–37. See Chapter 15 for the evidence for peasants'
perspectives.

[8] Bernold of St. Blasien, *Chronicle*, 333 (Latin: Bernold of St. Blasien, *Bernoldi Chronicon*,
533–34).

[9] For other examples, see Stieldorf, "Klöster," 64–67. There are also several confronta-
tions between the monastic community of Vézelay and its advocates in Hugh of Poitiers,
Vézelay Chronicle (see Chapter 10 below).

[10] The importance of the written word for churches' conflicts with their advocates is also
stressed in Stieldorf, "Klöster."

[11] See previous chapters and below for various examples. An especially interesting example
from the monastery of Prüm's *Liber Aureus* (DD H IV, 647–50, no. 476) includes the
abbot's speech at the imperial court, which is highly unusual for an authentic German
imperial charter. See also Stieldorf, "Klöster," 71–72.

a result, it is unsurprising that monks and other religious saw the written word as one of the most powerful weapons they could wield against their advocates. When the authentic privileges they possessed failed to stop advocatial abuses – as was often the case – many communities did not hesitate to turn to forgery as a next step in their efforts to limit their advocates' rights.

Historians have described the period from roughly 1050 to 1250 as a golden age for forgery.[12] While religious communities across Europe forged documents for any number of reasons, in those regions where advocacy was commonplace, the motivation behind forgeries was frequently the desire to alter a community's relationship with its advocates.[13] In some cases, religious houses forged entirely new documents, seeking to mimic the look of privileges issued by the imperial or papal chancery, and even removed seals from authentic documents and attached them to their forgeries to make them look as legitimate as possible. But this was only one form of forgery and document manipulation in this period.[14] Some forgers erased a small part of an authentic charter, changing just a few words to alter the terms of an agreement.[15] In other cases, actual forgeries do not survive; instead, monastic cartularies contain copies of documents that have clearly been manipulated or invented to rewrite the community's earlier history. Copies of supposedly authentic documents preserved in monastic chronicles similarly try to manipulate the historical record to the advantage of the religious community.[16] Regardless of what form they took, most forgeries concerning advocacy sought to define advocatial rights in ways comparable to authentic charters: by insisting that a community had the right to elect its own advocates, by defining how many times an advocate could hold court in a year and by listing how much the advocate was to receive as payment for providing justice and protection.[17]

---

[12] Constable, "Forgery," 12. For the broader context of many of the forgeries I will be discussing here, see especially *Fälschungen im Mittelalter*.

[13] Constable, "Forgery," 8. Numerous scholars have discussed forgeries in the context of advocacy; see, for example, Waas, *Vogtei*, 1:7–8 and 2:32–36; Acht, "Vogteifälschungen"; Nieus and Vanderputten, "Diplôme princier"; West, "Monks"; Koller, "Entvogtung"; Schreiner, "Hirsau."

[14] For the different forms forgery could take, see Constable, "Forgery"; Roach, *Forgery*, 13–20.

[15] See Chapter 9 for an example from the convent of Essen. For an example of a forger erasing almost the entire original text, see DD LdD 252–54, no. 177.

[16] The chronicle from the monastery of Petershausen includes a papal privilege supposedly from the late tenth century that is likely at least a partial forgery: Feger, ed., *Chronik*, 62–65, I.27. See also Zimmermann, ed., *Papsturkunden*, 639–40, no. 327.

[17] See, for example, DD H IV, 519–20, no. 393; 588–90, no. 439; and 622–23, no. 461; Fossier, ed., *Chartes*, 142–44, no. 10; Bridot, ed., *Chartes*, 37–41, no. 3; *Mainzer Urkundenbuch*, 1:154–56, no. 251.

Many of the most notorious forgers worked in ecclesiastical communities that traced their histories back to the Carolingian or Ottonian periods. When these communities came into conflict with their advocates in the late eleventh and twelfth centuries, they often had to assert their rights by relying on imperial privileges from the ninth or tenth centuries. However, in most cases, these did not delineate the role of the advocate as clearly as newer privileges did, especially those granted to reform-era communities.[18] As a result, some monasteries turned to forgeries to try to rewrite the outdated terms of their relationships with their advocates. These documents, many of which claim to be Carolingian and Ottonian privileges, often betray their post-1050 production by using language from this later period.[19] One supposedly granted to a convent by Emperor Henry II in 1015 uses an especially clever turn of phrase to try to make the forgery seem plausible: "Foreseeing the future tyranny of its advocates, lest they should burden the convent's household, we decree that no second advocate [i.e., subadvocate] may be placed above them."[20] Both the language of advocatial "tyranny" and the attempt to regulate subadvocates point less in the direction of Henry II's supposed prescience and more toward this document's twelfth-century origins.[21]

Clusters of forgeries demonstrate that monasteries were deeply invested in manipulating documents to improve their position vis-à-vis their advocates. The so-called "Reichenau forger," a monk working in the early-to-mid twelfth century, forged charters not only for his own community but also for numerous other monasteries in the southwest of the German kingdom.[22] One that he forged for Reichenau in the name of Emperor Charlemagne, which concerns the advocate's rights in a town, explains that the advocate was to bring with him "not more than thirty horses" when he came to hold court and regulates the goods and services owed to the advocate as well.[23] The same monk also forged two privileges issued in Charlemagne's name for another monastery, including one that focuses explicitly on regulating the role of the advocate at the monastery.[24] As with the forged charter of Emperor Henry II, there is little doubt from the language employed in this privilege that it was

---

[18] See previous chapters for changes in the language of imperial privileges from the eighth to the eleventh centuries.

[19] See, for example, DD Arn, 290–91, no. 188; DD O I, 613–15, no. 453; and DD O II, 378–79, no. 321.

[20] DD H II, 671–73, no. 521.

[21] See Chapter 7 for comparable language in twelfth-century sources.

[22] Jänichen, "Herkunft."

[23] DD Karol. I, 426–28, no. 285. See also Stieldorf, "Klöster," 74–75; Hägermann, "Urkundenfälschungen."

[24] DD Karol. I, 296–300, nos. 222–23.

written after 1050; the forger has Charlemagne announce that he had heard and knew to be true that "many of those men who are constituted advocates of churches misuse their proper power so greatly that they, who ought to be moderate defenders, have shamelessly become rapacious and harmful exactors."[25]

Alongside Reichenau, another leading center for forgery was the monastery of St. Maximin in Trier.[26] In the late eleventh century, the community forged a charter of Emperor Otto I, in which he supposedly granted St. Maximin's abbots the right to choose their own advocates.[27] This was the start of a lengthy forgery campaign at the community. A monk named Benzo, working in the mid-1110s, produced a whole collection of forged documents, including charters in the names of several Ottonian and Salian emperors.[28] One of his charters, supposedly a privilege of Emperor Henry II, decrees that the community's advocates were not to appoint subadvocates.[29] Another, this one in the name of Henry IV, focuses on regulating the lawcourts held by the advocates.[30] The rhetoric of these forgeries is not as dramatic as in the Reichenau ones, but they too highlight the ways in which religious communities used the written word to their own advantage in disputes over advocatial rights.[31]

How effective were these forgeries at altering the relationships between ecclesiastical communities and their advocates? In many cases, the sources do not permit a definitive answer. The persistent problems that many religious houses had with their advocates suggest that presenting an advocate with a forged imperial privilege was not in and of itself sufficient to stop advocatial abuses. Nobles knew that forgery was one of the weapons in the arsenal of religious houses and did not hesitate to accuse communities of manipulating privileges.[32] Nevertheless, there is evidence for some religious houses presenting forgeries at the imperial court and then successfully acquiring a new, authentic privilege from the ruler confirming what was in the forgery. All the monk Benzo's forgeries, for

---

[25] DD Karol. I, 299, no. 223. This same phrase appears almost verbatim in another of the Reichenau forger's charters: DD LdD, 252–54, no. 177.

[26] See especially Kölzer, *Studien*. Other discussions of these forgeries include Stieldorf, "Klöster," 73–74; Kölzer, "Fälschungen"; Mayer, *Fürsten*, 134–68.

[27] DD O I, 532–33, no. 391; Kölzer, *Studien*, 102–04.   [28] Kölzer, *Studien*, 159–60.

[29] DD H II, 641–44, no. 502. The text uses the unusual term *postadvocatus*.

[30] DD H IV, 206–208, no. 159.

[31] While these forgeries are not as critical of advocates as some other forgeries, there are hints of problems, especially with subadvocates: Kölzer, *Studien*, 299–303. Other sources from the monastery are more critical. See, for example, the now lost *liber aureus* from St. Maximin: Gudenus, ed., *Codex*, 3:1015 and Sauer, *Fundatio*, 287–92. Also important as a source for St. Maximin's advocates is its necrology; see Roberg, *Gefälschte Memoria*, 49–56.

[32] See, for example, *Passio*, 285. See also West, "Monks," 380.

example, culminated in St. Maximin receiving from Emperor Henry V in 1116 a new, authentic privilege, which regulated the rights of the community's advocates.[33]

In some cases, forgeries could have even more dramatic results. In 1234, Duke Otto I of Merania, who held the advocacies for the monasteries of Benediktbeuern and Tegernsee in Bavaria, died. His only son and heir was a minor at the time, and members of both religious communities, seeing this as an opportunity to end the hereditary control that Otto I's lineage had exerted over the advocacies for almost a century, traveled to the court of Emperor Frederick II's son, King Henry (VII). Benediktbeuern had received a privilege from Emperor Frederick I in 1155 that stated explicitly that "No one may be advocate [of the monastery] by hereditary right, but the abbot, receiving counsel from the brothers, may freely elect for himself a just and suitable defender."[34] Tegernsee did not possess a comparable legitimate privilege, but in the early thirteenth century, monks at the community had forged a charter of Emperor Henry VI, which borrowed almost verbatim the passage from the Benediktbeuern privilege of 1155.[35] When the two communities presented their privileges at the royal court and requested the right to appoint their own advocates, it was Tegernsee that succeeded in freeing itself from Otto I's lineage, whereas Benediktbeuern was pressured to accept the young Otto II as advocate.[36] A forgery had proven more effective than an authentic document in ending the power and influence of hereditary advocates.

Forgeries are evidence that advocates were not the only people interested in justice and protection on ecclesiastical estates who were willing to gain an advantage by employing methods we might consider corrupt or deceptive. The history of the Church between 1050 and 1250 is often framed in institutional terms: papal administration was expanding, canon law was being systematized, monastic orders were becoming better organized. Many historians are comfortable describing these developments with the language of government, constitutional structures and bureaucracy.[37] As a result, the Church in this period sometimes looks like a state, like a legitimate institution of quasi-public authority that rightly sought to quash private forms of power-holding.[38] However,

---

[33] DD H V, no. 186.   [34] DD F I, 179–81, no. 106.
[35] DD H VI, 236–40, no. BB 296; Acht, "Vogteifälschungen," 176.
[36] For Tegernsee, see *Historia Diplomatica Friderici Secundi*, 4.1:516–19. For Benediktbeuern, see *Tiroler Urkundenbuch*, 3:57–58, no. 1004. The house of canons at Diessen also forged a charter around this time because of the uncertain situation of the lineage of the dukes of Merania: Schlögl, ed., *Traditionen*, 127–35, no. 16.
[37] Melville, *Monasticism*, 146–51; Whalen, *Medieval Papacy*, 111–13; Robinson, *Papacy*, 1–291.
[38] See, for example, Morris, *Papal Monarchy*, 205–36.

ecclesiastics did not always play by a different set of rules than their advocates; they too could blur the line between their official responsibilities and more arbitrary claims to power and authority when fighting over local rights.

Rulers to the Rescue?

To understand ecclesiastical communities' strategies for undermining the power and influence of their advocates, the events that transpired at King Henry (VII)'s court in 1234 are significant beyond the issue of forgery. Part of the backdrop to this incident is the long history of religious houses sending members or representatives to the royal court to bring disputes with their advocates to the rulers' attention.[39] Ecclesiastical communities did not always get what they wanted when they went to court, as the monastery of Benediktbeuern's failure to free itself from its hereditary advocacy shows. Kings frequently needed to negotiate compromises between churches and their advocates, because they required the continuing support of both prelates and nobles to rule effectively.[40] Nevertheless, going to court to acquire new privileges and to ask rulers to address advocates' abuses was a commonplace strategy.

Here, it is important to draw a contrast between the French and German kingdoms between 1050 and 1250. As noted in previous chapters, advocacy had never featured as prominently in French royal privileges as in German ones, and as a general rule only some of the oldest religious houses in the kingdom of France – not the newer, reformed communities – still had advocates into the twelfth century. On rare occasions, disputes over advocacies could still make their way to the court of the Capetian kings. In 1110, King Louis VI (1108–37) settled a dispute between the abbot of St. Denis and one of its advocates and regulated how much the advocate was to be paid each year.[41] Almost a century later, in 1205, King Philip II Augustus (1180–1223) similarly confirmed the settlement of a dispute between the monastery of Saint-Germain-des-Prés by Paris and the advocate for one of its villages.[42] However, in the body of surviving French royal privileges from the twelfth and early thirteenth centuries, these are the exceptions that prove the rule that advocacy was waning in significance in the kingdom of France – at a time when it was demanding more and more ink and parchment further east.[43]

---

[39] For this point see previous chapters and Stieldorf, "Klöster," 71–73.
[40] Weiler, "King as Judge," 123–29.
[41] *Recueil des actes de Louis VI*, 1:76–78, no. 40. See also ibid., 2:348–51, no. 409.
[42] Delaborde, ed., *Recueil*, 2:477–78, no. 890.
[43] Bouchard, *Sword*, 128–30. For more on this point, see below and Chapter 11.

The century from roughly 1125 to 1225 witnessed a steadily growing number of religious communities complaining to the German kings and emperors about their advocates. In the year 1149, monks from the monastery of St. Remi in Reims went to King Conrad III's court at Frankfurt "and made a complaint against the advocates who were in the land belonging to [St. Remi], of whom there was a great number who were more prepared to inflict injury than to defend."[44] The king, acting in concert with the princes at court, then issued the judgment "that no one can hear and decide the cases and disputes pertaining to the advocates' rights, or hold advocatial courts, except one who has received the ban from the royal hand." In this case, St. Remi succeeded in receiving confirmation from the German king that the ruler had to approve the appointment of advocates for the monastery's German estates; nobles could not simply start calling themselves advocates and make demands of the monks and their dependents.

Obtaining clear judgments of this sort from the royal court was not always easy or straightforward, however. In the midst of the many conflicts between the monastery of Niederaltaich and its advocates, Abbot Poppo crossed the Alps in 1210 to go looking for the German ruler Otto IV in Italy. He reports that "Having reached Lombardy, immensely fatigued after the long journey, I found him in Alexandria ... I tearfully recounted to him the whole course of our case."[45] Rather than finding in the abbot's favor, however, Otto "delegated to the duke of Bavaria the ending of the whole case with rigorous justice." As a result, Poppo had to return to Bavaria empty-handed, and the dispute dragged on for months.[46]

Rulers could also intervene in disputes in less formal ways. In the second half of 1156 or early 1157, Emperor Frederick I wrote directly to Count Henry II of Wolfratshausen to inform him that he had confirmed the election of Rupert (1155–86) as the new abbot of Tegernsee; in his letter, he also warned the count not to commit any violent acts against the monastic community or to try to judge members of the monastery's household over whom he did not have judicial authority.[47] Around the same time, however, Duke Henry II of Austria wrote a letter to the abbot of Tegernsee on behalf of the count, reminding the abbot of the advocate's rights to exercise justice.[48] Thus, noble advocates could also turn to

---

[44] DD Ko III, 377–79, no. 210. See also West, "Monks," 392–93. For another example, Carré, "Avoueries," 321.

[45] *De Advocatis*, 374.   [46] Ibid., 374–76. See also Dendorfer, "Abtei," 119–21.

[47] *Tegernseer Briefsammlung*, 230, no. 198. See Chapter 7 for more about this dispute. For another example of a letter exchange, see Wibald of Stablo, *Briefbuch*, 2:388–91, no. 184; 2:396–98, no. 187; and 2:521–23, no. 243.

[48] *Tegernseer Briefsammlung*, 295–96, no. 266.

powerful friends and allies in these disputes; they did not sit by passively when religious communities sought to resist their power by bringing their disputes to the ruler.

Intervening on a case-by-case basis to help settle – or at least moderate – disputes between churches and advocates was only one way that rulers worked to support religious communities and limit advocatial abuses. When seeking to establish peace and order in their territories more generally, the German kings and emperors routinely addressed the issue of advocacy. In the general peace that Frederick I announced following his election in 1152, he decreed that anyone who had been stripped of an advocacy for misdeeds, "if afterwards by a rash effort he should seize the advocacy, ... let him be considered as a violator of the peace."[49] Three years later in 1155, when issuing a judgment for a monastery, he made it clear that his predecessors had long been opposed to all subadvocates and decreed, "so, in our times too, the judgment of our court has brought forth a sentence that subadvocates must be removed."[50] Grand pronouncements continued to appear in subsequent decades. To appease Pope Innocent III after his election in 1198, Philip of Swabia promised, among other things, "To the extent that I am able, I will compel advocates ... to cease from exactions."[51]

As impressive as all of this may appear, royal intervention, whether in individual cases or at the level of empire-wide pronouncements, frequently was not enough to stop advocatial abuses. The abundant evidence for conflicts between churches and advocates throughout the late twelfth and early thirteenth centuries highlights the enduring challenges of regulating these relationships. Some religious communities therefore turned increasingly to another option, asking the ruler himself to become the advocate. As discussed already, Cistercian houses are frequently cited in the scholarship as being at the forefront of this trend.[52] However, by the mid-twelfth century, communities from every religious order were employing this strategy.[53]

In 1149, for example, King Conrad III explained in a privilege for a Benedictine monastery that the abbot had given "the name of advocate" (*nomen advocati*) to the lay founder of the community; however, "neither he nor any of his successors could demand for themselves the advocacy of that place as if it were hereditary, because ... the king himself ought to be

---

[49] Const., 1:198, no. 140, chap. 17.
[50] DD F I, 210–11, no. 125. See also West, "Monks," 381.
[51] *Concilia Germaniae*, 3:468. As noted in the previous chapter, Emperor Frederick II also issued general proclamations against advocatial abuses.
[52] See Chapter 5.
[53] For the Premonstratensians, see Penth, "Kloster- und Ordenspolitik."

the legitimate advocate there."[54] Four years later in 1153, Frederick I issued a charter for a house of Augustinian canons, decreeing that "we receive this monastery, with everything it has acquired and will acquire, under our protection by royal authority and establish that the aforesaid place may have no other advocate except us and our successors as kings and emperors."[55] This is reminiscent of the same ruler's 1163 charter for Abbess Hildegard of Bingen's community of nuns and highlights the fact that his reign, in particular, saw this strategy flourish. He was especially interested in fostering strong relationships with the Premonstratensians and obtained the advocacies for thirty-nine of their houses during his lifetime.[56]

In some parts of the German kingdom, it was not the kings and emperors but the dominant princely family in the region to whom religious communities turned in their efforts to resist the influence of lesser nobles. These imperial princes were likewise increasingly interested by the late twelfth century in acquiring as many advocacies as possible to solidify their own territorial positions. The Wittelsbach dukes of Bavaria obtained the advocacies for numerous monasteries in the early thirteenth century when other noble lineages in the duchy died out. Abbot Herman of Niederaltaich saw the end of the lineage of the counts of Bogen and the Wittelsbachs' acquisition of his community's advocacy as an opportunity to end decades of advocatial abuses.[57]

Further east, the Babenberg dukes of Austria did not hesitate to clash with local elites as they tried to bring monastic advocacies under their own control. In 1235, for example, Duke Frederick II of Austria issued an extraordinarily blunt privilege for the monastery of Garsten:

We make known to everyone – and name by name the advocate Otto of Neulengbach, the brothers Liutold and Conrad of Altenburg, Otto and Ortulf of Graz and Gundakar of Steyr – that we received a complaint from Abbot Ulrich and the monks of Garsten about the injuries and troubles introduced by the aforesaid men and certain other lesser men, who called themselves advocates of their church. We therefore set a day for the said abbot and monks ... [to come] to our general court session, where the aforesaid abbot ... demonstrated sufficiently through many privileges that [his church] should have no advocate on any of its possessions except us. We therefore added the same advocacy to our power, as is right, ordering that no one may oppress or trouble [the monks] on their possessions on the pretext of advocacy.[58]

---

[54] DD Ko III, 379–81, no. 211.   [55] DD F I, 95–6, no. 56.

[56] Freed, *Frederick Barbarossa*, 21; Penth, "Kloster- und Ordenspolitik," 78–79. Penth refers to the Staufen rulers' accumulation of advocacies as a *Vogteipolitik*, but this downplays the case-by-case nature of their interventions.

[57] See Chapter 7. For the Wittelsbach acquisition of advocacies, see Kraus, "Herzogtum."

[58] BUB, 2:160–61, no. 322. See also Reichert, *Landesherrschaft*, 148–49. For the authority of the Babenberger dukes more generally, see Lutter, "Babenbergs."

Local advocates frequently resisted the Babenberg dukes' efforts to acquire advocacies in this fashion.[59] Indeed, following the end of the Babenberg lineage in 1246 and the acquisition of the duchy of Austria by Rudolf of Habsburg in 1278, the new duke would be forced to address questions about who rightfully possessed numerous advocacies.[60]

What did it mean in practice for a religious community to have the king or a leading imperial prince as its advocate? Obviously, the ruler of an expansive territory was not in a position to personally exercise justice and provide protection for every religious community for which he held the advocacy. Someone else had to do this for him. Essentially, though this is not always the language used in the sources, the king or duke as advocate had to appoint a subadvocate.[61] One might be tempted to see in this trend evidence for the growth of government and the rise of the state, with the ruler appointing an accountable official to fulfill those responsibilities which had previously belonged to hereditary "lordly" advocates. I will have much more to say about this in the coming chapters. Here, two brief examples from the late twelfth and early thirteenth centuries will suffice to highlight the fact that having the king as advocate was not necessarily a step toward centralized government – and certainly did not mean that a religious community's concerns about advocatial abuses suddenly disappeared.

At the monastery of Pegau in Saxony, the lineage of the community's founder became extinct in the male line in the 1130s, and there follows a gap of almost forty years when we know nothing about the community's advocates.[62] By the early 1170s at the latest, the advocacy had passed into the hands of Emperor Frederick I, who acknowledged in a privilege from 1172 that the monastery might need additional support. He decreed "that no one except the emperor of the Romans may be advocate of the said church without the consent of the abbot and brothers. If the brothers should need a subadvocate to defend them in the emperor's place, they are permitted to invite whatever person they want."[63] Immediately thereafter, the privilege recognizes that this could lead to a familiar set of problems: "If [the subadvocate] should be useless (*inutilis*) to the brothers by acting wickedly in the emperor's place, they are free to ask the emperor for a better subadvocate. In addition, no subadvocate's heirs should

---

[59] See Chapter 10.
[60] Reichert, *Landesherrschaft*, 90–104. For the authority of the early Habsburgs in Austria, see Stercken, "Dominion."
[61] Clauss, *Untervogtei*, 270–79; Penth, "Kloster- und Ordenspolitik," 82.
[62] *Annales Pegavienses*, 254–65. Various scholars have tried to guess what happened to the advocacy after the death of the founder's son in 1135, but the sources do not offer a definitive answer; see Schlesinger, *Anfänge*, 85; Patze, "Pegauer Annalen," 40–41; Baaken, "Verlorene Papst- und Kaiserurkunden," 555; Vogtherr, "Pegau," 1199.
[63] DD F I, 3:73–75, no. 594.

presume to demand for themselves any right to the advocacy." One is left with the impression that having the emperor as advocate could look very similar to noble advocacy, because it did not solve the basic problem of how to prevent abuses when someone accessed ecclesiastical estates to provide justice and protection at the local level.[64]

A quarter-century after Frederick I's privilege for Pegau, the community discovered there was another potential danger to having the emperor as advocate. The chronicle from a neighboring monastery reports that, although Frederick I and his son Henry VI had both decreed that the emperor could not give away the community's advocacy in fief, "After the death of Emperor Henry [VI], King Philip of Swabia – against the privileges of that church – granted the advocacy of Pegau to Count Dietrich of Sommerschenburg."[65] This is the same Count Dietrich who would go on to imprison the abbot of Pegau and mint coins in his own name at the monastery.[66] In other words, despite imperial privileges supposedly guaranteeing that a ruler could not give away the advocacy, Philip – in need of allies during the tumultuous years after his disputed election – decided the advocacy was too valuable not to use it to buy support.

King Philip earned the ire of the Premonstratensian canons of Ursberg for a similar reason. In need of money, he pawned the community's advocacy, which he refers to as "our advocacy" at one point, to a local noble in return for 200 marks.[67] According to the chronicler Burchard of Ursberg (or possibly a later interpolator), both the nobleman and his son "began to exercise such great tyranny there that the community of canons could in no way exist."[68] In 1202, the canons therefore paid the money in order to redeem the pledge and to free themselves from the exactions being squeezed out of them on account of the advocacy.[69] This proved to be only a short-term solution to the problem, however, because later rulers also pledged the community's advocacy in return for much-needed money.[70] By the early thirteenth century, the German emperors were just as likely as leading nobles to view their advocacies first and foremost through the lens of how much income they could generate – and which followers they could reward with the valuable prize of a subadvocacy.[71]

---

[64] For more on the Pegau advocacy in this period, see DD F I, 4:12–13, no. 813 and *Chronica Sereni Montis*, 275.

[65] *Chronica Sereni Montis*, 277–78.   [66] See Chapter 6.   [67] DD Phil, 152–54, no. 65.

[68] Burchard von Ursberg, *Chronik*, 254–57. For the authorship of this passage, see Neel, "Historical Work," 125–29.

[69] DD Phil, 152–54, no. 65.

[70] As discussed in the editors' comments for DD Phil, no. 65. See also Chapters 12 and 13.

[71] For the contrasting perspectives on good and bad "royal officials" in this period in Germany and England, see Weiler, "King as Judge," 121–22. Entries in the so-called "Reichssteuerliste" of 1241 issued under Frederick II for Swabia (Const., 3:1–6) make it

As all of this shows, when religious communities chose to involve the German rulers in disputes over their advocacies, they were playing with fire. If it served the ruler's interests, he could side with a church against its noble advocates and work to limit advocatial abuses, potentially by acquiring the advocacy for himself and his successors. However, the rulers were hardly detached observers of disputes over advocacies. They did not always side with the community and give it everything it wanted. Moreover, they could choose to privilege their own interests over the church's, because like nobles, rulers understood the political and economic value of church advocacies and recognized how beneficial they could be.[72] Thus, to label the ruler as an impartial representative of the state, as a benevolent agent of government or as a public authority figure is to misrepresent, at a fundamental level, how power worked in this period.

The Papacy and Canon Law

As discussed already, many religious communities sought Roman liberty and the protection of the Papal See in the decades after 1050 as a way to distance themselves from secular influence and authority.[73] However, by the mid-twelfth century, the countless conflicts between ecclesiastical communities and their advocates had laid bare the reality that the papacy could not adequately provide physical protection to religious houses and their estates north of the Alps. The steady stream of ecclesiastics traveling to the court of the German kings and emperors to seek support is evidence that their protection was increasingly seen as the better safeguard against abusive advocates. This does not mean, however, that the papacy and the institutional Church more generally had ceded all oversight of advocacy to secular rulers.[74]

From the early twelfth century, canon law increasingly offered religious communities a potential resource for challenging advocatial abuses. *The Harmony of Discordant Canons*, better known as Gratian's *Decretum*, was compiled in Bologna between the 1130s and 1150s and quickly became a foundational work for canon law.[75] Its author(s) collected and

clear that the emperor relied heavily on the income from advocacies. For a story of Frederick II's financial interests in acquiring an advocacy, see also *Chronicon Ottenburanum*, 623–24.
[72] For more on this point, see Chapter 11.   [73] See Chapter 5.
[74] Throughout the period, popes continued to reaffirm older papal privileges granting Roman *libertas* and the protection of the Roman See. See, for example, Horstkötter, ed., *Urkundenbuch*, 1:25–30, no. 2 and 44–54, no. 5.
[75] For the authorship of the *Decretum*, see Winroth, *Gratian's Decretum*. I take this overview of the early history of canon law from Brundage, *Canon Law*, 44–61; Duggan, "Master."

organized the mass of earlier Church laws and sought to root out incon-
sistencies. A series of scholars working in the years after the completion of
the *Decretum*, known as decretists, wrote glosses and commentaries on the
work, further refining the law. Pope Alexander III (1159–81) and the
circle around him embraced these new legal developments and wrote
hundreds of letters addressing questions from prelates seeking clarity on
unsettled points. Many of these letters became known as decretals
because they were integrated into canon law in formal collections of
papal addenda to the *Decretum*. Under Pope Gregory IX (1227–41), the
Liber Extra, which contained roughly 2,000 decretals, emerged as the
basis for much of subsequent canon law. Glosses and commentaries on
the decretals by so-called "decretalists" soon followed, further clarifying
difficult legal questions. Henry of Susa (ca. 1200–71), also known as
Hostiensis, proved to be one of the most prolific and influential of these
decretalists. Thus, between roughly 1150 and 1250, church law became
newly organized and systematized as the papacy and canon lawyers
increasingly sought to exert the Church's jurisdiction over countless
aspects of life.

Church advocacy occupies a complicated place in this body of canon
law. The compiler(s) of the *Decretum*, working in Bologna and heavily
influenced by the renewed interest there in ancient Roman law, had
a very different understanding of the word *advocatus* than did secular
and ecclesiastical elites north of the Alps. Advocates were first and
foremost Roman-style representatives at court (i.e., lawyers or barristers). Thus, in one passage drawn from early Church sources, the
Decretum notes, "In all cases, except criminal ones, bishops and priests
should have an advocate represent him."[76] Many of the references to
advocates in the works of the early decretists also describe advocates as
representing clients in court rather than exercising justice and providing
protection.[77]

The gap between the advocatial roles I have been analyzing in this book
and early canon law discussions of advocates is not solely the result of
a revival of interest in ancient Roman legal texts. In many parts of Italy by

---

[76] Gratian, *Decretum*, C 5.3.3, cols 547–48. For other evidence of Gratian's debt to Roman
Law discussions of the *advocatus*, see ibid., C 11.1.29, col. 634 and C. 11.3.71, col. 663.
See also Brundage, *Medieval Origins*, 169–70. Elsewhere, Gratian references Christ as
sinners' advocate with God: *Decretum*, C 33.3.40, cols. 1202–03. One place in Gratian's
Decretum where his use of the term aligns more with the advocates I am discussing here is
in a copy of a papal bull of Pope Urban II: C 1.3.8, col. 414.

[77] Brundage, *Medieval Origins*, 170–71. For these canonists, *advocatus*, *defensor* and *patronus*
were all synonymous terms for representatives in court proceedings. See, for example,
Rufinus, *Summa decretorum*, 278; Master Honorius of Kent *Summa*, 2:297; and another
decretist from either England or Normandy: *Summa "Omnis qui iuste iudicat,"* 2:84.

the mid-twelfth century, the term *advocatus* had largely become synony-mous with lawyer or barrister, further distancing Italian ideas about advocates from German ones.[78] In the Alpine regions, there were both northern-style church advocates and advocates who spoke at court on behalf of their clients.[79] But further south, the advocate who argued court cases was much more common. While there is some evidence for the existence of advocates who had responsibilities exercising justice, nothing suggests these were prominent nobles who also provided physical protection.[80] The difference between Italian advocates and those north of the Alps comes into especially sharp focus in sources tied to Emperor Frederick II. To read his privileges for German churches alongside the *Liber Augustalis*, the decrees he issued in 1231 as king of Sicily, is to see clearly that the term *advocatus* had taken on very different meanings north and south of the Alps by the early thirteenth century.[81]

As a result, not every part of canon law that refers to the position of advocate concerns the advocates who are the subject of this book. There is one particular strand of church law, however, that does acknowledge problems posed by advocates who exercised justice and provided protec-tion for religious communities. In the closing months of 1184, Pope Lucius III, in Emperor Frederick I's presence, issued the bull *Ad abolen-dam*. This bull is (in)famous for its lengthy discussion of heresy.[82] Most scholars, however, have not paid as much attention to what follows the section on heresy:

Because the advocates of churches are known to erupt with such insolence that they appoint and remove priests and other ecclesiastics in their churches by their own will and desire, and presume to transfer to others the right of advocacy (*ius advocationis*) under the title of gifting and selling . . ., extorting fodder, lodging . . . and similar things from those churches as if from their own peasants, . . . we establish by the present decree that they – either advocates (*advocati*), or patrons

---

[78] Brundage, *Medieval Origins*, 171–73. For the relationship between Roman law and the geography of advocacy, see also Depreux, "Ausprägungen," 351.
[79] See especially Riedmann, "Vescovi e Avvocati." For the counts of Görz as advocates of the patriarchal church of Aquileia, see for example, DD Ko III, 357–59, no. 198 and 361–63 no. 200. In contrast, in 1217, an advocate of Aquileia of lower social status was involved in a legal suit brought by the abbot of Moggio and spoke at court: *Die älteren Urkunden des Klosters Moggio*, 108, no. U 46. For the complexity of advocacy in this region, see also ibid., 93–94, U 19; and 104–07, nos. U 38 and U 41–44.
[80] See, for example, *Urkunden und Briefe der Markgräfin Mathilde*, 35–39, no. 2; 64–66, no. 12; 131–32, no. 39; 479–81, no. A 6; and 491–492, A 10. The Avvocati (or Avvogadri) family of Lucca, who took their surname from holding the position of legal *advocatus*, are one noteworthy exception to this general rule: see Schwarzmaier, *Lucca*, 310–18; Osheim, *Italian Lordship*, 33–37, 120–21; Wickham, *Community*, 16–17, 32, 182. More generally, Albertoni, "Evangelium."
[81] Const., 2:Supplementum, 257–59, I.83–84 (English translation: *Liber Augustalis*, 54–5).
[82] Moore, *War on Heresy*, 205–13; Morris, *Papal Monarchy*, 349–50.

(*patroni*), or lords' agents (*vicedomini*), or guardians (*custodes*) or . . . those called by any other name – cease from their impositions on churches and demand nothing from them except the ancient and moderate dues instituted by their bishops. And if they demand anything [else], let them be placed under excommunication.[83]

Here, the term *advocatus* is clearly being used to refer to the types of advocates that were causing so many problems for religious communities north of the Alps. The emperor's presence for the bull's promulgation is therefore telling; unlike the majority of works significant for the history of canon law, *Ad abolendam* was a text shaped by people familiar with the situation in the German kingdom.

The influence of this bull was far-reaching. There are clear echoes of it in Canon Forty-Five of the Fourth Lateran Council (1215), which expressly forbade "patrons, advocates and lords' agents . . . to appropriate more [from churches] than is determined to be permitted in law."[84] Especially significant is the fact both *Ad abolendam* and this canon mention advocates alongside other laymen who provided protection or other services for churches, especially "patrons" (*patroni*). By broadening the issue in this way, in order to make it apply to religious communities in Latin Christendom more generally, both texts folded advocacy in with other forms of secular interference in church affairs. As a result, church advocacy came to be discussed in canon law alongside the "right of patronage" (*ius patronatus*).[85] The section of *Ad abolendam* just cited appears in the *Liber Extra* under the heading *De iure patronatus* alongside a series of decretals that are mostly concerned with a church patron's right to present a new priest of his choosing to the bishop for appointment to that church (the right of advowson in England).[86] Church advocacy's location in the body of canon law thus suggests that canonists were not as focused on its specific challenges as rulers, prelates and nobles in the German kingdom were.

This is not to suggest that we can simply ignore canon law when analyzing church advocates. Hostiensis, for example, was careful in his *Summa* to explain the connection between the terms *patronus* and *advocatus*; he notes that the patron had "the obligation to defend and protect the church and so can be called advocate or defender . . . [H]e is bound therefore, to defend to the best of his ability the church from all

---

[83] *Decretalium Collectiones*, cols. 616–17 (*Liber Extra*, 3.38.23). See also Regesta Imperii Online, RI IV,4,4,2 no. 1247.

[84] *Constitutiones Concilii quarti Lateranensis*, 84–85, canon 45.

[85] See especially Willoweit, "Vogt, Vogtei," cols. 939–40; Willoweit, "Römische," 42–49; Landau, *Jus patronatus*; Wood, *Proprietary Church*, 883–904.

[86] *Decretalium Collectiones*, cols. 616–17 (*Liber Extra 3.38.23*).

oppressions."[87] Here, Hostiensis clearly recognizes that protection was central to the role of the advocate, evidence that he understood some advocates to be more than lawyers or barristers. Indeed, elsewhere in his writings on the right of patronage he acknowledged the problem of unjust exactions.[88] Comparable comments by other canonists are uncommon, however. From the perspective of canon law, church councils held at the level of the archdiocese or diocese in the German-speaking lands are the best place to find serious discussions of legal solutions to the problem of bad advocates.[89] Thus, a canon of the Council of Salzburg of 1274 decrees, "We publicly warn the advocates of churches, who burden churches with service beyond what is customary and owed, and in this way violate and infringe the liberties of churches, that they abstain from undue harassment of churches and their goods."[90]

While canon law at the level of the universal Church only rarely – and somewhat indirectly – touched on key issues at the heart of church advocacy, religious communities had another way to seek support from Rome in their conflicts with their advocates. Like kings and emperors, popes too could involve themselves in individual cases. Pope Gregory VII's intervention in a dispute over the advocacy for the convent of Sainte-Croix-en-Plaine in Alsace has already been discussed.[91] Almost a century-and-a-half later, in 1208, Pope Innocent III wrote to the archbishop of Magdeburg and two other ecclesiastics, asking them to intervene in a conflict between the abbess of Gandersheim and a local count over the advocacy for a village. The language of the document, which looks familiar from the perspective of religious communities' own complaints about their advocates, suggests that someone from Gandersheim was in Rome and had provided the pope with the details: the count, "on the pretext of advocacy, ... imposing undue exactions ..., entered the village three times a year with not a few knights and servants in his retinue."[92]

Papally mandated investigations of this sort gave religious communities the opportunity to direct the pope's authority against advocatial abuses. As with so many other strategies, however, papal intervention did not always succeed in improving the relationships between churches and advocates.[93] The Roman Church, backed by an increasingly

---

[87] Henry of Susa, *Summa*, Book 3, 180v–181v (here 181r).
[88] Henry of Susa, *In Tertium*, 145a–146.   [89] Willoweit, "Römische," 48–49.
[90] *Concilia Germaniae*, 3:643–44, chap. 24. See also Willoweit, "Römische," 49. For another example, see *Concilia Germaniae*, 3:635, chap. 10.
[91] See Chapter 5.   [92] *Urkundenbuch des Hochstifts Halberstadt*, 1:395–96, no. 443.
[93] For more on this point, see Chapter 11. I have found little evidence that threats of excommunication were an effective deterrent.

sophisticated body of canon law, was unable to bring church advocacy under its control. Advocates were simply too entrenched at the local level for a canonist writing in Bologna, a papal letter threatening excommunication or a brief visit by prelates conducting an investigation to impact their behavior over the long term. To limit their abuses of power, local solutions were necessary.

Money Talks

Religious communities forged documents, brought their disputes to the royal court and appealed to the papacy for support, yet the pace of complaints about bad advocates hardly slowed over the course of the late twelfth and early thirteenth centuries in the German kingdom. As a result, many churches increasingly turned to another strategy, one that had the potential to transform protection and justice at the local level in both the short and long term: purchasing their advocacies from their noble advocates.

To understand how and why this emerged as a viable strategy in the later twelfth century, let us return to the *Life* of Hildegard of Bingen and its claim that the abbess did not want a "lay advocate" (*laicus advocatus*).[94] The term *laicus* might seem unnecessary. Since the ninth century, the position of advocate had been tied to secular responsibilities on churches' estates. And yet, in the German kingdom, the dichotomy between lay and religious authority was never as sharp as one might think. Bishops, abbots and abbesses could hold rights that were typically held by lay nobles; some prelates even possessed ducal or comital authority – and with it, secular jurisdiction – on some of their lands.[95]

As a result, there are occasional references to bishops being referred to not only as defender but even as advocate for monasteries.[96] This means that the advocacy itself was in the hands of the bishop, and he could then appoint someone besides a local noble as lay advocate (essentially, a subadvocate) to exercise justice and provide protection. At Cologne, where the archbishops possessed extensive secular rights, some of their own ministerials were serving as local advocates already by the mid-twelfth

---

[94] See n. 2 of this chapter.

[95] Arnold, *Princes*, 99–105; Hoffmann, "Grafschaften," esp. 462–64.

[96] See, for example, Braun, ed., *Urkundenbuch*, 1:126–29, no. 109. See also: Carré, "Avoueries," 292, 408–13. Also interesting is a comment in a text from ca. 1000 about a saint in the midst of a property dispute: "In the end, it seemed proper to the blessed Servatius that he should be his own advocate" ("*Placuit tandem beato Seruatio, ut sibimet ipse aduocatus existeret*"). See *Gesta Sancti Servatii*, 136, chap. 58; Constable, "Religious Communities," 363.

century.[97] In other words, someone who belonged to a church's household, acting under the secular authority of their prelate, could be tasked with protecting ecclesiastical property and even acting as judge.

Thus, if a religious community could gain control of its advocacy, it could potentially avoid having to rely on hereditary noble advocates. We catch glimpses of this strategy in some twelfth-century privileges. In 1153, Emperor Frederick I granted his trusted adviser Abbot Wibald and his monastery of Stavelot "part of the advocacy of the same monastery … [such that] you and your successors as properly appointed abbots will deliver to us and the kingdom just as much in the way of provisions for our [Italian] expedition, both in men and arms, as the [previous] advocate and his predecessors."[98] A quarter-century later in the late 1170s, the duke of Austria granted the advocacies for two villages to the monastery of Garsten; to ensure that no one tried to usurp the right of advocacy, he insisted that the abbot should choose honest men to defend the proper-ties – but these men were not called advocates.[99] Thus, as the advocacy for a religious community or for a particular estate increasingly came to be viewed as something that could be held by a church, it became possible to imagine a world without noble advocates.

All of this helps to explain why religious communities began purchasing advocacies to free themselves from their troublesome advocates. There is evidence for this practice in the kingdom of France by the middle decades of the twelfth century at the latest.[100] It emerges in roughly the same period in the German kingdom as well, where bishops seem to have initially led the way.[101] Around 1180, Emperor Frederick I gave a privilege to the cathedral chapter of Hildesheim, which explains how one of the church's men, "coming to our court on yours and your church's behalf, conveyed to us that advocates are exercising great violence on your goods and do not cease to afflict your church with frequent plundering."[102] Frederick then decreed a solution to the problem of these bad advocates: "[W]e grant to you that, if in any way you are able to remove advocates from advocacies through your money and to free your goods from their unjust exactions, we concede and give to you henceforth the power to do so freely."

---

[97] Burkhardt, *Stab*, 303–04; Clauss, "Vogteibündelung," 188–93; Milz, "Die Vögte," 197–205; Aubin, *Entstehung*, 301–02. See also Chapter 9.

[98] DD F I, 74–5, no. 44.   [99] BUB, 1:64–65, no. 48.

[100] See, for example, *Cartulary of Notre-Dame of Homblières*, 120–22, no. 54 and 127–29, no. 59.

[101] For an especially good, concise overview of this trend, see Burkhardt, *Stab*, 359–62.

[102] DD F I, 3:353, no. 790. Though the original was probably not written in the imperial chancery, the charter is likely authentic.

This privilege provides context for a charter issued by Bishop Adelog of Hildesheim in 1181. It states that, because the advocate for one church's estates had died without any heirs, the bishop had decided to free the church "from every advocatial right and power."[103] In return, "forty measures of wheat should be paid from this advocacy on the feast of St. Martin each year to us and our successors."[104] Especially striking is the statement,

> Moreover, in order to ward off injuries from outsiders and to protect the properties of the church, any guardian (*tutor*) who ... acts in the provost's place in secular matters should be chosen by the provost and brothers of sounder counsel. If he should be a pious patron (*pius patronus*), he should administer the office of advocate (*advocati officium*) faithfully.[105]

Thus, the bishop dissolved the position of advocate, took some of the profits of the advocacy into his own hands and gave the church the right to choose someone else to handle secular affairs – a person who fulfilled the role of advocate, but without the title. Adelog's immediate successors were even more aggressive in seeking to eliminate advocates.[106] Bishop Conrad II (1221–46) is praised in one chronicle for his efforts along these lines: "A caring shepherd and diligent provider, he enriched our church and bishopric by purchasing properties and buying back advocacies."[107]

Hildesheim was not the only bishopric to pursue the strategy of using money to acquire advocacies. In 1226, Bishop Frederick of Halberstadt bought the advocacy and the jurisdiction over the town of Halberstadt and several other advocacies from the advocate: "We gave him 150 silver marks under the condition that he resign completely to us, into our hands, the advocacy and justice for our whole city and whatever is outside the city in our territory in the area of the city, as well as the advocacy for two villages."[108] The document states the advocate had three years to buy back the advocacy for the city, which suggests he may have been reluctant to resign it but needed the money. Other sources point to many nobles in the late twelfth and early thirteenth century struggling to maintain the lifestyle expected of the social elite and therefore needing to sell some of their rights.[109] It is

---

[103] *Urkundenbuch des Hochstifts Hildesheim*, 391–92, no. 402.   [104] Ibid.   [105] Ibid.
[106] *Chronicon Episcoporum Hildesheimensium*, 857–60. For charter evidence that confirms this chronicle's account, see, for example, *Urkundenbuch des Hochstifts Hildesheim*, 1:713–14, no. 762.
[107] *Chronicon Episcoporum Hildesheimensium*, 860.
[108] *Urkundenbuch des Hochstifts Halberstadt*, 1:521–22, no. 584.
[109] For the financial difficulties of lesser nobles and ministerials in this period, see Spiess, "Bäuerliche Gesellschaft," 400–01. See also Chapters 12 and 13 below.

unsurprising, therefore, that many bishoprics jumped at the opportunity to acquire their advocacies.[110]

Monastic communities also sought to buy advocacies or to obtain them through exchange. At Steterburg in the north of the German kingdom, Berthold, who was the community's provost in the 1210s, was praised as one "who, through many efforts and very large expenditures, freed our church from advocates, through whom it had been greatly oppressed."[111] In 1231, the abbot and community of St. Blasien gave the counts of Kyburg one of the monastery's properties in fief in return for the counts giving up all their advocatial rights on one of the house's other properties.[112] Around this time, Niederaltaich's principal advocate, Count Albert IV of Bogen, ceded all of his advocatial rights over the monastery for one year in return for a payment of 100 pounds from the abbot.[113] The women's community at Quedlinburg also spent large amounts of money purchasing advocacies from Count Hoier of Falkenstein, its principal advocate.[114] A document issued in the name of Abbess Gertrude (1233–70) leaves little doubt about the rationale behind this strategy:

> Because the people of our convent, on account of advocacy, endured such unjust and intolerable exactions that they were unable to pay us the dues they owed, and because we also feared that as in former times they were being hurt by their advocates' harsh injuries and pressure, ... we determined that the advocacy for [certain properties] had to be bought back from our faithful man Count Hoier of Falkenstein for 120 silver marks ... He transferred it freely into our hands with every right, which he was known to have had there.[115]

As popular as this strategy was by the middle decades of the thirteenth century, it did not necessarily solve the fundamental problem at the heart of advocacy, namely the fact that someone with indisputable power and authority needed to access ecclesiastical estates to provide effective protection and justice. While some advocacies are not well documented after they were purchased, which suggests that the religious community found

---

[110] For a pope confirming a bishop's purchase of an advocacy, see Rosenfeld and Schulze, eds., *Urkundenbuch*, 2:182–83, no. 158.

[111] *Gesta Praepositorum Stederburgensium continuata*, 720. For another example, see Rosenfeld and Schulze, eds., *Urkundenbuch*, 2:81, no. 67.

[112] Braun, ed., *Urkundenbuch*, 1:376–77, no. 287.

[113] *Monumenta Boica*, 11:203–04, no. 66. For a more detailed analysis of this document, see Dendorfer, "Abtei," 124–25. See also Chapter 6. For other examples from Niederaltaich, see Klose, ed., *Urkunden*, 326–27, no. 387; 482–83, no. 522; 600–02, no. 630.

[114] Erath, ed., *Codex*, 139–40, no. 30; 146, no. 41; 151–52, nos. 51–52; 154–55, no. 56.

[115] Ibid., 172, no. 87. See also Vollmuth-Lindenthal, "Äbtissin," 105–06. For another example of a monastery buying an advocacy, see Vanderputten, "Fulcard's Pigsty," 112.

ways to address this issue, others resurface in the hands of people designated as advocates within only a few years or decades.[116] At Quedlinburg,
for example, Count Siegfried of Blankenburg soon replaced Count Hoier
as the main advocate for the community, and there would continue to be
advocates for Quedlinburg for another 500 years.[117] Money may have
initially seemed like a good solution to the problem of corrupt advocates,
but without a viable alternative for exercising protection and justice,
advocacy would remain a fixture of many local landscapes.

Conclusion

By the mid-to-late twelfth century, many religious communities had seen
their relationships with their advocates fray badly. Violence, sometimes
spectacular but more often low level and quotidian, was a persistent
problem as the two sides wrestled over the scope of advocatial responsibilities. Increasingly, therefore, religious communities sought ways to
alter the rules of the game to their advantage. However, any strategy
designed to limit or even eliminate advocatial abuses had to include an
alternative to the local, noble advocate. As this chapter has shown, effective replacements were not easy to find. As religious houses turned to
kings and emperors, popes, their diocesan bishops and imperial princes
for support against their advocates, they pulled an ever-expanding group
of people into the competition over the economic benefits of providing
protection and justice for ecclesiastical properties – often with unintended
consequences.

---

[116] For more on this point, see Chapter 10.
[117] Erath, ed., *Codex*, 164, no. 74; 165–67, nos. 77–79; and 210, no. 152. See also below,
Chapter 14.

9   The Murder of Archbishop Engelbert

On November 7, 1225, knights from the entourage of Count Frederick of Isenberg violently attacked and killed the count's distant relative Archbishop Engelbert of Cologne. Although not as famous (or infamous) today as the murder fifty-five years earlier of the archbishop of Canterbury, Thomas Becket, at the hands of King Henry II of England's men, Engelbert's death sent shock waves through Latin Christendom. He had been one of the leading figures in the German kingdom throughout the early and mid-1220s, and at the time of his murder was serving as regent and guardian for the young King Henry (VII) while Emperor Frederick II was in Italy. A little over a year after the attack, on November 13, 1226, Count Frederick of Isenberg would be executed outside the walls of Cologne for his involvement, further evidence of the seriousness of the crime.[1] Indeed, like Becket, Engelbert was quickly seen as a martyr. The Cistercian monk Caesarius of Heisterbach began writing a *Life* of the archbishop within months of his death and continued to record miracles performed by the dead Engelbert into the late 1230s.

Unsurprisingly, contemporary accounts of Archbishop Engelbert's assassination are distinctly one-sided; killing a prelate rarely elicits sympathy from ecclesiastical authors. According to Caesarius in his *Life* of the saintly Engelbert, Count Frederick of Isenberg was a younger son who initially embarked upon a life as a church canon; however, when his older brother died childless and Frederick became his heir, "he was made a knight, and the more remote he became from grace, the more he inclined to wickedness."[2] For one chronicler, the archbishop was "father of our fatherland and splendor of Germany," but the count was a violent oppressor and tyrant who wretchedly cut Engelbert to pieces.[3] Another chronicle describes the archbishop as "most faithful in ecclesiastical affairs" before explaining how Frederick, "savage in appearance and mad in spirit," plotted to kill him.[4] The authors of these sources make

---

[1] For the basic outline of events, see Finger, "Tod"; Andermann, "Verschwörung"; Jung, "Jericho."
[2] Caesarius of Heisterbach, "Leben," 250, II.1.   [3] *Chronica Regia Coloniensis*, 255–56.
[4] *Emonis Chronicon*, 509.

every effort to present the events of the year 1225 as a conflict between good and evil, between the prelate's piety and the nobleman's baseness.[5]

The biased rhetoric of these ecclesiastical works obscures the complex dynamics of the relationship between Archbishop Engelbert of Cologne and Count Frederick of Isenberg. Numerous sources enable us to examine in detail some of the long- and short-term factors that led to the archbishop's death. Significantly, all of these texts agree about the root cause of the conflict between Frederick and Engelbert: the advocacy over a convent. When the dispute over this advocacy – rather than the dramatic and bloody assassination – is made the focus of analysis, the sharp line between the good archbishop and the bad count starts to blur. What emerges instead is a story that interweaves several strands of the history of advocates and advocacy I have discussed thus far. Archbishop Engelbert's assassination offers an especially compelling example of how advocates' efforts to profit from providing protection and justice, and religious communities' efforts to resist advocatial abuses, could transform local disputes into intractable conflicts that not even popes, rulers, prelates and prominent nobles could solve peacefully.

Murderous Advocates

European noble society during the period under investigation here was rife with violence. From the crusades to royal wars to local feuds, nobles and their military households frequently perpetrated violent acts of one sort or another.[6] While murders and assassinations of high-ranking members of the elite were not necessarily commonplace, they were not unusual either.[7] That said, nobles *in their roles as advocates* do not seem to have made a habit of killing either ecclesiastics or other nobles who challenged their control of an advocacy. Advocatial violence was typically of the sort I have discussed in the preceding chapters. This does not mean, however, that the case of Count Frederick and Archbishop Engelbert is unique. A small number of other incidents, though not as well-documented, can help us to better contextualize Engelbert's assassination within the history of church advocacy.

The chronicler Herman of Tournai, writing in the 1140s, tells the story of how the advocate Fastrad and the prior Tetbert came into conflict at the time of Bishop Radbod II of Tournai. Herman begins by explaining how "Tetbert was the prior [or business agent] of Bishop Radbod and

[5] For the ways in which modern historians have read these sources, see Wisplinghoff, "Kampf," 308–10.

[6] Brown, *Violence*, 167–92; Kaeuper, *Chivalry*, 155–60.

[7] Keupp, "Reichsministerialien"; Kaiser, "Mord."

showed himself faithful to him as if to his lord. Fastrad, the advocate, was angry with him for this reason, since he defended and protected the bishop's poor peasants everywhere."[8] As a result, "Fastrad first deceitfully struck up a friendship with Tetbert, accepting his son in baptism and becoming his [godfather]. A few days later . . ., Tetbert suspected no evil but was shadowed as he went to visit the lepers. As soon as he was treacherously kissed by [Fastrad], he was killed without any means of defending himself."[9] While Herman does not suggest that the advocate's actions were justified, he does acknowledge that Tetbert was interfering with Fastrad's ability to fulfill the role of advocate as he wanted to fulfill it; defending and protecting a church's peasants were normally the advocate's responsibility. That the prior, not the advocate, was performing these functions points to a clash over the advocate's proper rights and role.

The prose *Passion of St. Quirinus*, written at the monastery of Tegernsee in Bavaria in the 1170s, points to a dispute over advocatial rights as the motivation behind an advocate's attempted assassination of an abbot. According to the text, both Count Henry II of Wolfratshausen and Abbot Rupert of Tegernsee attended Emperor Frederick I's court in 1157 in the midst of their long-running dispute over the count's judicial authority as advocate.[10] The emperor and the princes at court issued a judgment that was mostly favorable to the abbot, an outcome that angered Count Henry. As the *Passion* explains, "Nevertheless, with the emperor bidding it, he kissed the abbot in his presence at the court and was reconciled, *but falsely*."[11] A short time later, as Henry and Rupert were returning home separately, the count sent assassins to try to murder the abbot; however, the abbot was warned in advance and fled. Here, the count's plot against the abbot is explained by Henry's anger at losing the court's judgment about his advocatial rights.

Dramatic incidents such as these demonstrate that the killing, or attempted killing, of a churchman or his agent by an advocate was not a casual act of violence. Underlying tensions over the role of the advocate occasionally drove nobles to take extreme measures.[12] The cases I have discussed in previous chapters of advocates imprisoning abbots are

---

[8] Herman of Tournai, *Restoration*, 83–84 (Latin: Herman of Tournai, *Liber*, 104–05, chap. 59).

[9] Herman of Tournai, *Restoration*, 84. See also the translator's endnotes to this passage (pp. 216–17).

[10] For the relationship between Count Henry and the monks of Tegernsee, see also Chapters 7 and 10.

[11] *Passio*, 284–85 (emphasis mine).

[12] Another example of an advocate ordering a prelate's death, apparently because he had not been consulted about that prelate's appointment, concerns Archbishop-Elect

additional evidence along these lines.[13] It is worth noting, too, that religious communities could employ violence in their disputes with their advocates. According to one chronicler, in the year 1094, "Herman, the advocate of Reichenau, a young man of good character, was ambushed and alas! cruelly hacked in pieces by the servants of the church of Reichenau on 25 September, while he was going to the church to pray."[14] Although the reasons for this attack are not entirely clear, one source suggests a disagreement over how much the advocate ought to be paid as the background to this violent act.[15]

Thus, murders and attempted assassinations involving advocates and ecclesiastics are explicable within the general framework of advocatial conflict I have discussed to this point. Disagreements over the extent of an advocate's rights to provide protection and exercise justice – and over how much they should benefit in return – could potentially turn violent if the two sides (and outside mediators) could not reach a compromise. This is important to keep in mind as we turn to Count Frederick of Isenberg and Archbishop Engelbert of Cologne.

The Advocacy for Essen

The sudden and violent death of Archbishop Engelbert of Cologne has attracted significant scholarly attention.[16] My interest here is less the act itself, however, than what the archbishop's death reveals about some of the intractable problems bound up with the history of church advocacy. I will therefore focus on the early thirteenth-century sources that provide the richest evidence for understanding both Count Frederick of Isenberg's and Archbishop Engelbert of Cologne's perspectives on the dispute between them.

The best and most detailed account of the events leading up to the archbishop's death in November of 1225 can be found in Caesarius of Heisterbach's *Life* of Engelbert. By the time this Cistercian monk began writing this text in 1226/27 at his monastery south of Cologne, he was already a prolific author, having completed several years earlier the work

<hr/>

Conrad of Trier in 1066: Lampert of Hersfeld, *Annals*, 112–13; *Triumphus Sancti Remacli*, 446, chap. 17; Robinson, *Henry IV*, 116–17; Kaiser, "Mord," 120, 123–24.

[13] See Chapters 6 and 7. Some scholars have also suggested that Count Frederick of Isenberg's aim in attacking Archbishop Engelbert was only to capture him, not kill him: Kleist, "Tod," 222–23.

[14] Bernold of St. Blasien, *Chronicle*, 321 (Latin: Bernold of St. Blasien, *Bernoldi Chronicon*, 514).

[15] Stieldorf, "Klöster," 64–65.

[16] See, for example, ibid., 77–78; *AufRuhr 1225!*; Jung, "Jericho"; Lothmann, *Erzbischof Engelbert*; Kleist, "Tod"; Ficker, *Engelbert*.

for which he is most famous, his *Dialogue on Miracles*. When Engelbert died, Caesarius was working on another collection of miracle stories as well as a collection of homilies.[17] His disdain for church advocates was already evident in both of these works. In one of the homilies, for example, he notes, "Our province, as you see, has been abandoned by its cultivators on account of the intolerable exactions made by advocates against the poor and the middling."[18] In his *Life* of Engelbert, he was equally critical of the advocate Count Frederick of Isenberg and painted a much more flattering portrait of the archbishop as the ideal prelate (which was not necessarily easy, as will be discussed further below). The text's obvious biases therefore complicate any analysis.[19] Nevertheless, Caesarius's account is invaluable, and there are enough other sources that discuss the conflict between archbishop and count that we do not have to rely on the *Life* exclusively.

At the beginning of the *Life*'s second book, which concerns the events surrounding Engelbert's murder, Caesarius introduces the story's antagonist, Count Frederick of Isenberg. He was the son of Matilda of Holland and Count Arnold of Altena-Isenberg (d. 1209), who was a first cousin of Archbishop Engelbert of Cologne. Frederick thus belonged to one of the leading noble lineages in the River Ruhr region northeast of Cologne. As noted above, he was not the firstborn son but became the heir after the death of his older brother. Frederick would eventually marry Sophia, the daughter of the duke of Limburg, whose lands lay to the west of Cologne, further entrenching the count in the uppermost echelons of the Rhineland nobility.[20] Frederick also had two younger brothers who were prelates at the time of his dispute with Archbishop Engelbert: Bishop Dietrich III of Münster (1218–26) and Bishop-Elect Engelbert of Osnabrück (1224–26), both of whom would be accused of conspiring with their older brother in the archbishop's murder.[21]

As impressive as Frederick's familial connections were, Caesarius of Heisterbach does not emphasize them when first introducing the count. Instead, the monk describes him in a way that foregrounds the count's conflict with the archbishop: "Count Frederick of Isenberg was advocate of the church of Essen."[22]

---

[17] Caesarius, "Leben," 229.
[18] Caesarius, *Wundergeschichten*, 1:117, no. 134. See also ibid., 96–97, no. 82. For a story about a wicked advocate in his *Libri miraculorum*, see Chapter 15.
[19] Finger, "Tod," 25–26.   [20] Janssen, "Adelsherrschaft."
[21] Lothmann, *Erzbischof Engelbert*, 59–65.
[22] Caesarius, "Leben," 249–50, II.1. Other chroniclers who recount Engelbert's death likewise emphasize this point: *Chronica Regia Coloniensis*, 255; *Emonis Chronicon*, 509. For Frederick as advocate, see also Leenen, "Stift Essen," 219–23.

The community of canonesses at Essen had been founded in the middle of the ninth century by a bishop of Hildesheim. Sometime before King Otto I issued a privilege for the community in 947, it had come into the possession of the East Frankish rulers.[23] As with Quedlinburg, Essen's close relationship to the rulers of the tenth and eleventh centuries led to it accumulating an impressive collection of rights and properties.[24] Typical of Ottonian privileges for most women's religious communities, Otto's 947 charter granting Essen immunity from secular judicial authority includes language granting the abbess the right to choose the community's advocate.[25] Otto II confirmed this privilege in 973, and twenty years later in 993, Otto III also approved this right.[26] Their two successors, Henry II and Conrad II, likewise confirmed this earlier grant.[27] Nevertheless, it is impossible to reconstruct with any certainty the line of advocates during these years.[28] By the second half of the twelfth century, however, the evidence points to Count Frederick of Isenberg's grandfather and father serving as advocates of Essen before him.[29]

It is only after labeling Count Frederick as advocate of Essen that Caesarius explains that he was a canon in the cathedral chapter of Cologne before his older brother's death.[30] According to the *Life*, "He was changed from a cleric into a count, and he was nominally made the advocate of the church of Essen, but in reality its enemy."[31] Employing other language that will be familiar to readers at this point, Caesarius goes on to state, "He did not learn to defend but rather to plunder."[32] More remarkable is the next sentence: "Although his father, Count Arnold of Altena, a man wholly prudent and sufficiently modest in his character, certainly injured the said church very unduly on account of the advocacy, that most recent one, Frederick, broke its bones."[33] Caesarius suggests here that Count Arnold's abuses were somehow more acceptable than those of his son, who "skinned ... the men" of the monastery "with such great exactions that that noble church ... would have been unable to subsist for much longer."[34] This language finds corroboration in other sources. One chronicle reports that the count, in his role as advocate,

---

[23] Wisplinghoff, "Kampf," 326–27; Schilp, "Gründungsurkunde," 153–57.
[24] Leenen, "Positionierung," 77–79; Bernhardt, *Itinerant*, 190–94; Leyser, *Rule*, 53–54.
[25] DD O I, 166–68, no. 85. See Chapter 3 for the language of Ottonian charters.
[26] DD O II, 58–59, no. 49 and DD O III, 525–26, no. 114.
[27] DD H II, 44–47, no. 39 and DD Ko II, 166–67, no. 121. For Henry II's privilege, see later in this section.
[28] Leenen, "Stift Essen," 214–19; Wisplinghoff, "Kampf," 327.
[29] Wisplinghoff, "Kampf," 327. For the poor survival rate of sources from Essen prior to ca. 1150, see Schilp, "Gründungsurkunde," 149–51. Even for the second half of the twelfth century, the number of extant charters from Essen is quite small: *Essener Urkundenbuch*, 24–29, nos. 37–45.
[30] Caesarius, "Leben," 250, II.1.   [31] Ibid.   [32] Ibid.   [33] Ibid.   [34] Ibid.

violently oppressed the community at Essen, "afflicting the people of the said church with the harshest of impositions and service demands."[35]

Two privileges, both apparently falsified at the convent of Essen in the early thirteenth century, seem to confirm the seriousness of the community's situation. The first is a charter that had initially been forged by the community in 1090.[36] This purports to be the foundation charter issued by Bishop Altfrid of Hildesheim in the year 870. The original forgery was intended to strengthen and legitimize the form of religious life practiced at the community in the midst of the various reform movements sweeping through Latin Christendom in the late eleventh century.[37] A little over a century later, as the community's advocacy increasingly became a point of contention, a sentence was then added to the privilege in a space before the dating clause: "We establish that no one, especially not any advocate, may have any jurisdiction in the aforesaid city [of Essen] except the abbess of Essen, excluding the cutting off of hands [i.e., for those guilty of theft] and the calling to arms."[38]

The community at Essen did something similar with the second falsified document, this one an authentic privilege originally issued by King Henry II in the year 1003. In this case, the forger erased part of the text and tried to mimic the hand of the 1003 scribe, but because the addition begins in the middle of a sentence, it makes nonsense of the original. The key added section reads, "We order that the abbess and convent by mutual consent may choose their own advocate. This advocate will not preside in judgment within the abbess's city of Essen but outdoors outside of the city ... Also, this advocate will usurp for himself no right on the properties belonging to the convent."[39] The forger even added a witness list, something we do not find in Henry II's authentic charters, and included an advocate in it.

Although the exact dates of the additions in these two falsified charters cannot be determined with certainty, the language of both strongly points to the context of the difficulties with Count Frederick of Isenberg.[40] Especially telling is the assertion added to Henry II's privilege that the abbess and the community had the right to choose their advocate, because this had already been stated earlier in the authentic part of the charter from 1003. Given that Frederick had apparently acquired the advocacy through inheritance from his father and older brother – without

[35] *Chronica Regia Coloniensis*, 255.
[36] For a detailed discussion of this forgery, see Schilp, "Gründungsurkunde."
[37] Ibid.; Leenen, "Urkunden," 286–87, no. A19.
[38] *Rheinisches Urkundenbuch*, 2:29–33, no. 159. See also Leenen, "Urkunden," 286, no. A19; *Essener Urkundenbuch*, 4–5, no. 6.
[39] DD H II, 44–47, no. 39a. See also *Essener Urkundenbuch*, 15–16, nos. 23–24.
[40] DD H II, 44, no. 39a. See also Leenen, "Urkunden," 286–87, no. A19. Frederick does not appear in the few surviving Essen charters from this period, which further suggests a strained relationship: *Essener Urkundenbuch*, 30–32, nos. 47–51.

any known involvement by the canonesses at Essen – the repetition of this free election clause was probably intended to stress the illegitimacy of Frederick's claims. As the previous chapter has shown, the early thirteenth century was precisely the period when many other religious houses were also pushing back against hereditary advocates and seeking ways to gain more control over the advocacies for their communities.

If these forgeries do indeed date from the early thirteenth century, they should be understood as only one aspect of a broader effort by the Essen canonesses to challenge their advocate. According to Caesarius, "The abbess and the sisters, frequently coming to Cologne, ... set forth with tears their miseries and Frederick's violent acts," first to Archbishop Dietrich I (1208–16) and subsequently to Archbishop Engelbert.[41] Since the community's appeals to the archbishops proved insufficient, Caesarius explains that the sisters brought their complaints to the attention of not only Pope Honorius III but also Emperor Frederick II, both of whom sent letters to Archbishop Engelbert urging him to intervene on Essen's behalf.[42] The dispute between the canonesses and Count Frederick of Isenberg had thus become much more than a local advocatial conflict. Increasingly, Archbishop Engelbert of Cologne became the focal point of events due to his position as head of the church province in which Essen was located.

As this brief overview has shown, there is relatively little in the lead-up to the events of the mid-1220s to suggest that Count Frederick of Isenberg's role as advocate was significantly different than the roles of the countless other church advocates who had harsh complaints leveled against them. Like many other religious houses, the women's community at Essen had privileges claiming the right to choose their own advocates, but these had failed to prevent a prominent local lineage from gaining control of the church's advocacy across multiple generations. As a result, the community used forgeries to strengthen its case and appealed to its archbishops, the pope and the emperor for support.[43] Since much of this looks typical of church–advocate relations in this period, it is essential to take a closer look at Archbishop Engelbert's role if we are to understand why the situation escalated in the way that it did.

Archbishop Engelbert of Cologne and Church Advocacy

Engelbert, who was probably born in the mid-1180s, was the son of Margaret of Guelders and Count Engelbert I of Berg (d. 1189). The

---

[41] Caesarius, "Leben," 251, II.1. The abbess was Adelheid, but she is not named in Caesarius's text.
[42] Ibid.   [43] For all of these strategies, see Chapter 8.

counts of Berg, a separate branch of the lineage to which Count Frederick of Isenberg also belonged, had exerted significant influence in the arch-bishopric of Cologne for decades before Engelbert rose to the position of archbishop.[44] Indeed, it was thanks to his family connections that Engelbert first became a canon in the cathedral chapter of Cologne around the age of thirteen, and he followed in the footsteps of a long line of relatives who had held prominent positions in that church, includ-ing his uncle Archbishop Bruno III (1191–93).[45]

When Engelbert was elected archbishop in 1216, he acquired a position that was much more than a religious one. The archbishops of Cologne had long been prominent political figures and landholders, especially since the fall of Duke Henry the Lion of Saxony and Bavaria in 1180, when Emperor Frederick I had granted the archbishops the duchy of Westphalia.[46] Many of Engelbert's predecessors had dedicated much of their energy to strengthening and expanding their control over the terri-tories of the archbishopric, and the title of duke seems to have suited many of them better than that of prelate.[47] Despite Caesarius of Heisterbach's best efforts to depict Engelbert as a peace-loving church-man, he too was often entangled with territorial rivals, especially local noble lineages, in disputes that made him look anything but saintly.[48]

Like many other bishops and archbishops in the early thirteenth century, Engelbert was especially interested in acquiring the advocacies for the churches and religious communities in his archdiocese.[49] In 1216, for example, while he was still archbishop-elect, Engelbert confirmed the transfer of the advocacy for a monastic estate from a nobleman into his own hands; he made it clear that he and his successors would not give the advocacy to another layman, "For we have learned from experience, and indeed it is known very clearly to all the world, how pernicious the works – or rather burdens – of advocates are in our times for all churches."[50] Five years later, Engelbert decreed for the same monastery, "Since we desire to provide for this long-oppressed church, we declare it hereafter free from the disturbances of any advocate."[51] Other religious communities received similar documents.[52] And in a charter from 1220, King

---

[44] Berner, *Kreuzzug*, 102–05; Lothmann, *Erzbischof Engelbert*, 1–5.
[45] Lothmann, *Erzbischof Engelbert*, 10–21. For his other relatives who were also archbishops, see Burkhardt, *Stab*, 35–36; Berner, *Kreuzzug*, 108–19.
[46] Weinfurter, "Erzbischof Philipp"; Arnold, *Princes*, 37–38, 101–03.
[47] Burkhardt, *Stab*, 90–96.
[48] Lothmann, *Erzbischof Engelbert*, 68–69. For Caesarius's difficulties making the decidedly unsaintly Engelbert into a saintly figure, see Jung, "Jericho."
[49] Lothmann, *Erzbischof Engelbert*, 105.
[50] *Westfälisches Urkunden-Buch*, 7:54–55, no. 122.   [51] Ibid., 7:89–90, no. 205.
[52] Lothmann, *Erzbischof Engelbert*, 105–23.

Frederick II decreed that the advocacy for a house of Premonstratensian canonesses in Dortmund would remain in his hands and those of his successors as kings and emperors; nevertheless, the text concedes that Frederick II was often in "remote places" and was therefore committing the community to Engelbert's protection to ensure that it would be safe when he was absent.[53] Thus, Engelbert appears in these sources as someone holding advocacies and providing protection in ways that secular nobles had traditionally done.

The complexity of the archbishop's relationship to advocacy is best seen at the religious community of Siegburg.[54] When Engelbert's older brother, Count Adolf III of Berg, died on crusade in Egypt in 1218, the archbishop inherited from him the advocacy for Siegburg.[55] In a privilege of 1221, he even refers to himself as "Engelbert, by the grace of God archbishop of Cologne, advocate of the monastery of Siegburg."[56] In 1223, he then issued a charter decreeing that he and his successors as archbishops had been chosen to be the advocates of Siegburg by the monastery and that they would not give the advocacy away again or appoint any subadvocates. Significantly, it also includes the statement that the *servitium* owed to the advocate, "that is, to us," would continue to be paid whenever the advocate held a court session for the monastery.[57] Here is clear evidence for the archbishop preserving the financial benefits of the advocacy after it had ceased to belong to his noble lineage.

However, sources written after Engelbert's death indicate that his possession of the advocacy for Siegburg was not as straightforward as he tried to make it appear.[58] In 1226, Duke Henry of Limburg, who claimed the vacant title of count of Berg through his wife, demanded compensation from Engelbert's successor for the advocacy as it had been held by Count Adolf III of Berg.[59] Then, in 1229, the duke, his wife and their children drew up an agreement with the monastery concerning what the advocates' rights would be, should the monastery reacquire the right to choose its own advocate.[60] Thus, Engelbert had acted less as an archbishop concerned about Siegburg's entanglements with secular advocates and more like one of the rival claimants to his brother's inheritance when

---

[53] DD F II, 3:358–59, no. 605.
[54] See Chapter 5 for the early history of Siegburg's advocacy.
[55] Berner, *Kreuzzug*, 147–57; Lothmann, *Erzbischof Engelbert*, 164–65.
[56] Wisplinghoff, ed., *Urkunden*, 194–95, no. 92. For this phrasing, see also Clauss, "Vogteibündelung," 191.
[57] Wisplinghoff, ed., *Urkunden*, 198–201, no. 95.
[58] Lothmann, *Erzbischof Engelbert*, 165–66; Berner, *Kreuzzug*, 150–51.
[59] Knipping, ed., *Regesten*, 91–92, no. 586.
[60] Wisplinghoff, ed., *Urkunden*, 207–08, no. 99.

he announced himself and subsequent archbishops to be the monastery's advocates.[61]

Although we might be inclined to question Engelbert's motivations, he had nevertheless received from Pope Honorius III strong ecclesiastical backing for his strategy of accumulating as many advocacies as he could for his archdiocese. In March of 1221, Honorius wrote to Engelbert and his suffragans on the subject and began with a noteworthy statement about the role of the advocate: "If the advocates of churches gave heed to the meaning of the title, as they ought, they would be zealous, on account of reverence for the heavenly advocate [i.e., Christ], ... to support those churches with good deeds and to defend them with strength."[62] Borrowing from the bull *Ad abolendam*, he then laments that advocates plunder ecclesiastical estates like thieves and insists that they should "be content with the just payments established from antiquity and rest from their molestations of churches."[63] He ends with an impressive rhetorical flourish:

But if, by chance, they should not acquiesce to your warnings, lest Peter's medicinal sword should seem to be dull with rust in your hand, you should aim forth against them according to the quantity and quality of their errors and cause them to return ... to the rigor of ecclesiastical discipline, so that the churches might recover from their oppression.

Two weeks later, in another letter to Engelbert and his suffragans, Honorius added a more specific suggestion:

[I]f it should happen that any advocacies become vacant, you should expressly forbid the churches, to which they pertain, from presuming to bestow them [again], but they should take care to adapt them for their own use, ... because the ministry (*ministerium*) of advocates of this sort, which is known to have been provided for the tranquility of churches, has invariably been turned toward churches' persecution through their usurpations.[64]

Thus, Engelbert, who had proven himself a powerful rival to local nobles in the struggle to control church advocacies, had papal support for limiting those same nobles' advocatial rights. As archbishop of Cologne, he was therefore in an unusually strong position to assert his right to intervene in any disputes over advocacies within his archdiocese – including the one for Essen.

---

[61] Lothmann, *Erzbischof Engelbert*, 166–67. For the subsequent history of the advocacy for Siegburg, see Lau, "Kampf."

[62] Lacomblet, *Urkundenbuch*, 2:51, no. 93. See also *Westfälisches Urkunden-Buch*, 5:139–40, no. 288. For Christ as advocate, see the Introduction.

[63] For the bull *Ad abolendam*, see Chapter 8.

[64] *Westfälisches Urkunden-Buch*, 5:141, no. 291. For the term *ministerium*, see Chapter 1.

The Importance of Honor – and Money

As noted above, Caesarius of Heisterbach reports that the abbess and canonesses of Essen traveled to Cologne on multiple occasions to complain about Count Frederick of Isenberg, first to Engelbert's predecessor as archbishop and then to Engelbert himself. The latter initially did nothing. According to the *Life*, familial love (*amor cognationis*) for his cousin Frederick led the archbishop to turn a blind eye toward any advocatial abuses.[65] Indeed, Engelbert and Frederick seem to have been on good terms for much of the archbishop's prelacy.[66] However, when the community at Essen involved Pope Honorius III and Emperor Frederick II in the matter, Engelbert could no longer ignore the situation: "He neither dared to, nor wanted to, neglect the injuries to the imperial church any longer and warned the count very earnestly, but he made no progress."[67] Caesarius explains that the archbishop continued to seek a solution and "offered him [Count Frederick] a fixed annual payment from his own income, provided that he was willing to make use of the advocacy lawfully."[68] Another chronicle reports that the archbishop promised "to enrich him with properties from his own [the archbishop's] patrimony."[69] Both texts agree that Frederick refused, setting the stage for the violent final act between count and archbishop.

Caesarius offers two different explanations for why Frederick rejected Engelbert's offer of an annual payment in return for the count tempering his advocatial demands at Essen. On the one hand, quoting the Bible, he states that Frederick did not accept, "because wisdom will not enter into a malevolent spirit."[70] However, he follows this statement immediately by explaining that "Frederick, discerning in the prelate's purpose that he wanted to disinherit (*exheredare*) him, complained to his friends and relatives."

At the center of scholarly interpretations of Engelbert's murder has long been the question of whether the archbishop had been initially reluctant to challenge his relative but was forced to do so by the pope and emperor, or whether he saw the pope and emperor's involvement as an excuse to seize the advocacy for Essen to advance his own territorial strategies for the church of Cologne.[71] Caesarius's use of the word *exheredare* strongly suggests that he thought the latter was a plausible explanation.[72] The verb is a surprising one for Caesarius to choose, because as the numerous legitimate imperial privileges for Essen attest,

---

[65] Caesarius, "Leben," 251, II.1.   [66] Finger, "Tod," 26.
[67] Caesarius, "Leben," 251, II.1.   [68] Ibid.   [69] *Emonis Chronicon*, 509.
[70] Caesarius, "Leben," 251, II.1 (Wis 1:4).   [71] Lothmann, *Erzbischof Engelbert*, 387.
[72] On this point, see also Wisplinghoff, "Kampf," 327–32 (esp. p. 329, n. 104).

the community had the right to choose its own advocate. Frederick therefore could not claim to hold the advocacy legitimately by hereditary right.[73] Nevertheless, even a Cistercian monk was willing to accept that the count's lineage had possessed the advocacy for enough generations by the early 1220s that it was for all intents and purposes a part of their inheritance.

As Caesarius notes, Frederick's fears about the archbishop disinheriting him led the count to seek the support of his friends and relatives. At this point, Caesarius puts an extraordinary speech into the advocate's mouth. It begins, "'I am,' he said, 'a count. I have land and strong castles. Two of my brothers are bishops. Duke Walram [of Limburg], the most powerful man in our land, is my father-in-law; his son is going to possess the county of Berg. I am the cousin of Count Dietrich of Cleves.'"[74] After establishing his standing in noble society in this way, Frederick tells his listeners, "[Archbishop Engelbert] has inflicted injuries on [you] and very many others; he has struck and offended [you] ... I will enrich all of you, I will protect and elevate you."[75] In this way, the count successfully rallied around him the group of conspirators who would plot the attack on the archbishop.

Rank and honor emerge from this speech as key factors in the conflict. By having Frederick of Isenberg insist that he was a prominent nobleman with extensive lands, strong castles and many high-status relatives, Caesarius makes it clear that the count considered himself of equal rank with his cousin, the archbishop of Cologne.[76] Engelbert therefore did not have the status or authority to disinherit him. By claiming that many other members of the local elite had also suffered from Engelbert's abuses of power, Caesarius's Count Frederick further suggests that the archbishop was not treating any of them with the respect they deserved. Honor was central to the noble ethos of this period, and any slights to one's honor could justifiably be met with violence.[77]

That said, we must be careful not to let the explanation for Engelbert's murder become too detached from the issue of advocacy. While Caesarius's description of Frederick's distrust of the archbishop is plausible, it is important to remember that Engelbert initially offered to pay the count in return for his being less aggressive as advocate of Essen. As noted previously, the early thirteenth century was a period when prelates and religious communities were increasingly offering advocates money or

[73] Ibid., 327–28.   [74] Caesarius, "Leben," 251–52, II.1.   [75] Ibid., 252, II.1.
[76] For the importance of rank in this society, see the articles in Peltzer, ed., *Rank*. See also Stieldorf, "Klöster," 83–85.
[77] For the importance of honor in this society, see Kaeuper, *Chivalry*, 52–56; Görich, *Ehre*, 2–11.

property if they consented to give up their advocatial rights.[78] In the majority of such cases, we know about these offers, because the advocates accepted them and the agreement was confirmed by a charter. The story of Frederick's refusal may hint that there was more tension in these negotiations than is apparent in the documentary evidence. The many conflicts between Duke Frederick II of Austria (1230–46) and the nobility in his lands, conflicts caused at least in part by ducal efforts to limit the advocatial rights of local nobles, may offer a parallel example of advocates pushing back on a powerful duke's interference in their traditional rights.[79] Perhaps other nobles were equally reluctant to part with their advocacies but – unlike Frederick – chose to accept the offer of money or other properties out of financial necessity or fear of losing the advocacy by force.

Frederick's refusal suggests that his position as advocate of Essen was valuable to him for reasons that extend beyond rank and honor. Two sources confirm this impression. They are referred to as "advocacy rolls" (*Vogteirollen*) in modern scholarship, and both concern Count Frederick of Isenberg's advocatial rights. One, known as the "small" roll, is the older of the two and was written shortly before 1220. The lengthier of the two, the "large" roll, dates from around 1220.[80] Both were therefore produced in the midst of the conflict over the Essen advocacy and provide clear evidence that the count was greatly interested in enumerating his advocatial rights at this pivotal moment.

The smaller and older of the two documents lists thirty-three estates for which the count held advocatial rights. In addition, it includes a list of the payments owed to him by the freemen in twenty-nine locations. Significantly, the highest amounts are from places belonging to the community at Essen.[81] The second of the two rolls begins with the scribe explaining the reason for his work: "So that no one can do injury to the count or his heirs, he had this written down."[82] Then follows, "This is the sum total of the [estates] belonging to Essen, which lie under my advocatial care (*sub mea ... advocatiali sollicitudine*); every year, they pay the compensation owed to me, plus exactions." The list of estates follows. This roll also mentions the count's advocatial rights over the properties of other religious communities, but significantly more than half of the total number are Essen properties.[83] All of this leaves little doubt that the

---

[78] See Chapter 8.   [79] See Chapter 8 and Reichert, *Landesherrschaft*.
[80] Leenen, "Vogteirollen," 283–85, no. A16. As noted in Chapter 6, sources that provide nobles' perspectives on their advocatial rights are rare around 1220.
[81] Ibid.   [82] "Vogteirollen des Stiftes Essen," 20. See also *Grosse Vogteirolle*.
[83] Leenen, "Vogteirollen."

advocacy for Essen was a major source of income for Count Frederick of Isenberg.

Thus, when Archbishop Engelbert of Cologne offered to pay the count (to buy him off, to be more precise), Frederick of Isenberg clearly saw this as a threat to an important and profitable right – especially if he thought (as Caesarius suggests) that this was the first step toward the archbishop seizing the Essen advocacy from him. It is unsurprising, therefore, that the count complained to his friends and relatives, many of them disgruntled local nobles who also feared the rising power of the duke-archbishop. According to one chronicle, "many counts conspired in his death," a sure sign that the advocacy for Essen was only one flashpoint in Engelbert's relations with his neighbors.[84] Whether Frederick's intention was to have the archbishop killed, or whether he simply wanted to put pressure on him, the count saw himself in need of allies, because he was locked in an increasingly tense competition over a set of rights that he did not want to lose. When Engelbert proposed a new round of discussions, Frederick had apparently decided already that he was done negotiating. Instead, his men attacked the archbishop while he was traveling and killed him.[85]

The Aftermath

Neither the archbishop's assassination nor the count's execution the following year settled the question of who ought to possess advocatial rights at Essen. In the immediate aftermath of Frederick's death, King Henry (VII) appointed a man named Arnold of Gymnich to hold the advocacy, evidence that the ruler had asserted royal claims over the position of advocate for Essen.[86] It would pass through various hands during the remainder of the century; in 1282, King Rudolf I of Habsburg would give possession of the advocacy to a canon of the church of Aachen – and would also order a thorough investigation into advocatial rights at Essen, a clear sign that the advocacy remained a vexed issue.[87] Eighty-five years after Engelbert's assassination in 1310, there continued to be so many lingering questions about the advocacy – including "about

---

[84] *Emonis Chronicon*, 509.   [85] Caesarius, "Leben," 259–63, II.7.
[86] *Essener Urkundenbuch*, 32–33, nos. 52–53. For the history of the advocacy in the century after Engelbert's death, see Leenen, "Stift Essen," 222–29. Engelbert's death meant that the advocacies he possessed as the last male member of the comital lineage of Berg also became vacant. For the fate of the advocacy of Werden, see Finger, "Kloster," 101–05; Gerchow, "Äbtissinnen," 73 and 78. For the fate of the advocacy of Siegburg, see Clauss, "Vogteibündelung," 191–93.
[87] Wisplinghoff, "Kampf," 328–29. Gerchow, "Äbtissinnen," 73–78. See also *Essener Urkundenbuch*, 63, no. 131 and Const., 3:320, no. 333.

the rights and dues of the same advocacy" – that the German king Henry VII had to intervene in an attempt to clarify the situation.[88]

Archbishop Engelbert's successors, meanwhile, continued his efforts to acquire other advocacies and to eliminate noble advocates in the archdiocese. Archbishop Conrad I (1238–61), for example, purchased various monastic advocacies from nobles as a way to strengthen his position inside the archbishopric.[89] By the thirteenth century, competition over advocacy had become too entrenched in the Rhineland and many other parts of Europe to be slowed by the dramatic events of November 1225.

Interestingly, in the stories recounting the miracles he performed posthumously, Archbishop Engelbert did not dislike all advocates, despite what Count Frederick of Isenberg and his henchmen had done to him. According to Caesarius of Heisterbach, Engelbert cured Herman, an advocate of Cologne, of his pain after Herman prayed, "'O lord archbishop, whom I loved above everyone else and who while living loved me in return even more, I ask of your kindness that you free me from this disease.'" When Herman did not immediately feel cured, he reminded Engelbert again "'that I served you and always loved you.'" This finally did the trick.[90] The whole story is a less-than-subtle reminder on Caesarius's part of what ecclesiastics thought to be the proper role of an advocate: to love and to serve.

Conclusion

If Count Frederick of Isenberg did not quite love and serve the abbess and canonesses of Essen in a way that Caesarius approved, he nevertheless cannot shoulder all the blame for what happened in 1225. The count, the canonesses of Essen, the archbishop of Cologne, the pope and the emperor all helped to set the fateful events in motion. There are at least two sides to every story. In this case, one can choose to view the situation like this: Engelbert, in his role as archbishop and head of the religious life in his archdiocese, followed the pope's and emperor's will and sought to limit Frederick's advocatial rights at Essen in order to free the community from his harshest forms of oppression. But if we look at this from Count Frederick's perspective, it is just as easy to argue that Engelbert, in his role as territorial prince, used the pope's and emperor's letters as justification to try to disinherit the count, strip him of an important source of income and weaken a local rival. The truth (always a dangerous term for historians) probably can be found somewhere in

---

[88] Const., 4:366–68, no. 420.   [89] Prößler, *Erzstift Köln*, 29–30.
[90] Caesarius, "Leben," 306–07, no. 40.

the middle, in that gray area where I have argued we must always go searching for the inner workings of church advocacy. No one in this story can be labeled the agent of public authority and good government fighting the forces of feudal lordship and private power. Everyone was looking to gain an advantage, in one way or another, by intervening in a dispute over the rights of the advocate.

10 Widening the Lens

It is time to take a step back. As the previous chapters have shown, disputes between advocates and religious communities were commonplace during the period from 1000 to 1250. While the murder of an archbishop is an especially dramatic example, numerous other conflicts could be analyzed at the same level of detail as Archbishop Engelbert of Cologne's clash with Count Frederick of Isenberg. However, we need to keep moving. The decades around 1250 are only the midpoint of this book. Another 500 years of disputes between advocates and local communities of various kinds still lie ahead of us. But before turning to the second half-millennium of my argument, it is necessary to first consider the question of why conflicts over advocacy had become such an intractable problem in many parts of Europe by the mid-thirteenth century.

I have already offered pieces of an answer. When religious communities granted secular elites access to their properties as their advocates in order to be provided with justice and protection, they gave them the opportunity to exploit that access for their own benefit. As advocates demanded more and more money, used the rights and properties of religious houses to support their own patron–client relationships and came to see their advocacies as hereditary, they steadily widened the gulf between their perception of the role and religious communities' expectations. Churches responded by turning to prelates, popes and kings for support in limiting advocatial authority: They sought to regulate how much they had to pay for protection, gain more control over the appointment of advocates and buy back their advocacies. Conflict frequently ensued because nobles had come to see advocacies as too valuable to their own power and influence to cede control of them without a fight. As a result, religious communities quickly learned that weakening or ending advocacy was not easy. Someone needed to access ecclesiastical properties to provide justice and protection, and by the thirteenth century, the advocate was too entrenched in local societies for the position to simply be eliminated.

In the Introduction, I suggested that *wrassling round* was a better way to understand all of this than such terms as feudalism, lordship, government, officeholding, bureaucracy and state-building. The phrase is not meant to be a technical term, of course, but an evocative one; it is intended to downplay the distinctive, "medieval" elements of advocatial relationships and to call attention to the more general problems that arise when property holders need to rely on someone else to provide justice and protection. This chapter builds on that point, contextualizing advocates' actions by drawing on evidence from both the ancient and modern periods in order to reflect more critically on advocates' motivations. Central to my argument here is that different advocates saw different kinds of opportunities in church advocacy. It oversimplifies the role of the advocate to assume that every noble had the same goals and pursued the same set of strategies in their attempts to profit from their advocacies. By taking a step back and thinking more broadly about how protection and justice work, we can better understand why secular elites were willing to invest so much of their time and energy fighting for their advocatial rights.

The Face of a Tyrant?

In March of 1287, the papal legate Bishop John of Tusculum presided over a church council in the town of Würzburg. King Rudolf I of Habsburg was also present, and the attendance of not only prelates but also many of the secular imperial princes from across the German kingdom means that the gathering doubled as a formal session of the imperial court.[1] On this august occasion, one of the numerous topics of discussion was church advocacy. The twenty-second canon issued by the council in the legate's name, "On Church Advocates" (*De Advocatis Ecclesiarum*), decries a familiar set of problems: "Some, who declare themselves the advocates of churches, ... not only do not defend those churches from oppressions, they also violently seize the properties of those churches ... And if the advocate should have four or more sons, ... they all count themselves advocates in plundering the churches' properties."[2] The canon goes on to insist that advocates, "whatever preeminent status they might be, should be content with the same rights, which have always been allowed to them or their predecessors ... And they should be eager to defend the churches, for which they are advocates, and to support them to the best of their ability." Otherwise, they should be removed from their position and, if necessary, excommunicated.

---

[1] Regesta Imperii Online, RI VI,1 no. 2063a.   [2] *Concilia Germaniae*, 3:730.

If we take Abbot Abbo of Fleury's *Collection of Canons* from the mid-990s as the earliest evidence for a prelate complaining about advocates who acted as plunderers rather than defenders of churches, the problems decried at the Council of Würzburg had been recurring for almost 300 years by the time this canon was written.[3] Since 1000, there had been a steady stream of decrees issued by kings and emperors addressing advocatial abuses at specific religious communities and within their realms more generally – as well as hundreds, if not thousands, of pronouncements by popes and prelates seeking to protect churches from their advocates. Nevertheless, conflicts between nobles and religious communities over advocacies continued unabated. As a result, it can be tempting to generalize about all the accusations of abuse and tyranny and to imagine that every advocate was basically the same. But if we are to better situate advocates within the broader framework of the history of protection and justice, we must set such generalizations aside and examine how individual nobles utilized church advocacies to advance their own interests.

Count Henry II of Wolfratshausen has already appeared on several occasions in the preceding pages. As advocate of the monastery of Tegernsee in Bavaria in the 1150s, he came under sharp criticism for his abuses, not only from the religious community but also Emperor Frederick I. The author of the prose *Passion of St. Quirinus*, writing at Tegernsee in the 1170s, dedicated significant space to Henry's misdeeds in the section of his work concerning how the saint punished the monastery's tyrannical advocates. According to the *Passion*, the count plotted the assassination of the abbot, seized shipments of wine intended for the community, demanded excessive exactions, treated the community's tenants unfairly when exercising justice and on one occasion gave his men free rein to eat, drink and revel in the monastery – including in the chapel, where they sang rowdy songs, to the horror of the praying monks.[4] It was seven days after this last incident that Henry was visited by a man in his dreams, who said, "Count Henry, rise, make satisfaction to God."[5] Realizing this was a sign that his days on earth were coming to an end, the advocate rushed to give property to Tegernsee and other monasteries to assist his soul before he died.

Not all of this can be dismissed as the overblown rhetoric of a hagiographer. Emperor Frederick I wrote a letter to the count urging him to refrain from committing any violence against the monastery, after Henry had sought to meddle in the election of a new abbot.[6] Moreover,

---

[3] See Chapter 4.   [4] *Passio*, 283–86.   [5] Ibid., 286.
[6] *Tegernseer Briefsammlung*, 230, no. 198.

the emperor's 1157 privilege for Tegernsee, in which he limited advocatial exactions and the advocates' judicial rights over the community, leaves little doubt that Count Henry had been seeking to benefit from the advocacy well beyond what the abbot and monks deemed his proper rights.[7] Thus, to read all of the Tegernsee sources together is to get the clear impression that Count Henry II of Wolfratshausen was a paradigmatic example of the bad advocate.

Only a few kilometers down the road from Tegernsee, however, the Augustinian canons and canonesses at the community of Diessen had an entirely different opinion of Count Henry II of Wolfratshausen. Henry was not the advocate for Diessen; rather, he belonged to the family that had founded this religious house. His parents, acting in concert with some of his more distant relatives, had established and endowed the community at Diessen in the 1120s.[8] They were buried there, as was his older brother, and he would choose to be buried there too. Unlike Tegernsee, for which Henry made only a single donation on his deathbed (apparently to try to make amends at the last minute for his abuses, if the *Passion of St. Quirinus* is to be believed), the canons and canonesses at Diessen received several gifts from him during his lifetime – the first coming more than a decade before his death.[9] In short, this community had a very different relationship with Count Henry than the monks at Tegernsee did.

Just how different that relationship was can be seen in a manuscript illumination produced at Diessen during the opening years of the thirteenth century (see Figure 10.1). It can be found in a codex that contains many of the community's most important texts: a copy of the Augustinian Rule, records of the house's property transactions and necrologies preserving the names of the community's dead as well as the names of donors to the community.[10] In the midst of the records of donations and exchanges, there is a half-page image of Mary enthroned, with Christ on her lap, surrounded by four members of the noble family that founded Diessen.[11] The most prominent of these four figures, the one who is facing the Virgin and Child and presenting them with a ring, is Count Henry II of Wolfratshausen. The reason for his preeminent position is explained by the text copied on the half-page below the image, which is a record of two separate donations Henry made to the community,

---

[7] DD F I, 274–76, no. 160. See also Chapter 7.
[8] Schütz, "Geschlecht," 49–59. Henry's cousins in the lineage of the counts of Andechs held the advocacy for Diessen: Lyon, "Noble Lineages."
[9] Schlögl, ed., *Traditionen*, 9–11, nos. 6–7; 21–23, no. 16; 25–26, nos. 17–18; and 28–31, no. 21. For his donation to Tegernsee: Acht, ed., *Traditionen*, 218–20, no. 290.
[10] Munich, Bayerische Staatsbibliothek, Clm 1018.   [11] Ibid., fol. 35v.

Figure 10.1 The face of a tyrant? Count Henry II of Wolfratshausen presenting a ring to the Virgin Mary. Bayerische Staatsbibliothek München, Clm 1018, fol. 35v

including one of his "principal estate" in Diessen itself.[12] Thus, at Diessen, Henry was not remembered as a tyrannical advocate but as the house's most generous benefactor.[13]

---

[12] Schlögl, ed., *Traditionen*, 11, no. 7.
[13] Because the count was childless, he made donations to several religious communities on his deathbed: Oefele, *Grafen*, 155–58; Dendorfer, "Verwandte," 80–86. As a result, he

The strikingly disparate pictures of Count Henry II of Wolfratshausen that emerge from the sources written at these two religious communities provide invaluable evidence for understanding why some advocates acted the way they did and sought to exploit their advocatial rights. No matter how much the monks of Tegernsee might have wanted Henry to be a useful advocate, one who served the monastery as a faithful official and committed himself to protecting its interests, there is no evidence to suggest that the count viewed the monks of Tegernsee as belonging to the network of friends, allies and supporters who were central to his own power and authority. His family's foundation of Diessen was much more significant to him as a religious community because it was there that he intended to be buried, that prayers would be said for his soul and that his memory as a righteous man would be preserved. Whether or not he had a good relationship with the abbot and monks of Tegernsee was not as important – in this life or the next. For Henry, the advocacy for Tegernsee was therefore first and foremost a source of income, to be exploited as much as possible for the benefit of himself and his followers.

The image of Count Henry II of Wolfratshausen preserved in the Diessen manuscript allows us to see, with unusual clarity, how one monastery's abusive advocate could be another's kind patron. Other examples of this phenomenon include Count Dietrich of Sommerschenburg (d. 1207), who as advocate for the monastery of Pegau imprisoned the abbot and usurped the community's minting rights.[14] He had a very different relationship with the monastery of Zschillen, which had been founded by his father and was the burial site of his parents; he and his brother donated several properties to this religious community.[15] Because Dietrich belonged to the Wettins, one of the foremost noble lineages in Saxony, he had connections to other regional monasteries as well.[16] In contrast, he likely saw his newly acquired advocacy for Pegau, which was not a community with long-standing ties to his family, principally as a source of revenue.

The significant gap that could exist between a religious community's interests and those of a prominent noble advocate explains an extraordinary story told about the advocacy of the monastery of St. Gall. In the early thirteenth century, Duke Berthold V of Zähringen reportedly

---

was remembered in the necrologies of several ecclesiastical houses: Oefele, *Grafen*, 26; Borgolte, "Stiftergedenken," 268. The relevant section of the oldest Tegernsee necrology is lost, meaning we do not know if or how his memory was initially preserved there.

[14] See Chapter 6.

[15] CDS I A, 3:98–99, no. 124. Dietrich would also be buried there: Pätzold, *Wettiner*, 209.

[16] *Chronica Sereni Montis*, 190–91, 196–97. See also Lyon, *Princely Brothers*, 47–48, 146; Pätzold, *Wettiner*, 132, 169–70 and 324–25.

offered 4,000 marks of silver to the monks of St. Gall and another 400
marks of silver to the community's most trusted ministerials, if they were
to grant him and his heirs the advocacy.[17] He also wanted the monastery
to confirm that the advocacy could never be taken from him. As the
St. Gall chronicler Conrad reports, "The abbot, disregarding the counsel
of the senior monks, rather agreed more with the ministerials, who feared
the power of the said duke," and refused the offer.[18] While it is noteworthy that the cloistered monks were apparently more than willing to accept
this deal, the ministerials' hesitation is more revealing. The dukes of
Zähringen had been accumulating church advocacies across the southwest of the German kingdom for a century by the time of Berthold V's
offer, and already had a well-established monastery that was
a multigenerational family burial center and prayer site.[19] The ministerials of St. Gall were therefore likely right to see Berthold V's efforts to
acquire the advocacy as being more about *potentia* – a power grab – than
about his desire to be a useful advocate.[20]

Nobles who viewed the position of advocate in largely exploitative
terms conform well to modern arguments about the many different
types of actors who seek to profit from a market rooted in the need for
protection.[21] Monasteries and other religious communities were substantial landholders, but in the regions that are the focus of this study, they
could not rely on rulers and well-developed governmental institutions to
protect those properties for them. As a result, they either had to provide
protection themselves with the help of their own dependents –
a possibility, but not one that aligned easily with Christian attitudes
about bloodshed – or enter the market and find someone else with

[17] Konrad of Pfäfers, *Casuum*, 169. Roughly two decades earlier, Count Dedo of Groitzsch
had reportedly paid 4,000 silver marks to Emperor Frederick I to obtain the march of
Lower Lusatia after his brother's death: Pätzold, *Wettiner*, 252 and 292. That the
advocacy of St. Gall had roughly the same value as this march highlights how valuable
the advocacies for prominent monasteries could be in this period.
[18] Konrad of Pfäfers, *Casuum*, 169. " ... *qui potenciam dicti ducis formidabant*." See also
Parlow, *Zähringer*, 378, no. 574; Zotz, *Zähringer*, 168. For an abbot needing to consider
the views of both his monks and his community's ministerials in situations such as this
one, see Schneidmüller, "Konsensuale Herrschaft," 56–59.
[19] See Chapter 5 and Zotz, *Zähringer*. See also Lyon, "Noble Lineages."
[20] According to the so-called "Reichssteuerliste" for Swabia drawn up in 1241 (Const., 3:1–
6), Emperor Frederick II expected to receive 100 marks annually for possessing the
advocacy for the town of St. Gall. However, extant sources do not indicate how much
St. Gall's monastic advocate was paid annually, meaning it is impossible to know how
long it would have taken the duke to recover his initial outlay if he was content with only
the customary advocatial payments.
[21] See the Introduction for more on this point. I take my argument here from, among other
works, Konrad and Skaperdas, "Market"; Mehlum, Moene, and Torvik, "Plunder";
Volkov, *Violent Entrepreneurs*.

sufficient power and influence to do it for them. However, once nobles were invited in as advocates to fulfill this role, religious communities often struggled to manage these "violent entrepreneurs," who made the position hereditary and extracted as much as they could when they accessed ecclesiastical estates.[22]

Controlling the people who provide protection is a universal challenge. One scholar analyzing the various violent groups who sought to profit from the absence of robust public authority after the fall of the Soviet Union notes, "Behind the differences in their origin and their legal and moral status, one could notice a puzzling similarity in their patterns of action and practice at the emerging markets. They intimidated, protected, gathered information, settled disputes, gave guarantees, enforced contracts, and taxed."[23] This is an apt description of many advocates as well, which helps us move their activities outside the standard paradigm of feudal lordship and to understand them in a more global historical context of organized violence by public, quasi-public and private actors.[24]

I am not proposing that scholars of medieval Europe adopt the term "violent entrepreneurs." Rather, much like *wrassling round*, I employ it here to escape stale teleologies and to reframe the question of why protection and justice proved to be such vexing issues for centuries. Violent entrepreneurship, more so than feudal lordship, acknowledges the agency of those nobles who chose to exploit their advocacies in every way possible – and who had little, if any, incentive to accept regulation. To see an advocate and his men as akin to an urban street gang (an uncomfortable comparison for many readers, I suspect) can help us to recognize more general patterns in their behavior. The subadvocate, for example, who is typically analyzed in a legal and constitutional framework as an advocate's local representative, begins to look more like the client in a patron–client relationship; his subadvocacy – and the local resource extraction that came with it – becomes a reward for a trusted follower who had earned his own source of revenue because of his loyalty.[25] This perspective offers insight into the countless complaints against subadvocates in our sources: They were the ones who were actually accessing ecclesiastical properties, physically exercising justice and finding creative new ways to increase their income through novel exactions. As long as

[22] For this term, see the Introduction.
[23] Volkov, "Political Economy," 709. For a similar point, see Joireman, *Government*, 121–23.
[24] My argument here also draws inspiration from Carocci and Collavini, "Cost"; McHaffie, "Law"; Bosl, "Schutz."
[25] Cf. Venkatesh, *Gang Leader*, 48–49; Stephenson, *Gangs*, 99–100. For views of subadvocates that take a more legal-constitutional perspective on their roles, see Clauss, *Untervogtei*; Scheyhing, *Eide*, 208–13. More nuanced is Clauss, "Vogteibündelung."

they continued to respect the authority of the "boss" advocate, they could innovate and keep the profits.[26]

More than a half-century ago, Frederic C. Lane observed,

> [A]n armed robber renders no service by his robbery; but the police that protect us from robbers, and the courts that protect the rights of the citizen even against the police, do, it is commonly agreed, render a service. Difficulties begin when we consider the racketeer who collects payments for "protection" against a violence that he himself threatens, and who actually supplies a sort of "black-market" protection in return, suppressing rival gangsters. Such borderline cases may not be important in analyzing the economic life of modern America, but they are far from negligible when we consider the violence-using and violence-controlling enterprises of Europe during the millennium between A.D. 700 and 1700. Which princes were rendering the service of police? Which were racketeers or even plunderers? A plunderer could be in effect the chief of police as soon as he regularized his "take," adapted it to the capacity to pay, defended his preserve against other plunderers, and maintained his territorial monopoly long enough for custom to make it legitimate.[27]

This is an apt description of the gray area in which Count Henry II of Wolfratshausen and his local agents operated. The author of the *Passion of St. Quirinus* concedes that Henry defended the monastery of Tegernsee from others – but mainly in order to use it as a source of plunder for himself and his followers.[28] Moreover, his conflict with the abbot of Tegernsee in the mid-1150s concerned his efforts to regularize what the monastery saw as the illegitimate expansion of his judicial authority and income. Critiques of advocates at many other religious communities suggest comparable situations; the annual advocatial payments owed by many churches had their roots in ad hoc exactions that had gradually become fixed and customary.[29] Following Lane and scholarship on violent entrepreneurs, I see all of this as conforming to much broader patterns in the history of protection and justice in Europe.

Count Henry II of Wolfratshausen, and other nobles who viewed their role as advocate as one that allowed them to squeeze as much profit as possible from a church's rights and properties, earned the label of tyrant for good reasons; they showed little interest in acting like accountable officials.[30] Nevertheless, as the relationship between Count Henry and the religious community at Diessen shows, advocates of this sort were not universally hated. Their violence was targeted and strategic. Moreover,

---

[26] Cf. Gambetta, *Sicilian Mafia*, 65–68. See also Vinci, "Like Worms," 321–27.

[27] Lane, "Economic," 403. See also Tilly, "War Making."

[28] For another example of an advocate threatening a potential rival in order to maintain his influence at a monastery, see Lampert of Hersfeld, *Annals*, 145–47.

[29] See Chapters 6 and 7.   [30] Lyon, "Tyrants."

not every advocacy was treated in such a transparently extractive fashion. In many ways, the case of Count Henry II of Wolfratshausen and Tegernsee is an extreme one from one end of the spectrum of advocatial behavior. Other nobles saw in their advocacies very different sorts of opportunities.

Hearts and Minds

Count William III of Nevers (1147–61) – at least as he is characterized by the monk Hugh of Poitiers in his history of the monastery of Vézelay in Burgundy – is representative of another type of advocate: one who sought to ingratiate himself with a religious community's dependents. Vézelay had been founded in 859. Three centuries later, it was an important pilgrimage site and a major landholder in its region; Bernard of Clairvaux even preached the Second Crusade there in 1146.[31] Like the *Passion of St. Quirinus*, Hugh's chronicle is a rich source for information on his religious community's struggles with its hereditary advocates, the counts of Nevers, across multiple generations. The work survives in a manuscript from the second half of the twelfth century, which also contains (among other material) a cartulary preserving some of the most important documents concerning the community's property rights – and its advocates.[32]

At the time of Hugh's writing in the mid-twelfth century, the monks of Vézelay were mired in a dispute with the counts of Nevers over advocatial rights.[33] In 1150–51, despite the abbot's numerous attempts to negotiate a settlement, Count William III and his men repeatedly attacked and plundered the monastery's lands, and Hugh of Poitiers refers to William as a tyrant throughout his narrative of this and other events.[34] Although Hugh clearly had a low opinion of the count, he nevertheless describes him as delivering a remarkably clever speech to the burghers of Vézelay in

---

[31] For the monastery in this period, see Romano, "Julian of Vézelay"; Hugh of Poitiers, *Vézelay Chronicle*, 1–14.

[32] For Latin editions of both Hugh's chronicle and the cartulary: *Monumenta Vizeliacensia*. For English translations of both: Hugh of Poitiers, *Vézelay Chronicle*. The manuscript has been dated to ca. 1170 (*Monumenta Vizeliacensia*, xix). See also Ward, "Memorializing."

[33] The abbot at this time, Ponce (1138–61), was the brother of Abbot Peter the Venerable of Cluny (1122–56), who had briefly served as prior of Vézelay before becoming abbot. This is a reminder that, although there is little direct evidence for advocates at Cluny, many of the monks there would have been familiar with advocacy. Cf. West, "Monks," 399. For advocacy and Cluny, see also Chapter 3; Constable, "Baume and Cluny," 422; Wibald of Stablo, *Briefbuch*, 2:351–54, no. 165.

[34] *Monumenta Vizeliacensia*, 425, 517 and 530 (Hugh of Poitiers, *Vézelay Chronicle*, 168, 233 and 246). For Vézelay's conflicts with the count, see also Ward, "Parchment" and Bouchard, *Sword*, 216–17.

the midst of this conflict. It was the monastery that possessed the town of Vézelay during this period, and disputes between the monks and the burghers over rights within the town were a frequent source of friction.[35] According to Hugh, Count William saw this friction as an opportunity to gain more influence. Realizing that he might be able to win the town of Vézelay to his side,

The count began: "You see how the abbot alone strives to hinder the welfare of you all, though I am the legitimate advocate and guardian of this church. In disdaining to answer his calumniators before me as judge and advocate, he is in fact demanding back from me the right of justice, he is seizing what belongs to another ... What case can I mount against those plundering your goods when the abbot retains, like a tyrant, judicial competence over them? In the final analysis," he said, "it is better to exercise power than to be always seeking it. In regard to the nature, extent, and scope of our power, however, nothing can be clearer than a proven case ... It is of some importance to you, therefore, how you vote on this issue. By favoring ourselves, by sharing our power, you need have no care for the now empty prayers of the monks or the futile resources of the abbot because ... you will enjoy security for your persons and your property forever."[36]

This speech, while unquestionably Hugh's invention in its extant form, is striking. Monastic authors typically do not report that noblemen called their own abbots tyrannical. The speech is also a rare example of an ecclesiastical author openly acknowledging one of the main dangers of advocacy for a religious community: namely, that the advocate could urge the community's dependents to become his own dependents and to view him as a better choice for their landlord.

This is a significantly different understanding of advocatial authority than Count Henry II of Wolfratshausen's. The *Passion of St. Quirinus* explicitly states of Henry, "[I]n every court session he was threatening more cruelly the men of the church than his own men."[37] Emperor Frederick I's privilege of 1157 for Tegernsee likewise insists that Henry, when holding court, "ought to impose correction and punishment without hatred."[38] In contrast, Hugh of Poitiers describes Count William III of Nevers as an advocate who recognized the potential advantages of providing good justice to a church's dependents. As different as these two perspectives on the advocate are, the extant sources use remarkably similar language in criticizing the counts. Both William and Henry are called tyrants by monastic authors at Vézelay and Tegernsee respectively. Emperor Frederick I's privilege for Tegernsee refers to Count Henry II's "insolence" and "violence," while Pope Anastasius IV in a letter to King

[35] Hugh of Poitiers, *Vézelay Chronicle*, 11.
[36] *Monumenta Vizeliacensia*, 428 (Hugh of Poitiers, *Vézelay Chronicle*, 173–74).
[37] *Passio*, 284. See Chapter 7 for this passage.   [38] DD F I, 274–76, no. 160.

Louis VII of France refers to Count William III as someone "who does not cease from raging against [Vézelay] with barbaric ferocity."[39] Here, we see clearly how the rhetoric of the extant sources can obscure the different strategies nobles pursued as advocates. What William is described as doing at Vézelay cannot be labeled a purely extractive protection racket based on plunder and extortion, or as an effort to squeeze everything he could from ecclesiastical property rights without any concern for the long-term impact. According to Hugh, the count offered the townspeople of Vézelay effective justice and real protection – with an eye toward winning their hearts and minds.

The situation at Vézelay aligns with a comment about organized crime supposedly made by a Neapolitan manufacturer to Max Weber: "Sir, the *Camorra* takes [ten] lire a month from me, but guarantees me security; the state takes ten times that amount, and guarantees me nothing."[40] More recent work on the Sicilian mafia confirms this impressionistic view: "[T]here are people who find it in their individual interest to buy mafia protection. While some may be victims of extortion, many others are willing customers."[41] Advocates who sought to disrupt the relationship between a religious community and that community's dependents by providing strong protection and fair justice on ecclesiastical estates were aiming to draw those dependents into their own sphere of influence. In the triangular set of ties that bound together a religious house, its dependents and its advocate, any advocatial strategy that effectively removed the religious house from the equation was bound to elicit harsh criticism from the members of that ecclesiastical community.

Modern organized crime is not the only place where we can find parallel strategies to Count William's. The fourth-century author Libanius (314–93), who spent much of his life at Antioch and Constantinople, wrote an illuminating oration on the subject of protection.[42] In it, he complains about Roman military officers profiting illicitly from local landowners in the provinces by demanding payment in return for protection. One of his specific concerns is that these men can interfere in the normal relationship between a master and his slaves. As he explains, it is not "right for a slave, if he demands justice for wrongs suffered, to look by chance to this man or that, and to present himself before anyone who is not his owner and implore his aid, while ignoring his master."[43] Libanius then expands on his point: "For [the slave] would no longer belong entirely to his master,

---

[39] *Monumenta Vizeliacensia*, 373–74, no. 61.   [40] Weber, *Economy*, 195.
[41] Gambetta, *Sicilian Mafia*, 2.
[42] For context, see Malosse, "Libanius' *Orations*," 86–87.
[43] Libanius, *Selected Orations*, 2:519, 47.21. I thank my colleague Jonathan Hall for suggesting some improvements to the published translation.

but he would present his protector with the lion's share in any division of his loyalty and personal services." His next comment is even more revealing:

"Well," it may be said, "what happens if the landlord is incapable of doing the job, and some more powerful personage is needed?" Then let the peasant tell the master, and he tell this other. You, my man, make your request to him, and let him pass it on. You would get help in this way, and he would suffer no harm, since the order of precedence in such matters remains firmly fixed . . . It is a different matter for the masters to make a contribution . . . for the sake of their tenants and for the tenants to do so to their masters' hurt. In the first case, the possessors are confirmed in their position; in the second, their confidence is undermined and it is as though the rot has set in.[44]

Libanius' complaints about military men upsetting the traditional master–slave/landowner–peasant relationship by sidelining the master/landowner are unusual for their frankness. I know of no ecclesiastical author of the eleventh to thirteenth centuries who expresses the advocate–church–dependent dynamic in quite the same way. Hugh of Poitiers, in the speech he places in the mouth of Count William III of Nevers in his history of Vézelay, may come the closest.

That having been said, once one recognizes this as a strategy that advocates could have pursued, some of the critiques leveled against them in the sources make more sense. In the early 1040s, the monk Andrew of Fleury complained about "a certain advocate ... [who] under the pretense of protection ruined [a] property very wickedly." Specifically, "he forced the dependents of St. Benedict within the halls of his house, [and] presiding over the court, issued public judgments against them. He attacked [them] with cunning tricks and then, having ripped away the monks' rights, joined [them] little by little to his will."[45] As at Vézelay, the law court appears here as a place where an advocate could sever the ties between a church and its dependents. This must have been one reason why, at the monastery of Garsten in Austria in the mid-twelfth century, the community insisted that "the abbot himself or his authorized messenger ought to sit at the advocate's side" when the advocate held court.[46] Other monasteries were equally insistent that advocates hold court at a site of their own choice, not within the confines of the advocate's own castle.[47] Was all of this solely out of a concern that the

---

[44] Libanius, *Selected Orations*, 2:518–21, 47.22. For this passage, see MacMullen, *Corruption*, 169; Bond, "Corrupting Sea," 52.

[45] *Miracula Sancti Benedicti*, 352–53, VI.3. See also Chapter 4.

[46] Haider, ed., *Traditionsurkunden*, 84–86, no. K 18. As noted in Chapter 7, this passage may also reflect concerns over the advocate abusing his position as judge in other ways.

[47] See Chapter 4.

advocates would unjustly extort excessive payments from a church's dependents? Or, was it also to limit the advocate's ability to exclude the ecclesiastical community in order to build his own relationships with those dependents?

While it is impossible to answer this question in most cases, posing it refocuses the scene of an advocate serving as judge on ecclesiastical estates. Although the advocate was expected to access church properties only for his court sessions – and occasionally when called upon to provide protection – there was a routine to these infrequent visits. He would come on important feast days and might stay for multiple days at a time, sleeping locally. He would typically appear with a large entourage, oftentimes a larger one than the ecclesiastical community would have liked. This show of force was surely threatening, but it also would have been a potent reminder to the dependents that this was a powerful man who protected and judged them, someone who had the influence and authority to keep the peace.[48] When the advocate and his entourage arrived, it was not simply the accused criminals and a few locals acting as agents of the court who were there to meet them; the expectation was that the entire community would be there. It is this group of dependents – not the bishop, abbot, abbess or other members of the religious house – who in most cases provided the advocate with a meal from its own resources.[49] While ecclesiastical communities sought to put strict limits on this meal, churches' dependents had clear incentives for wanting to give the advocate a lavish spread. If, in return, the advocate was a just judge, then the relationship between the advocate and the dependents could be a mutually beneficial one – without necessarily involving the religious community at all. Indeed, some dependents may even have been confused about who their real landlord was.[50]

That the meal prepared for an advocate by a religious community's dependents served the function of smoothing the relationship with their judge is suggested by twelfth-century sources from other parts of Europe. In his *Policraticus*, John of Salisbury (d. 1180) draws partly on Roman law when reflecting on the role of justices in England:

All duties should be freely performed so that nothing is either demanded or received beyond the fixed amount. But perhaps you ask what the fixed amount

---

[48] For much the same point, see Cheyette, *Ermengard*, 161, 165–66.

[49] Teuscher, *Lords' Rights*, 42; Willoweit, "Entwicklung," 69–70. See also Chapter 6. For a text that explicitly states that the *rustici* were to provide the advocate with a meal, see Haider, ed., *Traditionsurkunden*, 84–86, no. K 18. In contrast, for a text that insists the community's provost, not the monastery's dependents, would pay the *servitium*, see *Mainzer Urkundenbuch*, 2.1:556–58, no. 327.

[50] For similar observations, see Schreiner, "Grundherrschaft," 29–30; Chakrabarti, *Assembling the Local*, 141–42.

is. It is contained in the people's ordinance that none who governs is to accept a present or gift, except of food or drink, and this also is to be used in the days immediately following.[51]

He is quick to note, however, also following Roman law, "But these gifts are not to take on the character of remuneration." The *Dialogue of the Exchequer*, written a short time later, likewise concedes that it is not out of the ordinary to offer something to the king to obtain justice: "not to ensure that justice is done – lest you flare up and say that we sell justice for money – but rather to have it done without delay."[52] In other words, meals were not bribes but "gifts" intended to grease the wheels of justice.

For all of this to work effectively to the advocate's advantage, the church's dependents would have needed to see the religious community in a negative light. Hugh of Poitiers makes it clear that this was the case for the burghers of Vézelay, who considered the abbot unjust and abusive – and therefore saw an alliance with Count William III of Nevers as a viable alternative. Nevertheless, there is a tendency in the scholarship to assume that ecclesiastical landholders must have been more ethical and more concerned with the welfare of their dependents than secular elites were. Thomas Bisson argues, for example, "that clerical domains were comparatively, perhaps conspicuously, free of the harsh customs that accompanied the spread of lay lordship."[53] This was surely not the case. Between the eleventh and thirteenth centuries, prelates were routinely drawn from the leading noble families, and there is little evidence to suggest that most of them exercised their property rights much differently from their brothers who inherited the family's properties.[54]

Nor should we assume that religious communities' agents were universally respected by local populations. Carlo Ginzburg's famed sixteenth-century miller Menocchio regarded church officials, not secular ones, as the true oppressors of the poor.[55] Churchmen's vehement denunciations of so many advocates can plausibly be read as evidence that these advocates were a threat – not because they were destroying the community's properties but because they were forging strong ties with the church's dependents. Once we break down the assumption that the ecclesiastical–secular divide maps neatly onto a pious–impious, just–unjust divide, the complexity of local relationships comes into sharper focus – and the long history of corrupt practices of protection and justice becomes more legible.

---

[51] See John of Salisbury, *Policraticus*, 96–97, V.15.
[52] Richard fitzNigel, *Dialogus*, 180–81, chap. 23.   [53] Bisson, *Crisis*, 138–39.
[54] Stieldorf, "Klöster," 69–70.
[55] Ginzburg, *Cheese*, 14–15. See also Smail, *Legal Plunder*, 269.

The End, or Just the Beginning?

As different as the strategies pursued by Count Henry II of Wolfratshausen and Count William III of Nevers were, both grounded their actions in similar claims based on the language of rights. While Hugh of Poitiers makes it clear throughout his chronicle that the monks did not think the counts of Nevers had judicial authority over Vézelay or its dependents, he also concedes that the counts firmly believed they did. He has Count William II declare, "The church of Vézelay is in my advocacy."[56] And as noted above, Count William III complained in his speech to the burghers of Vézelay that the abbot was "demanding back from me the right of justice (*iusiusticie*)." Similarly, when Duke Henry II of Austria wrote to the abbot of Tegernsee about Count Henry II of Wolfratshausen, he warned him not "to take away his judicial authority, which he ought to have over your church from his advocatial right (*ex iure advocatie*)."[57] Thus, by the mid-twelfth century at the latest, nobles understood advocacy to be a right that could not be altered or taken away from them against their will. It was anything but an office controlled and regulated by the religious community.

Combining the high value that nobles placed on their advocacies with their strong views of their own advocatial rights helps to explain why the position of advocate proved to be such an enduring one. As discussed already, the late twelfth and early thirteenth centuries witnessed large numbers of churches buying advocacies from their advocates, and numerous rulers and leading secular princes acquiring advocacies from local nobles as well.[58] However, advocacy was such a widespread phenomenon that none of this led to advocates disappearing from local landscapes. Too many people recognized the advantages that came with being able to label oneself an *advocatus*.

On this point, my argument diverges significantly from the standard narrative of the decline of church advocacy in the thirteenth century. Since the late nineteenth century, historians have used the term *Entvogtung* to refer to the systematic acquisition of church advocacies by territorial princes, who agreed to defend religious communities in return for an annual payment – but who otherwise allowed churches to manage their own properties and rights.[59] The monastery of Kremsmünster in Austria offers an especially good example of this trend. It struggled with

---

[56] *Monumenta Vizeliacensia*, 420 ("'Aecclesia Vizeliacensis', inquit, 'in advocatione mea est'"); Hugh of Poitiers, *Vézelay Chronicle*, 160. For the differing opinions of monasteries and nobles in situations such as this one, see Brown, *Violence*, 107.
[57] *Tegernseer Briefsammlung*, 295–96, no. 266.   [58] See Chapter 8.
[59] The best overview is Reichert, *Landesherrschaft*, 128–35. While most work on this topic has focused on the German-speaking lands, a similar process was also taking place in

its local advocates until, in 1217, Duke Leopold VI of Austria freed the community from all secular jurisdiction.[60] The monks would remember this act fondly in a range of later sources, which praise the duke for ending advocatial abuses at the monastery.[61] In 1236, Duke Frederick II of Austria then "returned to [the monastery] every right of advocacy, which is commonly called *vogetreht* (*Vogtrecht*), such that it will pay ten pounds annually to our treasury for such a right."[62] Closely aligned with *Entvogtung* here is the concept of the "protective advocacy" (*Schirmvogtei*), which posits that the only aspect of the role of advocate that remained in the hands of the dukes was the protective one, similar to their more general responsibility to protect everyone under their ducal authority.[63]

It is not by accident that the example I have given here to explain *Entvogtung* concerns an Austrian monastery. The term originates in scholarship on Austria, and the most vigorous debates about how to understand the process of *Entvogtung* have concerned the Babenberg dukes of Austria and the distinctive nature of their ducal rights.[64] In more recent work, the term has also been applied to any case of a church purchasing its own advocacies in order to free itself from noble advocates and subadvocates.[65] Some of these religious communities maintained judicial authority over their estates, while at others, local or regional judges appointed by the territorial prince exercised justice. The term *Schirmvogtei* has likewise become a standard term across the German kingdom for the predominant form of church advocacy after 1250 – even though, as we will see, it is not a term that appears in the sources as frequently as it appears in modern scholarship.[66]

---

parts of France: Evergates, *Henry the Liberal*, 55–56. For more on this point, see Chapter 11.

[60] BUB, 2:8–11, no. 207.

[61] *Historiae Patavienses et Cremifanenses*, 634, 650 and 669–70.

[62] BUB, 2:163–64, no. 324.

[63] Clauss, *Untervogtei*, 168–71; Reichert, *Landesherrschaft*, 377–78; Hechberger, *Adel*, 484–87; Brunner, *Land*, 308–11.

[64] The origins of *Entvogtung* are traced to Heinrich Brunner, "Exemtionsrecht," 29–31. See Zehetmayer, "Vogtei," 225; Clauss, *Untervogtei*, 168; Reichert, *Landesherrschaft*, 128. Sources from Austria, especially ducal charters, are some of the richest sources for understanding the legal basis for advocacy in the thirteenth century. See, for example, BUB, 1:272–73, no. 195 for an early reference to a *Bettvogtei*, a term that arose to describe an advocacy that was uninheritable. See also Hageneder, "Lehensvogtei."

[65] Clauss, *Untervogtei*, 167–78; Willoweit, "Vogt, Vogtei," 940–41; Burkhardt, *Stab*, 359–62; West, "Monks," 402–03. See Chapter 8 for examples of churches purchasing their advocacies.

[66] Willoweit, "Vogt, Vogtei," 940. See also Chapter 3 for some of my hesitations regarding compound terms that aim to distinguish between different forms of advocacy.

As I have suggested above, eliminating local advocates and transforming the nature of advocatial rights was not as simple or straightforward as this narrative implies. The twenty-second canon of the Council of Würzburg, quoted earlier in this chapter, is clear evidence that church advocacy continued to attract the attention of kings, papal legates, prelates and secular princes during the late thirteenth century. Indeed, as my references to Libanius' oration on protection and to modern studies of the Sicilian mafia have been meant to show, providing protection and exercising justice are practices that invite too many complications for us to expect that the transition away from older ideas of advocacy could have been rapid or comprehensive.

Two points are therefore essential to emphasize here before I turn to the centuries after 1250 in the following chapters. First, the process that modern scholars label *Entvogtung* was not systematic but ad hoc.[67] Whether territorial princes were acquiring advocacies from noble advocates, or religious communities were purchasing the advocacies for particular ecclesiastical estates, this was done one advocacy at a time when the opportunity arose. Many other advocacies remained in nobles' hands. Moreover, in many cases, religious communities came to realize they were better off granting an advocacy back to a local nobleman rather than holding onto it themselves.[68] All of this means that *Entvogtung* was a slow and uneven process, not one that dramatically transformed the relationship between nobles and ecclesiastical property everywhere in the German-speaking lands by 1250.[69]

Abundant evidence survives for local nobles continuing to claim church advocacies into the late thirteenth century. An unusual but instructive example is a roll (*rotulus*), which preserves a series of documents relating to a lawsuit from 1275 to 1276. St. Bartholomew's Church in Frankfurt complained to the archbishop of Mainz that a man named Werner of Birnkeim and his co-heirs "oppressed and troubled ... with unjust exactions" the church's village of Kelkheim.[70] Werner and his co-heirs replied to the charge by insisting that their father had held the "right of advocacy" in the village peacefully for thirty-six years and that the family had justly acquired it from the lords of Eppstein.[71] The question of how, exactly, their father had come to possess the advocacy led to a lengthy investigation, and the archiepiscopal court eventually ruled that the family had never had a legitimate claim to the advocacy for Kelkheim.[72] This does not mean, however, that the advocacy came

---

[67] Cf. Clauss, *Untervogtei*, 169–70; Reichert, *Landesherrschaft*, 208–10.
[68] For this point, see Chapter 8.   [69] Cf. Reichert, *Landesherrschaft*, 329–30.
[70] Wettengel, *Streit*, 32–33, no. 1.   [71] Ibid., 36–39, no. 6. See also 38–41, no. 8.
[72] Ibid., 100–03, no. 25.

under the control of the church in Frankfurt; instead, it passed back into the hands of the lords of Eppstein, whose hereditary advocatial right had never been called into question during the trial.[73]

Elsewhere, too, nobles continued to claim the position of advocate. In 1280, the monastery of Prüm addressed a local nobleman's abuses by limiting some of his advocatial rights but also confirmed his and his heirs' judicial responsibilities as advocates on the monastery's estates.[74] A decade later, a knight made a donation of two properties to the monastery of St. Blasien for the sake of his soul but "retained the right of advocacy for me and my heirs."[75] It goes on to explain that he and his heirs would forfeit the right of advocacy to the monastery if "it should be troubled, against what is right, by the exaction of advocatial payments." Thus, not every church advocacy that appears in sources written between 1250 and 1500 (or between 1500 and 1800) can be designated a "protective advocacy" under the authority of the ruler or territorial prince. As we will see, some religious communities continued to struggle in later centuries with local advocates who look strikingly similar to advocates from the period 1000 to 1250.

The second point to emphasize is that, when an advocacy was acquired by the ruler or territorial prince or purchased by a religious community, the various forms of advocatial income that had become commonplace by 1200 did not simply disappear. As some historians of thirteenth-century France and England have noted in cautioning against teleological narratives of the rise of the state, kings frequently kept in place the harsh exactions of local nobles when they acquired new rights and properties.[76] Rulers and territorial princes – as well as bishops, abbots and abbesses – did not have a well-developed sense of the public good in this period. They were just as desperate for income as local advocates were.

Thus, when the count of Bogen agreed around 1225 not to demand any of his advocatial rights from the monastery of Niederaltaich for the span of one year in return for 100 pounds, these rights – including "any exactions" – did not lapse; they were to be "for the church's use" (*in usum ecclesiae*) during that year.[77] In a 1287 charter from a Cistercian monastery, we learn

---

[73] Ibid., 240–41.
[74] *Deutsches Wirtschaftsleben*, 79–85, no. 63. Many of the advocacies for Prüm's estates were held in fief by local lords: *Prümer Urbar*, 188, 200, 201, 237.
[75] Braun, ed., *Urkundenbuch*, 855–57, no. 646.
[76] Sabapathy, *Officers*, 125; Bartlett, "Impact," 88, 90. For a different perspective on the relationship between "the political economy of revenue extraction and the moral economy of justice" in roughly the same period, see Rustow, *Lost Archive*, 221–25.
[77] *Monumenta Boica*, 11:203–04, no. 66. For a more detailed analysis of this document, see Dendorfer, "Abtei," 124–25. By the later thirteenth century, 100 pounds seems to have been fixed as the advocatial payment at the monastery, and that money then started to circulate independently of whoever was actually performing the functions of advocate.

that each year the monastery's agents had been giving a widow named Adelheid "seven of the advocate's pennies, which are commonly called *voitespfenning*," from certain properties.[78] These Cistercians were apparently continuing to collect and benefit from an advocatial exaction decades after the German kings and emperors had begun issuing privileges insisting that Cistercian communities were free from advocatial authority.[79] In short, even in the case of advocacies that left the hands of local nobles in one way or another through the process labeled *Entvogtung*, the revenues that could be generated from advocatial rights continued to play a prominent role after 1250.

Conclusion

Exploring elements of continuity across the long history of advocacy before and after 1250 requires a different methodological approach from those scholars who have argued for a process of *Entvogtung*. Too often, sources that refer to rulers and princes acquiring advocacies in the thirteenth century, or to religious communities purchasing advocacies, are taken as a stopping point. Once many local nobles lost their advocatial rights, the type of advocate that had been commonplace between roughly 1000 and 1250 is thought to have disappeared. According to this line of argument, the sources for advocates and advocacies after 1250 are referring to different phenomena.[80] In contrast, as I have done throughout this book, my approach in the remaining chapters will be to continue to follow the word *advocatus* – and increasingly *Vogt* too – wherever it leads, rather than trying to fit it into legal or constitutional frameworks that assume the rise of officeholding and governmental institutions must have transformed advocacy into something that would have been unrecognizable to an eleventh-century duke or count. If we let the sources rather than modern constructs be our guide, an entirely different picture emerges, one that highlights the persistent challenges associated with the provision of protection and justice in European history.

Monumenta Boica, 11:253–54, no. 115, from 1277 explicitly states the abbot was to receive the 100 pounds instead of the duke.
[78] Krausen, ed., *Urkunden*, 338, no. 417.   [79] See Chapter 5 for more on this point.
[80] This argument has been shaped, at least in part, by the fact that the end of the Staufen dynasty and the subsequent "Interregnum" of the 1250s and 1260s form the dividing line between the "High" and "Late" medieval periods for many historians writing German history. See, for example, Schubert, *Fürstliche Herrschaft*, 104–08; Haverkamp, *Medieval Germany*; Keller, *Begrenzung*; Moraw, *Verfassung*.

11   The Emperor as *Vogt*, ca. 1000–1500

The epic Middle High German *Song of the Nibelungs* (*Nibelungenlied*), best known today as one of the inspirations for Richard Wagner's operatic *Ring* cycle, was first written down around the year 1200. A tale of loyalty, betrayal and vengeance, its first half centers on two couples: King Gunther, who rules from the town of Worms on the River Rhine, and the Icelandic queen Brünhild; and the heroic dragon-slayer Siegfried and Kriemhild, Gunther's sister.[1] Given the work's quasi-mythical setting in the fogs of time more than a half-millennium before its earliest surviving manuscript, and given its plotline that focuses on the bonds between royals and their leading magnates, it is not the sort of text in which one would necessarily expect to find advocates. Nevertheless, the word *Vogt* makes numerous appearances.[2] When Brünhild prepares to depart Iceland to become Gunther's queen and asks, "To whom can I entrust my lands?," the king replies that she should choose whomever she wants as advocate (*voget*) in her absence.[3] Later, after Siegfried has been killed and Kriemhild widowed, she says to her brother, "you should be the advocate for my person and property."[4] One of the most common uses of the word *Vogt* in the *Song of the Nibelungs* is a very different one, however. Gunther is typically given the title king (*künec*) in the text; he is *der künec Gunther* or *der künec von Rîne*.[5] But on occasion, he is also referred to as *der vogt von Rîne*: "the advocate of the Rhine."[6]

What does *Vogt* mean here? Although the period around 1200 saw countless churches complaining about their advocates, there is no

---

[1] Schulze, "Nibelungenlied"; Müller, "Contagious Violence."
[2] While the word *Vogt* first appears in Old High German in the Carolingian period, it only becomes commonplace from the mid-twelfth century in Middle High German texts. In dictionaries of Middle High German, the term can typically be found listed under *voget*, but there was a dizzying array of different spellings; see Lexer, *Mittelhochdeutsches Handwörterbuch*, 3:429–30; Kirschstein and Schulze, *Wörterbuch*, 3:2179–81. My thanks to Sheila Watts for discussing this issue with me.
[3] *Nibelungenlied*, ¶ 522. See also Reichert, *Konkordanz*, 2:963–64.
[4] *Nibelungenlied*, ¶ 1135: "beidiu lîbes unde guotes soltu mîn voget sîn."
[5] Ibid., ¶ 530 and ¶ 509.   [6] Ibid., ¶ 329, ¶ 473, and ¶ 607.

indication that the word carries a negative connotation in the *Song of the Nibelungs*. On the contrary, it seems to be almost interchangeable with "king" in some passages. This suggests a more expansive notion of the advocate's role than that of physically providing protection and executing justice on one particular church's estates. Significantly, the *Song* is not unique in applying the term "advocate" to a king in this way. The poem was first written down in a period when not only the German rulers and the intellectual circles around them but also popes and canon lawyers were increasingly linking church advocacy to the authority of kings – and especially of emperors. This connection first emerges in the 1150s before gaining even greater significance in the thirteenth and fourteenth centuries, when both the German rulers and the popes employed the term "advocate" in their ideological conflicts.[7]

As I will argue here, this strand of the history of advocacy is crucial for understanding why the position of advocate remained such an important one after 1250. When emperors and popes offered their own, competing characterizations of the proper role of the *advocatus*, they called attention to the fact that the position of advocate had never had one fixed definition. Advocacy was a malleable concept, which is why both secular and ecclesiastical elites would continue to try to shape it to their own advantage into the eighteenth century.

Three Advocates: Otto III, Godfrey of Bouillon and Charles of Flanders

The German kings and emperors frequently called themselves the advocates of specific religious communities. In 955, for example, Otto I's privilege for a newly founded convent decreed that the women of the community "should be subject to no secular dominion except ours, because we want to be their advocate and defender (*advocatus ac defensor*)."[8] Two centuries later, Emperor Frederick I Barbarossa continued to employ similar language in his privileges; in 1153, he decreed that a house of Augustinian canons "may have no other advocate except us and our successors as kings and emperors."[9] The end of the Staufen dynasty of German rulers in the mid-thirteenth century and the subsequent period of political upheaval and weak kings did not lead to the disappearance of royal claims of this sort. In 1299, King Albrecht

---

[7] See the section "Propaganda Wars" below.
[8] DD O I, 255-56, no. 174. See Chapter 3 for more on this point.
[9] DD F I, 95-96, no. 56. See Chapter 8 for more on this point.

236 11 The Emperor as Vogt, ca. 1000–1500

I insisted in one charter that "we are the advocate of the monastery of St. Blasien."[10]

Readers unfamiliar with the history of royal and imperial authority in the German-speaking lands might find this language confusing. Were a ruler's titles of *rex* and *imperator* insufficient for asserting authority over a monastery in the German kingdom? The short answer is *yes*. These rulers drew much of their power and authority from their own patchwork collection of rights and properties – including dynastic possessions – rather than from a legitimate and recognized claim to sovereignty over all territories in their kingdom.[11] As a result, they had to assert the right to be the advocate of a church or monastery in much the same way as nobles did. Kings likewise drew income from church advocacies in comparable ways, and their strategies for accumulating church advocacies were not so very different from the strategies pursued by many imperial princes.[12]

While the German kings and emperors could not assert effective, tangible authority everywhere in the German kingdom – or the Empire more broadly – on the basis of the titles of *rex* and *imperator*, they could use their preeminent position in society to make broad, ideological claims about their power and rights. Under Emperor Frederick I Barbarossa, the imperial chancery first began to use the position of advocate in this fashion in order to assert expansive claims to authority over the Roman Church, a point to which I will return below. Prior to his reign, there are few sources that suggest church advocacy had such ideological potential.[13] That said, three texts from the eleventh and early twelfth centuries are worth considering here because they help to contextualize later ideas about the roles of the *advocatus* and *Vogt*.

Writing in the 1010s, the chronicler Thietmar of Merseburg had surprisingly little to say about church advocacy, given that he was a bishop in Saxony with the right – granted to his see by Emperor Henry II – to appoint his own advocates.[14] Although he does not mention any local advocates, he does use the term *advocatus* twice in his chronicle in a different context. In his account of Otto III's imperial coronation in Rome in 996, Thietmar describes Otto as receiving imperial unction – and as being made "advocate of the church of St. Peter" (*advocatus ecclesie sancti Petri*).[15] Similarly, when Henry II arrived in Rome in 1014 for his

---

[10] Braun, ed., *Urkundenbuch*, 1:966–67, no. 743.
[11] For a good overview, see Arnold, *Medieval Germany*.
[12] Carocci and Collavini, "Cost," 139; Clauss, *Untervogtei*, 270–79.
[13] Tellenbach, "Kaiser," 65–66.   [14] DD H II, 78–80, no. 64.
[15] Thietmar of Merseburg, *Chronik*, 144–45, IV.27 (English translation: Thietmar, *Ottonian Germany*, 170–71).

own imperial coronation, Thietmar explains that "he was worthy to be made advocate of St. Peter."[16] This is an unusual turn of phrase. Other Ottonian-era sources occasionally refer to the ruler as patron (*patronus*) or defender (*defensor*) of the Roman Church, but there is no evidence to suggest these terms were understood to be synonymous with advocate in this period.[17] Thus, while Thietmar's uses of the phrase are difficult to interpret, they are early evidence for a connection between imperial authority and advocacy over the Roman Church, a connection that would become commonplace in later centuries.[18]

A second early example of the term *advocatus* being used to assert broad claims of authority appears in a source concerning Godfrey of Bouillon, duke of Lower Lorraine and the first ruler of the nascent kingdom of Jerusalem following the First Crusade. In a letter from September or October 1099, written in the name of several leaders of the crusade and addressed to the pope, he is identified as "Duke Godfrey, by the grace of God now advocate of the Church of the Holy Sepulchre" (*Godefridus dux, gratia Dei ecclesiae S. Sepulcri nunc advocatus*)."[19] Scholars have long puzzled over how to interpret this text.[20] As some historians have pointed out, Godfrey was not present when this letter was written, meaning that this may not have been the title he preferred to use.[21] Other historians, in contrast, have suggested that the title reflected Godfrey's desire to serve as a church official under the pope's authority rather than as a ruler of the Holy Land in his own right.[22] There is, however, no contemporary evidence to support this claim directly. Moreover, as I have argued in previous chapters, a prominent nobleman of the later eleventh century – especially one like Godfrey, who came from a region where church

[16] Thietmar of Merseburg, *Chronik*, 348–51, VI.101 (Thietmar, *Ottonian Germany*, 304). While the section referring to Otto III as advocate is missing from the oldest manuscript, this passage does appear in that manuscript. For more on these two passages: Goez, "Imperator," 319–20.

[17] Cf. Waas, *Vogtei*, 1:144-151, who argues that, already in the tenth century, we can speak of the imperial advocacy for the Roman Church. However, the evidence does not support this claim: Schramm, *Kaiser*, 175–76; Goez, "Imperator," 315. See also the section below "Rewriting History in the Mid-Twelfth Century."

[18] Tellenbach, "Kaiser," 51–52, 63. Tellenbach also notes that the Byzantine emperor referred to Henry V in 1120 as *advocato Romanae urbis* (pp. 66–67) to avoid calling him emperor.

[19] The original does not survive, but the earliest copies date from the opening decades of the twelfth century: *Codex Udalrici*, 2:449–53, no. 259; *Annales Sancti Disibodi*, 17.

[20] For discussions of this issue, see John, *Godfrey*, 180; Murray, "Title"; Riley-Smith, "Title"; Hagenmeyer, "Brief"; and from the perspective of church advocacy, Goez, "Imperator," 321–22.

[21] Riley-Smith, "Title," 84–85; John, *Godfrey*, 180. Both point out that there is evidence for the Crusaders discussing the idea of Jerusalem being overseen by an *advocatus* rather than a *rex*, but we know nothing about Godfrey's opinion of this idea.

[22] See, for example, Asbridge, *First Crusade*, 321.

advocacy was common at the time – almost certainly would not have understood the position of advocate in terms of officeholding anyway.

From the perspective of the history of advocacy, rather than the history of the Crusades (which is the lens through which this text has typically been read), two points are more significant than the question of whether Godfrey ever used this title. First, "advocate of the Church of the Holy Sepulchre" was a title understood by the letter's writers to be one that gave Godfrey his authority in the newly conquered territories in the Holy Land.[23] Second, the letter includes the phrase *gratia Dei*. As I have discussed previously, references to people being advocates "by the grace of God" are rare. If advocacy was (at least theoretically) an office granted by a prelate or religious community to a secular agent, the advocate really could not claim to hold that position "by the grace of God."[24] Thus, designating Godfrey *"gratia Dei ecclesiae S. Sepulcri nunc advocatus"* was highly unusual. Either the letter's writers were unfamiliar with the standard language of advocacy in most parts of Europe, or they were experimenting with a new idea of secular-religious authority.

Though we will probably never know what Godfrey's title was meant to convey, the timing of this text is noteworthy. The decades around the year 1100 witnessed a rapid increase in the use of the term *advocatus* across many parts of Europe because so many new religious foundations were appearing in this period. These same years were also when the terms *advocata*, *advocatrix* and *advocatissa* came into common use for some leading noblewomen.[25] Thus, this was clearly a time when people were testing the scope and limits of the role of the advocate. Members of both the secular and ecclesiastical elites were making a range of creative claims to power and influence over churches and their properties through the concept of advocacy in the late eleventh and early twelfth centuries, and Godfrey's title reflects this trend toward experimentation.

A final source demonstrates this point even better: Galbert of Bruges' contemporary account of the murder of Count Charles of Flanders in 1127. Galbert, who was shocked by the count's assassination at the hands of some of his own followers, routinely praises Charles as a just and valorous ruler. Early in his Prologue, when describing Charles's many virtues, Galbert refers to him as "father and advocate of the churches of God" (*pater et advocatus ecclesiarum Dei*).[26] A short time later, Charles is called "helper of the poor, advocate of the churches of God and defender

---

[23] Murray, "Title," 169–72.   [24] See Chapter 5.
[25] Lyon, "Advocata." See also Chapter 5.
[26] Galbert of Bruges, *De Multro*, 3, Prol. Translations are my own, but see also Galbert of Bruges, *Murder*. For this text, see Rider, *God's Scribe*.

of the fatherland."[27] This combination leaves little doubt that Galbert saw in the label *advocatus* the most succinct way of describing the count as someone who protected the interests of all the religious communities in his territories. Galbert goes one step further later in his text. When discussing how the men of Ghent accepted William Clito as the new count after Charles' death, he explains how they received him not only as count but also as "advocate of the whole land" (*terrae totius advocatum*).[28] Here, roughly seventy-five years before the *Song of the Nibelungs* refers to King Gunther as "the advocate of the Rhine," we see a leading nobleman being described similarly as the advocate of an entire territory – because he was responsible for all its churches.

While there is nothing to suggest a direct line connects the ideas of advocacy espoused by Thietmar of Merseburg, the Crusaders' letter and Galbert of Bruges with later ideas of the ruler as advocate, all three of these sources point to the ideological potential of the language of advocacy. Throughout the eleventh and early twelfth centuries, nobles and ecclesiastics at the local level struggled with one another over the rights and responsibilities attached to the role of advocate. As contentious as those disputes could be, new ideas about advocacy were developing simultaneously, ideas which saw in the position of advocate the basis for much broader claims to lay influence over churches – and even the Church as a whole. These ideas spread rapidly during the second half of the twelfth century – and increasingly became linked to the German kings and emperors, in particular, in ways that would have far-reaching consequences.

Rewriting History in the Mid-Twelfth Century

The conflict known as the Investiture Controversy had a profound impact on the relationship between emperor and pope. After it, the German rulers could no longer choose and approve candidates for the papacy, nor could they claim such broad authority over the churches in their territories as they had in the past. Nevertheless, the Concordat of Worms that settled the controversy in 1122 was not the end of the German kings' and emperors' efforts to assert the divine nature of their authority or their influence over the Church.[29] Emperor Frederick I and Frederick II's frequent clashes with the papacy from the late 1150s to the

---

[27] Galbert of Bruges, *De Multro*, 5, Prol. For similar examples, see ibid., 17, chap. 6 and 152, chap. 107.

[28] Ibid., 102, chap. 53; see also ibid., 131, chap. 79.

[29] For the impact of the Investiture Controversy on ideas of sacral kingship, see Dale, *Inauguration*, 17–20; Zey, *Investiturstreit*, 115–18.

latter's death in 1250 are evidence that many questions remained unre-
solved. Indeed, the precise nature of the relationship between emperor
and pope and between imperial authority and the Roman Church was no
more clearly defined after 1122 than it had been during the preceding
decades of open conflict.

The significance of the term *advocatus* for debates about empire and
papacy first becomes evident early in the reign of Frederick I Barbarossa.
Before turning to the German kings and emperors, however, it will be
helpful to take a final look westward to France to better understand why
my focus for the remainder of the book will be the German-speaking
lands. As I have noted in previous chapters, advocacy had never been as
commonplace or widespread in the French kingdom as in the German
kingdom. In the late twelfth and early thirteenth centuries, there were still
occasional references to church advocates in France – but far fewer than
further east. When King Philip II declared himself around the year 1200
to be "the highest lord and advocate" of all of the monastery of Corbie's
properties, he was using language that was rapidly becoming obsolete in
his kingdom.[30] Other terms for protection (including *tutela, protectio* and
custodia) were more common than "advocacy" in France for royal authority over churches.[31] In 1187, for example, Philip wrote "to all his provosts
(*prepositis*) and bailiffs (*ballivis*)," ordering that they "protect (*custodire*)
the properties of the monks of the Cistercian order ... as if they were our
own properties."[32] In contrast, a half-century later in a 1240 privilege
issued by the German king Conrad IV for the Cistercian monastery of
Ebrach, the language of advocacy was still prominent: "Just as the
Cistercian order has always been free and immune from every type of
advocate, ... so it follows that [Ebrach] may be subject to absolutely no
advocates except only the emperor of the Romans."[33] Thus, church
advocacy was largely disappearing from French royal privileges at a time
when it was becoming increasingly significant for German rulers' claims
to authority.

One reason for this divergence is that the position of advocate was, from
the 1150s onward, tied to ideological claims about the special relationship

---

[30] Delaborde, ed., *Recueil*, 2:142–43, no. 592; Depreux, "Ausprägungen," 378.
[31] See, for example, Delaborde, ed., *Recueil*, 1:194–95, no. 161; 224–25, no. 187; and 421–
22, no. 347. By my count, only 2 percent of Philip's roughly 1,800 charters reference
advocates or advocacy.
[32] Ibid., 1:260–61, no. 215. For provosts and bailiffs, see Baldwin, *Government*, 35–36, 126;
Jordan, "Anti-Corruption." In the county of Champagne, where there had been numerous advocacies in earlier periods, bailiffs and provosts also increasingly came to dominate
the administration: Evergates, *Aristocracy*, 45–46. See also Pergameni, *L'Avouerie*,
177–78.
[33] Goez, ed., *Urkunden*, 1:354–58, no. 174. See also Chapter 5.

between emperor and pope. Frederick I's imperial coronation holds the key to understanding this development.[34] His predecessor and paternal uncle, King Conrad III, had never been crowned emperor by the pope. As a result, Frederick sought to make the trip over the Alps as quickly as possible following his election as king in 1152 in order to assert the German rulers' lapsed rights in northern Italy and Rome. Pope Eugenius III (1145–53) was equally anxious to receive Frederick's support because of the growing threat of the Roman commune to papal authority in the city. Early in 1153, therefore, ruler and pope agreed to the Treaty of Constance to lay the groundwork for Frederick's imperial coronation. This treaty stipulated, among other things, that the king

will to the best of his ability preserve and defend the honor of the papal dignity and the worldly possessions of blessed Peter as a devoted and special advocate of the holy Roman church (*sicut devotus et specialis advocatus sanctae Romanae aecclesiae*) against [all] men … Moreover, those things which [the pope] does not now possess, he will help to recover as best he can, and he will defend whatever is recovered.[35]

While the claim that the emperor was the "special son" (*specialis filius*) of the Roman Church had deep roots, the phrase "special advocate" did not.[36] Its appearance here seemingly represents an attempt – in the wake of the Investiture Controversy and the Concordat of Worms – to establish the relationship between pope and emperor on fresh terms in a changing world. This was new language for the old idea that the German emperors, more so than the other rulers of Latin Christendom, were tasked with defending the popes and the Roman Church and its properties.

However, as I have argued in the previous chapters, members of the secular and ecclesiastical elites had struggled for centuries by the 1150s to find common ground on the rights and responsibilities attached to the role of advocate. Frederick I, as the son of a duke of Swabia, had been raised in an environment imbued with the German nobility's perspectives on church advocacy.[37] In contrast, Pope Eugenius III was not only an Italian from Pisa but a Cistercian monk; his successor, Pope Hadrian IV, who would perform the imperial coronation in 1155, was from England and had headed a house of canons in Avignon before his election. As

---

[34] Schludi, "*Advocatus*," 42.

[35] Const., 1:201–03, nos. 144–45. Tellenbach, "Kaiser," 66, lists this treaty as the earliest use of the term *advocatus* in this context as opposed to *defensor*, which had been used as recently as the 1130s and 1140s in papal documents.

[36] Schludi, "*Advocatus*," 42–43; Goez, "*Imperator*"; Schuster, "Kaiser," 114–60; Duggan, "Alexander," 43–44. For *specialis filius*, see Ullmann, *Papal Government*, 152–53; Schludi, "*Advocatus*," 48–73.

[37] Freed, *Frederick Barbarossa*, 29–45.

a result, there is no reason to think that these three men had a shared understanding of the duties of a "special advocate of the holy Roman church."[38] Different worlds collided in this phrase, and as the next 300 years of imperial and papal propaganda would show, what the title *specialis advocatus* actually meant was open to interpretation.[39]

Only a few years after the Treaty of Constance, in 1159, there was a split papal election, which saw the majority of the cardinals support Pope Alexander III rather than Emperor Frederick I's preferred candidate, Victor IV. Writing to Alexander III in October 1159, Frederick laid out his position on his relationship with the Church, explaining, "because we ought to act as patron (*patrocinari*) for all the churches established in our empire, we ought to be even more inclined to provide for the holy Roman Church, since its care and defense are believed to have been committed to us more specially by divine providence."[40] On these grounds, the emperor announced that it was his responsibility to call a general council of the Church to restore order and peace – and summoned Alexander III to attend. In his reply, Alexander conceded, "We recognize the lord emperor . . . [to be] advocate and special defender of the holy Roman Church," but he insisted that this did not give Frederick the power and authority to call a church council or usurp the role of judge in ecclesiastical matters.[41] Victor IV, in contrast, responded more positively to the emperor's claims, writing in one letter to the German princes, "[W]e earnestly and confidently entreat you all . . . that you ask and exhort our lord, the most invincible emperor, to watch over . . . the Church of God, the bride of Jesus Christ, of which he has been divinely appointed advocate and defender. Let him not delay to come to her aid."[42]

All of this was happening at a time when Frederick I's chancery was issuing numerous privileges asserting the emperor's right to be the advocate for individual religious communities in the German kingdom.[43] That the rhetorical strategies he and his allies were deploying in his conflict with Pope Alexander III were shaping – and being shaped by – their understanding of church advocacy more generally is evident in many of these documents. In one concerning ecclesiastical properties in the diocese of Liège, probably from 1162, we read, "Divine grace appointed us

---

[38] For the popes in this period, Morris, *Papal Monarchy*, 182–91.
[39] Schludi, "*Advocatus*," 43–47; Goez, "*Imperator*," 327–28. See also Ullmann, *Papal Government*, 71–73.
[40] Const., 1:255–56, no. 184.
[41] Ibid., 1:256–57, no. 185; Freed, *Frederick Barbarossa*, 264.
[42] Otto of Freising and Rahewin, *Gesta Friderici*, 298, IV.60. Other than my translation of *advocatus*, I follow the standard English translation: Otto of Freising and Rahewin, *Deeds*, 288.
[43] See Chapter 8.

advocate and defender of the churches of God so that we might defend them and their rights, full and uninjured, under our imperial protection, and so that we might not suffer them to be diminished in some way either in their possessions or in the privileges conferred by our predecessors as kings and emperors."[44] The phrase *"advocatus et defensor ẹcclesiarum deī"* in this privilege is an unusual one from the perspective of earlier sources and suggests that the emperor and his chancery were increasingly deploying the term "advocate" to make broad claims about imperial authority over the Church as a whole.

That the idea of the ruler as advocate was acquiring new ideological potency in this period is not only evident in imperial and papal documents but also in a variety of other types of sources. One of the best examples is the Middle High German verse *Kaiserchronik*, a narrative of the reigns of the Roman and German emperors probably produced around 1150.[45] In this work, Emperor Constantine is called "Roman advocate" (*rômiske voget*) in the context of the calling of a church council.[46] Emperor Heraclius is "advocate of Rome" (*Rôme voget*) in his dealings with a pagan king, including during their duel.[47] Emperor Theodosius, in the early days of the Arian heresy, states "I am called the Roman advocate and because of that I am hailed as judge."[48] Charlemagne speaks similar words – "I am called judge and advocate" (*ich haize rihtære unt voget*) – when Pope Leo comes to him to ask for help against the rebellious Romans.[49] And Otto I is "Roman advocate" (*Rômære voget*) when he calls a council at Aachen and the pope's messengers arrive.[50] In all of these scenes, the term *Vogt* is used at moments when the emperors are intervening in ecclesiastical matters and aiding the popes against their enemies, giving the clear impression that protection and justice were central to this author's conception of the emperor's role as advocate of the Roman Church.[51]

Other sources from this period similarly point in this direction. In *The Play of Antichrist* (*Ludus de Antichristo*), probably written around 1160 at

---

[44] DD F I, 2:253, no. 384.
[45] Chinca and Young, "Uses of the Past." See also Kaiserchronik Digital. I thank Mark Chinca, Christopher Young and Johanna Dale for discussing this text with me.
[46] *Kaiserchronik*, 237, line 8,489. Cf. *Book of Emperors*, 220, where the translator translates *Vogt* as "ruler."
[47] *Kaiserchronik*, 285, line 11,142. See also 287, line 11,267 (*der rômische voget*); cf. *Book of Emperors*, 263 and 265.
[48] *Kaiserchronik*, 324, lines 13,407–08 ("*ich haize Rômâre voget. unt bin durch daz ze rihtære gelobet*"); cf. *Book of Emperors*, 300.
[49] *Kaiserchronik*, 344, line 14,533. See also 341, line 14,358; cf. *Book of Emperors*, 322 and 324.
[50] *Kaiserchronik*, 368, line 15,869; cf. *Book of Emperors*, 353.
[51] Tellenbach, "Kaiser," 68–71.

the monastery of Tegernsee, the king of Jerusalem refers to "the king of the Germans" as advocate in a passage emphasizing the emperor's role as defender of the Church against heresy.[52] In the Middle High German version of the *Song of Roland* (*Das Rolandslied*), which was probably written around 1170, Charlemagne says of himself, "I am called the advocate of Rome" (*ich haize der uoget uon Rome*).[53] Given that conflict between Christendom and Islam is central to the *Song's* plot, this work too highlights the emperor's protection of the Church against non-Christians.[54] Charlemagne is also called advocate in two charters forged at the monastery of Fulda in the mid-twelfth century; in both, his titles include "advocate of the Romans" (*advocatus Romanorum*).[55] Charlemagne's authentic charters employed the title "patrician of the Romans" (*patricius Romanorum*), and the forger's decision to replace *patricius* with *advocatus* is almost certainly a reflection of the growing significance of the idea of the emperor as Roman advocate at the time he was working.[56]

Thus, starting in the mid-twelfth century, the term *advocatus* increasingly came to be applied to emperors (whether Roman, Frankish or German) to emphasize their special relationship with the popes and the Roman Church. From the papal perspective, the emperors held this office of advocate because they were to provide support – especially military support – when the pope summoned them to fight against the Church's enemies. We have already seen an example of how this was supposed to work: Pope Lucius III promulgated the bull *Ad abolendam* (1184) in Emperor Frederick I's presence, highlighting their shared responsibilities in combatting heresy and the abuses of corrupt church advocates.[57]

However, as both the pro-imperial arguments after the split papal election of 1159 and the *Kaiserchronik* indicate, the idea of the emperor as "special advocate" of the Roman Church could also be employed in order to assert his right to call church councils and to act as judge in ecclesiastical matters. Moreover, when chronicles recounting Emperor Frederick I Barbarossa's campaign during the Third Crusade refer to him

---

[52] *Ludus de Antichristo*, 16 (English translation: *Play of Antichrist*, 82). See also Tellenbach, "Kaiser," 68.

[53] *Rolandslied*, 270, line 7,653. See also ibid., 30, line 973 and 104, line 2,010.

[54] For an excellent discussion of the different ways this term might have been understood, see Richter, *Kommentar*, 206–07. Fifty years after the *Rolandslied*, Walther von der Vogelweide would use the phrase "*Von Rome voget*" to describe Frederick II: Walther von der Vogelweide, *Sämtliche Lieder*, 228, no. 74.5; Tellenbach, "Kaiser," 71–72.

[55] DD Karol. I, 433, no. 289 and 435–36, no. 292. In the latter, he is "Ego Karolus divina preordinante clementia Romanorum *advocatus* et Francorum et Longobardorum rex."

[56] Tellenbach, "Kaiser," 65. See also a charter of Henry I forged at Fulda: DD H I, 68–69, no. 34.

[57] See Chapter 8.

as "in the name of Our Lord Jesus Christ Roman emperor and special advocate of the land of Jerusalem" and as "the greatest and most excellent guardian and advocate of the holy mother church," it is clear that imperial supporters recognized the political potential of the title of *advocatus*.[58] Just as a local advocate for a single church or ecclesiastical estate could test the limits of his advocatial rights to protect and to judge, so too could the German ruler as advocate of the universal Church.

Propaganda Wars

Questions about the proper relationship between the German emperors and the Roman Church continued to generate tensions in the late twelfth and early thirteenth centuries. When Frederick I's son Emperor Henry VI died in 1197, his only son, the future Emperor Frederick II, was a child, which led the German princes to consider other candidates for the throne. One contemporary source describes how a group of princes called for the magnates of the German kingdom to gather in order to elect "an emperor, suitable and worthy to God, and an advocate of churches."[59] However, the election did not go smoothly. Two factions of imperial princes elected different kings: Henry VI's brother Philip of Swabia (d. 1208) and Duke Henry the Lion's son Otto IV (d. 1218). War soon followed. Otto IV's electors quickly wrote to the pope in 1198 to announce their choice: "we elected the lord Otto, most devoted cultivator of the Christian faith and most faithful advocate and defender of the holy Roman Church."[60] The language of the ruler as advocate thus remained central to arguments about the responsibilities of the German ruler vis-à-vis the papacy and the Church.

This can be seen even more clearly in Pope Innocent III's 1202 bull *Venerabilem*, one of the most important documents for papal claims to authority over the choice of a German king and future emperor. In it, the pope asserted the right to determine which of the two rival candidates ought to be king by arguing, "For if the [German] princes after due warning and delay cannot or will not agree, shall the apostolic see then lack an advocate and defender and be penalized for their fault?"[61]

---

[58] *Historia de Expeditione Friderici Imperatoris*, 87: "in nomine domini nostri Iesu Christi Romanus imperator et advocatus specialis Ierosolimitanę terrę." *Historia Peregrinorum*, 122: "maximo et excellentissimo sancte matris ecclesie tutore et advocato." English translations: *Crusade of Frederick Barbarossa*, 112 and 141. See also Tellenbach, "Kaiser," 67–68; Goez, "*Imperator*," 321–22.

[59] *Chronica Regia Coloniensis*, 162.   [60] Const., 2:24, no. 19.

[61] *Regestum Innocentii III*, 172, no. 62 (English translation: Tierney, *Crisis*, 133–34, no. 75). This particular section of the bull has not garnered as much attention as the section claiming that the papacy transferred Roman imperial authority from the Greeks to the

Because of the significance of Innocent III's claims in this bull, *Venerabilem* would be included in the *Liber Extra*, the decretal collection compiled at the behest of Pope Gregory IX.[62] This cemented its place in the body of canon law and ensured it would have a role to play in subsequent debates about empire and papacy.

From the beginning, however, canon lawyers recognized the dangers of misinterpreting the language of the bull. A mid-thirteenth-century gloss on the *Liber Extra* tries to clarify its meaning by explaining, "The *advocatus Ecclesiae* cannot be the church's patron (*patronus Ecclesiae*) but is like the guardian (*tutor*) who is given to an orphan, so that he may defend him from others' harassments."[63] The famed canonist of the late thirteenth century, Hostiensis, would repeat this point in his own commentary on *Venerabilem*.[64] Why was it so important to draw a sharp distinction between the role of advocate and that of patron in the context of this bull? In his discussion of the right of church patronage (*ius patronatus*), Hostiensis acknowledged that the terms *patronus, advocatus* and *defensor* could sometimes be synonymous.[65] However, the *ius patronatus* concerned (among other things) the right of a church's patron to present a new priest of his choosing to the bishop for appointment to that church. As a result, if one read advocate as a synonym for patron, one could potentially argue that the emperor, as patron/advocate of the Roman Church, had the right to interfere in papal elections.[66] Canonists' insistence on clarity on this point was therefore well founded.

Canon law was not the only place where the idea of the emperor as advocate of the Roman Church garnered attention in the thirteenth century. The papacy and members of the Staufen dynasty of kings and emperors also employed it in their propagandistic exchanges. In 1226, Pope Honorius III (1216–27) criticized Emperor Frederick II for his lack of gratitude toward the papacy and for his claim that he was *advocatus*: "the term advocacy (*advocatie vocabulum*) [is] frequently repeated in your

Germans. Indeed, most discussions of medieval political thought largely ignore the issue of advocacy and focus instead on such topics as the Two Swords theory. See, for example, Watt, "Spiritual" and Whalen, *Two Powers*. For the lack of attention paid to the idea of the emperor as advocate outside German historiography, see Goez, "*Imperator*," 315–16. Tellingly, the best discussion of this subject in English can be found in a work written by an Austrian émigré: Ullmann, *Papal Government*.

[62] *Decretalium Collectiones*, cols. 79–82 (*Liber Extra* 1.6.34). For the *Liber Extra*, see also Chapter 8. For *Venerabilem* and earlier references to the emperor as advocate in canon law, see Goez, "*Imperator*," 324–26.

[63] For this gloss, see the early modern printed edition: Gregory IX, *Decretales*, 121 (I. 6. 34).

[64] Henry of Susa, *In Primum*, 60a. He adds further that "The emperor ought to defend the church . . . and exalt the pope."

[65] Henry of Susa, *Summa*, Book 3, 180v–181v.

[66] See Chapter 8 and Landau, *Jus patronatus*, 8–15.

letters ... [However,] since the advocate of the church ought to be understood as a defender, if you disregard the office of defender, you improperly retain the name of advocate (*nomen advocati*)."[67] Nevertheless, two decades later in a letter to Pope Innocent IV (1243–54), Frederick II insisted that he had always acted as "special son of the church and foremost advocate (*precipuus advocatus*) for your person, your brothers, and the sacrosanct Roman Church, our mother."[68] Pope Alexander IV (1254–61) then reiterated the papal position in 1256 when expressing his concerns about the rule of the child Conradin, Frederick II's grandson. Following *Venerabilem*, he recognized that whoever was elected German king became the advocate of the Apostolic See, but Conradin was too young and therefore unsuitable and "useless (*inutilis*) for performing such an office or ministry of defense."[69]

After the end of the Staufen dynasty of kings and emperors in the mid-thirteenth century, popes continued to use the term *advocatus* to frame the German rulers' proper relationship with the Roman Church. Pope Urban IV (1261–64) wrote to the newly elected German king Richard of Cornwall that the one who "is presiding at the summit of the Roman Empire should hold the office of special advocate and foremost defender for the church."[70] In 1295, Pope Boniface VIII (1294–1303) called on the German ruler Adolf of Nassau to aid the Church, since "the king of the Romans is the peculiar son of the church and its special defender and advocate."[71] And Pope Clement V (1305–15), in his lengthy commentary on the coronation of Emperor Henry VII in 1312, was quite clear on what he saw the role of the emperor as advocate to be. In the midst of a lengthy passage insisting that the emperors cannot make any sort of claim on the properties of the Roman Church or in any way undermine ecclesiastical liberty, he writes that the emperor, "as catholic prince and advocate and defender of the said church, should assist it and stand by it with suitable counsel and aid against any who are disobedient or rebellious toward it,

---

[67] Epp. saec. XIII, 1:221, no. 296.

[68] *Innsbrucker Briefsammlung*, 97, no 17. For Frederick II, see also Const., 2:290–99, no. 215 (esp. pp. 294–95) and Tellenbach, "Kaiser," 67. The Romans, in a letter to Frederick II about his imperial coronation in 1220, refer to him as "*Romane ecclesie advocatus pariter et defensor*": Const., 2:103–04, no. 82. In 1253, Frederick II's son Conrad IV wrote to Innocent IV, asking for peace as a son and advocate of the church; see Regesta Imperii Online, RI V,1,2, no. 4607.

[69] Epp. saec. XIII, 3:399, no. 440. More work needs to be done on the competing uses of the term *advocatus* in the thirteenth-century disputes between papacy and Empire.

[70] Epp. Saec. XIII, 3:545, no. 560, pt. I. See also p. 547. While Tellenbach, "Kaiser," is invaluable for the Staufen period, he spends less than three pages (pp. 73–75) on the period post-1250. Goez, "*Imperator*," likewise does not go beyond 1250.

[71] Const., 3:516, no. 546: "*Romanorum rex peculiaris ecclesie filie et eius specialis defensor et advocatus existit.*"

especially the occupiers and disturbers of its lands and provinces, or any part of them."[72]

Despite the papacy's sustained efforts across almost two centuries to define the German rulers' role as advocate as first and foremost providing protection for the Roman Church and its properties, there remained into the fourteenth and fifteenth centuries no general agreement about this advocatial position. The German rulers continued to employ the language of advocacy to push their own ideological and political claims. In 1323, Pope John XXII (1316–34) questioned Ludwig IV "the Bavarian's" right to be German king, asserting that he could not exercise royal authority without the pope's approval.[73] Ludwig's initial response in December of 1323, known as the Nuremberg Appellation, at first echoes the papal ideal of the emperor as advocate: "As a faithful advocate and fervent zealot for the Christian faith, we want to pursue and destroy in every way possible [the Roman Church's] enemies and any rebels whom we know."[74] Later in the Appellation, however, Ludwig criticizes John for what he sees as the pope's many abuses of power and even accuses him of heresy; then, more provocatively, he calls himself "advocate of the sacrosanct Roman Church" when asserting his power to protect the apostolic see *from* John.[75] A short time later, Ludwig IV repeated much of the same language (but not the charge of heresy) when insisting that the king, because of his zeal and devotion "for the holy Church of God, whose defender, patron and advocate we are (*cuius defensor, patronus et advocatus existimus*)," was compelled to respond to John's abuses.[76] Here, the German ruler employed a range of terms – all of them, as noted above, terms in canon law for laymen with the obligation to support churches – to justify his actions. Who else but the defender, patron and advocate of the Roman Church could protect the faithful from a pope who had lost his way?[77]

The conflict between Ludwig IV and the papacy was the impetus behind a work that highlights the remarkable flexibility of the language of church advocacy. Lupold of Bebenburg (d. 1363), who studied law in Bologna, wrote his *Treatise on Royal and Imperial Rights* in 1338/39 for Archbishop Baldwin of Trier.[78] In it, he argues strongly against the idea that the pope at

---

[72] *Decretalium Collectiones*, cols. 1147–50 (*Constitutiones*, II.IX).
[73] Lord, "Golden Bull," 93.   [74] Const., 5:642, no. 824; Lord, "Golden Bull," 99.
[75] Const., 5:646, no. 824; Lord, "Golden Bull," 101.
[76] Const., 5:742-43, no. 909.32. In contrast, under the year 1324, an Austrian set of annals reports that the pope excommunicated Ludwig and then "chose [the Habsburg] Duke Leopold as advocate for himself" (*Annales Austriae*, 667).
[77] Ludwig IV did not employ the language of advocacy in the documents he issued in April of 1328 concerning the deposition of Pope John XXII: Const., 6.1:343–62, nos. 435–38. In these documents, he uses the imperial title and imperial authority to justify his actions.
[78] Wendehorst, "Lupold."

the imperial coronation imbued the German ruler with any authority; according to him, it was the election by the seven imperial electors that gave the ruler his authority in the Empire.[79] Lupold is especially pointed on the issue of how *Venerabilem* ought to be interpreted. A century earlier, Pope Innocent IV had used *Venerabilem* in his commentary on the *Liber Extra* to claim that the pope not only had a role to play in selecting the emperor but, more importantly: "the emperor is his advocate and swears an oath to him and holds the empire from him."[80] Lupold systematically discounts all of these points. Concerning the idea that the emperor is the pope's advocate, he argues, "It is not from him [i.e., the pope] that the emperor is the pope's advocate. For there are many prelates of churches and monasteries in Germany and other provinces, who have princes and nobles as advocates; [these advocates] are however accustomed to receive neither nomination nor approval from prelates in this way."[81] Here, Lupold explicitly references German church advocacy to explain what it meant for the emperor to be advocate of the Roman Church. Recognizing the heritability of the position of advocate in the German kingdom, he makes the case that the pope could no more choose his advocate than many German bishops and abbots could choose theirs.

One other aspect of Lupold's argument demands our attention. When attempting to define what the advocacy of the Roman Church was, Lupold claims, "Advocacy of the church is nothing else but the right of defending the church . . . [F]rom this, advocacy can be understood . . . as the *regimen* of the Roman Church conceded to the Germans."[82] He subsequently argues that *regimen* is not to be understood as *imperium*, which would imply that the emperors had indeed received the empire from the popes, but rather the "patricianship" (*patriciatus*) of the city of Rome, which was granted to Charlemagne and later Otto I.[83] He continues,

By this patricianship is to be understood either the dignity of punishing crimes and judging secular cases in the city or the advocacy of the Roman Church . . . The king of the Romans or emperor holds this patricianship or advocacy from the Roman Church . . . Whether this advocacy of the Roman Church possesses any added benefit (*emolumentum*), as the advocacies of churches and monasteries in Germany, or whether it possesses only the added onus of defense, I confess I do not know.[84]

---

[79] For Lupold's place in the broader context of debates about papal and imperial authority, see Scales, *German Identity*, 243–59.

[80] Innocent IV, *Commentaria*, 75v.: "*est imperator eius advocatus et iurat ei, et ab eo imperium tenet.*" See also Lupold of Bebenburg, *Tractatus*, 313, chap. 8.

[81] Lupold, *Tractatus*, 314, chap. 8.

[82] Ibid., 322, chap. 9. For the term *regimen*, see Goez, "*Imperator*," 326.

[83] Lupold, *Tractatus*, 375, chap. 13. For the place of Carolingian history in his arguments, see also ibid., 272, chap. 3 and Lupold of Bebenburg, *Libellus*, 499, chap. 15.

[84] Lupold, *Tractatus*, 375–76, chap. 13.

In seeking to downplay the significance of *Venerabilem* and its subsequent pro-papal interpretations, Lupold again turns to the contemporary German context to explain the position of advocate. He insists that advocacy could concern both exercising justice and providing protection – and even suggests that the emperors might profit from the role of advocate of the Roman Church in much the same way as the advocates of German churches did. Here, we see clearly how someone familiar with the role of advocate in the German kingdom could have a strikingly different understanding of the idea of the emperor as advocate of the Roman Church than Italian popes and canonists had.

Lupold's arguments did not carry the day. Others in the first half of the fourteenth century offered their own views on the advocacy for the Roman Church and the proper relationship between popes and emperors.[85] Nevertheless, Lupold's treatise demonstrates that nothing had been settled about the precise meaning of the word *advocatus* more than 500 years after church advocacies had first proliferated in Europe. In 1415, three-quarters of a century after Lupold wrote, King Sigismund could still refer to himself as advocate and protector of the Church when insisting that he had a role to play overseeing the Council of Constance and ending the Papal Schism.[86] Another quarter-century later in 1442, Frederick III and the imperial electors would employ the language of advocacy in their instructions to messengers going to Pope Eugenius IV and the Council of Basel; in calling for a new general council, they insisted that the Roman *princeps* was "advocate of the church" and that the pope "should not impede our most serene lord king from pursuing, by his right of advocacy (*jure advocacionis*), the calling and convening of a council of this kind."[87] Thus, throughout the long history of church advocacy, the proper role of the advocate continued to be open to interpretation – and to offer both ecclesiastical and secular elites the opportunity to advance a variety of political and ideological arguments.

Claims to Advocacy, Claims to Power

As the work of Lupold of Bebenburg shows, we cannot separate discussions about the emperor as advocate of the Roman Church from the

---

[85] See, for example, Konrad of Megenberg, *Ökonomik (Buch II)*, 33, 48, 54 and 72–73.

[86] Regesta Imperii Online, RI XI,1, nos. 1800 and 1807a.

[87] *Deutsche Reichstagsakten*, 16.2:590–91, no. 228, chaps. 10 and 15. For additional fifteenth-century examples of the emperor being labeled advocate of the Roman Church, see Piccolomini, *Pentalogus*, 130; Piccolomini, *Historia Austrialis*, 2:553; Ebendorfer, *Chronica*, 1:497 and 2:853. I have not pursued the language of the emperor as advocate past the year 1500.

broader history of church advocacy. Nor can we draw a sharp distinction between theories of imperial advocacy and the practices of local advocates. As various emperors' efforts to call and oversee church councils indicate, German rulers could use the label of *advocatus* to claim authority and influence over the Church in ways that parallel noble advocates' assertions of their own rights to interfere in churches' affairs. By the fourteenth and fifteenth centuries, when both emperors and nobles had been benefiting for almost a half-millennium from their positions as church advocates, the intermixing of theory and practice, of the imperial and the local, was so thorough that it becomes impossible to disentangle the different strands and to isolate the various forms of advocacy into discrete categories.

Two documents dating from the reign of Emperor Charles IV (1346–78) highlight this point. The first was issued in the name of Charles himself, who did not hesitate to use the title of advocate to press his own claims, referring to himself at one point as "general advocate of churches" (*advocatus generalis ecclesiarum*).[88] In 1357, he intervened in a dispute between the Teutonic Order and the burghers of Mühlhausen in Thuringia over the Order's parish rights in the town. The emperor appointed a bishop to hear the case and justified his intervention in this ecclesiastical matter by explaining in a letter that he was, as ruler, "an advocate of holy churches and protector of clerical freedom" (*ein voget der heiligen kirchen und beschirmer geistlicher friheit*) with the duty to defend churches' rights.[89] Thus, for Charles IV, the idea that the German kings and emperors were advocates for all churches gave him the authority to insert himself into even the most local and mundane of ecclesiastical affairs in his territories.[90]

The second document demonstrates that leading nobles also recognized in church advocacy the opportunity to assert broad-ranging rights when pursuing their own local interests. In 1361, the famed Italian Renaissance scholar Petrarch wrote to Charles IV to offer his assessment of an unusual document that had been presented to the imperial court a short time earlier. It was a privilege supposedly issued in the name of King Henry IV in 1058 for Margrave Ernst of Austria, and it included translations of two earlier privileges, "written in the language of the

---

[88] Const., 10:569–70, no. 753. For Charles IV's use of the title of advocate, see also Hölscher, *Kirchenschutz*, 79; Johanek, "Die 'Karolina,'" 805, 828–31.

[89] Const., 12:203–05, no. 187. See also Lindner, "Weitere Textzeugnisse."

[90] Similarly, in a 1473 letter concerning the monastery of Hersfeld, Emperor Frederick III refers to himself as "Obirster voyt" when describing his role as the protector of all churches in his lands: Marburg, Staatsarchiv Urk. 56, no. 1118.

pagans," concerning the region of Austria.[91] One of these was purport-edly issued by Julius Caesar, the other by Emperor Nero. Both limited the rights of the Roman emperors over Austria and guaranteed the rulers of this region a remarkable amount of authority. Needless to say, Petrarch had little trouble identifying these two documents as forgeries. Caesar's titulature incorrectly included the title *augustus*; the dating formulae in both texts did not follow ancient Roman practices; and the term used for Austria, *terra Orientalis*, was nonsensical from the perspec-tive of someone living in Rome.[92] One could add, as Eneas Silvius Piccolomini would note approximately a century after Petrarch's asses-sment, that it would have been unnecessary for someone to translate documents issued by Julius Caesar and Nero from "the language of the pagans" into Latin.[93] The forgers working at the court of the Habsburg Duke Rudolf IV of Austria in 1358/59, who produced this and several other forged privileges asserting that the rulers of Austria rivaled the status and rank of the (Holy) Roman Emperors, could not fool the Italian humanists.

For modern readers, the documents supposedly issued by Julius Caesar and Nero are so outrageous that they can easily lead us to overlook the other sections of King Henry IV's faked privilege. The forgers working for Duke Rudolf IV included in this charter additional claims, which were equally bold and assertive. Near the close of the document, they have Henry IV grant to Margrave Ernst and all his successors that "they ought to be advocates and lords (*advocati et domini*)" over the archbishopric of Salzburg, the bishopric of Passau and all of these churches' properties.[94] Given that the bishopric of Passau extended down the Danube river valley to Vienna and that the archbishopric of Salzburg was the dominant ecclesiastical power in the eastern Alps, asserting advocatial and lordly rights over these two churches was akin to the Habsburgs claiming total control over the ecclesiastical infrastructure in their Austrian territories. Like Emperor Charles IV, Duke Rudolf IV saw in the position of advocate the oppor-tunity to make expansive political and ideological claims. More than 300 years after advocacy first became a subject of forgeries produced by religious communities, an imperial prince had also come to recognize

---

[91] DD H IV, 1:52–54, no. 42. See also the more recent edition in *Privilegium maius*, 9–11, no. 1.

[92] Klecker, "Echtheitskritik," 194–95.   [93] Ibid., 195, n. 8.

[94] DD H IV, 1:52–54, no. 42. For the phrase *advocatus et dominus*, see Chapter 14. For the distinction in the fourteenth and fifteenth centuries between lords' rights and advocates' rights, see Schreiner, "Grundherrschaft."

how forging a document could help to shape the idea of advocatial authority to his own advantage.

Conclusion

In the late twelfth and early thirteenth centuries, a period some historians have described as a time when church advocacy was on the decline, the ideological and political significance of the advocate was increasing rapidly.[95] Both popes and emperors saw in the role of advocate a new way to characterize the relationship between imperial authority and the Roman Church. However, as I have argued throughout this book, there was not enough agreement between secular and ecclesiastical elites on the proper role of the advocate for church advocacy to be a neutral category with well-defined powers and authority. Like the countless nobles, bishops, abbots and abbesses who clashed over advocacies at the local level between 1000 and 1250, the German rulers and popes soon came into conflict over what it meant to be the "special advocate of the holy Roman church." Into the fourteenth and fifteenth centuries, advocacy remained an important issue in debates about the nature of papal and imperial authority precisely because its definition was so elusive. With the figure of the *advocatus*/*Vogt* playing such a prominent and contested role at the uppermost levels of politics, it is unsurprising that advocacy continued to be a vexed issue at the local level too. Indeed, as the next chapter will show, the position of advocate became even more capacious in the centuries after 1250 than it had been in the preceding ones, entangling advocates even more thoroughly in the contentious history of protection and justice in Europe.

---

[95] For this scholarship, see Chapter 10.

12   From Lordship to Government?

During the late 1420s, following the repeated failure of crusades launched into the Czech lands against them, the Hussites went on the offensive and began raiding the territories of some of their neighbors.[1] According to one annalist writing in the German archdiocese of Magdeburg, they first attacked Silesia, to the north, where they "killed Christians without mercy."[2] Then, in 1430, the Hussites turned their attention to the lands to the west of Bohemia in the German kingdom. As the author explains, "The Czechs entered the land of the advocates (*terram Advocatorum*) and destroyed the town of Plauen with its castle and the town of Hof, and entering into Franconia, they devastated ... very many towns."[3] What was this "land of the advocates"? As unfamiliar as the term may be for many readers, the author of this passage knew his geography well. He was referring to a small region located today in the corner of Germany where the federal states of Saxony, Thuringia and Bavaria come together along the border with the Czech Republic. It is a region that still bears the name "Advocate Land" in German: *das Vogtland*.

The term originates with a lineage whose leading members began to appear with the label "advocate of Weida" in the early thirteenth century.[4] The early history of these advocates and their authority is impossible to reconstruct with any certainty, but it seems that a church advocacy was not the basis for their advocatial position. Rather, the Staufen dynasty of German rulers apparently granted a local ministerial, Henry of Weida, judicial authority over imperial territories in the region.[5] Henry's lineage soon added the advocacies for two other towns, Gera and Plauen. However, its members did not obtain a more illustrious title – such as count – that might have led them to stop using *advocatus* as their principal

---

[1] Housley, *Later Crusades*, 256–57.   [2] *Gesta Archiepiscoporum Magdeburgensium*, 461.
[3] Ibid., 462.
[4] The lineage probably originated in the early twelfth century, but its members first began using the title *advocatus* in the early thirteenth century: Schmidt, ed., *Urkundenbuch*, 1:13–16, nos. 37–38. See also DD F II, 136–39, no. 234.
[5] Billig, *Pleissenland–Vogtland*, 23–30.

designation[6] As a result, by the early fourteenth century the lineage's charters place the position of advocate front and center. In one from 1306 (which also highlights the family's fondness for naming all of its male members Henry), the three leading men in the lineage are listed as "We, Henry the elder advocate of Weida, Henry the younger advocate of Plauen, and Henry the advocate of Gera."[7] This was clearly a region under the authority of advocates, a *terra advocatorum* or *Vogtland*.

Like the increasingly sophisticated claims of the German kings and emperors to be advocates of the Roman Church, the appearance of "the land of the advocates" highlights the vitality and mutability of the terms *advocatus* and *Vogt* in the period from the thirteenth to the fifteenth century. Despite the efforts of rulers, popes and prelates to limit advocatial abuses, the number of advocates did not decline after 1250; on the contrary, the terms *advocatus* and *Vogt* became attached to a variety of new positions in both ecclesiastical and secular administrative settings.[8] Evidence for church advocates, urban advocates (*advocatus civitatis* or *Stadtvogt*), territorial advocates (*advocatus terrae/provincialis* or *Landvogt*) and the advocates for individual villages, properties and estates abounds after 1250. One of the most extraordinary features of the terms *advocatus* and *Vogt* in the fourteenth and fifteenth centuries is that their usage extended across an enormous span of the social spectrum, from kings and emperors to the imperial princes to lesser nobles to non-nobles, including burghers. The quotidian character of advocacy is evident in the emergence of *Vogt* and its various spelling variations – *Voit*, *Voigt*, *Voight*, and so on – as surnames in this period.[9] From the lands of the Swiss Confederacy to the territories under the control of the Teutonic Order along the Baltic Sea coast, advocates were seemingly ubiquitous.

This chapter examines the proliferation of different types of advocates between the thirteenth and fifteenth centuries. In the opening sections, it provides brief overviews of the history of church advocacy, urban advocacy and territorial advocacy during this period in order to lay the groundwork for my broader arguments about advocates in the centuries

---

[6] See, for example, Schmidt, ed., *Urkundenbuch*, 1:31–32, no. 66; 37–38, no. 74 and 41–43, no. 83.

[7] Ibid., 1:187–88, no. 387: "*Wir Heinrich der alde voit von Wida und Heinrich der junge voit von Plawe und Heinrich der voit von Gera.*" See also ibid., 2:7–9, no. 7; 11–13, no. 12.

[8] Another lineage that used the title *advocatus/Vogt* throughout the later Middle Ages and into the early modern period was the lineage from Hunolstein in the archdiocese of Trier; see, for example, Toepfer, ed., *Urkundenbuch*, 1:21–22, no. 29 and 3:8–9, no. 11.

[9] See, for example, *Lübecker Niederstadtbuch*, 1:566, no. 4 ("*Johannis Voghet filii Hermanni Voghet*"). Various sources indicate that legal advocates who represented people without legal standing (typically an *Advokat* in German) could also be called *Vogt* in this period; see, for example, UB Strassburg, 2:410–11, no. 462, which concerns the *Vogt* for a dead knight's children and uses the term *vogtkint*. For the extraordinary diversity of late medieval advocates, see Teuscher, "Böse Vögte?," 90–91.

after 1250. The final section turns to the question of whether or not the spread of new forms of advocacy ought to be understood – as it often has been in scholarship on the subject – as a feature of the rise of the territorial state and the growth of bureaucratic forms of officeholding between 1250 and 1500. I will argue here that teleologies that posit a clear transition from lordship to government tend to downplay the rich evidence for these new advocates acting in ways that parallel earlier advocates' activities. The challenges and opportunities that arose from providing protection and exercising justice at the local level continued to shape the role of advocate – and to generate conflicts – into the fifteenth century.

Church Advocates

While new advocacies of various sorts proliferated between 1250 and 1500, the strategies pursued by churches in the twelfth and early thirteenth centuries to rein in their advocates' authority led to a reduction in the number of older ecclesiastical advocacies.[10] The term *advocatus* disappears from the sources for many religious communities as people with other labels took on responsibilities relating to protection and justice.[11] Moreover, the two most important new religious orders to appear in the thirteenth century, the Dominicans and Franciscans, did not as a general rule use advocates. They sought the protection of the rulers and territorial princes and used secular agents, who appear most often with the label *procurator*, to oversee their property regimes.[12] Thus, at the macro-level of the Church's infrastructure as a whole, advocacy was much less common in the German-speaking lands after 1250 than it had been in preceding centuries.

Nevertheless, every church advocacy has its own history, and some religious communities would continue to have advocates into the fifteenth century – and, in some cases, even the eighteenth. This does not mean that these advocacies remained unchanged. The reification and commodification of advocatial rights (and lords' landed rights more generally) from the thirteenth century onward altered the economic

---

[10] See Chapter 8.
[11] Andermann, "Aspekte"; Simon, *Grundherrschaft*, 41–42; Stievermann, *Landesherrschaft*, 25, 29; Fried, "Modernstaatliche," 303–06. For specific examples, see Klohn, *Entwicklung*, 74–97; Arnold, *Count*, 138–44.
[12] As with the Cistercians (see Chapter 5), to claim that Dominican and Franciscan houses did not have advocates is to oversimplify a complex situation. See the discussion of some Dominican women's houses in the Habsburg lands in today's Switzerland in Wehrli-Johns, "Stifter," 31–41, for a dispute between the Dominican convent at Töss and a count over advocatial rights. Moreover, the *procurator* could be just as complicated a figure at the local level as an *advocatus*: Neidiger, *Mendikanten*, 53–57, 73–85, 132–36. See also Stievermann, *Landesherrschaft*, 9–29. For the secular *Pfleger* who was responsible for, among other things, punishment of disobedient Beguines, see Degler-Spengler, "Beginen," 71–74.

significance of advocacy.[13] Increasingly, many church advocacies circulated among multiple, short-term holders as rulers and imperial princes sought to strengthen their patronage networks or gain short-term financial advantages.[14] In some cases, burghers acquired these church advocacies, which would have been unimaginable in 1000 or 1150.[15] Once advocacies became an object of exchange – meaning that the person who held the advocacy could receive the advocatial income from it without necessarily being the one exercising protection and justice – women too could hold them and appear with the label *Vögtin*.[16]

While church advocacy could look quite different after 1250, there is ample evidence for similarities with the preceding period too. One place where continuity can be seen clearly is royal and imperial privileges. In April of 1349, King Charles IV followed in the footsteps of his tenth-century predecessors, decreeing in a privilege for the bishop of Speyer that "no duke or count or any public judge or [anyone else] except only the bishop and his advocate for the church of Speyer . . . has the power . . . to hold a lawcourt or make a public judgment within the city of Speyer."[17] Two years later, he confirmed earlier privileges regulating the advocacy for a religious community belonging to the monastery of Siegburg.[18] And in 1357, he confirmed a pair of privileges issued earlier in the fourteenth century by the dukes of Brabant for a Cistercian convent; in one, he acknowledged the duke was "the highest advocate (*superior advocatus*) of the [convent] and of all the properties belonging to [it]" and was to defend the community from all violence.[19] Thus, the

---

[13] See Chapter 6 and Gillen, *Saint-Mihiel*, 144–55. For "*die Verdinglichung der Herrschaftsrechte*" more generally after 1250, see Fried, "Modernstaatliche," 301; Schubert, *Fürstliche Herrschaft*, 19–26.

[14] As I have insisted already (see especially Chapter 3), it is essential to avoid rigid structural and institutional approaches to advocacy. Distinguishing between the old, heritable advocacy over a church and the late medieval *Schirmvogtei* of the *Landesherr* is not always easy: Wehrli-Johns, "Stifter," 32–33; Stievermann, *Landesherrschaft*, 21.

[15] See the section "Urban Advocates" below and Stievermann, *Landesherrschaft*, 50–72; Hardy, *Political Culture*, 76; Hesse, *Amtsträger*, 473–82.

[16] For a countess's claims on an advocacy, see *Urkundenbuch des Stiftes Fischbeck*, 1:86–87, no. 84. For the term *Vögtin*, see Vienna, Stadt- und Landesarchiv, Bürgerspital – Urkunden, nos. 520 and 529. My thanks to Christina Lutter, Herbert Krammer and Daniel Frey for calling the latter two charters to my attention.

[17] Const., 9:178–79, no. 232. Cf. Duggan, *Bishop and Chapter*, 105–06. See also Chapter 3.

[18] Const., 10:196–99, no. 268. For Siegburg, see Chapter 5. Most prominent monasteries of the eleventh and twelfth century did not disappear after 1250 in the face of new orders like the Franciscans; many remained important: Mixson, *Poverty's Proprietors*, 1–9.

[19] Const., 12:19–22, no. 16. For the persistence into this period of the idea that nobles were responsible for providing protection to churches, see Schreiner, "Religiöse," 398–99. For the military responsibilities associated with a church advocacy into the fourteenth century, see Carré, "Avoueries," 48–51.

German rulers continued to treat some church advocacies in familiar ways.[20]

Similarly, leading nobles continued to recognize the value of the position of church advocate for both their status and their financial interests. Margrave Ludwig of Brandenburg (d. 1361), the son of King Ludwig IV "the Bavarian," included in his impressive list of titles a set of church advocacies he had acquired when he married his second wife; he was "margrave of Brandenburg, Landsberg and Lower Lusatia, high chamberlain of the Holy Roman Empire, count-palatine of the Rhine, duke in Bavaria and in Carinthia, count of Tyrol and Gorizia, and advocate of the churches of Aquileia, Trent and Brixen."[21] Accounts of the dues owed in cash and kind from lands and other rights (a type of work known as an *Urbar* in German) show many nobles continuing to record in detail what they received from their church advocacies.[22] *Weistümer*, which became increasingly common in the late fourteenth and fifteenth centuries, provide additional evidence along these lines. These were written confirmations of local customs and rights, formal acknowledgments by both the lord of a community and the members of that community of their reciprocal obligations.[23] If, as was often the case, the religious community that possessed a particular village or manor relied on an advocate to exercise its local rights, then the advocate would feature prominently in the *Weistum*. Discussions of how often the advocate should access the property, how long he should stay, how much he should be fed and the extent of his jurisdiction abound in these sources.

For example, Count-Palatine Stephen of Simmern-Zweibrücken (1410–59) issued a *Weistum* around the year 1445 to clarify his rights as advocate of the Augustinian house of Ravengiersburg. He was "chief hereditary advocate (*ein oberster Ehrbvaut*) and judge over capital crimes so long as the house of Ravengiersburg's court lasts."[24] After briefly listing his judicial rights, he turned to the subject of his income: "In mid-May, the provost or his chief [agent] should give to my honorable

[20] A treatise written in 1439, which claims to reflect the reforming interests of Charles IV's son Emperor Sigismund, insists that every religious community ought to have a *castenvogt*; see *Reformation Kaiser Siegmunds*, 180, 183, 190, 202 and 208.

[21] Const., 10:31–32, no. 42. See also *Preussisches Urkundenbuch*, 4:118–19, no. 130. His wife belonged to the lineage of the counts of Gorizia (Görz) and Tyrol, who had used this phrasing in their own titulature: see, for example, Const., 5:431, no. 541. For context, see Pfeifer, "Landwerdung."

[22] Gruber, ed., *Urkunden*, 26*–27*; 65*–66*; 189, no 206; 304, no. 1328; and 422, no. 3547. Numerous other *Urbare* and *Lehenbücher* also provide evidence for local church advocacies and the income they provided. See, for example, *Habsburgische Urbar*; *Reichenauer Lehenbücher*. See also *Salbuch*, 78 and 89.

[23] For an excellent discussion of *Weistümer*, see Teuscher, *Lords' Rights*, esp. 42–47.

[24] Wagner, "Weistum," 75.

lord, as legitimate advocate and protector of the monastery, sixty-seven and one-half heller [a type of coin], and also one pound, eighteen *albi* [silver pennies] as payment."[25] The same amount was due on the twenty-ninth of September. He was to receive other benefits as well: "Each house, as long as both husband and wife are alive, will give annually to my honorable lord, the advocate, so long as the monastery's court lasts, one measure of grain and one hen, called the *Vogthafer* and *Vogthuhn*."[26] While the terminology in this fifteenth-century German *Weistum* differs in some ways from that of twelfth-century Latin charters, the similarities are nevertheless clear: Exercising justice over the community's dependents remains front and center – as does what the advocate should be paid for doing it.[27]

While some scholars have suggested that the *Weistümer* were written versions of older oral traditions that had remained largely unchanged for centuries, more recent work has insisted that we read these documents as products of negotiation at the time they were written.[28] We cannot assume that the payments listed in this 1445 *Weistum* were the payments the canons and their dependents had always made since time immemorial. This particular *Weistum* seems to have been an attempt by Stephen, whose lineage had acquired this advocacy only two years before he became count-palatine, to clarify his rights. He was apparently quite successful in these negotiations, because other evidence suggests that the canons at Ravengiersburg had not recognized such wide-ranging advocatial rights in the past.[29] Regardless, what is most significant for my argument here is that the count-palatine was still asserting a right to collect grain and chickens from the religious house's dependents 400 years after these types of payments first appear in the sources. Clearly, local monastic advocacies remained important to even high-ranking secular nobles into the fifteenth century. These were not dusty old rights that had lost their value in a changing world; they were still vital and worth defining – and, as we will see, also worth fighting over.[30]

---

[25] Ibid., 76.   [26] Ibid., 82.

[27] For another example of a *Weistum* that echoes earlier sources about advocatial rights and responsibilities, see from 1495: Schrötter, ed., *Urkundenbuch*, 767–75, no. 948. See especially p. 772, where the *Vogtherr* is discussed in the context of ecclesiastical property transactions in ways that echo sources dating back to the ninth century (see Chapter 2).

[28] Teuscher, *Lords' Rights*.   [29] Wagner, "Weistum," 79–84.

[30] For a similar example, see Marburg, Staatsarchiv Urk. 56, no. 927. For the continuing importance of advocatial income for many rulers into the fifteenth and sixteenth centuries, see Körner, "Steuern"; Wild, "Herrenchiemsee," 143–44. For the importance more generally of agricultural products for noble finances in this period: Bünz, "Adlige Unternehmer?," 43–49; Andermann, "Grundherrschaften."

Church advocacy's enduring significance is also evident in regions east of the German kingdom. As previously noted, church advocacy had begun to spread in this direction in the late twelfth and early thirteenth centuries with the establishment of the march of Brandenburg east of the Elbe River.[31] The pattern was similar in Polish Silesia. Abbot Peter of the Cistercian monastery of Henryków, writing in the second half of the thirteenth century, insisted that only the dukes of Silesia were the monastery's advocates, though others had tried to claim the position.[32] Other prelates in this region relied on advocates too. In 1225, the bishop of Wrocław charged "Walter, our advocate," with settling Germans (*Teutonicos*) on some of the bishop's territories. Walter and his heirs were to be paid "for their expenses and labor" founding and administering the new settlement. Because the bishop also wanted Walter and his heirs to exercise justice in the region "as sole advocate in the German legal tradition" (*solum in iure Teutonico advocatum*), he gave them one-third of the judicial fines as well.[33] While Walter's role establishing a settlement is a novel one from the perspective of earlier sources about advocates, his responsibilities exercising justice had deep roots.

German expansion along the Baltic coast spread church advocacy even farther from the old Carolingian heartlands. The best early evidence for this phenomenon is Henry of Livonia's *Chronicle*, written in the first half of the thirteenth century and centering on the region around Riga in today's Latvia. Already in 1206/1207, within a decade of the start of sustained missionary efforts in the area, the new bishop of Riga had appointed "faithful men" to exercise justice through the "office of advocacy" (*officium advocacie*).[34] However, Henry reported that difficulties with advocates began shortly thereafter:

A certain pilgrim knight, Gottfried, was ... sent to Treiden [Turaida] to attend to the office of advocacy in secular law (*ad procurandum officium advocacie in iure seculari*). He went through the parishes, settling the disputes and quarrels of men, collected money and a great number of gifts, and, sending a little bit to the bishop, kept most of it for himself ... Because he had acted unjustly in perverting judgment and oppressing the poor, in justifying the iniquitous and despoiling the converts, by the just judgment of God it so happened that ... he afterwards died a shameful death, as some report.[35]

---

[31] See Chapter 5 and *Brandenburgisches Klosterbuch*, 335 and 865. Church advocacy did not spread to Bohemia: Wihoda, "Kirche."

[32] *Local Society*, 109–10.

[33] *Schlesisches Urkundenbuch*, 1:163–64, no. 225. For advocates in this region, see also *Local Society*, 153–54, 160–61, 169, 180, 186; Hoffmann, *Land*, 107, 114, 241 and 257.

[34] Henry of Livonia, *Livländische Chronik*, 46, X.15 (English translation: Henry of Livonia, *Chronicle*, 67). See also Stikāne, "Vogtei," 13.

[35] Henry of Livonia, *Livländische Chronik*, 50, XI.4. With some exceptions, I follow the translation in Henry of Livonia, *Chronicle*, 70, where the translator translates *advocatus* as

These are familiar accusations, but in a decidedly unfamiliar place – more than 1,000 kilometers from most of the sites I have discussed to this point in the book. Despite these early problems, advocacies continued to proliferate rapidly in the region around Riga, and Henry of Livonia frequently references advocates playing both judicial and military roles throughout his work.[36]

The arrival of the Teutonic Knights on the scene in Prussia and Livonia in the mid-thirteenth century further expanded the number of advocates active in the region.[37] Since the Order's members were drawn largely from German noble families, the position must have been a familiar one among the Teutonic Knights from the start. In the same period when many bishops in the German kingdom were purchasing and eliminating the advocacies over their bishoprics, the Order was appointing advocates for its newly founded bishoprics.[38] A privilege from April 1346 from the Prussian bishopric of Sambia looks similar in many ways to documents from German churches in earlier centuries: "We, brother John of Loensteyn, advocate of the church of Sambia, recognize and make known ... that we conveyed to [a man] and his true heirs two estates with the will and consent of our reverend lord Jacob, bishop of the same church."[39] Three years later, another advocate was present alongside the bishop of Sambia for the settlement of an inheritance dispute.[40] These church advocates played well-established roles within the bishopric's property regime – though as brothers of the Teutonic Order they combined military and monastic duties in ways that most advocates did not.[41]

During the fourteenth and fifteenth centuries, the position of advocate was a common one in the territories held by the Teutonic Knights. Members of the Order held most of these advocacies, and the sources

"magistrate." For churchmen's critiques of advocates in Livonia, see Stikāne, "Vogtei," 21.

[36] See, for example, Henry of Livonia, *Livländische Chronik*, 105, XVI.2; 107, XVI.3; 159, XXIII.7; 178–81, XXV.2; 185, XXV.5; and 189–90, XXVI.5–7. See also Stikāne, "Vogtei," 14–15.

[37] For advocacy in Livonia before and after the arrival of the Teutonic Knights, see Stikāne, "Vogtei." For a different approach to advocacy and the Teutonic Order, see Borchardt, "Vogtei."

[38] For an early example, see *Preussisches Urkundenbuch*, 2:35–36, no. 59.

[39] *Preussisches Urkundenbuch*, 4:16–17, no. 17. See also ibid., 26–29, nos. 26–28 and 216–17, no. 245.

[40] Ibid., 4:401–02, no. 442.

[41] The *advocatus* for the Prussian bishopric of Warmia (Ermland) at this time was also a member of the order: ibid., 4:12, no. 13: "*frater Bruno de Lutir eiusdem ecclesie advocatus.*" For him, see also ibid., 4:22–23, no. 23; 93–94, no. 99; and 98–99, no. 105. His successor in the position was a *frater Nicolaus de Bohemia* (ibid., 4:274–76, no. 309, esp. n. 2). For the bishopric of Pomesania, see ibid., 4:29–31, no. 29. For a member of the order as the advocate for some of the bishop of Kulm's territories, see ibid., 4:36–37, no. 36.

frequently show individual knights holding different advocacies at different times – while cycling through various other positions as well.[42] Between 1402 and 1455, for example, fifteen different brothers held "the office of advocate of Neumark."[43] As the representative of the Master of the Order in this region, the advocate was tasked with receiving homage from the people under the Order's authority, organizing the military resources of his region on behalf of the Order and settling local disputes.[44] Since they were also knights, they had responsibilities whenever the Order went to war, and many of these advocates were praised for their actions in battle.[45] In short, as different as this setting was from an eleventh-century monastic advocacy in Alsace or Austria, exercising justice and providing protection consistently surface in the sources as important responsibilities for these advocates too.

Thus, in many regions, church advocacy remained an important feature of local practices of protection and justice between the years 1250 and 1500. Its eastward spread in this period is evidence that it continued to serve a useful function in some places long after it had disappeared from other places farther west. Indeed, as the evidence from the territories controlled by the Teutonic Order demonstrates, the position of church advocate remained remarkably flexible and adaptable to new situations and needs. The blending of elements of continuity and novelty gave it much of its vitality between 1250 and 1500 – and gave those people who appear in the sources as *advocatus* and *Vogt* numerous opportunities to test the limits of their rights and responsibilities, much as their predecessors had done.

Urban Advocates

That advocates could exercise justice and provide protection for urban communities was well established by the year 1250. Already in the tenth century, the Ottonian rulers had issued privileges stipulating that bishoprics, monasteries and convents could appoint advocates for the towns and proto-towns under their authority.[46] Scattered examples from the

---

[42] Sarnowsky, *Wirtschaftsführung*, 116–35; Jähnig, "Vögte." In 1410, Michael Küchmeister briefly served as *Vogt* of the Neumark; he would later become head of the Order. For lists of the holders of different advocacies in Prussia and Livonia, see various articles in Czaja and Radzimiński, ed. *Teutonic Order*.

[43] Jähnig, "Vögte," 327.

[44] Neitmann, "Huldigung" (see especially the text editions on pp. 285–317).

[45] See, for example, the story of the *Vogt* of Goldingen in *Livländische Reimchronik*, lines 8,929–9,192.

[46] The case of Zurich in the late Carolingian period suggests the idea may be even older; see Chapters 2 and 3.

eleventh and early twelfth centuries similarly point to advocatial rights extending into urban communities.[47] As in the Ottonian period, most of these were the advocates of towns held by churches, and the early history of urban advocacy is therefore a component of the broader history of ecclesiastical advocacy. How an urban advocate in an episcopal town might have differed from a rural advocate for the same bishopric is difficult to know in most cases, because town advocates – as with so many other features of urban history in the eleventh and twelfth centuries – are only visible through occasional, brief references in the extant sources. It is not until the first half of the thirteenth century that the evidence improves, and the significance of urban advocates becomes more apparent.[48]

For the period 1250 to 1500, the starting point for any analysis of town advocacies is determining who held authority over the urban community. Was it under the direct authority of the German rulers (an imperial town)? Or that of a local noble lineage, bishop, abbot or abbess, who appointed agents to assert his or her rights of justice and protection inside the town? Or, was the burgher elite of the town able to staff its own courts and organize its own protection? In all of these cases, the person tasked with exercising justice and/or providing protection for the urban community might be labeled "town advocate" (*advocatus civitatis* or *Stadtvogt*) in the sources.[49] Unsurprisingly, given the different forms that authority over towns could take, these urban advocates came from a range of different social strata, noble and nonnoble.

Because rulers, prelates and leading nobles could all possess towns in the German kingdom, the history of some urban advocacies is traceable in sources produced at the highest levels of the secular and ecclesiastical elite. In 1197, Count-Palatine Henry of the Rhine (a son of Duke Henry the Lion) renounced his rights to the advocacy of the town of Trier and ceded them to the archbishops there, possibly in return for money to help fund his journey to the Holy Land later that year.[50] There is little evidence for what happened to the position of town advocate for the next 150 years – until, in the mid-1350s, Archbishop Baldwin of Trier asserted his claim to the title

---

[47] Nieus, "Vicomte"; Carré, "Avoueries"; Kupper, "L'avouerie"; Évrard, "Les avoueries."
[48] For towns' increased use of writing after 1200, see Bertrand, *Documenting*, 371–80. Bertrand's hesitancy to link this increase in writing to institutions and "administration" aligns well with many of my own arguments here.
[49] Not all towns had advocates. In many, a comparable role was played by the *scultetus/Schultheiß*. In Alsace, some towns employed one term, some the other; see Schmidberger, *Städtische Führungsgruppen*, 83. See also Stercken, *Städte*, 169–73; Isenmann, *Deutsche Stadt*, 216. *Schultheiß* is another position that would benefit from a wide-ranging study; see Buchholzer-Rémy, "Herrschaft."
[50] Ziwes, "Verzicht." See also Briechle, *Heinrich*, 197–200.

in a conflict with the burghers of the town. He insisted that he was lord and advocate (*voyt*) of Trier and that he possessed all secular and ecclesiastical judicial authority there. Emperor Charles IV agreed, issuing a privilege for the archbishops in 1364, which confirmed their possession of the town advocacy.[51]

The significance of an urban advocacy for political control over a town is also evident at Strasbourg in Alsace. As with many other episcopal towns, there are hints of advocates in twelfth-century sources, but no definitive conclusions about the role can be drawn from these.[52] The town advocacy first comes into clearer focus during the conflicts between Emperor Frederick II and the Papacy. In 1244, the pro-papal cathedral chapter decreed that "we will not concede, nor permit our bishop to concede, the advocacy of Strasbourg with its appurtenances to any illustrious or super-illustrious (*superillustri*) person, namely an emperor, a king, a duke, or the children of the same."[53] Five years later, the advocacy was held by a local noble family, and "Louis of Lichtenberg, advocate of Strasbourg," agreed, along with his sons, never to give the advocacy to anyone else in fief or by any other kind of transfer.[54] It was too important to the town's rule to allow it to fall into the wrong hands: in this case, those of the emperor or his allies.

The political upheaval in the German kingdom during the 1240s and 1250s was also a crucial period for the advocacy of Ulm, an imperial town on the upper Danube river.[55] The counts of Dillingen had held the advocacy from the emperors since the twelfth century but sided against Emperor Frederick II (and the burghers of Ulm) in the mid-thirteenth century. In 1255, after almost a decade of conflict, the urban community and Count Albert IV of Dillingen made peace and reached an agreement on the count's advocatial rights in the town.[56] For most cases that could not be handled by the town's court, the count was to receive one-third of the judicial fines; however, the agreement also stipulated: "our lord count shall celebrate a provincial court session in our city three times per year, and there, our agent shall sit with him at his side. From whatever money is

[51] Laufner, "Ausbildung," 127–28.
[52] See, for example, UB Strassburg, 1:467–76, no. 616. See also Dollinger, "Strassburg," 161.
[53] UB Strassburg, 1:220–21, no. 290. See also ibid., 1:235–36, no. 312.
[54] Ibid., 1:249–50, no. 334. See also Egawa, *Stadtherrschaft*, 46, 62 and 154–55. For more on the advocates of Strasbourg, see the section "The Rise of Bureaucratic Officialdom?" below, and Chapter 13.
[55] For imperial towns, see Meyer-Schlenkrich, "Imperial City"; Zeilinger, "Urban Lordships"; Isenmann, *Deutsche Stadt*, 295–311.
[56] Württembergisches Urkundenbuch online, 5:118–20, no. 1352. For this agreement, see also Layer, "Grafen," 80–85.

earned then from punishments, two parts of it go to our lord count, one-third to the agent of our city."[57] The count also was to receive other income from the town. Moreover, even when "for the good of peace" other people were prohibited from entering the town with swords and shields, the advocate and his men were permitted to do so. Much like a religious community, this urban community needed to grant its noble advocate special privileges, so he could effectively provide justice and protection.

The 1255 agreement between Albert IV and Ulm demonstrates how the position of urban advocate could be a way for members of the landed, secular elite to gain access to the growing wealth of towns. While rural advocacies remained important for many nobles after 1250, town advocacies rapidly gained in significance in this period – for obvious reasons. Urban life was booming.[58] The population density of towns, while still low in comparison with the modern world (most German towns had fewer than 10,000 inhabitants between 1250 and 1500), was much greater than it was in the countryside. Exercising justice and collecting fines at a court held in a town must have been much more profitable than advocatial courts were at the level of the village.[59] Moreover, advocates could also claim other perquisites and other kinds of urban income, which made these positions all the more attractive.

While counts, other nobles and also prelates frequently sought to control the position of town advocate, many urban communities succeeded in gaining the right to appoint their own advocates between the thirteenth and fifteenth centuries. One of the best examples is the town of Lübeck in the north of the German kingdom. In June of 1226, Emperor Frederick II gave the imperial town a privilege, in which he decreed "no outside advocate (*extraneus advocatus*) may presume to control the advocacy or exercise justice within the boundaries of the city."[60] Evidence from the years immediately following this privilege suggest the position of town advocate was an important one; during the second half of the thirteenth century, prominent members of the town council typically fulfilled the role.[61] These

[57] Württembergisches Urkundenbuch online, 5:118–20, no. 1352.
[58] Nicholas, *Medieval City*, 171–84.
[59] As noted in Chapter 6, we do not have records from rural courts in this period, which makes it impossible to know how much advocates typically collected in fines and other fees.
[60] DD F II, 5:653–58, no. 1197. In the first decade of the thirteenth century, King Waldemar II of Denmark had issued a privilege for Lübeck allowing its citizens in the markets of Skänor and Falsterbo (Sweden) to appoint their own *advocatus* to judge their crimes; see *Urkundenbuch der Stadt Lübeck*, 1:20–21, no. 13; Ebel, *Lübisches Recht*, 256.
[61] Lutterbeck, *Der Rat*, 45; Brandt, "Vogtei." For a good comparison between the advocates of Hamburg and Lübeck, see Bock, "Georg von Herwardeshude."

early advocates served as judges responsible for minor disputes and crimes and more generally oversaw the whole judicial process, including the jailing of the accused before the trial.[62] A text from the early fourteenth century lists the many executions carried out (on horse thieves, in particular) by the Lübeck advocate "Little" Conrad (*aduocatus Paruus Conradus*).[63]

The urban community at Lübeck apparently found the position of advocate to be both useful and versatile because advocates appear frequently in sources from the town during the fourteenth century. By 1325 at the latest, there were various advocates in and around Lübeck with responsibilities ranging from exercising justice and pursuing criminals to organizing military campaigns and escorting members of the town council. In the late fourteenth century, some of the town's advocates also played the familiar role of overseeing various property and financial agreements.[64] Lübeck employed advocates on some of its property holdings as well. In 1388, a man named Henry vander Wisch appears as "advocate of the lord consuls of Lübeck in Travemünde."[65]

While some of these advocates were burghers of the town, others (especially those with military responsibilities) were drawn from the local lesser nobility.[66] One source from the early fourteenth century suggests being an advocate for Lübeck was a well-paid position; it explains that the town council "will give eighty marks annually to the advocate Marquard Bome for his salary (*pro suo sallario*) and ten marks for his food and lodging. We will also give to him ten marks for an armed servant of his choice ... and will also give him [money] for his clothes."[67] Thus, not only churches but also burghers recognized the position of advocate to be a vital one that could serve numerous local needs – highlighting the similarities between landed and urban elites and their interests.

The history of advocacy in the imperial town of Goslar followed a different trajectory. Goslar had been an important center for the German rulers since the eleventh century, when it emerged as a key silver-mining site.[68] People identified as advocate for Goslar appear from roughly 1100 onward, and they were likely tasked by the rulers

---

[62] Ebel, *Lübisches Recht*, 256–57.

[63] *Urkundenbuch der Stadt Lübeck*, 2.1:351–52, no. 401.

[64] *Lübecker Niederstadtbuch*, 1:248, no. 4; 284, no. 3; 293, no. 1; 566, no. 3.

[65] Ibid., 1:649, no. 5: "*Hinricus vander Wisch advocatus dominorum consulum Lub in Trauenmunde.*" Because many other towns were heavily influenced by Lübeck law, advocates appear elsewhere in this region too; see, for example, *Preussisches Urkundenbuch*, 4:635, no. 707. See also Ebel, *Lübisches Recht*, 262–69.

[66] Ebel, *Lübisches Recht*, 261–62.

[67] *Urkundenbuch der Stadt Lübeck*, 2.2:1078, no. 1098. See also Ebel, *Lübisches Recht*, 261.

[68] Weinfurter, *Salian Century*, 108.

with exercising authority over the town on their behalf.[69] As late as 1252, King William of Holland still insisted that he would appoint the advocate there.[70] In 1290, however, the burghers acquired the advocacy; the count of Woldenberg, who held it from the duke of Saxony in fief, "sold our advocacy, which we had in the city and outside around the city, to the honorable consuls and to all the citizens in Goslar."[71] The town council then began appointing the advocates, and in the fourteenth century the position circulated among members of important Goslar burgher families, changing hands as frequently as every year or two.[72] These advocates typically adjudicated cases about the pawning or pledging of property. In 1358, "Conrad Romold, advocate of Goslar," confirmed an agreement between the Jewish community in the town and a local church; the Jewish community was to pay the church a measure of wine annually in return for burial rights in a particular location.[73] The surviving register for the advocacy of the town of Kraków in the years 1442–43 parallels the sources from Goslar in describing the role of one advocate, a burgher of Kraków, adjudicating mostly minor intra-urban court cases.[74]

As with church advocacies between 1000 and 1250, town advocacies between 1250 and 1500 were so abundant across such a wide geographical area that it is impossible to discuss more than a small fraction of them here.[75] Within the urban context, the term *advocatus* came with a broad range of responsibilities, and people from across a wide span of the social spectrum could hold the position. This diversity means that, in many

---

[69] Beyond their names, we know little about Goslar's advocates prior to the thirteenth century; for a similar problem, see Borchardt, "Vögte," 3–14. The best early sources for the advocacy are DD F II, 3:203–08, no. 528 and 5:130–31, no. 991. From this same period there survives a tomb effigy (today in the rebuilt imperial palace in Goslar) for the imperially appointed advocate Giselbert of Goslar. He is depicted holding a sword, which leans against his right shoulder, a common image for someone tasked with exercising justice. For this advocate, see also Bode, ed., *Urkundenbuch*, 1:478–80, nos. 486–87.

[70] DD Wilh, 238–39, no. 185. From this period, we have unusually detailed sources for the monetary aspects of the Goslar advocacy: Deich, *Goslarer Reichsvogteigeld.*

[71] Bode, *Urkundenbuch*, 2:389, no. 384; Schneidmüller, "Stadtherr," 172–74.

[72] Many of the fourteenth-century charters in Bode, ed., *Urkundenbuch*, reference the town's advocates. See also Wilke, *Goslarer Reichsgebiet*, 131–41.

[73] Bode, ed., *Urkundenbuch*, 4:476, no. 627. The advocate in the episcopal town of Hildesheim also oversaw minor judicial matters; see, for example, Hildesheim, Bistumsarchiv, Urkunden Stadtvogt zu Hildesheim B IV 2–1. For the different types of responsibilities urban advocates could have, see Kühnle, *Wir, Vogt*, 82.

[74] *Registrum domini advocati Cracoviensis*, 3. Especially noteworthy entries include p. 71, no. 975; 100, no. 1376; 139, no. 1715; 170, no. 1996; and 176, nos. 2054 and 2056. The advocate was Georg Arnsberg the Younger, whose father served on the town council in the early fifteenth century. For earlier evidence from Poland, see Hoffmann, *Land*, 259; Górecki, *Economy*, 269.

[75] For other town advocates, see for example Wackernagel, "Rudolf von Habsburg"; Zeilinger, "Procurator."

cases, it can be very difficult to know what the term meant in any given town at any given time.[76] Moreover, these positions were not static; town advocacies could pass from emperors and nobles to local burghers (and, as we will see, back to emperors and nobles in some cases).[77] Despite this diversity, justice and protection remained central to the position of town advocate, making it possible to draw parallels across time and place with church advocates and other types of advocacy as well. Indeed, while some town advocates may look like nothing more than judges over petty cases, one historian has described the career of Kraków's advocate in the early fifteenth century as being characterized by his "'flexibility' and his inclination toward political tug-of-war."[78] Even this type of advocate, in other words, could find opportunities to *wrassle round*.

Territorial Advocates

While urban advocacy can be traced back to the tenth century, the territorial advocate (*advocatus terrae/provincialis* or *Landvogt*) was a product of the thirteenth. Some scholars have seen this type of advocate as one of the first true imperial officials in the German kingdom (a point to which I will return later in this chapter). Its characterization as an office is reflected in the fact that the term "territorial advocacy" (*Landvogtei*) is sometimes translated as "bailiwick" to compare it to English administrative structures.[79] The oldest reference to a territorial advocate may date to the reign of King Philip of Swabia (1198–1208), but this evidence is problematic.[80] The sources improve in the middle decades of the thirteenth century, especially in the period of the so-called Interregnum after Emperor Frederick II's death in 1250.[81] However, not until the reign of the first Habsburg ruler of the German kingdom, Rudolf I (1273–91), does the territorial advocate emerge as a common position in some places. Rudolf relied on territorial advocates to oversee imperial possessions in the southwest of the German kingdom and along the lower and middle Rhine river.[82] He and his Habsburg descendants (whether kings or not) also used territorial advocates as their lead agents on their own family

---

[76] Ebel, *Lübisches Recht*, 254, where he refers to *"das ungemein beliebte Wort 'Vogt' für die unterschiedlichsten Amtsinhaber."*
[77] Kühnle, *Wir, Vogt*, 82–83.   [78] Starzyński, *Mittelalterliche Krakau*, 55–56.
[79] For institutional perspectives on the office of *Landvogt*, see Moraw, "Organisation," 50; Redlich, *Rudolf von Habsburg*, 454–64. See also, Scheyhing, *Eide*, 120–21. For "bailiwick," see Scott, *Swiss*, 179; Guenée, *States*, 215.
[80] DD Phil, 258–59, no. 114.
[81] Redlich, *Rudolf von Habsburg*, 454–55; Kaiser, "Mandat"; Weiler, "Image," 1126; Schnurrer, "Reichsstadt Rothenburg," 578–80.
[82] Willoweit, "Vogt, Vogtei," col. 941; Moraw, "Organisation," 50.

lands in what is now Switzerland after the lineage acquired the duchy of Austria.[83]

Why did thirteenth-century German rulers (and those around them) decide to call this new position territorial/provincial "advocate"? Other Latin terms could have been chosen instead. King Richard of Cornwall (1257–72) reportedly instituted someone as "advocate ... or governor" (*advocatus ... seu gubernator*) for a region in the southwest of the kingdom, yet "governor" seems to have gained little traction as an alternative.[84] By the fifteenth century, many authors and scribes recognized the term *balivus*, which was common in France, as being essentially synonymous with territorial advocate, yet it too failed to become the standard term for the position.[85] Why not? There is no way to answer this question definitively, but I suspect King Rudolf I's heavy reliance on territorial advocates is best explained by the fact that he started his political life as a count whose lineage had relied heavily on church advocacies to establish its position.[86] As with Frederick Barbarossa, whose own noble background clearly shaped his understanding of advocacy, we must not assume that Rudolf's view of advocacy changed significantly after he was elected king. For him, the role of territorial advocate may have been more akin to that of a noble church advocate than to that of a royal officeholder. As a result, some of the key features of earlier church advocacies – especially providing (and profiting from) justice and protection – may well have shaped the development of the position of territorial advocate.

Historians have analyzed the role of the territorial advocate in the southwest of the German kingdom in much greater detail than they have the territorial advocates who exercised authority in other places.[87] One reason for this is that the most famous advocate in the Western tradition, the tyrannical *Vogt* Gessler of the William Tell legend, plays a central role in the myth of the origins of the Swiss Confederacy.[88] Another reason is the relative richness of the sources for the territorial advocates in this region. They appear in many contemporary narrative histories; they issued various types of documents in their own names; and in some cases,

---

[83] Stercken, "Dominion," 338–39; Sablonier, *Gründungszeit*, 109–37.

[84] *Bellum Waltherianum*, 111.

[85] For *balivus*, see Chapter 13. For other terms used for comparable positions, see Stercken, "Dominion," 338–39; Willoweit, "Vogt, Vogtei," cols. 941–42; Keller, "Capitaneus."

[86] For the early Habsburgs and church advocacy, see Chapter 5. See also, Stercken, "Dominion," 330–31.

[87] Eneas Silvius Piccolomini, who spent time at the court of the Habsburg ruler Frederick III before becoming Pope Pius II, uses the term "Vogtland" to refer to this region where Habsburg territorial advocacies were so abundant: Piccolomini, *Europe*, 198. See also Tribolet, "Traités d'alliance." For territorial advocacy in the region just north of Frankfurt, see Schwind, "Ordnung."

[88] See Chapter 15 and Teuscher, "Böse Vögte?"; Köhn, "Tyrann der Untertanen."

they even had to provide accounts of their income and expenditures while holding the position.[89]

Some of the best sources from this region are the documents drawn up by the Habsburgs upon installing a new territorial advocate. In 1388, for example, Duke Albrecht III of Austria appointed Count Hugo of Montfort as territorial advocate in Aargau, Thurgau and the Black Forest; Hugo was to hold the position for one year in return for a salary of 3,000 gulden, payable in two installments.[90] Five years later, when appointing Engelhard VIII of Weinsberg as territorial advocate in Swabia and neighboring regions for 5 years in return for 7,000 gulden annually, Albrecht and his nephews made it clear that the new *lantfogt* "should hold, be responsible for, and protect our land and all of our towns, markets, villages, people, properties and dependents ... and especially all of our Jews" in the advocacy.[91]

The territorial advocates in the southwest of the German kingdom had a wide range of responsibilities. They defended those religious communities in their advocacy that were under the protection of the German rulers.[92] They also settled disputes, maintained the peace and oversaw judicial assemblies. In 1310, the territorial advocate of Alsace and the territorial advocate in the Speyergau were two of the men who confirmed a peace agreement between the town of Strasbourg and a rival.[93] Territorial advocates could also be responsible for assigning small fiefs on behalf of the rulers, arranging pledges and organizing military campaigns.[94]

Their role in warfare is evident in the diary of Johannes Knebel, a rich source for events in and around Basel in the 1470s, including the war against the duke of Burgundy in 1476–77. Knebel reports in August of 1476 that Count Oswald of Tierstein, whom he labels *balivus* when writing in Latin and *lantvogt* in German, summoned and organized the

---

[89] Narrative sources will be discussed later in this and in the next chapter. For a register of documents concerning one *Landvogt* in the 1390s, see Köhn, "Engelhard von Weinsberg," 32–48. See also pp. 49–119 for an accounting of the same advocate's income and expenditures.

[90] Thommen, ed., *Urkunden*, 2:221–22, no. 233. See also Köhn, "Abrechnungen," 122–26; Teuscher, "Böse Vögte?," 94.

[91] Köhn, "Engelhard von Weinsberg," 32–34, nos. 1–2. For a similar document from a different region, see Margrave Frederick IV of Meissen's 1422 letter appointing a new advocate: CDS I B, 4:107–08, no. 176.

[92] Planta, "Advocacy and 'Defensio.'" See Chapter 13 for more on this issue.

[93] UB Strassburg, 2:235–36, no. 286. See also ibid., 2:423–24, no. 474; 5:660–61, no. 847; and 5:664–65, no. 853. See also Freiburg im Breisgau, Staatsarchiv, StAF, U105/1, no.5 from 1367. For other examples of territorial advocates acting in comparable ways, see Hardy, *Political Culture*.

[94] See, for example, UB Strassburg, 2:221, no. 273 and Const., 4:1, 252, no. 289. See also Moraw, "Organisation," 50.

cavalry of nobles from his territory.[95] A couple of months later, William of Ropoltzstein replaced Oswald as territorial advocate: "Both of them, the old one and the new one, urged all knights, monasteries and churches in [the region] that they should, with all their strength, on foot and on horseback," rush to the aid of a besieged city.[96] A wide range of sources thus demonstrate that justice and protection were just as central to the position of territorial advocate as they had been to that of the church advocate.

While the evidence for territorial advocates is especially abundant in the southwest of the German kingdom, sources from elsewhere also point to the significance of the role. The march of Lower Lusatia, which lay to the south of Brandenburg, had territorial advocates throughout the fifteenth century, because it was frequently held by absentee margraves.[97] In 1481, the territorial advocate of Lower Lusatia freed a man and all his heirs from the "honey money" (honiggelder) he had previously been required to pay.[98] This document highlights the financial aspects of the position of territorial advocate, a point to which I will return later in this chapter, because as with church advocates, they were responsible for collecting various forms of income.[99] The role of territorial advocate also crossed the Oder river into Silesia, an indication that, like other forms of advocacy, it was considered an important part of the administrative framework that German settlers brought with them as they traveled eastward.[100]

As with ecclesiastical and urban advocacies, territorial advocacies proved to be flexible as their use spread. In some places, the term Unterlandvogt, or "territorial subadvocate," appears in the fourteenth century, because the high-ranking nobles who served as territorial advocates sometimes delegated the role to others.[101] Over the course of the fifteenth century, various towns in today's Switzerland gained control of territorial advocacies as they acquired more and more land. Rather than seeing them as vestiges of the bad old days of Habsburg rule, they incorporated them into their own administrative structures. The Swiss town of Bern, for example, appointed Bernese burghers – as opposed to prominent nobles, as the Habsburgs had done – to be the new territorial advocates.[102] The town council of Zurich likewise was responsible for

[95] Knebel, Tagebuch, 3:41.   [96] Ibid., 3:63.
[97] Lehmann, Geschichte der Niederlausitz, 99–100.
[98] Lippert, ed., Urkundenbuch, 175, no. 180.   [99] Moraw, "Organisation," 50.
[100] Hoffmann, Land, 20. See also Local Society, 185, 236 and 237.
[101] This seems to have been especially common in Alsace; see, for example, UB Strassburg, 5:792, no. 1029 and Hilsch, "Bořiwoj von Swinaře," 439–40. For the term subadvocatus, see especially Chapter 7.
[102] Hübner, Dienste, 225–28; Teuscher, "Threats"; Teuscher, Bekannte, 27; and Schreiner, "Religiöse," 426.

272 12 From Lordship to Government?

appointing various territorial advocates in neighboring regions during the fifteenth century.[103] In Lower Lusatia too, the status of the role changed over the course of the fifteenth century, but there the territorial advocacy increasingly attracted the attention of high-ranking nobles.[104] Despite this variety, protection, justice, and the profits to be had from them remained central features of all of these territorial advocacies down to the end of the fifteenth century – and sometimes beyond.

The Rise of Bureaucratic Officialdom?

Advocates appear in too many settings between 1250 and 1500 to discuss all of them here.[105] Their proliferation unfolded against the backdrop of increased oversight of territories and people at all levels of society during this period. The Latin terms *officium* and *officialis* and the German terms *Amt* and *Amtmann*, "office" and "officer," became increasingly common in sources from the thirteenth century onward as rulers, imperial princes and towns all began expanding the scope of their local control. Moreover, juridical texts from this period refer to judicial institutions and judicial officeholders in increasingly ordered and organized ways, further evidence for top-down efforts to administer lands more effectively.[106] These developments occurred with varying levels of intensity across Europe, and historians have typically interpreted this broad trend in one of two ways. For many scholars of earlier generations, this was evidence for the rise of the "state" and of the bureaucratic forms of officeholding that have been central to the state's success.[107] Other scholars, however, have been more cautious in their assessments of the changes unfolding in this period; they insist that, while there is unquestionably evidence for new and more efficient techniques of administration from the thirteenth century onwards, Europe still had a long road to travel before the state and bureaucracies truly took shape.[108]

Evidence for advocacy between 1250 and 1500 can be used to support both of these positions. Some sources seem to depict the advocates of this

---

[103] Dütsch, *Zürcher Landvögte*, 20–21.   [104] See Chapter 13.

[105] For advocacy in territorial administrations in different regions, see Hesse, *Amtsträger*; Willoweit, "Vogt, Vogtei," cols. 941–42.

[106] Brown, *Violence*, 237–38. For Germany, the key text is the *Sachsenspiegel*. The increased oversight and organization made proxy power holders of various sorts (not only advocates) an essential feature of political, legal and economic life: Signori, "Stellvertreter."

[107] See, for example, Wolter, "Amt und Officium"; Guenée, *States*, 114–17; and various articles in *Der deutsche Territorialstaat*. More cautious is Moraw, *Verfassung*, 183–94. See the Introduction for more on this point.

[108] Willoweit, "Entwicklung," 81–92; Hardy, *Political Culture*, 82–83; Schubert, *Fürstliche Herrschaft*, 14–19; Watts, *Polities*, 238–44; Tilly, *Coercion*, 25.

period as officeholders. A privilege issued by King Charles IV in 1352 concerning a grant to a Cistercian monastery includes advocates in the list of agents – *vicariis, burggraviis, advocatis, capitaneis, nobilibus ac civitatum et locorum judicibus, officialibus ac ceteris* – who were to respect the grant.[109] Here, advocates are seemingly indistinguishable from every other high- and mid-ranking member of the royal administration. In addition, by the early fourteenth century, some advocates were being paid an annual salary.[110]

There is also evidence from this period of new strategies for holding advocates accountable. Some urban and territorial advocates served for fixed periods of time, limiting their ability to claim the position as a heritable family possession.[111] Habsburg territorial advocates could also be called to account, with their income and expenses documented and examined by other members of the Habsburg administration to ensure they had done their job properly.[112] An especially striking description of accountability can be found in the mid-fourteenth-century *Chronicle of Holstein*: "Count Nicholas [of Holstein] was mild and humble toward his subjects. When peasants were harmed by his advocates, they visited the count personally, setting forth their case before him ... And whatever they said to him, he heard, and he often delivered a sentence in their favor against his advocates."[113]

All of this evidence reinforces scholarly arguments about the growth of government and bureaucratic officeholding from the thirteenth century onward. Annual salaries, fixed terms in office and the rendering of account were all strategies employed across Europe in this period to try to limit the types of problems that arose when people treated their positions of authority as personal and familial property rather than public offices.[114] Nevertheless, we must be careful not to draw too sharp a dichotomy between "officeholding" advocates and the "lordly" advocates of the preceding chapters.

---

[109] Const., 10:347, no. 452. See, similarly, John of Viktring, *Liber*, 2:17.

[110] See, for example, *Schleswig-Holsteinische Regesten*, 13:20, no. 609, chap. 46: "*solvimus advocato nostro sallarium suum de integro anno.*"

[111] For territorial advocates, see Köhn, "Abrechnungen." For town advocates, see above. For a reference to an *advocatus temporalis*, see *Schlesisches Urkundenbuch*, 1:227–28, no. 308.

[112] Köhn, "Abrechnungen," 117–20. The same is also true of advocates in the Teutonic Order's administration: Jähnig, "Vögte," 328. In some other regions, comparable monitoring of advocates' accounts did not come until the second half of the fifteenth century; see Auge, *Handlungsspielräume*, 190–92.

[113] *Chronicon Holzatiae*, 285. For a similar example, see Korner, *Chronica Novella*, 400–01. I thank my student Tristan Sharp for this latter reference.

[114] Sabapathy, *Officers*; Jordan, "Anti-corruption"; and various articles in *Anticorruption*.

Because most scholarship on advocacy does not analyze the church advocates of the period 1000 to 1250 alongside the urban and territorial advocates of the period 1250 to 1500, advocates of the earlier period are frequently treated as a separate phenomenon from the later ones.[115] We have already encountered a comparable situation in scholarship that assumes a sharp dichotomy between Carolingian "officeholding" advocates and the "lordly" advocates of the period after the year 1000.[116] But the imaginary dividing lines that historians create to separate the past into manageable blocks must not mislead us into thinking entirely new structures and institutions replaced older ones when we shift from an "early Middle Ages" to a "central Middle Ages" to a "later Middle Ages" – and then to a "Renaissance" or "early modern period." If we ignore categories that people in the past knew nothing about, we can start to understand the history of advocacy in a new way, one that focuses less on apparent differences and more on the key similarities between advocates before and after the year 1250.

There is abundant evidence that many advocates in the period 1250 to 1500 pursued familiar strategies when seeking to benefit from their positions. In a letter the new German king Rudolf I wrote to one of his advocates in April of 1274, he warned, "you should be content with the ancient dues and approved tolls in [that] village; besides these, you should demand or require nothing from those passing through, if you want to avoid offending our majesty."[117] While the veiled threat at the end suggests a new level of royal attention to how local agents were profiting from their advocacies, this letter fits a centuries-old pattern of royal attempts to limit advocatial abuses. The wording of a document from fifty years later is even more telling. In 1323, Count Adolf VII of Holstein and Schaumburg and his wife Heilwig gifted a convent the advocacy over an estate and insisted "that none of our advocates or officials (*nullus advocatorum seu officialium nostrorum*) ought henceforth to attack the said properties for any reason or demand provisions (*servitia*) or exactions (*exactiones*) from the properties' inhabitants."[118] While the term "officials" could be read as evidence that the count had a more sophisticated administrative apparatus for his lands than nobles of preceding centuries

---

[115] German scholarship has tended to draw a clear distinction between the new administrative advocates of post-1250 and the noble church advocates of the earlier period. See on this point Clauss, *Untervogtei*, 172; Sablonier, *Adel im Wandel*, 214; Scheyhing, *Eide*, 113–27. It is rare, however, for any modern works, other than dictionary and encyclopedia entries on the *Vogt*, to consider pre-1250 church advocates together with post-1250 urban and territorial ones; see, for example, Schmidt, "Vogt, Vogtei"; Willoweit, "Vogt, Vogtei."

[116] See the Introduction and Chapters 1–4.   [117] Const., 3:48, no. 52.

[118] *Urkundenbuch des Stiftes Fischbeck*, 1:86–87, no. 84.

possessed, the linkage here of advocacy with claims to *servitium* and *exactiones* suggests advocatial roles had not changed so dramatically between 1050 and the early fourteenth century.[119]

Other evidence also cautions against trying to fit advocacy within a framework of bureaucratic officeholding. Many local noble families – and, in some cases, burgher families – continued to regard their advocatial positions as hereditary property.[120] The urban advocacy at Strasbourg, after being given to the local lord Louis of Lichtenberg in the late 1240s, quickly became a family possession in the eyes of the Lichtenberg lineage. When Louis's two sons in 1256 wrote in support of the burghers of Strasbourg regarding a general peace in the region, they titled themselves "We, the brothers Henry and Louis, lords of Lichtenberg [and] advocates of Strasbourg" (*advocati Argentinenses*).[121] This was a period when brothers frequently shared the inheritance of family property rather than dividing it, and Henry and Louis clearly did not view the position of town advocate as an office that only one of them could hold.[122] Additional evidence along these lines dates from a quarter-century later; in 1283, despite earlier promises by the lords of Lichtenberg that they would never alienate the advocacy, they sold it to King Rudolf I.[123]

Almost 200 years later, on the opposite side of the German kingdom, the territorial advocacy for Lower Lusatia was similarly treated like hereditary property. Held by the von Polenz lineage across at least two generations in the fifteenth century, two brothers, both of them, confusingly, named Jacob, jointly claimed the position of territorial advocate in the 1440s; in one document, they title themselves "We, Jacob and Jacob, brothers von Polenz, advocates of Lusatia" (*Voigte czu Lusiz*).[124] Thus, the heritability of at least some urban and territorial advocacies was considered the norm throughout the period 1250 to 1500 – much as the heritability of church advocacies had been the expectation of many noble lineages since the late tenth and early eleventh centuries.

Many of the new advocacies to appear between 1250 and 1500 had other characteristics that made them look more like noble assets than bureaucratic offices. In 1299, according to one source, "The *advocatissa* of Alsace came to Colmar with many ladies, and there also came the lord John of Lichtenberg, . . . advocate of the king of the Romans . . . over the

---

[119] Another term that continues to be linked to advocacy in the fourteenth century is *utilis*: Const., 4.1:121, no. 149. For this term, see Chapter 4.
[120] The lineage of the advocates of Weida, Gera and Plauen, which exercised authority in the *Vogtland*, has already been mentioned above.
[121] UB Strassburg, 1:299, no. 398. See also ibid., 1:249–50, no. 334; Egawa, *Stadtherrschaft*, 46, 62 and 154–55.
[122] Lyon, *Princely Brothers*, 199–206. [123] *Annales Colmarienses Maiores*, 210.
[124] Riedel, ed., *Codex*, 5:10, no. 773.

land of Alsace, wearing on his head a hat decorated with silver, gold and precious stones worth many marks of silver."[125] John of Lichtenberg belonged to the same lineage as the aforementioned town advocates of Strasbourg, evidence that a small number of well-connected noble families tended to control many of the advocacies in the southwest of the German kingdom.[126] The description of his expensive hat similarly emphasizes his noble status rather than an identity shaped by an ethos of officeholding. Equally noteworthy is the term *advocatissa*; sources designating the wife of an advocate in this fashion first became commonplace around the year 1100, when church advocacy was emerging as a significant feature of many noble lineages' claims to power and authority.[127] This brief passage thus points in several ways to an advocatial position defined by noble interests.

One additional feature of advocacy between 1250 and 1500 helps to distance it even more from the framework of the state, government and accountable officeholding. As has already been discussed, during the thirteenth century some church advocacies became objects of exchange because of their economic value.[128] This trend continued into later centuries, when the appointment of an advocate frequently had less to do with his qualifications than with a ruler, prince or prelate's need for money. Pledging, in particular, was a commonplace practice, one that had more to do with short-term financial gain and patron–client relationships than the idea that an advocate was a governmental official.[129] The Premonstratensian canons of Ursberg, for example, saw the advocacy for their house passed around frequently from the early thirteenth century onward.[130] The German kings and emperors had held the advocacy since the twelfth century and routinely pledged it to various nobles – and jointly to three burghers of Ulm in 1347 – during difficult financial moments.[131] In 1446, the nobleman who held the advocacy in fief from the emperor sold it to the urban government of Ulm, but even this was not the end of the advocacy's complicated history.[132]

---

[125] *Annales Colmarienses Maiores*, 224–25.
[126] For John's familial interests, see Planta, "Advocacy and 'Defensio,'" 196–97.
[127] Lyon, "Advocata." For the importance of clothing at such moments, see Sablonier, "Zur wirtschaftlichen Situation," 9–10.
[128] See Chapters 6 and 8.
[129] Hardy, *Political Culture*, 78–83; Bittmann, *Kreditwirtschaft*, 111–23. For pledges in late medieval Europe more generally, Smail, *Legal Plunder*, 116 and 134.
[130] See Chapter 8.
[131] Kreuzer, "Ursberg," 70–71. The German rulers did continue to insist throughout this period that no advocate for the monastery was to abuse their position; see, for example, Const., 10:445–47, no. 598.
[132] Kreuzer, "Ursberg," 73. For the advocacy after 1446, see Chapter 13.

The town advocacy for Ulm itself is another example of this trend. The urban community sided with the Habsburg candidate after the split royal election of 1314, a decision which came back to haunt the town when the Wittelsbach Ludwig IV "the Bavarian" secured the kingship instead. After returning from Italy in 1330, Ludwig gave Count Berthold von Graispach the town in pledge, granting him the rights of advocate there. The count was given the keys to the town and was allowed to keep the exactions owed to the emperor. He even seized the properties of the former mayor. When he died, Ludwig gave the position to his son.[133] There is little evidence here to suggest that this advocacy ought to be understood as an office in the fourteenth century.

Pledging also played an important role in the history of the Habsburg territorial advocates in the southwest of the German kingdom. At first glance, many look like government officials since they served for a limited time and had to render account. However, a list of known territorial advocates from the late fourteenth and early fifteenth centuries indicates that the actual amount of time nobles held these positions varied significantly, from under a year to five years.[134] This suggests the Habsburgs had problems with many of their advocates – unsurprising, given that they frequently had to assign territorial advocacies to their creditors as a way to repay their debts.[135] Many of these advocates seem to have been mostly interested in exploiting their position for profit, prompting the Habsburgs to question many of their expenses when they rendered account.[136] The German rulers Charles IV and Wenzel (1378–1400) similarly had to pawn the territorial advocacy for Alsace on several occasions for financial reasons.[137] Once we dig below the surface and take a closer look at what the sources for advocacy between 1250 and 1500 tell us, we see that the advocates of this period, like their predecessors in earlier centuries, recognized the position as a source of potential profit, status and rank rather than as an accountable office with a routine set of responsibilities.

Conclusion

In the year 1000, there was already significant variety to advocates' roles, with some responsible for protecting religious communities themselves and others providing protection and justice on rural estates or inside

---

[133] Frauenknecht, "Reichsstädte," 38–39; Keitel, "Städtische Bevölkerung," 98–105.

[134] Köhn, "Abrechnungen," 122–26.   [135] Ibid., 127–28.

[136] Ibid., 131–49. Köhn does note, however, that it is difficult to determine on the basis of the surviving sources how much these advocates could enrich themselves (pp. 156–59). See also Máthé, "Österreich," 8; Niederhäuser, "Landvogt."

[137] Hilsch, "Bořiwoj von Swinaře," 439–40.

towns. However, surviving sources from the period before 1250 rarely permit us to see how any of these advocates did their jobs on the ground. This changes from the mid-thirteenth century onward, when there is increasingly detailed evidence for how ecclesiastical, territorial, urban and local advocates carried out their responsibilities. Much of this material demonstrates that – despite some variations – protection and justice remained key features of the advocatial position across the German-speaking lands between 1250 and 1500. In many ways, therefore, the advocate of the late fifteenth century would have looked familiar to the advocate of the early eleventh. The similarities among advocates across this period become even more pronounced when we turn to a subject that I have left for the next chapter: the violent competition for the profits from advocacy.

13   Reframing the History of Violence

At some point before the end of the thirteenth century, the Alsatian monastery of Marmoutier (German: Maursmünster) acquired a house and courtyard inside the nearby town of Strasbourg. This was not at all unusual; by 1300, many religious communities held real estate in the rapidly growing urban centers of Europe in order to advance their own economic interests. Marmoutier's Strasbourg property did not only present opportunities for the monks but also challenges, however, which prompted them to go to the bishop of Strasbourg in 1296 to seek his help. Apparently, although the monastery's advocates were to have no authority whatsoever over the community's real estate in the town, multiple members of the family that held the advocacy for Marmoutier were claiming to be the advocates and showing up in Strasbourg to use the property.[1] The monastery's list of complaints to the bishop includes both familiar and novel advocatial abuses: These advocates used violence to take food and fodder for themselves and their horses (the terms *violenter, multas violencias* and *per violenciam* all appear only a few clauses apart), took advantage of the members of the monastic household who worked there, and forced the abbot and monks to sleep elsewhere in the town because they were using the house and stable for their own entourages. The bishop, in an effort to support the community, confirmed that the monastery's property in Strasbourg could only be used by the abbot, the monks and their messengers. While there is nothing surprising about an advocate (or his family) seeking to access monastic property, Marmoutier's complaints demonstrate that urbanization and the changing world of the late thirteenth century offered advocates a new setting to play an old game.

According to many scholars, that old game had already been gathering dust on a shelf for decades by the years around 1300. Standard narratives of the Feudal Revolution/Mutation/Transformation focus on the period from the late tenth to the early twelfth centuries as the time when the

[1] UB Strassburg, 2:162–64, no. 206.

violence associated with unregulated forms of lordship was at its worst. In this teleology, the growth of government and the state gradually put an end to such practices over the course of the thirteenth century.[2] However, most historians who have made arguments of this sort do not extend their studies into the fourteenth and fifteenth centuries or carefully compare evidence from around 1300 or 1400 with the evidence from around 1000 or 1100. Moreover, scholars who specialize in the later period, especially those influenced by the work of the Austrian historian Otto Brunner (1898–1982), have tended to frame noble violence as a legitimate, constitutive element of political order in the fourteenth and fifteenth centuries, rather than as a destabilizing force.[3] Historians who have challenged this position and emphasized the unrestrained character of the violence committed by nobles between 1250 and 1500, especially against peasants, are in the minority.[4]

As I have done throughout this book, I will set aside these scholarly debates here and focus instead on the sources for advocates from the late thirteenth to the fifteenth century. What does the evidence from this period reveal about the actions of those people who held the position of *advocatus* and *Vogt*? As we will see, numerous sources point to advocates continuing to take advantage of their roles in familiar ways.

Violence took many forms in Europe between 1250 and 1500. From the Hundred Years' War to attacks on Jewish communities in the midst of the Black Death, from peasant uprisings to the infamous Vlad the Impaler's campaigns along the Ottoman frontier, one does not need to look far to find examples of violent actions of various kinds. Moreover, the growth of administration at the level of the kingdom, principality and town did not necessarily create more peace and stability as the period progressed; as one historian has pointed out, "The political entities that were beginning to gel across Europe from the fourteenth century onward ... were capable of being spectacularly violent toward those within their jurisdictions."[5] Because advocates continued throughout these centuries to provide protection and exercise justice at the local level, they were thoroughly enmeshed in this culture of violence.

---

[2] See the Introduction and Chapters 3 and 8.
[3] Brunner's *Land und Herrschaft* was originally published in 1939 and went through several subsequent editions. English translation: Brunner, *Land*. For Brunner's influence, see Kaminsky, "Noble Feud"; Hechberger, *Adel*, 454–62.
[4] The sharpest critique of Brunner along these lines is Algazi, *Herrengewalt*. See also Wright, *Knights and Peasants*. For nuanced overviews of violence in this period, see Kaeuper, *Chivalry*, 181–205; Brown, *Violence*, 223–87.
[5] Smail, *Legal Plunder*, 254. See also Smail, "Violence"; Tilly, *Coercion*, 98–99; Parker, *French Absolutism*, 59–64.

Indeed, to claim that advocates between 1250 and 1500 initiated or experienced a wide array of violent acts is to state the obvious.

As a result, my aim in this chapter is not simply to catalogue every kind of violence linked to advocacy in the sources. The numerous examples of advocates who led armed men into battle to defend their advocacies or attack their enemies – while unquestionably informative to the history of advocacy writ large – lie outside the scope of my argument here.[6] Instead, my focus will be the evidence for those forms of advocatial violence (or, in some cases, accusations of advocatial violence) that provide clear parallels with the abuses and violent acts described in sources from the centuries prior to 1250. I will argue that, throughout the thirteenth to fifteenth centuries, advocates' claims of access to other people's property and dependents in order to exercise justice and provide protection continued to generate specific kinds of abuses and violent behavior. The precise limits of advocatial responsibilities and authority were just as contested after 1250 as they had been in earlier centuries, which calls into question narratives of increased state-building and rising official accountability during this period.

Continuity and Change

The monastery of Tegernsee in Bavaria has appeared frequently in the preceding chapters.[7] Its conflicts with its twelfth-century advocates generated a rich body of narrative and archival sources. These include a forged imperial privilege, which convinced Emperor Frederick II in 1234 to transfer the advocacy for the monastery from the noble lineage that had held it for generations. This was not the end of Tegernsee's conflicts with local advocates, however. In 1299, the abbot of the monastery issued a document concerning "a war between us and our advocate, Lord Leutold of Kuenring, who is our hereditary advocate over our monastery's property at Loiben by Dürnstein."[8] This property was located roughly 300 kilometers from Tegernsee in the Danube river valley west of Vienna, and supplied the community with its wine.[9] As the abbot

---

[6] See Chapter 12 for advocates in the Teutonic Order leading raids. For other examples of advocates' military roles, see Rothe, *Düringische Chronik*, 614–15, 639 and 648. Also outside my scope here is the interesting case of the Kraków *advocatus* Albert, who in 1311/12 led an attempt to transfer the German burghers' allegiance from one member of the ruling Piast dynasty to another; see *Annales Capituli Cracoviensis*, 607; Długosz, *Annals*, 260–62 (where the term for *advocatus* is "Starosta"); Peiper, "Gedicht."

[7] See Chapters 7, 8 and 10.

[8] Chmel, *Urkunden*, 283–85, no. 117: "ain chriek zwischen vns vnd vnsern voget was hern Liutolden von Chvnring … der vnser erib voget ist vber vnsers goteshuses aigen ze Livben pei Tyrnstain."

[9] For these estates and their advocates, see Gneiß, "Kloster," 194–96 and 199–204; Reichert, *Landesherrschaft*, 200–02; Becker and Scheiber, *Zur Landeskunde*, 96–101.

explains, the reason for the war centered squarely on the issue of the advocate's judicial rights concerning this property, namely the question of "what [belongs] to our right and our officials' right (*vnserr amptlaeut recht*) to judge [there] and what matters belong to our aforementioned *voget* to judge." Roughly 150 years after sources from Tegernsee first described disputes between the community and its advocates over judicial authority, tensions remained, especially on estates distant from the monastery itself.

Other types of conflicts between churches and advocates are evident across the German-speaking lands between 1250 and 1500. Around the year 1300, a monk (or monks) at the Benedictine monastery of Rastede to the northwest of Bremen wrote a history of the community. This text is one of the richest sources for an unusual crusade launched in the early thirteenth century against the Stedinger, a group of (possibly heretical) free peasants from the region.[10] According to this history, the origins of the crusade against the Stedinger lay in the later twelfth century, when these peasants had begun to rebel. The reason for the rebellion was "two castles in their land, ... in which there lived knights, whose advocates (*advocati*), on account of their insolence, strove to commit very many evils."[11] The peasants, meeting secretly at night, banded together and attacked the two castles, burning them to the ground and killing many people. From there, the rebellion grew quickly, leading in 1234 to the calling of a crusade and the start of a violent campaign to crush the Stedinger.[12]

That the monk(s) who wrote this history laid the blame for the entire Stedinger uprising at the feet of wicked advocates is noteworthy, because a second fourteenth-century text from this monastery, the *Miraculous Acts at the Monastery of Rastede*, delights in describing the divine vengeance orchestrated against various advocates who harmed the community. One story begins, "There was a certain count of Oldenburg, who through his advocates inflicted very many injuries on the estate managers of this church."[13] Another concerns "a certain malicious advocate of this church."[14] And a third opens, "There were two advocates of this monastery, father and son, who did very many immoderate things, both in our manor court and against the estate managers of this village, demanding whole pork hocks through violence."[15] While scholars have dedicated significantly more attention to the rhetoric of violence in tenth- and eleventh-century hagiographical works than to the rhetoric of similar

[10] Cassidy-Welch, "Stedinger Crusade."
[11] *Historia Monasterii Rastedensis*, 504, chap. 18.   [12] Ibid., 506, chap. 27.
[13] *Miracula in Monasteria Rastedensi*, 513, chap. 2.   [14] Ibid., 514, chap. 5.
[15] Ibid., 514, chap. 6. For these stories, see also Chapter 15.

texts from later periods, monastic authors clearly continued to find this language an effective tool for shaping the narratives of their conflicts with their advocates.

Into the fifteenth century, a range of sources describe intractable disputes over rights relating to church advocacies. The Premonstratensian house of Ursberg had seen its advocacy bought, sold and pawned on numerous occasions from the late twelfth century onward.[16] In 1446, the town council of Ulm purchased the advocacy and subsequently interfered in the abbatial election, supporting its own candidate and sparking conflict inside the community.[17] Not only Emperor Frederick III but also the papal legate for Germany – and eventually Pope Pius II (1458–64) as well – were drawn into this dispute. The emperor stripped Ulm of the advocacy and gave it to a local nobleman, Ber von Rechberg, which prompted the pro-Ulm faction in the community of canons to insist that past rulers had given them the right to choose their own advocate. This argument failed. Ber was present when a cardinal conducted a visitation in the monastery, and in 1459, the new head of the monastery was a candidate he supported.[18] A decade later, in July of 1469, Emperor Frederick III granted Ursberg the right to appoint its own advocates for the next twenty years – as well as the right to remove them – acknowledging as he did so that the community continued to suffer damage to its properties on account of its advocates.[19] This is a familiar narrative from the perspective of the late twelfth and early thirteenth centuries and extends the history of conflicts over church advocacies to the period around 1500.

There is also abundant evidence for urban and territorial advocates abusing their positions and committing violence that parallels the behavior of church advocates. Sources for the Lübeck town advocates are especially rich. They appear frequently as military leaders for the urban community.[20] However, they also became embroiled in various low-level disputes, where it is not always clear whether they were acting as agents of the town. Around the year 1300, one advocate ran into trouble with the town council, because he was (among other things) "secretly" (*occulte*) and "against justice" (*contra iusticiam*) inventing charges against and then demanding fines from people who came before him as judge.[21] In 1343, a knight had to intervene between Lübeck and two men to settle a dispute

---

[16] See Chapters 8 and 12.   [17] Kreuzer, "Ursberg," 73–75.   [18] Ibid., 75–80.
[19] Regesta Imperii Online, [RI XIII] H. 2, no. 117. See also Kreuzer, "Ursberg," 80–81. For other fourteenth- and fifteenth-century disputes over church advocacies, see Wild, "Herrenchiemsee," 143–44; Algazi, *Herrengewalt*, 68; Lau, "Kampf."
[20] See, for example, *Annales Lubicenses*, 417; Koppmann, ed., *Chroniken*, 1:378 and 386–87; Demski, *Adel und Lübeck*, 75–77; Brandt, "Vogtei," 183.
[21] *Urkundenbuch der Stadt Lübeck*, 3:40–41, no. 43; Ebel, *Lübisches Recht*, 1:260–61.

involving "the town advocate of Lübeck," who had destroyed the men's castle.[22] And five years later in 1348, agents of the king of Denmark and duke of Saxony wrote to the town council of Lübeck to ask for the return of "those eight horses, which your advocate took and led to your city."[23] While it is impossible to know to what extent these last two advocates might have been overstepping their authority, we should not assume that they were properly fulfilling their roles as urban representatives.

An excellent example of violence erupting over a town advocacy occurred at Halberstadt. In 1401/2, Pope Boniface IX delegated three churchmen to intervene in a dispute between the cathedral chapter there and the town council.[24] This was one aspect of a much larger conflict between the burghers and some of the religious communities in the town over urban rights and properties.[25] According to the pope's letter, which relies heavily on information given to the papal chancery by representatives of the Halberstadt cathedral chapter, "the proconsul, consuls and burghers" of the town had seized the Halberstadt advocacy over the objections of the chapter. The letter makes it clear from the outset that the advocacy had significant value; the canons reportedly "were accustomed to receive very many benefits and provisions (*utilitates et servitia quamplurima*)" from some of the people living within the advocacy. Both the cathedral chapter and the town council therefore had good reasons to press their own claims to the urban advocacy.

Boniface's letter reports that, when the cathedral canons gathered to discuss the usurpation, a group of armed men sent by the urban community accosted them and threatened "that, if they did not immediately pledge the advocacy to the burghers, ... they would kill them with [their] swords." Terrified, the cathedral canons were forced to comply, giving up all of their rights within the advocacy. The papal account of events then employs some familiar language:

[A]fter this, the proconsul, consuls and burghers ... compelled the men residing in the advocacy to render to them unaccustomed provisions (*servitia inconsueta*) and then extorted from them every year certain sums of money. They also hindered, as they still hinder, ... the chapter from being able to receive the benefits and provisions owed to them from the advocacy and the men [in it].[26]

[22] *Urkundenbuch der Stadt Lübeck*, 2.2:736, no. 786; Demski, *Adel und Lübeck*, 132. The knight tasked with settling the dispute ruled against Lübeck, which suggests the advocate's actions had been unjust.
[23] *Urkundenbuch der Stadt Lübeck*, 2.2:834, no. 902; Demski, *Adel und Lübeck*, 135–37.
[24] *Urkundenbuch des Hochstifts Halberstadt*, 4:460–63, no. 3179. See also *Urkundenbuch der Stadt Halberstadt*, 2:11–14, nos. 697–98.
[25] For this so-called *Pfaffenkrieg*, see Averkorn, "Bischöfe von Halberstadt," 34–37.
[26] *Urkundenbuch des Hochstifts Halberstadt*, 4:461, no. 3179.

Pope Boniface IX insisted that his delegates should work to restore the advocacy to the cathedral chapter and should threaten the urban community with excommunication if necessary. Despite the pope's efforts, however, the dispute dragged on for several more years.[27] Control of the town advocacy was too important an element of urban authority (and urban income) for either side to give up its claims quickly or quietly.[28]

Much like church advocacies across the centuries, urban advocacies offered an opportunity to benefit from someone else's rights over property and people. By holding court, exercising military authority and collecting revenues, town advocates performed a set of roles that had been associated with the advocate since the year 1000, if not earlier. It is therefore unsurprising that sources frequently claim that these types of advocates abused their positions in familiar ways. Indeed, we must be careful not to fall into the trap of assuming fourteenth- and fifteenth-century urban communities were the seedbeds of modern, bourgeois, democratic society; urban elites could be just as intent on extracting income from those under their authority as noble elites.[29] Town advocacies had too much potential value for their holders not to consider employing violence in order to reap extra benefits from their "office" whenever they could.

Because of its expansiveness, the position of territorial advocate could also be exploited in a variety of ways.[30] A territorial advocate appointed by the German king or emperor to oversee all of the imperial rights and properties in a particular region essentially functioned as an urban advocate for the imperial towns in that region and a church advocate for the imperial monasteries there. We get a clear picture of what this might have meant in practice in a document from the monastery of St. Gall. The Habsburg king Frederick, one of the two rivals elected to the German throne in 1314, wrote to the religious community in 1315 to confirm that "Henry, [abbot] of St. Gall ..., made satisfaction to Count Werner of Homberg, provincial advocate ..., for all the payments and exactions, which the abbot is known to have received from the men of the advocacy of St. Gall – which advocacy belongs to us and the empire – from the time of the imperial vacancy until now."[31] This text demonstrates how some

---

[27] Averkorn, "Bischöfe von Halberstadt," 36–37.
[28] For another example of violence erupting over control of a town advocacy, see Wackernagel, "Rudolf von Habsburg," 191–92.
[29] On the place of urbanization in teleologies of the rise of modernity, see Boone, "Cities"; Moraw, "Cities." For the language of "sophisticated" urban structures versus "primitive" princely ones, see Isenmann, "Holy Roman Empire," 246. For a critique of such dichotomies, see Bünz, "Adlige Unternehmer?"
[30] For the disputes when some Habsburg territorial advocates rendered account, see Chapter 12.
[31] Const., 5:257, no. 295.

monasteries would continue to collect advocatial exactions on their estates even when there was no advocate.[32] Just as significantly, it also points to the territorial advocate being responsible for gathering the income that was rightfully owed by St. Gall's dependents to the proper holder of the church advocacy, the German king. The territorial advocate could thus access the monastery's properties in ways comparable to earlier church advocates.

The territorial advocates for Alsace offer especially good evidence of how these imperial agents could abuse their roles – at least according to many of their critics – in ways that fit well-worn patterns. In 1280, King Rudolf I appointed his nephew Otto of Ochsenstein to govern Alsace and part of southwestern Germany "in the name of the empire and in our name."[33] Although Otto is not explicitly designated as advocate for these regions in the document confirming his appointment, local sources refer to him as the territorial advocate (*advocatus terrae*).[34] He soon intervened in affairs in the imperial town of Colmar, angering at least some members of the urban community in the process. According to one chronicle,

[King Rudolf] made Walter [Rossilman] ... the judge (*scultetus*) in Colmar. Rudolf placed Otto of Ochsenstein ... in the position of advocate of Alsace. But the judge and the territorial advocate did not see eye to eye on everything. The advocate, with the king ordering it (or rather conniving in it), made very many exactions. The judge and the people paid unwillingly.[35]

Their reluctance angered the king, who besieged Colmar and removed Walter from his position, thereby backing his territorial advocate Otto – and his exactions. Another accusation leveled against a territorial advocate in a text from Colmar also follows familiar lines: "The lord of Hohenstein, advocate of Alsace, violently seized eight containers of wine from the sisters of St. John."[36] As we will see, advocatial violence of this sort persisted in this region into the later fifteenth century.[37]

---

[32] See Chapter 10 for more on this point. For a town apparently doing something similar, see Schnurrer, ed., *Urkunden*, 1:331, no. 809 and 339, no. 828; Schnurrer, "Reichsstadt Rothenburg," 579.

[33] Const., 3:257, no. 264.

[34] *Annales Colmarienses Maiores*, 207. For Otto, see also ibid., 212 and for his successor, ibid., 222–24. For an overview of the narrative sources from Colmar, see Schmidberger, *Städtische Führungsgruppen*, 50–61.

[35] *Chronicon Colmariense*, 254. For this incident, see Buchholzer-Rémy, "Herrschaft," 180. For Otto in the *Chronicon*, see also p. 257 and for his successor p. 262. See also Scheyhing, *Eide*, 118–19.

[36] *Annales Colmarienses Maiores*, 210. See also ibid., 211.

[37] For an excellent discussion of some of the accusations leveled against the territorial advocates working for Bern in the fifteenth century, see Teuscher, "Threats," 107, 111. This is not to suggest that all territorial advocates were violent all the time, a point stressed by Teuscher, "Böse Vögte?" A good example of a *Landvogt* (mostly) doing his

Across the period 1250 to 1500, some rulers and princes intervened to try to rein in their advocates and regulate behavior deemed excessive. In 1350, King Charles IV wrote in support of a Cistercian convent, because he had learned that the nuns "and their properties are – on account of the advocates of Bautzen, who are temporary (*qui sunt pro tempore*), and many other neighboring nobles, vassals and faithful men of ours – suffering from frequent and onerous [demands for] nighttime lodging; unaccustomed troubles, payments and exactions; diverse sorts of harassment and endless, unreasonable expenses."[38] In 1384, Margrave William I of Meissen ordered his advocates, subadvocates and other agents to stop seizing the property of dead priests, a strategy advocates had been employing since the late twelfth century to enhance their income.[39] Advocates' rights and responsibilities remained fluid throughout this period, with many of their administrative roles and functions never clearly defined and delineated, giving advocates frequent opportunities to press their claims to authority – with or without the knowledge of those for whom they ostensibly worked.

As abundant as the evidence is for comparable forms of advocatial violence before and after 1250, continuity should not be confused with stasis. Sources from the thirteenth to fifteenth century also reveal advocates devising new ways to benefit from their positions. For example, while there were no formal prisons in this period, advocates increasingly came to play the role of jailer and to be responsible for overseeing prisoners.[40] In 1345, one man wrote a letter acknowledging that, in the midst of a feud, "he had been seized by the town advocate of Lübeck and led by him to the same city."[41] Five years later, during another feud, a second man likewise wrote that Lübeck's advocate had captured him and "placed him in a tower."[42] As we will see, critiques of advocates' actions as jailers grew rapidly from the fourteenth century onward.

A second type of advocatial violence that first surfaces in the sources after 1250 is sexual assault. In the above-mentioned history of the monastery of Rastede, the explanation for the origins of the crusade against the

---

job properly is Stislav von der Weitenmühl, who worked to arrange a peace between Strasbourg and one of its rivals; see UB Strassburg, 5:651, no. 835; 664–65, no. 853; 669, no. 860; 672–673, no. 865; and 677–79, nos. 872–74.

[38] Const., 10:148, no. 188. For similar complaints, see CDS II, 2:164–65, no. 647 and *Gesta Praepositorum Stederburgensium continuata*, 729.

[39] CDS I B, 1:77, no. 115. For this form of advocatial abuse, see also Chapters 7 and 14.

[40] The earliest reference I know to this role is *Deutsches Wirtschaftsleben*, 22, no. 14. For prisons in this period, Smail, *Legal Plunder*, 156–60; Dean, *Crime*, 120–24; Peters, "Prison," 33–34.

[41] *Urkundenbuch der Stadt Lübeck*, 2.2:779, no. 841. See also, ibid., 779–80, no. 842.

[42] Ibid., 2.2:893, no. 967.

Stedinger is quite specific; in two castles, "there lived knights, whose advocates, on account of their insolence, strove to commit very many evils through their violent taking of girls and women (*per oppressionem puellarum et mulierum*)."[43] The legend of William Tell also places the sexual assault of women at the center of its story of the Swiss uprising against the Habsburgs around 1300.[44] And in the first edition of the Grimm brothers' collection of German legends (*Deutsche Sagen*), published in the mid-1810s, the one story about an "evil and cruel advocate of the emperor" (*der böse und grausame Vogt des Kaisers*) also concerns this topic: "Once per year, in the still of the night, thunder shakes the ruins [of the castle of Schwanau] and a loud lament sounds in the tower; around the walls, the advocate is pursued by the virgin clothed in white, whom he had dishonored, until with a howl he throws himself into the lake."[45] While it is impossible to know how common this type of advocatial violence was, this legend shows that the stereotype of the advocate as sexual predator would persist for centuries.[46]

Thus, throughout the period 1250 to 1500, the position of advocate still brought with it access to other people's lands and rights, access that could easily lead to abuses – and precipitate violence. Advocates, whether ecclesiastical, urban, territorial or other, maintained a great deal of freedom to profit from their roles in various ways, even as some rulers and princes experimented with new strategies to try to hold them accountable. The odds of suffering serious consequences for trying to extract as much profit as possible from providing protection and exercising justice remained too low to convince many advocates to refrain from their violent abuses. Narratives that posit a shift from lordship to government and argue for the rise of the state from the thirteenth century onward thus ignore – or, at the very least, undervalue – the ongoing efforts by local "officeholders" to take advantage of their positions for personal gain.

Three Case Studies from the Fifteenth Century

The volume of surviving sources for the history of advocacy increases rapidly in the years after 1250, as does the level of detail in many of those sources. By the fifteenth century, it is possible to analyze advocatial abuses and violence in much greater depth than in any preceding century. In the remainder of this chapter, I will therefore provide three case studies from different regions of the German-speaking lands in order to

---

[43] *Historia Monasterii Rastedensis*, 504, chap. 18.   [44] See Chapter 15.
[45] Grimm and Grimm, *Deutsche Sagen*, 1:427, no. 330.
[46] For a similar observation, see Kaeuper, *Chivalry*, 204–05.

demonstrate more clearly the continuities in advocates' actions across the period from roughly 1000 to 1500.

Conrad Brückner

By the end of it all, in July of 1407, five prominent burghers of the town of Zwickau in Saxony – including a six-term mayor and a five-term town council member – had been executed. The first of the five was beheaded in the market square of Zwickau by order of that year's town council; the others were hanged in Meissen by order of the margrave who ruled the region. Conrad Brückner, whose actions had precipitated the whole series of unfortunate events, was nowhere to be found. Brückner too had been a leading citizen of Zwickau, serving three terms on the town council and one term as mayor in earlier years. In a list of Zwickau town council members from 1404, he is identified as "the advocate Brückner" (*advocatus Bruckener*), and contemporary sources are clear that his actions as advocate lay at the heart of the conflict that cost some of his fellow burghers their lives.[47]

What sort of advocate was Conrad Brückner? He was appointed to the position of *voyt* (*Vogt*) by Margrave William I of Meissen (d. 1407), who was the lord of the town of Zwickau. Brückner's advocacy did not include the town, however, but rather the surrounding territories outside its walls, which also belonged to the margrave.[48] His responsibilities included exercising justice (which was still closely connected to the collection of exactions as well), mustering and commanding the troops from the district for the margrave and performing what we would call policing duties.[49] Although his advocacy is referred to in sources from this period as the *Amt* Zwickau (the Zwickau "office" of the margrave's administration), Brückner should not be viewed as an officer in an emerging professional bureaucracy.[50] Margrave William's fourteenth-century predecessors had frequently treated advocatial positions such as Brückner's as objects to be pawned for their own financial benefit, and family connections and other personal networks – not specific educational or administrative qualifications – were typically the key factors in the selection of the advocate.[51] It is therefore unsurprising that

---

[47] For Conrad, see *Urkundenbuch der Stadt Zwickau*, 2:41, no. 117; 45, no. 128; and 54, no. 155. See also Oelsner and Stoye, "Zwickauer Ereignisse," 72.

[48] For an overview, see Kunze, "Verhältnis," 28–46. The exercising of justice and related responsibilities inside the town walls were a different matter; see, for example, *Urkundenbuch der Stadt Zwickau*, 1:27–28, no. 29.

[49] Kunze, "Verhältnis," 31–33.   [50] Ibid., 30. For the *Amt* Zwickau, ibid., 42–43.

[51] See, for example, *Urkundenbuch der Stadt Zwickau*, 1:20–22, nos. 19–22 for thirteenth-century advocates in Zwickau. In 1297, there were two advocates: "Nos Cunradus et Fridericus advocati in Zwikowe" (ibid., 28–29, no. 31). In 1335, Margrave Frederick II

Brückner was accused of abusing his position. As in so many other places and times, it was a dispute about the proper reach of an advocate's authority that would, in the end, lead to violence.

During his time as the margrave's advocate, Brückner continued to maintain close links to the urban community of Zwickau. Ties of friendship and kinship and patron–client bonds were just as important for the burgher elite of a town like Zwickau as they were for the noble elite of the period. Factionalism among the burghers, as well as the various networks that bound together the town's lord and his agents on the one hand and the urban community on the other, shaped the political life of the town in important ways.[52]

The key source for understanding Conrad Brückner's role in the events that led to the five executions is an unusually detailed list of complaints against him. They are preserved in a 1407 document addressed to the margrave in the name of the Zwickau town council as well as "the whole community, all handworkers, rich and poor, of the town of Zwickau ... against Conrad Brückner, *voite* [*Vogt*]."[53] The nineteen articles that follow leave little doubt that, although the town of Zwickau itself lay outside of his advocacy, Brückner had routinely used his position to expand his own authority at the expense of his fellow townsmen. The opening articles complain that Brückner had frequently spoken against the town before Margrave William; he claimed that the town did not legitimately hold some of its rights beyond the town walls (to fields and fisheries, for example) and then usurped those rights for himself.[54]

With Article Six, we find ourselves in familiar territory in the sphere of judicial authority. The town council's words echo those of many monastic authors of earlier centuries: "Moreover, he held court with his helpers ... against the will of our city, ... and he did this more through his own pleasure than for the good of his lord."[55] Equally noteworthy is Article Eight: "Moreover, he wrested from us the city's rights and freedoms concerning some things, such that he and his men ran wild against people in their houses and committed evil therein, all of which he did against his honor and the oath he swore as our fellow burgher."[56] Other articles

---

of Meissen pawned the advocacy for Zwickau to Henry the Elder, *Vogt* of Gera (ibid., 71–72, no. 86; see also 72–73, no. 87). Margrave Frederick III pawned it in 1358 to two brothers (ibid., 119–20, no. 133).

[52] For the complexity of intra-urban networks as well as the networks connecting urban communities to neighboring religious communities and noble families, see Lutter, *Hof und Kloster*; Lutter, "Soziale Räume"; and various articles in *Mittler zwischen Herrschaft und Gemeinde*. See also Schmidberger, *Städtische Führungsgruppen*, 15.

[53] *Rechtfertigungsschrift*, 290. See also pp. 298–310 for a photographic reproduction of this text.

[54] Ibid., 290, Articles I–III.   [55] Ibid., 290, Article VI.   [56] Ibid., 290, Article VIII.

complain about "his violence" (*syner Gewalt*): He sent his men to murder a burgher of the town in the burgher's own house, and – a complaint against him which shows a clear attempt by the town council to win the margrave to their side – he plundered the margravial castle following the death of the previous margrave.[57]

The final complaint against Brückner is that he installed Franz Stuchsing in the position of town judge against the will of the town. At this point, the text shifts to a list of fourteen articles against Stuchsing.[58] Franz Stuchsing had been mayor of Zwickau in 1404 and had also served on the town council. The first several articles complain about his earlier misdeeds in these positions. The sixth article then tells the story of how the judicial court in Zwickau, for which the town council had previously had the right to appoint the judge, had been taken out of the town council's hands.[59] According to Article Seven, Stuchsing was then given the position of judge "with the help and advice of Conrad Brückner, the advocate."[60]

Although the town council avoids criticizing the margrave in this list of complaints, it is clear that he was at least tacitly supportive of all of this. Brückner and Stuchsing had chosen to align with the margrave against other leading members of the town, perhaps because of long-simmering factional tensions, in order to gain more power and influence for themselves.[61] Brückner's position of advocate, though it technically came with no authority within the town, provided him with the opportunity to press claims of various sorts, especially judicial ones, over Zwickau. Whether he did this principally for the margrave's benefit or his own is open to debate.

When, in early 1407, the town council of Zwickau made the decision to reassert its long-standing right to exercise high justice in the town, it found Franz Stuchsing guilty of breaking the peace and beheaded him in the town square. By this point, Margrave William I of Meissen was dead; his heirs were the ones who refused to recognize the reassertion of Zwickau's right. Instead, they viewed the town council as having illegitimately executed an official acting on behalf of the town's lord. Unsurprisingly, therefore, four of the leading townsmen were found

---

[57] Ibid., 291, Articles XIII–XV.
[58] Ibid., 292–95. Stuchsing is never referred to as *Stadtvogt* in the text, probably because to label him the town advocate would have been to acknowledge he had legitimate judicial authority in Zwickau. Nevertheless, he was clearly acting like a *Stadtvogt*: Oelsner and Stoye, "Zwickauer Ereignisse," 73, 104.
[59] *Rechtfertigungsschrift*, 293, Article VI.
[60] Ibid., 293–94, Articles VII–VIII: "mit hulfe und mit rate Conrad Brugkener, des voites."
[61] Oelsner and Stoye, "Zwickauer Ereignisse," 96, 104.

guilty and hanged by the margravial court in Meissen.[62] No extant source tells us what happened to Conrad Brückner.

Dramatic incidents such as this one can be viewed through a variety of contextual lenses. Disagreements between the margraves of Meissen and the town council of Zwickau over who had the right to exercise justice within the town walls shaped the course of events in important ways. Competition within the burgher elite of the town was clearly another crucial factor; the list of complaints against Brückner and Stuchsing does little to hide the personal animosities that some members of the 1407 town council had for their two fellow burghers. We cannot, however, focus purely on local contexts.[63] The fact that Conrad Brückner held the position of advocate ties this incident to a much larger history of advocatial efforts to press their claims aggressively. None of the accusations leveled against him – or his agent, Franz Stuchsing – are unusual for someone labeled an advocate in our sources. Both men used their positions to assert the right to exercise justice over people outside their advocatial authority in much the same way as other advocates had been doing for centuries.

Lower Lusatia

A dispute over the territorial advocacy for Lower Lusatia highlights nobles' continued willingness to wrestle over control of the position of *advocatus* across the fifteenth century. Unlike the preceding case study, which involved different factions within one small town, the case of Lower Lusatia belongs to the sphere of high politics in the Holy Roman Empire. It concerned the Habsburg emperor Frederick III (1440–93), rival claimants to the throne of Bohemia and members of two of the leading lineages of the Empire – a Wettin duke of Saxony and a Hohenzollern margrave of Brandenburg.[64] Though a complex case, it is one that takes us to the heart of advocacy's utility for gaining access to other people's rights and properties.

The march of Lower Lusatia to the south of Berlin was frequently in the hands of absentee margraves, who installed territorial advocates to exercise authority for them in the region.[65] Emperor Charles IV had acquired

---

[62] Ibid., 104–06. Although the town lost the right to exercise high justice in 1407, the council bought it back in 1444; see Bräuer, *Wider den Rat*, 54, 59.

[63] While Oelsner and Stoye, "Zwickauer Ereignisse," 107, label this case unique when assessed alongside the histories of other towns in the march of Meissen, this is too limited a comparative framework.

[64] For the broader context of the dispute I am discussing here, see Eibl, "Lausitzen."

[65] See Chapter 12.

the march for the kingdom of Bohemia in the 1360s, and his sons Wenzel (German king, 1378–1400; died 1419) and Sigismund (German king and emperor, 1410–37) held the title of margrave in subsequent years. Under both Wenzel and Sigismund, from the 1410s to the mid-1430s, a man named Hans von Polenz appears consistently in documents from the region as the territorial advocate.[66]

The situation in Lower Lusatia grew significantly more complicated in 1437, when both Emperor Sigismund and Hans von Polenz died. Sigismund's son-in-law Albrecht, the Habsburg duke of Austria who would be elected German king in 1438, followed Sigismund as king of Bohemia and margrave of Lower Lusatia. He gave the position of advocate to Nickel von Polenz, a cousin of Hans, while also granting him Lower Lusatia in pledge.[67] As both advocate and lord, Nickel effectively exercised full authority in the region on behalf of the king of Bohemia. However, Bohemia was thrown into political turmoil only two years later when King Albrecht died. Albrecht's wife gave birth to a son a short time after his death, Ladislaus "Posthumus," but the question of who would govern Bohemia until he came of age was a vexed one. In 1440, the newly elected German king Frederick III, a Habsburg cousin of Albrecht, designated himself Ladislaus's guardian and thus claimed a right to intervene in Bohemian affairs. At the same time, two of the seven electors of the Empire, Duke Frederick II of Saxony (d. 1464) and Margrave Frederick II of Brandenburg (d. 1471), saw in all of this an opportunity to intervene in Lower Lusatia, which bordered both of their territories.

In the midst of the turmoil, in January of 1441, "Nickel von Polenz, knight, advocate of Lusatia and lord of the people and cities of the same land of Lusatia," agreed to pay Margrave Frederick II of Brandenburg 500 "good Rhineland gulden" per year for three years in return for Frederick taking him "into his protection and safeguard" (*In seinen schucz vnd beschermunge*).[68] The document confirming this agreement makes it clear that the king and Crown of Bohemia were the true hereditary lords (*erbherren*) of the region. However, the dynastic uncertainty following the death of King Albrecht apparently led Nickel to worry that he would receive no help from Bohemia in case of trouble.

Adding to an already complicated political situation in Lower Lusatia, Nickel von Polenz was not the only person in the 1440s with a claim to the

---

[66] Lippert, ed., *Urkundenbuch*, 39–40, no. 50; 48–50, nos. 58–59; 52–54, nos. 63–64; 55–56, no. 66.

[67] Eibl, "Lausitzen," 317; Lehmann, *Geschichte der Niederlausitz*, 80.

[68] Riedel, ed., *Codex*, 4:227–29, no. 1615: "Ich nickel von polenczk, Ritter, voit zcu lusicz und heren manne vnd stete des selbin landes zcu lusicz." See also Lehmann, *Geschichte der Niederlausitz*, 80–81.

territorial advocacy. His predecessor, Hans von Polenz, had two sons, both named Jacob.[69] In May of 1439, "Nickel von Polenz, territorial advocate of Lusatia," was acting as guardian for these two young boys.[70] They must have reached the age of majority by 1446, because in that year Duke Frederick II of Saxony intervened to settle an inheritance dispute between Nickel and the two brothers.[71]

Everything finally boiled over in 1448. On September 29, King Frederick III, using his guardianship of Ladislaus Posthumus as justification, intervened in the affairs of Lower Lusatia and pledged the march to Duke Frederick II of Saxony after the duke had settled with the members of the von Polenz family over their own rights to hold the march in pledge.[72] The same day, however, Margrave Frederick II of Brandenburg referred to himself in a document "as an advocate and administrator of the land of Lusatia" (als ein voyt und verweser des lands zu Lusicz), leaving little doubt that he intended to press his own claims to exercise authority in the march.[73] In the ensuing weeks, both sides sent armies into the field. The duke of Saxony, supported by the various members of the von Polenz family, had some initial success.[74] By mid-October, however, the tide had turned. Margrave Frederick II of Brandenburg started to gain ground, and Nickel von Polenz was badly injured in battle when he attempted to intercept the Hohenzollern forces.[75]

On October 18, 1448, the two Jacobs von Polenz agreed to sell the town and castle of Lübben, one of the most important sites in Lower Lusatia, to Margrave Frederick II.[76] The following day, "We, Jacob and Jacob, brothers von Polenz, advocates of Lusatia," acknowledged receiving a substantial sum of money from the margrave in return for all their rights in the march.[77] Only three days later, on October 22, a Lower Lusatian town promised "to receive no other advocate or administrator" except Margrave Frederick II and his heirs.[78] Other places in the march soon followed suit.[79] A few

---

[69] See Chapter 12.

[70] Lippert, ed., *Urkundenbuch*, 60–61, no. 72. See also ibid., 62–65, nos. 76–77 and 69–71, nos. 82–83.

[71] Ibid., 71–75, no. 84. See also Lehmann, *Geschichte der Niederlausitz*, 81–82.

[72] Regesta Imperii Online, [RI XIII] H. 11, no. 82. See also Eibl, "Lausitzen," 318–19.

[73] Lehmann, ed., *Quellen*, 1:212, no. 15.

[74] Lippert, ed., *Urkundenbuch*, 85–86, no. 92 and 87–88, no. 94. See also Lehmann, *Geschichte der Niederlausitz*, 83.

[75] Lippert, ed., *Urkundenbuch*, 88–89, no. 95.

[76] Lehmann, ed., *Quellen*, 1:212, no. 16; Lippert, ed., *Urkundenbuch*, 89–90, no. 96.

[77] Riedel, ed., *Codex*, 5:10, no. 773. See also ibid., 4:417, no. 1695.

[78] Ibid., 4:413, no. 1689.

[79] Ibid., 4:413–16, nos. 1690–94. A letter of October 24 to the duke of Saxony indicates the margrave had conquered much of the march by this point: Lippert, ed., *Urkundenbuch*, 93–94, no. 99. See also Lehmann, *Geschichte der Niederlausitz*, 84–85.

months later, in July of 1449, Margrave Frederick II and his brothers wrote to the Crown of Bohemia, explaining that a crowned king of Bohemia could purchase the advocacy for Lower Lusatia back from them; but until that happened, Frederick and his heirs would hold onto it – and exercise effective authority in the march.[80]

Unsurprisingly, the margrave had no intention of fulfilling the responsibilities of a territorial advocate of Lower Lusatia himself. In the early months of 1449, sources name Otto von Schlieben as the territorial advocate acting on Frederick's behalf there.[81] Then, in November of 1449, the margrave designated Botho von Ileburg as territorial advocate for three years. The document concerning his installation as advocate includes a detailed list of his responsibilities; these included fortifying and defending Lübben, protecting the march militarily as necessary and maintaining bridges.[82] The last sentence before the dating clause is a reminder that the role of advocate had not changed significantly since the eleventh century: "We have also committed to him and given to his administration, for these three years, the courts in the land; however, he should not burden anyone with unaccustomed exactions, but he should rather let everyone remain unthreatened in their old and traditional rights."[83]

The case of the territorial advocacy of Lower Lusatia demonstrates the political potential of the position of advocate into the fifteenth century. At no point in the 1440s did Margrave Frederick II of Brandenburg or anyone else call into question the Crown of Bohemia's rightful possession of the region.[84] After Frederick II's military victory over the Habsburg ruler's proxy, the duke of Saxony, he did not title himself the new margrave of Lower Lusatia.[85] What he wanted was to be able to call himself the legitimate "advocate and administrator" (*voyt und verweser*).[86] As the document installing Botho von Ileburg makes clear, the territorial advocate was the one who provided protection and exercised justice – and collected the income that was the reward for fulfilling these responsibilities. Thus, advocacy was anything but an antiquated institution in this period. It remained a valuable source of authority and profit for even the highest-ranking members of the

---

[80] Riedel, ed., *Codex*, 4:417–20, no. 1696. King Albrecht II's daughter Anna, one of the claimants to Bohemia, confirmed all of this on July 10, 1449: Eibl, "Lausitzen," 325, n. 69.

[81] Lippert, ed., *Urkundenbuch*, 102, no. 107 and 114–15, no. 116.

[82] Ibid., 115–116, no. 117. To give a sense of the level of detail, when the advocate completed his three years and moved out of the residence in Lübben, the text stipulates that he was not to take with him any of the bed linens, dishes, benches or other moveables.

[83] Ibid.   [84] Lehmann, *Geschichte der Niederlausitz*, 84–85.

[85] In 1461, Frederick returned Lower Lusatia to Bohemia. Territorial advocates would remain at the center of the back and forth in the region into the time of Matthias Corvinus; see Lehmann, *Geschichte der Niederlausitz*, 86–94.

[86] For the importance that lords attached to the legitimacy of their claims to rights, see Schreiner, "Religiöse."

empire's elite. For that reason, just as in earlier centuries, advocacies were still worth fighting over.

Peter of Hagenbach

The story of Peter (or Pierre) of Hagenbach, who served as territorial advocate in Alsace between 1469 and 1474, highlights the dangers of assuming a teleology of the rise of bureaucratic forms of officeholding between 1250 and 1500. Peter is well known in some scholarly circles, because his trial and subsequent execution in 1474 have sometimes been labeled "the first international war crimes trial in history."[87] While this is a misleading characterization of these events, there is no question that Peter's actions as territorial advocate elicited a dramatic response; he was captured, tried and killed by a group of local power holders in and around Alsace for what they considered to be his tyrannical behavior and his abuse of his position.

Peter of Hagenbach belonged to the lesser nobility of southern Alsace. The castle of Hagenbach was a fief held from the Habsburgs, and although Peter is the most famous member of his lineage, he was not the first to serve in princely administrations in the region.[88] While his father's side of the family had strong Habsburg ties, his mother was from Burgundy, and through her he inherited rights and property in the Franche-Comté (Free County of Burgundy). At some point, Peter became connected to the court of the dukes of Burgundy, one of the leading political and cultural centers of Europe in the mid-fifteenth century. By the early 1460s, he was a loyal supporter of the future Duke Charles the Bold of Burgundy (1467–77), serving him in different positions in the Burgundian army as well as on diplomatic missions.[89] Then, in May of 1469, Duke Charles acquired the Habsburg territories on the Upper Rhine in pledge through the Treaty of Saint-Omer. At the end of the year, he appointed Peter of Hagenbach as his representative in Alsace and neighboring properties held through the treaty. Because of the multilingual setting, Peter appears with various titles in sources from the ensuing years: *balivus, bailli, Amtmann* and *Landvogt.*[90]

---

[87] Gordon, "Trial," 13. He convincingly argues against this characterization of the trial.
[88] Ibid., 25. Unsurprisingly for a lesser noble family from this region, the Hagenbachs also held a monastic advocacy over some of the dependents of Masmünster (Masevaux).
[89] Brauer-Gramm, *Landvogt*, 11–21. Like Count Henry of Wolfratshausen (see Chapter 10), Peter of Hagenbach is depicted in starkly different ways in different sources; he was clearly much more than just a tyrannical advocate. See, for example, Hardy, "Burgundian Clients," 34–37; Paravicini, "Un amour malheureux"; *Court and Civic Society*, 119–29.
[90] Hardy, *Political Culture*, 220–21. For the different versions of his title, see for example Chmel, ed., *Aktenstücke*, 1:30–32, no. 9 and 114–19, nos. 25–26; Knebel, *Tagebuch*, 2:3.

As with other territorial advocacies in this period, Hagenbach's did not give Peter control over all people and property in the entire region. The Habsburg's lands and rights were extensive but scattered, and Hagenbach's authority extended over not only parts of Alsace but also a few places east of the Rhine, including the town of Breisach. His wide-ranging responsibilities included keeping the roads and waterways safe and overseeing forest and mining rights. Similar to other advocates, he also mustered troops from his advocacy, exercised some kinds of justice and had the authority to collect dependents' customary dues.[91] In one document from 1472, "Peter von Hagenbach, knight, ... territorial advocate and master of the court" of Duke Charles granted various types of revenue to a burgher from an Alsatian town, highlighting one of the more mundane aspects of his position.[92]

From the beginning of his term as territorial advocate, Peter of Hagenbach aggressively enforced the duke of Burgundy's claims. Since Charles the Bold held the region in pledge, Hagenbach was not overseeing the duke's own properties and dependents but someone else's. It is therefore unsurprising that the Burgundian ruler and his administration were keen to profit as much as possible during the period of the pledge.[93] Indeed, at his trial in 1474, Peter of Hagenbach would insist that all he did was follow ducal orders and that he therefore could not be accused of abusing his position.[94]

For many people living in and around Alsace in the early 1470s, however, Peter of Hagenbach's actions were an extreme form of the advocatial violence the region had experienced intermittently for centuries. Several of the best sources for his activities deploy critiques of advocacy that by this time were almost half a millennium old. One of the richest texts for the closing months of Peter of Hagenbach's life is the diary of Johannes Knebel, a churchman in Basel. From the start of this work, Knebel makes it clear what local attitudes toward territorial advocates were. When recounting an attempt by Emperor Frederick III to convince the Swiss Confederacy to restore Habsburg rule over their territories, Knebel describes the Swiss embassy as responding brusquely: In the days when the Habsburgs held their lands, "they ruled through noble advocates and bailiffs (*advocatos et balivos nobiles*) of that country, not in a suitable manner, but tyrannically; they permitted the land to be plundered, committing against those whom

---

In another text, he is *gubernator et rector.* Niklaus Gerung, "Flores Temporum," 71. Peter was also a paid councilor to the Habsburg duke Sigmund at the time: Hardy, *Political Culture*, 219.

[91] Brauer-Gramm, *Landvogt*, 82. For the military aspects of his role, see, for example, Knebel, *Tagebuch*, 2:36.

[92] Freiburg im Breisgau, Staatsarchiv, U 100/2 No. 11: "Ich Peter von Hagenpach Ritter . . . Lanntvogt und Hofmeister."

[93] Hardy, *Political Culture*, 221–22.

[94] Knebel, *Tagebuch*, 2:87; Brauer-Gramm, *Landvogt*, 308–17.

they should have nourished disgraceful and unlawful acts; and they imposed on them unaccustomed payments, tallages and exactions and countless other intolerable and heinous things."[95] Knebel would repeat much of this language in the passages of his diary concerning Peter of Hagenbach – evidence that, for him, Hagenbach's time as advocate conformed in many ways to much broader patterns of advocatial corruption.

For example, Knebel reported that it came to the attention of the duke of Burgundy that Peter of Hagenbach "stripped (*excoriaret*) the people of that country and exacted extraordinary amounts from them."[96] Specifically, he required people to pay an exaction on wine known locally as "the bad penny" (*malum denarium*).[97] Knebel also claimed that Hagenbach "exercised great tyranny" against the burghers of the town of Breisach, repeating his earlier language that "he exacted from them and stripped them."[98] In the villages around Breisach, Hagenbach forced the inhabitants to provide him with "straw and hay, grain, wine, and all sorts of other food."[99] All of this supposedly led the people in and around Alsace to cry, "When will we be free ... from the diabolical tyranny of the duke of Burgundy and the accursed Peter of Hagenbach?"[100]

Knebel also accused Hagenbach of sexual violence: The "most heinous business of that most vile man, Peter of Hagenbach," concerned his treatment of women. Knebel tells one story of "a young nun of exceptional beauty" in a convent in Breisach, whom Hagenbach lusted after. When the territorial advocate told her that he would send some of his men to bring her to his house, she went to the abbess, who called on her friends and relatives to take her from the convent and hide her to keep her safe. Hagenbach then threatened death to anyone whom he discovered to be hiding her, but eventually her family succeeded in smuggling her out of the town.[101] Knebel immediately followed this story with one about Hagenbach kissing a woman at the altar in the middle of Mass, when the priest was in the midst of trying to raise the host.[102] Elsewhere in his diary, Knebel also accused him of "violently taking a virgin" (*opprimens virginem*).[103] As noted above, this type of accusation was more commonplace in the fourteenth and fifteenth centuries than in earlier periods, and it would prove in the long run to be one of the harshest critiques that could be leveled against advocates who abused their power at the local level.[104]

---

[95] Knebel, *Tagebuch*, 2:5. See also Chapter 15.   [96] Ibid., 2:61.   [97] Ibid., 2:63.
[98] Ibid., 2:64.   [99] Ibid., 2:70.
[100] Ibid., 2:67. Note that on pp. 84–85 he also uses the language of tyranny for other people. See also Hardy, *Political Culture*, 222–28.
[101] Knebel, *Tagebuch*, 2:69–70.
[102] Ibid., 2:70. For this story, see also Teuscher, "Böse Vögte?," 105.
[103] Knebel, *Tagebuch*, 2:40.   [104] See also Chapter 15.

While much of the rhetoric in Johannes Knebel's diary may seem overwrought, numerous other sources confirm his accusations against the territorial advocate. A letter written by the Habsburg duke Sigmund to Duke Charles of Burgundy in 1474 repeats many of the same complaints about the improper use of "violence and force" (*gewalt und gedrang*).[105] In another letter, this one from the town council of Basel to the towns of Bern and Solothurn, Hagenbach's seizure of Breisach in December of 1473 is described in especially evocative terms; the territorial advocate entered the town accompanied by a large number of troops, "and when they came into the city, they burst in on the honest townspeople in their houses and courtyards and treated them badly."[106] When the people complained, they were told, "You've been sold (*ir sind verkoufft*) and must be made to suffer," a claim that points to the helplessness that many dependents must have felt when their town or village was held in pledge by someone who cared little for their well-being.

In the spring of 1474, the burghers of Breisach were able to expel Hagenbach and his troops from the town, and as the territorial advocate fled, they captured him and put him in chains.[107] During the ensuing trial, which took place at an ad hoc court comprised of judges nominated by various local powers (including Breisach and several other towns), there were four principal charges leveled against Peter. The extant sources differ on some of the precise details, but in general terms these were (1) his unjust execution of four burghers of the town of Thann; (2) his failure to abide by the oath he took when he became territorial advocate to respect local customs and rights; (3) his mistreatment of the people of Breisach, including his quartering of troops in their homes; and (4) his violence against women.[108]

According to Johannes Knebel in his summary of the charges, Hagenbach "imposed unaccustomed tallages, payments and exactions" and "took with force and against their will many women in the city of Breisach, married and virgin – including nuns."[109] A second contemporary account of the trial describes the executions of the burghers of Thann as the result of Hagenbach's "outrageous violence" and decried the lack of proper justice.[110] The anonymous author of this text also singles out Hagenbach's demanding of the "bad penny" without the duke of Burgundy's permission as an especially egregious type of unaccustomed

---

[105] Chmel, ed., *Aktenstücke*, 1:117–19, no. 26.
[106] Knebel, *Tagebuch*, 3:366 (Beilagen). For a short description of all his bad deeds, see also Niklaus Gerung, "Flores Temporum," 71–72.
[107] Knebel, *Tagebuch*, 2:74–75.   [108] Gordon, "Trial," 33.
[109] Knebel, *Tagebuch*, 2:86–87.   [110] Sieber-Lehmann, "Beschreibung," 148.

Figure 13.1 The execution of the territorial advocate Peter of Hagenbach. Conrad of Pfettisheim, *Geschichte Peter Hagenbachs: Reimchronik der Burgunderkriege* (1477), 1v. Staatsbibliothek zu Berlin, Digitalisierte Sammlungen.

exaction.[111] Despite mounting a vigorous defense, Hagenbach was found guilty and beheaded in a field outside the town of Breisach (see Figure 13.1).

Numerous scholars have written accounts of Peter of Hagenbach's life and career, some more sympathetic to the territorial advocate than

[111] Ibid., 148–49. The verse history of Conrad of Pfettisheim, another early source for the trial, also focuses on the issue of the "bad penny": Pfettesheim, *Geschichte Peter Hagenbachs*, Kommentar, 20.

others.[112] Because our most detailed accounts of his activities were all written by people in and around Alsace who were highly critical not only of him but also the Burgundian administration more generally, there is no question that the vivid descriptions of his tyrannical behavior must be approached cautiously. Nevertheless, his highly unusual trial and execution strongly suggest that Hagenbach had crossed a line and had acted in ways that were completely unacceptable to people in the region.

Regardless of one's assessment of his actions, it is essential to recognize that many of the accusations leveled against Peter had very deep roots in the history of advocacy. While we might be tempted to read them as formulaic complaints against bad lordship in general, they are too closely related to advocates' traditional responsibilities to dismiss them in this way. Peter of Hagenbach used his position of territorial advocate to access other people's lands and dependents in order to exercise justice and provide protection – and to profit from a range of advocatial rights. When he abused his position, he did so in ways that must have looked very familiar to the inhabitants of the region, because advocates of various kinds had been abusing their positions in a comparable fashion for centuries.[113] To debate the question of just how tyrannical Peter of Hagenbach really was therefore only gets us so far. The tyrannical advocate was a stock figure by this time – for very good reason – because certain types of advocatial abuses had persisted at the local level since time immemorial. The more important question is why some people in the region reacted to Peter's advocatial violence in a surprising new way: by killing him.[114]

Conclusion

Just how similar were the violent advocates of the period 1250 to 1500 to their predecessors in earlier centuries? This is a difficult question to answer in the case of urban advocates, territorial advocates and the other types of advocates who began to play roles in newly developing local administrations from the mid-thirteenth century, because the sources for their activities are in many ways quite different from the earlier sources for church advocates. The town council of Zwickau's long, detailed list of complaints against Conrad Brückner and the numerous

---

[112] Gordon, "Trial"; Brauer-Gramm, *Landvogt*. Especially sympathetic is Claerr-Stamm, *Pierre de Hagenbach*.

[113] Knebel, much like Hugh of Poitiers 300 years earlier (see Chapter 10), puts into the advocate's mouth a speech justifying his actions: Knebel, *Tagebuch*, 2:59–60. Like Hugh's Count William of Nevers, Knebel's Hagenbach suggests that the local people would be better off under his authority than that of the traditional powers in the region.

[114] See Chapter 15.

contemporary accounts of Peter of Hagenbach's trial have no clear parallels in sources from previous centuries. That said, once we focus on the types of violence that advocates are described as committing, clear continuities emerge. From asserting far-reaching judicial authority to demanding excessive exactions, many of these advocates acted in ways that would have looked familiar to people in the eleventh and twelfth centuries.

This makes sense. Advocates of the thirteenth to fifteenth centuries were still tasked with exercising justice, providing protection and collecting revenue from someone else's lands and dependents. There is nothing to indicate that ideas of government and accountable officeholding had meaningfully transformed the position, or that advocates of this later period felt a newfound responsibility to respect the rights of the people who fell under their advocatial authority. Nor should we assume that the lords for whom they worked expected or demanded ethical, bureaucratic behavior from them. Rulers and other property holders had been talking about making advocates accountable since the later tenth century, yet even into the fifteenth century there is little evidence to suggest that lords aggressively pursued most complaints about violent advocates. The line between legitimate and illegitimate advocatial behavior remained much more blurred than teleologies of the rise of the state might lead us to expect. Advocacy continued to be what it had always been: an opportunity to press claims, assert rights and profit as much as possible from someone else's property. Unsurprisingly, therefore, the end of the so-called Middle Ages did not see the end of the violent advocate.

14 Crossing the False Divide
Advocates after 1500

Published in 1725, Johann Gottfried Lange's dissertation for the law faculty of the University of Leipzig, *On German Advocates and Advocacies*, claims to be the first comprehensive study dedicated to the subject.[1] From the beginning, Lange acknowledges the remarkable diversity of different types of advocates, and over the course of his sixty-four-page work he discusses not only church advocates but also territorial and urban advocates, among others. Despite this variety, Lange insists that protection, justice and administration lay at the heart of advocacy in all its many forms. He supports this account by citing many of the sources I have referenced in this book, including Carolingian capitularies, papal bulls and imperial privileges. The same decade that Lange's work appeared, the first German-language dictionary of Latin legal terms was also published; its fourth edition, from 1753, includes more than a dozen variants of the terms *advocatus, advocatia* and *advocatio*, each with a clear and concise definition.[2] Thus, over the course of the eighteenth century, advocacy and the documents central to its history increasingly became objects of academic inquiry. Research into them has not stopped since.

None of this means, however, that advocates had abandoned the monastery, town and village for the university by 1700 – or even 1800. The earliest scholarship on advocacy emerged at a time when advocates were still exercising justice and providing protection in many places in the German-speaking lands. Indeed, some of the people who undertook research into the history of advocacy in this period did so for very practical reasons; conflict – and violence – continued to erupt between advocates and local communities throughout the sixteenth to eighteenth centuries because of disputes over the proper limits of advocatial rights.[3] Advocacy still generated such an enormous body of source material in this period

---

[1] Lange, *De Advocatis*.   [2] *Lexicon Juridicum*, 35–36.

[3] This same period saw the origins of diplomatics, the scientific study of documents; this discipline came into being in part because there were questions about the authenticity of the many medieval documents that still carried legal force in the early modern period. See Roach, *Forgery*, 3–5; Dorna, *Mabillon*, 17.

that a book-length study would be necessary to do the subject justice. My goal here is more modest: to offer sufficient evidence to support my argument for continuity in many advocatial practices across the millennium from roughly 750 to 1800.

Medieval and Early Modern

The Austrian National Library in Vienna preserves today a handwritten book bearing the date of 1714 and entitled *The Order and Process of a Praiseworthy Advocate's Court of the Town of Schaffhausen.*[4] It is quite a small volume, almost pocket-sized, with only eighty-three numbered pages plus an index and a table of contents; unfortunately, it contains no illustrations. The first chapter begins with the oath that the imperial advocate (*der Herr Vogt des Reichs*) was to swear, including his promises "to be a fair judge" and to hold court regularly.[5] Subsequent sections discuss (among other topics) the oaths sworn by the other agents of the court, the crimes that fell under the court's jurisdiction (including breaking the peace and other high crimes), the calling and questioning of witnesses, and the punishments to be meted out to those who were found guilty. The eighth and final chapter concerns what the imperial advocate was to receive annually in compensation.[6]

While the level of detail this little book provides about an advocate's judicial role is remarkable, especially in comparison with the paltry evidence from earlier centuries for such proceedings, nothing here is surprising. Advocates had been responsible for judging violent crimes in some parts of Europe for three-quarters of a millennium by the time this text was written. There had been advocates at Schaffhausen in the north of Switzerland, the site of an important monastery, since the eleventh century.[7] According to the work's subtitle, this volume had been compiled in 1714 on the basis of older accounts of the court's organization and processes, which points to the significant role tradition and custom played in judicial proceedings of this sort. In short, *The Order and Process of a Praiseworthy Advocate's Court of the Town of Schaffhausen* is tangible evidence that the line historians like to draw between a "medieval" period and an "early modern" one is often unhelpful – if not downright misleading.

As I argued in the Introduction, dividing European history into a "Middle Ages," a subsequent "Renaissance" and then a "modern"

---

[4] Vienna, Österreichische Nationalbibliothek, Cod. 12875. The date is given on p. 83. The complete title is *Ordnung und Process eines lobl[ichen] Vogtgerichts der Statt Schaffhausen. Aus den alten Ordnungen und bisher geführten Process zusahmen gezogen und erneuert.*
[5] Ibid., 1–2.   [6] Ibid., 81–83.   [7] See Chapter 5.

period has never been a politically neutral act. Since its origins in four-teenth-century Italy, the idea of an ignorance-filled "middle" period between Antiquity and an imagined new, modern age has always been part of a narrative of European progress and improvement.[8] Religion, superstition and feudalism are co-travelers with the concept of the medi-eval, while secularism, capitalism and democracy are inherent to the notion of the modern.[9] The story of Europe, in other words, is the story of how the continent overcame a millennium of "medieval" backwardness to create a better "modern" world. To draw a dividing line sometime around the year 1500 is therefore to decree that is when Europe reached a tipping point and began moving inexorably in the right direction.

For my purposes here, the key issue in this narrative of European progress concerns the transition from feudalism and lordship to government, bureauc-racy and the state. As I have discussed, some historians who specialize in medieval European history are comfortable speaking of a Carolingian state in the ninth century, or of the thirteenth century as the period when the modern state first took shape.[10] Outside the field of medieval history, however, many scholars prefer to align the origins of the state with the concept of sovereignty and the birth of modernity from the sixteenth century onward.[11] According to this line of argument, government, officeholding and bureaucracy as we understand them today are products of the period after 1500, when the administrative apparatus of the state expanded rapidly, as evidenced by the explosion of administrative documents in government archives.[12]

As compelling as this narrative is, recent generations have been more cautious than some earlier ones in their assessments of the nature of the state between the sixteenth and eighteenth centuries. Many scho-lars insist that the sovereign state was not an all-encompassing institu-tion in this period. Patrimonial forms of officeholding continued to predominate in many places (including not only Europe but also the American colonies).[13] Government before 1800 was not impersonal in the Weberian sense; the administrative reforms that led to modern ideas of bureaucracy mostly postdate the French Revolution.[14] Into

---

[8] Le Goff, *History*, 13–16.   [9] Davis, *Periodization*, 3–4; Fasolt, "Hegel's Ghost."
[10] See Chapters 1 and 12 and Lyon, "State"; Guenée, *States*; Strayer, *Medieval Origins*.
[11] For a good overview, see Hont, "Permanent Crisis," 178–83. There is an enormous historiography on this topic, not only in history but also many other disciplines. For examples of works that discuss the medieval period but see the state as emerging in later centuries, see Tilly, *Coercion*; Spruyt, *Sovereign State*.
[12] Useful here are Castelnuovo, "Offices"; Head, "Knowing." See also Brady, *German Histories*, 97–104; McGlynn, "Written Record."
[13] Adams, *Familial State*; Lind, "Great Friends," esp. 145–47; Whaley, *Germany*, 1:486–91; Bailyn, "Politics"; Billings, "Growth."
[14] Especially helpful here is Holenstein, "Introduction." See also Bernard, "Water-Spout," 131–32.

the eighteenth century, even in countries today considered models for good government, there remained frequent problems associated with controlling how protection was provided, justice was exercised and revenue was collected at the local level.[15] As a result, some scholars have argued that a "feudal" logic persisted in many places into the eighteenth century.[16] These historians have stressed that throughout this period some lords continued to rely on customary labor services and dues owed by their dependents – including advocatial payments tied to justice and protection – rather than general taxes to fund their administrations.[17]

All of this work is evidence that we must not let the traditional medieval/modern dividing line around 1500 shape our expectations for the history of advocacy between the sixteenth and eighteenth centuries. The advocates of this period were no more bureaucratic officeholders than their predecessors in earlier periods had been. To be sure, the growth of princely administration in the German-speaking lands can, at times, make advocates look more accountable and more integrated into official networks after 1500 than they had been before.[18] Nevertheless, as was the case already in the Carolingian period, if we dig below the surface of prescriptive sources about proper advocatial behavior, we quickly uncover evidence for advocates creatively pushing the limits of their roles as judges and defenders to profit from their positions in any way they could.

Church Advocates after 1500

The Reformation transformed the ecclesiastical landscape of the German-speaking lands. Martin Luther's critiques of monastic vows and the ascetic life led to the shuttering of large numbers of religious institutions across the regions where his reforms took root.[19] As a result, many church advocacies disappeared as well, though scholars have cautioned against the idea that Lutheran princes simply seized for themselves all the monastic estates and rights in their territories under the pretense of secularization.[20] As with so many other aspects of the history of the Reformation, there was a remarkable amount of local variation in how

---

[15] Bågenholm, "Corruption"; Head, "Shared Lordship"; Waquet, *Corruption*.
[16] Wickham, "Feudal Economy," 37.
[17] Whaley, *Germany*, 2:252–53; Blickle, *Leibeigenschaft*, 236–38; Simon, *Grundherrschaft*, 46–75; Körner, "Steuern"; Bosl, "Schutz," 49.
[18] For more on this point, see below.
[19] Brady, *German Histories*, 172–77; Whaley, *Germany*, 1:185–86.
[20] Cohn, "Church Property," 166–69.

Protestant reform ideals impacted advocacy. Quedlinburg became a house for Lutheran noblewomen living pious lives, and the advocacy for the community remained in existence until 1803.[21] The Cistercian convent of Nonnenmünster survived the Reformation inside the walls of the Lutheran town of Worms – with the urban administration holding its advocacy.[22] In Austria, where the Catholic Counter-Reformation would ultimately prove successful, there were several decades in the mid-and late sixteenth century when much of the population had become Protestant; this led to many a Lutheran nobleman appointing a Lutheran preacher to a parish church over which he held advocatial rights – even if that parish belonged to one of the many Catholic monasteries in the region.[23] Thus, as in previous centuries, each church advocacy continued to have its own unique history.

An excellent example of an advocacy for an ecclesiastical property surviving for centuries on both sides of the year 1500 concerns the village of Pfalzfeld west of the Rhine. The village is first referenced in an extant source in 820, when Emperor Louis the Pious granted it to the monastery of Prüm.[24] In the late eleventh and twelfth centuries, the advocacy for Pfalzfeld was probably in the hands of the counts of Arnstein, who held extensive advocatial rights over Prüm's properties in the region. In 1185, when the Arnstein lineage died out in the male line, the counts of Katzenelnbogen acquired their advocatial rights in the region.[25] Then, at some point in the mid-fourteenth century, while still holding the advocacy for Pfalzfeld as a fief from Prüm, a count of Katzenelnbogen gave it in fief to the lords of Braunshorn. When this family died out in the male line in 1360 and the count tried to reclaim it, a dispute ensued with the legal heirs of the lords of Braunshorn, the lords of Winneburg-Beilstein. In 1367–68, these lords were forced to renounce all claims, and the advocacy returned to the hands of the counts of Katzenelnbogen.[26] By the mid-fifteenth century, Count Philip of Katzenelnbogen (1444–79) was effectively exercising authority as lord in Pfalzfeld, and there is little evidence that Prüm's rights in the village were being respected. On Philip's death without a male heir, however, Landgrave Henry of Hessen-Kassel acquired the advocacy for Pfalzfeld. Although Prüm sold its other rights in Pfalzfeld to the archbishopric of Trier in 1576, the advocacy remained under the landgraves' control.[27]

---

[21] See the section "The Advocacy for Quedlinburg, 936–1803," later in this chapter.

[22] Kemper, "Vogteirechte." For another example of the complexity of the Reformation's impact on church advocacy, see Finger, "Kloster," 104–05.

[23] Winkelbauer, *Ständefreiheit*, 2:106–08; Eder, *Glaubensspaltung*, 360–75.

[24] Reimold, *Chronik*, 34.   [25] Ibid., 39.   [26] Ibid., 40–42.   [27] Ibid., 43.

The situation changed little until the arrival of French troops in the mid-1790s, when the advocacy was finally dissolved.[28]

That the landgraves of Hessen-Kassel considered the Pfalzfeld advocacy to be valuable after they acquired it is evidenced by a detailed description of a court session held there in 1548. This text preserves what is clearly a highly formalized dialogue between the advocate and the representatives of the village of Pfalzfeld. It begins with the advocate asking whether it is the correct day of the year to hold the court session in the village. A series of questions then follow about proper court procedures and the crimes that ought to be judged there. The advocate then asks, "What in the advocacy is our merciful Prince and Lord's to enjoy, and what are his rents and levies?" A detailed list of the amounts of various grains and the number of lambs and chickens owed by the community and the individual households then follows. The next question makes it even clearer that the collection of these advocatial rights and dues was still important: "How should one teach obedience to those who are late in the delivery of the above-mentioned goods?" The villagers reply, "If one or the other person is late, my merciful Prince may punish him however he wants."[29] The formulaic and ritualistic nature of this account suggests that these court sessions were performative and were designed, at least partly, to remind the village every year of the power and authority of its advocate.[30] Nevertheless, the emphasis on the advocate's income also shows that nobles continued into the sixteenth century to pay close attention to the profits they accrued from providing protection and justice to someone else's dependents.[31]

There is also evidence throughout the period from 1500 to 1800 of religious communities coming into conflict with their advocates. At several of the monasteries I have discussed repeatedly in this book, including Siegburg, Benediktbeuern and St. Maximin in Trier, the question of who was advocate and/or who held advocatial rights to collect certain exactions continued to be a vexed one.[32] At the Premonstratensian house of Ursberg, which had been granted the right to appoint its own advocates for twenty years by Emperor Frederick III in 1469, tensions erupted in the early sixteenth century after the community lost this right. After the

---

[28] Ibid., 110–11. See also pp. 107–08 for the story of the French capturing the *Vogt* of Pfalzfeld in 1734 and demanding a ransom, only to discover that no one was willing to pay for the advocate's release.

[29] Ibid., 141–44, no. 11.   [30] Teuscher, *Lords' Rights*, 42.

[31] Trier's so-called *Feuerbuch* of 1563, which recorded the number of hearths in the archbishopric's territories for tax purposes, indicates that numerous advocates continued to hold rights on individual Trier estates: Brommer, *Ämter Kurtriers*, 166, 181 and 252.

[32] Wisplinghoff, *Benediktinerabtei Siegburg*, 95–100; Lau, "Kampf," 72–73; Hemmerle, *Benediktbeuern*, 203–05; Resmini, *St. Maximin*, 582–87.

election of a new head of the monastery in 1522, the advocate for the community, the count of Helfenstein, clashed with him and tried to have him removed, even entering the monastery by force.[33] Less than a decade later at the Augustinian house of Ravengiersburg, the count-palatine and duke Johann II of Simmern, acting as advocate, became involved in a dispute over judicial rights with the community. In 1531, his soldiers stormed the religious house, leading to decades of conflict.[34] In the next century, a disagreement involving the emperor, the canonesses at Lindau and the urban administration of Lindau over the advocacy for some of the canonesses' properties led to a long-running legal dispute; central to the disagreement was a debate about the authenticity of the community's foundation privilege, a debate that is illuminating for the early history of diplomatics.[35]

Abbatial elections, judicial rights and forged documents: The flash-points for many of these disputes are similar to those of earlier centuries. As I stressed in the previous chapter, however, evidence for continuity should not be interpreted to mean that advocacy had become a static and hoary institution by 1500. Advocates were always looking for opportunities to press their claims in new ways in order to gain more access to the people and property in their advocacies.

In the Habsburgs' Austrian lands, the issue of advocates' rights over dead churchmen's properties became an increasingly vexed one during the sixteenth and seventeenth centuries. This subject had first surfaced in the mid-twelfth century, when Emperor Frederick I had sought to stop advocates from claiming "for themselves the personal goods of dying priests."[36] Thirteenth-century church councils, including the Council of Vienna in 1267, addressed this problem too.[37] Nevertheless, many advocates continued to insist this was their right, and in 1544, the Habsburg ruler Ferdinand I issued for the territory of Lower Austria a "general mandate concerning the interference of lord-advocates in the properties of dead ecclesiastics."[38] The mandate complained that it had become common practice for advocates to seize the property of dead priests before the priests' debts had been paid off and their legitimate

---

[33] Kreuzer, "Ursberg," 83–84. See also Chapter 13.
[34] Wagner, "Weistum," 78 and 84.   [35] Dorna, *Mabillon*, 55–88.
[36] DD F I, 2:143–44, no. 320. See Chapter 7.
[37] *Concilia Germaniae*, 3:635, chap. 10. See also Chapter 8 above and Eder, *Land ob der Enns*, 39–40.
[38] Vienna, Österreichische Nationalbibliothek, Cod. 8084, fol. 78v–80r. For the context, Eder, *Glaubensspaltung*, 57. Other texts from this period also reveal a great deal of concern with advocacies in Lower Austria; see, for example, Vienna, Österreichische Nationalbibliothek, Cod. 7710 and Cod. 8714.

heirs had received anything. Ferdinand I insisted that advocates ought to inventory dead priests' property and protect it – not benefit from it.

And yet, 125 years later, an advocate's claim to the personal property of a dead priest would be one of the focal points of a fascinating dispute at the Austrian monastery of Seitenstetten in Lower Austria.[39] The rich documentation for this dispute deserves close scrutiny. Seitenstetten had been founded in 1112 by a local noble lineage. The advocacy was initially in the hands of members of this founding lineage, but by the later twelfth century it had passed to other nobles in the region, which likely explains why the monastery, like so many other communities, turned to forgery sometime in the late twelfth or early thirteenth century in an attempt to limit the rights of its local advocates.[40] By 1240 at the latest, when Duke Frederick II of Austria issued a privilege for the monastery, it had come under the influence of the Babenberg dukes.[41] But local nobles continued to press claims to advocatial rights over Seitenstetten in subsequent years until the first Habsburg king, Rudolf I, acquired Austria and claimed the advocacy.[42] This was not a case of *Entvogtung*, however. In 1359, the lord of the nearby castle of Steyr was in possession of the advocacy for Seitenstetten, and in subsequent centuries, the Habsburgs would continue to grant the holders of Steyr the advocacy for the monastery.[43]

In 1663, Emperor Leopold I pledged the Lordship (*Herrschaft*) of Steyr to one of his loyal supporters, Count Johann Maximilian of Lamberg. Three years later in 1666, the emperor sold it to him outright.[44] The move prompted five years of conflict over the advocacy for Seitenstetten, because Abbot Gabriel Sauer (1648–74) took the position that the monastery did not owe the traditional advocatial rights to the count.[45] The issue of dead priests' property would become one of the main points of contention, but it was another advocatial right that first started the dispute between the monastery and its new advocate. Every year on the

---

[39] For the history of this community, see Ortmayr and Decker, *Benediktinerstift Seitenstetten*; Reichert, *Landesherrschaft*, 194–99.

[40] *Niederösterreichisches Urkundenbuch*, 2.1:450–53, no. 12². See also pp. 461–62. This forgery includes familiar language: "[I]f the advocate should be *inuttilis* [sic] and should oppress the monastery through any violence, the abbot and the brothers possess the privilege of removing him."

[41] BUB, 2:198–99, no. 354. See also 282–83, no. 429.

[42] Raab, ed., *Urkundenbuch*, 95–97, no. 80 and 103, no. 86. See also Ortmayr and Decker, *Benediktinerstift Seitenstetten*, 211.

[43] In 1438, King Albrecht II granted the advocacy to Hans Neidegger, who held the castle of Steyr on his behalf; see Regesta Imperii Online, RI XII no. 137. I thank Herwig Weigl and Roman Zehetmayer for their generosity in guiding me through the evidence for Seitenstetten.

[44] Ortmayr and Decker, *Benediktinerstift Seitenstetten*, 210.   [45] Ibid.

feast of St. Martin (November 11), the monastery was expected to give to the lord of Steyr the "advocate's sword" (*Vogtschwert*) as a token of gratitude for the protection and justice he provided to the community as holder of the advocacy.[46] It was a custom that dated back to at least the late sixteenth and early seventeenth centuries, and November of 1666 was apparently to be the first time that the "advocate's sword" would be given to the new lord.[47] But the delivery never occurred, leading to a legal back and forth between the two sides that was not settled until 1670, when the abbot agreed to pay the count 300 Gulden in return for the count's abandoning of his claim to the sword.[48]

As was so often the case in past centuries too, when an advocate retreated on one type of advocatial claim, he sought an opportunity to press his rights in a new direction. Within a year of the end of the dispute over the sword, the focus of the dispute between Steyr and Seitenstetten had already shifted to their competing rights over the parish church in a village called Asbach (Aschbach-Markt). This parish had belonged to the monastery of Seitenstetten since 1116, and it had been a source of friction between the abbots and their advocates long before the early 1670s. A century earlier, when the lord of Steyr was Lutheran, he had prevented the abbot from installing a Catholic pastor or promoting Catholicism there.[49] In 1671, conflict erupted for a different reason: advocatial efforts to claim the property of a dead priest.

On June 22, 1671, the pastor of Asbach died. Only three days later, the abbot of Seitenstetten, Gabriel Sauer, wrote a letter to his neighbor, the count of Steyr, to complain about the behavior of some of the count's agents in the wake of the pastor's death.[50] The letter begins with the abbot assuring the count that he does not want to bother him but that his monastery has recently suffered an unexpected wrong "against ecclesiastical immunity on the pretext of advocatial right." In a letter otherwise written almost entirely in German, these words stand out clearly, because they were written in Latin (*contra immunitatem Ecclesiasticam . . . praetextu*

---

[46] Ibid.

[47] Ibid., 184. In 1626, during a peasant uprising, the castle of Steyr had been plundered and the "advocates' swords" (*Vogtschwerter*) seized.

[48] Documents concerning the *Vogtschwert* are in Linz, Oberösterreichisches Landesarchiv, Herrschaft Steyr, Schachtel No. 313, 40b. See also Ortmayr and Decker, *Benediktinerstift Seitenstetten*, 211–12. Other religious communities throughout the period 1500 to 1800 also sought to free themselves from customary advocatial payments by offering lump sums of money. See, for example, Horstkötter, ed., *Urkundenbuch*, 2:681, no. 283 (commentary). For more on this practice, see Chapter 8.

[49] Ortmayr and Decker, *Benediktinerstift Seitenstetten*, 160–61. For more on Protestants and Catholics at Asbach, see ibid., pp. 185–89.

[50] All of the documents for this dispute are in Linz, Oberösterreichisches Landesarchiv, Herrschaft Steyr, Schachtel No. 313, 40c, Faszikel 187.

Iuris Advocatiae) and in a clearer and larger hand than the scribe's typical cursive. The letter goes on to explain how the monastery's vicar in the small town of Aspach had died a short time earlier. On the day of his funeral, many of the monks of Seitenstetten, members of their household and other local community members came together for his burial and a modest meal thereafter. His vicarage (*Pfarrhof*) had been locked, and there was no one there on that day except the abbot's local judge (*Hofrichter*), who had left the funeral early.

Unannounced, one of the count's agents, Johann Baptista Chriegsauer, arrived at the vicarage along with another man. Chriegsauer declared he was there in the name of the Lordship of Steyr on account of its advocatial authority (*Voggt Obrigkheit*) and demanded entrance to the vicarage. The *Hofrichter* explained that he would have to be patient and wait, since the prior and everyone else were still at the funeral. Chriegsauer refused to wait and demanded the vicarage be opened immediately – or else he would use force to break the door down. As the letter complains, the advocatial office (*Voggteylichen officii*) was meant to provide protection "against disturbers of churches and their properties" (*contra turbatores Ecclesiarum earumque rerum*), but Chriegsauer himself had become the disturber threatening force "against the ecclesiastical immunity." When the *Hofrichter* persisted in refusing to grant access, Chriegsauer broke down one of the doors and entered the vicarage. A short time later, the prior with three of his priests arrived back at the vicarage. The prior immediately began to criticize Chriegsauer for his actions – on the day of the vicar's funeral, no less.

At this point, the letter finally starts to shed light on why Chriegsauer's presence at the vicarage had sparked such anger on the part of the monastic community. The prior insisted that all of the dead vicar's property belonged by right to the monastery of Seitenstetten and that the lords of Steyr had no claim to any part of his inheritance by their advocatial authority. Chriegsauer refused to accept this. The prior then asked if he was in possession of a written mandate, sealed by the lord of Steyr, explaining the advocate's claims to the vicar's property. Chriegsauer replied that he had no such mandate but that he was simply to be believed since he was an officer of the lordship. The prior still refused to give anything to him. At this point, the narrative ends. The letter once again addresses the count of Steyr, asking him to do something about his agent's improper behavior.

This dispute did not drag on as long as the one over the "advocate's sword." It was settled two months later in mid-August of 1671 as part of a broader agreement between the count and the abbot.[51] While the count

---

[51] Linz, Oberösterreichisches Landesarchiv, Herrschaft Steyr, Schachtel No. 313, 40b, Faszikel 186.

insisted that his "advocatial jurisdiction" (*voggtheyliche Jurisdiction*) gave him the right to impound and inventory the property of any deceased pastor of Asbach, out of "neighborly goodwill" (*nachbarlichen Guetwilligkeit*) he agreed to allow Seitenstetten to oversee this process in the case of a pastor who was a member of the monastic community – but not when the pastor was from outside of it. Thus, as far as the count was concerned, his rights as advocate (as he chose to define them) remained intact. After this, the volume of archival evidence about the Seitenstetten advocacy declines, suggesting that this compromise eased tensions.

That count and monastery fought over advocatial rights for five years after the count acquired the advocacy is noteworthy. Roughly 550 years after Seitenstetten's foundation, there were still questions about what, precisely, it meant for the monastery's advocate to exercise justice and provide protection – and to be paid for fulfilling these responsibilities. Even imperial mandates could not place definitive limits on advocates' roles or stop advocates and their agents from trying to profit in any way they could. The actions of Johann Baptista Chriegsauer, who quite literally broke the door down in order to gain access to a dead priest's property, are an especially vivid – if hardly unusual – example of the quotidian, violent assertions of advocatial rights across centuries of European history.

Advocates and Secular Administration after 1500

If you ride the U2 line of the Berlin subway system, you will come to a station called "Hausvogteiplatz." Take the stairs up from the station platform, and you will find yourself in a gentrified and rather sleepy corner of downtown. This was not always the case, however. The plaza takes its name from a jail built there in 1750 by King Frederick the Great of Prussia (1740–86). The "house advocate" (*Hausvogt*), a position which dated to the early decades of Hohenzollern rule in Brandenburg in the fifteenth century (if not earlier), initially was responsible for collecting certain dues and for provisioning the princely palace in Berlin.[52] During the sixteenth and seventeenth centuries, the position's policing functions grew in significance. In contrast to the Berlin city jail run by the urban administration, the jail overseen by the house advocate was for those people who were under the direct legal authority of the Hohenzollerns (including Jewish residents of the city) and those whose crimes – especially political crimes – made them answerable to Hohenzollern princely agents.[53] As one scholar has

---

[52] Raumer, ed., *Codex*, 1:179–80, no. 30.
[53] Luuk, *Berlin-Handbuch*, 546. For an excellent description of the *Hausvogt*'s wide-ranging responsibilities, see Schmoller and Krauske, *Die Behördenorganisation*, 2:53–54, no. 17.

observed, "The *Hausvogt* . . . was the most important and feared person for the Jews of Berlin, . . . the most visible symbol of the state's omnipotence."[54] Thus, not only church advocates but also other types of advocates remained key figures with significant power and authority at the local level after 1500.

While advocates were not used everywhere in the German-speaking lands in princely and urban administrations, in many regions they fulfilled a wide range of functions. In the territories ruled by the Hohenzollerns, advocates were even more commonplace in Prussia than they were in and around Berlin. As discussed already, advocates had played prominent roles in the Teutonic Order's administration in Prussia during the fourteenth and fifteenth centuries, and this continued into the later period.[55] Under the first duke of Prussia after the Order's dissolution, the Hohenzollern Albrecht (d. 1568), advocates appear frequently. In 1562, for example, the *Hausvogt* of Memel (Klaipėda in modern Lithuania) was one of three agents sent by Albrecht to meet with the *Vogt* of Grobin (Grobiņa in modern Latvia) to discuss concerns about the mishandling of the advocacy's finances and other types of mismanagement.[56] These agents were to restore order and remind the advocate of Grobin of his oath and duty (*eide und pflicht*) to serve the duke well.[57]

Far to the southwest of Prussia, another region where advocates were commonplace in local administration was the duchy of Württemberg.[58] Every town and village in the duchy was located within an administrative district, and each had a *Vogt* as the local head of the territorial administration. This advocate presided over the court in the main town in his district and also presided, once per year, over advocatial courts in the other towns in his district.[59] In 1514 there were forty-three of these districts, an impressive number that suggests a well-developed and defined administrative apparatus.

And yet, in 1514, approximately half of these advocatial positions were in the hands of only nine families.[60] This can be explained by the fact that

---

[54] Stern, *Preussische Staat*, 1.1:30–31. The *Hausvogt* also collected the "protection money" (*Schutzgelder*) from the Jews for the Hohenzollern. See also Geiger, *Geschichte*, 2:33–34.
[55] See Chapter 12.
[56] Berlin, Geheimes Staatsarchiv Preußischer Kulturbesitz, XX. HA, HBA, D, No. 2943. For advocates in the early modern Baltic region, see Stikāne, "Vogtei."
[57] For the significance of advocates' oaths, see Chapters 5 and 7.
[58] For the importance of church advocacies for the development of the territorial power of the dukes of Württemberg, see Stievermann, *Landesherrschaft*, 173–91. For advocates in southwestern Germany in this period, see also Simon, *Grundherrschaft*.
[59] Hirbodian, "Konrad Breuning," 206; Vann, *State*, 38–41; Trugenberger, "Vogt," 39, 51–52. For the challenges of presiding over these courts, see Fritz, "Diener," 139.
[60] Kühnle, *Wir, Vogt*, 116; Hirbodian, "Konrad Breuning," 207.

these positions had to be purchased, as was typical of many administrative positions in this period. Because the buyer was expected to be well educated and to have followers in the district where he would be advocate, the holders of these and many other key positions tended to be related to each other and to belong to a fairly closed functional elite (*Funktionselite*).[61] One advocate in the early sixteenth century, Konrad Breuning, came from a leading family in Tübingen with strong ties to the dukes of Württemberg. Despite being in the duke's inner circle for a time, he was caught up in the political turmoil after the duke called for a new tax; he was beheaded on the duke's orders in 1517.[62] Thus, while at first glance the administration of the duchy of Württemberg might look much more "modern" than any of the princely administrations of the preceding centuries in the German-speaking lands, we must be careful not to assume that a bureaucratic officialdom had already taken shape in this period.[63]

Indeed, it is impossible to separate these advocates' judicial and administrative roles from their roles as leading members of local society. Evidence that many of these advocates treated their positions as family property, not as a public office, takes various forms. Some declared their marriages (or those of their daughters) "official" events and demanded wedding "gifts" from those in their advocacy; others invested taxes supposedly collected for the dukes in their own business enterprises.[64] These Württemberg advocates clearly followed in the footsteps of their predecessors from earlier centuries in seeing their positions as opportunities to profit by any means possible. Even into the late eighteenth century, despite ongoing attempts to make advocates more accountable, many of these dynamics persisted.[65]

The same is true to the south of Württemberg in the Swiss lands. Since the Carolingian period, this region had been central to the history of advocacy. At the monastery of St. Gall, the site of one of the best ninth-century source collections for advocates anywhere in Europe, advocates remained central figures in the administration of the community's territories for three-quarters of a millennium. In 1583, the prince-abbot of St. Gall tasked the territorial advocate Georg Reding with overseeing the administrative and judicial aspects of the re-Catholicization of the

---

[61] Hirbodian, "Konrad Breuning," 207. See also Fritz, "Diener," 124.
[62] Hirbodian, "Konrad Breuning."
[63] Most scholars tend to focus on the evidence for nascent government structures and ignore the evidence for corruption: Fritz, "Diener," 120.
[64] Fritz, "Diener," 129 and 135.
[65] Ibid. To be fair, some early modern advocates seem to have had good reputations. I thank my colleague Alice Goff for sharing with me her work on an advocate of the town of Sinzig, whose body was treated as a mascot of sorts by the townspeople.

monastery's dependents.[66] Four decades later in 1621, an investigation into the murder of one of St. Gall's officials (an *Amtmann*) involved several advocates.[67] The territorial advocate Dietrich Reding initially organized the manhunt, offered money for information about the murderers and threatened any dependents who remained silent.[68] Nevertheless, eight years passed before the murderers were identified. The territorial advocate at that time, Dietrich's son Hans Rudolf Reding, oversaw their arrest and incarceration.[69] At the court called in 1629 to hear the case, the presiding judge was the imperial advocate (*Reichsvogt*) from nearby Wil, and the advocate of Iberg (who was Hans Rudolf's brother) sat on the court as well.[70] While the level of detail for advocatial involvement in this case far exceeds anything we have for earlier centuries, advocacy at St. Gall in the early seventeenth century clearly maintained several familiar features, including control of the position by a prominent local family and the intermingling of both policing and judicial responsibilities.

As Habsburg authority in the Swiss lands declined over the course of the fourteenth and fifteenth centuries, other local powers besides the monastery of St. Gall also acquired and maintained the use of a variety of advocatial positions.[71] The town of Bern relied heavily on territorial advocates to administer the lands outside its walls; these advocates tended to be prominent burghers whom one historian has described as "independent co-entrepreneurs" whose "success depended on their ability to create synergies in the simultaneous pursuits of their own and their lord's interests."[72] At Zurich, which also employed territorial advocates appointed for fixed terms from among the burghers of the town, the advocates still drew much of their income from payments in grain, chicken and other agricultural goods. In 1553, the town administration agreed to increase the pay for some of these advocates in return for their keeping their accounts more accurately. Nevertheless, into the eighteenth century, Zurich's territorial advocates continued to find ways to profit from their positions beyond their "official" income.[73] Paralleling the dynamics between churches and noble advocates that had existed since at least the eleventh century, these town-appointed burgher advocates

---

[66] Z'Graggen, *Tyrannenmord*, 179.   [67] Ibid., 63.   [68] Ibid., 65–66.   [69] Ibid., 71.
[70] Ibid., 83. Josef Lussi, *Vogt* in Schwazenbach, was also there. For the different advocates in the St. Gall territories, see ibid., 131 and 155.
[71] See also Chapter 12 and Head, "Shared Lordship."
[72] Teuscher, "Threats," 103–04. For the argument that Bern's territorial advocates should be understood through patron–client networks rather than bureaucratic officeholding, see also Teuscher, *Bekannte*, 27, 207–10.
[73] Dütsch, *Zürcher Landvögte*, 50–64.

repeatedly sought creative ways to extend their reach beyond the limits placed on them by their employers.

Unsurprisingly, therefore, if we look past the façade of the formal features of the position of territorial advocate between 1500 and 1800, we quickly discover familiar accusations of advocatial misbehavior.[74] This is best seen in sources from Basel. There, territorial advocates were appointed by the town to an eight-year term, and the position was, at least in theory, tightly regulated: The advocate was to be a Basel burgher and was answerable to the urban administration.[75] In the 1790s, however, locals frequently complained to the town about the territorial advocate Hans Franz Hagenbach. In 1795, for example, the people living in and around one village were outraged, because for no reason he raised the amount of money they owed as the equivalent for providing the *Fastnachtshühner* (Fat Tuesday chickens).[76] The same year, a man from another village complained in general about the territorial advocate's oppressive demands. In 1796, Hagenbach was accused of being overly aggressive and threatening in the interrogation of a fourteen-year-old girl, whom he slapped and left in a "cold pit" (he would later also be accused of mishandling a pregnant woman during an interrogation). The following year, a villager refused to go to Hagenbach's castle to have his case heard, because the territorial advocate was notorious for his unfair judgments; the man suspected that Hagenbach would simply lock him in a tower.[77] This is only a small sample of the many accusations leveled against this one territorial advocate.[78]

All of these were typical complaints about advocates. Indeed, some of them were 800 years old by this time. The urban administration of Basel apparently paid attention to at least some of these accusations; in 1796, the advocate was reprimanded for demanding too much in judicial fines.[79] We might be tempted to argue, therefore, that Hagenbach was more of an accountable officeholder than his predecessors. But rulers and lords of various sort (ecclesiastical, noble, urban) had been hearing complaints about misbehaving advocates since at least the year 1000, and as with most other cases, Basel's actions never went beyond admonishment.

---

[74] On this point, see also Head, "Shared Lordship," esp. 496–97.

[75] Simon, *Untertanenverhalten*, 201–02.

[76] For all of the following complaints against him, see ibid., 207. By this time, the Fat Tuesday chicken was a customary payment made to many advocates: Head, "Shared Lordship," 503; Dütsch, *Zürcher Landvögte*, 50.

[77] For similar complaints in Württemberg, see Fritz, "Diener," 143 and 158.

[78] Hagenbach's wife was equally unpopular. One man called her a "thunder-shooting" (*donnerschiessige*) woman, and another complained that she had "a nasty mouth" (*ein böse Maul*) and was always present during interrogations.

[79] Simon, *Untertanenverhalten*, 207.

Hagenbach was neither summoned to a judicial proceeding nor removed from office, because the town needed him and other advocates like him to help it administer its territories.[80] As in other places and times, the advocate's role inevitably came with a certain amount of flexibility, and the town had no choice but to accept that low-level corruption was an intrinsic part of exercising justice and providing protection beyond its walls.[81] In and around Basel, locals only succeeded in putting an end to this feature of advocatial authority from January of 1798, when a group of villagers went to Hagenbach's castle to demand their traditional rights. A short time later, they destroyed the castle.[82] The spirit of the French Revolution had reached the Swiss lands.

The Advocacy for Quedlinburg, 936–1803

The property regime that emerged in many parts of Europe during the Carolingian period, which required large landholders (ecclesiastical ones, in particular) to "contract out" to someone else the provision of justice and protection, led to a millennium of advocates testing the limits of their position. With access came opportunity, and so long as the role of advocate existed, members of local elites and their followers found ways – some of them as old as advocacy itself, others creatively new – to profit from other people's rights and properties. The blending of continuity and change that characterized the long history of advocacy down to the eighteenth century can be seen especially well at a religious community that has appeared on numerous occasions in the preceding pages.

The canonesses at Quedlinburg had had advocates since their community's foundation in 936.[83] In the mid-twelfth century, when the advocacy passed from the German rulers' hands to those of local nobles, the convent's coinage frequently depicted the community's sword-wielding advocate alongside its abbess.[84] In the thirteenth century, following in the footsteps of many other religious houses of the time, the canonesses pursued an aggressive strategy of purchasing the advocacies for many of their properties.[85] Nevertheless, the advocacy for the community itself survived into subsequent centuries and was held by a series of prominent princely lineages in the region.[86] The advocacy for the town of Quedlinburg

---

[80] Ibid. On this point, see also Teuscher, "Threats."
[81] Simon, *Untertanenverhalten*, 206.   [82] Ibid., 207.   [83] See Chapter 3.
[84] See Chapter 6.   [85] See Chapter 8.
[86] Vollmuth-Lindenthal, "Äbtissin," 105. The most detailed history of the advocacy remains Arnstedt, "Schirmvogtei."

remained in existence as well, with a separate history from that of the convent's advocacy.[87]

A new chapter in the story of both the ecclesiastical and urban advocacies at Quedlinburg began in the mid-fifteenth century. In 1422, following the death of the last duke of Saxony-Wittenberg of the Ascanian lineage (whose line had held the advocacy for the Quedlinburg community of canonesses since 1320), the church advocacy fell vacant for a time.[88] The advocacy for the town of Quedlinburg, meanwhile, was held by the bishops of Halberstadt but had been pledged to the town of Quedlinburg, giving the urban community a great deal of autonomy. Indeed, by the mid-fifteenth century, the canonesses had lost virtually all influence over the town and were no longer collecting their traditional revenues there. This is likely one reason why, in 1458, the community chose an abbess from a powerful family: Hedwig, daughter of the elector and duke Frederick II of Saxony of the Wettin lineage – and niece of Emperor Frederick III.[89] She was twelve at the time. Her father was therefore to serve as her guardian and as overseer of Quedlinburg's secular affairs until she turned twenty and became abbess in 1465. In the years until the duke's death in 1464, he started the process of pulling Quedlinburg into the Wettin family's orbit.[90]

In the 1470s, Abbess Hedwig, backed by her two brothers Dukes Ernst and Albert of Saxony, began to press her convent's claims to the advocacy over the town of Quedlinburg. Both the bishop of Halberstadt and the urban community contested this, and the dispute eventually involved various prominent princes in the region as well as the emperor. In 1477, following a brief but bloody conflict between the town and Wettin troops, Dukes Ernst and Albert of Saxony forced the town to sue for peace. The community of canonesses, which had first been granted the advocacy for the town in the tenth century, reacquired it as part of the peace negotiations.[91] Two years later in 1479, Abbess Hedwig enfeoffed her two brothers with the advocacy for the religious community and its estates – and also included advocatial rights over the urban community.[92]

---

[87] Vollmuth-Lindenthal, "Äbtissin," 106–07. The bishopric of Halberstadt acquired this advocacy between 1332 and 1338, but in 1396, the financially strapped bishop pledged it to the town.

[88] Ibid., 111.   [89] Ibid., 108–09. For this duke of Saxony, see also Chapter 13.

[90] Arnstedt, "Schirmvogtei"; Lorenz, ed., *Quellen*, xvi–xxx.

[91] Lorenz, ed., *Quellen*, 349–53, no. 67, esp. n. 2. See also Arnstedt, "Schirmvogtei," 195–97. Representatives of the bishopric of Halberstadt would continue to dispute this agreement in subsequent decades. In 1511, the pope sided with the bishopric and demanded the abbess return the advocatial rights she had seized from Halberstadt, but his pronouncement had no effect: ibid., 200–02.

[92] *Urkundenbuch der Stadt Quedlinburg*, 2:9–12, no. 572. See also Vollmuth-Lindenthal, "Äbtissin," 113–14. Following the division of the Wettin lands between the brothers in

For the next 300 years, Abbess Hedwig's 1479 privilege for her brothers served as the model for the privileges confirming first a series of Wettin rulers of Saxony and then, from 1698, a series of Hohenzollern rulers of Brandenburg and Prussia as "our community's hereditary advocates" (*unserm stiffs erbvoigte*).[93] Not even the introduction of the Protestant Reformation at the community in the 1540s impacted the nature of the relationship between the abbesses and their advocates in any meaningful way.[94] Language from the 1479 document was still being repeated in 1798, when Abbess Sophia Albertina confirmed King Frederick William III of Prussia's possession of the "*Voigtey zu Quedlinburg.*"[95]

The repetition of the same formulaic language in privileges from the fifteenth to the late eighteenth century might give the impression that the advocacy over Quedlinburg became an increasingly antiquated right, one that carried little of the value and significance it had possessed in earlier periods. This is, however, anything but the case. Some of the most powerful princes in the Holy Roman Empire continued to take a great deal of interest in local advocatial rights at Quedlinburg. Elector Johann Georg II of Saxony (1656–80) issued a lengthy document as the advocate in 1661, in which he clearly defined the rights of his agent in Quedlinburg, the *Stiftshauptmann*, vis-à-vis the urban community; as was so often the case in past centuries with agreements of this sort, one of the key issues was the question of which crimes fell under the advocate's judicial authority.[96] Seven years later in 1668, the elector wrote to the town council, warning it to respect his rights and to abide by earlier agreements, suggesting that there continued to be disputes about the nature of Wettin authority in the town.[97] The same year, Abbess Anna Sophia I of Quedlinburg (1645–80) wrote to Johann Georg II about the collection of ordinary and extraordinary "taxes," insisting that he be satisfied with his customary sources of income and not demand anything new – evidence that disagreements over the revenue attached to the advocacy persisted as well.[98]

1485, the advocacy over Quedlinburg went to the Albertine line. In subsequent decades, when the abbess was no longer the advocate's sister, tensions surfaced over the limits of advocatial authority; see, for example, Lorenz, ed., *Quellen*, 35–38, no. 10; 153–55, no. 23; and 259–62, no. 38. For an excellent overview of all these sources, see Lorenz, ed., *Quellen*, xvi–xxx.

[93] See, for example, Berlin, Geheimes Staatsarchiv Preußischer Kulturbesitz, VII. HA, Geistliche Fürsten, Abtei Quedlinburg, Nos. 23, 27 and 45.

[94] For the Reformation at Quedlinburg, see Wiesner-Hanks, "Ideology."

[95] Berlin, Geheimes Staatsarchiv Preußischer Kulturbesitz, VII. HA, Geistliche Fürsten, Abtei Quedlinburg, No. 59.

[96] Lorenz, ed., *Quellen*, 393–98, no. 71 (esp. p. 395).   [97] Ibid., 419–21, no. 79.

[98] Ibid., 421–22, no. 80. The abbess and the elector also clashed in 1677, when she issued a "*Policey-Ordnung*" to regulate proper behavior in the town, only to have the elector insist

Conflict over advocatial rights at Quedlinburg intensified in the years following the Hohenzollerns' acquisition of the advocacy. The change in control came in 1697–98, a product of the Wettin Elector Frederick Augustus I's enormous debts after his election as Polish king.[99] He agreed to sell his rights over Quedlinburg to the Hohenzollern Elector Frederick III of Brandenburg.[100] As a result, on January 30, 1698, a contingent of Frederick III's troops arrived at the gates of the town. The commander ordered the town to billet the troops in burghers' homes and also demanded the keys to the town.[101] Abbess Anna Dorothea (1684–1704) objected to the town giving the keys to the Hohenzollern commander but was unable to stop the transfer. Access, in short, was the first priority of the new advocate, and it quickly became clear that Frederick III intended to demand much more from the town and the convent than the Wettins had.[102] Already in October of 1698, he issued a detailed list of the different "taxes" that the Hohenzollern administration would collect.[103]

Abbess Anna Dorothea soon clashed with her new advocate. In 1701, she ordered the publication of a 300-page work, addressed to the Holy Roman Emperor, defending her community's rights against the Hohenzollern elector.[104] Carefully researched, it contains copies of dozens of documents relating to the history of the convent and its advocacy, including King Otto I's privilege of 936.[105] One of the more striking arguments in the work is a response to Frederick III's claim that his Wettin predecessors had held not only the title of hereditary advocate (*Erbvogt*) but also that of territorial prince (*Landesfürst*) of Quedlinburg, giving them complete authority over the canonesses and their properties. As the text notes, however, "it must be remembered that it is impossible

that it had to be issued by both of them jointly; see Göse, "Beschränkte Souveränität," 133. Göse notes (pp. 137–39) that some of the disputes between *Vogt* and abbess clearly revolved around issues of status and rank rather than rights. See also pp. 140–41, where he discusses various complaints in the late seventeenth century about the Wettins' failure to provide protection in times of war.

[99] Lorenz, ed., *Quellen*, 470–84, nos. 96–98.

[100] Berlin, Geheimes Staatsarchiv Preußischer Kulturbesitz, VII. HA, Geistliche Fürsten, Abtei Quedlinburg, No. 20. As part of this agreement, Frederick III also acquired the advocacy for the town of Nordhausen, which his son Frederick William I then sold to the town in 1715: Lauerwald, "Nordhausen."

[101] Lorenz, ed., *Quellen*, 470–73, no. 96. The billeting of troops was based on the claim that the advocates had possessed complete authority over military matters in the town since 1477: ibid., xxiii.

[102] Göse, "Beschränkte Souveränität," 145.   [103] Lorenz, ed., *Quellen*, 473–81, no. 97.

[104] *Wohlgegründete Anmerckungen*. The work is a response to a *Streitschrift* published by the elector in 1700: Arnstedt, "Schirmvogtei," 206–07. For context, see also Göse, "Beschränkte Souveränität," 143–45.

[105] *Wohlgegründete Anmerckungen*, 173–74.

to be both a true territorial prince and a true hereditary advocate in the same jurisdiction and concerning the same object – just as someone cannot be the true lord of a property and at the same time a true subject on the same property."[106] Here, the abbess was pushing back against centuries of advocates trying to blur the line between their advocatial responsibilities as representatives on the one hand and the rights of the actual landholder on the other.[107] Only the abbess was the rightful territorial ruler in Quedlinburg; the hereditary advocate, in contrast, was there to serve the community as "a protector, defender and guardian" (*Schützer, Schirmer und Vertheidiger*).[108]

Disputes between the abbesses of Quedlinburg and the Prussian rulers over the advocacy continued for the next four decades. Finally, in 1742, Abbess Maria Elizabeth (1718–55) and King Frederick the Great settled many of their differences.[109] The king refused to eliminate entirely the "taxes" first implemented in 1698, but he did agree to give the abbess some of the revenue he collected. In addition, he promised to regulate the garrison of Prussian troops at Quedlinburg more tightly in order to end the accusations that his soldiers were extorting money from the burghers. The king also recognized the right of free election of an abbess, though he insisted that he had the right to approve the selection. Only two years later, Frederick's own sister Anna Amalia would be appointed to the position of *Koadjutorin* of the community of Quedlinburg; with her brother's help, she would become Abbess in 1755. Conflict between the community and the king subsided thereafter.[110]

Given Frederick the Great's role in his sister's election, one might be tempted to conclude that this "Enlightened" monarch had found a very "medieval" solution to disputes over Hohenzollern rights at Quedlinburg. After all, the Ottonian rulers, acting as advocates of the community, had appointed their own relatives as abbesses too – 800 years earlier.[111] This is, however, the wrong perspective to take. There was nothing distinctly "medieval" about Frederick's actions. He was using his position of authority to his own advantage to ensure that he could profit as much as possible from his dynasty's recently acquired advocatial rights over the community of canonesses and the town. In other words, he was playing in the gray area between "lordship" and "government" in ways that should look familiar not only to scholars who study medieval European history but those who study other places and times too. Indeed, if we take

[106] Ibid., 3.   [107] For more on this point, see Lorenz, ed., *Quellen*, xvii–xviii.
[108] *Wohlgegründete Anmerckungen*, 12.   [109] Lorenz, ed., *Quellen*, 580–82, no. 120.
[110] Göse, "Beschränkte Souveränität," 146; Küppers-Braun, "Kanonissin," 85–86; Heinrich, *Friedrich II.*, 113.
[111] Bernhardt, *Itinerant*, 143.

seriously Robert Penn Warren's Governor Willy Stark, the American Founding Fathers would be doing something similar just a few years later: *I bet things were just like they are now. A lot of folks wrassling round.*

Conclusion

When did advocacy in all its many forms finally come to an end? There is no easy answer to this question. From the beginning, I have used the millennium from roughly 750 to 1800 as my chronological frame, but that does not mean that advocacy had disappeared completely by the opening years of the nineteenth century. To be sure, the changes unleashed by the French Revolution and the Napoleonic Wars led to a dramatic decline in the number of advocacies. The secularization of Quedlinburg began in 1802, when the king of Prussia acquired all of the community's rights and properties as part of a treaty with France.[112] In Bavaria, the secularization of the monasteries in 1803 was likewise the end of the remaining advocacies, including that of Benediktbeuern.[113] As most of the remaining monasteries in the German-speaking lands saw their houses shuttered and their territorial rights seized by various rulers, for the first time in a millennium they no longer needed advocates to help them defend their properties and communities.

Nevertheless, advocacy survived in ways that suggest we must be cautious not to assume the start of the nineteenth century saw a sharp break with Europe's past. Into the early 1820s, agents of the Lordship of Steyr in Austria were still recording the annual collection of advocatial oats (*Vogthaber*) from some of the lordship's dependents.[114] During the same decade, figures opposed to the Prussian regime feared being detained indefinitely in the *Hausvogtei* prison in Berlin because of the harsh conditions; in 1834, the novelist Fritz Reuter (1810–74) would spend a brief time there for his ties to a university student political organization.[115] In Switzerland, the imperial advocate (*Reichsvogt*) continued to supervise executions until the year 1872, a legacy of the long-standing recognition by the Swiss that the emperor was the source of all legitimate authority.[116] Even into the twentieth century, one can still find occasional acknowledgments of advocacy's lingering impact. In 1915, the editor of some of Quedlinburg's documents dryly observed that the town

---

[112] Breywisch, "Quedlinburgs Säkularisation."
[113] Hemmerle, *Benediktbeuern*, 204. For the end of advocacy around Liège, see Carré, "Avoueries," 403–07.
[114] Linz, Oberösterreichisches Landesarchiv, Herrschaft Steyr, Schachtel No. 311, 39a.
[115] Schmidt, "Fritz Reuters Brief," 85; Williamson, "Thought," 291–92.
[116] Maissen, "Inventing," 129–30.

of Quedlinburg was still owed 12,000 florins by the Hohenzollerns, who had agreed to take on the debt when they purchased the advocacy in 1698.[117]

These are only scattered references, however. In the years after 1800, advocates clearly did not have the impact on local life that they had had in previous centuries. The archive, the library and the university are now where most knowledge of advocacy resides. Most – but not all. To appreciate fully the enduring impact of advocacy, it is necessary to turn to one last corpus of sources, one where the legacy of the long history of advocatial violence can still be found today. From the tenth to the twenty-first century, the literary and cultural figure of the "bad advocate" who suffers a terrible death has persisted as a reminder of what ought to happen to those who benefit from corrupt practices of protection and justice.

---

[117] Lorenz, *Quellen*, ed., xviii, n. 1. For Peter of Hagenbach's enduring infamy, see Heimpel, "Mittelalter und Nürnberger Prozeß."

15 A Cultural History of the Rapacious Advocate, or: William Tell's Revenge

Popular culture has not been kind to the legend of the Swiss national hero William Tell. Many people today know it only as the story of a man who shoots an apple from his son's head. Others, upon hearing Rossini's famous *William Tell Overture*, think not of a legend set in the Swiss countryside but of the Lone Ranger riding across the American West. That the story has been told and retold countless times since the late fifteenth century, above all because of the enduring value of its political lessons, has largely been forgotten. So too the fact that the villain, Gessler, whose misdeeds and subsequent assassination by Tell set in motion the uprising that leads to Swiss independence, was an advocate.

In the best-known version of the legend, Friedrich Schiller's 1804 play *Wilhelm Tell*, it is William Tell himself, while he is lying in wait with his crossbow to kill Gessler, who comments upon the proper role of the advocate:

> You are my lord and my emperor's advocate.
> But the emperor would not permit
> What you do. He sent you into these lands
> In order to judge the law – sternly, for he is angry –
> But not in order, with murderous lust,
> To commit every iniquity yourself and to go unpunished.
> There lives a God to punish and avenge.[1]

Because Gessler has abused the judicial authority granted to him as the ruler's representative, he must be made to suffer. Elsewhere in the play, Schiller uses even stronger words to call attention to Gessler's abuses. He and the other advocates in the region place the people under "the tyrants' yoke" (*das Tyrannenjoch*); they wield "the tyrants' sword" (*das Tyrannenschwert*); and they employ "tyrannical violence" (*der tyrannischen Gewalt*).[2] Such dramatic

---

[1] Schiller, *Wilhelm Tell*, lines 2590–96. My translation here draws partly on the Project Gutenberg eBook translation of the play (eBook, no. 6788).
[2] Schiller, *Wilhelm Tell*, lines 634, 679 and 788.

rhetoric, commonplace throughout the play, helps to justify the Swiss people's rebellion against their Habsburg lords.

Schiller was inspired by earlier versions of the legend, which use comparable language. However, by the time the story of William Tell was first
written down in the later fifteenth century, much of this rhetoric was
already a half-millennium old. Indeed, it is tempting to argue that Schiller
owed his nationalistic rallying cry to eleventh- and twelfth-century
monks, who had already drawn the connection between wicked advocates
and tyranny – albeit in a decidedly different cultural context than
Germany in the Napoleonic era. The parallels run even deeper. William
Tell's words in Schiller's play, "There lives a God to punish and avenge,"
point to the equally old tradition of stories about advocates who supposedly suffered divine vengeance for their wicked deeds.

This tradition has much to teach us. As I will argue here, the history of
advocates is much more than the story of a largely forgotten local agent in
the German-speaking lands. Standard progress narratives of European
history, which posit a shift from the "medieval" to the "modern" and from
feudal particularism to the sovereign state's universalism, need "government" to replace "lordship" at some point. As the previous chapters have
shown, however, the history of advocates does not reveal a clear transition
from one to the other at any point between 750 and 1800. That Friedrich
Schiller would choose the legend of William Tell to say something about
his political present in 1804 suggests that the transition was not evident to
him either. Thus, the enduring fantasy of the wicked advocate suffering
divine punishment is neither distinctly "medieval" nor really about "lordship." It speaks instead, at a much deeper level, to the ceaseless tensions
between those who wield power over others and those who experience
that power.

Monastic Fantasies of Divine Vengeance

Shortly after the year 946, monks at the monastery of St. Bavo in Ghent
compiled a collection of miracles.[3] According to one of the stories in this
compendium,

A dependent of St. Bavo, called to account by his advocate, was compelled to pay
thirty shillings. On the appointed day, he prayed with humble devotion to his saint
that he might find that same man milder towards him. And so he went, so that he
might pay his debt. But he discovered that the advocate was dead. Rejoicing at this
fact, he offered half of what he owed to the merciful St. Bavo.[4]

---

[3] For the dating of the collection, see Vanderputten, *Monastic Reform as Process*, 73–74.
[4] *Ex Miraculorum*, 596, III.9.

The modern scholar is not given very much to work with here. It is not even clear that anything particularly miraculous lies at the heart of this story. Nevertheless, since it appears in a miracle collection, its author presumably wanted his readers to picture St. Bavo interceding on behalf of one of the monastery's dependents, punishing this advocate with death for demanding an unjust exaction. Admittedly, the text's brevity and opacity make it difficult to draw even this conclusion with any real confidence. This story is noteworthy, nonetheless, because it is the earliest one I know in which an advocate appears to suffer divine punishment for his bad behavior.

The date of this text is therefore worth considering more closely. As discussed previously, there is abundant evidence for advocates gaining prominence at many monastic communities around the year 950 – at the time when this miracle was recorded.[5] Advocates had been acting as religious communities' agents on ecclesiastical estates since the eighth century, and there are occasional critiques of their behavior in Carolingian sources dating back to the years around 800. However, accusations of advocatial abuses do not become commonplace until after the year 1000.[6] The story of St. Bavo's miraculous punishment of an unjust advocate is therefore an early piece of evidence that advocates' rising influence was beginning to generate tensions at the local level.

Stories about advocates suffering divine punishment become more numerous and more detailed over the course of the eleventh century. One of the most vivid was written by the monk Aimo at the monastery of Fleury around the year 1000. Like the St. Bavo story, it too was included in a collection of miracles concerning the community's patron saint: in this case, St. Benedict. The story is set near Troyes, at a village held by Fleury.[7] As Aimo explains, although the advocate, a man named Gauzfredus, "defended it from outsiders, he ravaged it more violently than any stranger." The monks warned him to end his wicked ways, but he refused. St. Benedict therefore prevailed upon God to intervene. And so, "one day, when [the advocate] was residing in his own house within the walls of Troyes, judging the peasants' legal cases, a frenzied black dog entered. Injuring none of the people who were standing around, it attacked him, mutilating his nose and face with its bites. Then, it left." The advocate's friends took him, senseless, to a local church, where he gradually recovered, though not fully. Later, when "he added worse things to the evils he had inflicted on the poor of St. Benedict, he was seized by a demon" and died soon thereafter. Aimo ends the story by

[5] See Chapter 3.   [6] See Chapter 4.
[7] *Miracula Sancti Benedicti*, 274–75, III.13. For this collection, see also Chapter 4.

noting, "Everyone who had known him professed openly that he had suffered such things on account of his cruelty toward the peasants of the dear confessor Benedict."

Another Fleury monk, Andrew, wrote a second version of this same story a generation later in the early 1040s.[8] While it follows Aimo's in many ways, its language is even more vivid in several places. The court scene is especially dramatic: "And so, one day, when very many of the blessed Benedict's inhabitants had gathered in the customary way, while the cruel man subjected them cruelly to his examination, demanding more than was reasonable of money that did not belong to him, behold!, in the midst of everyone there entered a terrifying dog, covered in black fur." The advocate's demonic possession and death are also recounted with zeal: "Seized in the mind, he became the plaything of demons. He who had exercised unfavorable domination over the peasants of beloved God was never again freed from the domination of the ancient enemy until he died." Andrew does not stop there. He reports that Gauzfredus's brother and successor, Rotbert, also suffered divine punishment for his misdeeds. This Rotbert claimed monastic property unjustly, demanded undue exactions and terrorized one of the religious community's dependents. St. Benedict therefore intervened again, striking him down as well. His body was turned over to another monastery for burial, but the sacred ground of the cemetery refused to accept it. Three times, his body was ejected from the earth. Only after the monks at Fleury had agreed to pardon his sins was it possible to bury him.[9]

Like the story of St. Bavo's miracle, these two versions of St. Benedict's miraculous work at Fleury focus specifically on advocatial abuses directed against the monastery's dependents. Here, however, the advocate's suffering is emphasized to a much greater degree, with his divine/supernatural punishment coming in two different forms: a black dog and demonic possession. Both monastic authors explicitly describe all of his suffering as punishment for his wicked deeds. Moreover, the *Schadenfreude* is difficult to miss, as both monks take a certain perverse pleasure in recounting in detail Gauzfredus's end. If there was nothing the monks and their peasants could do against wicked advocates in life, at least they could revel in their suffering in death – and, in the process, warn others about what would happen if they crossed their patron saint.[10]

Although stories such as this one never became commonplace between 1000 and 1250, there are enough others to suggest that many religious communities found them compelling.[11] An excellent example from the

[8] Ibid., 352–55, VI.3.   [9] Ibid.   [10] Barthélemy, *Chevaliers*, 153.
[11] For other examples, see Henry of Livonia, *Chronicle*, 197–98, and more generally, Stieldorf, "Klöster."

Benedictine monastery of Tegernsee dates to the years around 1170. Like the stories just discussed, it is preserved in a collection of miracle stories about the community's patron saint: in this case, Quirinus.[12] The story opens with complaints about Tegernsee's advocate during the early 1130s, Count Otto II of Wolfratshausen, who "continuously injured this place in many ways and injured its household with harsh exactions."[13] Otto also sent cruel agents to carry out his will on the monastery's estates, and these men "levied the count's rights from the people by going door to door through the villages and homes." The death of one of these agents, who supposedly had devised new ways of extracting goods from the people on Tegernsee's estates, "was the occasion for a wondrous and terrible spectacle on account of the demons playing at his funeral." As the text explains, "In the hour he died, it was heard to resound, as if from every corner of this monastery and every joint and crack of the walls and tables, from every window and opening, 've, ve, ve.'" Initially, the monks and the monastery's dependents were reluctant to bury him in the monastic church because he had violently extracted so much from so many people. In the end, he was finally allowed to be buried. However,

For a long time after this, he was seen nights, as he had been accustomed while living, approaching some people's homes and demanding cows and oxen through threats and fear. Sometimes [he was seen] chasing the cattle he found in the pastures, or the plow-oxen, or the men who encountered him. Also, some people always observed him before the hour of nocturn being carried around by a whirling, malignant spirit, and, when a signal sounded, he returned to his grave, sometimes driving a great herd of cattle. There, before he threw himself down in his tomb, he cried out, bellowing horribly, and thus was shut up again.[14]

The monastic author of this text does not draw as direct a line between this man's suffering and divine vengeance as Aimo and Andrew of Fleury did in their stories of their community's wicked advocates. Nevertheless, given that this story can be found in a section of the text dedicated to "celebrat[ing] the perpetual victory of our most unconquerable patron over the advocates' tyranny," the connection is clear.[15] At Tegernsee, it was not any and all people who committed violence against the monastic community and its dependents who required saintly intervention; the advocates and their agents were the main targets of St. Quirinus's wrath.[16] Indeed, while there are obvious similarities between this story and the ones from

---

[12] For this collection, and Tegernsee's difficulties with its advocates more generally, see Chapters 7, 8 and 10.

[13] *Passio*, 280.

[14] Ibid. See also Metellus of Tegernsee, *Quirinalien*. For other, contemporary stories about rampaging revenants, see Bruce, ed., *Undead*, 129–36.

[15] *Passio*, 275.   [16] For more on this point, see Lyon, "Rulers."

Fleury, we should not assume that this is simply a stock story that can be separated from its local context. Conflicts between monasteries and their advocates were so commonplace in the eleventh and twelfth centuries that we must allow for the possibility of independent traditions with their own organic origins based on distinctive fantasies about the horrible deaths of local representatives. This author and his audience of fellow Tegernsee monks clearly had a specific advocatial agent in mind here, whom they imagined suffering even after death because they were so outraged by his actions in life.

In contrast, a few decades later Caesarius of Heisterbach recounted a miraculous story about a bad advocate taken by the devil, which he labels an *exemplum*: a short moral story stripped of its specificity to teach a more general lesson.[17] It is entitled "About an advocate, whom the devil took while he was going to make an exaction."[18] Caesarius reports that he heard this story from a Cistercian abbot in the diocese of Bremen a few years earlier but otherwise provides no context. As he explains, "a certain knight was the advocate of various villages. He was a merciless and greedy man, making frequent and severe exactions against those subject to him." One day, when he was on his way to a village to demand exactions, the devil, disguised as a man, joined him on the road. The advocate easily recognized him, but neither praying nor making the sign of the cross would make the devil leave. As they continued down the road, they saw a peasant with his pig. The peasant was having a great deal of trouble controlling the pig and angrily shouted at it, "May the devil have you!" The advocate, trying to free himself, said to the devil, "'Listen, friend, that pig has been given to you. Go and take him.' The devil replied, 'By no means did he give it to me willingly, so I cannot take it.'"

The advocate and the devil continued on and came to a village. A baby was crying, and its mother said to it in frustration, "May the devil have you! Why do you bother me with your weeping and wailing?" The advocate again tried to distract the devil by suggesting the mother had offered the baby to him, but the devil dismissed the idea, explaining that that was just how people talked when angry. Finally, they approached the village where the advocate had been going to make his exactions. The people of the village saw them and knew exactly why the advocate was coming. They shouted in one voice, "May the devil have you. Come safely to the devil!" The devil, laughing, said to him, "Behold, they have given you to me most willingly, and for that reason you are mine." The devil seized

---

[17] For the popular, folkloric elements of medieval *exempla*, see McGuire, "Cistercians."
[18] Caesarius of Heisterbach, "Die beiden ersten Bücher," 106–07, II.25: "De advocato, quem dyabolus tulit, dum iret facere exactionem." For Caesarius, see also Chapter 9.

him, and no one knew what happened to him after that. Caesarius closes by explaining the moral to the story: "Listen to this example, exactors of the poor (*pauperum exactores*), of whom there are countless numbers today. What is more horrible than an impenitent man, caught in the criminal act, being led from life to the infernal torment of eternal punishment?"

Two aspects of this story are important to emphasize, because they will have a direct bearing on arguments made later in this chapter. First, the advocate's attempts to convince the devil to take the pig from the peasant and the baby from its mother highlight – much more than the general accusation of this advocate demanding exactions – how advocatial abuses frequently struck at the heart of peasant life, at their most valuable possessions and cherished family relationships. At Tegernsee, it was cows rather than pigs that were central to the story of the divinely punished advocatial agent, but the idea is the same.[19] As we will see below, livestock and children are critical to the legend of William Tell too. Second, unlike the earlier miracle stories discussed above, Caesarius's *exemplum* clearly gives agency to the villagers rather than a saint; they are the ones who free themselves from their wicked advocate by sending him to the devil. Caesarius was a Cistercian monk, so I am not suggesting that we hear in this story an authentic peasant voice. Nevertheless, the idea that the suffering people, rather than the suffering saint, had it in their own power to end their advocate's tyranny is another theme at the heart of the legend of William Tell.

These few examples demonstrate that vivid stories of divinely punished advocates (or their agents) appeared across a wide swath of Europe between approximately 950 and 1250. To be clear, none of the language of suffering and demonic torture in these texts is unique to advocates.[20] Various scholars have done excellent work examining the miraculous violence perpetrated against all sorts of people by saints in defense of monastic properties and rights.[21] Indeed, if this book were only a study of the tenth to thirteenth centuries, my analysis would add little to scholarly arguments about the active roles played by saints in monastic narratives of divinely punished enemies. However, as I have insisted throughout the previous chapters, it is essential that we not let artificial divisions of history – such as the one around 1250 supposedly separating a "central Middle Ages" from a "late Middle Ages" – shape our perceptions of local practices of protection and justice. When we follow the term *advocatus* into sources written after 1250, we discover that these collective fantasies

---

[19] For the significance of livestock for accusations about advocatial abuses, see Chapter 7.
[20] Lyon, "Rulers."   [21] See especially Brown, *Violence*, 111–16; Barthélemy, *Chevaliers*.

about vengeance and punishment continue. While at first glance the earliest miracle stories about bad advocates might seem to be explicable as byproducts of the lack of strong centralized authority and government in the centuries immediately following the collapse of the Carolingian empire, their enduring popularity after 1250 points to much deeper tensions within the history of power and authority in Europe.

Old Monks Telling Old – and New – Stories

The field of late medieval religious history suffers from a scholarly inclination to fetishize the new. Franciscans, Dominicans, Beguines and other post-1200 religious movements suck up so much of the oxygen in studies of the period that it is easy to forget that hundreds upon hundreds of monastic houses founded in earlier centuries continued to exist after 1250.[22] In the face of all the new forms of religious life that emerged from the thirteenth century onward, these traditional communities inevitably look rather dull. One side effect of this lack of interest among historians in older religious houses is a shortage of detailed research on church advocacy after 1250 since (most) Franciscan and Dominican houses did not have advocates.[23] This can easily lead to the false impression that religious critiques of advocates declined in the later period. However, there are numerous sources that point to the enduring appeal of fantasies of divine vengeance directed against bad advocates.

The miracle collection compiled at the Benedictine monastery of Rastede near Oldenburg around the year 1300 is an especially rich source.[24] It opens by explaining, "Nowhere in this country did the blessed mother of God, the Virgin Mary, shine with the glory of such great miracles as in this place."[25] It continues, "For she smites all the despoilers of the goods of this church, both advocates and oppressors, punishing them greatly and making them perish by a miserable death, so that they recognize in the present life – on account of the afflictions and adversities they are made to suffer – that they have transgressed against this church."[26] The author then explains that he will offer examples of counts, vassals and advocates who were punished in this way, but in truth, advocates dominate in the subsequent miracle stories. One reports, "A

---

[22] A good example of this problem is the community of canonesses at Quedlinburg. Historians produce scholarship on Quedlinburg in the tenth and early eleventh century at a truly prodigious rate, yet remarkably little work has been done on the community in the fourteenth and fifteenth centuries.
[23] See Chapter 12.   [24] For this collection, see also Chapter 13.
[25] *Miracula in Monasterio Rastedensi*, 513, chap. 1. For the Marian elements of these texts, see Cassidy-Welch, "Stedinger Crusade," 166–67.
[26] For Mary as terrifying warrior, see Fulton Brown, *Mary*, 206–07.

certain malicious advocate of this church, after he had captured a certain man and went to strip off the garment in which he was clothed, was killed by that captive with his own knife, which he had in its sheath."[27] According to a second, "There were two advocates of this monastery, father and son, who did very many immoderate things. . . . The blessed virgin mercifully freed us from malefactors of this sort, because they were miserably killed in a certain swamp. And their bodies remained unburied, devoured by the beasts of the earth and the birds of the sky."[28] The text ends with the monastic author pithily reaffirming the lesson of all these stories: "[D]ivine vengeance smites the advocates and disturbers of this monastery."[29]

As these stories show, monastic fantasies about divinely punished advocates were not confined to the bad old days of tyrannical local lordship during the so-called Feudal Revolution/Mutation/Transformation.[30] By the early fourteenth century, princely administrations were increasingly taking shape across the German-speaking lands, and fewer and fewer monastic advocates were local nobles operating independently of higher authorities. Nevertheless, the types of advocatial abuses that monastic communities had been complaining about since the turn of the first millennium continued.[31] If religious communities still could not stop these abuses, at least they could keep imagining horrible punishments for their wicked advocates in the next life.

One particularly vivid fantasy was handed down as an *exemplum* in a collection of "fables for the people" (*Fabule ad populum*) preserved in a fifteenth-century manuscript originally compiled at the Benedictine monastery of Benediktbeuern in Bavaria.[32] This *exemplum*, entitled "Concerning a certain advocate (*De advocato quodam*)," opens simply, "A certain advocate harassed his poor people unduly and unjustly with arbitrary demands, taxes and exactions." It then goes on to explain how, after this advocate had died, a multitude of crows gathered on the roof of his house and cawed loudly. They only dispersed after one of the advocate's followers chased them off with holy water. It continues, "Then, when his family and friends gathered on the night before his funeral (as was custom) to hold a vigil by his body, around midnight a multitude of black cows, dogs and other monstrous animals gathered around the bier

---

[27] *Miracula in Monasterio Rastedensi*, 514, chap. 5.   [28] Ibid., 514, chap. 6.
[29] Ibid., 514, chap. 7: "ultio divina advocatos et turbatores huius monasterii percutit."
[30] See Chapter 4.   [31] For more on this point, see Chapter 13.
[32] Rostock, Universitätsbibliothek, Mss. theol. 37a, fols. 55r–55v. This *exemplum* does not appear in Tubach's *Index Exemplorum*. To date, I have not found an earlier version of it, but one likely exists. On the difference between a monastic *exemplum* and a fable, and the issue of genre more generally, I find useful Green, *Elf Queens*, 71–75.

and wallowed about, confusing the eyes and disturbing the spirits of everyone watching them." Eventually, they too were chased off with the help of holy water. But that was not the end of the mourners' night:

Behold, a horrible man, terrible in appearance, suddenly entered and said, 'You, who are holding vigil, why do you not entertain yourselves as is customary at a funeral?' Everyone was silent with fear. He spoke again: 'I will make you have fun. But first, remove that cross near the bier at once, lest it impede us.' When that was done, he said to the dead advocate, 'Rise, my friend N., and we will divide evenly all this meat.' As he [i.e., the advocate] rose again, everyone who had been present fled, and standing before the doors, they waited for the pair to exit. Then, in frustration [that everyone had fled], the man ripped apart the corpse of the dead advocate and scattered the pieces, which – oh the pain! – were found that way the next morning.[33]

The text offers no moral to the story, but the point seems clear enough: The desecration of the advocate's body at the hands of his demonic guest leaves little doubt that we are to understand that the advocate suffered this supernatural punishment after death for his wicked behavior during life.[34]

A second fifteenth-century manuscript, this one from Cologne, also calls attention to the fact that stories about the eternal punishment of bad advocates continued to garner interest throughout the period 1250 to 1500. In this case, Caesarius of Heisterbach's above-cited story was added to the end of an extensive collection of his *exempla*. The scribe copied the entirety of the collection while making only a very small number of marginal notations and corrections. The story of the greedy advocate taken by the devil is the only one to have a rubricated title included in the margin: "On the advocate whom the devil carried off while still living."[35] Although it is impossible to know why the scribe highlighted this particular *exemplum* in this way, its placement at the end of the collection and the addition of a title in the margin mark it off from the other *exempla*, which suggests this story was still a popular or meaningful one more than 200 years after Caesarius first included it in his work.

---

[33] Rostock, Universitätsbibliothek, Mss. theol. 37a, fols. 55r–55v. For other examples of monastic ghost stories from this period, see Bruce, ed., *Undead*, 204–15.
[34] Holy water and crosses were both commonplace strategies to protect the bodies of the recently deceased. See Schmitz-Esser, *Der Leichnam*, 464–67. Dismemberment and desecration of criminals' corpses were not uncommon punishments in this period, especially for crimes such as treason, and were frequently carried out in public. See ibid., 538–52.
[35] Vienna, Österreichische Nationalbibliothek, Cod. 4556, fol. 140v–141r: "de aduocato quem diabolus vivum rapuit." I thank Julia Burkhardt for calling this manuscript to my attention.

Myths and legends about members of the elite suffering after death for the crimes they committed in this life against the weak and the poor are certainly not limited only to advocates – or even to European elites more generally. They are a global phenomenon.[36] Wherever they appear, they are not as simple and straightforward as they might seem. Some are smear campaigns by one side in a dispute, an attempt to discredit an opponent by making him look as tyrannical as possible.[37] Others function as cautionary tales meant to remind the elites of the long-term damage that can be done to their reputations by the circulation of such stories after their deaths;[38] this is almost certainly one explanation for those tales about wicked advocates that name names – and mention their family and friends too. The *exempla*, in contrast, because they lack specificity in order to offer broader moral lessons, clearly have another purpose: They warn all who would walk in these bad advocates' footsteps of the mortal dangers they could face for abusing their positions of power and authority. It is with this in mind that we can return to the origin story of the Swiss Confederacy.

The Legend of William Tell

The earliest known version of the William Tell legend appears in the *White Book of Sarnen (Das Weisse Buch von Sarnen)*, which was written around the years 1470/1471 by a local scribe active in central Switzerland.[39] The setting for the legend is the late thirteenth and early fourteenth centuries. Prior to this period, the counts of Habsburg had been the dominant lords in the region that is now Switzerland. However, with the election of Rudolf of Habsburg as German king in 1273 and his subsequent acquisition of the duchies of Austria and Styria for his lineage, the focus of Habsburg attention increasingly shifted eastward toward Vienna and the Danube river valley in modern Austria. As a result, the Habsburgs spent less and less time directly ruling their lands in the southwest of the German kingdom and began appointing territorial advocates to govern these regions for them.[40] The *White Book* opens in the thirteenth century with the counts of Habsburg as the lords of the three Swiss communities of Uri, Schwyz and Unterwalden. It then

---

[36] See, for example, Tubach, *Index Exemplorum*, 40, nos. 451–55. More broadly, Scott, *Weapons*, 18.

[37] Teuscher, "Böse Vögte?," 91, 104–05.   [38] Scott, *Weapons*, 23–24, 178.

[39] *Weiße Buch*. Despite countless attempts, no one has ever been able to prove the historicity of William Tell. The *White Book of Sarnen* is the first surviving source to name him, yet it was written almost 200 years after he supposedly existed. See Teuscher, "Böse Vögte?"; Guenée, *States*, 212–16.

[40] For more on these advocates, see Chapters 12–14.

recounts how Rudolf, after he became king, was a good ruler, who
protected and defended everyone's traditional rights and liberties and
always kept his promises, including giving Uri, Schwyz and
Unterwalden only pious men as territorial advocates.[41] This is the narrative trope of the "good old days" of the righteous ruler and of just
administration, and its use is intended to sharpen the contrast with the
subsequent period.

According to the *White Book*, after King Rudolf I died in 1291, the
territorial advocates started to behave poorly and to be cruel to the people
of the three lands of Uri, Schwyz and Unterwalden. At some point in the
following years, a minor nobleman from southern Germany named
Gessler became the territorial advocate of Uri and Schwyz, and another
minor lord from Landenberg, also in southern Germany, became territorial advocate for Unterwalden. The *White Book* reports that both Gessler
and this other territorial advocate promised to be true to the empire in
serving as administrators for their territories. But they failed to keep their
promise. They immediately began oppressing the people of the three
lands – all day and all night, according to the text – and they tried to
remove the three lands from the empire's control in order to bring them
under their own control.[42]

Though the original version of the William Tell legend in the *White
Book of Sarnen* is quite brief, it already contains the main features of the
story of these bad territorial advocates.[43] The most famous part of the
legend begins with Gessler placing his hat on a pole in a village and
stationing one of his knights by the hat to make sure that anyone who
passes by bows to the hat as if it were Gessler himself.[44] William Tell,
a well-respected local townsman, passes by but fails to bow to the hat. The
knight detains him and summons Gessler. The territorial advocate, who
has heard of Tell's prowess with a crossbow, demands that he shoot an
apple off his son's head, or else he will be executed.[45] Tell's shot strikes
the apple, but Gessler notices that Tell is holding a second crossbow bolt

---

[41] *Weiße Buch*, 3–5. Teuscher, "Böse Vögte?," argues there is no evidence to suggest the
Habsburg's advocates were actually wicked in this period, but see Chapter 13 above for
my own arguments about territorial advocates more generally.
[42] *Weiße Buch*, 5–7.
[43] Ibid., 7–19. See also Knebel, *Tagebuch*, 2:5. Knebel, writing in the same period as the
White Book was written, also discusses the bad Habsburg advocates of the early fourteenth century, evidence that the author of the *White Book* did not invent this framing
element of the Tell legend.
[44] For a similar story, though with a different meaning, see Teuscher, "Threats," 101. For
earlier accounts of the Swiss Confederacy's origins, which also emphasize the involvement of bad advocates, see Teuscher, "Böse Vögte?," 101.
[45] This is not the earliest story with this plot element; see Saxo Grammaticus, *Gesta
Danorum*, 1:696–97, X.7.1.

in his hand. When asked to explain himself, Tell states bluntly that he was planning to shoot Gessler if his first shot had accidentally struck his son. For this insolence, Tell is arrested. However, as Gessler's men transport Tell by boat across a lake in order to bring him to the territorial advocate's prison, a storm blows up. Tell is able to jump from the boat and escape to shore. He then tracks down Gessler and kills him with a shot from his crossbow.

While the story of Tell shooting the apple from his son's head is undoubtedly the best-known part of the myth of the origins of the Swiss Confederacy, it is important to note that, already in the *White Book*, there are three additional stories about the advocates and their agents behaving badly, all of them intended to set the stage for the Swiss coming together to form an alliance to drive out their oppressors.[46]

The first concerns the other territorial advocate, the one for Unterwalden, who one day sees one of the local farmers with a pretty plow and team of oxen. The territorial advocate orders one of his knights to seize the animals. When the farmer's son tries to resist and even strikes the knight, the knight flees and reports the incident to the advocate. The territorial advocate is unable to arrest the son, who has disappeared, but he imprisons and blinds his elderly father and takes all his possessions.[47]

The second story concerns a different kind of criminal behavior. In its opening discussion of the cruelty of the territorial advocates, the *White Book* notes that those who held the position of territorial advocate frequently seized the pretty wives and daughters of the locals and took them away to their castles to do with them as they wished.[48] Then, after recounting the story of the father and son and their oxen, the *White Book* tells the story of a local lord (*herr*) who lusts after the pretty wife of a simple, honest farmer. While the husband is out chopping wood, the lord enters their house and demands that the wife draw him a bath and bathe with him. But the husband returns, his wife tells him what is happening and the husband kills the lord.[49]

The third story that travels with the William Tell legend from the very beginning concerns the community of Schwyz and a man named Stoupacher, who has just built a pretty stone house. Gessler is the territorial advocate for Schwyz, and one day he sees the house and asks Stoupacher whose it is. Stoupacher, fearing what would happen if he says the house belongs to him, states that the house belongs to Gessler as the ruler's representative and that he holds it in fief. This satisfies Gessler, who rides away, but both Stoupacher and his wife are concerned

---

[46] On this point, see also Teuscher, "Böse Vögte?," 101–02.   [47] *Weiße Buch,* 6–9.
[48] Ibid., 6–7.   [49] Ibid., 8–11.

that Gessler has plans for their house. Stoupacher therefore joins together with angry farmers from the other two lands and they all swear an oath, which is start of the Swiss Confederacy.[50] After this, Gessler comes to Uri, and the Wilhelm Tell part of the legend unfolds, culminating in Gessler's death.

The many parallels between the William Tell legend and earlier stories of wicked advocates should by now be obvious. Demands for livestock and other property, unjust imprisonment, violence against women: The corrupt behavior of these territorial advocates is largely indistinguishable from the behavior described by our sources throughout the preceding half-millennium. Clearly, any kind of division between the "lordly" monastic advocates of the period 1000 to 1250 and the "official" administrative advocates of the period 1250 to 1500 is misleading. Indeed, I do not think it unreasonable to see in William Tell's murder of Gessler an act of divine vengeance, not one committed by a saint, but one committed by a mythical hero who, like a saint, embodied a societal fantasy about the punishment of those who mistreated the weak and the poor. Confronted with noblemen who felt they could do whatever they wanted to other people's dependents over whom they had some sort of authority, those same dependents imagined a world in which a supernatural defender could intervene to act in a way that they could not (at least not without facing severe consequences).

The legend of William Tell was first written down at a time when many of the towns of the Swiss Confederacy were employing territorial advocates of their own to administer the lands outside their walls.[51] As a result, the critique of the Habsburg advocates at the heart of the legend – and Gessler's murder, especially – provided a pointed lesson about the proper role of the territorial advocate, a lesson clearly directed at a late fifteenth-century audience. The fact that the legend's popularity grew rapidly in the decades after the appearance of the *White Book* is evidence that subsequent generations also recognized the value of this morality tale.

Two sixteenth-century versions of the Swiss origin myth are worth considering in this context. Both include slight variations to the story as it is told in the *White Book of Sarnen*. In the case of Petermann Etterlin's *Chronicle* of 1507, it is noteworthy that Etterlin explicitly identifies the territorial advocate for Unterwalden as the one who insists that the wife draw him a bath and bathe with him. When the husband comes home and kills the advocate, we end up with a version of the legend in which both of the territorial advocates who are the main antagonists of the story are killed. Significantly, Etterlin also includes references to officials

---

[50] Ibid., 10–13.   [51] See Chapters 12 and 14.

(*Amtleute*) in his work, references that are absent in the *White Book*. We read of "advocates or officials" (*vögtte oder amplütte*) on multiple occasions in this text.[52] At one point, Etterlin explicitly states that, had "the officials and advocates of the three lands" (*die amptlütte und vögt der Dryer Lenderen*) behaved better, it never would have come to war between the Swiss Confederacy and the Habsburgs. In other words, not just advocates but all local officials needed to do their jobs properly – or they would face the consequences.

Aegidius Tschudi (1505–72), writing his *Swiss Chronicle* a half century later, adds another revealing story to the legend. According to him, ambassadors from Uri, Schwyz and Unterwalden went to the Habsburg King Albrecht I in the year 1305 in order to complain about the territorial advocates. In a lengthy passage, these ambassadors describe all the cruel and unjust things that Gessler and the other territorial advocate had been doing to the people. They ask the king to remove them from office – in other words, to hold them accountable for their actions – but the king refuses to listen.[53] Given that it was commonplace by this time for people to bring their complaints about their territorial advocates to the urban administrations of the Swiss Confederacy, this story seems to be another reminder to those in power to pay attention to their dependents.[54] It was only because the king failed to act that the inhabitants of Uri, Schwyz and Unterwalden were forced to take matters into their own hands.[55]

Tschudi's work also fits within a growing trend in sixteenth-century retellings of the legend to describe the advocates' behavior as tyrannical, something that the author of the *White Book of Sarnen* had not done. Already in the 1510s, a version written for the stage includes numerous extended critiques of the position of advocate and employs the words tyrant/tyranny a half-dozen times over the course of its brief 800 lines.[56] Tschudi uses comparable language even more often in his *Swiss Chronicle*. He refers to "the territorial advocates' tyranny" (*der landtvögten tyrannij*), their "tyrannical violence" (*tirannischen gwalt*) and "the tyrant's yoke" (*das tirannisch joch*).[57] Tyranny was central to humanist conversations about politics at this time, and this language therefore links these stories about wicked advocates to much broader contemporary debates about good and bad rulers.[58] However, it also links these stories back to earlier monastic complaints about wicked advocates, where references to

---

[52] Etterlin, *Kronica*, 99.   [53] Tschudi, *Chronicon Helveticum*, 3:210.
[54] Teuscher, "Threats." See also Chapter 14.
[55] See, for the growing solidarity of village communities more generally, Sablonier, "Zur wirtschaftlichen Situation," 22.
[56] *Urner Tellenspiel*, 70–99.   [57] Tschudi, *Chronicon Helveticum*, 3:221–25.
[58] For humanist debates about tyranny, see Schadee, "Tyrants."

tyranny also abound, evidence that this was a remarkably durable idea across a half-millennium of European history.

Despite these variations, the main stories at the heart of the Swiss origin myth do not change significantly across these texts written in the century from approximately 1470 to 1570. Combined, they paint a vivid picture of where local Swiss communities drew the line between acceptable and unacceptable official behavior.[59] A father is punished because he and his son resist when the territorial advocate wants to steal their plow and oxen. A husband murders a man who has attempted to rape his wife in their own home. A husband and wife fear that their house is going to be taken away from them. And William Tell is asked to risk the life of his own son (see Figure 15.1). Both the *White Book of Sarnen* and Petermann Etterlin's chronicle leave little doubt that these stories are all closely connected, because they describe the plow and oxen, the wife, the house and William Tell's son as all being "pretty" (*hübsch*). Drawing such an explicit link between the four targets of advocatial violence calls attention not only to their value but to the cruelty of the people who would threaten them. Do not harm our most prized possessions – our pretty children, our pretty wives and our pretty homes and plow teams – or we will kill you. These stories are a warning that those tasked with accessing Swiss territories to exercise justice and provide protection must not cross the line into the personal and the familial.[60]

The timeless qualities of these stories help to explain why the William Tell legend was told and retold so many times. The most famous later retelling of the legend is unquestionably Friedrich Schiller's play *Wilhelm Tell*, first performed in 1804 and still performed occasionally today. It opens dramatically, with the peasant Konrad Baumgarten fleeing the horsemen of the territorial advocate because he has just killed the advocate for entering his house and forcing his wife to draw him a bath. This scene has its roots in the *White Book of Sarnen*, as do many of the other scenes in the play about the abuses perpetrated by Gessler and other advocates – including scenes about the stolen team of oxen and Stoupacher's house. In some ways, however, Schiller diverges quite dramatically from the original legend.

Gessler's death scene, for example, is a drawn-out affair. Act 4, Scene 3 opens with Tell – hiding in wait for Gessler – delivering his lengthy monologue, partially quoted at the beginning of this chapter. Later in the scene, Gessler is speaking to a local woman who has stopped him on the road to plead on behalf of her unjustly imprisoned husband. Gessler refuses to grant her request and is announcing that he will institute a new

---

[59] On this point, see Head, "William Tell."   [60] Ibid., 531.

Figure 15.1 The territorial advocate Gessler forces William Tell to shoot an apple from his son's head. Petermann Etterlin, *Kronica von der loblichen eydtgnoschaft* (Basel, 1507), 13r. Universitätsbibliothek Basel, A lambda IV 14 (e-manuscripta)

law to punish the people even more harshly when Tell's shot to the heart interrupts him mid-sentence.[61] Gessler himself exclaims, "This is Tell's shot" before falling from his horse.[62] Locals gather around to watch as the advocate slowly bleeds to death. The woman who had stopped Gessler in the road lifts up one of her children and says, "Look, children, how a tyrant dies!"[63] To this, one of the advocate's men replies,

[61] Schiller, *Wilhelm Tell*, lines 2732–85.   [62] Ibid., line 2791.   [63] Ibid., line 2811.

> "Crazy woman, have you no feelings
> That you revel in looking on this horror?
> Help me – lay your hands on him – Does no one stand by me
> To pull this painful bolt from his chest for him?"[64]

The women standing around step back and exclaim, "We, touch him, whom God has struck down!"[65] Gessler's man draws his sword to threaten them, but one of the locals stops him:

> "Watch it, Lord!
> Your power is at an end. The tyrant
> Of the land is dead. We will suffer
> No more violence. We are free men."[66]

Schiller leaves little doubt here that God has acted through William Tell, and that Tell is the agent of divine vengeance.

The parallels between Schiller's version of Gessler's death and earlier accounts of wicked advocates being divinely punished are striking. Whereas the *White Book of Sarnen* has Tell kill Gessler on an isolated stretch of road, Schiller includes a public, who participate in the audience's *Schadenfreude* at watching Gessler die slowly and painfully. Likewise, the stories by Aimo and Andrew of Fleury and the anonymous monk at Tegernsee as well as the fifteenth-century *exemplum* from Benediktbeuern all emphasize the presence of witnesses who observe the arrival of supernatural figures delivering divine vengeance. Moreover, in the Fleury miracle stories, the wicked advocate Gauzfredus is described as being attacked while holding court and handing out unjust sentences; Schiller similarly includes a woman pleading for her unjustly imprisoned husband at the precise moment of Tell's attack. She is there to remind the audience that Tell's murderous act is justified. Divine vengeance does not lurk in the dark, or in secluded places; it shines forth in public, with the victims present to see the price the advocate has paid for his wicked deeds.

I am certainly not the first person to call attention to the ideas of divine vengeance in Schiller's work, nor the first to compare Tell's shot that kills Gessler to a miracle.[67] However, it is essential to recognize that William Tell has *always* played the role of a saint – from his earliest appearance in the *White Book of Sarnen*. By framing the legend in terms of unjust acts committed against peasants and then describing the wicked advocate's violent end, the author of the *White Book* was following a pattern that was already evident in the earliest miracle stories about divine vengeance directed against advocates. Schiller, while unquestionably adding nuance

---

[64] Ibid., lines 2812–15.   [65] Ibid., line 2816.   [66] Ibid., lines 2817–20.
[67] Meulen, "Theological." For an overview of scholarship on the play, see Guthke, "Wilhelm Tell."

and multiple layers of richness to the legend, nevertheless does not change this essential feature of the myth. In his play, an eleventh- and twelfth-century monastic fantasy has become a nineteenth-century revolutionary one.

The Wicked Advocate after 1800

Schiller was not the last author to place an advocate at the center of a story about local injustice. In Heinrich von Kleist's novella *Michael Kohlhaas* (1810), a bad castle advocate (*Burgvogt/Schlossvogt*), who demands unjust exactions from travelers, drives the protagonist to rebel and to set fire to the castle, killing the advocate.[68] A few years later, the Grimm brothers published the first edition of their collection of German legends (*Deutsche Sagen*), which includes the story of an "evil and cruel advocate."[69] The nineteenth and early twentieth centuries would see many other Europeans avidly collect similar myths and legends, including others about wicked advocates. Some of these are very specific in their descriptions of the advocatial actions at the root of the stories. One concerning the Teutonic Order's advocate for Sambia in Prussia describes his unjust demand for all of the amber that has washed ashore in his advocacy, even though the custom had long been that anyone who found amber was allowed to keep it. Because of this injustice, we are told, the advocate's soul has found no rest, and he can still be seen wandering the beach on stormy nights.[70]

Some of these stories remain popular down to our own day. I close with one that can be found on the website *Sagenhaftes Ruhrgebiet*, part of an initiative to preserve the Ruhr region's cultural heritage in the digital world of the twenty-first century.[71] It is called "The wicked advocate of Kamen" ("Der böse Vogt von Kamen") and is set just east of Dortmund.

In Kamen, there was a fortified house, and "in this fortified house there lived a harsh advocate, who feared neither man, nor God, nor the devil." The only thing he was afraid of was lightning. One day, a monk from the

---

[68] Kleist, *Michael Kohlhaas*, 31–32. The novella is based on the feud conducted between 1534 and 1540 by Hans Kohlhase, a merchant from Cölln in Brandenburg, against Saxony. The conflict began when people working for a noble lord seized Hans's horses. However, in the original story, there is no mention of a wicked advocate; see Dießelhorst and Duncker, *Hans Kohlhase*.

[69] Grimm and Grimm, *Deutsche Sagen*, 1:427, no. 330. See Chapter 13 for this story.

[70] Bechstein, *Deutsches Sagenbuch*, 204–5, no. 231. For the Teutonic Order's attempts to control the valuable amber trade, see Bliujienė, *Northern Gold*, 12.

[71] www.sagenhaftes-ruhrgebiet.de/Der_böse_Vogt_von_Kamen (July 31, 2021). The website with this story has had over 1.6 million hits, a testament to the popularity of these stories in Germany even today.

nearby Premonstratensian house of Cappenberg knocked on his door and announced that he had been sent by the head of his house to discuss "the release of one of the monastery's servants, whom the advocate had unjustly imprisoned." The advocate refused to listen to the monk and chased him away. But the monk shouted, "Beware, advocate, evil is already standing behind you!," because a storm was gathering. Then, "the advocate laughed scornfully, but the thunder was already rolling across town, and his ridicule turned to fear." He fled to a secure room in his tower, but "fire from the sky engulfed the tower, and those who saw it thought that they had looked upon the devil himself in the flames." The advocate's followers rushed to help him but found him dead. The legend then continues: "The consecrated ground of the cemetery would not take the body of the sinner. Every time he was buried, the earth threw him back out. Finally, the people buried him hastily outside the walls of the city under linden trees and covered his tomb with enormous millstones. Thereafter, during every storm, lightning struck the lindens." Thus, thanks to the Internet, the wicked advocate still cannot escape his divine punishment.

Conclusion

Demons, black dogs, ghost cows, bodies that cannot be buried: These are only some of the themes that reoccur in fantasies about advocates suffering in death for their wicked acts in life. The roots of this tradition can be traced back to religious communities at the turn of the first millennium, when monastic authors first crafted miracle stories about their patron saints punishing bad advocates. These stories captured the imagination of subsequent generations, who reworked them in various ways while maintaining the core ideas of divine vengeance and supernatural punishment. But why were these stories so appealing and powerful that they eventually made their way into central European folklore traditions? Why, in other words, was the figure of the wicked advocate one that resonated so deeply for so long?

As previous chapters have demonstrated, part of the answer to these questions lies in the nature of the position of advocate from the Carolingian period to the end of the eighteenth century. Throughout this period, the advocate was someone who interacted directly with local communities, specifically local communities under someone else's authority. These advocates exercised justice and provided protection, but these two roles also included a whole set of related responsibilities that gave advocates wide-ranging access to these communities. They functioned as the police, apprehending criminals and running jails; they held court, collecting judicial fines and performing executions; and they and their men collected payments in money and in kind to support their work as defenders. Thus, whether we choose to frame their activities in terms of "lordship" in the "medieval" period or "government" in the "modern" period, they represented – in intensely local and personal terms – the power and influence of political and economic elites over subject populations. This is why the wicked behavior mentioned in the sources is described in such intimate terms: unjust court decisions and fines; unjust imprisonment; going door to door to press unjust claims to cows and other valuable property. It is this intimacy, I would argue, that helps to explain why stories of bad advocates being divinely punished have survived for a millennium.

There is also another part to the answer, one I stressed at the outset of this book. The Holy Roman Empire, Germany, Austria and Switzerland inevitably hold up poorly when compared to England and France in historical arguments about the development of the state and efficient governmental bureaucracies. The question of whether or not the English and French states were as precocious as some scholars have suggested does not concern us here.[72] However, there is little doubt that the enduring stereotype of the wicked advocate confirms that the relative weakness of the state in the German-speaking lands was a very real problem. The fact that a set of monastic complaints about nobles abusing their authority on churches' estates could persist for three-quarters of a millennium as an apt description of the abuses of all sorts of advocates points to persistent tensions tied to practices of power and authority at the local level. That so many generations of writers have delighted in imagining tyrannical advocates and their henchmen suffering eternal punishments in the afterlife for their cruel behavior during this life highlights, in sometimes uncomfortable ways, the deeply entrenched problem of capricious, unaccountable "official" behavior in European history.

---

[72] There are, however, reasons to be skeptical of this narrative; for England, see O'Neill, "Counting"; Sabapathy, *Officers*, esp. 222–60; Amt, "Reputation."

Conclusion

> In the coming months, I learned that Officer Jerry was a notorious presence in the building. I heard dozens of stories from tenants who said they'd suffered all forms of harassment, abuse, and shakedowns at the hands of Officer Jerry. It was hard to corroborate these stories, but based on what I'd seen with my own eyes, they weren't hard to believe. And to some degree, it probably didn't much matter whether all the reports of his abusive behavior were true. In the projects, the "bad cop" story was a myth that residents spread at will out of sheer frustration that they lived in a high-crime area where the police presence was minimal at best, unchecked at worst.   – Sudhir Venkatesh, *Gang Leader for a Day*[1]

The Chicago Police Department's "Officer Jerry," much like Robert Penn Warren's Governor Willy Stark, with whom I began, is a reminder that the themes of this book are not specifically "medieval" – or European. The people labeled "advocate" in the sources from the eighth to eighteenth centuries were hardly unique in their efforts to take advantage of their positions as local authorities overseeing justice and protection. Especially in places as vast and heterogeneous as the Holy Roman Empire before 1806, or the United States today, it is difficult to imagine that professional bureaucrats could ever fully replace people exercising less formal power and authority at the local level. This becomes even more difficult to imagine when we consider that the various elites who benefit from less formal means of exercising power and authority have little if any incentive to support an efficient bureaucracy.[2] Put simply, the state has never successfully regulated human ingenuity – or our propensity to act in our own self-interest. So long as people are capable of thinking creatively, some will always find cracks in the system and choose to privilege private gain over public good.

As a result, it might be tempting to shrug off the actions of corrupt advocates and the near-permanent competition over the profits of

---

[1] Venkatesh, *Gang Leader*, 236.
[2] For the argument that the United States is moving in the direction of *more* privatized power and authority, not less, see Cordelli, *Privatized State*, esp. 298–302.

protection and justice at the center of this book as a ubiquitous phenomenon, as a structural problem as old as human civilization itself. There is
unquestionably some truth in this line of thought. Corruption is stub-
bornly persistent, despite countless anticorruption efforts, some of them
dating back centuries in various parts of the world.[3] Nevertheless, I will
conclude by suggesting two reasons why we should avoid trivializing the
history of advocates and advocacy between 750 and 1800 in this way.

First, the story I have told here of advocates wrestling with rulers,
prelates, princes, burghers and peasants over the profits of protection
and justice across a millennium is not the traditional story told about
Europe. The European story has been one of progress, of the
"Renaissance" and "modernity" gradually liberating the continent from
the dark days of its "medieval" past. Government, bureaucracy and the
state overcame the evils of lordship and feudalism ("a system where
money and muscle matters") to set Europe on a course toward political
freedom and democracy.[4] To be sure, I am not the first person to be
skeptical of this narrative; many others have recognized the latent
assumptions lurking in the medieval/modern periodization scheme's
teleology.[5] In line with my arguments here, some scholars have insisted
that corruption of various sorts was much more common in the early
modern period than older narratives of the rise of the sovereign state and
rational bureaucracy suggested they were.[6] Other scholars have recognized that the road to the modern nation-state was not as smooth and
straight as Joseph Strayer argued it was in his *On the Medieval Origins of the
Modern State*, when he wrote that "during the thirteenth century it
became clear that the basic loyalty of the English people (or at least of
the people who were politically active) had shifted from family, community, and Church to the state."[7]

Nevertheless, most grand narratives of the history of European progress
downplay the types of corrupt, abusive and violent practices that have
been central to this book.[8] As I have argued throughout, continuity does
not mean stasis; the advocates of the fourteenth and sixteenth centuries
did not behave in exactly the same ways as advocates in the ninth or
eleventh centuries. Instead, across the period from 750 to 1800, the
position of advocate served as the entry point for members of secular

---

[3] See the articles in *Anticorruption*.   [4] As quoted in Davis, *Periodization*, 133.
[5] See, for example, Freedman and Spiegel, "Medievalisms"; Ganim, *Medievalism*; Fasolt,
"Hegel's Ghost"; Davis, *Periodization*; Symes, "Modernity"; Le Goff, *History*.
[6] Waquet, *Corruption*; Bernard, "Water-Spout"; Durand, "Corruption." Also helpful is
MacMullen, *Corruption*.
[7] Strayer, *Medieval Origins*, 45. Cf. Tilly, *Coercion*; Adams, *Familial State*.
[8] For more on this point, see the Introduction.

elites to access other people's properties and rights – and to devise creative ways of profiting from their responsibility to provide protection and exercise justice. From the beginning, there were attempts to hold these representatives accountable in one way or another. However, the advocate and his agents – the people on the ground who knew local conditions best – frequently found ways to stay one step ahead of whatever authority was tasked with holding them accountable. Whether this game really ended around the year 1800, when this study stops, is a question for others to address.[9] I suspect that an approach to the history of Europe that sidelines narratives of progress and emphasizes instead the constant struggle of polities to govern effectively at the local level would be a fruitful approach to the study of the nineteenth, twentieth and twenty-first centuries as well.

My second point follows from the first but turns to the question of what lessons we can learn from the history of advocacy. As I made clear in the Introduction, one goal of this book has been to write a history of Europe that makes it look less "special" and more "normal" from a global perspective. To analyze advocates' abuses of the roles of protector and judge, abuses that were deep-rooted for a millennium across large parts of Europe, is to appreciate the significant challenges to instilling good governance anywhere in the world. Indeed, situating the rise of bureaucratic mentalities and accountable officeholding too early in the history of Europe is not simply wrong from a historical perspective. It is also dangerous. It makes the implementation of government and strong state structures look too easy, too straightforward and most importantly, too permanent. As this book has shown, even in the heart of Europe, it was a slow, difficult process for public institutions and civil society to gain a foothold in the struggle against particularism and private interests – and there is no reason to think that struggle has ended.[10] The long history of advocates' corrupt practices of protection and justice is, I hope, a reminder that anticorruption campaigns can never rest on their laurels. Some local official somewhere is inevitably looking for an opportunity to profit from their position in some new (or old) way.

As members of local elites who operated in the gray area between the just and unjust, the legitimate and the illegitimate, advocates call attention to a problem that has confronted people throughout history and still does so across much of the globe today: the difficulty of controlling representatives who lack a clear sense of official accountability or

---

[9] For one perspective on this issue, see Barreyre and Lemercier, "Unexceptional State."

[10] This argument is partly a response to a call for more work on the history of anticorruption efforts in countries that today have a reputation for effectively controlling corruption: Mungiu-Pippidi, *Quest*, 57.

a bureaucratic work ethic – but who are nevertheless granted access to people and property because someone needs to provide protection and exercise justice. To be clear, local advocates were not the only ones who sought to exploit the people they were supposed to judge and defend – kings, emperors, princes and prelates (some of them calling themselves advocates) were often no more or less ethical than they were. However, because many advocates and their agents operated in villages and small towns, their corrupt activities left a lasting impression on generations of Europeans. Seizing families' chickens, pigs and cows as payment for "protection"; imprisoning fathers, husbands and sons for no good reason until they paid "fines"; sexually assaulting mothers, wives and daughters because they had little if any fear of reprisal: These were the types of abuses that came to define the bad advocate across a millennium of European history.

Today, when taxes and fines are increasingly paid electronically and local officials no longer go door to door demanding access to our property, the rapacious advocate can easily look like an antiquated figure. The physical distance between the governed and those who govern is typically much greater now than it was before 1800. But the example of "Officer Jerry" cautions against the view that the specific kinds of abuses perpetrated by advocates are a thing of the past. There are still many places where accountable officials are the exception rather than the norm. The path to establishing (reasonably) good government has been a long and arduous one, and as the world reminds us daily, *maintaining* (reasonably) good government presents just as great a challenge.

Works Cited

Manuscripts and Archival Materials

Berlin, Geheimes Staatsarchiv Preußischer Kulturbesitz
   VII. HA, Geistliche Fürsten, Abtei Quedlinburg, Nos. 20, 23, 27, 45 and 59
   XX. HA, HBA, D, No. 2943
Freiburg im Breisgau, Staatsarchiv
   U 100/2 No. 11 and U 105/1 No. 5
Hildesheim, Bistumsarchiv
   Urkunden Stadtvogt zu Hildesheim B IV 2–1 (digitized at monasterium.net)
Linz, Oberösterreichisches Landesarchiv
   Herrschaft Steyr, Schachtel No. 313
Marburg, Staatsarchiv
   Urk. 56 (alt: M I Reichsabtei Hersfeld), nos. 927 and 1118 (digitized at
      monasterium.net)
Munich, Bayerisches Hauptstaatsarchiv
   KL Niederaltaich Lit. 39
Munich, Bayerische Staatsbibliothek
   Clm 1018 (digitized at Münchener DigitalisierungsZentrum)
   Clm 18571
   Clm 22501 (digitized at Münchener DigitalisierungsZentrum)
Rostock, Universitätsbibliothek
   Mss. theol. 37a
Vienna, Haus-, Hof- und Staatsarchiv
   Hs. R 83/1 and Hs. R 83/2 (digitized at manuscripta.at)
Vienna, Österreichische Nationalbibliothek,
   Cod. 413, Cod. 4556, Cod. 7710, Cod. 8084, Cod. 8714 and Cod. 12875
Vienna, Stadt- und Landesarchiv
   Bürgerspital – Urkunden, nos. 520 and 529 (digitized at monasterium.net)
Vorau, Stiftsbibliothek
   Cod. 277
Wolfenbüttel, Herzog August Bibliothek
   Cod. Guelf. 97 Weiss. (digitized at Wolfenbütteler Digitale Bibliothek)
Zwettl, Stiftsbibliothek
   Cod. 15 (digitized at manuscripta.at)

Websites Consulted

Deutsches Wörterbuch von Jacob Grimm und Wilhelm Grimm (http://dwb.uni-trier de/de/)
Diplomatica Belgica Online (www.diplomata-belgica.be/colophon_fr.html)
Douay-Rheims Bible Online (http://drbo.org/)
Kaiserchronik Digital (https://doi.org/10.11588/edition.kcd)
kenom Virtuelles Münzkabinett (www.kenom.de/)
Manuscripta.at (https://manuscripta.at/)
Monasterium.net (www.monasterium.net/mom/home)
Monumenta Germaniae Historica (https://mgh.de) and (www.dmgh.de/)
Münchener DigitalisierungsZentrum (www.digitale-sammlungen.de/)
"Nomen et Gens" Database (https://escience-center.uni-tuebingen.de/neg/gast/ startseite.jsp)
Oxford English Dictionary Online (www.oed.com/)
Project Gutenberg (www.gutenberg.org/)
Regesta Imperii Online (https://regesta-imperii.de)
Sagenhaftes Ruhrgebiet (www.sagenhaftes-ruhrgebiet.de/Hauptseite)
Wolfenbütteler Digitale Bibliothek (www.hab.de/digitale-bibliothek-wdb/)
Württembergisches Urkundenbuch Online (www.wubonline.de/)

Published Primary Sources

Abbo of Fleury. *Canones*. In *Patrologia Latina*. Ed. J.-P. Migne. Vol. 139 (Paris, 1853), cols. 473–508.
Acht, Peter, ed. *Die Traditionen des Klosters Tegernsee 1003–1242* (Munich, 1952).
Acta Murensia: Die Akten des Klosters Muri mit der Genealogie der frühen Habsburger. Ed. Charlotte Bretscher-Gisiger and Christian Sieber (Basel, 2012).
Aimo of Fleury. *Vita et Passio Sancti Abbonis*. In *L'abbaye de Fleury en l'an mil*, ed. Robert-Henri Bautier and Gillette Labory (Paris, 2004), pp. 9–137.
Die älteren Urkunden des Klosters Moggio (bis 1250). Ed. Reinhard Härtel (Vienna, 1985).
Die älteren Urkunden des Klosters S. Maria zu Aquileia (1036–1250). Ed. Reinhard Härtel (Vienna, 2005).
Ambrose of Milan. *De Officiis*. Ed. Ivor J. Davidson. 2 vols. (Oxford and New York, 2001).
Die Annalen des Klosters Einsiedeln. Ed. Conradin von Planta. MGH SSrG 78 (Hanover, 2007).
Annales Austriae. Ed. Wilhelm Wattenbach. In MGH SS 9 (Hanover, 1851), pp. 479–843.
Annales Capituli Cracoviensis. Ed. Richard Roepell and Wilhelm Arndt. In MGH SS 19 (Hanover, 1866), pp. 582–607.
Annales Colmarienses Maiores. Ed. Philipp Jaffé. In MGH SS 17 (Hanover, 1861), pp. 202–32.
Annales Fuldenses sive Annales Regni Francorum Orientalis. Ed. Georg Heinrich Pertz and Friedrich Kurze. MGH SSrG 7 (Hanover, 1891).

Annales Hildesheimenses. Ed. Georg Waitz. MGH SSrG 8 (Hanover, 1878).

Annales Lubicenses. Ed. Johann Martin Lappenberg. In MGH SS 16 (Hanover, 1859), pp. 411–29.

Annales Pegavienses et Bosovienses. Ed. Georg Heinrich Pertz. In MGH SS 16 (Hanover, 1859), pp. 232–70.

Annales Reicherspergenses. Ed. Wilhelm Wattenbach. In MGH SS 17 (Hanover, 1861), pp. 443–76.

Annales Sancti Disibodi. Ed. Georg Waitz. In MGH SS 17 (Hanover, 1861), pp. 4–30.

Annales Sancti Quintini Veromandensis. Ed. Georg Heinrich Pertz. In MGH SS 16 (Hanover, 1859), pp. 507–8.

The Annals of Fulda. Trans. Timothy Reuter (Manchester and New York, 1992).

Augustine of Hippo. *Enarrationes in Psalmos 51–100*. Ed. Hildegund Müller. Vol. 1 (Vienna, 2004).

Babrius and Phaedrus: Newly Edited and Translated into English. Trans. Ben Edwin Perry (Cambridge, MA and London, 1975).

Balderich of Trier. *Gesta Alberonis Archiepiscopi*. Ed. Georg Waitz. In MGH SS 8 (Hanover, 1848), pp. 243–60.

  A Warrior Bishop of the Twelfth Century: The Deeds of Albero of Trier. Trans. Brian A. Pavlac (Toronto, 2008).

Beccaria, Cesare. *On Crimes and Punishments*. Trans. David Young (Indianapolis, 1986; orig. 1764).

Bechstein, Ludwig. *Deutsches Sagenbuch* (Leipzig, 1853).

Becquet, Jean, ed. *Actes des évêques de Limoges des origines à 1197* (Paris, 1999).

Bede. *In Marci Evangelium Expositio*. In *Opera Exegetica*. Ed. David Hurst. Vol. 3 (Turnhout, 1960).

Bellum Waltherianum. Ed. Philipp Jaffé. In MGH SS 17 (Hanover, 1861), pp. 105–14.

"Das Benediktbeurer Traditionsbuch." Ed. Franz Ludwig von Baumann. *Archivalische Zeitschrift* 20 (1914): 1–82.

Bern of Reichenau. *Tractatus liturgici*. Ed. Henry Parkes (Turnhout, 2019).

Bernard of Clairvaux. "De Consideratione ad Eugenium Papam." In *Sancti Bernardi Opera, vol. 3: Tractatus et Opuscula*, ed. Jean Leclercq and Henri-Maria Rochais (Rome, 1963), pp. 381–493.

Bernold of St. Blasien. *Chronicle*. In *Eleventh-Century Germany: The Swabian Chronicles*, trans. Ian Stuart Robinson (Manchester and New York, 2008), pp. 245–337.

  Bernoldi Chronicon. Ed. Ian Stuart Robinson. In *Die Chroniken Bertholds von Reichenau und Bernolds von Konstanz, 1054–1100*. MGH SSrG NS 14 (Hanover, 2003), pp. 383–540.

Berthold of Reichenau. *Bertholdi Chronicon*. Ed. Ian Stuart. Robinson. In *Die Chroniken Bertholds von Reichenau und Bernolds von Konstanz, 1054–1100*. MGH SSrG NS 14 (Hanover, 2003), pp. 161–381.

  Chronicle: The Second Version. In *Eleventh-Century Germany: The Swabian Chronicles*, trans. Ian Stuart Robinson (Manchester and New York, 2008), pp. 108–244.

Beyer, Heinrich, ed. *Urkundenbuch zur Geschichte der mittelrheinischen Territorien.* Vol. 1 (Coblenz, 1860).

Biblia Sacra: iuxta Vulgatam versionem. Ed. Roger Gryson. 4th ed. (Stuttgart, 1994).

Bloch, Hermann, ed. "Die älteren Urkunden des Klosters S. Vanne zu Verdun." *Jahrbuch der Gesellschaft für lothringische Geschichte und Altertumskunde* 10 (1898): 338–449.

Bode, Georg, ed. *Urkundenbuch der Stadt Goslar.* Vols. 1–4 (Halle, 1893–1905).

The Book of Emperors: A Translation of the Middle High German Kaiserchronik. Trans. Henry Allen Myers (Morgantown, WV, 2013).

Braun, Johann Wilhelm, ed. *Urkundenbuch des Klosters Sankt Blasien im Schwarzwald: Von den Anfängen bis zum Jahr 1299.* Vol. 1 (Stuttgart, 2003).

Breviarium Alaricianum: Römisches Recht im fränkischen Reich. Ed. Max Conrat (Leipzig, 1903).

Bridot, Jean, ed. *Chartes de l'abbaye de Remiremont des origines à 1231* (Turnhout, 1997).

Burchard von Ursberg. *Die Chronik des Propstes Burchard von Ursberg.* Ed. Matthias Becher. In *Quellen zur Geschichte der Welfen und die Chronik Burchards von Ursberg* (Darmstadt, 2007), pp. 100–311.

Caesarius of Arles. *Sermones.* Ed. Germain Morin. Vol. 1 (Turnhout, 1953).

Caesarius of Heisterbach. "Die beiden ersten Bücher der Libri VIII Miraculorum." In *Die Wundergeschichten des Caesarius von Heisterbach,* ed. Alfons Hilka. Vol. 3 (Bonn, 1937), pp. 1–222.

Die Wundergeschichten des Caesarius von Heisterbach. Ed. Alfons Hilka. Vol. 1 (Bonn, 1933).

"Leben, Leiden und Wunder des heiligen Engelbert, Erzbischofs von Köln." Ed. Fritz Zschaeck. In *Die Wundergeschichten des Caesarius von Heisterbach,* vol. 3 (Bonn, 1937), pp. 223–328.

Capitularia regum Francorum. MGH Leges. Ed. Alfred Boretius and Victor Krause. 2 vols. (Hanover, 1883–97).

The Cartulary and Charters of Notre-Dame of Homblières. Ed. Theodore Evergates, Giles Constable and William Mendel Newman (Cambridge, MA, 1990).

The Cartulary of Montier-en-Der, 666–1129. Ed. Constance B. Bouchard (Toronto, 2004).

Casuum S. Galli Continuatio II. Ed. Ildefons von Arx. In MGH SS 2 (Hanover, 1829), pp. 148–63.

Chartae Latinae Antiquiores: Facsimile-Edition of the Latin Charter Prior to the Ninth Century. Ed. Albert Bruckner and Robert Marichal. Vol. 15 (Zurich, 1986).

Chevrier, Georges, and Maurice Chaume, eds. *Chartes et documents de Saint-Bénigne de Dijon: prieurés et dépendances des origines à 1300.* Vol. 2 (Dijon, 1943).

Chmel, Joseph, ed. *Aktenstücke und Briefe zur Geschichte des Hauses Habsburg im Zeitalter Maximilians I.* Vol. 1 (Hildesheim, 1968; orig. 1854).

——— ed. *Urkunden zur Geschichte von Österreich, Steiermark, Kärnten, Krain, Görz, Triest, Istrien, Tirol.* Fontes Rerum Austriacarum II.1 (Vienna, 1849).

Chronica Regia Coloniensis. Ed. Georg Waitz. MGH SSrG 18 (Hanover, 1880).

Chronica Sereni Montis auctore Conrado presbytero. Ed. Klaus Nass. MGH SSrG 83 (Wiesbaden, 2020).

Chronicon Benedictoburanum. Ed. Wilhelm Wattenbach. In MGH SS 9 (Hanover, 1851), pp. 210–38.

Chronicon Colmariense. Ed. Philipp Jaffé. In MGH SS 17 (Hanover, 1861), pp. 240–70.

Chronicon Episcoporum Hildesheimensium. Ed. Georg Heinrich Pertz. In MGH SS 7 (Hanover, 1846), pp. 845–73.

Il Chronicon Farfense di Gregorio di Catino. Ed. Ugo Balzani (Rome, 1903).

Chronicon Holzatiae. Ed. Johann Martin Lappenberg. In MGH SS 21 (Hanover, 1869), pp. 251–306.

Chronicon Laureshamense. Ed. Karl August Friedrich Pertz. In MGH SS 21 (Hanover, 1869), pp. 334–453.

Chronicon Ottenburanum. Ed. Ludwig Weiland. In MGH SS 23 (Hanover, 1874), pp. 609–30.

Der Codex Eberhardi des Klosters Fulda. Ed. Heinrich Meyer zu Ermgassen. Vol. 1 (Marburg, 1995).

Codex Diplomaticus Saxoniae Regiae. Part I. Section A. Ed. Otto Posse and Hubert Ermisch. 3 vols. (Leipzig, 1882–1898).

Codex Diplomaticus Saxoniae Regiae. Part I. Section B. Ed. Hubert Ermisch et al. 4 vols. (Leipzig and Dresden, 1899–1941).

Codex Diplomaticus Saxoniae Regiae. Part II. Ed. Ernst Gotthelf Gersdorf et al. 21 vols. (Leipzig, 1864–2021).

Codex Falkensteinensis: Die Rechtsaufzeichnungen der Grafen von Falkenstein. Ed. Elisabeth Noichl (Munich, 1978).

Codex Laureshamensis. Ed. Karl Glöckner. 3 vols. (Darmstadt, 1929–36).

Codex Udalrici. Ed. Klaus Nass. 2 vols. MGH Briefe der deutschen Kaiserzeit 10 (Wiesbaden, 2017).

Codice diplomatico Longobardo. Ed. Luigi Schiaparelli, Carlrichard Brühl and Herbert Zielinski. 5 vols. (Rome, 1929–2003).

Collectio Dacheriana. In *Spicilegium sive Collectio veterum aliquot scriptorum qui in Galliae bibliothecis delituerant.* Ed. Luc d'Archery and L. F. J. de la Barre. Vol. 1 (Paris, 1723), pp. 509–64.

Collectio Sangallensis Salomonis III. tempore conscripta. In MGH Leges Formulae. Ed. Karl Zeumer (Hanover, 1886), pp. 390–433.

Concilia Aevi Karolini. MGH Leges: Concilia 2. Ed. Albert Werminghoff. 2 vols. (Hanover and Leipzig, 1906–8).

Concilia Africae, a. 345–a. 525. Ed. Charles Munier (Turnhout, 1974).

Concilia Galliae, a. 511–a. 695. Ed. Charles de Clercq (Turnhout, 1963).

Concilia Germaniae. Ed. Josephus Hartzheim. 11 vols. (Cologne, 1759–1790).

Constitutiones Concilii Quarti Lateranensis una cum Commentariis Glossatorum. Ed. Antonio García y García (Vatican City, 1981).

Constitutiones et Acta Publica Imperatorum et Regum. Ed. Ludwig Weiland et al. MGH. 14 vols. (Hanover, 1893–2020).

Court and Civic Society in the Burgundian Low Countries c. 1420–1530. Trans. Andrew Brown and Graeme Small (Manchester and New York, 2007).

The Crusade of Frederick Barbarossa: The History of the Expedition of the Emperor Frederick and Related Texts. Trans. Graham A. Loud (Farnham and Burlington, VT, 2010).

De Advocatis Altahensibus. Ed. Philipp Jaffé. In MGH SS 17 (Hanover, 1861), pp. 373–76.

Decretalium Collectiones. Ed. Emil Friedberg. Corpus Iuris Canonici, vol. 2 (Graz, 1959).

Deeds of the Bishops of Cambrai. Trans. Bernard S. Bachrach, David S. Bachrach and Michael Leese (London and New York, 2018).

The Deeds of Count Ludwig of Arnstein. Trans. Jonathan R. Lyon. In *Noble Society: Five Lives from Twelfth-Century Germany* (Manchester, 2017), pp. 220–48.

The Deeds of Margrave Wiprecht of Groitzsch. Trans. Jonathan R. Lyon and Lisa Wolverton. In *Noble Society: Five Lives from Twelfth-Century Germany* (Manchester, 2017), pp. 22–91.

Delaborde, Henri-François et al., eds. *Recueil des actes de Philippe Auguste, roi de France*. 6 vols. (Paris, 1916–2005).

Despy, Georges, ed. *Les chartes de l'abbaye de Waulsort*. Vol. 1 (Brussels, 1957).

Deutsche Reichstagsakten. Ed. Hermann Herre and Ludwig Quidde. Vol. 16: 2 (Göttingen, 1957).

Deutsches Wirtschaftsleben im Mittelalter III: Quellensammlung. Ed. Karl Lamprecht (Leipzig, 1885).

d'Herbomez, Armand, ed. *Cartulaire de l'abbaye de Gorze* (Paris, 1898).

Dietrich von Amorbach [Thierry de Fleury]. *Illatio Sancti Benedicti*. In *Acta Sanctorum Ordinis Sancti Benedicti*, ed. Jean Mabillon and Luc d'Achery. Saec. 4, Part 2, 2nd ed. (Venice, 1738), pp. 362–67.

Diplomata Belgica ante annum millesimum centesimum scripta. Ed. Maurits Gysseling and Anton C. F. Koch. Vol. 1 (Brussels, 1950).

I Diplomi di Berengario I. Ed. Luigi Schiaparelli (Rome, 1903).

I Diplomi di Guido e di Lamberto. Ed. Luigi Schiaparelli (Rome, 1906).

I Diplomi di Ugo e di Lotario, di Berengario II e di Adalberto. Ed. Luigi Schiaparelli (Rome, 1924).

I Diplomi Italiani di Lodovico III e di Rodolfo II. Ed. Luigi Schiaparelli (Rome, 1910).

Długosz, Jan. *The Annals of Jan Długosz*. Trans. Maurice Michael (Chichester, 1997).

Dufour-Malbezin, Annie, ed. *Actes des évêques de Laon des origines à 1151* (Paris, 2001).

Ebendorfer, Thomas. *Chronica Regum Romanorum*. Ed. Harald Zimmermann. 2 vols. MGH SSrG NS 18 (Hanover, 2003).

Einhard. *Einhards Briefe: Kommunikation und Mobilität im Frühmittelalter*. Ed. Annette Grabowsky, Christoph Haack, Thomas Kohl and Steffen Patzold (Seligenstadt, 2018).

Vita Karoli Magni. Ed. Oswald Holder-Egger, G. H. Pertz and Georg Waitz. MGH SSrG 25, 6th ed. (Hanover and Leipzig, 1911).

Ekkehard IV. *Casus Sancti Galli*. Ed. Hans F. Haefele and Ernst Tremp. MGH SSrG 82 (Wiesbaden, 2020).

Emonis Chronicon. Ed. Ludwig Weiland. In MGH SS 23 (Hanover, 1874), pp. 465–523.

Erath, Anton Ulrich von, ed. *Codex Diplomaticus Quedlinburgensis* (Frankfurt, 1764).

Erconrad of Le Mans. *Translatio Sancti Liborii: Eine wiederentdeckte Geschichtsquelle der Karolingerzeit und die schon bekannten Übertragungsberichte.* Ed. Alfred Cohausz (Paderborn, 1966).

Escher, Jakob, and Paul Schweizer, eds. *Urkundenbuch der Stadt und Landschaft Zürich.* Vol. 1 (Zurich, 1888–90).

Essener Urkundenbuch: Regesten der Urkunden des Frauenstifts Essen im Mittelalter. Ed. Thomas Schilp. Vol. 1 (Düsseldorf, 2010).

Etterlin, Petermann. *Kronica von der loblichen Eydtgnoschaft, jr harkommen und sust seltzam strittenn und geschichten.* Quellenwerk zur Entstehung der Schweizerischen Eidgenossenschaft, 3:3 (Aarau, 1965).

Évrard, Jean-Pol, ed. *Actes des princes Lorrains. Les évêques de Verdun: A – des origines à 1107* (Nancy, 1977).

Ex Miraculorum Sancti Bavonis libri III. Ed. Oswald Holder-Egger. In MGH SS 15:2 (Hanover, 1888), pp. 589–97.

Ex Vita Sancti Willibrordi auctore Thiofrido abbate. Ed. Ludwig Weiland. In MGH SS 23 (Hanover, 1874), pp. 23–30.

Feger, Otto, ed. *Die Chronik des Klosters Petershausen* (Sigmaringen, 1978).

Fleck, Michael, ed. *Leben und Wundertaten des heiligen Wigbert* (Marburg, 2010).

Flodoard of Reims. *Historia Remensis Ecclesiae.* Ed. Martina Stratmann. MGH SS 36 (Hanover, 1998).

Folcuin. *Gesta Abbatum S. Bertini Sithiensium.* Ed. Oswald Holder-Egger. MGH SS 13 (Hanover, 1881), pp. 607–35.

Formulae Augiensis. In MGH Leges Formulae. Ed. Karl Zeumer (Hanover, 1886), pp. 339–77.

Formulae Imperiales e curia Ludovici Pii. In MGH Leges Formulae, pp. 285–327.

Formulae Salicae Lindenbrogianae. In MGH Leges Formulae, pp. 265–82.

Formulae Senonenses Recentiores. In MGH Leges Formulae, pp. 211–20.

Fossier, Robert, ed. *Chartes de coutume en Picardie (XIe–XIIIe siècle)* (Paris, 1974).

Froumund. *Die Tegernseer Briefsammlung.* Ed. Karl Strecker. MGH Epp. sel. 3 (Berlin, 1925).

Fulbert of Chartres. *The Letters and Poems of Fulbert of Chartres.* Ed. Frederick Behrends (Oxford, 1976).

Fundatio Monasterii Gratiae Dei. Ed. Hermann Pabst. In MGH SS 20 (Hanover, 1868), pp. 683–91.

Galbert of Bruges. *De Multro, Traditione, et Occisione Gloriosi Karoli, Comitis Flandriarum.* Ed. Jeff Rider (Turnhout, 1994).
  The Murder, Betrayal, and Slaughter of the Glorious Charles, Count of Flanders. Trans. Jeff Rider (New Haven, CT and London, 2013).

Gerhard of Augsburg. *Vita Sancti Uodalrici: Die älteste Lebensbeschreibung des heiligen Ulrich.* Ed. and trans. Walter Berschin and Angelika Häse, 2nd ed. (Heidelberg, 2020).

Gesta Abbatum Gemblacensium auctore Sigeberto. Ed. Georg Heinrich Pertz. In MGH SS 8 (Hanover, 1848), pp. 523–42.

Gesta Archiepiscoporum Magdeburgensium. Ed. Wilhelm Schum. In MGH SS 14 (Hanover, 1883), pp. 361–486.

Gesta Episcoporum Cameracensium. Ed. L. C. Bethmann. In MGH SS 7 (Hanover, 1846), pp. 393–525.

Gesta Praepositorum Stederburgensium continuata. Ed. Georg Waitz. In MGH SS 25 (Hanover, 1880), pp. 719–35.

Gesta Sancti Servatii episcopi Tungrensis et confessoris. Ed. Friedrich Wilhelm. In *Sanct Servatius, oder wie das erste Reis in deutscher Zunge geimpft wurde* (Munich, 1910), pp. 3–147.

Gilcher, Birgit, ed. *Die Traditionen des Augustiner-Chorherrenstifts Herrenchiemsee* (Munich, 2011).

Goez, Elke, ed. *Die Urkunden der Zisterze Ebrach 1127–1306.* 2 vols. (Neustadt and Aisch, 2001).

Gonzo of Florennes. *Ex Miraculis S. Gengulfi.* Ed. Oswald Holder-Egger. In MGH SS 15:2 (Hanover, 1888), pp. 790–96.

Graber, Tom, ed. *Urkundenbuch des Zisterzienserklosters Altzelle.* Vol. 1. CDS II:19 (Hanover, 2006).

Grat, Félix, Jacques de Font-Réaulx, Georges Tessier and Robert-Henri Bautier, eds. *Recueil des actes de Louis II le Bègue, Louis III et Carloman II, rois de France (877– 884)* (Paris, 1978).

Gratian. *Decretum magistri Gratiani.* Ed. Emil Friedberg. Corpus Iuris Canonici, vol. 1 (Leipzig, 1879).

Gregory IX, Pope. *Decretales D. Gregorii Papae IX. svae integritati vna cvm glossis restitvtae.* 2 vols. (Venice, 1605).

Die große Vogteirolle des Grafen Friedrich von Isenberg-Altena um 1220. Ed. Moritz zu Bentheim Tecklenburg Rheda (Bielefeld, 1955).

Gruber, Johann, ed. *Die Urkunden und das älteste Urbar des Stiftes Osterhofen* (Munich, 1985).

Gudenus, Valentin Ferdinand von, ed. *Codex Diplomaticus Anecdotorum.* Vol. 3 (Frankfurt and Leipzig, 1751).

Guérard, Benjamin, ed. *Polyptyque de l'abbaye de Saint-Remi de Reims* (Paris, 1853).

Guyotjeannin, Olivier, ed. *Le chartrier de l'abbaye prémontrée de Saint-Yved de Braine (1134–1250)* (Paris, 2000).

Das Habsburgische Urbar. Ed. Rudolf Maag. Vol. 1 (Basel, 1894).

Haider, Siegfried, ed. *Die Traditionsurkunden des Klosters Garsten: Kritische Edition* (Vienna and Munich, 2011).

Haimo of Hirsau. *Vita Willihelmi Abbatis Hirsaugiensis.* In MGH SS 12. Ed. Wilhelm Wattenbach (Hanover, 1856), pp. 209–25.

Halkin, Joseph, and C.-G. Roland, eds. *Recueil des chartes de l'Abbaye de Stavelot-Malmedy.* Vol. 1 (Brussels, 1909).

Halphen, Louis, ed. *Recueil des actes de Lothaire et de Louis V, Rois de France (954–987)* (Paris, 1908).

Hanquet, Karl, ed. *La chronique de Saint-Hubert dite Cantatorium* (Brussels, 1906).

Heeg-Engelhart, Ingrid, ed. *Das älteste bayerische Herzogsurbar: Analyse und Edition* (Munich, 1990).

Henry of Livonia. *The Chronicle of Henry of Livonia*. Trans. James A. Brundage (New York, 2003). *Heinrichs Livländische Chronik*. Ed. Leonid Arbusow and Albert Bauer. MGH SSrG 31, 2nd ed. (Hanover, 1955).

Henry of Susa (Hostiensis). *In Primum Decretalium Librum Commentaria* (Turin, 1965; repr. of Venice, 1581).

In Tertium Decretalium Librum Commentaria (Turin, 1965; repr. of Venice, 1581).

Summa. Ed. Niccolò Soranzo (Aalen, 1962; repr. of Lyon, 1537).

Herman of Tournai. *Liber de Restauratione Ecclesie Sancti Martini Tornacensis*. Ed. R. B. C. Huygens (Turnhout, 2010).

The Restoration of the Monastery of Saint Martin of Tournai. Trans. Lynn H. Nelson (Washington, DC, 1996).

Herquet, Karl, ed. *Urkundenbuch des Prämonstratenser-Klosters Arnstein an der Lahn* (Wiesbaden, 1883).

Heuwieser, Max, ed. *Die Traditionen des Hochstifts Passau* (Munich, 1930; repr. Aalen, 1969).

Hincmar of Reims. *De presbiteris criminosis: Ein Memorandum Erzbischof Hinkmars von Reims über straffällige Kleriker*. Ed. Gerhard Schmitz (Hanover, 2004).

Quaterniones (Pro Ecclesiae Libertatum Defensione, Expositio Prima). In *Patrologia Latina*, ed. J.-P. Migne. Vol. 125 (Paris, 1879), cols. 1035–60.

Historia de Expeditione Friderici Imperatoris. Ed. Anton Chroust. In MGH SSrG NS 5 (Berlin, 1928), pp. 1–115.

Historia Diplomatica Friderici Secundi. Ed. Jean Louis Alphonse Huillard-Bréholles. 6 vols. (Paris, 1852–61).

Historia Monasterii Rastedensis. Ed. Georg Waitz. In MGH SS 25 (Hanover, 1880), pp. 495–511.

Historia Peregrinorum. Ed. Anton Chroust. In MGH SSrG NS 5 (Berlin, 1928), pp. 116–72.

Historiae Patavienses et Cremifanenses. Ed. Georg Waitz. In MGH SS 25 (Hanover, 1880), pp. 610–78.

Honorius of Kent, Master. *Magistri Honorii Summa "De iure canonico tractaturus."* Ed. Rudolf Weigand, Peter Landau and Waltraud Kozur. 3 vols. (Vatican City, 2004–10).

Honselmann, Klemens, ed. *Die alten Mönchslisten und die Traditionen von Corvey*. Vol. 1 (Paderborn, 1982).

Höppl, Reinhard, ed. *Die Traditionen des Klosters Wessobrunn* (Munich, 1984).

Horstkötter, Ludger, ed. *Urkundenbuch der Abtei Hamborn mit Übersetzung und Kommentar*. 2 vols. (Münster, 2008).

Hugh of Fleury. *Opera Historica*. Ed. Georg Waitz. In MGH SS 9 (Hanover, 1851), pp. 337–406.

Hugh of Poitiers. *The Vézelay Chronicle and Other Documents from MS. Auxerre 227 and Elsewhere*. Trans. John Scott and John O. Ward (Binghamton, NY, 1992).

Innocent IV, Pope. *Commentaria in Quinque Libros Decretalium* (Lyons, 1554).

Die Innsbrucker Briefsammlung. Ed. Josef Riedmann. MGH Briefe des späteren Mittelalters 3 (Wiesbaden, 2017).

Isidore of Seville. *Etymologiae VII (Étymologies Livre VII)*. Ed. Jean-Yves Guillaumin and Pierre Monat (Paris, 2012).

Jacobsen, Peter Christian, ed. *Die Geschichte vom Leben des Johannes, Abt des Klosters Gorze*. MGH SSrG 81 (Wiesbaden, 2016).

ed. *Miracula s. Gorgonii: Studien und Texte zur Gorgonius-Verehrung im 10. Jahrhundert*. MGH Studien und Texte 46 (Hanover, 2009).

John of Salisbury. *Policraticus*. Trans. Cary J. Nederman (Cambridge, 1990).

John of Viktring. *Liber Certarum Historiarum*. Ed. Fedor Schneider. 2 vols. MGH SSrG 36 (Hanover and Leipzig, 1909–10).

Die Kaiserchronik eines Regensburger Geistlichen. Ed. Edward Schröder. MGH Deutsche Chroniken, 1:1 (Hanover, 1895).

Die Kapitulariensammlung des Ansegis. Ed. Gerhard Schmitz. MGH Capit. Nova Series 1 (Hanover, 1996).

Die Reichenauer Lehenbücher der Äbte Friedrich von Zollern (1402–1427) und Friedrich von Wartenberg (1428–1453). Ed. Harald Derschka (Stuttgart, 2018).

Kleist, Heinrich von. *Michael Kohlhaas*. In *Sämtliche Werke und Briefe*, ed. Helmut Sembdner, 2nd ed. (Munich, 1961), pp. 9–103.

Klose, Josef, ed. *Die Urbare Abt Hermanns von Niederaltaich*. 2 vols. (Munich, 2003).

Die Urkunden Abt Hermanns von Niederaltaich (1242–1273) (Munich, 2010).

Knebel, Johannes. *Johannis Knebel Capellani Ecclesiae Basiliensis Diarium [Tagebuch des Kaplans am Münster zu Basel]*. In *Basler Chroniken*, ed. Wilhelm Vischer. Vols. 2–3 (Leipzig, 1880–7).

Knipping, Richard, ed. *Die Regesten der Erzbischöfe von Köln im Mittelalter*. Vol. 3 (Bonn, 1909–13).

Koch, A. C. F., ed. *Oorkondenboek van Holland en Zeeland tot 1299*. Vol. 1 (The Hague, 1970).

Konrad of Megenberg. *Die Werke des Konrads von Megenberg: Ökonomik (Buch II)*. Ed. Sabine Krüger. MGH Staatsschriften 3:2 (Stuttgart, 1977).

Konrad of Pfäfers. *Casuum Sancti Galli Continuatio III*. Ed. Ildefons von Arx. In MGH SS 2 (Hanover, 1829), pp. 163–83.

Koppmann, Karl, ed. *Die Chroniken der niedersächsischen Städte: Lübeck*. Vol. 1 (Leipzig, 1884).

Korner, Hermann. *Die Chronica Novella des Hermann Korner*. Ed. Jakob Schwalm (Göttingen, 1895).

Krausen, Edgar, ed. *Die Urkunden des Klosters Raitenhaslach 1034–1350* (Munich, 1959).

Krimm-Beumann, Jutta, ed. *Die ältesten Güterverzeichnisse des Klosters Sankt Peter im Schwarzwald* (Stuttgart, 2011).

Lacomblet, Theodor Josef, ed. *Urkundenbuch für die Geschichte des Niederrheins*. 4 vols. (Düsseldorf, 1840–58).

Lambert of Ardres. *The History of the Counts of Guines and Lords of Ardres*. Trans. Leah Shopkow (Philadelphia, PA, 2001).

Lampert of Hersfeld. *The Annals of Lampert of Hersfeld*. Trans. Ian Stuart Robinson (Manchester, 2015).

Lange, Johann Gottfried. *De Advocatis et Advocatiis Germanicis* (Leipzig, 1725).

Lauer, Philippe, ed. *Recueil des actes de Charles III le Simple, Roi de France (893–923)* (Paris, 1949).

Lehmann, Rudolf, ed. *Quellen zur Geschichte der Niederlausitz*. Vol. 1 (Cologne and Vienna, 1972).

Leo IX, Pope. *Epistolae et Decreta Pontificia*. In *Patrologia Latina*, ed. J.-P. Migne. Vol. 143 (Paris, 1882), cols. 591–798.

Lesort, André, ed. *Chronique et chartes de l'abbaye de Saint-Mihiel* (Paris, 1909–12).

Levillain, Léon, ed. *Recueil des actes de Pépin Ier et de Pépin II rois d'Aquitaine (814–848)* (Paris, 1926).

Lex familiae Wormatiensis ecclesie. Ed. Lorenz Weinrich. In *Quellen zur deutschen Verfassungs-, Wirtschafts- und Sozialgeschichte bis 1250* (Darmstadt, 1977), pp. 88–105.

Lexicon Juridicum Romano-Teutonicum. Ed. Samuel Oberländer and Rainer Polley, 4th ed. (Nuremberg, 1753; repr. Cologne, Weimar and Vienna, 2000).

Libanius. *Selected Orations*. Trans. A. F. Norman. 2 vols. (Cambridge, MA and London, 1969–77).

The Liber Augustalis, or Constitutions of Melfi. Trans. James M. Powell (Syracuse, NY, 1971).

Liber Memorialis von Remiremont. Ed. Eduard Hlawitschka, Karl Schmid and Gerd Tellenbach. 2 vols. MGH Libri Memoriales 1 (Dublin and Zurich, 1970).

The Life of Hildegard. Trans. Anna Silvas. In *Jutta and Hildegard: The Biographical Sources* (University Park, PA, 1998), pp. 118–210.

The Life of Pope Leo IX. Trans. Ian Stuart Robinson. In *The Papal Reform of the Eleventh Century: Lives of Pope Leo IX and Pope Gregory VII* (Manchester and New York, 2004), pp. 97–157.

Lippert, Woldemar, ed. *Urkundenbuch der Stadt Lübben*. Vol. 3 (Dresden, 1933).

Livländische Reimchronik. Ed. Leo Meyer (Paderborn, 1876).

A Local Society in Transition: The Henryków Book and Related Documents. Trans. Piotr Górecki (Toronto, 2007).

Lorenz, Hermann, ed. *Quellen zur städtischen Verwaltungs-, Rechts- und Wirtschaftsgeschichte von Quedlinburg vom 15. Jahrhundert bis zur Zeit Friedrichs des Grossen*. Vol. 1 (Halle, 1916).

Das Lübecker Niederstadtbuch (1363–1399). Vol. 1. Ed. Ulrich Simon (Cologne, Weimar and Vienna, 2006).

Der Ludus de Antichristo. Ed. Friedrich Wilhelm (Munich, 1912).

Lupold of Bebenburg. *Libellus de Zelo Christiane Religionis Veterum Principum Germanorum*. Ed. Jürgen Miethke and Christoph Flüeler. In MGH Staatsschriften 4 (Hanover, 2004), pp. 411–505.

   Tractatus de Iuribus Regni et Imperii. Ed. Jürgen Miethke and Christoph Flüeler. In MGH Staatsschriften 4 (Hanover, 2004), pp. 233–409.

Mai, Hardo-Paul, ed. *Die Traditionen, die Urkunden und das älteste Urbarfragment des Stiftes Rohr, 1133–1332* (Munich, 1966).

Mainzer Urkundenbuch. Ed. Peter Acht and Manfred Stimming. 2 vols. (Darmstadt, 1932–71).

Marculfi Formulae. Ed. Karl Zeumer. In MGH Leges: Formulae. (Hanover, 1886), pp. 32–106.

Metellus of Tegernsee. *Die Quirinalien des Metellus von Tegernsee: Untersuchungen zur Dichtkunst und kritische Textausgabe*. Ed. Peter Christian Jacobsen (Leiden and Cologne, 1965).

Miracles de Saint Gorgon. Ed. and trans. Monique Goullet, Michel Parisse and Anne Wagner. In *Sources hagiographiques de l'histoire de Gorze (Xᵉ siècle)* (Paris, 2010), pp. 152–203.

Miracula in Monasterio Rastedensi Acta. Ed. Georg Waitz. In MGH SS 25 (Hanover, 1880), pp. 513–14.

Miracula Sancti Benedicti: Les Miracles de Saint Benoît. Trans. and ed. Anselme Davril, Annie Dufour and Gillette Labory (Paris, 2019).

Monumenta Boica. Vol. 11 (Munich, 1771).

Monumenta Vizeliacensia: Textes relatifs à l'histoire de l'abbaye de Vézelay. Ed. R. B. C. Huygens (Turnhout, 1976).

Das Nibelungenlied: I. Teil. Ed. Helmut Brackert (Frankfurt and Hamburg, 1970).

Niederösterreichisches Urkundenbuch. Ed. Roman Zehetmayer, Dagmar Weltin and Maximilian Weltin. Vol. 2 (St. Pölten, 2013).

Niklaus Gerung (Blauenstein). "Flores Temporum 1417–1475." In *Basler Chroniken*, ed. August Bernoulli. Vol. 7 (Leipzig, 1915), pp. 38–74.

Notker the Stammerer. *The Deeds of Emperor Charles the Great*. In *Charlemagne and Louis the Pious*, trans. Thomas F. X. Noble (University Park, PA, 2009), pp. 51–118.

  Karoli Magni Imperatoris. Ed. Hans F. Haefele. MGH SSrG NS 12 (Berlin, 1959).

Oediger, Friedrich Wilhelm, ed. *Die Regesten der Erzbischöfe von Köln im Mittelalter*. Vol. 1 (Bonn, 1954–61).

Otto of Freising. *Chronica sive Historia de Duabus Civitatibus*. Ed. Adolf Hofmeister. In MGH SSrG 45 (Hanover and Leipzig, 1912).

  The Two Cities. Trans. Charles Christopher Mierow (New York, 2002).

Otto of Freising, and Rahewin. *The Deeds of Frederick Barbarossa*. Trans. Charles Christopher Mierow (New York, 2004).

  Gesta Friderici I. Imperatoris. Ed. Georg Waitz and Bernhard von Simson. In MGH SSrG 46 (Hanover, 1997).

Pahud, Alexandre, ed. *Le cartulaire de Romainmôtier (XIIe siècle): Introduction et édition critique* (Lausanne, 1998).

Parisse, Michel, ed. and trans. *La vie de Jean, abbé de Gorze* (Paris, 1999).

Passio Secunda Sancti Quirini. Ed. Johann Weissensteiner. In *Tegernsee, die Bayern und Österreich: Studien zu Tegernseer Geschichtsquellen und der bayerischen Stammessage* (Vienna, 1983), pp. 247–87.

Pfettesheim, Conradus. *Geschichte Peter Hagenbachs und der Burgunderkriege*. Ed. Rolf Müller and Lilli Fischel. 2 vols. (Plochingen, 1966).

Piccolomini, Eneas Silvius. *Europe (c. 1400–1458)*. Trans. Robert D. Brown (Washington, DC, 2013).

  Historia Austrialis. Ed. Julia Knödler and Martin Wagendorfer. In MGH SSrG NS 24. 2 vols. (Hanover, 2009).

  Pentalogus. Ed. Christoph Schingnitz. In MGH Staatsschriften 8 (Hanover, 2009).

I placiti del "Regnum Italiae." Vol. 1. Ed. Cesare Manaresi (Rome, 1955).

The Play of Antichrist. Trans. John Wright (Toronto, 1967).

Poupardin, René, ed. *Recueil des chartes de l'abbaye de Saint-Germain-des-Prés des origines au début des XIIIᵉ siècle*. Vol. 1 (Paris, 1909).

Pradié, Pascal, ed. *Chronique des abbés de Fontenelle (Saint-Wandrille)* (Paris, 1999).

Preussisches Urkundenbuch. Vols. 2 and 4. Ed. Max Hein, Erich Maschke and Hans Koeppen (Königsberg, 1932–39 and Marburg, 1960).

Prou, Maurice, ed. *Recueil des actes de Philippe Iᵉʳ, roi de France (1059–1108)* (Paris, 1908).

Prou, Maurice, and Alexandre Vidier, eds. *Recueil des chartes de l'abbaye de Saint-Benoît-sur-Loire*. Vol. 1 (Paris, 1900–7).

Das Prümer Urbar. Ed. Ingo Schwab (Düsseldorf, 1983).

Das Register Gregors VII. Ed. Erich Caspar. 2 vols. In MGH Epp. sel. 2 (Berlin, 1920–3).

Raab, Isidor, ed. *Urkundenbuch des Benedictiner-Stiftes Seitenstetten*. Fontes Rerum Austriacarum, II.33 (Vienna, 1870).

Raoul of St. Trond. *Epistulae*. Ed. Paul Tombeur. Corpus Christianorum Continuatio Medieavalis 257 (Turnhout, 2013).

Ratpert. *St. Galler Klostergeschichten (Casus sancti Galli)*. Ed. Hannes Steiner. MGH SSrG 75 (Hanover, 2002).

Raumer, Georg Wilhelm von, ed. *Codex diplomaticus Brandenburgensis continuatus: Sammlung ungedruckter Urkunden zur Brandenburgischen Geschichte*. 2 vols. (Berlin, Stettin and Elbing, 1831).

Rechtfertigungsschrift des Rates. Ed. Michael Hofmann and Jens Kunze. In *1407: Rat kontra Landesherr?*, ed. Wilfried Stoye and Silva Teichert (Zwickau, 2011), pp. 290–310.

Recueil des actes de Louis VI roi de France (1108–1137). Ed. Jean Dufour. 2 vols. (Paris, 1992).

Recueil des actes de Robert 1ᵉʳ et de Raoul rois de France (922–936). Ed. Jean Dufour (Paris, 1978).

Redlich, Oswald, ed. *Die Traditionsbücher des Hochstifts Brixen vom 10. bis in das 14. Jahrhundert* (Innsbruck, 1886).

Reformation Kaiser Siegmunds. Ed. Heinrich Koller. MGH Staatsschriften 6 (Stuttgart, 1964).

Regestum Innocentii III papae super negotio Romani imperii. Ed. Friedrich Kempf (Rome, 1947).

Regino of Prüm. *De Ecclesiasticis Disciplinis*. In *Patrologia Latina*, edited by J.-P. Migne, Vol. 132 (Paris, 1880), cols. 175–400.

Registrum Domini Advocati Cracoviensis 1442–1443 [Księga Wójtowska Krakowska 1442–1443]. Ed. Mieczysław Niwiński, Krystyna Jelonek-Litewka and Aleksander Litewka (Krakow, 1995).

Rheinisches Urkundenbuch: Ältere Urkunden bis 1100. Ed. Erich Wisplinghoff. Vol. 2 (Düsseldorf, 1994).

Richard fitzNigel. *Dialogus de Scaccario: The Dialogue of the Exchequer*. Ed. Emilie Amt (Oxford, 2007).

Richer of Saint-Rémi. *Historiae*. Ed. Hartmut Hoffmann. MGH SS 38 (Hanover, 2000).

Riedel, Adolph Friedrich, ed. *Codex Diplomaticus Brandenburgensis*. Part 2, vols. 4–5 (Berlin, 1847–8).

Roland, C.-G., ed. *Recueil des chartes de l'Abbaye de Gembloux* (Gembloux, 1921).

Das Rolandslied des Pfaffen Konrad. Ed. Carl Wesle, 3rd ed. (Tübingen, 1985).

Rosenfeld, Felix, and Hans K. Schulze, eds. *Urkundenbuch des Hochstifts Naumburg*. 2 vols. (Magdeburg, 1925–2000).

Roth, Charles, ed. *Cartulaire du Chapitre de Notre-Dame de Lausanne*. Vol. 1 (Lausanne, 1948).

Rothe, Johann. *Düringische Chronik*. Ed. R. v. Liliencron (Jena, 1859).

Rufinus of Bologna. *Summa Decretorum*. Ed. Heinrich Singer (Paderborn, 1902; repr. Aalen, 1963).

Salbuch des Stiftes Niedermünster in Regensburg. Ed. Franz Christian Höger (Landshut, 1888).

Salzburger Urkundenbuch. Ed. Willibald Hauthaler. Vol. 1 (Salzburg, 1910).

Saxo Grammaticus. *Gesta Danorum: The History of the Danes*. Ed. Karsten Friis-Jensen. Vol. 1 (Oxford, 2015).

Schiller, Friedrich. *Wilhelm Tell: Schauspiel*. In *Schillers Werke: Nationalausgabe*, ed. Siegfried Seidel. Vol. 10 (Weimar, 1980), pp. 127–277.

Schlesisches Urkundenbuch. Vol. 1. Ed. Heinrich Appelt (Vienna, Cologne and Graz, 1971).

Schleswig-Holsteinische Regesten und Urkunden. Ed. Wolfgang Prange. Vol. 13 (Neumünster, 1994).

Schlögl, Waldemar, ed. *Die Traditionen und Urkunden des Stiftes Diessen 1114–1362* (Munich, 1967).

Schmidt, Berthold, ed. *Urkundenbuch der Vögte von Weida, Gera und Plauen*. 2 vols. (Jena, 1885–92).

Schnurrer, Ludwig, ed. *Die Urkunden der Reichsstadt Rothenburg 1182–1400*. Vol. 1 (Neustadt and Aisch, 1999).

Schöpflin, Johann Daniel, ed. *Alsatia Aevi Merovingici, Carolingici, Saxonici, Salici, Suevici Diplomatica*. Vol. 1 (Mannheim, 1772).

Schrötter, Georg, ed. *Urkundenbuch der Benediktiner-Abtei St. Stephan in Würzburg*. Vol. 2 (Würzburg, 1932).

Sigeberti Gemblacensis Chronica cum Continuationibus. Ed. L. C. Bethmann. In MGH SS 6 (Hanover, 1844), pp. 268–474.

Simon of Ghent. *Gesta Abbatum Sancti Bertini Sithiensium*. In MGH SS 13. Ed. Oswald Holder-Egger (Hanover, 1881), pp. 635–63.

Solothurner Urkundenbuch. Ed. Ambros Kocher. Vol. 1 (Solothurn, 1952).

Sonzogni, Daniel, ed. *Les actes du fonds d'archives de Saint-Denis, VIe–Xe siècle: étude critique et catalogue raisonné*. Vol. 1 (Paris, 2015).

Stengel, Edmund Ernst, ed. *Urkundenbuch des Klosters Fulda*. Vol. 1 (Marburg, 1958).

Stephan, Michael, ed. *Die Urkunden und die ältesten Urbare des Klosters Scheyern* (Munich, 1988).

Summa "Omnis qui iuste iudicat" sive Lipsiensis. Ed. Rudolf Weigand, Peter Landau and Waltraud Kozur. 3 vols. (Vatican City, 2007–10).

Die Tegernseer Briefsammlung des 12. Jahrhunderts. Ed. Helmut Plechl. MGH Die Briefe der deutschen Kaiserzeit 8 (Hanover, 2002).

Tessier, Georges, ed. *Recueil des actes de Charles II le Chauve, Roi de France*. 3 vols. (Paris, 1943–55).

The Theodosian Code and Novels and the Sirmondian Constitutions. Trans. Clyde Pharr (Princeton, NJ, 1952).

Theodosiani Libri XVI cum Constitutionibus Sirmondianis et Leges novellae ad Theodosianum pertinentes. Ed. Theodor Mommsen and Paul M. Meyer (Berlin, 1905).

Thiel, Matthias, and Odilo Engels, eds. *Die Traditionen, Urkunden und Urbare des Klosters Münchsmünster* (Munich, 1961).

Thietmar of Merseburg. *Chronik.* Ed. Werner Trillmich (9th ed., Darmstadt, 2011). *Ottonian Germany: The Chronicon of Thietmar of Merseburg.* Trans. David Warner (Manchester and New York, 2001).

Thommen, Rudolf, ed. *Urkunden zur Schweizer Geschichte aus österreichischen Archiven.* Vol. 2 (Basel, 1900).

Tiroler Urkundenbuch. Section 1, vol. 3. Ed. Franz Huter (Innsbruck, 1957).

Tock, Benoît-Michel, ed. *Les chartes de l'abbaye cistercienne de Vaucelles au XIIe siècle* (Turnhout, 2010).

Toepfer, Friedrich, ed. *Urkundenbuch für die Geschichte des graeflichen und freiherrlichen Hauses der Voegte von Hunolstein.* 3 vols. (Nuremberg, 1866–72).

Die Traditionen des Hochstifts Freising. Ed. Theodor Bitterauf. 2 vols. (Munich, 1905–1909; repr. Aalen, 1967).

Traditiones Wizenburgenses: Die Urkunden des Klosters Weissenburg, 661–864. Ed. Anton Doll (Darmstadt, 1979).

Triumphus Sancti Remacli de Malmundariensi coenobio. Ed. Wilhelm Wattenbach. In MGH SS 11 (Hanover, 1854), pp. 433–61.

Tschudi, Aegidius. *Chronicon Helveticum.* Ed. Bernhard Stettler. Quellenwerk zur Entstehung der Schweizerischen Eidgenossenschaft, Neue Folge, Part 1, vol. 7.3 (Bern, 1980).

Die Urkunden Arnolfs. Ed. Paul Kehr. MGH DD Deutsche Karolinger 3 (Berlin, 1940).

Die Urkunden der Arnulfinger. Ed. Ingrid Heidrich. MGH DD (Hanover 2011).

Die Urkunden der burgundischen Rudolfinger. Ed. Theodor Schieffer. MGH DD (Munich, 1977).

Die Urkunden Friedrichs I. Ed. Heinrich Appelt. 5 vols. MGH DD Deutsche Könige und Kaiser 10 (Hanover, 1975–1990).

Die Urkunden Friedrichs II. Ed. Walter Koch et al. 6 vols. MGH DD Deutsche Könige und Kaiser 14 (Hanover, 2002–2021).

Die Urkunden Heinrich Raspes und Wilhelms von Holland. Ed. Dieter Hägermann and Jaap G. Kruisheer. 2 vols. MGH DD Deutsche Könige und Kaiser 18 (Hanover, 1989–2006).

Die Urkunden Heinrichs des Löwen. Ed. Karl Jordan. MGH DD Laienfürsten und Dynastenurkunden 1 (Leipzig, 1949).

Die Urkunden Heinrichs II. und Arduins. Ed. Harry Bresslau et al. MGH DD Deutsche Könige und Kaiser 3 (Hanover 1900–1903).

Die Urkunden Heinrichs III. Ed. Harry Bresslau and Paul Kehr. MGH DD Deutsche Könige und Kaiser 5 (Berlin, 1931).

Die Urkunden Heinrichs IV. Ed. Dietrich von Gladiss and Alfred Gawlik. 3 vols. MGH DD Deutsche Könige und Kaiser 6 (Berlin, Weimar and Hanover, 1941–1978).

Die Urkunden Heinrichs V. und der Königin Mathilde. Ed. Matthias Thiel et al. MGH DD Deutsche Könige und Kaiser 7. Online Pre-edition at www.mgh.de.

Die Urkunden Heinrichs VI. und der Kaiserin Konstanze. Ed. Heinrich Appelt et al. MGH DD Deutsche Könige und Kaiser 11. Online Pre-edition at www.mgh.de.

Die Urkunden Konrad I., Heinrich I. und Otto I. Ed. Theodor von Sickel. MGH DD Deutsche Könige und Kaiser 1 (Hanover, 1879–1884).

Die Urkunden Konrads II. Ed. Harry Bresslau. MGH DD Deutsche Könige und Kaiser 4 (Hanover and Leipzig, 1909).

Die Urkunden Konrads III. und seines Sohnes Heinrich. Ed. Friedrich Hausmann. MGH DD Deutsche Könige und Kaiser 9 (Vienna, Cologne and Graz, 1969).

Die Urkunden Lothars I. und Lothars II. Ed. Theodor Schieffer. MGH DD Karolinger 3 (Berlin and Zurich, 1966).

Die Urkunden Lothars III. und der Kaiserin Richenza. Ed. Emil von Ottenthal and Hans Hirsch. MGH DD Deutsche Könige und Kaiser 8 (Berlin, 1927).

Die Urkunden Ludwigs II. Ed. Konrad Wanner. MGH DD Karolinger 4 (Munich, 1994).

Die Urkunden Ludwigs des Deutschen, Karlmanns und Ludwigs des Jüngeren. Ed. Paul Kehr. MGH DD Deutsche Karolinger 1 (Berlin, 1934).

Die Urkunden Ludwigs des Frommen. Ed. Theo Kölzer. 2 vols. MGH DD Karolinger 2 (Wiesbaden, 2016).

Die Urkunden der Merowinger. Ed. Theo Kölzer. 2 vols. MGH DD (Hanover, 2001).

Die Urkunden Otto des II. Ed. Theodor von Sickel. MGH DD Deutsche Könige und Kaiser 2:1 (Hanover, 1888).

Die Urkunden Otto des III. Ed. Theodor von Sickel. MGH DD Deutsche Könige und Kaiser 2:2 (Hanover, 1893).

Die Urkunden Philipps von Schwaben. Ed. Andrea Rzihacek and Renate Spreitzer. MGH DD Deutsche Könige und Kaiser 12 (Wiesbaden, 2014).

Die Urkunden und Briefe der Markgräfin Mathilde von Tuszien. Ed. Elke Goez and Werner Goez. MGH DD Laienfürsten und Dynastenurkunden 2 (Hanover, 1998).

Die Urkunden Zwentibolds und Ludwigs des Kindes. Ed. Theodor Schieffer. MGH DD Deutsche Karolinger 4 (Berlin, 1960).

Urkundenbuch der Abtei Sanct Gallen. Ed. Hermann Wartmann, Placid Bütler, Traugott Schiess, Paul Staerkle and Joseph Müller. 6 vols. (Zurich and St. Gall, 1863–1955).

Urkundenbuch der Stadt Halberstadt. Ed. Gustav Schmidt. Vol. 2 (Halle, 1879).

Urkundenbuch der Stadt Lübeck. Ed. Johann Friedrich Böhmer and Friedrich Techen. 11 vols. (Lübeck, 1843–1905).

Urkundenbuch der Stadt Quedlinburg. Ed. Karl Janicke. Vol. 2 (Halle, 1882).

Urkundenbuch der Stadt Strassburg. Ed. Wilhelm Wiegand et al. 7 vols. (Strassbourg, 1879–1900).

Urkundenbuch der Stadt Zwickau. Ed. Jens Kunze and Henning Steinführer. CDS II:20–21 (Hanover and Peine, 2012–14).

Urkundenbuch des Hochstifts Halberstadt und seiner Bischöfe. Ed. Gustav Schmidt. Vols. 1 and 4 (Leipzig, 1883 and 1889).

Urkundenbuch des Hochstifts Hildesheim und seiner Bischöfe. Ed. Karl Janicke. Vol. 1 (Leipzig, 1896).

Urkundenbuch des Klosters Frauensee 1202–1540. Ed. Waldemar Küther (Cologne and Graz, 1961).

Urkundenbuch des Stiftes Fischbeck. Ed. Heinrich Lathwesen and Brigitte Poschmann. 2 vols. (Rinteln, 1978–79).

Urkundenbuch zur Geschichte der Babenberger in Österreich. Ed. Heinrich Fichtenau et al. 4 vols. (Vienna and Munich, 1950–97).

Das Urner Tellenspiel. Ed. Max Wehrli. Quellenwerk zur Entstehung der Schweizerischen Eidgenossenschaft, Part 3, vol. 2.1 (Aarau, 1952), pp. 55–99.

Van Mingroot, Erik, ed. *Les chartes de Gérard Ier, Liébert et Gérard II, évêques de Cambrai et d'Arras, comtes du Cambrésis (1012–1092/93)* (Leuven, 2005).

Vita Annonis minor/Die jüngere Annovita. Ed. Mauritius Mittler (Siegburg, 1975).

Vita Annonis Archiepiscopi Coloniensis. Ed. Rudolf Koepke. In MGH SS 11 (Hanover, 1854), pp. 462–518.

Vita Meinwerci Episcopi Patherbrunnensis: Text, Übersetzung, Kommentar. Ed. Guido M. Berndt (Munich, 2009).

Vita Sanctae Hildegardis. Ed. Monica Klaes (Turnhout, 1993).

"Die Vogteirollen des Stiftes Essen." Ed. Moritz zu Bentheim Tecklenburg Rheda. In *Die Geschichte der Grafen und Herren von Limburg und Limburg-Styrum und ihrer Besitzungen.* Vol. 4 (Assen and Münster, 1968), pp. 16–41.

Walther von der Vogelweide. *Sämtliche Lieder.* Ed. Friedrich Maurer (Munich, 1972).

Wampach, Camille, ed. *Geschichte der Grundherrschaft Echternach im Frühmittelalter. Quellenband* (Luxembourg, 1930).

——— ed. *Urkunden- und Quellenbuch zur Geschichte der altluxemburgischen Territorien bis zur burgundischen Zeit.* Vol. 1 (Luxembourg, 1935).

Weinrich, Lorenz, ed. *Quellen zur deutschen Verfassungs-, Wirtschafts- und Sozialgeschichte bis 1250* (Darmstadt, 1977).

Das Weiße Buch von Sarnen. Ed. Hans Georg Wirz. In *Quellenwerk zur Entstehung der Schweizerischen Eidgenossenschaft,* Vol. 3:1 (Aarau, 1947).

Weissthanner, Alois, ed. *Die Urkunden und Urbare des Klosters Schäftlarn* (Munich, 1957).

Westfälisches Urkunden-Buch. Ed. Heinrich Finke and Theodor Ilgen. Vols. 5 and 7 (Münster, 1888 and 1908).

Wibald of Stablo. *Das Briefbuch Abt Wibalds von Stablo und Corvey.* Ed. Martina Hartmann. 3 vols. MGH Briefe der deutschen Kaiserzeit 9 (Hanover, 2012).

Widemann, Josef, ed. *Die Traditionen des Hochstifts Regensburg und des Klosters S. Emmeram* (Munich, 1943; repr. Aalen, 1969).

Widukind of Corvey. *Rerum Gestarum Saxonicarum Libri Tres (Sachsengeschichte).* Ed. Georg Waitz, Karl Andreas Kehr, Paul Hirsch and Hans-Eberhard Lohmann. MGH SSrG 60, 5th ed. (Hanover, 1935).

Wisplinghoff, Erich, ed. *Urkunden und Quellen zur Geschichte von Stadt und Abtei Siegburg.* Vol. 1 (Siegburg, 1964).

Wohlgegründete Anmerckungen Auf die In Druck gegebene Allerunterthänigste Fernere Anzeige und Exceptiones Nullitatis, ... (1701; digitized by the Universitäts- und Landesbibliothek Sachsen-Anhalt).

Zimmermann, Harald, ed. *Papsturkunden 896–1046.* Vol. 2 (Vienna, 1985).

Die Zwiefalter Chroniken Ortliebs und Bertholds. Ed. Luitpold Wallach, Erich König and Karl Otto Müller (Sigmaringen, 1978).

Secondary Sources

Acht, Peter. "Die Tegernseer-Ebersberger Vogteifälschungen." *Archivalische Zeitschrift* 47 (1951): 135–88.

Adams, Julia. *The Familial State: Ruling Families and Merchant Capitalism in Early Modern Europe* (Ithaca, NY and London, 2005).

Ahram, Ariel, and Charles King. "The Warlord as Arbitrageur." *Theory and Society* 41 (2012): 169–86.

Airlie, Stuart. "The Aristocracy in the Service of the State in the Carolingian Period." In *Staat im frühen Mittelalter*, ed. Stuart Airlie, Walter Pohl and Helmut Reimitz (Vienna, 2006), pp. 93–111.

Albertoni, Giuseppe. "Mit dem Evangelium und dem Schild: Anmerkungen zur Rolle der Vögte im hochmittelalterlichen Italien." In *Kirchenvogtei und adlige Herrschaftsbildung*, pp. 329–43.

Algazi, Gadi. *Herrengewalt und Gewalt der Herren im späten Mittelalter* (Frankfurt and New York, 1996).

Althoff, Gerd. *Die Ottonen: Königsherrschaft ohne Staat*, 3rd ed. (Stuttgart, 2013).

——— "Gandersheim und Quedlinburg: Ottonische Frauenklöster als Herrschafts- und Überlieferungszentren." *Frühmittelalterliche Studien* 25 (1991): 123–44.

Amt, Emilie M. "The Reputation of the Sheriff, 1100–1216." *Haskins Society Journal* 8 (1996): 91–98.

Andermann, Kurt. "Aspekte von Kirchenvogtei und adliger Herrschaftsbildung im spätmittelalterlichen Südwestdeutschland." In *Kirchenvogtei und adlige Herrschaftsbildung*, pp. 197–223.

——— "Grundherrschaften des spätmittelalterlichen Niederadels in Südwestdeutschland. Zur Frage der Gewichtung von Geld- und Naturaleinkünften." *Blätter für deutsche Landesgeschichte* 127 (1991): 145–90.

Andermann, Kurt, and Enno Bünz. "Kirchenvogtei und adlige Herrschaftsbildung im europäischen Mittelalter: Eine Einführung." In *Kirchenvogtei und adlige Herrschaftsbildung*, pp. 9–20.

Andermann, Ulrich. "Die Verschwörung gegen Engelbert I. von Köln am 7. November 1225 und ihre Folgen." In *AufRuhr 1225!*, pp. 35–46.

Anderson, Perry. *Passages from Antiquity to Feudalism* (London and New York, 1978).

Anticorruption in History: From Antiquity to the Modern Era. Ed. Ronald Kroeze, André Vitória and G. Geltner (Oxford, 2018).

Arias, Enrique Desmond. "The Dynamics of Criminal Governance: Networks and Social Order in Rio de Janeiro." *Journal of Latin American Studies* 38 (2006): 293–325.

Arnold, Benjamin. *Count and Bishop in Medieval Germany: A Study of Regional Power, 1100–1350* (Philadelphia, PA, 1991).

Medieval Germany, 500–1300: A Political Interpretation (Toronto and Buffalo, 1997).

Princes and Territories in Medieval Germany (Cambridge, UK, 1991).

Arnstedt, Friedrich Adrian von. "Schirmvogtei über das Stift und die Stadt Quedlinburg." *Zeitschrift des Harzvereins für Geschichte und Alterthumskunde* 4 (1871): 169–208.

Asbridge, Thomas S. *The First Crusade: A New History* (Oxford and New York, 2004).

Aubin, Hermann. *Die Entstehung der Landeshoheit nach niederrheinischen Quellen. Studien über Grafschaft, Immunität und Vogtei* (Berlin, 1920).

"Immunität und Vogteigerichtsbarkeit." *Vierteljahrschrift für Sozial- und Wirtschaftsgeschichte* 12 (1914): 241–57.

AufRuhr 1225! Ritter, Burgen und Intrigen: Das Mittelalter an Rhein und Ruhr. Ed. Tim Bunte and Brunhilde Leenen (Mainz, 2010).

Auge, Oliver. *Handlungsspielräume fürstlicher Politik im Mittelalter: Der südliche Ostseeraum von der Mitte des 12. Jahrhunderts bis in die frühe Reformationszeit* (Ostfildern, 2009).

"*Hominium, Tributum, Feudum*. Zu den Anfängen des Lehnswesens im Nordosten des Reiches bis 1250." In *Das Lehnswesen im Hochmittelalter*, pp. 195–215.

Averkorn, Raphaela. "Die Bischöfe von Halberstadt in ihrem kirchlichen und politischen Wirken und in ihren Beziehungen zur Stadt von den Anfängen bis zur Reformation." In *Bürger, Bettelmönche und Bischöfe in Halberstadt*, ed. Dieter Berg (Werl, 1997), pp. 1–79.

L'Avouerie en Lotharingie. Actes des 2es Journées Lotharingiennes (Luxembourg, 1984).

Baaken, Katrin. "Verlorene Papst- und Kaiserurkunden für Kloster St. Jakob zu Pegau." DA 44 (1988): 544–61.

Bachrach, David S. "The Benefices of Counts and the Fate of the Comital Office in Carolingian East Francia and Ottonian Germany." *ZRG GA* 136 (2019): 1–50.

"Exercise of Royal Power in Early Medieval Europe: The Case of Otto the Great 936–73." *Early Medieval Europe* 17 (2009): 389–419.

"Inquisitio as a Tool of Royal Governance under the Carolingian and Ottonian Kings." *ZRG GA* 133 (2016): 1–80.

Bågenholm, Andreas. "Corruption and Anticorruption in Early-Nineteenth-Century Sweden: A Snapshot of the State of the Swedish Bureaucracy." In *Anticorruption in History*, pp. 239–50.

Bailyn, Bernard. "Politics and Social Structure in Virginia." In *Seventeenth-Century America: Essays in Colonial History*, ed. James Morton Smith (Chapel Hill, 1959), pp. 90–115.

Baldwin, John W. *The Government of Philip Augustus: Foundations of French Royal Power in the Middle Ages* (Berkeley, Los Angeles and Oxford, 1986).

Balzer, Manfred. "Vornehm – reich – klug: Herkunft, Königsdienst und Güterpolitik Bischof Meinwerks." In *Für Königtum und Himmelreich: 1000*

Jahre Bischof Meinwerk von Paderborn, ed. Christoph Stiegemann and Martin Kroker (Regensburg, 2009), pp. 88–99.

Barraclough, Geoffrey. *The Origins of Modern Germany*, 2nd ed. (Oxford, 1947).

Barreyre, Nicolas, and Claire Lemercier. "The Unexceptional State: Rethinking the State in the Nineteenth Century (France, United States)." *AHR* 126 (2021): 481–503.

Barrow, Julia. "Ideas and Applications of Reform." In *The Cambridge History of Christianity*, vol. 3, ed. Julia M. H. Smith and Thomas F. X. Noble (Cambridge, 2008), pp. 345–62.

Barth, Rüdiger E. *Der Herzog in Lotharingien im 10. Jahrhundert* (Sigmaringen, 1990).

Barthélemy, Dominique. *Chevaliers et miracles: La violence et le sacré dans la société féodale* (Paris, 2004).

"Debate: The 'Feudal Revolution.'" *Past and Present* 152 (1996): 196–205.

The Serf, the Knight, and the Historian. Trans. Graham Robert Edwards (Ithaca, NY and London, 2009).

Bartlett, Robert. "The Impact of Royal Government in the French Ardennes: The Evidence of the 1247 *Enquête*." *Journal of Medieval History* 7 (1981): 83–96.

The Making of Europe: Conquest, Colonization, and Cultural Change, 950–1350 (Princeton, NJ, 1993).

Barton, Richard E. *Lordship in the County of Maine, c. 890–1160* (Woodbridge, 2004).

Beach, Alison I. *The Trauma of Monastic Reform: Community and Conflict in Twelfth-Century Germany* (Cambridge, UK, 2017).

Becker, Anton, and Artur Maria Scheiber. *Zur Landeskunde des Raumes von Strengberg in Niederösterreich* (Vienna, 1946).

Becker, Jan-Erik. "Die Pegauer Brakteatenprägung Abt Siegfrieds von Rekkin (1185–1223): Kriterien zu deren chronologischer Einordnung." In *Proceedings of the XIVth International Numismatic Congress*, ed. Nicholas Holmes (Glasgow, 2011), pp. 1372–81.

Bedos-Rezak, Brigitte. "Diplomatic Sources and Medieval Documentary Practices: An Essay in Interpretative Methodology." In *The Past and Future of Medieval Studies*, ed. John Van Engen (Notre Dame and London, 1994), pp. 313–43.

Below, Georg von. *Der deutsche Staat des Mittelalters: Ein Grundriß der deutschen Verfassungsgeschichte* (Leipzig, 1914).

Berkhofer, Robert F. *Day of Reckoning: Power and Accountability in Medieval France* (Philadelphia, PA, 2004).

Bernard, G. W. "'A Water-Spout Springing from the Rock of Freedom'? Corruption in Sixteenth- and Early-Seventeenth-Century England." In *Anticorruption in History*, pp. 125–38.

Berner, Alexander. *Kreuzzug und regionale Herrschaft: Die älteren Grafen von Berg 1147–1225* (Cologne, Weimar and Vienna, 2014).

Bernhardt, John W. *Itinerant Kingship and Royal Monasteries in Early Medieval Germany, c. 936–1075* (Cambridge, UK, 1993).

Bertrand, Paul. *Documenting the Everyday in Medieval Europe: The Social Dimensions of a Writing Revolution, 1250–1350.* Trans. Graham Robert Edwards (Turnhout, 2019).

Beumann, Helmut, and Walter Schlesinger. "Urkundenstudien zur deutschen Ostpolitik unter Otto III." *Archiv für Diplomatik* 1 (1955): 132–256.

Bierbrauer, Katharina. *Die vorkarolingischen und karolingischen Handschriften der Bayerischen Staatsbibliothek.* 2 vols. (Wiesbaden, 1990).

Bijsterveld, Arnoud-Jan A. "Conflict and Compromise: The Premonstratentians of Ninove (Flanders) and the Laity in the Twelfth Century." In *Negotiating Secular and Ecclesiastical Power,* ed. Arnoud-Jan A. Bijsterveld, Henk Teunis and Andrew Wareham (Turnhout, 1999), pp. 167–83.

Billig, Gerhard. *Pleissenland–Vogtland: Das Reich und die Vögte* (Plauen, 2002).

Billings, Warren M. "The Growth of Political Institutions in Virginia, 1634 to 1676." *William and Mary Quarterly* 31 (1974): 225–42.

Bischoff, Bernhard. *Manuscripts and Libraries in the Age of Charlemagne.* Trans. Michael M. Gorman (Cambridge, UK and New York, 1994).

Bisson, Thomas N. *The Crisis of the Twelfth Century: Power, Lordship, and the Origins of European Government* (Princeton, NJ and Oxford, 2009).

"Debate: The 'Feudal Revolution' (Reply)." *Past and Present* 155 (1997): 208–25.

"The 'Feudal Revolution.'" *Past and Present* 142 (1994): 6–42.

"Medieval Lordship." *Speculum* 70 (1995): 743–59.

Tormented Voices: Power, Crisis, and Humanity in Rural Catalonia, 1140–1200 (Cambridge, MA and London, 1998).

Bittmann, Markus. *Kreditwirtschaft und Finanzierungsmethoden: Studien zu den wirtschaftlichen Verhältnissen des Adels im westlichen Bodenseeraum 1300–1500* (Stuttgart, 1991).

Blaydes, Lisa, and Eric Chaney. "The Feudal Revolution and Europe's Rise: Political Divergence of the Christian West and the Muslim World before 1500 CE." *American Political Science Review* 107 (2013): 16–34.

Blickle, Peter. *Von der Leibeigenschaft zu den Menschenrechten: Eine Geschichte der Freiheit in Deutschland* (Munich, 2003).

Bliujienė, Audronė. *Northern Gold: Amber in Lithuania (c. 100 to c. 1200)* (Leiden and Boston, 2011).

Bloch, Marc. *Feudal Society.* Trans. L. A. Manyon. 2 vols. (Chicago, 1961).

Bock, Günther. "Georg von Herwardeshude, Vogt zu Hamburg – Zur Frage der städtischen Führungsorgane im 13. Jahrhundert." *Zeitschrift des Vereins für Hamburgische Geschichte* 103 (2017): 1–34.

Bois, Guy. *The Transformation of the Year One Thousand: The Village of Lournand from Antiquity to Feudalism.* Trans. Jean Birrell (Manchester and New York, 1992).

Bond, Sarah E. "The Corrupting Sea: Law, Violence and Compulsory Professions in Late Antiquity." In *Anticorruption in History,* pp. 49–61.

Boone, Marc. "Cities in Late Medieval Europe: The Promise and the Curse of Modernity." *Urban History* 39 (2012): 329–49.

Borchardt, Karl. "Vögte, Truchsesse, Küchenmeister: Stauferzeitliche Ministerialen zwischen Rothenburg und Würzburg." In *Herbipolis. Studien zu Stadt und Hochstift Würzburg in Spätmittelalter und Früher Neuzeit*, ed. Dorothea Klein, Markus Frankl and Martina Hartmann (Würzburg, 2015), pp. 1–58.

"Vogtei und Schutz bei geistlichen Ritterorden des 12. und 13. Jahrhunderts." In *Kirchenvogtei und adlige Herrschaftsbildung*, pp. 87–141.

Borgolte, Michael. "Stiftergedenken in Kloster Dießen. Ein Beitrag zur Kritik bayerischer Traditionsbücher." *Frühmittelalterliche Studien* 24 (1990): 235–89.

Boshof, Egon. "Untersuchungen zur Kirchenvogtei in Lothringen im 10. und 11. Jahrhundert." *ZRG KA* 65 (1979): 55–119.

Bosl, Karl. "Ruler and Ruled in the German Empire from the Tenth to the Twelfth Century." Trans. Miriam Sambursky. In *Lordship and Community*, pp. 357–75.

"Schutz und Schirm, Rat und Hilfe als Voraussetzung von Steuer, Abgabe und Dienst im Mittelalter." In *Steuern, Abgaben und Dienste vom Mittelalter bis zur Gegenwart*, ed. Eckart Schremmer (Stuttgart, 1994), pp. 43–51.

Bouchard, Constance B. *Strong of Body, Brave and Noble: Chivalry and Society in Medieval France* (Ithaca, NY and London, 1998).

Sword, Miter, and Cloister: Nobility and the Church in Burgundy, 980–1198 (Ithaca, NY and London, 1987).

Bougard, François. "Public Power and Authority." In *Italy in the Early Middle Ages 476–1000*, ed. Cristina La Rocca (Oxford and New York, 2002), pp. 34–58.

Boussard, Jacques. "Actes royaux et pontificaux des Xe et XIe siècles, du chartrier de Saint-Maur des Fossés." *Journal des Savants* (no. 2, 1972): 81–113.

Brady, Thomas A. *German Histories in the Age of Reformations, 1400–1650* (Cambridge, UK, 2009).

Brandenburgisches Klosterbuch: Handbuch der Klöster, Stifte und Kommenden bis zur Mitte des 16. Jahrhunderts. Ed. Heinz-Dieter Heimann et al., 2 vols. (Berlin, 2007).

Brandt, Georg Wilhelm von. "Vogtei und Rektorat in Lübeck während des 13. Jahrhunderts." *Blätter für deutsche Landesgeschichte* 107 (1971): 162–201.

Bräuer, Helmut. *Wider den Rat: Der Zwickauer Konflikt 1516/17* (Leipzig, 1999).

Brauer-Gramm, Hildburg. *Der Landvogt Peter von Hagenbach* (Göttingen, Berlin and Frankfurt, 1957).

Braunmüller, Benedikt. "Drangsale des Klosters Nieder-Altaich im Jahre 1226." *Wissenschaftliche Studien und Mittheilungen aus dem Benedictiner-Orden* 2 (1881): 99–108.

Breywisch, Walter. "Quedlinburgs Säkularisation und seine ersten Jahre unter der preußischen Herrschaft 1802–1806." *Sachsen und Anhalt* 4 (1928): 207–49.

Briechle, Andrea. *Heinrich Herzog von Sachsen und Pfalzgraf bei Rhein* (Heidelberg, 2013).

Brommer, Peter. *Die Ämter Kurtriers: Grundherrschaft, Gerichtsbarkeit, Steuerwesen und Einwohner. Edition des sogenannten Feuerbuchs von 1563* (Mainz, 2003).

Brown, Elizabeth A. R. "The Tyranny of a Construct: Feudalism and Historians of Medieval Europe." *AHR* 79 (1974): 1063–88.

Brown, Warren C. "Conflict, Letters, and Personal Relationships in the Carolingian Formula Collections." *Law and History Review* 25 (2007): 323–44.

"Laypeople and Documents in the Frankish Formula Collections." In *Documentary Culture and the Laity in the Early Middle Ages*, ed. Warren Brown, Marios Costambeys, Matthew Innes and Adam Kosto (Cambridge, UK, 2013), pp. 125–51.

Unjust Seizure: Conflict, Interest, and Authority in an Early Medieval Society (Ithaca, NY, 2001).

Violence in Medieval Europe (Harlow, 2011).

Brown, Warren C., and Piotr Górecki. "What Conflict Means: The Making of Medieval Conflict Studies in the United States, 1970–2000." In *Conflict in Medieval Europe*, pp. 1–35.

Bruce, Scott G., ed. *The Penguin Book of the Undead: Fifteen Hundred Years of Supernatural Encounters* (New York, 2016).

Brühl, Carlrichard. "Servitium Regis." In *Lexikon des Mittelalters*, vol. 7 (Munich, 1995), cols. 1796–97.

Studien zu den Merowingischen Königsurkunden. Ed. Theo Kölzer (Cologne, Weimar and Vienna, 1998).

Brundage, James A. *Medieval Canon Law* (London and New York, 1995).

The Medieval Origins of the Legal Profession: Canonists, Civilians, and Courts (Chicago and London, 2008).

Brunner, Heinrich. "Das gerichtliche Exemtionsrecht der Babenberger." In *Abhandlungen zur Rechtsgeschichte: Gesammelte Aufsätze*, ed. Karl Rauch (Weimar, 1931; orig. 1864), pp. 1: 3–81.

Deutsche Rechtsgeschichte. 2 vols. (Leipzig, 1887–92).

"Zeugen- und Inquisitionsbeweis der karolingischen Zeit." In *Forschungen zur Geschichte des deutschen und französischen Rechtes: Gesammelte Aufsätze* (Aalen, 1969; orig. 1865), pp. 88–247.

Brunner, Karl. *Österreichische Geschichte 907–1156: Herzogtümer und Marken* (Vienna, 1994).

Leopold, der Heilige: ein Portrait aus dem Frühling des Mittelalters (Vienna, Cologne and Weimar, 2009).

Brunner, Otto. "Feudalism: The History of a Concept." In *Lordship and Community*, trans. Miriam Sambursky, pp. 32–61.

Land and Lordship: Structures of Governance in Medieval Austria. Trans. Howard Kaminsky and James Van Horn Melton (Philadelphia, PA, 1992).

Brunt, P. A. "The 'Fiscus' and Its Development." *The Journal of Roman Studies* 56 (1966): 75–91.

Buc, Philippe. "What Is Order? In the Aftermath of the 'Feudal Transformation' Debates." *Francia: Forschungen zur westeuropäischen Geschichte* 46 (2019): 281–300.

Buchholzer-Rémy, Laurence. "Von der Herrschaft zur Gemeinde? Der Schultheiß, eine ambivalente Figur (Elsass, 12–15. Jahrhundert)." In *Mittler zwischen Herrschaft und Gemeinde*, pp. 177–99.

Bünz, Enno. "Adlige Unternehmer? Wirtschaftliche Aktivitäten von Grafen und Herren im späten Mittelalter." In *Grafen und Herren in Südwestdeutschland vom 12. bis ins 17. Jahrhundert*, ed. Kurt Andermann and Clemens Joos (Epfendorf, 2006), pp. 35–69.

Bur, Michel. *La formation du comté de Champagne v. 950 – v. 1150* (Nancy, 1977).

Burbank, Jane, and Frederick Cooper. *Empires in World History: Power and the Politics of Difference* (Princeton, NJ and Oxford, 2010).

Burkhardt, Stefan. "Lehnsrechtliche Ordnungsvorstellungen in den Urkunden der Erzbischöfe von Mainz und Köln." In *Das Lehnswesen im Hochmittelalter*, pp. 177–93.

Mit Stab und Schwert: Bilder, Träger und Funktionen erzbischöflicher Herrschaft zur Zeit Kaiser Friedrich Barbarossas (Ostfildern, 2008).

The Cambridge History of Medieval Monasticism in the Latin West. Ed. Alison I. Beach and Isabelle Cochelin. 2 vols. (Cambridge, UK, 2020).

Carocci, Sandro, and Simone M. Collavini. "The Cost of States: Politics and Exactions in the Christian West (Sixth to Fifteenth Centuries)." In *Diverging Paths? The Shapes of Power and Institutions in Medieval Christendom and Islam*, ed. John Hudson and Ana Rodríguez (Leiden and Boston, MA, 2014), pp. 125–58.

Carpenter, Christine, and Olivier Mattéoni. "Offices and Officers." In *Government and Political Life in England and France, c.1300–c.1500*, ed. Christopher Fletcher, Jean-Philippe Genet and John Watts (Cambridge, UK, 2015), pp. 78–115.

Carré, Pascal. "Les Avoueries des églises liégeoises, XIᵉ–XVᵉ siècles" (PhD diss., University of Liège, 2009).

Cassidy-Welch, Megan. "The Stedinger Crusade: War, Remembrance, and Absence in Thirteenth-Century Germany." *Viator* 44 (2013): 159–74.

Castelnuovo, Guido. "Offices and Officials." In *The Italian Renaissance State*, ed. Andrea Gamberini and Isabella Lazzarini (Cambridge, UK, 2012), pp. 368–84.

Chakrabarti, Upal. *Assembling the Local: Political Economy and Agrarian Governance in British India* (Philadelphia, PA, 2021).

Chakrabarty, Dipesh. *Provincializing Europe: Postcolonial Thought and Historical Difference* (Princeton, NJ and Oxford, 2000).

Cheyette, Fredric L. *Ermengard of Narbonne and the World of the Troubadours* (Ithaca, NY and London, 2001).

"Georges Duby's *Mâconnais* after Fifty Years: Reading It Then and Now." *Journal of Medieval History* 28 (2002): 291–317.

"Introduction." In *Lordship and Community*, pp. 1–10.

"Some Reflections on Violence, Reconciliation, and the 'Feudal Revolution.'" In *Conflict in Medieval Europe*, pp. 243–64.

Chinca, Mark, and Christopher Young. "Uses of the Past in Twelfth-Century Germany: The Case of the Middle High German *Kaiserchronik*." *Central European History* 49 (2016): 19–38.

Chittolini, Giorgio. "The 'Private,' the 'Public,' the State." *Journal of Modern History* 67, Supplement (1995): S34–61.

Claerr-Stamm, Gabrielle. *Pierre de Hagenbach: Le destin tragique d'un chevalier sundgauvien au service de Charles le Téméraire* (Riedisheim, 2004).

Clanchy, Michael T. *From Memory to Written Record: England 1066–1307*, 3rd ed. (Chichester, 2013).

Clauss, Martin. *Die Untervogtei: Studien zur Stellvertretung in der Kirchenvogtei im Rahmen der deutschen Verfassungsgeschichte des 11. und 12. Jahrhunderts* (Siegburg, 2002).

"Vogteibündelung, Untervogtei, Landesherrschaft: Adlige Herrschaft und Klostervogtei in den Rheinlanden." In *Kirchenvogtei und adlige Herrschaftsbildung*, pp. 169–96.

Cohn, Henry J. "Church Property in the German Protestant Principalities." In *Politics and Society in Reformation Europe: Essays for Sir Geoffrey Elton*, ed. E. I. Kouri and Tom Scott (Basingstoke, 1987), pp. 158–87.

Colet, Anna, et al. "The Black Death and Its Consequences for the Jewish Community in Tàrrega: Lessons from History and Archeology." *Medieval Globe* 1 (2014): 63–96.

Collins, Randall. "Patrimonial Alliances and Failures of State Penetration: A Historical Dynamic of Crime, Corruption, Gangs, and Mafias." *Annals of the American Academy of Political and Social Science* 636 (2011): 16–31.

Conflict in Medieval Europe: Changing Perspectives on Society and Culture. Ed. Warren C. Brown and Piotr Górecki (Aldershot and Burlington, VT, 2003).

Constable, Giles. "Baume and Cluny in the Twelfth Century." In *The Abbey of Cluny: A Collection of Essays to Mark the Eleven-Hundredth Anniversary of Its Foundation* (Berlin, 2010), pp. 405–35.

"Cluny in the Monastic World of the Tenth Century." In *Il Secolo di Ferro: Mito e Realtà del Secolo X*. Vol. 1 (Spoleto, 1991), pp. 391–437.

"Forgery and Plagiarism in the Middle Ages." *Archiv für Diplomatik* 29 (1983): 1–41.

The Reformation of the Twelfth Century (Cambridge, UK, 1996).

"Religious Communities, 1024–1215." In *NCMH*, vol. 4:1, ed. David Luscombe and Jonathan Riley-Smith (Cambridge, 2004), pp. 335–67.

Corcoran, Simon. "Hincmar and His Roman Legal Sources." In *Hincmar of Rheims: Life and Work*, ed. Rachel Stone and Charles West (Manchester, 2015), pp. 129–55.

Cordelli, Chiara. *The Privatized State* (Princeton, NJ and Oxford, 2020).

Costambeys, Marios, Matthew Innes and Simon MacLean. *The Carolingian World* (Cambridge, UK, 2011).

Crook, John A. *Legal Advocacy in the Roman World* (Ithaca, NY, 1995).

Czaja, Roman, and Andrzej Radzimiński, eds. *The Teutonic Order in Prussia and Livonia: The Political and Ecclesiastical Structures 13th–16th Century* (Torún and Vienna, 2015).

Dachowski, Elizabeth. *First Among Abbots: The Career of Abbo of Fleury* (Washington, DC, 2008).

Dale, Johanna. *Inauguration and Liturgical Kingship in the Long Twelfth Century* (York, 2019).

Davies, Rees. "The Medieval State: The Tyranny of a Concept?" *Journal of Historical Sociology* 16 (2003): 280–300.

Davis, Jennifer R. *Charlemagne's Practice of Empire* (Cambridge, UK, 2015).

"Charlemagne's Settlement of Disputes." In *Streit am Hof im frühen Mittelalter*, ed. Matthias Becher and Alheydis Plassmann (Göttingen, 2011), pp. 149–73.

Davis, Kathleen. *Periodization and Sovereignty: How Ideas of Feudalism and Secularization Govern the Politics of Time* (Philadelphia, PA, 2008).

De Jong, Mayke. "Carolingian Monasticism: The Power of Prayer." In *NCMH*, vol. 2, ed. Rosamond McKitterick (Cambridge, UK, 1995), pp. 622–53.

De Long, J. Bradford, and Andrei Shleifer. "Princes and Merchants: European City Growth before the Industrial Revolution." *Journal of Law & Economics* 36 (1993): 671–702.

Dean, Trevor. *Crime in Medieval Europe, 1200–1550* (London and New York, 2001).

Declercq, Georges. "Originals and Cartularies: The Organization of Archival Memory (Ninth–Eleventh Centuries)." In *Charters and the Use of the Written Word in Medieval Society*, ed. Karl Heidecker (Turnhout, 2000), pp. 147–70.

Degler-Spengler, Brigitte. "Die Beginen in Basel." *Basler Zeitschrift für Geschichte und Altertumskunde* 69 (1969): 5–83.

Deich, Werner. *Das Goslarer Reichsvogteigeld: Staufische Burgenpolitik in Niedersachsen und auf dem Eichsfeld* (Lübeck, 1974).

Demski, Rainer. *Adel und Lübeck: Studien zum Verhältnis zwischen adliger und bürgerlicher Kultur im 13. und 14. Jahrhundert* (Frankfurt, 1996).

Dendorfer, Jürgen. "Die Abtei und ihre Vögte im frühen und hohen Mittelalter." In *Die Abtei Niederaltaich*, ed. Roman Deutinger and Stephan Deutinger (St. Ottilien, 2018), pp. 93–127.

Adelige Gruppenbildung und Königsherrschaft: Die Grafen von Sulzbach und ihr Beziehungsgeflecht im 12. Jahrhundert (Munich, 2004).

"Verwandte, Freunde und Getreue – Adelige Gruppen in der klösterlichen Memoria des 12. Jahrhunderts in Bayern." In *Adlige – Stifter – Mönche. Zum Verhältnis zwischen Klöstern und mittelalterlichem Adel*, ed. Nathalie Kruppa (Göttingen, 2007), pp. 63–105.

Depreux, Philippe. "The Development of Charters Confirming Exchange by the Royal Administration (Eighth-Tenth Centuries)." In *Charters and the Use of the Written Word in Medieval Society*, ed. Karl Heidecker (Turnhout, 2000), pp. 43–62.

"Unterschiedliche Ausprägungen der Kirchenvogtei in Frankreich. Ein regionaler Vergleich (9.–12. Jahrhundert)." In *Kirchenvogtei und adlige Herrschaftsbildung*, pp. 345–79.

Despy, Georges. "Serfs ou libres? Sur une notice judiciaire cambrésienne de 941." *Revue belge de philologie et d'histoire* 39 (1961): 1127–43.

Deutinger, Roman. "Aus dem verlorenen Traditionsbuch des Klosters Niederaltaich." *Studien und Mitteilungen zur Geschichte des Benediktinerordens und seiner Zweige* 124 (2013): 207–18.

Der deutsche Territorialstaat im 14. Jahrhundert. Ed. Hans Patze. 2 vols. (Sigmaringen, 1970–71).

Deutsche Verwaltungsgeschichte. Ed. Kurt G. A. Jeserich, Hans Pohl and Georg-Christoph von Unruh. Vol. 1 (Stuttgart, 1983).

Dickau, Otto. "Studien zur Kanzlei und zum Urkundenwesen Kaiser Ludwigs des Frommen. Ein Beitrag zur Geschichte der karolingischen Königsurkunde im 9. Jahrhundert. Erster Teil." *Archiv für Diplomatik* 34 (1988): 3–156.

Dicke, Gerd, and Klaus Grubmüller. *Die Fabeln des Mittelalters und der frühen Neuzeit: Ein Katalog der deutschen Versionen und ihrer lateinischen Entsprechungen* (Munich, 1987).

Dierkens, Alain. *"Carolus monasteriorum multorum eversor et ecclesiasticarum pecuniarum in usus proprios commutator?* Notes sur la politique monastique du maire du palais Charles Martel." In *Karl Martell in seiner Zeit*, ed. Jörg Jarnut, Ulrich Nonn and Michael Richter (Sigmaringen, 1994), pp. 277–94.

Dierkens, Alain, and Jean-Pierre Devroey. "L'avouerie dans l'Entre-Sambre-et-Meuse avant 1100." In *L'Avouerie en Lotharingie*, pp. 43–94.

Dießelhorst, Malte, and Arne Duncker. *Hans Kohlhase: Die Geschichte einer Fehde in Sachsen und Brandenburg zur Zeit der Reformation* (Frankfurt, 1999).

Dohrmann, Wolfgang. *Die Vögte des Klosters St. Gallen in der Karolingerzeit* (Bochum, 1985).

Dollinger, Philippe. "Strassburg in salischer Zeit." In *Die Salier und das Reich*, ed. Stefan Weinfurter (Sigmaringen, 1991), pp. 3: 153–64.

Dopsch, Alfons. "Die Grundherrlichkeit der Karolingerzeit (Immunität und Vogtei)." In *Verfassungs- und Wirtschaftsgeschichte des Mittelalters: Gesammelte Aufsätze* (Vienna, 1928; repr. Aalen, 1968), pp. 11–50.

Dopsch, Heinz. "Die Grafen von Lebenau (ca. 1130–1229), bescheidener Zweig einer großen Dynastie." In *Hochmittelalterliche Adelsfamilien in Altbayern, Franken und Schwaben*, ed. Ferdinand Kramer and Wilhelm Störmer (Munich, 2005), pp. 509–37.

Dorna, Maciej. *Mabillon und Andere: Die Anfänge der Diplomatik*. Trans. Martin Faber (Wiesbaden, 2019).

Duby, Georges. *The Early Growth of the European Economy: Warriors and Peasants from the Seventh to the Twelfth Century*. Trans. Howard B. Clarke (London, 1974).

"The Evolution of Judicial Institutions: Burgundy in the Tenth and Eleventh Centuries." In *The Chivalrous Society*, trans. Cynthia Postan (Berkeley and Los Angeles, 1980), pp. 15–58.

Guerriers et paysans, VII–XIIe siècle: premier essor de l'économie européenne (Paris, 1973).

Duggan, Anne J. *"Alexander ille meus*: The Papacy of Alexander III." In *Pope Alexander III (1159–81): The Art of Survival*, ed. Peter D. Clarke and Anne J. Duggan (Farnham and Burlington, VT, 2012), pp. 13–50.

"Master of the Decretals: A Reassessment of Alexander III's Contribution to Canon Law." In *Pope Alexander III (1159–81): The Art of Survival*, ed. Peter D. Clarke and Anne J. Duggan (Farnham and Burlington, VT, 2012), pp. 365–417.

Duggan, Lawrence G. *Bishop and Chapter: The Governance of the Bishopric of Speyer to 1552* (New Brunswick, NJ, 1978).

Dümmler, Ernst. "Über Leben und Schriften des Mönches Theodorich (von Amorbach)." *Abhandlungen der Königlichen Akademie der Wissenschaften in Berlin* (1894): 1–38.

Dümmler, Ernst, and Hermann Wartmann. "St. Galler Todtenbuch und Verbrüderungen." *Mitteilungen zur vaterländischen Geschichte St. Gallen* 11 (Neue Folge, 1) (1869): 1–124.

Dupont, Christian. "Violence et avouerie au XIe et au début du XIIe siècle en Basse-Lotharingie: notes sur l'histoire des abbayes de Saint-Hubert et de Saint-Trond." In *L'Avouerie en Lotharingie*, pp. 115–28.

Durand, Stéphane. "Corruption and Anticorruption in France between the 1670s and the 1780s: The Example of the Provincial Administration of Languedoc." In *Anticorruption in History*, pp. 153–64.

Dütsch, Hans-Rudolf. *Die Zürcher Landvögte von 1402–1798: Ein Versuch zur Bestimmung ihrer sozialen Herkunft und zur Würdigung ihres Amtes im Rahmen des zürcherischen Stadtstaates* (Zurich, 1994).

Ebel, Wilhelm. *Lübisches Recht*. Vol. 1 (Lübeck, 1971).

Ebling, Horst. *Prosopographie der Amtsträger des Merowingerreiches von Chlothar II. (613) bis Karl Martell (741)* (Munich, 1974).

Eder, Karl. *Glaubensspaltung und Landstände in Österreich ob der Enns 1525–1602* (Linz, 1936).

Das Land ob der Enns vor der Glaubensspaltung (Linz, 1932).

Egawa, Yuko. *Stadtherrschaft und Gemeinde in Straßburg vom Beginn des 13. Jahrhunderts bis zum Schwarzen Tod (1349)* (Trier, 2007).

Eibl, Elfie-Marita. "Die Lausitzen zwischen Böhmen, Brandenburg und Sachsen in der Zeit Kaiser Friedrichs III. (1440–1493)." In *Akkulturation und Selbstbehauptung: Studien zur Entwicklungsgeschichte der Lande zwischen Elbe/Saale und Oder im späten Mittelalter*, ed. Peter Moraw (Berlin, 2001), pp. 311–46.

Eldevik, John. *Episcopal Power and Ecclesiastical Reform in the German Empire: Tithes, Lordship and Community, 950–1150* (Cambridge, UK, 2012).

Empowering Interactions: Political Cultures and the Emergence of the State in Europe 1300–1900. Ed. Wim Blockmans, André Holenstein and Jon Mathieu (Farnham and Burlington, VT, 2009).

Endemann, Traute. *Vogtei und Herrschaft im alemannisch-burgundischen Grenzraum* (Constance and Stuttgart, 1967).

Epstein, Steven. *An Economic and Social History of Later Medieval Europe, 1000–1500* (Cambridge, UK, 2009).

Esders, Stefan. "Amt und Bann. Weltliche Funktionsträger (*centenarii, vicarii*) als Teil ländlicher Gesellschaften im Karolingerreich." In *Kleine Welten. Ländliche Gesellschaften im Karolingerreich*, ed. Thomas Kohl, Steffen Patzold, and Bernhard Zeller (Ostfildern, 2019), pp. 255–307.

Römische Rechtstradition und merowingisches Königtum: Zum Rechtscharakter politischer Herrschaft in Burgund im 6. und 7. Jahrhundert (Göttingen, 1997).

Esders, Stefan, and Gunnar Folke Schuppert. *Mittelalterliches Regieren in der Moderne oder Modernes Regieren im Mittelalter?* (Baden-Baden, 2015).

Evergates, Theodore. *The Aristocracy in the County of Champagne, 1100–1300* (Philadelphia, PA, 2007).

Henry the Liberal: Count of Champagne, 1127–1181 (Philadelphia, PA, 2016).

Évrard, Jean-Pol. "Les avoueries de l'évêché de Verdun (du milieu du Xe au milieu du XIIe siècle)." In *L'Avouerie en Lotharingie*, pp. 175–87.

Fälschungen im Mittelalter: Diplomatische Fälschungen. MGH Schriften 33: 3–4 (Hanover, 1988).

Fasolt, Constantin. "Hegel's Ghost: Europe, the Reformation, and the Middle Ages." *Viator* 39 (2008): 345–86.

Feist, Valerie, and Karl Helleiner. "Das Urkundenwesen der Bischöfe von Augsburg von den Anfängen bis zur Mitte des XIII. Jahrhunderts (897–1248)." *Archivalische Zeitschrift* 37 (1928): 38–88.

Felten, Franz J. *Äbte und Laienäbte im Frankenreich: Studie zum Verhältnis von Staat und Kirche im früheren Mittelalter* (Stuttgart, 1980).

Ferguson, Yale H. et al. "What Is the Polity? A Roundtable." *International Studies Review* 2 (2000): 3–31.

Fichtenau, Heinrich. *Lebensordnungen des 10. Jahrhunderts: Studien über Denkart und Existenz im einstigen Karolingerreich.* 2 vols. (Stuttgart, 1984).
  Living in the Tenth Century: Mentalities and Social Orders. Trans. Patrick J. Geary (Chicago and London, 1991).

Ficker, Julius. *Engelbert der Heilige, Erzbischof von Köln und Reichsverweser* (Cologne, 1853).

Finger, Heinz. "Der gewaltsame Tod des Kölner Erzbischofs Engelbert und die Vorgeschichte." In *AufRuhr 1225!*, pp. 21–33.

"Das Kloster und die Vögte: Die 'Schutzherren' von Werden." In *Das Jahrtausend der Mönche. KlosterWelt Werden 799–1803*, ed. Jan Gerchow (Cologne, 1999), pp. 99–105.

Firnhaber-Baker, Justine. *Violence and the State in Languedoc, 1250–1400* (Cambridge, UK, 2014).

Fischer, Balthasar. "Die Entwicklung des Instituts der Defensoren in der römischen Kirche." *Ephemerides Liturgicae* 48 (1939): 443–54.

Fischer, Eugen. "Das Monasterium der heiligen Märtyrer Felix und Regula in Zürich." *Zeitschrift für schweizerische Kirchengeschichte* 53 (1959): 161–90.

Flammarion, Hubert. "Les sources narratives en Lorraine autour de l'an Mil." In *Religion et culture autour de l'an Mil*, ed. Dominique Iogna-Prat and Jean-Charles Picard (Paris, 1990), pp. 301–8.

Fouracre, Paul J. *The Age of Charles Martel* (Harlow, 2000).
  "Carolingian Justice: The Rhetoric of Improvement and Contexts of Abuse." In *Frankish History: Studies in the Construction of Power* (Farnham and Burlington, VT, 2013), XI: 771–803.
  "Eternal Light and Earthly Needs: Practical Aspects of the Development of Frankish Immunities." In *Property and Power in the Early Middle Ages*, ed. Wendy Davies and Paul J. Fouracre (Cambridge, UK, 1995), pp. 53–81.
  "'Placita' and the Settlement of Disputes in Later Merovingian Francia." In *The Settlement of Disputes*, pp. 23–43.

Fräss-Ehrfeld, Claudia. *Geschichte Kärntens.* Vol. 1 (Klagenfurt, 1984).

Frauenknecht, Erwin. "Reichsstädte im Dilemma. Königliche Verpfändungen im 14. Jahrhundert am Beispiel südwestdeutscher Reichsstädte." *ZWLG* 77 (2018): 31–42.

Freed, John B. "Bavarian Wine and Woolless Sheep: The *Urbar* of Count Sigiboto IV of Falkenstein (1126–ca. 1198)." *Viator* 35 (2004): 71–112.
  The Counts of Falkenstein: Noble Self-Consciousness in Twelfth-Century Germany (Philadelphia, PA, 1984).

Frederick Barbarossa: The Prince and the Myth (New Haven, CT and London, 2016).

Noble Bondsmen: Ministerial Marriages in the Archdiocese of Salzburg, 1100–1343 (Ithaca, NY and London, 1995).

Freedman, Paul H. *The Origins of Peasant Servitude in Medieval Catalonia* (Cambridge, UK, 1991).

Freedman, Paul H., and Gabrielle M. Spiegel. "Medievalisms Old and New: The Rediscovery of Alterity in North American Medieval Studies." *AHR* 103 (1998): 677–704.

Freeman, Elizabeth. "Nuns." In *The Cambridge Companion to the Cistercian Order*, ed. Mette Birkedal Bruun (Cambridge, UK, 2013), pp. 100–111.

Fried, Pankraz. "'Modernstaatliche' Entwicklungstendenzen im bayerischen Ständestaat des Spätmittelalters. Ein methodischer Versuch." In *Der deutsche Territorialstaat*, pp. 2: 301–41.

"Zur Geschichte der Steuer in Bayern." In *Forschungen zur bayerischen und schwäbischen Geschichte: Gesammelte Beiträge von Pankraz Fried* (Sigmaringen, 1997), pp. 41–66.

Fritz, Gerhard. "Des Herzogs ungetreue Diener. Vögte und Amtleute in Altwürttemberg zwischen Legitimität, Korruption und Untertanenprotest." *ZWLG* 63 (2004): 119–67.

Fulton Brown, Rachel. *Mary and the Art of Prayer: The Hours of the Virgin in Medieval Christian Life and Thought* (New York, 2018).

Gamberini, Andrea, and Isabella Lazzarini. "Introduction." In *The Italian Renaissance State*, ed. Andrea Gambertini and Isabella Lazzarini (Cambridge, 2012), pp. 1–6.

Gambetta, Diego. *The Sicilian Mafia: The Business of Private Protection* (Cambridge, MA, and London, 1993).

Ganim, John M. *Medievalism and Orientalism: Three Essays on Literature, Architecture and Cultural Identity* (New York, 2005).

Ganshof, François Louis. *Feudalism*. Trans. Philip Grierson (London, New York and Toronto, 1952).

Frankish Institutions Under Charlemagne. Trans. Bryce Lyon and Mary Lyon (New York, 1968).

Ganz, David, and Walter Goffart. "Charters Earlier Than 800 From French Collections." *Speculum* 65 (1990): 906–32.

Gaudemet, Jean. "Le Bréviaire d'Alaric et les Epitome." In *La formation du droit canonique médiéval* (London, 1980), pp. 1: 3–57.

Geary, Patrick J. "Living with Conflicts in Stateless France: A Typology of Conflict Management Mechanisms, 1050–1200." In *Living with the Dead in the Middle Ages* (Ithaca, NY, 1994), pp. 125–60.

Phantoms of Remembrance: Memory and Oblivion at the End of the First Millennium (Princeton, N.J., 1994).

Gebrekidan, Selam, Matt Apuzzo and Benjamin Novak. "The Money Farmers: How Oligarchs and Populists Milk the EU for Millions." *The New York Times*, Nov. 3, 2019, www.nytimes.com/2019/11/03/world/europe/eu-farm-sub sidy-hungary.html (last accessed 29 July 2021).

Geiger, Ludwig. *Geschichte der Juden in Berlin.* Vol. 2 (Berlin, 1871).

Gelting, Michael H. "Reflections on the Insertion of Bureaucratie Structures in Médiéval Clientelic Societies." In *Law and Power in the Middle Ages. Proceedings of the Fourth Carlsberg Academy Conference on Medieval Legal History,* ed. Per Andersen, Mia Münster-Swendsen and Helle Voght (Copenhagen, 2008), pp. 257–68.

Genicot, Léopold. "Sur le vocabulaire et les modalités de l'avouerie avant l'an mil dans la Belgique actuelle." In *L'Avouerie en Lotharingie,* pp. 9–32.

Gerchow, Jan. "Äbtissinnen auf dem Weg zur Landesherrschaft im 13. Jahrhundert: Das Beispiel der Frauenstifte Essen und Herford." In *Reform, Reformation, Säkularisation: Frauenstifte in Krisenzeiten,* ed. Thomas Schilp (Essen, 2004), pp. 67–88.

Gillen, Anja. *Saint-Mihiel im hohen und späten Mittelalter: Studien zu Abtei, Stadt und Landesherrschaft im Westen des Reiches* (Trier, 2003).

Ginzburg, Carlo. *The Cheese and the Worms: The Cosmos of a Sixteenth-Century Miller.* Trans. John Tedeschi and Anne C. Tedeschi (Baltimore, 2013).

Glitsch, Heinrich. *Untersuchungen zur mittelalterlichen Vogtgerichtsbarkeit* (Bonn, 1912).

Gneiß, Markus. "Kloster und Klientel: Fallstudien zum Verhältnis des rittermäßigen Gefolges der Kuenringer zum Klarissenkloster Dürnstein mit einigen Bemerkungen zur Herrschaftsentwicklung in der Wachau." In *Adel und Verfassung im hoch- und spätmittelalterlichen Reich,* ed. Christina Mochty-Weltin and Roman Zehetmayer (St. Pölten, 2018), pp. 187–245.

Goetz, Hans-Werner. *Moderne Mediävistik: Stand und Perspektiven der Mittelalterforschung* (Darmstadt, 1999).

"Protection of the Church, Defense of the Law, and Reform: On the Purposes and Character of the Peace of God, 989–1038." In *The Peace of God,* pp. 259–79.

"Die St. Galler Tauschurkunden (und der alemannische Raum)." In *Tauschgeschäft,* pp. 171–200.

Goez, Werner. "*Imperator advocatus Romanae ecclesiae.*" In *Aus Kirche und Reich: Studien zu Theologie, Politik und Recht im Mittelalter,* ed. Hubert Mordek (Sigmaringen, 1983), pp. 315–28.

Goffart, Walter. *The Le Mans Forgeries: A Chapter from the History of Church Property in the Ninth Century* (Cambridge, MA, 1966).

Goldberg, Eric J. "*Dominus Hludowicus Serenissimus Imperator Sedens pro Tribunali*: Conflict, Justice, and Ideology at the Court of Louis the German." In *Streit am Hof im frühen Mittelalter,* ed. Matthias Becher and Alheydis Plassmann (Göttingen, 2011), pp. 175–202.

Struggle for Empire: Kingship and Conflict under Louis the German, 817–876 (Ithaca, NY and London, 2006).

Gordon, Gregory S. "The Trial of Peter von Hagenbach: Reconciling History, Historiography and International Criminal Law." In *The Hidden Histories of War Crimes Trials,* ed. Kevin Jon Heller and Gerry Simpson (Oxford and New York, 2013), pp. 13–49.

Górecki, Piotr. *Economy, Society, and Lordship in Medieval Poland, 1100–1250* (New York and London, 1992).

Görich, Knut. *Die Ehre Friedrich Barbarossas: Kommunikation, Konflikt und politisches Handeln im 12. Jahrhundert* (Darmstadt, 2001).

Göse, Frank. "Beschränkte Souveränität: Das Verhältnis zwischen Stift und Schutzherrschaft im 17. und 18. Jahrhundert." In *Kayserlich*, pp. 130–50.

Graulau, Jeannette. *The Underground Wealth of Nations: On the Capitalist Origins of Silver Mining, AD 1150–1450* (New Haven, CT and London, 2019).

Green, Judith A. *The Government of England Under Henry I* (Cambridge, UK, 1986).

Green, Richard Firth. *Elf Queens and Holy Friars: Fairy Beliefs and the Medieval Church* (Philadelphia, PA, 2016).

Greer, Sarah. *Commemorating Power in Early Medieval Saxony: Writing and Rewriting the Past at Gandersheim and Quedlinburg* (Oxford, 2021).

Grimm, Jacob, and Wilhelm Grimm. *Deutsche Sagen*. 2 vols. (Berlin, 1816–18).

Guenée, Bernard. *States and Rulers in Later Medieval Europe*. Trans. Juliet Vale (Oxford and New York, 1985).

Guthke, Karl S. "Wilhelm Tell." In *A Companion to the Works of Friedrich Schiller*, ed. Steven D. Martinson (Rochester, NY and Woodbridge, 2005), pp. 247–67.

Hageneder, Othmar. "Lehensvogtei und Defensorenamt in den babenbergischen Herzogsurkunden." *Jahrbuch für Landeskunde von Niederösterreich* 42 (1976): 70–94.

Hagenmeyer, Heinrich. "Der Brief der Kreuzfahrer an den Papst und die abendländische Kirche vom Jahre 1099 nach der Schlacht bei Askalon." *Forschungen zur deutschen Geschichte* 13 (1873): 400–412.

Hägermann, Dieter. "Die Urkundenfälschungen auf Karl den Großen: Eine Übersicht." In *Fälschungen im Mittelalter*, pp. 3: 433–43.

Harding, Alan. *Medieval Law and the Foundations of the State* (Oxford and New York, 2002).

Hardy, Duncan. *Associative Political Culture in the Holy Roman Empire: Upper Germany, 1346–1521* (Oxford, 2018).

"Burgundian Clients in the South-Western Holy Roman Empire, 1410–1477: Between International Diplomacy and Regional Political Culture." In *Practices of Diplomacy in the Early Modern World c. 1410–1800*, ed. Tracey A. Sowerby and Jan Hennings (London and New York, 2017), pp. 25–43.

Harries, Jill. *Law and Empire in Late Antiquity* (Cambridge, UK, 1999).

Haussherr, Reiner, and Christian Väterlein, eds. *Die Zeit der Staufer: Geschichte, Kunst, Kultur*. 5 vols. (Stuttgart, 1977).

Haverkamp, Alfred. *Medieval Germany, 1056–1273*. Trans. Helga Braun and Richard Mortimer (Oxford, 1988).

Haverkamp, Eva. "Jewish Images on Christian Coins: Economy and Symbolism in Medieval Germany." In *Jews and Christians in Medieval Europe*, ed. Philippe Buc, Martha Keil and John Tolan (Turnhout, 2015), pp. 189–226.

Head, Randolph C. "Knowing Like a State: The Transformation of Political Knowledge in Swiss Archives, 1450–1770." *The Journal of Modern History* 75 (2003): 745–82.

"Shared Lordship, Authority, and Administration: The Exercise of Dominion in the *Gemeine Herrschaften* of the Swiss Confederation, 1417–1600." *Central European History* 30 (1997): 489–512.

"William Tell and His Comrades: Association and Fraternity in the Propaganda of Fifteenth- and Sixteenth-Century Switzerland." *The Journal of Modern History* 67 (1995): 527–57.

Head, Thomas. *Hagiography and the Cult of Saints: The Diocese of Orléans, 800–1200* (Cambridge, UK, 1990).

Hechberger, Werner. *Adel im fränkisch-deutschen Mittelalter: Zur Anatomie eines Forschungsproblems* (Ostfildern, 2005).

Hedwig, Andreas. "Precaria." In *Lexikon des Mittelalters*, vol. 7 (Munich, 1995), cols. 170–71.

Heidecker, Karl. "Charters as Texts and as Objects in Judicial Actions: The Example of the Carolingian Private Charters of St Gall." In *Medieval Legal Process. Physical, Spoken and Written Performance in the Middle Ages*, ed. Marco Mostert and P. S. Barnwell (Turnhout, 2011), pp. 39–53.

Heilmann, Alfons. *Die Klostervogtei im rechtsrheinischen Teil der Diözese Konstanz bis zur Mitte des dreizehnten Jahrhunderts* (Cologne, 1908).

Heimpel, Hermann. "Mittelalter und Nürnberger Prozeß." In *Festschrift Edmund E. Stengel zum 70. Geburtstag am 24. Dezember 1949* (Münster and Cologne, 1952), pp. 443–52.

Heinrich, Gerd. *Friedrich II. von Preußen* (Berlin, 2009).

Hemmerle, Josef. *Die Benediktinerabtei Benediktbeuern* (Berlin and New York, 1991).

Hennebicque-Le Jan, Régine. "Prosopographica neustrica: Les agents du roi en Neustrie de 639 à 840." In *La Neustrie*, pp. 1: 231–69.

Herlihy, David. "Church Property on the European Continent, 701–1200." *Speculum* 36 (1961): 81–105.

Herzberg-Fränkel, Siegmund. "Wirtschaftsgeschichte des Stiftes Niederaltaich." *MIÖG: Ergänzungsband* 10 (1928): 81–235.

"Die wirtschaftsgeschichtlichen Quellen des Stiftes Niederaltaich." *MIÖG: Ergänzungsband* 8 (1911): 1–130.

Hesse, Christian. *Amtsträger der Fürsten im spätmittelalterlichen Reich: Die Funktionseliten der lokalen Verwaltung in Bayern-Landshut, Hessen, Sachsen und Württemberg, 1350–1515* (Göttingen, 2005).

Heydemann, Gerda. "*Nemo militans Deo implicat se saecularia negotia*: Carolingian Interpretations of II Timothy II.4." *Early Medieval Europe* 29 (2021): 55–85.

Hill, Boyd H., Jr., *Medieval Monarchy in Action: The German Empire from Henry I to Henry IV* (London and New York, 1972).

Hilsch, Peter. "Bořiwoj von Swinaře als Landvogt im Elsaß. Zur königlichen Politik Wenzels gegenüber Straßburg und der elsäßischen Landvogtei." *ZWLG* 40 (1981): 436–51.

Hirbodian, Sigrid. "Konrad Breuning und die Bedeutung der städtischen Führungseliten für Württemberg." In *1514 – Macht, Gewalt, Freiheit. Der Vertrag zu Tübingen in Zeiten des Umbruchs*, ed. Götz Adriani and Andreas Schmauder (Ostfildern and Tübingen, 2014), pp. 206–10.

Hirsch, Hans. "The Constitutional History of the Reformed Monasteries during the Investiture Contest." In *Mediaeval Germany 911–1250*, pp. 2: 131–73.

Die Klosterimmunität seit dem Investiturstreit: Untersuchungen zur Verfassungsgeschichte des deutschen Reiches und der deutschen Kirche (Weimar, 1913; 2nd ed., Cologne and Graz, 1967).

"Studien über die Vogtei-Urkunden süddeutsch-österreichischer Zisterzienserklöster." *Archivalische Zeitschrift* 37 (1928): 1–37.

Hirschfeld, Otto. *Die kaiserlichen Verwaltungsbeamten bis auf Diocletian*, 2nd ed. (Berlin, 1905).

Hlawitschka, Eduard. *Studien zur Äbtissinnenreihe von Remiremont (7. – 13. Jh.)* (Saarbrücken, 1963).

Hoffmann, Hartmut. *Bücher und Urkunden aus Helmarshausen und Corvey* (Hanover, 1992).

"Grafschaften in Bischofshand." *DA* 46 (1990): 375–480

"Der König und seine Bischöfe in Frankreich und im Deutschen Reich 936–1060." In *Bischof Burchard von Worms 1000–1025*, ed. Wilfried Hartmann (Mainz, 2000), pp. 79–127.

"Theoderich von Fleury / Amorbach / Trier." *DA* 71 (2015): 475–526.

Hoffmann, Richard C. *Land, Liberties, and Lordship in a Late Medieval Countryside: Agrarian Structures and Change in the Duchy of Wrocław* (Philadelphia, 1989).

Holenstein, André. "Introduction." In *Empowering Interactions*, pp. 1–31.

Hollister, C. Warren, and John W. Baldwin. "The Rise of Administrative Kingship: Henry I and Philip Augustus." *AHR* 83 (1978): 867–905.

Hölscher, Wolfgang. *Kirchenschutz als Herrschaftsinstrument: Personelle und funktionale Aspekte der Bistumspolitik Karls IV.* (Warendorf, 1985).

Holzfurtner, Ludwig. "Ebersberg–Dießen–Scheyern: Zur Entwicklung der oberbayerischen Grafschaft in der Salierzeit." In *Die Salier und das Reich*, ed. Stefan Weinfurter (Sigmaringen, 1991), pp. 1: 549–77.

Hont, Istvan. "The Permanent Crisis of a Divided Mankind: 'Contemporary Crisis of the Nation State' in Historical Perspective." *Political Studies* 42 (1994): 166–231.

Hough, Dan. *Corruption, Anti-Corruption and Governance* (Basingstoke, 2013).

Housley, Norman. *The Later Crusades, 1274–1580: From Lyons to Alcazar* (Oxford and New York, 1992).

Howe, John. *Before the Gregorian Reform: The Latin Church at the Turn of the First Millennium.* (Ithaca, NY and London, 2016).

Hübner, Klara. *Im Dienste ihrer Stadt: Boten- und Nachrichtenorganisationen in den schweizerisch-oberdeutschen Städten des späten Mittelalters* (Ostfildern, 2012).

Humfress, Caroline. "Advocates." In *Late Antiquity: A Guide to the Postclassical World*, ed. G. W. Bowersock, Peter Brown and Oleg Grabar (Cambridge, MA and London, 1999), pp. 277–78.

"Defensor Ecclesiae." In *Late Antiquity: A Guide to the Postclassical World*, pp. 405–06.

Hummer, Hans J. *Politics and Power in Early Medieval Europe: Alsace and the Frankish Realm, 600–1000* (Cambridge, UK, 2005).

"Reform and Lordship in Alsace at the Turn of the Millennium." In *Conflict in Medieval Europe*, pp. 69–84.

Visions of Kinship in Medieval Europe (Oxford, 2018).

Huyghebaert, Nicolas. "Pourquoi l'eglise a-t-elle besoin d'avoués?" In *L'Avouerie en Lotharingie*, pp. 33–42.

Innes, Matthew. *State and Society in the Early Middle Ages: The Middle-Rhine Valley, 400–1000* (Cambridge, UK and New York, 2000).

Isenmann, Eberhard. *Die deutsche Stadt im Mittelalter 1150–1550*, 2nd ed. (Cologne, Weimar and Vienna, 2014).

"The Holy Roman Empire in the Middle Ages." In *The Rise of the Fiscal State in Europe, c. 1200–1815*, ed. Richard Bonney (Oxford and New York, 1999), pp. 243–80.

Jahn, Joachim. *Ducatus Baiuvariorum: Das bairische Herzogtum der Agilolfinger* (Stuttgart, 1991).

Jähnig, Bernhart. "Die Vögte des Deutschen Ordens in der Neumark und ihr Verhältnis zu Preußen." In *Landesherr, Adel und Städte in der mittelalterlichen und frühneuzeitlichen Neumark*, ed. Klaus Neitmann (Berlin, 2015), pp. 319–30.

Jakobs, Hermann. *Der Adel in der Klosterreform von St. Blasien* (Cologne, 1968). *Die Hirsauer: Ihre Ausbreitung und Rechtsstellung im Zeitalter des Investiturstreites* (Cologne and Graz, 1961).

Jänichen, Hans. "Zur Herkunft der Reichenauer Fälscher des 12. Jahrhunderts." In *Die Abtei Reichenau*, ed. Helmut Maurer (Sigmaringen, 1974), pp. 277–87.

Janssen, Roman. "Papst Leo IX., Graf Adalbert von Calw und die Weihe von St. Maria und Markus in Althengstett." In *Text und Kontext. Historische Hilfswissenschaften in ihrer Vielfalt*, ed. Sönke Lorenz and Stephan Molitor (Ostfildern, 2011), pp. 59–73.

Janssen, Wilhelm. "Adelsherrschaft und Herzogsgewalt – Politische Strukturen und Entwicklungen zwischen Ruhr und Lippe 1180–1300." In *AufRuhr 1225!*, pp. 47–58.

Johanek, Peter. "Die 'Karolina de ecclesiastica libertate': Zur Wirkungsgeschichte eines spätmittelalterlichen Gesetzes." *Blätter für deutsche Landesgeschichte* 114 (1978): 797–831.

John, Simon. *Godfrey of Bouillon: Duke of Lower Lotharingia, Ruler of Latin Jerusalem, c. 1060–1100* (London and New York, 2018).

Joireman, Sandra Fullerton. *Where There Is no Government: Enforcing Property Rights in Common Law Africa* (Oxford and New York, 2011).

Jordan, Karl. *Henry the Lion: A Biography*. Trans. P. S. Falla (Oxford, 1986).

Jordan, William Chester. "Anti-Corruption Campaigns in Thirteenth-Century Europe." *Journal of Medieval History* 35 (2009): 204–19.

Jung, Jacqueline Elaine. "From Jericho to Jerusalem: The Violent Transformation of Archbishop Engelbert of Cologne." In *Last Things: Death and the Apocalypse in the Middle Ages*, ed. Caroline Walker Bynum and Paul Freedman (Philadelphia, PA, 2000), pp. 60–82, 283–92.

Kaeuper, Richard W. *Medieval Chivalry* (Cambridge, UK, 2016).

Kaiser, Hans. "Ein unbekanntes Mandat König Richards und die Anfänge der Landvogtei im Elsaß." *Zeitschrift für die Geschichte des Oberrheins* 58/NF 19 (1904): 337–39.

Kaiser, Reinhold. "'Mord im Dom': Von der Vertreibung zur Ermordung des Bischofs im frühen und hohen Mittelalter." *ZRG KA* 79 (1993): 95–134.

Kaminsky, Howard. "From Lateness to Waning to Crisis: The Burden of the Later Middle Ages." *Journal of Early Modern History* 4 (2000): 85–125.

"The Noble Feud in the Later Middle Ages." *Past and Present* 177 (2002): 55–83.

Kamp, Norbert. *Moneta Regis: Königliche Münzstätten und königliche Münzpolitik in der Stauferzeit* (Hanover, 2006).

Kasten, Brigitte, and Katharina Gross. "Tausch- und Prekarieurkunden in Lotharingien bis 1100." In *Tauschgeschäft*, pp. 325–80.

Kayserlich – frey – weltlich: Das Reichsstift Quedlinburg im Spätmittelalter und in der Frühen Neuzeit. Ed. Clemens Bley (Halle, 2009).

Keitel, Christian. "Städtische Bevölkerung und Stadtregiment bis 1397." In *Die Ulmer Bürgerschaft auf dem Weg zur Demokratie*, ed. Hans Eugen Specker (Stuttgart, 1997), pp. 87–118.

Keller, Hagen. "Capitaneus." In *Lexikon des Mittelalters*, vol. 2 (Munich and Zurich, 1983), col. 1475.

Zwischen regionaler Begrenzung und universalem Horizont: Deutschland im Imperium der Salier und Staufer, 1024 bis 1250 (Frankfurt and Berlin, 1986).

Kemper, Joachim. "Vogteirechte als Hebel der Reformation." In *Kirche und Politik am Oberrhein im 16. Jahrhundert. Reformation und Macht im Südwesten des Reiches*, ed. Ulrike A. Wien and Volker Leppin (Tübingen, 2015), pp. 387–95.

Keupp, Jan. "Reichsministerialien und Bischofsmord in staufischer Zeit." In *Bischofsmord im Mittelalter*, ed. Natalie Fryde and Dirk Reitz (Göttingen, 2003), pp. 273–302.

Kirchenvogtei und adlige Herrschaftsbildung im europäischen Mittelalter. Ed. Kurt Andermann and Enno Bünz (Ostfildern, 2019).

Kirschstein, Bettina, and Ursula Schulze, eds. *Wörterbuch der mittelhochdeutschen Urkundensprache*. Vol. 3 (Berlin, 2010).

Kittell, Ellen E. *From Ad Hoc to Routine: A Case Study in Medieval Bureaucracy* (Philadelphia, PA, 1991).

Klecker, Elisabeth. "Echtheitskritik–Invektive–Selbstinzenierung. Francesco Petrarca über die pseudoantiken Inserte im Heinricianum (Sen. 16, 5)." In *Privilegium maius*, pp. 193–212.

Kleist, Wolfgang. "Der Tod des Erzbischofs Engelbert von Köln. Eine kritische Studie." *Zeitschrift für vaterländische Geschichte und Altertumskunde* 75 (1917): 182–249.

Klohn, Otto. *Die Entwicklung der Corveyer Schutz- und Vogteiverhältnisse* (Hildesheim, 1914).

Kluge, Bernd. *Deutsche Münzgeschichte von der späten Karolingerzeit bis zum Ende der Salier (ca. 900 bis 1125)* (Sigmaringen, 1991).

Kluge, Friedrich and Elmar Seebold. *Etymologisches Wörterbuch der deutschen Sprache* (24th ed., Berlin and New York, 2002).

Kohl, Thomas. "Besitzübertragungen, Kirchweihen, verprügelte *servi* und das Schwein des Bischofs." In *Grenzen des Rituals. Wirkreichweiten – Geltungsbereiche – Forschungsperspektiven*, ed. Andreas Büttner, Andreas

Schmidt and Paul Töbelmann (Cologne, Weimar and Vienna, 2014), pp. 73–86.

"Groß- und Kleinfamilien im frühmittelalterlichen Bayern." In *Verwandtschaft, Name und soziale Ordnung (300–1000)*, ed. Steffen Patzold and Karl Ubl (Berlin and Boston, 2014), pp. 161–75.

Lokale Gesellschaften: Formen der Gemeinschaft in Bayern vom 8. bis zum 10. Jahrhundert (Ostfildern, 2010).

Köhn, Rolf. "Die Abrechnungen der Landvögte in den österreichischen Vorlanden um 1400. Mit einer Edition des *Raitregisters* Friedrichs von Hattstatt für 1399–1404." *Blätter für deutsche Landesgeschichte* 128 (1992): 117–78.

"Der Landvogt in den spätmittelalterlichen Vorlanden. Kreatur des Herzogs und Tyrann der Untertanen?" In *Die Habsburger im deutschen Südwesten*, ed. Franz Quarthal and Gerhard Faix (Stuttgart, 2000), pp. 153–98.

"Der österreichische Landvogt Engelhard von Weinsberg und die für ihn von Mai 1395 bis Juli 1356 geführten Abrechnungen." *Argovia* 106 (1994): 1–129.

Koller, Heinrich. "Die Entvogtung bei den Zisterziensern." *Archiv für Diplomatik* 23 (1977): 209–23.

Kölzer, Theo. *Kaiser Ludwig der Fromme (814–840) im Spiegel seiner Urkunden* (Paderborn, 2005).

Studien zu den Urkundenfälschungen des Klosters St. Maximin vor Trier (10.–12. Jahrhundert) (Sigmaringen, 1989).

"Zu den Fälschungen für St. Maximin in Trier." In *Fälschungen im Mittelalter*, pp. 3: 315–26.

Konrad, Kai A., and Stergios Skaperdas. "The Market for Protection and the Origin of the State." *Economic Theory* 50 (2012): 417–43.

Körner, Martin. "Steuern und Abgaben in Theorie und Praxis im Mittelalter und in der frühen Neuzeit." In *Steuern, Abgaben und Dienste vom Mittelalter bis zur Gegenwart*, ed. Eckart Schremmer (Stuttgart, 1994), pp. 53–76.

Körntgen, Ludger. "Zwischen Herrschern und Heiligen: Zum Verhältnis von Königsnähe und Eigeninteresse bei den ottonischen Frauengemeinschaften Essen und Gandersheim." In *Herrschaft, Liturgie und Raum: Studien zur mittelalterlichen Geschichte des Frauenstifts Essen*, ed. Katrinette Bodarwé and Thomas Schilp (Essen, 2002), pp. 7–23.

Koziol, Geoffrey. *Begging Pardon and Favor: Ritual and Political Order in Early Medieval France* (Ithaca, NY and London, 1992).

"Monks, Feuds, and the Making of Peace in Eleventh-Century Flanders." In *The Peace of God*, ed. Thomas Head and Richard Landes, pp. 239–58.

The Peace of God (Leeds, 2018).

The Politics of Memory and Identity in Carolingian Royal Diplomas: The West Frankish Kingdom (840–987) (Turnhout, 2012).

Kraus, Andreas. "Das Herzogtum der Wittelsbacher: Die Grundlegung des Landes Bayern." In *Wittelsbach und Bayern*, ed. Hubert Glaser. Vol. 1:1 (Munich, 1980), pp. 165–200.

Kreuzer, Georg. "Das Prämonstratenserstift Ursberg zwischen Abhängigkeit und Selbstbehauptung. Zur Rolle der Vogtei im Spätmittelalter und in der

Frühen Neuzeit." In *Suevia Sacra: Zur Geschichte der ostschwäbischen Reichsstifte im Spätmittelalter und in der Frühen Neuzeit.*, ed. Wilhelm Liebhart and Ulrich Faust (Stuttgart, 2001), pp. 69–90.

Kroeschell, Karl A. "Herrschaft." In *Handwörterbuch zur deutschen Rechtsgeschichte*, ed. Adalbert Erler and Ekkehard Kaufmann. Vol. 1 (Berlin, 1971), pp. 103–08.

Kroeze, Ronald, André Vitória and G. Geltner. "Introduction." In *Anticorruption in History*, pp. 1–17.

Krumwiede, Hans-Walter. *Das Stift Fischbeck an der Weser* (Göttingen, 1955).

Kühnle, Nina. *Wir, Vogt, Richter und Gemeinde: Städtewesen, städtische Führungsgruppen und Landesherrschaft im spätmittelalterlichen Württemberg (1250–1534)* (Ostfildern, 2017).

Kunze, Jens. "Das Verhältnis von Stadt und Amt Zwickau im 14. und 15. Jahrhundert." In *1407. Rat kontra Landesherr?*, ed. Wilfried Stoye and Silva Teichert (Zwickau, 2011), pp. 26–49.

Kupper, Jean-Louis. "L'avouerie de la cité de Liège au haut moyen âge." In *L'Avouerie en Lotharingie*, pp. 95–113.

Küppers-Braun, Ute. "Kanonissin, Dechantin, Pröpstin und Äbtissin – Quedlinburger Stiftsdamen nach der Reformation." In *Kayserlich*, pp. 30–104.

Küss, Tobias. *Die älteren Diepoldinger als Markgrafen in Bayern (1077–1204)* (Munich, 2013).

Landau, Peter. *Jus patronatus: Studien zur Entwicklung des Patronats im Dekretalenrecht und der Kanonistik des 12. und 13. Jahrhunderts* (Cologne and Vienna, 1975).

Landes, Richard. "The Fear of an Apocalyptic Year 1000: Augustinian Historiography, Medieval and Modern." *Speculum* 75 (2000): 97–145.

Lane, Frederic C. "Economic Consequences of Organized Violence." *Journal of Economic History* 18 (1958): 401–17.

Lau, Friedrich. "Der Kampf um die Siegburger Vogtei 1399–1407." *Zeitschrift des Bergischen Geschichtsvereins* 38 (1905): 60–134.

Lauerwald, Paul. "Die Reichsstadt Nordhausen und ihr münz- und geldpolitisches Engagement nach dem dauerhaften Erwerb des Schultheißen- und Vogteiamtes im Jahre 1715 bis zum Ende der Reichsfreiheit." *Harz-Zeitschrift* 67 (2015): 50–62.

Laufner, Richard. "Die Ausbildung des Territorialstaates der Kurfürsten von Trier." In *Der deutsche Territorialstaat*, pp. 2:127–47.

Lauwers, Michel. "La 'Vie du seigneur Bouchard, comte vénérable': Conflits d'avouerie, traditions Carolingiennes et modèles de sainteté à l'abbaye des Fossés zu XIe siècle." In *Guerriers et moines: conversion et sainteté aristocratiques dans l'occident médiéval (IXe-XIIe siècle)* (Antibes, 2002), pp. 371–418.

Layer, Adolf. "Die Grafen von Dillingen." *Jahrbuch des Historischen Vereins Dillingen an der Donau* 75 (1973): 46–101.

Le Goff, Jacques. *Must We Divide History into Periods?* Trans. M. B. DeBevoise (New York, 2015).

Le Jan, Régine. "L'Aristocratie Lotharingienne: Structure interne et conscience politique." In *Lotharingia: Eine europäische Kernlandschaft um das Jahr 1000*, ed. Hans-Walter Herrmann and Reinhard Schneider (Saarbrücken, 1995), pp. 71–88.

Leenen, Brunhilde. "Positionierung zwischen den Mächten – Die Landesherrschaft der Äbtissin von Essen." In *AufRuhr 1225!*, pp. 77–91.

"Das Stift Essen und seine Vögte." In *Aus der Nähe betrachtet: Regionale Vernetzungen des Essener Frauenstiftes in Mittelalter und früher Neuzeit*, ed. Jens Lieven and Birgitta Falk (Essen, 2017), pp. 213–30.

"Vogteirollen Graf Friedrichs von Isenberg." In *AufRuhr 1225!*, pp. 283–85.

"Zwei interpolierte Urkunden des Stiftes Essen." In *AufRuhr 1225!*, pp. 286–87.

Lehmann, Rudolf. *Geschichte der Niederlausitz* (Berlin, 1963).

Das Lehnswesen im Hochmittelalter. Forschungskonstrukte – Quellenbefunde – Deutungsrelevanz. Ed. Jürgen Dendorfer and Roman Deutinger (Ostfildern, 2010)

Levillain, Léon. *Examen critique des chartes mérovingiennes et carolingiennes de l'abbaye de Corbie* (Paris, 1902).

Lexer, Matthias. *Mittelhochdeutsches Handwörterbuch*. Vol. 3 (Leipzig, 1878).

Leyser, Karl. "Ottonian Government." *EHR* 96 (1981): 721–53.

Rule and Conflict in an Early Medieval Society: Ottonian Saxony (London, 1979).

Liebaert, Paul. "Règlement d'avouerie en faveur de l'abbaye de St-Denys en France." *Revue bénédictine* 30 (1913): 70–78.

Liebhart, Wilhelm. "'*Advocatiae super possessiones beati Udalrici*'. Zur mittelalterlichen Klostervogtei in Schwaben und Baiern am Beispiel von St. Ulrich und Afra." In *Aus Schwaben und Bayern: Festschrift für Pankraz Fried*, ed. Peter Fassl, Wilhelm Liebhart and Wolfgang Wüst (Sigmaringen, 1991), pp. 169–77.

Lind, Gunner. "Great Friends and Small Friends: Clientelism and the Power Elite." In *Power Elites and State Building*, ed. Wolfgang Reinhard (Oxford and New York, 1996), pp. 123–47.

Lindner, Michael. "Weitere Textzeugnisse zur *Constitucio Karolina super libertate ecclesiastica*." *DA* 51 (1995): 515–38.

Little, Lester K. *Benedictine Maledictions: Liturgical Cursing in Romanesque France* (Ithaca, NY and London, 1993).

Lord, Kevin Lucas. "Toward the Golden Bull and Against the Pope: The Role of Custom and Honor in King Ludwig IV's Nuremberg and Frankfurt Appellations (1323–24)." *Austrian History Yearbook* 51 (2020): 91–113.

Lordship and Community in Medieval Europe: Selected Readings, ed. Fredric L. Cheyette (New York, 1968).

Lothmann, Josef. *Erzbischof Engelbert I. von Köln (1216–1225): Graf von Berg, Erzbischof und Herzog, Reichsverweser* (Cologne, 1993).

Loud, Graham A. "A Political and Social Revolution: The Development of the Territorial Principalities in Germany." In *Origins of the German Principalities*, pp. 3–22.

Lutter, Christina. "The Babenbergs: From Frontier March to Principality." In *Origins of the German Principalities*, pp. 312–28.

"Geteilte soziale Räume und gemeinsame Zugehörigkeiten: Die Wiener Zisterzienserinnen um 1300." In *Konstanz und Wandel. Religiöse Lebensformen im europäischen Mittelalter*, ed. Gordon Blennemann, Christine Kleinjung and Thomas Kohl (Affalterbach, 2016), pp. 199–216.

Zwischen Hof und Kloster: Kulturelle Gemeinschaften im mittelalterlichen Österreich (Vienna, Cologne and Weimar, 2010).

Lutterbeck, Michael. *Der Rat der Stadt Lübeck im 13. und 14. Jahrhundert* (Lübeck, 2002).

Luuk, Ernst, ed. *Berlin-Handbuch: Das Lexikon der Bundeshauptstadt* (Berlin, 1992).

Lyon, Bryce, and Adriaan E. Verhulst. *Medieval Finance: A Comparison of Financial Institutions in Northwestern Europe* (Providence and Bruges, 1967).

Lyon, Jonathan R. "Advocata, Advocatrix, Advocatissa. Frauen als Vögtinnen im Hochmittelalter." In *Kirchenvogtei und adlige Herrschaftsbildung*, pp. 143–68.

"The Medieval German State in Recent Historiography." *German History* 28 (2010): 85–94.

"Nobility and Monastic Patronage: The View from Outside the Monastery." In *Cambridge History of Medieval Monasticism*, pp. 2:848–64.

"Noble Lineages, *Hausklöster*, and Monastic Advocacy in the Twelfth Century: The Garsten Vogtweistum in its Dynastic Context." *MIÖG* 123 (2015): 1–29.

"Otto of Freising's Tyrants: Church Advocates and Noble Lordship in the Long Twelfth Century." In *Christianity and Culture in the Middle Ages: Essays to Honor John Van Engen*, ed. David Mengel and Lisa Wolverton (Notre Dame, 2015), pp. 141–67.

Princely Brothers and Sisters: The Sibling Bond in German Politics, 1100–1250 (Ithaca, NY and London, 2013).

"Rulers, Local Elites and Monastic Liberties. Tegernsee and Bury St Edmunds Under the Staufens and Plantagenets." In *Staufen and Plantagenets: Two Empires in Comparison*, ed. Alheydis Plassmann and Dominik Büschken (Göttingen, 2018), pp. 151–82.

MacLean, Simon. *Kingship and Politics in the Late Ninth Century: Charles the Fat and the End of the Carolingian Empire* (Cambridge, UK, 2003).

"Shadow Kingdom: Lotharingia and the Frankish World, c.850–c.1050." *History Compass* 11 (2013): 443–57.

MacMullen, Ramsay. *Corruption and the Decline of Rome* (New Haven, CT and London, 1988).

Magnou-Nortier, Elisabeth. *Le Code Théodosien, livre XVI et sa réception au Moyen Âge* (Paris, 2002).

"The Enemies of the Peace: Reflections on a Vocabulary, 500–1100." In *The Peace of God*, pp. 58–79.

"Note sur l'expression *iustitiam facere* dans les capitulaires carolingiens." In *Haut Moyen-Age: Culture, éducation et société. Etudes offertes à Pierre Riché*, ed. Michel Sot (Garenne-Colombes, 1990), pp. 249–64.

Maissen, Thomas. "Inventing the Sovereign Republic: Imperial Structures, French Challenges, Dutch Models and the Early Modern Swiss Confederation." In *The Republican Alternative*, ed. Thomas Maissen, André Holenstein and Maarten Prak (Amsterdam, 2008), pp. 125–50.

Malosse, Pierre-Louis. "Libanius' *Orations*." In *Libanius: A Critical Introduction*, ed. Lieve Van Hoof (Cambridge, UK, 2014), pp. 81–106.

Mancia, Lauren. "Sources for Monasticism in the Long Twelfth Century." In *Cambridge History of Medieval Monasticism*, pp. 2: 667–83.

Manganaro, Stefano. "Forme e lessico dell'immunità nei diplomi di Ottone I: La mediazione cancelleresca tra Regno ed enti religiosi attraverso il privilegio scritto." *Studi Medievali* 51 (2010): 1–93.

"Royal Rulership in the Tenth and Early Eleventh Centuries: German and Italian Approaches in Dialogue." *Reti Medievali Rivista* 20 (2019): 157–85.

Mann, Jill. *From Aesop to Reynard: Beast Literature in Medieval Britain* (Oxford, 2009).

Margue, Michel. "Klostervogtei zwischen monastischem Diskurs und bilateraler Aushandlung am Beispiel des zentralen lotharingischen Raums (10. bis Anfang 12. Jahrhundert)." In *Kirchenvogtei und adlige Herrschaftsbildung*, pp. 381–422.

Marten, Kimberly. "Warlordism in Comparative Perspective." *International Security* 31 (2006/7): 41–73.

Warlords: Strong-Arm Brokers in Weak States (Ithaca, NY and London, 2012).

Martin, Franz. "Die kirchliche Vogtei im Erzstifte Salzburg." *Mitteilungen der Gesellschaft für Salzburger Landeskunde* 46 (1906): 339–436.

Marx, Karl, and Friedrich Engels. *The Marx-Engels Reader.* Ed. Robert C. Tucker (2nd ed., New York, 1978).

Máthé, Piroska Réka. "'Österreich contra Sulz 1412'. Verwaltung und Politik im Aargau unter Landvogt Graf Hermann von Sulz und der Streit um das Laufenburger Erbe." *Argovia* 99 (1987): 5–39.

May, Alfred N. "An Index of Thirteenth-Century Peasant Impoverishment? Manor Court Fines." *Economic History Review* 26 (1973): 389–402.

Mayer, Theodor. *Fürsten und Staat: Studien zur Verfassungsgeschichte des deutschen Mittelalters* (Weimar, 1950).

"The State of the Dukes of Zähringen." In *Mediaeval Germany 911–1250*, pp. 2: 175–202.

Mazel, Florian. "Amitié et rupture de l'amitié. Moines et grands laïcs provençaux au temps de la crise grégorienne (milieu XIe – milieu XIIe siècle)." *Revue Historique* 307 (2005): 53–95.

L'évêque et le territoire: l'invention médiévale de l'espace (Paris, 2016).

McGlynn, Margaret. "From Written Record to Bureaucratic Mind: Imagining a Criminal Record." *Past and Present* 250 (2021): 55–86.

McGuire, Brian Patrick. "The Cistercians and the Rise of the Exemplum in Early Thirteenth-Century France." In *Friendship and Faith: Cistercian Men, Women, and Their Stories, 1100–1250* (Aldershot and Burlington, VT, 2002), pp. V:211–67.

McHaffie, Matthew. "Law and Violence in Eleventh-Century France." *Past and Present* 238 (2018): 3–41.

McKeon, Peter R. *Hincmar of Laon and Carolingian Politics* (Urbana, IL, 1978).

McKitterick, Rosamond. *The Carolingians and the Written Word* (Cambridge, UK, 1989).

Charlemagne: The Formation of a European Identity (Cambridge, UK, 2008).

"Charlemagne's *Missi* and Their Books." In *Early Medieval Studies in Memory of Patrick Wormald*, ed. Stephen Baxter, Catherine Karkov, Janet L. Nelson and David Pelteret (Farnham and Burlington, VT, 2009), pp. 253–67.

"Some Carolingian Law-Books and Their Function." In *Authority and Power: Studies on Medieval Law and Government Presented to Walter Ullmann*, ed. Brian Tierney and Peter Linehan (Cambridge, UK, 1980), pp. 13–27.

McNair, Fraser. "Governance, Locality and Legal Culture: The Rise and Fall of the Carolingian Advocates of Saint-Martin of Tours." *Early Medieval Europe* 29 (2021): 201–24.

Mediae Latinitatis Lexicon Minus. Ed. Jan Frederik Niermeyer, C. van de Kieft and J. W. J. Burgers, 2nd ed. (Leiden and Boston, MA, 2002).

Mediaeval Germany 911–1250: Essays by German Historians. Trans. Geoffrey Barraclough. 2 vols. (Oxford, 1938).

Mehl, Manfred. *Die Münzen des Stiftes Quedlinburg* (Hamburg, 2006).

Mehlum, Halvor, Karl Ove Moene, and Ragnar Torvik. "Plunder & Protection Inc." *Journal of Peace Research* 39 (2002): 447–59.

Meier, Matthias. *Gründung und Reform erinnern: Die Geschichte des Klosters Muri aus der Perspektive hochmittelalterlicher Quellen* (Ostfildern, 2020).

Meloy, John L. "The Privatization of Protection: Extortion and the State in the Circassian Mamluk Period." *Journal of the Economic and Social History of the Orient* 47 (2004): 195–212.

Melville, Gert. *The World of Medieval Monasticism: Its History and Forms of Life*. Trans. James D. Mixson (Athens, OH, 2016).

Mersiowsky, Mark. *Die Urkunde in der Karolingerzeit: Originale, Urkundenpraxis und politische Kommunikation*. 2 vols. (Wiesbaden, 2015).

"Regierungspraxis und Schriftlichkeit im Karolingerreich: Das Fallbeispiel der Mandate und Briefe." In *Schriftkultur und Reichsverwaltung unter den Karolingern*, ed. Rudolf Schieffer (Opladen, 1996), pp. 109–66.

"Tauschgeschäfte und Tauschurkunden in Westfalen bis 1125." In *Tauschgeschäft*, pp. 239–71.

Meulen, Ross Vander. "The Theological Texture of Schiller's *Wilhelm Tell*." *Germanic Review* 53 (1978): 56–62.

Meyer-Schlenkrich, Carla. "The Imperial City: The Example of Nuremberg." In *Origins of the German Principalities*, pp. 68–82.

Milz, Joseph. "Die Vögte des Kölner Domstiftes und der Abteien Deutz und Werden im 11. und 12. Jahrhundert." *Rheinische Vierteljahrsblätter* 41 (1977): 196–217.

Mitterauer, Michael. *Why Europe? The Medieval Origins of Its Special Path*. Trans. Gerald Chapple (Chicago and London, 2010).

Mittler zwischen Herrschaft und Gemeinde: Die Rolle von Funktions- und Führungsgruppen in der mittelalterlichen Urbanisierung Zentraleuropas. Ed. Elisabeth Gruber, Susanne Claudine Pils, Sven Rabeler, Herwig Weigl and Gabriel Zeilinger (Innsbruck, Vienna and Bozen, 2013).

Mixson, James D. *Poverty's Proprietors: Ownership and Mortal Sin at the Origins of the Observant Movement* (Leiden and Boston, MA, 2009).

Moore, R. I. *The War on Heresy* (Cambridge, MA, 2012).

Moraw, Peter. "Cities and Citizenry as Factors of State Formation in the Roman-German Empire of the Late Middle Ages." *Theory and Society* 18 (1989): 631–62.

"Organisation und Funktion von Verwaltung im ausgehenden Mittelalter (ca. 1350–1500)." In *Deutsche Verwaltungsgeschichte*, pp. 21–65.

Von offener Verfassung zu gestalteter Verdichtung: Das Reich im späten Mittelalter 1250 bis 1490 (Berlin, 1985).

Mordek, Hubert. *Bibliotheca capitularium regum Francorum manuscripta: Überlieferung und Traditionszusammenhang der fränkischen Herrschererlasse* (Munich, 1995).

Morris, Colin. *The Papal Monarchy: The Western Church from 1050 to 1250* (Oxford, 1989).

Morris, Rosemary. "The Problems of Property." In *The Cambridge History of Christianity*, vol. 3, ed. Thomas F. X. Noble and Julia Smith (Cambridge, UK, 2008), pp. 327–44.

Mostert, Marco. *The Political Theology of Abbo of Fleury* (Hilversum, 1987).

Mukhopadhyay, Dipali. *Warlords, Strongman Governors, and the State in Afghanistan* (New York, 2014).

Müller, Jan-Dirk. "Circa 1200: Contagious Violence." In *A New History of German Literature*, ed. David E. Wellbery et al. (Cambridge, MA and London, 2004), pp. 87–91.

Mungiu-Pippidi, Alina. *The Quest for Good Governance: How Societies Develop Control of Corruption* (Cambridge, UK, 2015).

Murray, Alan V. "The Title of Godfrey of Bouillon as Ruler of Jerusalem." In *The Franks in Outremer: Studies in the Latin Principalities of Palestine and Syria, 1099–1187* (Farnham and Burlington, VT, 2015), pp. VII: 163–78.

Naz, Raoul. "Avouerie, Avoué." In *Dictionnaire de droit canonique*, ed. Raoul Naz. Vol. 1 (Paris, 1935), cols. 1561–1578.

Neel, Carol Leigh. "The Historical Work of Burchard of Ursberg, I: The Ursberg 'Chronicon' Text." *Analecta Praemonstratensia* 58 (1982): 96–129.

Neidiger, Bernhard. *Mendikanten zwischen Ordensideal und städtischer Realität: Untersuchungen zum wirtschaftlichen Verhalten der Bettelorden in Basel* (Berlin, 1981).

Neitmann, Klaus. "Huldigung und Privilegienbestätigung: Die Ausbildung der landständischen Verfassung der Neumark unter der Herrschaft des Deutschen Ordens und der frühen Hohenzollern." In *Landesherr, Adel und Städte in der mittelalterlichen und frühneuzeitlichen Neumark*, ed. Klaus Neitmann (Berlin, 2015), pp. 245–317.

Nelson, Janet L. *Charles the Bald* (Harlow and New York, 1992).

"Dispute Settlement in Carolingian West Francia." In *The Settlement of Disputes*, pp. 45–64.

"Kingship and Royal Government." In *NCMH*, vol. 2, ed. Rosamond McKitterick (Cambridge, UK, 1995), pp. 383–430.

La Neustrie: Les pays au nord de la Loire de 650 à 850. Ed. Hartmut Atsma. 2 vols. (Sigmaringen, 1989).

Newman, Martha G. "Foundation and Twelfth Century." In *The Cambridge Companion to the Cistercian Order*, ed. Mette Birkedal Bruun (Cambridge, UK, 2013), pp. 25–37.

Nicholas, David. *The Growth of the Medieval City: From Late Antiquity to the Early Fourteenth Century* (London and New York, 1997).

Niederhäuser, Peter. "'Der Landvogt kam nie gen Baden ... ': Baden – ein habsburgisches Verwaltungszentrum nach 1400?" *Badener Neujahrblätter* 78 (2003): 139–49.

Nieus, Jean-François. "Avouerie et service militaire en Flandre au XIe siècle" (in press).

"Vicomte et avoué: les auxiliaires laïcs du pouvoir épiscopal (XIe-XIIIe siècle)." In *Le diocèse de Thérouanne au Moyen Âge*, ed. Jeff Rider and Benoît-Michel Tock (Arras, 2010), pp. 119–33.

Nieus, Jean-François, and Steven Vanderputten. "Diplôme princier, matrice de faux, acte modèle. Le règlement d'avouerie du comte Baudouin V pour Saint-Bertin (1042) et ses réappropriations sous l'abbatiat réformateur de Lambert (1095–1123)." *The Medieval Low Countries* 1 (2014): 1–59.

Nightingale, John. *Monasteries and Patrons in the Gorze Reform: Lotharingia c. 850–1000* (Oxford, 2001).

Nikolay-Panter, Marlene. "Siegburg: Stadt–Abtei–Grundherrschaft." In *Grundherrschaft – Kirche – Stadt zwischen Maas und Rhein während des hohen Mittelalters*, ed. Alfred Haverkamp and Frank G. Hirschmann (Mainz, 1997), pp. 191–218.

Nirenberg, David. *Communities of Violence: Persecution of Minorities in the Middle Ages* (Princeton, NJ, 1996).

Noble, Thomas F. X. "The Place in Papal History of the Roman Synod of 826." *Church History* 45 (1976): 434–54.

The Republic of St. Peter: The Birth of the Papal State, 680–825 (Philadelphia, PA, 1984).

North, Douglass C., John Joseph Wallis and Barry R. Weingast. *Violence and Social Orders: A Conceptual Framework for Interpreting Recorded Human History* (Cambridge, UK and New York, 2013).

Ó Riain, Diarmuid. "The *Magnum Legendarium Austriacum*: A New Investigation of one of Medieval Europe's Richest Hagiographical Collections." *Analecta Bollandiana* 133 (2015): 87–165.

Oefele, Edmund von. *Geschichte der Grafen von Andechs* (Innsbruck, 1877).

Oelsner, Norbert, and Wilfried Stoye. "Die Zwickauer Ereignisse anno 1407 und die Hinrichtung ' ... etzlich Erbarn bürger der stat ... ' am 10. Juli selbigen Jahres in der Burg zu Meißen." In *1407. Rat kontra Landesherr?*, ed. Wilfried Stoye and Silva Teichert (Zwickau, 2011), pp. 68–109.

O'Neill, Rosemary. "Counting Sheep in the C Text of *Piers Plowman*." *The Yearbook of Langland Studies* 29 (2015): 89–116.

Oostebrink, Edo Wilbert. "Der Drache und die Vögte von Geldern." *Annalen des Historischen Vereins für den Niederrhein* 211 (2008): 191–267.

The Origins of the German Principalities, 1100–1350. Essays by German Historians. Ed. Graham A. Loud and Jochen Schenk (London and New York, 2017).

Ortmayr, Petrus, and Aegid Decker. *Das Benediktinerstift Seitenstetten: Ein Gang durch seine Geschichte* (Wels, 1955).

Osheim, Duane J. *An Italian Lordship: The Bishopric of Lucca in the Late Middle Ages* (Berkeley, Los Angeles and London, 1977).

Otto, Eberhard F. *Die Entwicklung der deutschen Kirchenvogtei im 10. Jahrhundert* (Berlin-Grunewald, 1933).

Owens, Patricia. "Distinctions, Distinctions: 'Public' and 'Private' Force?" *International Affairs (Royal Institute of International Affairs 1944-)* 84 (2008): 977–90.

Paravicini, Werner. "Un amour malheureux au XVe siècle: Pierre de Hagenbach et la dame de Remiremont." *Journal des Savants* (2006): 105–81.

Parisse, Michel. "Les règlements d'avouerie en Lorraine au XIe siècle." In *L'Avouerie en Lotharingie*, pp. 159–73.

"Lotharingia." In *NCMH*, vol. 3, ed. Timothy Reuter (Cambridge, UK, 1999), pp. 310–27.

"Noblesse et monastères en Lotharingie du IXe au XIe siècle." In *Religieux et religieuses en Empire du Xe aux X^{iie} siècle*, ed. Michel Parisse (Paris, 2011), pp. 32–54.

"Restaurer un monastère au Xe siècle. L'exemple de Gorze." In *Religieux et religieuses*, pp. 55–71.

Parker, David. *The Making of French Absolutism* (New York, 1983).

Parlow, Ulrich. *Die Zähringer: Kommentierte Quellendokumentation zu einem südwestdeutschen Herzogsgeschlecht des hohen Mittelalters* (Stuttgart, 1999).

Patze, Hans. "Die Pegauer Annalen, die Königserhebung Wratislaws von Böhmen und die Anfänge der Stadt Pegau." *Jahrbuch für die Geschichte Mittel- und Ostdeutschlands* 12 (1963): 1–62.

Pätzold, Stefan. *Die frühen Wettiner: Adelsfamilie und Hausüberlieferung bis 1221* (Cologne, Weimar and Vienna, 1997).

Patzold, Steffen. *Das Lehnswesen* (Munich, 2012).

"Ein klösterliches Lehnswesen? Der Zusammenhang von Besitz und personalen Bindungen im Spiegel von Klosterchroniken des 12. Jahrhunderts." In *Das Lehnswesen im Hochmittelalter*, pp. 103–24.

"Human Security, fragile Staatlichkeit und Governance im Frühmittelalter. Zur Fragwürdigkeit der Scheidung von Vormoderne und Moderne." *Geschichte und Gesellschaft* 38 (2012): 406–22.

Ich und Karl der Große: Das Leben des Höflings Einhard (Stuttgart, 2013).

"Warlords oder Amtsträger? Bemerkungen zu Eliten im Frankenreich um das Jahr 700 aus der Perspektive der Geschichtswissenschaft." In *Warlords oder Amtsträger? Herausragende Bestattungen der späten Merowingerzeit*, ed. Sebastian Brather, Claudia Merthen and Tobias Springer (Nuremberg, 2018), pp. 10–18.

The Peace of God: Social Violence and Religious Response in France around the Year 1000. Ed. Thomas Head and Richard Landes (Ithaca, NY and London, 1992).

Pearson, Kathy Lynne Roper. *Conflicting Loyalties in Early Medieval Bavaria: A View of Socio-Political Interaction, 680–900* (Aldershot, 1999).

Peiper, Rudolf. "Gedicht auf den Vogt Albert von Krakau." *Forschungen zur deutschen Geschichte* 17 (1877): 372–75.

Peltzer, Jörg, ed. *Rank and Order: The Formation of Aristocratic Elites in Western and Central Europe, 500–1500* (Ostfildern, 2015).

Penth, Sabine. "Kloster- und Ordenspolitik der Staufer als Gegenstand einer vergleichenden Ordensforschung: Das Beispiel der Prämonstratenser, die Vogteiregelungen Friedrich Barbarossas und viele offene Fragen." *Analecta Praemonstratensia* 81 (2005): 64–93.

Pergameni, Charles. *L'Avouerie ecclésiastique belge des origines a la période Bourguignonne* (Ghent, 1907).

Peters, Edward M. "Prison before the Prison: The Ancient and Medieval Worlds." In *The Oxford History of the Prison*, ed. Norval Morris and David J. Rothman (Oxford and New York, 1998), pp. 3–43.

Peters, Ralf. *Die Entwicklung des Grundbesitzes der Abtei Saint-Denis in merowingischer und karolingischer Zeit* (Aachen, 1993).

Petersen, Stefan. "Die Rechtsstellung des Prämonstratenserinnenstifts Hausen gegenüber Bischof, Vogt und Vaterabt." *Mainfränkisches Jahrbuch für Geschichte und Kunst* 66 (2014): 89–99.

Petit, Roger. "L'avouerie de l'abbaye de Stavelot du IXe au XIIe siècle." In *L'Avouerie en Lotharingie*, pp. 129–57.

Pfeifer, Gustav. "Landwerdung durch 'Übervogtung': Überlegungen zu einem zentralen Deutungsmuster der Tiroler Landesgeschichte am Beispiel der Brixner Hochstiftsvogtei." In *Kirchenvogtei und adlige Herrschaftsbildung*, pp. 261–96.

Pischek, Adolf. *Die Vogtgerichtsbarkeit süddeutscher Klöster in ihrer sachlichen Abgrenzung während des früheren Mittelalters* (Stuttgart, 1907).

Pitz, Ernst. *Verfassungslehre und Einführung in die deutsche Verfassungsgeschichte des Mittelalters* (Berlin, 2006).

Planck, Julius Wilhelm von. *Das deutsche Gerichtsverfahren im Mittelalter: Nach dem Sachsenspiegel und den verwandten Rechtsquellen*. 2 vols. (Brunswick, 1879).

Planta, Conradin von. "Advocacy and 'Defensio' – The Protection of the Houses of the Teutonic Order in the Region of the Upper Rhine during the Thirteenth and Fourteenth Centuries." In *The Military Orders*, vol. 6.2, ed. Jochen Schenk and Mike Carr (London and New York, 2017), pp. 193–202.

Pohl, Walter. "Staat und Herrschaft im Frühmittelalter: Überlegungen zum Forschungsstand." In *Staat im frühen Mittelalter*, ed. Stuart Airlie, Walter Pohl and Helmut Reimitz (Vienna, 2006), pp. 9–38.

Poly, Jean-Pierre, and Eric Bournazel. *The Feudal Transformation: 900–1200.* Trans. Caroline Higgitt (New York and London, 1991).

Pomeranz, Kenneth. *The Great Divergence: Europe, China, and the Making of the Modern World Economy* (Princeton, NJ and Oxford, 2000).

Powicke, F. M. "Presidential Address: Reflections on the Medieval State." *Transactions of the Royal Historical Society*, Ser. 4, 19 (1936): 1–18.

Privilegium maius. Autopsie, Kontext und Karriere der Fälschungen Rudolfs IV. von Österreich. Ed. Thomas Just, Kathrin Kininger, Andrea Sommerlechner and Herwig Weigl (Vienna, Cologne and Weimar, 2018).

Prößler, Robert. *Das Erzstift Köln in der Zeit des Erzbischofs Konrad von Hochstaden: organisatorische und wirtschaftliche Grundlagen in den Jahren 1238–1261* (Cologne, 1997).

Raaijmakers, Janneke. *The Making of the Monastic Community of Fulda, c. 744–c. 900* (Cambridge, 2012).

Redlich, Oswald. *Rudolf von Habsburg: Das deutsche Reich nach dem Untergange des alten Kaisertums* (Innsbruck, 1903).

"Ueber bairische Traditionsbücher und Traditionen." *MIÖG* 5 (1884): 1–82.

Reichert, Folker. *Landesherrschaft, Adel und Vogtei: Zur Vorgeschichte des spätmittelalterlichen Ständestaates im Herzogtum Österreich* (Cologne and Vienna, 1985).

Reichert, Hermann. *Konkordanz zum Nibelungenlied nach der St. Galler Handschrift*. Vol. 2 (Vienna, 2006).

Reimold, Walter. *Chronik der Vogtei Pfalzfeld* (Boppard, 1965).

Reinhard, Wolfgang. "Introduction." In *Power Elites and State Building*, ed. Wolfgang Reinhard (Oxford and New York, 1996), pp. 1–18.

Rembold, Ingrid. *Conquest and Christianization: Saxony and the Carolingian World, 772–888* (Cambridge, UK, 2018).

Rennie, Kriston R. *Freedom and Protection: Monastic Exemption in France, c. 590–c. 1100* (Manchester, 2018).

Resmini, Bertram. *Die Benediktinerabtei St. Maximin vor Trier*. Vol. 1 (Berlin and Boston, 2016).

Reuter, Timothy. "All Quiet Except on the Western Front? The Emergence of Pre-modern Forms of Statehood in the Central Middle Ages." In *Medieval Polities and Modern Mentalities*, ed. Janet L. Nelson (Cambridge, UK, 2006), pp. 432–58.

"Debate: The 'Feudal Revolution.'" *Past and Present* 155 (1997): 177–95.

"Forms of Lordship in German Historiography." In *Pour une anthropologie du prélèvement seigneurial dans les campagnes médiévales (XIᵉ-XIVᵉ siècles)*, ed. Monique Bourin and Pascual Martínez Sopena (Paris, 2004), pp. 51–61.

Germany in the Early Middle Ages, c. 800–1056 (London, 1991).

"The 'Imperial Church System' of the Ottonian and Salian Rulers. A Reconsideration." *Journal of Ecclesiastical History* 33 (1982): 347–74.

"Introduction: Reading the Tenth Century." In *NCMH*, vol. 3, ed. Timothy Reuter (Cambridge, UK, 2000), pp. 1–24.

"'Kirchenreform' und 'Kirchenpolitik' im Zeitalter Karl Martells: Begriffe und Wirklichkeit." In *Karl Martell in seiner Zeit*, ed. Jörg Jarnut, Ulrich Nonn and Michael Richter (Sigmaringen, 1994), pp. 35–59.

"The Medieval German *Sonderweg*? The Empire and Its Rulers in the High Middle Ages." In *Medieval Polities and Modern Mentalities*, ed. Janet L. Nelson (Cambridge, UK, 2006), pp. 388–412.

"Nobles and Others: The Social and Cultural Expression of Power Relations in the Middle Ages." In *Medieval Polities*, pp. 111–26.

"Property Transactions and Social Relations between Rulers, Bishops and Nobles in Early Eleventh-Century Saxony." In *Property and Power in the Early Middle Ages*, ed. Wendy Davies and Paul Fouracre (Cambridge, UK, 1995), pp. 165–99.

Reynolds, Susan. *Fiefs and Vassals: The Medieval Evidence Reinterpreted* (Oxford, 1994).

"Government and Community." In *NCMH*, vol. 4:1, ed. David Luscombe and Jonathan Riley-Smith (Cambridge, UK, 2004), pp. 86–112.

"The Historiography of the Medieval State." In *The Routledge Companion to Historiography*, ed. Michael Bentley (London and New York, 1997), pp. 117–38.

"There were States in Medieval Europe: A Response to Rees Davies." *Journal of Historical Sociology* 16 (2003): 550–55.

Richter, Horst. *Kommentar zum Rolandslied des Pfaffen Konrad Teil I* (Bern and Frankfurt, 1972).

Rider, Jeff. *God's Scribe: The Historiographical Art of Galbert of Bruges* (Washington, DC, 2001).

Riedmann, Josef. "Vescovi e Avvocati." In *I poteri temporali dei Vescovi in Italia e in Germania nel Medioevo*, ed. Carlo Guido Mor and Heinrich Schmidinger (Bologna, 1979), pp. 35–76.

Riley-Smith, Jonathan. "The Title of Godfrey of Bouillon." *Bulletin of the Institute of Historical Research* 52 (1979): 83–86.

Rio, Alice. *Legal Practice and the Written Word in the Early Middle Ages: Frankish Formulae, c. 500–1000* (Cambridge, UK, 2009).

Roach, Levi. *Forgery and Memory at the End of the First Millennium* (Princeton, NJ and Oxford, 2021).

Roberg, Francesco. *Gefälschte Memoria: Diplomatisch-Historische Studien zum ältesten "Necrolog" des Klosters St. Maximin vor Trier* (Hanover, 2008).

Roberts, Edward. "Hegemony, Rebellion and History: Flodoard's *Historia Remensis Ecclesiae* in Ottonian Perspective." *Journal of Medieval History* 42 (2016): 155–76.

Robinson, Ian Stuart. *Henry IV of Germany, 1056–1106* (Cambridge, UK, 1999).

The Papacy 1073–1198: Continuity and Innovation (Cambridge, UK and New York, 1990).

Röckelein, Hedwig. *Reliquientranslationen nach Sachsen im 9. Jahrhundert: Über Kommunikation, Mobilität und Öffentlichkeit im Frühmittelalter* (Stuttgart, 2002).

Rolker, Christof. "The *Collection in Seventy-Four Titles*: A Monastic Canon Law Collection from Eleventh-Century France." In *Readers, Texts and Compilers in the Earlier Middle Ages*, ed. Martin Brett and Kathleen G. Cushing (Farnham and Burlington, VT, 2009), pp. 59–72.

Romano, John F. "Julian of Vézelay, a Twelfth-Century Critic of His Monastery's Worldly Success." *Medieval Sermon Studies* 50 (2006): 51–69.

Rosenwein, Barbara H. *Negotiating Space: Power, Restraint, and Privileges of Immunity in Early Medieval Europe* (Ithaca, NY, 1999).

Rosenwein, Barbara H., Thomas F. Head and Sharon Farmer. "Monks and Their Enemies: A Comparative Approach." *Speculum* 66 (1991): 764–96.

Rustow, Marina. *The Lost Archive: Traces of a Caliphate in a Cairo Synagogue* (Princeton, NJ and Oxford, 2020).

Sabapathy, John. *Officers and Accountability in Medieval England 1170–1300* (Oxford, 2014).

Sablonier, Roger. *Adel im Wandel: Eine Untersuchung zur sozialen Situation des ostschweizerischen Adels um 1300* (Göttingen, 1979).

Gründungszeit ohne Eidgenossen: Politik und Gesellschaft in der Innerschweiz um 1300 (Baden, 2008).

"Zur wirtschaftlichen Situation des Adels im Spätmittelalter." In *Adelige Sachkultur des Spätmittelalters*, ed. Heinrich Appelt (Vienna, 1982), pp. 9–34.

Sarnowsky, Jürgen. *Die Wirtschaftsführung des Deutschen Ordens in Preussen (1382–1454)* (Cologne, Weimar and Vienna, 1993).

Sassier, Yves. *Royauté et idéologie au moyen âge: Bas-Empire, monde franc, France (IVᵉ–XIIᵉ siècle)* (2nd ed., Paris, 2012).

Sauer, Christine. *Fundatio und Memoria: Stifter und Klostergründer im Bild, 1100 bis 1350* (Göttingen, 1993).

Scales, Len. *The Shaping of German Identity: Authority and Crisis, 1245–1414* (Cambridge, UK, 2012).

Schadee, Hester. "'I Don't Know Who You Call Tyrants': Debating Evil Lords in Quattrocento Humanism." In *Evil Lords. Theories and Representations of Tyranny from Antiquity to the Renaissance*, ed. Nikos Panou and Hester Schadee (New York, 2018), pp. 172–90.

Scheyhing, Robert. "Bann (Part I)." In *Lexikon des Mittelalters*, vol. 1 (Munich and Zurich, 1980), cols. 1414–15.

Eide, Amtsgewalt und Bannleihe: Eine Untersuchung zur Bannleihe im hohen und späten Mittelalter (Cologne and Graz, 1960).

Schieffer, Rudolf. "Das Lehnswesen in den deutschen Königsurkunden von Lothar III. bis Friedrich I." In *Das Lehnswesen im Hochmittelalter*, pp. 79–90.

Schilp, Thomas. "Die Gründungsurkunde der Frauenkommunität Essen: Eine Fälschung aus der Zeit um 1090." In *Studien zum Kanonissenstift*, ed. Irene Crusius (Göttingen, 2001), pp. 149–83.

Schlesinger, Walter. *Die Anfänge der Stadt Chemnitz und anderer mitteldeutscher Städte* (Weimar, 1952).

Die Entstehung der Landesherrschaft: Untersuchungen vorwiegend nach mitteldeutschen Quellen (Dresden, 1941; repr. 1969).

Schludi, Ulrich. "*Advocatus sanctae Romanae ecclesiae* und *specialis filius beati Petri*: Der römische Kaiser aus päpstlicher Sicht." In *Staufisches Kaisertum im 12. Jahrhundert*, ed. Stefan Burkhardt, Thomas Metz, Bernd Schneidmüller and Stefan Weinfurter (Regensburg, 2010), pp. 41–73.

Schmeidler, Bernhard. "Die Briefsammlung Froumunds von Tegernsee: Bemerkungen zur Beschaffenheit frühmittelalterlicher Briefsammlungen überhaupt." *Historisches Jahrbuch* 62/69 (1942/49): 220–38.

Schmid, Karl. "Adel und Reform in Schwaben." In *Investiturstreit und Reichsverfassung*, ed. Josef Fleckenstein (Sigmaringen, 1973), pp. 295–319.

"Zur Problematik von Familie, Sippe und Geschlecht, Haus und Dynastie beim mittelalterlichen Adel." *Zeitschrift für die Geschichte des Oberrheins* 105/NF 66 (1957): 1–62.

Schmidberger, Christopher. *Städtische Führungsgruppen im Konflikt: Zur Struktur und Funktion persönlicher Beziehungen in Colmar im 13. und 14. Jahrhundert* (Stuttgart, 2015).

Schmidt, Adolf. "Mittheilungen aus Darmstädter Handschriften." *Neues Archiv der Gesellschaft für ältere deutsche Geschichtskunde* 13 (1888): 603–22.

Schmidt, Charles. *Les seigneurs, les paysans et la propriété rurale en Alsace au moyen âge* (Paris and Nancy, 1897).

Schmidt, Hans-Joachim. "Vogt, Vogtei." In *Lexikon des Mittelalters*, vol. 8 (Munich, 1997), cols. 1811–14.

Schmidt, Walter. "Fritz Reuters Brief an Wilhelm Wolff vom 12. Januar 1864." *International Review of Social History* 27 (1982): 85–96.

Schmitz, Gerhard. "The Capitulary Legislation of Louis the Pious." In *Charlemagne's Heir: New Perspectives on the Reign of Louis the Pious (814–840)*, ed. Peter Godman and Roger Collins (Oxford, 1990), pp. 425–36.

"Wucher in Laon. Eine neue Quelle zu Karl dem Kahlen und Hinkmar von Reims." DA 37 (1981): 529–58.

Schmitz-Esser, Romedio. *Der Leichnam im Mittelalter* (Ostfildern, 2014).

Schmoller, Gustav von, and Otto Krauske, eds. *Die Behördenorganisation und die allgemeine Staatsverwaltung Preußens im 18. Jahrhundert*. Vol. 2 (Berlin, 1898).

Schneider, Herbert. "Karolingische Kapitularien und ihre bischöfliche Vermittlung. Unbekannte Texte aus dem Vaticanus latinus 7701." DA 63 (2007): 469–96.

Schneidmüller, Bernd. "Konsensuale Herrschaft. Ein Essay über Formen und Konzepte politischer Ordnung im Mittelalter." In *Reich, Regionen und Europa in Mittelalter und Neuzeit*, ed. Paul-Joachim Heinig, Sigrid Jahns, Hans-Joachim Schmidt, Rainer Christoph Schwinges and Sabine Wefers (Berlin, 2000), pp. 53–87.

"Stadtherr, Stadtgemeinde und Kirchenverfassung in Braunschweig und Goslar im Mittelalter." ZRG KA 79 (1993): 135–88.

Schnurrer, Ludwig. "Die Reichsstadt Rothenburg im Zeitalter Karls IV. 1346–1378." In *Kaiser Karl IV. 1316–1378: Forschungen über Kaiser und Reich*, ed. Hans Patze (Neustadt and Aisch, 1978), pp. 563–612.

Schramm, Percy Ernst. *Kaiser, Rom und Renovatio: Studien und Texte zur Geschichte des römischen Erneuerungsgedankens vom Ende des karolingischen Reiches bis zum Investiturstreit* (Leipzig and Berlin, 1929).

Schreiner, Klaus. "*Grundherrschaft*: Entstehung und Bedeutungswandel eines geschichtswissenschaftlichen Ordnungs- und Erklärungsbegriffs." In *Die Grundherrschaft im späten Mittelalter*, ed. Hans Patze (Sigmaringen, 1983), pp. 1: 11–74.

"Hirsau, Urban II. und Johannes Trithemius: Ein gefälschtes Papstprivileg als Quelle für das Geschichts-, Reform- und Rechtsbewußtsein des Klosters Hirsau im 12. Jahrhundert." DA 43 (1987): 469–530.

"Religiöse, historische und rechtliche Legitimation spätmittelalterlicher Adelsherrschaft." In *Nobilitas. Funktion und Repräsentation des Adels in Alteuropa*, ed. Otto Gerhard Oexle and Werner Paravicini (Göttingen, 1997), pp. 376–430.

Schroeder, Jean. "Avoués et sous-avoués en Luxembourg." In *L'Avouerie en Lotharingie*, pp. 189–200.

Schubert, Ernst. *Fürstliche Herrschaft und Territorium im späten Mittelalter* (Munich, 1996).

Schulze, Ursula. "Nibelungenlied (und Klage)." In *Lexikon des Mittelalters*, vol. 6 (Munich and Zurich, 1993), cols. 1120–25.

Schuster, Hermine. "Der Kaiser als Vogt der Römischen Kirche" (PhD diss., University of Vienna, 1968).

Schütz, Alois. "Das Geschlecht der Andechs-Meranier im europäischen Hochmittelalter." In *Herzöge und Heilige*, ed. Josef Kirmeier and Evamaria Brockhoff (Munich, 1993), pp. 21–185.

Schwarzmaier, Hansmartin. *Lucca und das Reich bis zum Ende des 11. Jahrhunderts* (Tübingen, 1972).

Schwind, Fred. "Zur staatlichen Ordnung der Wetterau von Rudolf von Habsburg bis Karl IV." In *Der deutsche Territorialstaat*, pp. 2: 199–228.

Scott, James C. *Weapons of the Weak: Everyday Forms of Peasant Resistance* (New Haven, CT and London, 1985).

Scott, Tom. *The Swiss and Their Neighbours, 1460–1560: Between Accommodation and Aggression* (Oxford, 2017).

Screen, Elina. "Lothar I in Italy, 834–40: Charters and Authority." In *Problems and Possibilities of Early Medieval Charters*, ed. Jonathan Jarrett and Allan Scott McKinley (Turnhout, 2013), pp. 231–52.

Seibert, Hubertus. "*Non predium, sed beneficium esset* … Das Lehnswesen im Spiegel der bayerischen Privaturkunden des 12. Jahrhunderts (mit Ausblicken auf Tirol)." In *Das Lehnswesen im Hochmittelalter*, pp. 143–62.

Semmler, Josef. "Saint-Denis: Von der bischöflichen Coemeterialbasilika zur königlichen Benediktinerabtei." In *La Neustrie*, pp. 2: 75–123.

"Traditio und Königsschutz. Studien zur Geschichte der königlichen monasteria." *ZRG KA* 45 (1959): 1–33.

"Verdient um das karolingische Königtum und den werdenden Kirchenstaat: Fulrad von Saint-Denis." In *Scientia veritatis. Festschrift für Hubert Mordek zum 65. Geburtstag*, ed. Oliver Münsch and Thomas Zotz (Ostfildern, 2004), pp. 91–115.

Senn, Félix. *L'Institution des avoueries ecclésiastiques en France* (Paris, 1903).

The Settlement of Disputes in Early Medieval Europe. Ed. Wendy Davies and Paul Fouracre (Cambridge, UK, 1986).

Sieber-Lehmann, Claudius. "Eine bislang unbekannte Beschreibung des Prozesses gegen Peter von Hagenbach." *Basler Zeitschrift für Geschichte und Altertumskunde* 93 (1993): 141–54.

Signori, Gabriela. "Der Stellvertreter." *ZRG GA* 132 (2015): 1–22.

Simon, Christian. *Untertanenverhalten und obrigkeitliche Moralpolitik: Studien zum Verhältnis zwischen Stadt und Land im ausgehenden 18. Jahrhundert am Beispiel Basels* (Basel and Frankurt, 1981).

Simon, Thomas. *Grundherrschaft und Vogtei: Eine Strukturanalyse spätmittelalterlicher und frühneuzeitlicher Herrschaftsbildung* (Frankfurt, 1995).

Smail, Daniel Lord. *The Consumption of Justice: Emotions, Publicity, and Legal Culture in Marseille, 1264–1423* (Ithaca, NY and London, 2003).

Legal Plunder: Households and Debt Collection in Late Medieval Europe (Cambridge, MA, and London, 2016).

"Violence and Predation in Late Medieval Mediterranean Europe." *Comparative Studies in Society and History* 54 (2012): 7–34.

Smith, Andrew. "Pope Leo IX: A Reforming Pope?" *History Compass* 17, no. 9 (2019): 1–13.

Spiess, Karl-Heinz. "Bäuerliche Gesellschaft und Dorfentwicklung im Hochmittelalter." In *Grundherrschaft und bäuerliche Gesellschaft im Hochmittelalter*, ed. Werner Rösener (Göttingen, 1995), pp. 384–412.

Spruyt, Hendrik. "Institutional Selection in International Relations: State Anarchy as Order." *International Organization* 48 (1994): 527–57.

The Sovereign State and Its Competitors: An Analysis of Systems Change (Princeton, NJ, 1994).

Spufford, Peter. *Money and Its Use in Medieval Europe* (Cambridge, UK, 1988).

Stahleder, Helmuth. *Hochstift Freising (Freising, Ismaning, Burgrain)*. Historischer Atlas von Bayern (Munich, 1974).

Starflinger, Hermann. *Die Entwickelung der Domvogtei in den altbayerischen Bistümern* (Ludwigshafen, 1908).

Starzyński, Marcin. *Das mittelalterliche Krakau: Der Stadtrat im Herrschaftsgefüge der polnischen Metropole* (Cologne, Weimar and Vienna, 2015).

Steinbach, Sebastian. *Das Geld der Nonnen und Mönche: Münzrecht, Münzprägung und Geldumlauf der ostfränkisch-deutschen Klöster in ottonisch-salischer Zeit (ca. 911–1125)* (Berlin, 2007).

Steiner, Hannes. *Alte Rotuli neu aufgerollt: Quellenkritische und landesgeschichtliche Untersuchungen zum spätkarolingischen und ottonischen Zürich* (Freiburg and Munich, 1998).

Stengel, Edmund Ernst. *Diplomatik der deutschen Immunitäts-Privilegien vom 9. bis zum Ende des 11. Jahrhunderts* (Innsbruck, 1910).

"Zur Geschichte der Kirchenvogtei und Immunität." *Vierteljahrschrift für Sozial- und Wirtschaftsgeschichte* 10 (1912): 120–37.

Stephenson, Svetlana. *Gangs of Russia: From the Streets to the Corridors of Power* (Ithaca, NY and London, 2015).

Stercken, Martina. "Shaping a Dominion: Habsburg Beginnings." In *Origins of the German Principalities*, pp. 329–46.

Städte der Herrschaft: Kleinstadtgenese im habsburgischen Herrschaftsraum des 13. und 14. Jahrhunderts (Cologne, Weimar and Vienna, 2006).

Stern, Selma. *Der preussische Staat und die Juden*. Vol. 1:1 (Tübingen, 1962).

Stieldorf, Andrea. "Klöster und ihre Vögte zwischen Konflikt und Interessenausgleich im 11. und 12. Jahrhundert." In *Kirchenvogtei und adlige Herrschaftsbildung*, pp. 53–86.

"Zum 'Verschwinden' der herrscherlichen Placita am Beginn des 9. Jahrhunderts." *Archiv für Diplomatik* 53 (2007): 1–26.

Stievermann, Dieter. *Landesherrschaft und Klosterwesen im spätmittelalterlichen Württemberg* (Sigmaringen, 1989).

Stikāne, Vija. "Die Vogtei im mittelalterlichen Livland. Ihre Funktionen und Zuständigkeiten im Bistum und Erzbistum Riga." *Forschungen zur baltischen Geschichte* 11 (2016): 11–39.

Stoclet, Alain J. "Evindicatio et petitio. Le recouvrement de biens monastiques en Neustrie sous les premiers Carolingiens. L'exemple de Saint-Denis." In *La Neustrie*, pp. 2: 125–49.

"Fulrad de St. Denis (v. 710–784) abbé et archprêtre de monastères 'exempts.'" *Le Moyen Âge* 88 (1982): 205–33.

Störmer, Wilhelm. *Früher Adel: Studien zur politischen Führungsschicht im fränkisch-deutschen Reich vom 8. bis 11. Jahrhundert.* 2 vols. (Stuttgart, 1973).

Strange, Susan. *The Retreat of the State: The Diffusion of Power in the World Economy* (New York, 1996).

Strayer, Joseph R. "Feudalism in Western Europe." In *Lordship and Community*, pp. 12–21.

On the Medieval Origins of the Modern State (Princeton, NJ and Oxford, 1970; repr. 2016).

Svensson, Roger. *Renovatio Monetae: Bracteates and Coinage Policies in Medieval Europe* (London, 2013).

Symes, Carol. "When We Talk about Modernity." *AHR* 116 (2011): 715–26.

Tabuteau, Emily Zack. "Punishments in Eleventh-Century Normandy." In *Conflict in Medieval Europe*, pp. 131–49.

Tauschgeschäft und Tauschurkunde vom 8. bis zum 12. Jahrhundert. Ed. Irmgard Fees and Philippe Depreux (Cologne, Weimar and Vienna, 2013).

Taylor, Alice. "Formalising Aristocratic Power in Royal *Acta* in Late Twelfth- and Early Thirteenth-Century France and Scotland." *Transactions of the Royal Historical Society*, Ser. 6, 28 (2018): 33–64.

The Shape of the State in Medieval Scotland, 1124–1290 (Oxford, 2016).

Tebruck, Stefan. "Kirchenvogtei und adlige Herrschaftsbildung. Eine Zusammenfassung." In *Kirchenvogtei und adlige Herrschaftsbildung*, pp. 423–40.

Tellenbach, Gerd. *The Church in Western Europe from the Tenth to the Early Twelfth Century.* Trans. Timothy Reuter (Cambridge, UK, 1993).

"Der Kaiser als Vogt der römischen Kirche." In *Mittelalter und Gegenwart: Vier Beiträge aus dem Nachlaß*, ed. Dieter Mertens, Hubert Mordek and Thomas Zotz (Freiburg and Munich, 2003), pp. 51–75.

Libertas: Kirche und Weltordnung im Zeitalter des Investitursstreites (Stuttgart, 1936).

Teschke, Benno. "Geopolitical Relations in the European Middle Ages: History and Theory." *International Organization* 52 (1998): 325–58.

Teuscher, Simon. *Bekannte – Klienten – Verwandte. Sozialität und Politik in der Stadt Bern um 1500* (Cologne, Weimar and Vienna, 1998).

"Böse Vögte? Narrative, Normen und Praktiken der Herrschaftsdelegation im Spätmittelalter." In *Habsburger Herrschaft vor Ort – weltweit (1300–1600)*, ed. Jeanette Rauschert, Simon Teuscher and Thomas Zotz (Ostfildern, 2013), pp. 89–108.

Lords' Rights and Peasant Stories: Writing and the Formation of Tradition in the Later Middle Ages. Trans. Philip Grace (Philadelphia, PA, 2012).

"Threats from above on Request from below: Dynamics of the Territorial Administration of Berne, 1420–1450." In *Empowering Interactions*, pp. 101–14.

Thieme, Klaus. *Brakteaten der Markgrafschaft Meißen und ihrer Nachbarn zwischen Saale und Neiße: Bestandskatalog* (Leipzig, 2011).

Thompson, James Westfall. *Feudal Germany* (Chicago, 1928).

Tierney, Brian. *The Crisis of Church and State 1050–1300* (Toronto, Buffalo and London, 1988).

Tilly, Charles. *Coercion, Capital, and European States, AD 990–1992* (Cambridge, MA and Oxford, 1992).

"War Making and State Making as Organized Crime." In *Bringing the State Back In*, ed. Peter B. Evans, Dietrich Rueschemeyer and Theda Skocpol (Cambridge, UK and New York, 1985), pp. 169–91.

Tribolet, Maurice de. "Traités d'alliance et avouerie: quelques aspects inédits des relations entre villes et seigneurs dans la région jurassienne au XIIIe siècle." In *Kommunale Bündnisse Oberitaliens und Oberdeutschlands im Vergleich*, ed. Helmut Maurer (Sigmaringen, 1987), pp. 153–64.

Trugenberger, Volker. "Vogt, Gericht und Gemeinde: Württembergische Amtsstädte im späten Mittelalter." In *Württembergische Städte im späten Mittelalter*, ed. Sigrid Hirbodian and Peter Rückert (Ostfildern, 2016), pp. 37–60.

Tubach, Frederic C. *Index Exemplorum: A Handbook of Medieval Religious Tales* (Helsinki, 1969).

Twellenkamp, Markus. "Das Haus der Luxemburger." In *Die Salier und das Reich*, ed. Stefan Weinfurter (Sigmaringen, 1991), pp. 1: 475–502.

Ullmann, Walter. *The Growth of Papal Government in the Middle Ages*, 3rd ed. (London and New York, 2010).

Vanderputten, Steven. "Crises of Cenobitism: Abbatial Leadership and Monastic Competition in Late Eleventh-Century Flanders." *EHR* 127 (2012): 259–84.

"Fulcard's Pigsty: Cluniac Reformers, Dispute Settlement, and the Lower Aristocracy in Early Twelfth-Century Flanders." *Viator* 38 (2007): 91–115.

Monastic Reform as Process: Realities and Representations in Medieval Flanders, 900–1100 (Ithaca, NY and London, 2013).

"Monastic Reform from the Tenth to the Early Twelfth Century." In *Cambridge History of Medieval Monasticism*, pp. 1: 599–617.

"Monks, Knights, and the Enactment of Competing Social Realities in Eleventh- and Early Twelfth-Century Flanders." *Speculum* 84 (2009): 582–612.

Vann, James Allen. *The Making of a State: Württemberg 1593–1793* (Ithaca, NY and London, 1984).

Veach, Colin. *Lordship in Four Realms: The Lacy Family, 1166–1241* (Manchester, 2014).

Venarde, Bruce L. *Women's Monasticism and Medieval Society: Nunneries in France and England, 890–1215* (Ithaca, NY and London, 1997).

Venkatesh, Sudhir. *Gang Leader for a Day: A Rogue Sociologist Takes to the Streets* (New York, 2008).

Verdon, Jean. "Recherches sur les monastères féminins dans la France du nord aux IXe–XIe siècles." *Revue Mabillon* 59 (1976): 49–96.

Vidier, Alexandre. *L'Historiographie à Saint-Benoît-sur-Loire et les miracles de saint Benoît* (Paris, 1965).

Vinci, Anthony. "'Like Worms in the Entrails of a Natural Man': A Conceptual Analysis of Warlords." *Review of African Political Economy* 34 (2007): 313–31.

Vogtherr, Thomas. *Die Reichsabteien der Benediktiner und das Königtum im hohen Mittelalter (900–1125)* (Stuttgart, 2000).

"Die Reichsklöster Corvey, Fulda und Hersfeld." In *Die Salier und das Reich,* ed. Stefan Weinfurter (Sigmaringen, 1991), pp. 2: 429–64.

"Pegau." In *Die Mönchsklöster der Benediktiner in Mecklenburg, Vorpommern, Sachsen-Anhalt, Thüringen und Sachsen,* ed. Ulrich Faust (St. Ottilien, 2012), pp. 1195–1224.

Volkov, Vadim. "The Political Economy of Protection Rackets in the Past and the Present." *Social Research* 67 (2000): 709–44.

Violent Entrepreneurs: The Use of Force in the Making of Russian Capitalism (Ithaca, NY and London, 2002).

"Who Is Strong When the State is Weak? Violent Entrepreneurship in Russia's Emerging Markets." In *Beyond State Crisis? Postcolonial Africa and Post-Soviet Eurasia in Comparative Perspective,* ed. Mark R. Beissinger and Crawford Young (Washington, DC, 2002), pp. 81–104.

Vollmuth-Lindenthal, Michael. "Die Äbtissin von Quedlinburg als Stadt- und Landesherrin im Spätmittelalter." In *Kayserlich,* pp. 105–19.

Vones-Liebenstein, Ursula. "Similarities and Differences between Monks and Regular Canons in the Twelfth Century." In *Cambridge History of Medieval Monasticism,* pp. 2: 766–82.

Vregille, Bernard de. "Moines de Romainmôtier, sires de Joux, sires de Salins." In *Romainmôtier: Histoire de l'abbaye,* ed. Jean-Daniel Morerod (Lausanne, 2001), pp. 107–14.

Waas, Adolf. *Vogtei und Bede in der deutschen Kaiserzeit.* 2 vols. (Berlin, 1919–23).

Wackernagel, Jacob. "Rudolf von Habsburg und die Basler Stadtvogtei." *Basler Zeitschrift für Geschichte und Altertumskunde* 19 (1921): 175–92.

Wagner, Willi. "Das Weistum über die Rechte des Pfalzgrafen Stephan als Erbvogt der Propstei Ravengiersburg." In *Kultur- und Geschichtslandschaft Nahe-Hunsrück,* ed. Joachim Füllmann, Heinz Herrmann and Wolfgang H. München (Kirn, 1994), pp. 75–86.

Waitz, Georg. *Deutsche Verfassungsgeschichte.* 1st ed. 8 vols. (Kiel, Berlin, 1844–78).

Wangerin, Laura E. *Kingship and Justice in the Ottonian Empire* (Ann Arbor, MI, 2019).

Waquet, Jean-Claude. *Corruption: Ethics and Power in Florence, 1600–1770.* Trans. Linda McCall (University Park, PA, 1992).

Ward, John O. "Memorializing Dispute Resolution in the Twelfth Century: Annal, History and Chronicle at Vézelay." In *The Medieval Chronicle: Proceedings of the 1st International Conference on the Medieval Chronicle,* ed. Erik Kooper (Amsterdam and Atlanta, 1999), pp. 269–84.

"Parchment and Power in Abbey and Cathedral: Chartres, Sherborne and Vézelay, c. 1000–1175." In *Negotiating Secular and Ecclesiastical Power,* ed. Arnoud-Jan A. Bijsterveld, Henk Teunis and Andrew Wareham (Turnhout, 1999), pp. 149–65.

Warren, Robert Penn. *All the King's Men* (San Diego, New York and London, 1984).

Watt, J. A. "Spiritual and Temporal Powers." In *The Cambridge History of Medieval Political Thought c.350–c.1450*, ed. J. H. Burns (Cambridge, UK, 1988), pp. 367–423.

Watts, John. *The Making of Polities: Europe, 1300–1500* (Cambridge, UK, 2009).

Weber, Max. *Economy and Society: An Outline of Interpretive Sociology*. Ed. Guenther Roth and Claus Wittich. 2 vols. (Berkeley, Los Angeles and London, 1978).

Wehrli-Johns, Martina. "Stifter und Landesherr: Das Kloster Töss unter dem Schirm der Habsburger." In *Alter Adel – neuer Adel? Zürcher Adel zwischen Spätmittelalter und früher Neuzeit*, ed. Peter Niederhäuser (Zurich, 2003), pp. 31–41.

Weidemann, Margarete. *Geschichte des Bistums Le Mans von der Spätantike bis zur Karolingerzeit*. Vol. 2 (Mainz, 2002).

Weiler, Björn. "Image and Reality in Richard of Cornwall's German Career." *EHR* 113 (1998): 1111–42.

"The King as Judge: Henry II and Frederick Barbarossa as Seen by Their Contemporaries." In *Challenging the Boundaries of Medieval History: The Legacy of Timothy Reuter*, ed. Patricia Skinner (Turnhout, 2009), pp. 115–40.

Weinfurter, Stefan. "Erzbischof Philipp von Köln und der Sturz Heinrichs des Löwen." In *Gelebte Ordnung – Gedachte Ordnung: Ausgewählte Beiträge zu König, Kirche und Reich*, ed. Helmuth Kluger, Hubertus Seibert and Werner Bomm (Ostfildern, 2005), pp. 335–59.

"Die kirchliche Ordnung in der Kirchenprovinz Salzburg und im Bistum Augsburg 1046–1215." In *Handbuch der bayerischen Kirchengeschichte*, ed. Walter Brandmüller (St. Ottilien, 1998), pp. 1: 271–328.

The Salian Century: Main Currents in an Age of Transition. Trans. Barbara Bowlus (Philadelphia, PA, 1999).

Salzburger Bistumsreform und Bischofspolitik im 12. Jahrhundert (Cologne and Vienna, 1975).

Wendehorst, Alfred. "Lupold III. von Bebenburg." In *Lexikon des Mittelalters*, vol. 6 (Munich and Zurich, 1993), col. 14.

West, Charles. "Lordship in Ninth-Century Francia: The Case of Bishop Hincmar of Laon and His Followers." *Past and Present* 226 (2015): 3–40.

"Monks, Aristocrats, and Justice: Twelfth-Century Monastic Advocacy in a European Perspective." *Speculum* 92 (2017): 372–404.

Reframing the Feudal Revolution: Political and Social Transformation between Marne and Moselle, c. 800–c. 1100 (Cambridge, UK, 2013).

"The Significance of the Carolingian Advocate." *Early Medieval Europe* 17 (2009): 186–206.

Wettengel, Michael. *Der Streit um die Vogtei Kelkheim 1275–1276: Ein kanonischer Prozess* (Frankfurt, Bern and Cirencester, 1981).

Whalen, Brett Edward. *The Medieval Papacy* (Basingstoke, 2014).

The Two Powers: The Papacy, the Empire, and the Struggle for Sovereignty in the Thirteenth Century (Philadelphia, PA, 2019).

Whaley, Joachim. *Germany and the Holy Roman Empire*. 2 vols. (Oxford, 2012).

White, Stephen D. "Debate: The 'Feudal Revolution.'" *Past and Present* 152 (1996): 205–23.

"Repenser la violence: de 2000 à 1000." *Médiévales* 37 (1999): 99–113.

"Tenth-Century Courts at Mâcon and the Perils of Structuralist History: Re-reading Burgundian Judicial Institutions." In *Conflict in Medieval Europe*, pp. 37–68.

Wickham, Chris. *Community and Clientele in Twelfth-Century Tuscany* (Oxford, 1998).

"Debate: The 'Feudal Revolution.'" *Past and Present* 155 (1997): 196–208.

Framing the Early Middle Ages: Europe and the Mediterranean, 400–800 (Oxford and New York, 2005).

"How Did the Feudal Economy Work? The Economic Logic of Medieval Societies." *Past and Present* 251 (2021): 3–40.

Medieval Europe (New Haven, CT and London, 2016).

Sleepwalking into a New World: The Emergence of Italian City Communes in the Twelth Century (Princeton, NJ and Oxford, 2015).

Wiesner-Hanks, Merry E. "Ideology Meets the Empire: Reformed Convents and the Reformation." In *Germania Illustrata: Essays on Early Modern Germany Presented to Gerald Strauss*, ed. Andrew C. Fix and Susan C. Karant-Nunn (Kirksville, 1992), pp. 181–95.

Wihoda, Martin. "Kirche und adlige Herrschaftsbildung in den böhmischen Ländern zur Zeit der Premysliden." In *Kirchenvogtei und adlige Herrschaftsbildung*, pp. 297–328.

Wild, Joachim. "Herrenchiemsee im Spätmittelalter 1218–1520." In *Herrenchiemsee. Kloster – Chorherrenstift – Königsschloss*, ed. Walter Brugger, Heinz Dopsch and Joachim Wild (Regensburg, 2011), pp. 123–48.

Wilke, Sabine. *Das Goslarer Reichsgebiet und seine Beziehungen zu den territorialen Nachbargewalten* (Göttingen, 1970).

Williamson, George S. "'Thought Is in Itself a Dangerous Operation': The Campaign Against 'Revolutionary Machinations' in Germany, 1819–1828." *German Studies Review* 38 (2015): 285–306.

Willoweit, Dietmar. "Die Entwicklung und Verwaltung der spätmittelalterlichen Landesherrschaft." In *Deutsche Verwaltungsgeschichte*, pp. 66–143.

"Römische, fränkische und kirchenrechtliche Grundlagen und Regelungen der Vogtei." In *Kirchenvogtei und adlige Herrschaftsbildung*, pp. 21–52.

"Vogt, Vogtei." In *Handwörterbuch zur deutschen Rechtsgeschichte*, ed. Adalbert Erler, Ekkehard Kaufmann and Dieter Werkmüller (Berlin, 1998), cols. 5: 932–46.

Wilson, Peter H. *Heart of Europe: A History of the Holy Roman Empire* (Cambridge, MA, 2016).

Winkelbauer, Thomas. *Österreichische Geschichte 1522–1699: Ständefreiheit und Fürstenmacht*. 2 vols. (Vienna, 2003).

Winroth, Anders. *The Making of Gratian's Decretum* (Cambridge, UK, 2000).

Wisplinghoff, Erich. *Die Benediktinerabtei Siegburg* (Berlin and New York, 1975).

"Der Kampf um die Vogtei des Reichsstifts Essen im Rahmen der allgemeinen Vogteientwicklung des 10.–12. Jahrhunderts." In *Aus Geschichte und*

Landeskunde. Festschrift für Franz Steinbach, ed. Max Braubach, Franz Petri and Leo Weisgerber (Bonn, 1960), pp. 308–32.

Wolter, Udo. "Amt und Officium in mittelalterlichen Quellen vom 13. bis 15. Jahrhundert. Eine begriffsgeschichtliche Untersuchung." *ZRG KA* 74 (1988): 246–80.

"Verwaltung VI. Mittelalter." In *Geschichtliche Grundbegriffe*, ed. Otto Brunner, Werner Conze and Reinhart Koselleck, vol. 7 (Stuttgart, 1992), pp. 28–47.

Wolverton, Lisa. *Cosmas of Prague: Narrative, Classicism, Politics* (Washington, DC, 2015).

Wood, Ian N. "The Code in Merovingian Gaul." In *The Theodosian Code: Studies in the Imperial Law of Late Antiquity*, ed. Jill Harries and Ian Wood (London, 1993), pp. 161–77.

The Merovingian Kingdoms: 450–751 (London and New York, 1999).

Wood, Susan. *The Proprietary Church in the Medieval West* (Oxford and New York, 2006).

Woods, Andrew R. "From Charlemagne to the Commercial Revolution (c.800–1150)." In *Money and Coinage in the Middle Ages*, ed. Rory Naismith (Leiden and Boston, 2018), pp. 93–121.

Wright, Nicholas. *Knights and Peasants: The Hundred Years War in the French Countryside* (Woodbridge, 1998).

Zehetmayer, Roman. "Vogtei und Herrschaftsausbau des österreichischen und steirischen Adels im Hochmittelalter." In *Kirchenvogtei und adlige Herrschaftsbildung*, pp. 225–60.

Zeilinger, Gabriel. "Procurator, Schaffner und Vogt in der Urbanisierung der Herrschaft Rappoltstein (13.–15. Jahrhundert)." In *Mittler zwischen Herrschaft und Gemeinde*, pp. 201–16.

"Urban Lordships." In *Origins of the German Principalities*, pp. 60–67.

Zeller, Bernhard. "Writing Charters as a Public Activity: The Example of the Carolingian Charters of St Gall." In *Medieval Legal Process. Physical, Spoken and Written Performance in the Middle Ages*, ed. Marco Mostert and P. S. Barnwell (Turnhout, 2011), pp. 27–37.

Zey, Claudia. *Der Investiturstreit* (Munich, 2017).

Z'Graggen, Bruno. *Tyrannenmord im Toggenburg: Fürstäbtische Herrschaft und protestantischer Widerstand um 1600* (Zurich, 1999).

Ziwes, Franz-Josef. "Der Verzicht des rheinischen Pfalzgrafen Heinrich auf die Trierer Stadtvogtei. Randbemerkungen zur Quellenlage." In *Liber Amicorum necnon et Amicarum für Alfred Heit*, ed. Friedhelm Burgard, Christoph Cluse and Alfred Haverkamp (Trier, 1996), pp. 43–54.

Zorzi, Andrea. "Justice." In *The Italian Renaissance State*, edited by Andrea Gamberini and Isabella Lazzarini (Cambridge, UK, 2012), pp. 490–514.

Zotz, Thomas. "Burg und Amt – zur Legitimation des Burgenbaus im frühen und hohen Mittelalter." In *Burgen im Breisgau. Aspekte von Burg und Herrschaft im überregionalen Vergleich*, ed. Erik Beck, Eva-Maria Butz, Martin Strotz, Alfons Zettler and Thomas Zotz (Ostfildern, 2012), pp. 141–51.

"In Amt und Würden. Zur Eigenart 'offizieller' Positionen im früheren Mittelalter." *Tel Aviver Jahrbuch für deutsche Geschichte* 22 (1993): 1–23.

"*Turegum nobilissimum Sueviae oppidum*. Zürich als salischer Pfalzort auf karolingischer Basis." *Frühmittelalterliche Studien* 36 (2002): 337–54.

Die Zähringer: Dynastie und Herrschaft (Stuttgart, 2018).

"Zürich, Freiburg in Burgund, Bern. Zum Umgang der Zähringer mit einer alten und zwei neuen Städten." In *Archäologie und Geschichte der Stadt in der Zähringerzeit*, ed. Stephan Kaltwasser and Heinz Krieg (Freiburg and Munich, 2019), pp. 101–19.

Index

Aachen, map 2, 34, 211, 243
Aargau, map 4, 270
Abbo, abbot of Fleury, 96–98, 100, 106, 216
accountability, 1, 3, 7, 10, 15, 16, 53, 82, 104, 173, 175, 185, 222, 270, 273, 276, 277, 281, 288, 302, 306, 315, 317, 339, 345, 348, 349
Ad abolendam, 189, 190, 207, 244
Adalbert (Babenberg), advocate, 126
Adalbert II, count of Calw, 112–115
Adelheid, abbess of Essen, 204 n. 41
Adelheid III, abbess of Quedlinburg, 148–50
Adolf of Nassau, German king, 247
advocacy
    definitions of, 4 n. 12, 52, 53, 257 n. 14
advocate
    definitions of, 4, 6, 18, 19, 26 n. 14, 40
    devil's (*advocatus diaboli*), 19 n. 73
    fiscal (*advocatus fisci*), 41, 42, 80 n. 83
    gratia Dei, 125, 128, 237, 238
    significance of, 5, 15, 17, 22
    special (of the Roman Church), 121 n. 60, 241–50, 253
    types of, 17–22, 35, 62, 68, 69, 79 n. 78, 80, 142, 188, 230, 255, 274 n. 115, 303, 313
    women as, 90, 126, 238, 257, 275
advocatia/advocatio. *See* advocacy
advocatus. *See* advocate
advowson, 190
Aimo of Fleury, 98, 327–29, 342
Albert III, count of Bogen, 171, 172
Albert IV, count of Bogen, 195
Albert IV, count of Dillingen, 264, 265
Albrecht I, German king, 235, 236, 339
Albrecht II, German king, 293, 310 n. 43
Albrecht III, duke of Austria, 270
Albrecht of Sommerschenburg, count-palatine of Saxony, 148–50
Alexander II, pope, 112

Alexander III, pope, 188, 242
Alexander IV, pope, 247
All Saints (Allerheiligen). *See* Schaffhausen
Alsace, map 3, 108, 135, 262, 263 n. 49, 270, 271 n. 101, 275, 277, 286, 296–98, 301
Amalbert, abbot of St. Denis, 27 n. 18, 29
Amalung, advocate of St. Gall, 68
Amalung, count and advocate of Paderborn, 89
Amorbach, map 3, 86
Amt, 19, 272, 289
Anastasius IV, pope, 224
Andechs, counts of, 217 n. 8
Andrew of Fleury, 226, 328, 329, 342
Aniane, 52 n. 39
Anna Amalia, abbess of Quedlinburg, 322
Anna Dorothea, abbess of Quedlinburg, 321
Anna Sophia I, abbess of Quedlinburg, 320
Anno II, archbishop of Cologne, 118, 124, 134, 135
Aquileia, 88 n. 7, 189 n. 79, 258
Aquitaine, map 1, 41 n. 78, 42, 45, 72, 98, 101
Arn, archbishop of Salzburg, 37, 39
Arnold, count of Altena-Isenberg, 201, 202
Arnold of Dollendorf, advocate of Cologne, 124
Arnstein, map 6, 120, 307
Arnulf, East Frankish ruler, 71
Asbach, map 5, 311, 313
Atto, bishop of Freising, 37–39
Augsburg, maps 3 and 5, 77, 78 n. 76, 81
Augustinians, 110, 119, 120, 167, 184, 217, 235, 258, 309
Austria, map 5, 87, 88, 126, 136, 146, 184, 185, 193, 210, 229, 230, 252, 262, 269, 307, 309, 310, 335, 345
Autun, 72 n. 46

409